Congratulations!
Welcome to HLS.

Competition Policy and Price Fixing

LOUIS KAPLOW

Competition Policy
and Price Fixing

PRINCETON UNIVERSITY PRESS
PRINCETON AND OXFORD

Library of Congress Cataloging-in-Publication Data

Kaplow, Louis.

Competition policy and price fixing / Louis Kaplow.

pages cm

Includes bibliographical references and index.

ISBN 978-0-691-15862-4 (alk. paper)

1. Competition—Government policy.   2. Antitrust law.   3. Price fixing.   I. Title.

HD41.K37 2013

338.6′048–dc23   2012047888

British Library Cataloging-in-Publication Data is available

This book has been composed in Minion Pro

Printed on acid-free paper. ∞

Printed in the United States of America

1 3 5 7 9 10 8 6 4 2

For Irene, Leah, and Jody

Summary of Contents

𝒇

PART III: COMPARISON OF APPROACHES

Contents

PART III: COMPARISON OF APPROACHES

Preface

🕊

Competition policy toward price fixing presents an unrecognized paradox. Commentators, competition agencies, and competition laws throughout the world unanimously condemn the practice, treating it as the field's most important transgression, subject to its harshest sanctions. Yet further scrutiny reveals the prohibition's definition to be incoherent, its practical reach uncertain, and its fit with fundamental economic principles obscure.

Consensus has bred complacency. This book aims to be an antidote. Efficacy demands starting from scratch on two fronts: legal doctrine and economic policy analysis. Misunderstandings about the former constitute a straightjacket that has aborted progress on the latter. Accordingly, the plan of attack is to exhaustively examine the law so as to clear the way for a ground-up assessment of optimal competition policy toward price fixing.

The root of the legal problem lies in competition law's agreement requirement, which demarcates the domain of liability for price fixing. This precondition is examined from multiple perspectives, many underappreciated and some overlooked entirely: basic definitions of key terms, the concept of communications that many see as constitutive of a violation, statutory provisions, higher court interpretations, lower court practice, and basic oligopoly theory. Each inquiry undermines the conventionally endorsed view but is harmonious with the law's reaching all successful coordinated price elevation by oligopolistic firms. This broad convergence should fully extinguish existing inhibitions and stimulate broader study, but it does not suffice to dictate policy because internal coherence does not guarantee optimal consequences for welfare.

A systematic economic investigation of price-fixing policy has three elements: articulating the problem in terms of social welfare, assessing how to detect harmful behavior, and designing appropriate sanctions. Familiar static and often-ignored dynamic effects are examined, followed by the presentation of the appropriate framework for decision-making, a subject that has been largely neglected in the analysis of optimal enforcement quite generally as well as with regard to competition law. Detection is the most challenging element of the analysis. Various techniques are examined with a particular eye to their potential contribution to deterrence and also their tendency to generate false positives, the prospect of which chills desirable conduct. The appropriate magnitude and type of sanctions are determined by reference to the benefits and costs of penalizing underlying conduct.

Finally, the emergent direct economic approach toward price fixing is compared to the traditionally favored proscription that focuses on particulars of firms' communications—a subset of means to an end rather than the end itself. This familiar method is inferior on a priori grounds due to its formalistic nature and poor nexus with the social objective. Unfortunately, it is even worse. The commonly endorsed proscription constitutes a dominated strategy: Compared to the direct approach, it targets cases that generate relatively small deterrence gains and high chilling costs, while exonerating cases where the social danger is greatest and chilling costs are comparatively modest. In addition, contrary to widely held beliefs, it is more complex and costly to implement because it requires an additional, subtle inquiry with little evidence to guide it.

Despite the power of the foregoing conclusions, this book should largely be understood as advancing conceptual understanding rather than specific policy prescriptions. First, it is unavoidably preliminary because it covers so much new territory—indeed, there is remarkably little subject matter overlap with most contemporary literature on the topic. Second, existing empirical knowledge provides limited illumination of many key issues. Third, optimal competition policy, particularly due to its economic complexity, is highly institutionally dependent, and institutions vary widely across the globe and even within some individual jurisdictions, notably, the United States. In sum, this book seeks to invigorate debate, redirect thinking, and guide future research, with the hope of improving the quality of subsequent discourse and, ultimately, of competition policy toward price fixing.

• • •

My interest in competition law and policy began as a student. During the course of my education, I have been tremendously lucky in my instructors and mentors: Mike Scherer, Mike Spence, Dick Caves, Mike Porter, and Phil Areeda. I have also benefited from my collaborations with co-authors—Phil Areeda and Aaron Edlin on *Antitrust Analysis* (a casebook for law students) and Carl Shapiro on *Antitrust* (a survey aimed at economists).

From the outset of my academic career, the traditional treatment of the price-fixing prohibition has bothered me, and I have always found it difficult to teach material that I could not make sense of for myself. The exception in extant scholarship is Richard Posner's 1969 article, followed by a chapter in his book on antitrust, which famously endorses a more economically based strategy for addressing oligopoly pricing. Although these writings have been widely cited, their substance has been largely ignored. The present investigation goes beyond Posner's work and departs in many respects, which can hardly be surprising in light of the decades of theoretical and empirical work in industrial organization in the interim. Yet the spirit of his argument as well as some key insights provide invaluable illumination.

In addition to my intellectual forebears, I wish to acknowledge the substantial support I have received over the years working on this project. For helpful discussions and comments, I am grateful to Jon Baker, Ryan Bubb, Aaron Edlin, Joe Harrington, Oliver Hart, Al Klevorick, Carl Shapiro, Steve Shavell, Kathy Spier, reviewers for the Princeton University Press, editors and referees at journals, and workshop and conference participants at Chicago, Columbia, Georgetown, Harvard, Michigan, NYU, Virginia, Yale, the Antitrust Division of the U.S. Department of Justice, Northwestern's Searle Center Antitrust Economics and Competition Policy Conference, and the American Law and Economics Association Annual Meeting. Molly Eskridge, Matt Seccombe, and the team at Princeton University Press provided terrific administrative, editorial, and other assistance. I have also benefited substantially from the efforts of many talented research assistants (with apologies to any accidently omitted): Shobitha Bhat, Josh Branson, Jamison Davies, Danielle D'Onfro, Michael Doore, Ariel Fox, Joseph Gay, David Geiger, Barbara Glowacka, David Gottlieb, Jason Green-Lowe, Jesse Gurman, Kinga Guzdek, Anat Holtzman, James Ianelli, Daniel Jacobsen, Noam Lerer, Lauren Merrell, William Milliken, Soojin Nam, Balaji Narain, Max Nicholas, Maria Parra-Orlandoni, Robert Ritchie, Cody Rockey,

Krysten Rosen, Michael Sabin, Dorothy Shapiro, and Joseph Vardner. Generous financial support was provided by Harvard Law School's John M. Olin Center for Law, Economics, and Business; Harvard Law School; the Kaufmann Foundation; and the Leeds Research Fund. Finally, I wish to acknowledge that, in the course of writing this book, I published the following articles drawn from the manuscript: "On the Meaning of Horizontal Agreements in Competition Law," *California Law Review*, vol. 99(3), 683–818 (2011); "An Economic Approach to Price Fixing," *Antitrust Law Journal*, vol. 77(2), 343–449 (2011); and "Direct versus Communications-Based Prohibitions on Price Fixing," *Journal of Legal Analysis*, vol. 3(2), 449–538 (2011).

A brief note is in order regarding the extensive footnotes. Most of them present further analysis, qualifications, or illustrations that may be of great interest to some readers (perhaps those most inclined to disagree at various points) but would disrupt the flow if placed in the main body. A few serve to elaborate economic ideas, often subtleties, for those with less background. And, in the first part of the book, many contain significant legal detail, in some instances to document claims that may otherwise seem far-fetched or to illustrate the prominent endorsement of views that some might otherwise think to be straw men.

Competition Policy and Price Fixing

1

Introduction

The rule against price fixing is the least controversial prohibition in competition law throughout the world, and the practice is universally subject to the law's harshest penalties. There is, however, far less consensus than meets the eye on what constitutes price fixing and on how legal regimes should determine its presence. More surprising, prevalent understandings are not grounded in oligopoly theory even though modern competition policy is widely taken to rest on economic substance rather than legal formalism.

This book's central aim is to provide an analytical foundation for designing policy toward coordinated price elevation in oligopolistic industries. In rough terms, the proper methodology is straightforward. First, one articulates the problem and undertakes welfare-based analysis to specify the benefits and costs of attempts to control it. Next, one examines how coordinated price elevation is best detected, attending to the error costs associated with different types of proof. Finally, one sets appropriate sanctions.

These elements of a direct approach have received remarkably little attention in the literature. Instead, commentators, government agencies, and courts display some tendency to focus on penalizing certain sorts of interfirm communications that facilitate coordinated oligopoly pricing. Although such punishment has great value for unmasked cartels, systematic comparison with a more direct, functional approach reveals conventional means to be inferior and in important respects counterproductive in cases without smoking-gun evidence. In those settings, a direct approach dominates the conventionally favored communications-based prohibition in that the former targets situations that involve both greater social harm and less risk of chilling desirable behavior than those most likely to generate liability under the latter. The direct approach is also less difficult to administer, contrary to conventional wisdom.

On reflection, these conclusions are hardly unexpected. Direct approaches tend to be superior to indirect, circumscribed ones. Analysts, enforcers, and adjudicators usually do best by asking the right question—the one of direct social concern—rather than by attempting to answer a different one. Sometimes indirect tactics turn out to be superior, but this can be ascertained only after sustained analysis that articulates the competing methods and explicitly assesses their differences. It is therefore striking that many of the topics investigated here have been so neglected.

This book proceeds in three parts. Part I offers a fresh, in-depth exploration of competition law's horizontal agreement requirement. Many commentators and, to a degree, courts see this command as imposing a constraint on the inquiry and largely dictating the use of a communications-based prohibition rather than a direct approach to the problem of coordinated oligopolistic price elevation. This conventional view is shown to be incoherent, with the key statutory terms and underlying concepts actually being more in accord with a direct approach. Furthermore, much doctrine as well as practice, both in court and outside, is more consistent with a broader view of the law's prohibition. Finally, it is explained that the narrower interpretation of the agreement requirement has no analogue in modern oligopoly theory, so any attempt to maintain such a legal rule really has to be highly formalistic, divorced from economic precepts.

With much underbrush having been removed, part II analyzes the problem of coordinated oligopolistic price elevation, starting from first principles. The initial step is to assess—more explicitly, carefully, and completely than is usually done—the nature of the social problem, including the possible costs of regulation in terms of chilling desirable behavior through the risk of false positives. The second step is detection, which, it is emphasized, can be done in a number of ways that vary across contexts in their availability and accuracy. Third, one must apply sanctions, another topic that has suffered from too little attention. Contrary to much existing commentary, emphasis here is placed on the deterrent role of remedies, rather than on their ex post ability to restore competition, because a well-functioning system will discourage most violations and prospective compliance is best achieved through the threat of sanctions, not legal injunctions that are more akin to command-and-control regulation.

Part III explicitly compares a direct approach to the orthodox one, a communications-based prohibition. There is an important sense in which this part is not logically necessary, for part II undertakes a ground-up analysis of the problem and a communications-based prohibition is not what emerges. However, given the nearly exclusive focus on this method by commentators as well as the belief that it reflects existing law, a systematic, side-by-side comparison seems valuable and proves instructive. Setting aside cases with sharp, conclusive evidence—in which the two approaches would both assign liability—the communications-based prohibition is seen to be defective in ways that are an immediate consequence of its design: aiming at a subset of symptoms rather than at the problem itself. Specifically, this indirect method requires addressing the same detection question as under the direct approach—identifying whether oligopolistic coordination has taken place—as well as tackling the further question of whether such was accomplished by particular means, prohibited communications. This explains why decision-making is rendered more rather than less complicated. Worse, if one accepts conventional views about aspects of this analysis (which views will be questioned), the consequence is to focus liability on situations involving less social danger and a greater risk of chilling costs.

Because the exposition of all three parts is extensive, it is helpful at the outset to provide a more detailed overview of the analysis, beginning with part I, on the law of horizontal agreements. To set the stage, suppose that firms in a concentrated industry are able to charge the monopoly price and maintain it at this level because those that contemplate cheating (cutting price to enhance market share) fear sufficiently swift and substantial retaliation to render deviation unprofitable. The firms' actions and inactions are interdependent in that each firm's strategic assessment is notably influenced by how it expects the other firms to react.

A central question for competition law is whether such oligopolistic interdependence that produces supracompetitive prices should in itself be deemed a violation or whether something additional—perhaps secret negotiations producing a signed cartel agreement, perhaps less formal arrangements—should be a prerequisite to liability. Most contemporary writers believe that the law does and should require more than interdependence. It is obscure, however, just what supplement is necessary. Moreover, as many appreciate, this bounded view of the law is in tension with a rejection of formalism and an embrace of economically based competition regulation because coordinated price elevation leads to essentially the same economic consequences regardless of the particular manner of interactions that generates this outcome.

Chapter 2 begins the investigation of the horizontal agreement question by presenting scenarios that illustrate the difficulty of defining agreement in a coherent fashion that successfully distinguishes pure interdependence (firms refrain from price cutting because of an expectation of retaliation derived from a shared appreciation of their circumstances)—deemed to be insufficient for liability—from classic cartels (firms meet secretly in hotel rooms to discuss prices and the consequences of cheating)—widely accepted to be more than sufficient. Of course, most legal categories give rise to line-drawing problems; it is notoriously difficult to distinguish similar shades of gray. The examples presented, however, are more corrosive because they demonstrate how hard it is to distinguish what many regard to be polar-opposite cases, analogous to black and white.

This chapter also scrutinizes the concepts used in discussing horizontal agreements. Initial examination suggests that the standard meaning of terms like agreement, concerted practice, and conspiracy—each of which contemplates a mutual understanding or meeting of the minds—readily encompasses interdependence, although under some alternative definitions this is not the case. There is widespread use of a number of terms having potentially different meanings, which generates substantial confusion. Even more dysfunctional, certain words associated with one category of behavior are sometimes used to denote the opposite category. Interpreting both court opinions and commentary can be almost impossible, and there is room for interpreters to depict key passages, including important canonical statements of the doctrine, as having whatever meaning is desired, especially when these pronouncements are taken out of context. More broadly, intelligent dialogue about the agreement requirement is undermined, perhaps without the participants recognizing the extent of misunderstanding that their statements may cause or their readings may involve. To some degree, this state of affairs reflects inattention. But it also is symptomatic of underlying substantive challenges; after all, it never is easy to state with precision ideas that themselves are foggy, inconsistent, or incoherent.

Chapter 3 examines interfirm communications that many, sometimes implicitly, take to be central in defining the law's concept of agreement. The core problem with making the existence of communications determinative is that communication is ubiquitous, among other reasons because most actions, certainly including the sale of a good at a price, themselves communicate pertinent information. If the use of communications constitutes agreement, then pure interdependence (indeed, less) would trigger liability. Therefore, if agreement is to depend on communications and yet be more restrictive, it is necessary to specify some subcategory of communications, perhaps based on the mode of communication or its content, the use of which is necessary and sufficient to constitute agreement. It is explained that this approach is tantamount to declaring the result of price fixing to be per se legal while designating as illegal only the use of certain means—and, moreover, suspending the agreement requirement with respect to the decision to use such means, despite the fact that the same agreement requirement is what exonerates price coordination when such means are not employed. Furthermore, if regulation is to be restricted to a particular subcategory of communications, it is necessary to decide whether firms' use of functional equivalents also gives rise to liability. If it does not, circumvention is invited. But if it does—which one might expect under a modern, nonformalistic view of the law—one returns to a prohibition on all successful interdependent coordination, for the function that is meant to be served by the communications in question is to succeed at coordination.

The discussion of communications also considers a range of theories and bodies of evidence about language that seem pertinent but have not previously been applied to the present context. Human language is extremely flexible and adaptable, resisting efforts at regulation. It also can be difficult for outsiders to understand what is being communicated. These and other points are sharply highlighted by sign language—the very existence of which is deeply problematic for those who implicitly seek to prohibit communication that uses language and yet freely permit the use of signs (like price signaling). It is also observed that standard approaches to defining agreement, which require the presence of particular, purely symbolic communications while excluding tangible behavior that communicates, have as their underlying logic the notion that "words speak louder than actions." Of course, the more familiar, opposite maxim is better rooted in common sense and, not surprisingly, in the teaching of scholars of strategy, including business strategy with regard to the interaction of firms in an oligopoly.

Chapters 4 and 5 examine how the agreement requirement is reflected in existing doctrine. The provision of U.S. Sherman Act Section 1, which is rarely elaborated directly, does suggest some guidance, particularly through its use of the word "conspiracy." This term had and continues to have an established legal meaning that is rather expansive. In fact, some of the earlier Supreme Court cases that provide seminal interpretations of Section 1 are also regarded as leading pronouncements on the more general law of conspiracy, and precisely for some of its broader features. More recent Supreme Court opinions contain more restrictive interpretations, although the agreement question was not formally before the Court in these cases and the statements themselves are difficult to give meaning. Practice in the lower courts is quite mixed. In spite of some direct pronouncements that are ambiguous or to the contrary, actual practice is often as if the law regarded successful interdependence to be illegal. Notable in this regard are the "plus factors" deemed sufficient to establish agreement, jury instructions on what must be found to establish an agreement, and damages rules that necessarily reflect a standard of liability due to the requisite causal nexus between liability and compensable injury. Interpretation of EU Article 101 (formerly 81) is also briefly considered. Although the details differ, it is not surprising that similar difficulties arise because the underlying economic problem is identical and the structure of the legal prohibition is almost the same.

Chapter 6 explores what is referred to here as the paradox of proof, a phenomenon that some have previously noted but none have analyzed in depth. This paradox grows out of the interplay of two starting points: (1) deeming agreement to require more than demonstration of success-

ful interdependence—such as by also using certain sorts of communications—and (2) needing to infer the existence of agreement from circumstantial evidence, out of a recognition that parties hide their actions
from legal scrutiny. Think about the demand that these factors jointly
impose. It is assumed that, in adjudication, it frequently will be impossible to observe the communications that the defendant firms employed. Nevertheless, the factfinder must infer whether or not certain
means of communication were used, based on what can be observed
about market conditions, notably, how conducive they are to successful
oligopolistic coordination and whether such successful coordination
appears to have occurred. Because the outcome, interdependent oligopoly pricing, might have come about in any number of ways, the process
of making inferences about whether the unobserved communications
employed by the defendants were of one type rather than another is
challenging, to say the least.

There is also a particular feature of the inference process that seems
paradoxical: Evidence indicating that the conditions are more conducive to successful coordination—which makes successful price elevation more likely—may reduce the likelihood of the existence of an
agreement, defined for present purposes as the use of specified means
of communication rather than others. Conventional wisdom suggests
that, beyond some point, the greater the danger of coordinated oligopoly pricing, the stronger will be defendants' claim that they were able to
accomplish it without using any prohibited means. Chapter 6—with
later elaboration in chapter 17—explores this logic and a number of important variations in detail. The conclusion is that the information,
about both oligopoly behavior in general and the particular nature of
the industry and its firms, that is necessary to assess the likelihood of
the use of prohibited communications is highly complex and subtle,
posing a serious obstacle to factfinding. Moreover, the implications for
parties' litigation strategies are jarring. It will be highly case-dependent
which party should be on which side of many factual disputes, and
whichever side does make sense for each party could readily flip midstream, such as if some witness proves to be more or less powerful than
the parties had anticipated. In all, careful analysis of the paradox of
proof has a whimsical feel, seemingly far removed from what appears to
be the standard practices of firms, their lawyers, and adjudicators. It is

thus difficult to reconcile, on one hand, the reasoned implications of what many claim that the law on agreement is and should be with, on the other hand, what the law in action is in fact or with what one might ever imagine it could be.

Chapter 7 closes part I by assessing the relationship between modern oligopoly theory and the meaning of the agreement requirement. Because competition law seeks to regulate oligopoly behavior and, moreover, to ground such regulation in modern economic understandings, it would seem to follow that, if the law's notion of agreement reflects economic substance, the agreement requirement would correspond to a core distinction drawn in oligopoly theory. As it turns out, that theory, which is an application of game theory (particularly, that of repeated games), does have an explicit notion of agreement. But this notion refers to binding agreements and thus is irrelevant for present purposes because competition law renders horizontal price-fixing agreements void ab initio. When agreements are not taken to be automatically enforced by an outside authority, another branch of game theory is applicable. But the pertinent theory, models, and analysis are applicable equally to successful oligopolistic coordination accomplished through pure interdependence and to that effectuated in the form of a classic cartel. That is, the distinction that many would have the law make central is, as a first approximation, nonexistent in the relevant economic theory.

Modern oligopoly theory does, however, have a central concept—whether parties' strategies constitute an equilibrium—that may be applicable in a somewhat different manner. The concept of equilibrium is closely related to the idea of a meeting of the minds that both is at the very essence of interdependent oligopolistic coordination and constitutes a standard definition of agreement and related terms. Equating the concept of equilibrium with agreement is not without its problems, but it really is the only concept in the relevant theory that relates in a significant way to the notion of an agreement. This chapter also considers the roles of communications and of promises in oligopoly theory, finding each of potential relevance but neither hinging critically on a notion of agreement.

It is hoped that the first part of the book advances thought on the best way to regulate coordinated oligopoly behavior through competition law. Because the near consensus of present opinion centers on a criterion—or, more likely, numerous differing criteria—of uncertain meaning and fails to appreciate many implications of the dominant view, it is important to clarify terminology, eliminate much underbrush, and begin the task of using modern oligopoly theory to analyze the problem directly. It is difficult to compare, say, liability based on interdependence with a rule requiring more if we do not know what that more is, how to identify its existence, or how it relates to the justification for limiting oligopolistic interaction. And even simple points about terminology are critical, for it is hard to assess competing arguments when they are couched in language susceptible to multiple, even opposite, interpretations. In addition, a partial but possibly substantial explanation for the almost complete avoidance of direct policy analysis in this realm seems to be the belief that existing law in most jurisdictions dictates a particular, immutable solution. Accordingly, showing that such is not the case in a number of important respects should free analysts and policy-makers to consider the problem anew.

It is tempting to go further and conclude from the analysis in part I that a different, concrete normative conclusion is established: that the horizontal agreement requirement is best interpreted as applicable to all interdependent behavior that is successful in producing elevated prices. After all, from each of the angles considered, virtually every difficulty derives from attempting to define agreement as requiring something more, whatever that may be. But such a conclusion would be premature. Competition policy is not best advanced by relying on a formal, interpretive enterprise, even when that undertaking seems to yield an outcome that is in accord with modern economic teachings. Instead, the thesis advanced here is that competition policy should be grounded directly in economic analysis of the pertinent issues, which the remaining two parts of this book undertake.

Part II comprises a three-step inquiry, focusing on articulation of the social problem, detection of its presence, and the application of sanctions. The first step begins in chapter 8 by examining the social welfare consequences of coordinated oligopolistic price elevation. From the outset, it is notable that none of the pertinent theory directly distinguishes between successful coordination due merely to recognized interdependence and that resulting from classic cartel behavior, or various cases in between. The harm from price coordination in terms of allocative inefficiency or loss in consumer welfare depends most directly on the extent and duration of supracompetitive pricing, not on the means of reaching or maintaining an understanding to charge the heightened price.

From a dynamic perspective, price elevation may also cause production inefficiency on account of excessive entry. There are some settings in which additional entry could be efficient due to insufficient product variety or other difficulties in recovering fixed costs. Such benefits might sometimes justify some price elevation, but—crucially for present purposes—do not directly distinguish the means by which it is accomplished. The expectation of above-marginal-cost prices also induces a number of other kinds of investments, many (but not all) of which are efficient. Such investment tends to be encouraged by the prospect of unilateral exercises of the market power created by such activity rather than by collective price elevation that is independent of it; indeed, incentives for efficient investment may be dampened by the presence of coordinated price elevation. This distinction provides the core rationale for prohibiting price fixing while ordinarily permitting unilateral price elevation by individual firms.

Chapter 9 presents a framework for assessing competition rules. An economic approach to limiting coordinated oligopolistic price elevation seeks to determine liability and apply sanctions based primarily on the deterrence benefits that result as well as any chilling of desirable behavior that may ensue, while also considering the expense of operating the regime. In assessing the cost of false positives, attention focuses on incidental negative behavioral effects, not on mistakes that are defined by reference to proxy legal standards and then given arbitrary weight. An example that will prove important involves imposing sanctions on firms that actually charged elevated oligopoly prices, the prospect of which deters such behavior. This outcome is favorable in terms of social welfare but under some legal standards would be deemed to be an undesirable error in cases in which the firms did not employ forbidden modes of communication. It will also be seen that examining the rate of false positives (properly conceived) provides a highly incomplete and potentially misleading (even backward) indication of how well a system is functioning, particularly with regard to achieving deterrence. In addition, the optimal legal policy depends heavily on empirical matters, such as the extent of coordinated price elevation in the economy and the potential success of various means of detecting it; some evidence is reviewed, but important gaps in knowledge remain.

Chapters 10 and 11 explore the problem of detection, the greatest challenge in the control of interdependent oligopoly pricing. Firms naturally seek to hide illegal aspects of their behavior, and reliable indicators are not always readily obtainable by enforcers. One approach is to employ market-based evidence to identify successful oligopolistic coordination. Price elevation may be inferred from pricing changes over time, such as the observation of significant industry price increases not accompanied by corresponding changes in cost or of sharp price drops associated with price wars. Alternatively, markups might be determined from measures of price and marginal cost or inferred from the elasticity of firms' demand curves. Note that, as with most of the analysis throughout, these inquiries do not depend on whether detected price elevation originated through classic cartel behavior.

Also relevant to detection is the degree to which conditions are conducive to coordinated oligopoly pricing. Highly conducive conditions make inferences of successful interdependent pricing more credible whereas unconducive conditions cast doubt on its plausibility. However, due to the noisy empirical relationship between industry structure and performance as well as the possibility that conditions are highly conducive yet oligopolistic pricing is effectively deterred, conducive conditions do not in themselves strongly indicate coordinated price elevation—whereas highly unconducive conditions do significantly negate the inference. Conducive conditions also favor liability because false positives and concomitant chilling effects are less likely; unconducive conditions are more often associated with fairly competitive behavior and thus situations in which chilling effects are a greater concern. To preview chapter 17, this feature of sound detection strategy differs importantly from the results of focusing on the existence of particular interfirm communications because, under certain assumptions, more conducive conditions reduce the likelihood that such communications occurred even though they increase the magnitude of the net expected social harm from a failure to apply sanctions.

Another route to detection looks for internal evidence of whether coordinated oligopolistic price elevation took place. In addition to attempts to observe behavior directly or to infer it from market activity, one can examine firms' internal understandings as reflected in their agents' thinking and actions. Yet another, more familiar form of evidence, often deriving from similar sources, concerns interfirm communications, the existence of which may likewise indicate what firms actually did. When such evidence is clear and powerful, it will generally be sufficient to establish liability, just as under a narrower communications-based prohibition. (The approaches to liability differ when such evidence is unavailable.)

Chapter 12 emphasizes that these internal sources of information are complementary to each other and to market-based techniques. In deciding whether to assign liability in a particular case, all such evidence on detection should be considered in light of the decision-theoretic approach articulated previously. Some forms of proof are more reliable than others and give rise to different risks of particular types of errors. For example, some market-based techniques that attempt to determine firms' marginal costs could result in adverse incentive effects in the case of underestimation, making it optimal to find liability only if the measured price elevation is substantial or other confirming evidence is present. The chapter also considers two additional matters: liability for attempts and the problem of determining which firms should be held liable.

The analysis of sanctions in chapter 13 concentrates primarily on deterrence. In many instances, reflecting current practice, the most important instruments are fines levied by government enforcers and, where permitted, damages collected by injured parties. If the probability of sanctions and their magnitude are sufficient, most coordinated price elevation will be deterred. A major challenge in setting monetary sanctions is determining the extent of price elevation, although this magnitude will often be indicated by much of the evidence on detection considered in chapters 10 and 11. The measurement problem is conceptually the same whether price elevation was accomplished through secret meetings, mere recognition of interdependence, or in any other manner. The threat of imprisonment as well as fines assessed against individual actors can be a useful supplement, particularly in light of agency problems within firms. Injunctions are also considered. Although much academic commentary fixates on injunctive relief, it is not evident that it is important in controlling coordinated oligopoly pricing.

Chapter 14 examines unilateral market power, a possibility set to the side in the rest of the book and ignored in most prior work on the subject. The exercise of such power sometimes constitutes a competing explanation for price elevation in oligopolistic industries. This possibility raises three questions: whether exercising unilateral market power is also usually socially undesirable and thus should be prohibited by competition law; if it is not, how one can distinguish it from coordinated price elevation; and how one should err in cases of uncertainty. Analysis focuses both on industries with homogeneous goods and on those with differentiated products, the former of which are more relevant for present purposes because coordinated pricing is generally thought to be difficult when differentiation is substantial.

Chapter 15 addresses two additional subjects. Institutional issues, which influence the cost and accuracy of investigation and adjudication, are important in fashioning competition rules. Second, coordinated behavior may involve not only price—the focus of this book—but also nonprice terms, such as product characteristics, territories, and other dimensions of competitive strategy. The logical structure of the analysis presented throughout is largely relevant to nonprice coordination, although, as will be discussed, the relative importance of different considerations, particularly concerning detection, can differ significantly depending on the nature of the coordination involved.

As suggested at the outset of this introduction, part II would seem to offer a complete analysis of the regulation of price fixing by considering the nature of the problem, how to detect its presence, and what remedies to apply. In the course of this investigation, the commonly advocated approach of attacking only express and perhaps also tacit agreements, variously defined, barely surfaces. That is, it does not emerge from a systematic consideration of how best to address coordinated oligopolistic price elevation. Nevertheless, it is useful to compare these methods more explicitly, which is done in part III.

Chapter 16 begins by defining the conventional prohibition in an operational fashion. As we know from part I, this is a daunting task. Most views can be captured by supposing that the price-fixing prohibition is

limited to certain sorts of interfirm communication, whether designated by mode, content, or otherwise. This formulation on its face
seems problematic because it focuses not on whether the means employed in fact caused harm in a given case but rather on whether one
versus another means was employed. Preliminary consideration of social welfare consequences suggests a negative assessment, for the distinction drawn has little relationship to welfare.

Moreover, making this type of distinction central to the prohibition
suggests that detection will often prove difficult, which chapter 17 indicates is indeed the case. The essential contrast with the direct approach
outlined in part II is that the communications-based prohibition uses a
large portion of the most relevant evidence indicative of undesirable behavior in an indirect way and also counts evidence concerning conduciveness of conditions backward, generating what chapter 6 already ex-
pounds, the paradox of proof. Specifically, under certain assumptions
that many endorse, evidence of a high danger of successful coordinated
oligopoly pricing exonerates firms instead of raising the likelihood that
they will be subject to sanctions. It is explained in chapter 17 that, if one
calibrates the burden of proof under the direct approach to find liability
in the same number of situations as under the communications-based
prohibition, then the direct approach dominates. The cases it targets involve both greater social danger and less risk of chilling desirable behavior than those most likely to generate liability under commentators'
favored rule.

This comparison can be further illuminated from another perspective. If the major concern with too aggressive an approach toward coordinated oligopolistic price elevation is the risk of chilling desirable activity as a consequence of the anticipation of false positives, then the
best response would naturally be to raise the burden of proof under a
direct approach. The communications-based prohibition does not take
this route. Instead, it requires demonstration of particular behavior that
not only is hard to identify but also is not well correlated with high deterrence benefits and low chilling costs—indeed, in certain ranges, it
may be negatively correlated with both. If one attempts to optimize the
proof burdens (adjust the liability/no liability boundaries) under this
circumscribed prohibition, one is led to reshape it into the direct
approach.

In addition, the communications-based prohibition raises the cost and complexity of investigation and adjudication. The rule requires that one not only determine the presence of interdependent oligopoly pricing—the focus of the direct approach elaborated in part II—but also identify the means by which it was accomplished. The latter compels additional effort. Also, because the difference between permitted and prohibited means is formally rather than functionally determined, there is little empirical evidence that can guide the necessary inference process, so substantial conjecture is required. As a consequence, the conventional approach—in addition to producing inferior substantive outcomes—is significantly more challenging to apply, which is ironic in light of its widely being favored on administrability grounds.

Chapter 18 considers a number of additional subjects: the determination of sanctions under a communications-based prohibition; an alternative rule under which liability cannot be based on circumstantial evidence, contrary to the long-standing norm in competition law; implications of the contrasting approaches for other areas of competition law, such as the stringency of limits on horizontal mergers and the regulation of practices that might facilitate oligopolistic coordination; and the manner in which rapid evolution in communications technology might influence the analysis, particularly concerning detection.

Finally, the leading three arguments offered in favor of the traditional view—although responded to in substance at various points earlier in the book—are related explicitly to the foregoing analysis. One argument asserts a difficulty in attacking purely interdependent behavior because such would involve commanding firms to behave irrationally. This criticism is mistaken because it omits consideration of deterrence: applying heavy sanctions to certain choices will change what firms find it rational to do. Another objection is that making price elevation by oligopolists illegal is inconsistent with the legality of price elevation by monopolists. This point ignores the aforementioned purpose of separate, more stringent prohibitions on group behavior and, moreover, the notion implies that classic cartels should be legal. Third, it is argued that remedies, particularly injunctive relief, directed at price elevation are problematic because they amount to price regulation. This claim is misconceived because, as mentioned, effective control is best accomplished through penalties that achieve deterrence rather than by relying on directive legal commands. However, the argument is suggestive of an important concern with competition policy regarding price fixing that is underdeveloped in the existing literature, namely, that the detection of violations can be quite difficult, raising the problem of false positives, the prospect of which chills desirable behavior. As emphasized throughout part II, this concern should indeed be central in shaping the optimal legal regime, but the analysis shows that it does not imply the desirability of the conventional approach over a direct method that takes explicit account of possible chilling costs.

Parts II and III of this book, which contain the policy analysis, are qualitatively different from most prior work on what rule should govern coordinated oligopolistic price elevation. Indeed, as noted earlier, there is little overlap even in the topics that are addressed. The central reason for this divergence is that the focus here is not on the question that has preoccupied much previous discussion: "How should we define the term 'agreement'?" Instead, this book concentrates on the question: "What approach toward coordinated oligopoly pricing best promotes social welfare?" In answering the latter, it is natural to proceed by examining the nature of the problem and then determining how to identify its presence and to remedy it.

Modern competition law emphasizes real economic effects over legalistic formalities, has an open-ended, flexible expression, and could be amended. Also, as part I argues at length, a more substantive approach conforms better to the statutory language, much of the relevant precedent, and aspects of existing practice than does the more formalistic method that is widely endorsed. Even if prevailing doctrine does impose significant constraints, it is best to start by trying to determine what in principle is the most sensible way to address coordinated price elevation.

Coming to a firm conclusion on the best competition policy toward price fixing remains quite difficult even when the problem is properly formulated and analyzed. The optimal rule depends greatly on empirical evidence in realms where existing understanding is incomplete. One set of issues concerns the extent of coordinated oligopolistic price elevation that would prevail under various regimes. Another involves the manner in which such coordinated pricing is achieved—for example, with resort to what sorts of communication—and, more broadly, how much of it can be detected, by which methods, and at what error cost. Without further knowledge, it is difficult to identify the best rule with any confidence. However, the proffered framework not only guides that decision in the interim but also sharpens the research agenda so that better strategies might be devised in the future.

PART I

HORIZONTAL AGREEMENTS

2

Defining the Problem

🦋

To understand the meaning of horizontal agreement, it is necessary to juxtapose abstract categories and concrete situations. Accordingly, this chapter begins by offering two examples that illustrate how difficult it is to define the notion of agreement as it is conventionally understood in the competition policy literature.[1] Next, frequently used terms are defined, which is necessary given the unusually wide variance in usage, including the extreme of employing a single key term to denote opposite conceptions. Once terminology is clarified, it is possible to describe commentators' views and thereby articulate the core questions that occupy the analysis in the remainder of the book.

A. Illustrations

In some instances, it is straightforward to determine the existence of an agreement, however that notion might be defined within a fairly broad range. When two parties sign a formal, legally binding contract for the sale of an object, there is undoubtedly an agreement. When two individuals, unconnected in any way, each choose which glove to put on first, there is no agreement, even if they both start with the same hand.

Regarding horizontal agreements in competition law, the challenge is not merely that there is a line-drawing problem as with any categorical distinction. Rather, fairly common interactions raise difficult questions.

---

[1] The conventional view, which de facto tends to focus on the presence or absence of certain sorts of interfirm communications that facilitate coordinated oligopoly pricing, is prominently advanced by Turner (1962) and Areeda and Hovenkamp (2003).

Firms in an oligopolistic industry would like to raise prices above the competitive level,[2] ideally to a mutually optimal monopoly-like price, and to keep the price elevated—avoiding the problem of cheating to the extent possible and quickly identifying and punishing any defections that occur (the prospect of which, the firms hope, will deter cheating in the first place).[3] Such firms may reap great profits if they are on the legal side of the line (even if just barely) but suffer stiff penalties if they are on the other side (even slightly). As a consequence, their strategic anticipatory behavior places great pressure on the boundary, wherever it is drawn. This section presents two sets of related scenarios in order to illustrate the tensions that arise.

Example 1

As the curtain opens, our two competitors are staring intently at each other. Each sees the other's gaze. Each is thinking (and is pretty darn sure that the other is thinking): "This is ridiculous. We've each been charging the competitive price of $3.00 for months. We'd both make a ton more money if we were charging something higher."

And each thinks: "Should I break the staring contest and just shout out to my competitor that this is so? Nah, why bother? It's so obvious as to be pathetic, embarrassing. A good primal scream might get it off my chest, but the name of the game is *communication* and reaching an *agreement* to move forward, not a therapy session."

One of the two, who will be called the Initiator, decides that it's time to act. Initiator thinks that a good price would be $3.40 but doesn't want to be too aggressive. So Initiator decides to go with $3.25 as an opening suggestion. Initiator proclaims, "As of this very instant, until further notice, I'm going to charge all of my customers $3.25. By the way, if I change my mind, I can assure you

---

[2] If prices would otherwise be supracompetitive due to the exercise of unilateral market power, explored in chapter 14, the challenge is to elevate prices above that baseline. For ease of exposition, the equilibrium in the absence of successful coordination will be taken to be competitive.

[3] For further elaboration, see section 7.A.

that you will be among the first to know. There will be no secret price cuts. Never."

The other, who will be called the Responder, is delighted. Responder thinks: "Should I just go right along, accepting this invitation? Or, since I think that the ideal price is higher, should I raise the offer? Hey, why not go for it while the going's good." Responder answers: "As of this moment, until further notice, I'm going to charge all of my customers $3.35. And, if I change my mind, you will certainly be among the first to know. I will never secretly cut my price."

Initiator is ecstatic. Initiator had hoped and suspected that Responder would answer positively. But one never knows for sure. And Responder has done one better by going up to $3.35. So, Initiator wonders: "Do I respond quickly and match the offer, closing the deal, or should I go for it and press for $3.40, my view of the ideal price? What the heck, today is a good day and Responder is obviously in the spirit of cooperation. And $3.40 is hardly an in your face rejection!" Initiator then declares: "As of now, until further notice, I'm going to charge all of my customers $3.40. And . . . ."

Responder answers quickly this time. Responder wasn't sure if the right price was $3.35, $3.40, or perhaps $3.45. "But hey, Initiator must think it's $3.40, and we're nearly symmetrically situated, so why not close the deal?" Responder announces: "As of now, until further notice, I'm going to charge all of my customers $3.40. . . ."

And there our story ends. Initiator and Responder live happily, and profitably, ever after. Of course, their customers do not.

At this point, one should ask whether the foregoing depicts an agreement. (Also consider variants, such as an express agreement.) Most, I suspect, will have little reluctance answering in the affirmative.

But what of the fact that there is no binding contract? No signed document? No language of offer and acceptance, of agreement, of promises, and so forth? These questions do not create serious reservations. Agreements subject to competition law's prohibition need not be binding contracts; indeed, this is an impossibility because, for agreements that involve forbidden behavior like pure price fixing, they as a consequence cannot be legally binding. Nor is writing required. Nor the use of magic

words. Stating "There will be no secret price cuts" rather than "I promise that there will be no secret price cuts" is not taken to be an important distinction, and it may be viewed as meaningless in this context
because, as just noted, no promise is binding in any event. Furthermore,
as a practical matter, if a finding of agreement could be avoided merely
by phrasing communications in the language of declarations of unilateral intent—perhaps adding for good measure formal disclaimers of
any agreement—then parties, coached by lawyers as necessary, would
be free to fix prices with impunity. Accordingly, our story of the two
competitors would generally be regarded to involve an undoubted
agreement.[4]

Suppose now that we change the story. Instead of a secret meeting of
the principals of (the only) two competitors in a market, consider the
interaction of two gas station owners located on adjacent corners in an
otherwise isolated area.[5] No words are spoken. We begin with each selling at $3.00 per gallon. Then, one morning, the owner playing the role
of initiator changes the numbers displayed on the station's large sign—
visible from a block away and thus impossible to miss for the competing
station owner across the street—to show a new price of $3.25. Shortly
thereafter, the owner of the competing station posts $3.35 on its large
sign. And so forth, until the price that each charges settles at $3.40 and
remains there indefinitely. Suppose further that each entertains precisely the same thoughts as in our original story—that is, they both
think it ridiculous to be selling at the competitive price, the initiator
initially thought that $3.40 would be a good price but out of caution
began by posting $3.25, and so on.

---

[4] Nevertheless, of the many individuals who have read this story in draft or heard it presented, a couple viewed it as not involving an agreement, apparently because specific words
of assurance were not included, despite the seemingly open invitation to circumvention provided by this approach. Furthermore, it seems that they would also be willing to infer agreements from circumstantial evidence, a task that chapters 6 and 17 indicate is quite daunting
if there must be some sort of express agreement, but one that seems impossible if subtle differences in phrasing must be inferred from marketplace behavior. Indeed, even proof of a
hundred secret meetings may not suffice to establish an agreement under this view if there
were no transcripts—or, if there were, but they revealed that the participants carefully
avoided certain words and phrases.

[5] The presentation of this example expands on that in Kaplow and Shapiro (2007,
1122–23).

Does this new scenario depict an agreement? It is almost universally accepted that it does not. Even though the consequence in terms of supracompetitive pricing is the same as in our original setting, this unfortunate result is attributed to the structural character of the market in question, not to an agreement. After all, because no agreement exists, how could it be otherwise?

Although there is near consensus on the outcomes, this harmony does not extend to the articulation of which distinctions between the two scenarios are responsible for the demarcation: an undoubted agreement in the first and none in the second. Some would emphasize the inevitability of an oligopoly outcome in the second case, making an agreement unnecessary. Some might note the lack of any exchange of words or other forms of explicit communication in the latter setting. But, regardless of which factors are mentioned, it obviously is necessary to be able to identify one or more differences that explain why there is an agreement in one case but not in the other. Furthermore, because neither case is generally regarded to be a close call, the distinguishing features should be fairly sharp.

Upon reflection, however, any proposed answer must be deficient. One way to see this point is to entertain the suggestion that the exposition of the second case involved a sleight of hand: specifically, the introductory sentence was inaccurate. Suppose that the two gas station owners are not players in a changed, second story. Instead, imagine that they were the principals in the original version; that is, the second story can be interpreted as just a retelling of the first, which can be seen by reviewing that play closely: At the outset, the two competitors were staring intently at each other—from across the street. Each thought the situation of two gas stations in a remote area charging the competitive price was foolish. Each would have had to "shout out to the other" because they were across the street, not in a hotel room. The Initiator "proclaims" (that is, declares publicly, gives an outward indication, to mention some standard definitions of the term)[6] a new price of $3.25 in the clearest and most convincing manner possible, by posting that price on the station's price sign. Obviously, any subsequent change in this

---

[6] For a discussion of the use of dictionary definitions in this chapter and throughout, see note 12.

price would result in the competing owner being among the first to know, and there cannot be a secret price cut in this setting. The Responder "answers" (acts in response to an action performed by another) and later "announces" (makes known publicly) its own prices, using its own price signs.

One could augment the story and suppose that the price signs, in addition to displaying the price in large numerals, also contain, in standard-form smaller print, the words: "The above price is this gas station's price from this very instant and will continue in force until further notice. And if the owner of this station should ever wish to change the price, this can be done only by replacing this price sign with a sign showing such different price. In addition, the owner is bound to charge the price posted on this sign and no other price, that is, unless and until this sign is changed." In such a fashion, each word in the original scenario could be included. Of course, because this is the plain, unambiguous meaning of the simple sign that contains merely the price, no meaningful difference is entailed.[7]

This example therefore poses a sharp challenge. The simple, straightforward scenario is properly characterized in two ways: a classic, undoubted agreement, and a clear case of no agreement. Whatever distinctions one might have hypothesized to be sufficient to rationalize this difference in legal characterization must be mistaken because there is only one situation after all. Therefore, even before examining particular definitions of and variations on agreement and related terms in section B, it is apparent that the categorization problem, as conventionally understood, is quite difficult to solve, if indeed any solution is possible.

Example 2

Version A. Individuals with price-setting authority at each of the firms in a fairly concentrated industry meet in a hotel room and

---

[7] The ordinary meaning of the term "sign" includes, rather pertinently, a posted command, warning, or direction. The reason that price signs at gas stations (and in many other settings) contain only numerals is that the further verbal elaboration in the story has been conventional and unambiguous for so long as to render restatement redundant. Indeed, charging a customer more than the posted price violates some consumer protection laws and may be regarded as fraud because the meaning of price postings is so well established. Consider also the discussion of language, including of sign language, in section 3.C.

hash out an explicit agreement on pricing: future prices, penalties for deviation, and so forth. They all speak directly, and all concur on the final outcome, which includes increasing each firm's price from the current, competitive level to a monopoly level in one month, and this result occurs on schedule.

Version B. This variant is the same as version A except that the language is lawyered, which is to say that there is no use of magic words like "agreement" or "promise"; instead, all statements are carefully phrased as expressions of thoughts, wishes, or unilateral intentions. No one's understanding, however, is influenced by this adjustment, and the same result transpires.

Version C. Same as version B except that each individual is in a conference room at his or her respective home office and the meeting is conducted by video conference.

Version D. Same as version C except that members of the news media are present in each conference room.

Version E. Same as version D except that the media crews supply and operate the video equipment.

Version F. Same as version E except that the meeting is decreed by each firm to be a press conference, with the broadcast made public (live) through the Internet rather than kept private (limited to the other firms).

Version G. Same as version F except that there is some time lag between statements. The same statements are made in the same order with the same tones and gestures, and precisely the same understanding is reached. Indeed, because even in version A the price increase was not to take effect for a month, there is not even any delay in the time of the eventual price rise.

Version A of this example[8] is the stereotypical express agreement, no doubt about it. By contrast, sequential press conferences of the sort depicted in version G are not ordinarily regarded as involving agreements.[9] The question, therefore, is whether this difference can be

---

[8] For precursors, see Areeda and Kaplow (1988, 346–48), Areeda and Hovenkamp (2003, 210, 254–55), and Kaplow and Shapiro (2007, 1122).

[9] See, for example, Areeda and Hovenkamp (2003, 29, 37, 254–57). In this light, however, it is curious that such behavior, at least of a highly explicit sort, is not commonly observed

rationalized by one or more of the changes introduced in moving from A to G.[10]

The move from A to B—lawyering the phrasing to remove magic words of agreement, substituting the language of thoughts, wishes, and intentions—is, as noted when discussing example 1, not generally regarded to matter. All of the other steps, from B through G, involve seemingly inconsequential shuffles: changing rooms, inviting the media, switching who operates the cameras, and so forth. Since these details are unrelated both to the harm involved (consumers being charged monopoly prices) and to most conceptions of agreement (see section B), it is difficult to see how these tweaks should matter. It is possible that in practice the lack of magic words, close proximity, privacy, and immediacy will erode firms' ability to reach consensus. Yet it was posited that, in this instance, such is not the case. Furthermore, cultural differences, personality clashes, and other difficulties might make a meeting of the minds more rather than less difficult at a secret meeting, but it is not imagined that such possibilities, even if demonstrated in a particular case, would negate the existence of an agreement when the meeting was successful.

In example 1, two interpretations of the same story led to opposite outcomes. In the present example, there are differences but not ones that appear to be important for the notion of agreement. As a result, it is not easy in example 2 to determine either where the characterization switches—i.e., if version A is an agreement and version G is not, which step along the way causes the result to change?—or what would be the rationale for reversing the outcome at the specified step. Furthermore, even if certain adjustments are given some weight, it is not clear that they can bear the burden of explaining the difference between version A, which is the clearest of possible agreements, and version G, which most view as definitely not an agreement. That is, versions A and G do

---

rather than being widespread. For discussion of this and other disjunctions between conventional views of the agreement requirement and behavior in the world, see section 6.F.

[10] One could also take the steps in a different order: for example, after version B, first inviting in the press before moving to different rooms. Or, perhaps more interesting would be to retain the language of agreement, promise, and so forth through to the press conference stage, removing it only as the final step. The same question could be asked regarding any such ordering.

not merely have different outcomes, perhaps each being ever so close to the line; instead, they are seen as being a great distance apart on the agreement spectrum. These two examples, taken together, suggest at a minimum that substantial work needs to be done in articulating and defending a concept of horizontal agreement if that concept is indeed to distinguish among situations like those presented here.

B. Terminology

It is remarkable, on one hand, how much weight legal and economic commentary and also court opinions place on the meaning of particular terms and, on the other hand, how inconsistent is the usage—the combination being a recipe for misunderstanding.[11] Although it is usually unhelpful to dwell on dictionary-like definitions of terms in an exploration of matters of economic policy, the present subject seems exceptional. Not only are terms frequently used as if their meanings are self-evident, despite a century of contest on the matter, but a particular

---

[11] The logical structure of some of the problem is as follows. It is commonly argued that some term describes X, the category of behavior or situations that constitutes an agreement (and thus is per se illegal if it involves simple price fixing) whereas another term describes X′, the category that does not. However, it is often the case that neither the term identifying X nor that for X′ is defined. Even worse, the terms used to depict the two categories may be synonyms under standard definitions, or one term may be viewed as a subset of the other. At best, one can attempt to infer the intended meaning of the terms for X and X′ from the context, such as the arguments given, but this may leave open multiple interpretations, or sometimes none at all, such as when two arguments implicitly entail inconsistent assumptions about the situations in each category. The difficulties escalate with multiple authors (whether courts or commentators) due to the need to compare one author's term for X (or X′) to the term for X (or X′) of another.

A conjecture is that present confusion is due in part to a series of motivated interpretations over an extended period, some of which have become commonplace. For example, it may be that terms like independent or parallel (conscious or otherwise) had clear meanings when first employed but were described by subsequent litigants, courts, or commentators as if they had other meanings in order to advance their own agendas. See note 37, exploring origins of alternative usages for the term independent. Since, as will be seen, many of the terms in common usage have multiple meanings that allow key passages to be given different (sometimes opposite) interpretations, this process may have been easier than is ordinarily the case.

key term, as we shall see, is sometimes used to denote opposite conceptions. Substantive discourse is significantly impeded, and attempts to make sense of legal doctrine are often confusing or incoherent: After all, if the central word in a canonical statement of the law can take many meanings, including opposite ones, there is essentially no constraint on the interpretive exercise. It is difficult to state existing law in an operational way, one that conveys the same meaning to firms, their lawyers, judges, and commentators and that readily distinguishes cases by their facts. Related, it is difficult to assess various arguments about the proper scope of the law when they consider the relative virtues of competing legal formulations that are highly ambiguous and not necessarily distinct. Most commentators advance a notion of agreement that is narrower than interdependence, but it is hard to evaluate their position if we have little idea what agreement or the other key words used to define it actually encompass. An examination of commonly used terms cannot resolve all these problems or indicate how the law should be given content. But it does serve to clarify subsequent discussion, legal and economic.

Before proceeding, it is useful to offer a brief preview of the taxonomy employed in the next section, which discusses commentators' views. It is conventional to distinguish independent behavior from interdependent behavior and, within the latter category, to identify a subset constituting express agreement or perhaps some broader notion of agreement. All variants and interpretations of section A's examples involve interdependent behavior, as distinguished from independent behavior (which would consist, for example, of competitive gas stations raising their prices in response to an increase in the wholesale price they must pay). What is at issue in those examples, and in the doctrinal debate more broadly, is whether and how one might delineate some subset of interdependent behavior that will be deemed to constitute illegal agreement, with all other interdependent behavior deemed not to constitute such agreement and hence to be legal.

AGREEMENT.—Since the term agreement is, as a matter of blackletter law, the legally relevant determinant of the applicability of Sherman Act Section 1 and is also one of the terms in EU Article 101 (formerly 81), its definition might be regarded as particularly central. Yet, as will be discussed in chapter 4, not only do these edicts fail to define what is meant by agreement, but the term does not even appear in the Sherman Act: instead, under Section 1, the word agreement is employed to capture the composite concept embodied in the statutory language of contract, combination, and conspiracy.

The most pertinent standard definition of agreement is a harmony of opinion, action, or character.[12] A harmony of opinion exists when there is a meeting of the minds in the sense discussed below with regard to interdependent behavior, including that of oligopolistic firms behaving so as to coordinate their prices. It, along with harmony of action or character, may also be taken more broadly, as incorporating common behavior even when it arises independently (such as when competitors pass along changes in input prices). Thus, we might say that two individuals who never interacted are in agreement that Jones is a terrific author if both actually believe this to be so. We would not require their thought processes to be interdependent to say that they agree on the matter. Yet we also may not be inclined to describe them as having reached an agreement on a view of Jones by mere coincidence of opinion.

There are also narrower definitions of agreement, such as viewing it as synonymous with a compact, treaty, or a legally binding contract. But the legal notion of agreement in the present context is surely broader. After all, "contract" is just one of the listed terms in the Sherman Act that agreement is taken to capture. Moreover, as mentioned, because the statute itself renders price-fixing contracts legally void, if binding contracts were all that was illegal, the statute would not punish even classic, express, price-fixing cartels.

It seems that if the term agreement is to be given a standard meaning—and one that does not nullify the statute (as the narrower one just given does) or expand it vastly (as the broader one encompassing mere commonality does)—it would have to encompass interdependent behavior, certainly including behavior involving coordinated oligopolistic

---

[12] Throughout, proffered standard definitions are taken from the CD-ROM version of *Merriam-Webster's Collegiate Dictionary* (11th ed., 2007). Some definitions are direct quotations and others are paraphrases. Since dictionary definitions vary somewhat and lack canonical status for present purposes in any event, quotation marks will be dispensed with. Irrelevant or unhelpful senses are omitted. (For example, in defining agreement, this dictionary also includes "the act or fact of agreeing," which is circular.)

price elevation. This approach is hardly novel. Donald Turner (1962, 671), despite arguing that interdependent oligopolistic behavior should not be a sufficient basis for Section 1 liability as a matter of policy, states that, as a matter of language usage, "there are far better grounds for saying that though there may be 'agreement' it is not unlawful agreement."[13] Earlier, he observes (665) that "[i]t is not novel conspiracy doctrine to say that agreement can be signified by action as well as by words." Turner (683) concludes on the matter as follows:[14]

> I also find considerable appeal, as a general matter, in defining "agreement" for purposes of Sherman Act law in terms of interdependence of decisions, if for no other reason than that it seems to me to be a clearer and more workable standard than any other standard, of acceptable scope, which requires something more. Once one goes beyond the boundaries of explicit, verbally communicated assent to a common course of action—a step long since taken and from which it would not seem reasonable to retreat—it is extraordinarily difficult if not impossible to define clearly a plausible limit short of interdependence.

An alternative (not necessarily inconsistent with giving agreement its standard meaning) is to take agreement to be a term of art. This approach may have added appeal under U.S. law because, as mentioned, the term is not in the Sherman Act itself.[15] Once this course is taken, it is not clear whether the path becomes clearer or more obscure. The former would hold if the usage were consistent or if canonical definitions were accepted, neither of which appears to be the case. Instead, the term

---

[13] The notion that a category of behavior may be deemed to involve agreements but be subject to further analysis to determine whether there is liability—that is whether it constitutes a "restraint of trade"—will be considered further in section 3.B.

[14] See also note 53 in chapter 4, discussing the Supreme Court's citation of Turner on the agreement question.

[15] This approach may be less available with other terms, such as conspiracy, which do appear in the statute, and with regard to other statutes, like EU Article 101, that do contain the language under consideration. Such terms may still be terms of art, but the approach to interpreting them may differ when they are part of an enacted provision rather than chosen by courts and commentators as a convenience.

is often used by different writers in a conclusory fashion that often does little to convey meaning on the question at hand.

To summarize, the term agreement may, consistent with wider usage, readily be defined to embrace interdependent oligopolistic price elevation, which entails the required meeting of the minds. A narrower definition limited to legally binding contracts is possible in a vacuum but not useful in the present context. Accordingly, if a narrower but different construction is desired, it would have to be a term of art constructed for the specific purpose at hand—and some definition of that term would need to be articulated.

CONSPIRACY.—The term conspiracy appears in Sherman Act Section 1 and, moreover, is a legal term of art with a long history that might illuminate its meaning, as further elaborated in subsection 4.A.2. For the present, attention will be confined to standard definitions, one of which refers to agreements among conspirators. This definition is reassuring because it suggests that the term agreement is an appropriate summary of this component of the statutory language, and it leaves us with the result from the preceding discussion. Another standard definition is that a conspiracy involves action in harmony toward a common end, a close fit with the concept of interdependent behavior.[16]

CONCERTED PRACTICES.—EU Article 101 employs the term concerted practices. The most pertinent meaning of concerted is that which is mutually contrived or agreed on. The latter, equivalent to the term agreement itself, readily encompasses interdependent behavior involving a meeting of the minds, whereas the notion of contrived even more clearly carries this meaning. Concerted can also, like agreement, have a broader meaning that includes all acts in unison, but one that is rejected for present purposes.

COLLUSION.—The term collusion is often used in discussions of oligopoly and price fixing, especially by economists. Interdependent

---

[16] Conspiracy often refers to secret agreements, presumably because the context, like the present one with price fixing, is one in which the agreement is illegal, inducing parties to act clandestinely. However, just as with conspiracy to rob a bank, it is not the case that immunity from conspiracy prosecution arises if word leaks out or if others are alerted for this purpose (unless a party is withdrawing and offering to assist the government in the prosecution of other conspirators in exchange for a grant of immunity).

oligopolistic behavior is often regarded to be encompassed by the term, which seems to be used to describe the economic nature of the behavior rather than how it might be categorized under the law. The standard, general definition of collusion is that it is an agreement, adding that it may well be regarded as one undertaken for illegal purposes—which supplement would be redundant in the present context because price-fixing agreements are already considered to be illegal. In addition, collusion is often taken to denote secrecy, which would make it narrower than agreement.[17]

MEETING OF THE MINDS.—Meeting of the minds is a metaphorical phrase that directs attention to parties' subjective states (even if objectively determined). It readily covers behavior that is interdependent (on which more in a moment), such as the standard scenario in which firms in an oligopoly are able to coordinate their prices by understanding each other's thought processes, which forms the basis for predicting their reactions to different prices that each firm may charge. The term is used sufficiently often to have its own entry in dictionaries, where it is defined as a synonym for agreement or concord—which itself is defined as involving agreement or harmony, the latter being one of the terms used to define agreement. The phrase is also a legal term of art used in determining the existence of a contract, particularly under the subjective theory of contractual agreement.[18] And, as discussed in subsection 7.A.3, it is a concept that economists sometimes use in elaborating the notion of equilibrium in a noncooperative game.

EXPRESS.—Using ordinary definitions, an agreement would be express if it were directly, firmly, and explicitly stated. The term explicit (itself sometimes used in discussions of agreements prohibited by competition law) is a reasonably close synonym; it indicates an absence of

---

[17] It is ironic that, in describing oligopolistic behavior, the term collusion would be used in place of agreement to avoid the legal term that indicates illegality when the ordinary meaning of collusion is narrower than (a subset of) agreement. (The terms would be coincident if avoiding secrecy conferred immunity, as mentioned in the preceding note.)

[18] See *Black's Law Dictionary* (2009, 1072–73) and also http://www.legal-explanations .com/definitions/meeting-of-the-minds.htm (last accessed November 22, 2010): "The phrase 'Meeting of the mind' is used to represent the state of mind of the parties that the parties involved are thinking and understanding a situation, provision or stipulations etc [*sic*] in the correct and similar meaning."

vagueness or ambiguity. On one hand, this articulation of express agreement might include what some mean to exclude. In example 1 just above, for the interpretation with the two gas station owners, everything was explicit and unambiguous, even though many would not count it as an agreement, much less an express one.[19] On the other hand, if taken literally, then lawyered language, as discussed in example 2, would be sufficient to remove a wide range of activity from the category that few if any courts or commentators would in fact exonerate. One might also ask how much explicitness is required to be in this category. If the answer were functional, then an agreement would be express when what transpired was sufficient to produce oligopolistic coordination, that is, successful interdependent behavior.[20] If not, it would be necessary to specify what degree of precision was necessary but in a manner not tethered to the function of the communication: That is, some formalistic distinction would have to be delineated.

The adjective express seems to be used also (or instead) to refer to a communicative dimension, which would be more naturally indicated if the verb form were used (that is, if "express agreement among the parties" were taken as a shorthand for "an agreement among the parties that they expressed to each other"). However, in all variants and interpretations of the two previous examples—including those not generally regarded as involving express agreements—there was expression. The verb express is broad, not being limited to expressions in words and not specifying the nature of words, signs, or symbols that need to be involved. Because the notion that the definition of agreement should distinguish communications, either by mode or content, is central to many understandings of the agreement concept, it is explored at length, in chapter 3.

It is worth keeping in mind that, even if express (or, more fully, express agreement) is defined, the legal inquiry is not concluded because

---

[19] If the ground for distinction is that given in the next paragraph—perhaps interpreting express agreement as requiring words to be expressed—it is not clear that the situation changes, unless a sign indicating "$3.40" is deemed not to be words (just numerals), whereas a sign indicating "three dollars and forty cents" would count. See also the prior discussion of how adding details to the sign should be viewed as immaterial and the discussion in section 3.C on language.

[20] See the elaboration in section 3.A of functional equivalents regarding communication.

the legal category of agreement need not be coincident with one or any particular notion of express agreement. For example, as considered further momentarily, tacit agreements might also be included. Thus, one might grant that express agreements are, by definition, highly explicit and accordingly declare the use of lawyered language that communicates effectively to establish instead a tacit (but not an express) agreement, which in turn would be deemed to be sufficient for liability in the case of price fixing.

TACIT.—By contrast to the adjective express, the term tacit indicates the negation, so that a tacit agreement would be any agreement that is not an express agreement. More specifically, tacit is taken to refer to that which is implied or indicated, but not actually expressed. On reflection, this more direct definition of the term tacit does little to help pin down the boundary between tacit and express. In just about any setting involving possible communication, something must be conveyed if a mutual understanding is to be reached, but it is never the case that every conceivable ambiguity is excluded. Thus, if one is told that tacit and express agreements will be treated differently, one knows that a line will be drawn somewhere between zero and infinity on the communications spectrum, but the terms by themselves tell us little about where that boundary is located.

If agreements under Sherman Act Section 1, EU Article 101, or other jurisdictions' prohibitions must be express agreements, then express agreements need to be defined carefully in order to know what triggers liability. Tacit agreement might just be a convenient term to refer to those agreements not giving rise to liability. On the other hand, if it is agreements that give rise to liability, then tacit agreements would suffice because they are a type of agreement.[21] In that case, there would be no significance to the demarcation between express and tacit agreements, so this line-drawing difficulty would be moot. Nevertheless, if tacit as well as express agreements are covered by Section 1 or Article 101, certain narrow interpretations of the term agreement would be ruled out.

---

[21] Since many would take it to be an undisputed point of blackletter law that agreements trigger Section 1 and Article 101, to exclude tacit agreements would strain language. Consider proclaiming that a brown cow, a mere type of cow, is not a cow, perhaps after expounding on how the black-and-white cow is the quintessential cow.

INDEPENDENT.—The oft-used term independent is, unfortunately, one that has given rise to much confusion. For a long period, and still most of the time, its conventional usage in the present context tracks a standard definition—not looking to others for guidance in conduct, or not relying on others—a definition that can be juxtaposed with its opposite, interdependent, on which more in a moment. (Another standard definition, self-governing, allows the alternative and almost opposite meaning discussed in section C that leads to confusion because interdependent action, including highly express price-fixing agreements, can be understood as independent in this sense.)

Independent behavior—sometimes referred to as purely or entirely independent behavior for clarity—includes behavior by two or more parties that has no relationship whatsoever as well as behavior that has similarities yet is motivated by considerations that do not depend on others' reactions. The latter is of greater relevance for assessing horizontal agreements in competition law. When it begins to rain, two individuals might simultaneously raise and open their umbrellas, but each may not care at all about the other's actions. Moreover, this indifference may exist even if each sees the other or is able to infer what the other is going to do. Likewise, when the price of some input rises or falls (say, the price gasoline stations are charged for gasoline delivered to them in tank trucks), we would expect even perfect competitors to raise or reduce their prices accordingly. Each may be aware of the other's actions or be able to predict them, but those actions are not the explanation for why each adjusts its own retail price. Similarly, if industry demand shifts upward for some reason, competitive firms with rising marginal costs would all raise their prices and outputs. Each firm sells at the new market equilibrium price because that price indicates what the market will bear (not because of how a firm expects other firms to react to its own decisions), and each raises its output because this decision is profitable given the higher price.

There are some complications regarding this elaboration because perfect competitors, in responding to the prevailing market price, are implicitly responding to the behavior of their peers. If a firm noticed that for some reason all of its competitors raised their prices, the firm would find it profitable to raise its price as well, and likewise if they all lowered their prices. Nevertheless, the perfect competitor takes other firms' behavior (in particular, their prices) as given when deciding how it should behave.[22]

A further variation arises in the case in which a firm refuses to deal with a supplier, say, because the quality of its product is substandard. The firm predicts that its competitors will behave likewise, but this expectation is not the reason for its decision. Indeed, if some or all of its competitors purchased the deficient input, the firm would benefit from their divergent behavior. Thus, the firm's best choice is to desist regardless of what its competitors do. Its fate may not be entirely independent of competitors' behavior, but its decision in this case is.[23]

INTERDEPENDENT.—Conventional definitions focus on the possible meanings of the prefix "inter," which may then be combined with definitions of dependent, which refers to that which is determined or conditioned by another.[24] This prefix relevantly means between or among, reciprocal, or carried on between—all of which denote the linkages among parties, such as coordinating oligopolists.

Accordingly, interdependent behavior for present purposes is taken to refer to behavior that involves coordination with others.[25] Operators of

---

[22] Not only perfect competitors take other firms' behavior as given. For example, in Cournot interaction or Bertrand competition with differentiated products, firms take others' quantities or prices, respectively, as given, and the result is that prices are higher than under perfect competition. Hence, behavior that is independent in the sense described in the text is not necessarily perfectly competitive. For further exploration of this point and references, see note 16 in chapter 7 and also chapter 14. As will emerge, it is common for courts and commentators (especially legal commentators) to equate independent behavior and competitive behavior.

[23] This example captures the situation in *Theatre Enterprises*, discussed in subsection 4.B.1. One can also imagine variations in which pure independence no longer holds. For example, if competitors use the subpar input, a firm may want to emphasize the superiority of its own product in its marketing. In this case and others, there may be some interdependence, but it is not of the sort that raises the concerns addressed by competition law's regulation of horizontal agreements.

[24] Dependent may also be defined as subject to the jurisdiction of another, which corresponds to the alternative meaning of independent discussed below that produces confusion and thus is avoided here. In practice, usage of the term interdependence seems fairly uniform and has not, by itself, given rise to that problem.

[25] Although of little relevance in the present setting, interdependent behavior viewed more broadly need not be cooperative in this sense. In the examples in the text, drivers all hope to avoid collisions, individuals want to meet for lunch rather than fail to connect, and firms wish to maintain supracompetitive prices. But there are other possibilities, including

motor vehicles choosing whether to drive on the right or the left side of the road in a remote, unregulated area will make their choice in light of what they expect others to do. When meeting someone for lunch, a rendezvous point may have significance only because of where the other is expected to appear. Thus, parties may meet at the information booth at Grand Central Station not because they need any information but purely because it is an easily identified place at the station.[26] Note further that the thought process involved in such cases is iterative. One party is thinking about what the other is thinking; the second is thinking about what the first is thinking; each is aware that the other is thinking about what it is thinking; ad infinitum. This subjective state is commonly termed a meeting of the minds, noted just above. In game-theoretic parlance, the situation constitutes an equilibrium.

More relevant for present purposes is the situation in which firms coordinate not their driving or lunch dates but their marketplace behavior—notably, their prices. Specifically, we are interested in pricing behavior that takes into account how other firms are expected to react. The Initiator in example 1 first raised its price because it expected that the Responder would do likewise. If the Responder did not, the result of the price increase would merely be to lose business until the increase was rescinded. Additionally, once prices settled at $3.40, neither firm would cut its price, say, to $3.35 in attempt to steal business from its rival. This reluctance is not because stealing business at $3.35 would not be profitable. To the contrary, grabbing perhaps the entire market at a profit of $0.35 per unit would be more lucrative than taking half the

---

interdependent behavior that is rivalrous. Two race car drivers may adjust their positions on the track, the leader trying to block passage and the follower attempting to slip by. A baseball team may use a pinch hitter, and the opposing team may substitute pitchers, each hoping to gain an edge (in a zero-sum game). Firms trying to grab market share may devise new products or marketing campaigns hoping to take advantage of other firms' weaknesses or to catch them off guard. These situations involve interdependence because each player attempts to anticipate others' reactions, but unlike the examples in the text, the purpose is to outperform rivals rather than act harmoniously to everyone's mutual benefit. Instead of a meeting of the minds, players attempt a beating of the minds.

[26] And, as in one of Schelling's (1960, 54–57) famous examples, individuals might coordinate on such a meeting place without having specifically discussed it in advance. For present purposes, such discussion is immaterial; in either case, the decision to appear at the information booth at a given time is made because of expectations about each other's behavior.

market at a per unit profit of $0.40. Rather, each firm assumed that, if it did cut its price, its rival would quickly follow, rapidly enough that little would be gained in the interim—not enough to compensate for the fact that it would earn less profit going forward than if prices remained at $3.40. If either firm did not think this to be so, it would indeed cut its price.

In this standard coordinated oligopoly setting, in which firms succeed in raising prices to and maintaining them at a supracompetitive level, the thought process is much like that in the examples of driving and lunch dates. Each firm is thinking about what the other firm is thinking and how that firm will react; each recognizes that the other thinks similarly; and so forth. The firms' minds have met; they are in an equilibrium that is favorable (for them). Parties' mental states and behavior contrast with those in independent, competitive situations.[27]

Notice that, in all of these settings, there generally needs to be some flow of information. For example, for parties to meet for lunch, something must have happened to make them aware of each other's existence and their mutual desire to meet, and something more that leads each to think of a common place and time to meet.[28] In the oligopoly setting, more substantial information transmission and exchange are involved. Firms typically know much in common about their industry and about each other from a variety of sources including prior interactions. For a price increase to induce others to follow, the price increase must be ob-

----

[27] See also section 7.A, which elaborates on these ideas as they are developed more precisely in a game-theoretic formulation. In some cases of independent behavior, as previously noted, parties might be aware of what others are thinking, but because this awareness is incidental to their own behavior, the behavior is independent and their thought processes would not ordinarily be depicted as a meeting of the minds.

[28] In some of Schelling's famous examples, mentioned in note 26, some of this information is constructed by the parties, but they do know of each other, their desire to meet, and something about the meeting place and time. One could envision a blind date, but in that situation everything but the identity of the other party is known and there is some information even about that fact conveyed implicitly through intermediaries. A more extreme example (closer to choosing whether to drive on the left or right side of the road) would be where two individuals show up at a singles bar some evening. Here, the thought process has some parallels (people know that others are thinking similarly, which is why they expect some prospect of meeting someone at the bar); one might say that they have a probabilistic meeting with various individuals (the probability depending on the demographics of the jurisdiction, number of bars, and other factors).

served by the others. For cheating to be deterred, it must be observable
or capable of being inferred from other observable information.[29] In example 1, taking the interpretation involving two gas stations, they are
constantly sending their current price—and thus all price movements,
and failures to react—to each other. In the oligopoly setting, the concept of interdependence and the related notions of a meeting of the
minds or of an equilibrium in a game thus involve a fair amount of
communication. Nothing, however, has yet been said about what sorts
of communication are required for successful interdependence; presumably, the answer will depend on the context.

PARALLELISM, CONSCIOUS PARALLELISM.—These terms, frequently
used in discussions of oligopoly pricing in the competition law context,
unfortunately lend themselves to opposite meanings, referring to that
which is merely and purely independent (yet common) and that which is
interdependent. Beginning with the former, a range of independent yet
similar behavior, from two individuals raising their umbrellas when it
starts raining to cars moving in the same direction all driving on the
same side of the road to firms changing their sales prices in response to
changes in input prices, is described as parallel. In each instance, if the
relevant players are also aware of each other's behavior, it might be called
consciously parallel, even though it is independent. Highly interdependent behavior, such as successful oligopolistic price coordination, is also
parallel as well as consciously parallel. By itself, parallelism refers to that
which resembles or corresponds, which is consistent with purely independent behavior but does not rule out interdependent behavior. But
parallelism may also be defined as interdependent. In that sense, behavior exhibiting parallelism could not be independent. The pertinent
definition of parallel (as an adjective) is that which is similar or analogous—or interdependent—in tendency or development. This range of
definitions also reinforces this dual, opposed set of possibilities.

It would seem that adding the term conscious does not necessarily
do anything to move one from independent (if one starts there to begin
with) to interdependent, because conscious can variously be defined as
perceiving, apprehending, noticing, or having awareness, all of which

---

[29] Stigler (1964) presents the seminal statement, with subsequent development appearing,
for example, in Spence (1978) and Green and Porter (1984). See subsection 7.A.2.

suggest that, if the behavior is independent, the parties cannot be entirely isolated, but none of which indicates much more than that. (Strangers raising umbrellas may well be conscious of their parallel behavior.) Nevertheless, it seems as though commentators adding this adjective to parallelism often contemplate exactly that switch. Why add the adjective if no further refinement is intended? On the other hand, if adding an adjective, why employ one that is almost always redundant in context, if taken literally? Furthermore, if adding the adjective is done to indicate that interdependent rather than independent behavior is contemplated, can we then safely assume that all references to parallelism by itself refer to independent behavior? Apparently not.

Existing usage is especially problematic because often the immediate context (and lack of elaboration) does not remove potential ambiguity. Sometimes it is apparent that one or the other meaning must be intended—that may be the whole point of a passage—but to determine which meaning is correct requires broad inferences (for example, one interpretation might be inconsistent with later arguments) or, in some cases, guesswork. Furthermore, even when the intended message can be ascertained with reasonable confidence, the language may be quoted elsewhere with a different import. The most important instance of this problem involves interpretations of the U.S. Supreme Court's opinion in *Theatre Enterprises*. As elaborated in subsection 4.B.1, this opinion gave the term conscious parallelism its prominence in discussions of competition law, but there is serious irony and confusion since the Court clearly used the terms to refer to independent behavior, as distinguished from that which was coordinated in any way—precisely opposite to the just-described usage—which, to make matters worse, is sometimes used specifically to (mis)characterize *Theatre Enterprises*'s holding, as will be discussed.

To summarize, behavior exhibiting parallelism in many senses of the term excludes merely disparate, unrelated behavior, a type of independent behavior that is of no interest in examining possible price fixing. Ordinary competitive behavior is parallel in this sense of the term. And consciously parallel behavior, while adding another word, does not itself distinguish between independent and interdependent parallel behavior. However, both parallel and consciously parallel are sometimes used to refer to interdependent, as distinguished from independent, behavior.

COMPETITION.—The term competition does not figure as directly as the others in articulating the agreement requirement under Sherman Act Section 1 or EU Article 101. However, it often appears in discussions of the agreement requirement, so it is helpful to have likely meanings in mind. In general usage, the term is taken to refer to rivalrous interactions. This meaning is consistent with the particular application to the marketplace, one of the common domains of the term (that is, even outside competition law): the effort of two or more parties acting independently to secure the business of a third party by offering the most favorable terms. There exists a further, more precise notion of perfect textbook competition, an idea widely viewed as an abstraction that may be approached rather than actually observed.

Relating this definition to the foregoing discussion, behavior that is competitive matches well with that which is independent. Successful interdependent behavior in an oligopoly, producing a monopoly-like price, is widely regarded as exhibiting a lack of competition. The resulting price is described as supracompetitive, and behavior that facilitates such an outcome is described as anticompetitive or involving a suppression of competition. Of course, competition may not be completely eliminated—firms may still try to attract business through better service, for example. Nevertheless, crudely speaking, competition typically refers to independent behavior, and an absence (or limitation) of competition to interdependent behavior.

C. Commentators' Views

Courts and commentators have used varying numbers of categories, described using the terms just elaborated, to classify different situations with regard to the interaction among firms. The potential for confusion runs deep: The division between some categories is mysterious (see section A), different terms may be used to describe a given category, and, worst of all, a single term might be used to describe different (even mutually exclusive) categories. This section employs the clarifications in section B to describe commentators' views. It then discusses the most frequent and problematic of the terminological difficulties, the use of the term independent behavior to encompass the opposite category of interdependent behavior.

Most in the field recognize and purport to distinguish behavior that is purely independent (undertaken without regard to how others might react), behavior that is interdependent (undertaken in light of how others are expected to react), and behavior that is the product of an agreement, perhaps an express agreement. Importantly, the three types of behavior are not symmetric classifications; rather, there is a hierarchy. The first two categories, independent and interdependent, can be thought of as a mutually exclusive and exhaustive partition of possible behavior. That is, behavior is independent or it is not, and if it is not (but only if it is not), it is deemed to be interdependent. Within the category of interdependent behavior, that resulting from agreement, perhaps from express agreement, is typically taken to be a subset. The subset of interdependent behavior that is not deemed to result from express agreement is not ordinarily given its own name.

Using this taxonomy, it is possible to describe the range of commentators' views. Independent behavior—in the sense used here—is universally regarded as not constituting an agreement for purposes of competition law, regardless of how similar firms' independent behavior might be. That is, behavior must (at least) be interdependent.

The greater difficulty is in determining how the law subdivides this second category. Among modern commentators, there is little sympathy for the view that all interdependent behavior constitutes an agreement under competition law, which would render such subdivision unnecessary. Richard Posner's (1969, 2001) academic writing is the main exception.[30] For others, it is necessary to divide the category of interdependent behavior between that which is sufficient under Section 1 of the Sherman Act or Article 101 of the EU Treaty, for example, and that which is not. At various points below, it proves useful to avoid the usual terminology altogether and refer to the former category simply as be-

---

[30] Posner's (1969, 1562) introduction to his original article summarized his view as follows: "The heart of the suggested approach is a questioning of the prevailing view that monopoly pricing by oligopolists, when unaccompanied by any detectable acts of collusion, constitutes an economically and legally distinct problem requiring new doctrines and new remedies for its solution.... The employment of section 1 against purely tacit collusion would do no violence to the statutory language or purpose; and while difficult problems of proof and of remedy would be involved, I am not convinced that they would be insuperable." See also page 32 discussing Turner's views.

havior involving acts in the set X and the latter as in the set X'. That is, any acts or clusters of acts that are legally deemed to constitute an agreement compose set X, and all others, set X'.

Everyone concurs that express agreements are a subset of interdependent behavior that counts, that is, triggers liability. There is, however, little clear consensus on the boundaries of this subset. We know that it includes at least the canonical (one might say extreme) example of firms meeting in person, engaging in extensive, direct, and un-lawyered discussions, and coming together on an explicit plan of action that is encapsulated in a precise verbal formula such as may be contained in a fleshed-out written document signed by each party. But we also know that all who use the term express agreement would include within the category cases involving less, possibly far less, explicitness.

Moreover, it is uncertain whether, in addition to express agreements, perhaps others, notably tacit agreements, also suffice. As explained in section B, these sorts of questions are interrelated. For example, if express agreements are defined broadly, to include what others might deem to be tacit agreements, then express agreements might be viewed as exhausting the space of interdependent behavior that suffices (which would be true if the only other candidate behavior involves tacit agreements). Many, including the U.S. Supreme Court in both earlier decisions and its most recent ones (discussed in sections 4.A and 4.B), do in fact state that tacit agreements are sufficient, yet it is hard to know what to make of these proclamations given the great ambiguity of the terms.[31] Indeed, the examples in section A reveal how hard it is to distinguish clear, traditional express agreements from interdependence alone, so it should be all the more challenging to articulate an intermediate category, notably broader than express agreement but distinctly narrower than interdependence. This task is not aided by the general failure of courts and commentators to define any of these categories with even modest precision.

For purposes of the law, assuming that interdependent behavior is not deemed to be sufficient, it is necessary and sufficient to articulate a single further division. In subdividing interdependent behavior, there

---

[31] Hay (2006, 891–95) discusses the lack of clarity in courts' use of the term tacit agreement, and Kovacic (1993, 14–21) examines courts' varying usage of this term.

are various dimensions along which one might draw distinctions. One could look to parties' mental states, identifying various respects in which their minds have met, a concept that has roots in ordinary language (as mentioned), and also in Supreme Court opinions and conspiracy law more generally, as will be seen in chapter 4. Many modern commentators (legal scholars and economists) and some court opinions would instead draw lines based on the presence of communications, the modes of communications employed, or the types of information communicated,[32] a subject elaborated in chapter 3. It would also be possible to consider what sort of assurances or commitments, if any, have been conveyed.[33] Any of these or other features might be deemed to constitute the relevant boundaries, or they might be factors considered in defining such terms as express agreement.

Yet another way that one might attempt to draw the line is functionally, based not on what types of communication or other activities are employed but instead on whether those used in a particular setting are successful in producing oligopolistic coordination that leads to higher prices. This approach, however, essentially replicates the distinction between independent and interdependent behavior: Successful coordination is interdependent whereas failed coordination leaves the firms to go their own way, behaving as competitors.[34] Thus, if not all successful interdependent behavior is deemed to be sufficient to trigger liability,

---

[32] See, for example, Page (2009, 451–64), and Judge Posner's opinion in In re High Fructose Corn Syrup Antitrust Litigation, 295 F.3d 651, 654 (7th Cir. 2002): "This statutory language [of Sherman Act Section 1] is broad enough . . . to encompass a purely tacit agreement to fix prices, that is, an agreement made without any actual communication among the parties to the agreement. . . . Nevertheless, it is generally believed . . . that an express, manifested agreement, and thus an agreement involving actual, verbalized communication, must be proved in order for a price-fixing conspiracy to be actionable under the Sherman Act." Economists include Kühn (2001), advocating that liability for oligopoly pricing be based exclusively on the use of particular sorts of communication; Porter (2005, 147–48), suggesting a distinction between direct and indirect communication; and Whinston (2006, 20), referring to the law as prohibiting "talking" between firms. See also Motta (2007, 315) and note 6 in chapter 3, discussing Werden's views. Black (2005, 341) and Jones (1993, 276) offer similar depictions of the law in the European Union.

[33] Areeda and Hovenkamp are leading proponents of this view, as discussed in note 67 in chapter 7.

[34] Note that the text for convenience refers to unsuccessful (attempted) interdependent behavior as (de facto) independent.

this instrumental approach cannot be the basis for determining the legal boundary. The use of a substantially formal rather than purely functional inquiry, in turn, helps to explain why the two examples in section A, both involving successful interdependence, pose difficulties for conventional methods of categorization.

Finally, it is useful to offer a clarification regarding the fact that what is referred to throughout this book (and elsewhere) as interdependent behavior is sometimes described as independent behavior.[35] Naturally, this practice can be terribly confusing because it is so common to use the terms independent and interdependent to demarcate mutually exclusive categories of behavior. The intention behind this alternative usage of the term independent is clearest when the two terms are joined, such as by describing firms' decisions as interdependent yet independently determined.[36] The meaning seems to be that, although the behavior in question is indeed interdependent, it is determined by each firm on its own. That is, however interdependent and perfectly aligned may be the firms' thought processes in deciding what prices to charge, at the end of the day each firm has chosen the price that it deems to be in its own best interest, all things (including other firms' reactions) considered.

This clarification is helpful and may not cause too much befuddlement or misdirection when the terms independent and interdependent are combined in the manner just described. However, this is not always the case, making it hard for a reader to know when "independent" means purely independent, and when it also includes the opposite of

---

[35] To this author's knowledge, Chamberlin (1929, 65, 83) is the first to use the term independent to refer to interdependent behavior in the oligopoly context.

[36] See, for example, Areeda and Hovenkamp (2003, 207): "In short, each firm is aware of its impact upon the others. Though each may independently decide upon its own course of action, any rational decision must take into account the anticipated reaction of the other two firms. Whenever rational decision making requires an estimate of the impact of any decision on the remaining firms and an estimate of their response, decisions are said to be 'interdependent.' Because of their mutual awareness, oligopolists' decisions may be interdependent although arrived at independently." But in fact the stand-alone usage of "independent" in contexts in which it appears to mean purely independent and competitive is sometimes interpreted as encompassing interdependent oligopolistic behavior. Posner (2001, 100) laments that "[m]ost courts mistakenly regard tacitly collusive behavior as independent" in applying *Monsanto*'s test (which is discussed in subsection 4.B.2).

purely independent. Interdependent seems to be a much better short-hand for "interdependent yet independently determined" than does independent, especially given the back and forth information flows and behaviors as well as the interconnected thought processes, not to mention that the term independent is also being used to refer to the distinct type of behavior described earlier.[37] Of course, when the term independent is clearly defined and used only in one sense, typically that followed here, confusion does not arise.[38]

There is also a deeper problem that remains despite this semantic clarification. Whether decisions are independent in the alternative sense just described is generally proposed as a means of distinguishing between interdependent behavior that does involve express (or some other legally sufficient sort of) agreement and interdependent behavior that does not. But the proffered distinction is illusory. The notion advanced is that, in the case of so-called independent interdependence, each firm ultimately makes its own decision based on its own calculation of interests, however much its calculations reflect expectations of other firms' reactions. And, so the argument goes, this fact renders the behavior plainly legal, for the law is deemed to permit independent actions, as we all know, and the permitted independent actions are taken under this view to include highly interdependent ones, as long as each firm ultimately makes its own decision at the end of the day.

The sophistry of this chain of reasoning is made obvious by recognizing that this depiction is equally apt in the case of an express price-fixing agreement once one recalls that such agreements are legally void ab initio. Even if the price-fixing agreement is in writing, signed in blood, and attested to by reliable witnesses, it provides absolutely no basis for legal enforcement. Hence, when a firm decides whether or not

---

[37] It is interesting to speculate on why this usage of the term independent has emerged despite the confusion it creates. As will be discussed in section 4.B, numerous U.S. Supreme Court cases have stated that behavior that is "independent" does not give rise to liability (and is insufficient to survive defendants' motion for summary judgment, and so forth). Accordingly, if the word independent can successfully be attached to a type of behavior that a party, a commentator, or a court wishes to exonerate, victory would appear to follow automatically.

[38] For example, Turner (1962, 681) refers to "'independent' decision [as] a decision that would have been taken regardless of what competitors decided to do."

to adhere to such an express agreement, it accords no weight whatsoever to being legally bound (it isn't). It does, to be sure, take into account the consequences of defection by, say, lowering its price. That is, it considers that other firms may react by matching its price cut or otherwise administering punishment, which reaction may render the decision to deviate unprofitable. But this characterization is likewise true of interdependent behavior more generally. In either case—that is, with or without an express agreement—the firm's decision is, in the final analysis, entirely its own (presumably to be made by a calculation of its own best interest). That is, all firms' decisions in the relevant settings are independent under the proffered usage. Indeed, under this interpretation, a victim's decision at gunpoint to hand a wallet to a mugger is aptly described as independent: It is in the victim's best interest, taking into account the mugger's possible reaction if the wallet is instead withheld.[39] This simple observation is not meant to suggest that there cannot exist other distinctions within the category of interdependent behavior, but only to indicate that the broadened notion of independence under consideration is not one of them, once legally enforceable agreements are off the table.[40]

---

[39] Nor would this strained usage be rendered natural if the attacker was silent, leaving implicit, from the act of pulling the gun, the threat "your money or your life," and the victim likewise merely handed over the wallet without any utterance of submission.

[40] This lack of conceptual distinction within the category of interdependent behavior is mirrored in the discussion of game-theoretic terminology, as discussed in subsection 7.A.1.

3

Communications

In determining what sort of interaction is sufficient to trigger liability under Sherman Act Section 1, EU Article 101, or other such provisions, many focus on the nature of communications among the firms, as mentioned just above.[1] The present chapter examines reliance on communications as a means of articulating a subdivision within interdependent behavior and, relatedly, of attempting to give content to the notion of an express agreement. The reader should keep in mind that, as chapters 4 and 5 will indicate, it is unclear the extent to which such an approach is supported by statutory provisions, higher court interpretations, or lower court practice. Also, it should be noted that most of the analysis of the legal requirement in this book does not depend on the boundary between agreements and nonagreements being defined by reference to communications. (As a final alert to the reader, communications are discussed as well in subsection 7.B.2, which further addresses the ways that they can facilitate oligopolistic coordination. It is explained there that this feature of communications is largely distinct from how they might relate to the definition of agreement, the focus of the current chapter.)

The use of a communications requirement in formulating the legal test might be implicit, so that, in determining whether an express agreement (or whatever else might be demanded) exists, the factual inquiry might pay significant attention to communications. Alternatively, a test could be explicit, inquiring directly whether particular modes of communication were employed (face-to-face discussions? writings? only public announcements?) or what types of information were transmitted

---

[1] See the sources cited in note 32 in chapter 2.

(past prices? future prices? assurances?); all manner of combinations are likewise possible. Furthermore, the existence of requisite communications might be proved directly or inferred from other circumstances.

Additional questions are raised by the relationship, or lack thereof, between communications and agreement. Recall that a standard definition of agreement considers whether parties' minds have met, whereas examining communications may be more informative about how such a meeting of minds came about, if indeed one did. Of course, a complete disjunction is hardly necessary. Communications might be a basis for inferring the existence of an understanding, or agreement may by stipulation be deemed to constitute certain types of communication (for example, an exchange of verbal promises).

Although communications are the focus in commentary and some court opinions, it is largely taken for granted what the notion of communication means and what sorts of communication count. This chapter begins by showing that these suppositions are deeply problematic. In any event, there is substantial sentiment for condemning certain sorts of communications because they undesirably facilitate coordinated oligopolistic pricing, without regard to the precise relationship between the communications and some particular notion of agreement. This approach is elaborated next. Finally, in light of the attention devoted to communications, it seems appropriate to examine common but often implicit assumptions about the nature of human expression and interpretation. Accordingly, a final section briefly considers some pertinent ideas from studies of language in a variety of disciplines.

A. Nature of Communications

Communication generally refers to a process by which information is exchanged between individuals through some common system of symbols, signs, or behavior. The concept is clearly a broad one, including, for example, communication between insects using pheromones.[2] More

---

[2] Lest the reader think this example farfetched, the dictionary used throughout (see note 12 in chapter 2) presents this as its sole illustration of the just-stated definition of communication.

importantly, it clearly encompasses all variants of the two examples in section 2.A as well as generic versions of oligopolistic price coordination because pricing moves constitute behavior and, even in the absence of advance announcements through press conferences, are ordinarily conveyed through some sort of sign or symbol. In particular contexts, the intended mode may be more specific. For example, if one asks whether a communication has been received from Smith, it may be clear that the questioner has in mind a letter, a phone call, or perhaps an email or text message. By contrast, on a submarine or ship, especially in the past, Morse code or signal flags may have been meant, and a baseball pitcher or batter would be referring to hand signals from the catcher or third base coach, respectively. In the American Revolution, the most famous communication involved two lanterns in Boston's Old North Church.

The standard definition of communication and this range of examples indicate that making communications the prerequisite to triggering liability is tantamount to covering all interdependent behavior, certainly including coordinated oligopoly pricing—and seemingly much more unless it is further required that the communications be successful in producing supracompetitive prices. Yet those invoking a communications requirement seem to believe that it involves a significant limitation, selecting only a subset of interdependent behavior.

One possibility is that only certain communications—those in some set X—count. Communications might be limited by mode: Face-to-face meetings, letters, phone calls, and emails matter, whereas hand or smoke signals—those in X'—do not.[3] Or they might be limited by content: Future prices may be a forbidden subject whereas present prices would be permissible; assurances might be prohibited whereas declarations of intentions or predictions would be allowed. Or they might be limited by the setting: Statements in smoke-filled hotel rooms could be prosecuted whereas public announcements would be tolerated; permissible methods of price announcements may be more circumscribed

---

[3] To remind, for convenience and because it seems in accord with what most have in mind, this book uses the language of communications when referring to the sorts of acts that are in the sets X and X'. The analysis that makes reference to these sets, however, does not depend on this interpretation. Rather, the set X includes all acts or combinations of acts of whatever sort that are deemed to constitute an agreement, and the set X' includes all others.

when there are a few large buyers who occasionally place large orders than when there are significant numbers of small purchasers.

Some combination of these sorts of prohibitions and permissions often seems to be contemplated, but the basis for singling out some types while excluding others generally is unspecified and the rationale is hardly self-evident.[4] Regardless of the justification, it is not apparent even approximately where the division is thought to lie. The difficulty in articulating such a classification can be understood by reference to the flexibility and substitutability of modes of communication (on which, more in section C on language). If one prohibits talking, individuals can write. If writing is unavailable, there are hand signals, even full sign languages. The parties in question, firms competing in an industry, may know each other well and interact over extended periods of time, allowing for the development of effective means of communication. They have strong incentives to find some way to communicate and may do so if any channels are left open.

To help understand this challenge, consider the problem of functional equivalents. One option is to limit the triggering category X to a prespecified list of modes, content, or various combinations, meaning that there will inevitably exist fairly close functional equivalents that are omitted. This approach invites circumvention.[5] On the other hand, if functional equivalents are included, then there is no real limitation. After all, the function in question is to communicate sufficiently well to accomplish successful interdependent behavior. Thus, when effective interdependence is present, the function has been served and liability would be triggered. A functional approach therefore implies no limit to the inclusion of all successful interdependent oligopolistic behavior, which is contrary to the apparent intention of those who would impose a communications requirement.[6]

---

[4] The possible policy basis for such a demarcation is the subject of part III of the book, and it is discussed with regard to the definitional problem in section 16.A.

[5] If the list is sufficiently inclusive, circumvention may be difficult, but the result would be little different from the inclusion of functional equivalents. Also, the rationale for such a list is difficult to imagine. For example, if English, French, and even American Sign Language are on the prohibited list, why bother excluding languages with smaller vocabularies or less developed systems of hand signals? Or if winks, nods, smiles, intonations, and hand signals are on the list, what would be gained by excluding grunts?

[6] To illustrate the resulting tension, consider Werden's (2004, 780) views. He concludes that there must be "some evidence of communications of some kind among the defendants

Requiring that certain modes of communication have been employed or that certain messages have been sent also creates serious proof problems if inferences are allowed to be based on circumstantial evidence.[7] To take a far-fetched but logically apt example, suppose that two individuals are accused of conspiracy to rob a bank. The bank's videotapes reveal tight teamwork, but no words are recorded. How could a prosecutor establish the mode of communication at the planning stage? (Can we infer that they used telephones or face-to-face meetings rather than something else?) Or what was communicated? (Which details? In what language—say, mere suggestions of possibilities or a commitment to a particular plan?) In the absence of smoking-gun evidence—not of successfully coordinated interdependent behavior, which is obvious, but of whether this result came about through at least some communications in set X and not solely through others in set X'—how is this determination possible?[8] This obstacle, which seems potentially greater with oligopolistic behavior than with bank robbery, has largely been ignored, perhaps because writers imagine that all that must be inferred is the use of some sort of communication. But we have seen that this route, although coherent, is tantamount to covering all successful interdependent behavior (or more).

Focusing on only a limited subset of communications might be justified in other ways. First, communications may be examined not because

---

through which an agreement could have been negotiated." Although "communications of some kind" is all-encompassing, he restates this (using the phrase "[i]n other words") as requiring that evidence must support a "spoken agreement." Ibid. This, in turn, seems to exclude exchanges by letters or email, among other things. However, he had previously stated that "[a] 'spoken agreement' results from communications using anything akin to language . . . ." Ibid. (735). He notes that this can include "winks, nods, and the like," that "the law does not require the exchange of explicit mutual assurances," and thus that "there are no legally important distinctions among essentially linguistic means of communication." Ibid. He nevertheless distinguishes and thus excludes "communications purely in the form of marketplace actions," granting that such is within the meaning of the term communications. Ibid. Such a distinction may be rationalized under a result-oriented approach that views communications as facilitating practices, which is discussed here at the end of section B, but it is hard to make sense of these views as an attempt to define the terms in question so as to articulate what constitutes an agreement. See also note 67 in chapter 7, discussing Areeda and Hovenkamp's requirement that interdependence be supplemented by some evidence of commitment.

   [7] For elaboration, see chapters 6 and 17.

   [8] As explained in subsection 4.A.2, conspiracy law in the United States does not require such determinations; it is blackletter law that express agreement is not required.

they have any significance in their own right but instead because they may be a means of determining whether interdependence is likely to have occurred, as explored in section 11.C. All manner of evidence can be helpful, particularly in settings where interdependence is difficult to ascertain directly. For this purpose, some sorts of communication are more probative than others. For example, a seller's quoting a price to a buyer is a form of communication, and one that, depending on the setting, has a varying probability of reaching competing sellers, which probability the particular seller likely knows. But such price transmission occurs in some fashion in all sales transactions and hence cannot be probative of interdependence; therefore, it is uninformative, beyond reaffirming the existence of business activity.[9] On the other hand, a price planning session among competitors is highly probative of interdependence because it serves few other functions.

Second, deterring certain types of communication may be more or less costly. Taking the preceding examples, because sellers must eventually communicate a price at which they are willing to sell to buyers, it would be absurd to penalize such behavior in and of itself, whereas there may be little risk of social loss in prohibiting firms from meeting to discuss future pricing policy. This distinction is particularly important if communications are not considered as constitutive of agreement or as a basis for inferring one, which has been the focus thus far, but rather as a direct basis for liability, the subject of the next section.

B. Communications as Facilitating Practices

To the extent that liability comes to depend on the presence of certain types of communication, the prohibition might be viewed as applying to those forms of communication rather than to price fixing itself. Some commentators make this connection explicit.[10] Nor is the approach

---

[9] Other forms of price transmission, such as gasoline stations posting prices on signs, may be more or less necessary on other grounds (or may be subject to varying extrinsic legal requirements), so sometimes certain inferences about interdependence might be possible.

[10] See, for example, Areeda and Hovenkamp (2003, ¶¶1407, 1435, 1436); Carlton, Gertner, and Rosenfield (1997); DeSanti and Nagata (1994); and Kühn (2001, 180): "Enforcing primarily against such 'secondary' activities or 'facilitating practices' may then be a much more powerful enforcement strategy than an attempt to infer behaviour directly."

doctrinally radical. It is well established that agreements which facilitate price fixing but do not themselves constitute price fixing may nevertheless be violations.[11] For example, Sherman Act Section 1 prohibits not just price fixing but all agreements that unreasonably restrain trade. Thus, if an agreement facilitates price fixing (and has no important redeeming virtues), it will be condemned.[12] Accordingly, it seems unsurprising that types of communication that serve primarily to assist coordinated oligopolistic pricing would be regarded to be prohibited.

Furthermore, this perspective makes the fixation on communications easier to understand: If certain communications are separately prohibited as facilitating practices, it is important to ascertain their existence. The inability to sort out the relationship between communications and concepts of agreement emphasized in the preceding section then seems less problematic.[13] All that is necessary is knowledge of which communications are targeted. Although determining this set is no easy task, as already suggested, no formal demarcation is necessary. Instead, the analysis would be functional, involving a determination of the competitive consequences, without regard to how the behavior in question might linguistically be categorized.

Two features of this approach warrant emphasis. First, its relationship to the breadth of the direct prohibition on price fixing should be explored. If successful interdependent behavior leading to supracom-

---

The activities that seem to be most closely associated with collusion tend to centre around communication."

[11] Section 10.C further examines facilitating practices more generally, both as acts that might be prohibited and as possible bases for inferences about coordinated behavior with regard to pricing.

[12] Aspects of this position find support in cases holding illegal a variety of practices, including American Column & Lumber Co. v. United States, 257 U.S. 377 (1921), condemning the exchange of detailed pricing information through a trade association; United States v. Container Corp. of America, 393 U.S. 333 (1969), finding illegal telephone verification of competitors' price quotes on particular transactions; National Society of Professional Engineers v. United States, 435 U.S. 679 (1978), striking down an agreement to refrain from price negotiations until a particular engineer is selected; and Catalano, Inc. v. Target Sales, Inc., 446 U.S. 643 (1980), forbidding an agreement not to offer credit to buyers.

[13] Taken to the limit, this notion could be viewed as rendering the question irrelevant. Doubts, however, are raised in the text to follow as well as in section 5.D (on determining damages attributable to illegal as distinguished from legal behavior).

petitive pricing is deemed an illegal agreement, then the separate attack on communications as facilitating practices is less important. It is not entirely unimportant because it may not always be possible to prove interdependence even when it exists and because communications may be designed to elevate prices but fail. Regarding the latter, just as it is often sensible to punish attempts as distinct from completed offenses in other contexts,[14] so it might be good policy to attack certain types of communications directly.[15] Unless most interdependent behavior is difficult to identify while prohibited communications are easy to detect, however, it does not seem that this sort of attack on facilitating practices should be the core solution to the problem of coordinated oligopolistic price elevation.

Most who advance a prohibition on communications as facilitating practices, however, do not regard successful interdependent pricing behavior to be illegal. If coordinated oligopolistic activity is by itself lawful, it seems all the more important to attack practices that facilitate it, and this need is an important justification offered for the approach. Note, however, that there is a certain irony involved: Aiding and abetting is heavily punished, but undertaking the act one is trying to facilitate is freely permitted if such aids are unnecessary or cannot be proved to have been employed. This tension is explored further in chapters 6 and 17.

Second, in the case in which successful interdependence is not, without more, deemed to be an agreement, it is worth reflecting on the implication of the agreement requirement for the posited prohibition of certain communications. If manifest interdependence is not in itself an

---

[14] See Shavell (1990). Liability for attempts at price fixing is discussed in section 12.B.

[15] This approach, however, is not without costs. Importantly, if many forms of communication that facilitate coordinated oligopoly pricing also have legitimate uses in other instances (and, moreover, the maintained assumption of the present argument is that it is difficult to tell whether such communication really is facilitating oligopoly pricing), there may be significant costs to a separate prohibition on communications. The easiest cases for independent liability would be activities such as secret meetings that have little procompetitive justification. The risks escalate, however, when their existence is demonstrated not by smoking-gun evidence but by inferences from behavior that, in isolation, is more innocuous or ambiguous. Section 18.C further discusses the relationship between liability for coordinated price elevation and for facilitating practices.

agreement, what is the basis for finding an agreement regarding facilitating practices, namely, communications themselves? Many commentators take the answer to be sufficiently self-evident as to require no explanation.[16] But this is hardly the case.[17]

It is difficult to untangle this question in the absence of any clear sense of what constitutes an agreement. To focus the immediate inquiry, we might hold constant the legal meaning of agreement (whatever that may be) when considering both coordinated oligopolistic pricing and the communications on which there is posited to be an agreement. To do this, let us derive guidance from examples like those in section 2.A. In the first example, consider the interpretation under which two gas stations signal their prices to each other iteratively using price signs. We are supposing for present purposes that this process and result do not constitute an agreement. The question, then, is why conducting a discussion in a hotel room is itself an agreement. There is interdependent behavior: What one party says at the meeting takes into account what others have said and how others are expected to react. But such interdependence, we are supposing, is not enough. In addition, the discussion may reach a successful conclusion. But so did the gas stations' price signaling exchange, and we are assuming that this too is insufficient.[18]

---

[16] See, for example, Areeda and Hovenkamp (2003, 6, 24–25, 54), whose views are further discussed in note 18.

[17] Interestingly—and, many commentators would assert, incorrectly—the FTC lost a case, E.I. du Pont de Nemours & Company v. Federal Trade Commission, 729 F.2d 128 (2nd Cir. 1984), in which it argued that various facilitating practices that may have been adopted unilaterally in an oligopolistic industry should be reached by Section 5 of the Federal Trade Commission Act, which statute does not require an agreement. See Baker (1993, 210–15) and Posner (2001, 98), both criticizing *du Pont*, and Turner (1962, 682), who stated two decades prior to *du Pont* that "I have little doubt that an FTC decision condemning as an 'unfair method of competition' any of the conduct which I have suggested be condemned [that facilitates oligopoly pricing but may involve no agreement] would, assuming an adequate statement of reasons, be readily upheld by the Supreme Court."

[18] To illustrate the difficulty, consider the stance of Areeda and Hovenkamp. On one hand, they argue that interdependent oligopoly pricing behavior is not an agreement, as they would define it, because firms may well be willing to risk price announcements or moves that can quickly be rescinded without advance commitments from their rivals. Areeda and Hovenkamp (2003, 22, 96). On the other hand, they also argue that meetings themselves, and the willingness to attend such meetings, are agreements. Ibid. (25). But they do not attempt to explain (which would seem difficult, to say the least) why a firm willing to risk a price move

In response, some who advance the view under consideration suggest that an agreement can be found in the willingness to attend a meeting in a hotel room.[19] But that simply moves the question back a stage. For example, Initiator emails Responder, "I think it would be a good idea to talk about prices next Wednesday at 7 p.m. I'll rent a room at the Stardust Motel and leave my room number at the reception desk. I'm not agreeing to anything, mind you, not even to meet. But I'll be there. P.S.: Don't reply to this message." Responder (not using "reply" but sending a separate message), "I'll be at the Stardust next Thursday at 8 p.m." Etc. (They ultimately settle on Thursday at 7:30 p.m.) If the price signaling game with unilateral declarations is not an agreement, it is hard to see why iterating to a common meeting time (rather than to a common selling price) is.[20] Of course, it is quite easy to characterize the price discussion meeting as involving an agreement as well as the

---

without an advance assurance would be unwilling to risk talking and listening at a meeting without advance assurances about how others would respond to various proposals and other remarks. If interdependent pricing decisions are deemed to be unilateral because each firm, at the end of the day, makes its own decisions, why are meeting attendance and speaking any different as long as each retains control of its own voice? Surely it is in every firm's interest to attend, to listen, to think, and even to take the risk of saying something that might produce successful oligopolistic coordination. Compare ibid. (27–28), offering as a "simple[] justification for finding an agreement"—regarding telephone calls in United States v. Container Corp. of America, 393 U.S. 33 (1969), in which competing firms verified price quotes to buyers—that the calls involved "consensual and collaborative activity" so that "[n]othing more is needed"; concluding that "[t]he respondent forms an agreement to give information to its interrogator when it answers the question"; ignoring that elsewhere they repeatedly insist that matching a leader's price increase and all manner of other consensual and collaborative, that is, interdependent activity does not constitute an agreement (see also page 81 in chapter 4 for further discussion of this aspect of *Container*); and ibid. (265), stating that, "[m]oreover, the requisite conspiracy can be found when several firms take active steps to exchange *unilaterally* adopted manuals with each other" (emphasis added)—despite insisting that so-called unilateral adoption of each other's suggested prices cannot be deemed a conspiracy.

[19] See, for example, Areeda and Hovenkamp (2003, 29, 34, 36, 120, 155). Likewise, when engaging in direct discussions, one can ask whether the firms' representatives need any agreement to speak in the same language. (Consider even the case where all are fluent in more than one common language.) It is easy to answer this question affirmatively, but once again by treating successful interdependent interaction as agreement. See also the discussion in section C on the use of common language.

[20] One could assert that they agreed to send the emails, but the same question arises, and the argument is even more attenuated.

hypothesized exchange to arrange the meeting, but the present discussion is supposing that we have a narrow definition of agreement that excludes even highly coordinated interdependent behavior.

One answer to this challenge is simply to define agreement, by stipulation, as including the meeting but not the meeting's outcome.[21] This conclusory approach works mechanically, but it eliminates the notion that some concept of agreement embodied in various statutory provisions is doing any of the work.

Another approach is more frank but perhaps less satisfactory. One could admit that all are agreements and then assert further that some arrangements are prohibited and others allowed. Doctrinally, under Sherman Act Section 1's rule of reason, one would say that some are and others are not unreasonable restraints of trade. However, the rule-of-reason test asks whether the restraint in question promotes or suppresses competition.[22] Thus, implicitly, the approach amounts to asserting that successfully charging elevated oligopoly prices rather than competitive ones is promoting competition, or at least is competitively benign, rather than suppressing competition, whereas talking or meeting constitutes suppression of competition—indeed, precisely because it makes more likely the oligopolistic price elevation that was just stipulated not to involve a suppression of competition.

This juxtaposition, it should be recognized, really just restates the core idea behind approaches that exonerate successful interdependent pricing but seek to capture various means that facilitate it. If a necessary

---

[21] Areeda and Hovenkamp (2003, 269, 272), despite devoting much of volume 6 of their treatise to the elaboration of the agreement requirement and what they regard to be its implications (interdependent oligopolistic pricing by itself is not an agreement, but engaging in communications often is), also offer occasional remarks indicating that they endorse a result-oriented approach to the interpretation of the term agreement. See also ibid. (292–93), expressing reservations regarding liability for unilaterally adopted facilitating practices, but not seeing these concerns as sufficient to deny liability under Section 5 of the FTC Act, under which there are no private suits, treble damages, or criminal penalties; yet implicitly limiting their reluctance to practices ordinarily discussed under the rubric of facilitating practices, which do not include communications that facilitate coordinated oligopolistic price elevation. Turner (1962, 673–78), as mentioned in section 2.B, is willing to view interdependent oligopoly pricing as an agreement yet not condemn it, and he is also willing to condemn certain facilitating practices in the absence of an agreement.

[22] See Chicago Board of Trade v. United States, 246 U.S. 231, 238 (1918), and National Society of Professional Engineers v. United States, 435 U.S. 679, 690–91, 693–96 (1978).

condition for liability is the existence of certain sorts of communication, then there is an important sense in which naked price fixing is not per se illegal, as blackletter law consistently holds. Indeed, the opposite is the case: Truly naked price fixing is per se legal. Illegality flows from acts that clothe it using certain types of communication.[23]

The present section is meant to elucidate the view that certain communications should be prohibited as illegal agreements to engage in facilitating practices even though that which is facilitated—coordinated oligopoly pricing—is not in itself deemed to be illegal because no agreement is said to exist. In particular, the point is to state the doctrinal structure of the idea and to relate it to the agreement concept as applied to price fixing itself. Whether one or another approach, no matter how formalistically congenial or strained, is superior in advancing social welfare or some other objective is not under consideration at this point, but is deferred to parts II and III of the book.

C. Remarks on Language

Section A emphasizes a broad view of the concept of communication as well as the challenge posed by functional equivalents that underlines the difficulty of disrupting effective information transmission through the regulation of some forms of communication but not others. These ideas are reinforced by a wide range of scholarship on a number of subjects and from a variety of disciplinary perspectives, including anthropology, evolution, linguistics, philosophy of language, and sign language studies.[24] Philosophers of language, linguists, and social and natural scientists with similar interests debate many issues, but it seems

---

[23] Put another way, price fixing is per se legal, but facilitated price fixing is illegal (illegal per se for certain forms of communication that facilitate price fixing, but subject to a rule of reason for many other types of facilitation). A semantic response would be to state that only the facilitated version is really "price fixing." However, that term is not in the leading statutes. Moreover, its meaning must then be ascertained, which begs the question. (Interestingly, a dictionary definition of price fixing is the setting of prices artificially, contrary to free market operations, which definition itself encompasses successful interdependent price elevation, keeping in mind that a free market is defined as one that operates competitively, a term discussed in section 2.B.)

[24] See Bonvillain (2003), Corballis (2003), Fisher and Marcus (2006), Hauser, Chomsky, and Fitch (2002), Jackendoff (2002), and Pinker (1994, 2007).

uncontroversial that language and communication are ultimately taken to constitute an intersubjective phenomenon in which what counts is the ability to transmit thoughts through whatever means (broadly, symbols) are successful.[25]

Consider a number of features that seem common in human language. In ordinary, unregulated interactions, there exists a variety of modes of expression, of which words are only one. Others include behavior, facial expressions, body language, and tone. Language is seen by many as having gestural origins, partly evidenced by other primates' use of gestures,[26] and these nonverbal channels remain an important component of human expression today. An instructive example is provided by sign languages, whose richness approaches that of spoken languages.[27] Note that some of these features suggest that face-to-face interchanges allow for richer communication whereas other aspects (including notably behavior) may require no direct contact at all.

Another trait of communication is its symbolic nature, and, in both elaborate modern human languages and other forms of expression, most of the symbols are arbitrary.[28] Although written/spoken languages and sign languages all have similar grammars, each may employ its own particular words or signs to represent various content. Accordingly, it is unclear the extent to which prohibiting certain magic words (like agreement, promise, assurance, or commitment) or even entire forms of speech or writing would inhibit effective communication.[29]

---

[25] Hauser's (1996, 7) table offers a sampling of definitions of communication in different fields.

[26] See, for example, Corballis (2003, 203), noting further that "[n]early all [such gestures] included reference to another individual, usually in a way that invited reciprocation." In addition to what develops naturally, each species of great ape "has been taught to communicate quite well using visual and manual signals. . . . [T]he bonobo Kanzi[] has invented gestures to add to the repertoire . . . ." Ibid. (204).

[27] Corballis (2003, 208) explains that American Sign Language "incorporates such features as tense and mood[; at] Gallaudet University, . . . students learn all the usual subjects, even poetry, without a word being spoken." (Interestingly, Darwin suggested that the main advantage of spoken language was that it freed individuals' hands. Ibid. (213).)

[28] See, for example, Bonvillain (2003, 34–35), discussing sign language. This trait is related to the notion in the economic theory of "cheap talk" that there is an inessential multiplicity of equilibria because there is an infinite variety of ways of signaling; all that is required is that the parties employ some common system. See, for example, Crawford (1998, 289).

[29] This reservation is not to suggest that all methods of communication are perfect substi-

Additional features of human language compound the challenge. Words or other symbols can be recombined to produce countless messages that a receiver can readily understand even though the combination has never been experienced previously.[30] Strangers can converse without any prior agreement and, especially if they have similar backgrounds, can understand each other readily.[31] It is also a familiar feature of written and spoken languages that messages, even central ones, are sent indirectly, requiring the receiver to read between the lines.[32] Steven Pinker (2007, 22, ch. 8) offers a variety of colorful examples indicating how frequent and widespread this phenomenon is, and he points out that indirection is often used precisely when there is legal regulation— for example, bribes and threats may be communicated through euphemisms or innuendo.[33] Although in these instances the meaning is often crystal clear to the parties and to observers despite the message being implicit, in other cases outsiders to a language community may find it difficult to recognize aspects of communication that are taken for granted by insiders.[34]

Even worse for attempts at crafting language regulation is the fact that language evolves readily and functionally to meet individuals' needs. The underlying structures (aspects of grammar, the combinatoric

---

tutes. As mentioned in the text, disallowing face-to-face (or equivalent) encounters may reduce the ability to convey certain nuance through gestures, although the importance of these modes in oligopolistic interaction is unclear. (One might have thought that these methods mattered most in settings such as early-stage courtship; however, the rapid and successful evolution of Internet matchmaking, in which electronic written communication dominates, provides evidence, supplementing that in the text to follow, of the ability of language to evolve functionally even when subject to significant constraints.)

[30] See Hauser (1996, 38), Hauser, Chomsky, and Fitch (2002, 1571, 1573), Jackendoff (2002, xiv), and Wade (2006, 38).

[31] See Fisher and Marcus (2006, 10).

[32] "In everyday life we anticipate our interlocutor's ability to listen between the lines and slip in requests and offers that we feel we can't blurt out directly." Pinker (2007, 22).

[33] Pinker explains that this method is also common in dating, particularly with regard to sexual suggestiveness.

[34] For example, misunderstandings in interpreting nonverbal behavior can be produced by cultural diversity. See Bonvillain (2003). Furthermore, it was only after extensive study of sign languages that scholars eventually discovered that the height of a sign for perceived motion might reveal signer perspective. See Fischer and Siple (1990, 1, 3).

quality) are innate in humans[35] and give language great flexibility in overcoming incompleteness; language is dynamic and adaptive.[36] Shared meanings emerge within groups that need to interact.[37] Powerful evidence for these features is offered by observed instances in which elaborate languages spontaneously emerged. Thus, when two groups with no common language are combined, pidgins (simplified speech often drawn from both languages) readily arise; the next generation of such groups may transform this base into a full-blown language, referred to as a creole.[38] A similar process is widely observed among the deaf.[39] Deaf children (even in their early years) develop their own sign language if they are not taught one.[40] Groups of deaf individuals invent and develop elaborate sign languages if they are isolated from already existing systems.[41] In a school that attempted to teach deaf children in a standard spoken and written language, the children invented their own sign language and passed it on to future generations of students.[42]

Against this background, one should expect firms in an industry that interact over long periods and that are run by individuals who share common languages, backgrounds, and understandings of their strategic situation to develop means of communicating even if certain statements

---

[35] See Fisher and Marcus (2006, 15, 17).

[36] See Wade (2006, 38).

[37] See Bonvillain (2003, 2–4).

[38] See Bickerton (1990, 118–22, 169–71, 181–85), and Wade (2006, 40–41).

[39] It has also been observed among "religious communities sworn to silence, people working in extremely noisy environments, [and] indigenous peoples involved in rituals of silence." Corballis (2003, 208). Furthermore, existing sign languages have been shown to be capable of importing words from the surrounding spoken language. Fischer and Siple (1990, 4).

[40] See Corballis (2003, 209), Fisher and Marcus (2006, 9), and Jackendoff (2002, 99–100).

[41] For example, Sandler et al. (2005) describe the spontaneously created Al-Sayyid Bedouin Sign Language in an isolated community.

[42] Senghas, Kita, and Özyürek (2004, 1780): "Although instruction in school was conducted in Spanish (with minimal success), these first children began to develop a new, gestural system for communicating with each other. The gestures soon expanded to form an early sign language. Through continued use, both in and out of school, the growing language has been passed down and relearned naturally every year since, as each new wave of children entered the community."

or techniques are off-limits.[43] The relevant actors as well as consultants they hire may have taken similar courses on competitive strategy at business school, attended conferences on the subject, and read the same literature.[44] When competitors have access to a common play book, which in a sense offers a two-way translation between pertinent moves and standard signals, communication may flow easily.[45] One could even consider extreme versions: Suppose that a consulting firm creates and sells to all the firms in an industry a detailed signaling system using, say, the fifteenth and sixteenth decimal place of a price announcement or the number of milliseconds that elapse between electronic transmissions of dollars and cents, reconstructing all forbidden magic words or anything else that may prove useful.[46] Lest these hypotheticals seem

---

[43] Drug dealers speak in a code of sorts to help avoid detection and prosecution, and their language has many of the characteristics described in this section. "Dealers don't just sound like rappers, but actually structure a variation of language and sophisticated codes that nearly anyone would have trouble translating. Rather than hiring an Ebonics expert to understand the lingo of drug dealers, the DEA would be better off hiring a former drug dealer. Urban language, in general, has a very dynamic dimension to it that changes with the release of every new album, the start of every new school year and with each new season on *BET*." Watkins (2010).

[44] For example, Porter's (1980, chs. 4, 5) prominent business text includes chapters on "Market Signals" and "Competitive Moves." In those chapters, there is substantial discussion of the means of obtaining the sort of mutual understanding that will result in behavior that redounds to the firms' advantage, but little if any discussion of (much less fixation on) what those commenting on the law would characterize as express agreement. See also Besanko et al. (2007, ch. 8), and Dranove and Marciano (2005, chs. 5, 6), with chapters titled "The Cancer of Competition: How to Diagnose It" and "The Cancer of Competition: How to Cure It." Compare Heil, Day, and Reibstein (1997, 288): "When rivals follow similar strategies, use similar structures, and the managers have similar backgrounds, they understand each other and usually make correct attributions of each other's moves. Difficulties arise with new competitors that go unrecognized because they are members of a divergent strategic group."

[45] "[O]ne explanation [for successful coordination] is that [firms'] market moves are interpretable as messages. They converse in a code, as it were." Friedman (1971, 11).

[46] An analogy that may be familiar to some readers is the use of bidding conventions in the game of bridge, which must be shared before play with opponents in duplicate bridge tournaments through the use of convention cards. See "The Bridge World: Bridge Glossary," http://www.bridgeworld.com/default.asp?d=bridge_glossary&f=glossc.html (last accessed November 22, 2010). In addition, defenders employ signaling systems when playing a hand. In both instances, the players are not allowed to speak, wink, or nod once play commences: All communication is undertaken using preexisting signaling systems that players learn from

far-fetched, similar behavior was employed through an electronic price-posting system in the *Airline Tariff* case and the use of trailing digits in FCC spectrum auctions.[47]

Another interesting feature of communication relates to the overwhelming tendency of proposed competition law regulation to focus on the use of words. As noted, communication takes many forms, including, importantly, behavior—that is, actions. To restrict words but freely permit actions would make sense if the former were a distinctively more powerful means of effectuating coordinated oligopolistic understandings and outcomes.[48] But one should wonder whether this is the case. The familiar adage, after all, is that "actions speak louder than words," not vice versa.[49] Consider also numerous cousins: "All talk, no action." "Put your money where your mouth is." "Practice what you preach." "Walk the talk."[50] This idea relates to the point that successful interdependent behavior in many settings—including coordinated oligopoly pricing—requires that players have reason to believe that others will behave cooperatively, and actions themselves either constitute the cooperative behavior that mere words promise or at a minimum demonstrate a higher level of commitment.[51]

---

books, other media, and experience, including direct discussions with their partners before the competition.

[47] See Borenstein (2004), Porter (2005, 153, 158), and Werden (2004, 766).

[48] This seems to be the view, for example, of Areeda and Hovenkamp (2003, 65), who believe that a crucial question is the credibility of commitment and assert that "expressly exchanged views . . . convey more assurance about the future than mere marketplace behavior." Their views are further discussed in note 67 in chapter 7.

[49] See GoEnglish.com Pocket English Idioms, http://www.goenglish.com/ActionsSpeak LouderThanWords.asp (last accessed November 22, 2010): "'Actions speak louder than words' means that your actions (what you do) communicate more clearly than your words (what you say). It is as if they were louder than words. 'Actions speak louder than words' means that if you want people to believe your words, you should 'speak' with your actions. Example: 'Don't tell me how to do this; show me! Actions speak louder than words.'"; and The New Dictionary of Cultural Literacy (3rd ed., 2005) http://dictionary.reference.com/browse/ Actions+speak+louder+than+words (last accessed November 22, 2010): "People are more impressed with our sincerity if we act on our beliefs than if we merely talk about them."

[50] On the origins of "walk the talk," see Paul Brians, "Walk the Talk," in Common Errors in English (2nd ed., 2008), http://www.wsu.edu/~brians/errors/walk.html (last accessed November 22, 2010).

[51] An important caveat, of course, is that actions may be louder but more ambiguous. Whether this is so will depend on the context. Ordinary language is often misunderstood or,

Nor is it novel to apply this principle in the present context. Thomas Schelling (1960, 107), in his seminal investigation, *The Strategy of Conflict*, stated, "Even with full verbal communication, the situation may not be greatly different [from that without any]; patterns of action may speak louder than words." In discussing communication, cheap talk, and promises (and thus anticipating some modern developments in game theory), he elaborated (117, emphasis omitted),

> This is one of the reasons why talk is not a substitute for moves. Moves can in some way alter the game, by incurring manifest costs, risks, or a reduced range of subsequent choice; they have an information content, or evidence content, of a different character from that of speech. Talk can be cheap when moves are not . . . .[52]

Michael Porter (1980, 103) echoes similar sentiments in *Competitive Strategy*: "Announcements or leaks of the intention to carry out a commitment are also communicating devices, although they do not usually communicate with the seriousness of past behavior."[53] One can also consider this question in the context of the gas stations parable. Suppose that the Initiator points to a not-yet-posted sign with a higher price, and that the Responder gives a "thumbs-up" reply. Such symbolic action is obviously pretty close to verbal expression. But isn't putting "signs-up" rather than "thumbs-up" at least as compelling an indication of a willingness to charge the new price?

---

importantly, understood but not believed, that is, not taken at face value. Compare Pinker's point noted in the text that meaning is often what is interpreted between the lines of even clear words. Likewise, many actions, such as initiation of a price increase, like in the illustration with two gas stations, are quite clear. For further discussion, see subsection 7.B.2.

[52] The ellipsed material is "(except for the 'talk' that takes the form of *enforcible* threats, promises, commitments, and so forth, and that is to be analyzed under the heading of *moves* rather than communication anyway)." See subsection 7.A.1, distinguishing cooperative game theory, in which promises are enforceable, from noncooperative game theory, relevant to competition law, in which they are not.

[53] See Heil, Day, and Reibstein (1997, 285): "However, since announcements are so easy and inexpensive, bluffing is more likely. As a result, a manager needs to choose between the fast, low-cost announcement or the slower, more expensive but often more credible action."; and also compare Porter (1980, 77 n.3): "Competitors can also comment on their pleasure or displeasure *directly* through interviews, speeches to security analysts, and so on. But announcing that they will do something, in response to a firm's move, is usually a more binding commitment to their position than mere statements of pleasure or displeasure."

Determining the implications of the foregoing observations about language is left to chapters 6 and 7 and to subsequent research. However, a few clarifying notes are in order. First, it certainly need not be supposed that a ban on some subset of communications will be meaningless. Even so, defining any such subset will be difficult, and inferring from circumstantial evidence whether the communications that transpired were or were not in the subset will often be harder still. Indeed, even with perfect recordings of all interactions, some possibly significant ambiguity will remain in interpreting what transpired.[54] Second, predicting the effect of any such regulation will be also be challenging. The result will vary greatly by context, and it also may change over time as parties' language, broadly viewed, evolves in response. Innovation in communications technology, which is becoming increasingly rapid, will further complicate the picture.[55] Third, outside observers—such as courts, regulators, and academics—are at a disadvantage in determining what is actually happening if parties attempt to be clever and subtle in their methods of communication.

---

[54] The problem is compounded by the very difficulty of defining the concept of agreement and the existence of widely divergent usages. For example, courts sometimes refer to evidence of the existence of an "understanding," which is most relevantly defined as being in harmonious relationship, having an agreement of opinion or feeling, or more specifically a mutual agreement not formally entered into but in some degree binding on each side—definitions consistent with a variety of meanings of the term agreement (including interdependent behavior without more) and not clearly distinguishing among them. See section 5.A. How is one to determine how the term was used in context? And if only meetings of the minds that are achieved through specific modes of communication count, how can one tell how such were achieved? And even if those modes are directly in evidence, how does one know whether they were necessary or sufficient in achieving the understanding? For further discussion, see sections 5.A and 5.E and chapter 6.

[55] See section 18.D.

4

Statutory Provisions and Higher Court Interpretations

❦

In examining competition law's doctrine on horizontal agreements, this chapter begins by addressing the U.S. statute, Sherman Act Section 1.[1] Although such attention may seem conventional because the legal question is one of statutory interpretation, in fact the language of Section 1 is not much discussed. Indeed, as previously mentioned, the core term agreement does not even appear in the provision. Given the difficulty in making sense of the agreement requirement, it seems appropriate to examine the statute for what illumination it may offer.

The leading Supreme Court precedents on Section 1 are examined next. These are the primary source of U.S. antitrust law in general and specifically in delineating what constitutes a horizontal agreement. Here, there is more conflict than meets the eye. Key older decisions that continue to receive frequent, favorable citation appear to state the rule in a way that includes any interdependent coordination on price (or related matters), which contradicts what most commentators deem the law to be. More recent decisions present a mixed picture: They state rules in canonical language, but the key terms are some of those shown in section 2.B to have multiple, even opposite, meanings. The latest cases seem to be most supportive of commentators' views that demand more than interdependent behavior, yet these opinions accord little direct attention to the central question and they also reaffirm, draw support from, and employ to state their holding the earlier cases that endorse a

---

[1] Federal Trade Commission Act Section 5 broadly reaches unfair competition, without specifically requiring an agreement, although the provision was interpreted more narrowly in *du Pont*, a decision commentators have criticized. See note 17 in chapter 3.

broad view of the agreement requirement. How this tension plays out in lower court practice is deferred to chapter 5.

Finally, the corresponding provision in the European Union, Article 101, is examined. Because the underlying questions and the relevant economic theory of oligopolistic coordination are the same, it is natural to expect similar challenges to arise, and they do.

A. Sherman Act Section 1

1. Contract, Combination, or Conspiracy

Sherman Act Section 1 declares to be illegal "[e]very contract, combination in the form of trust or otherwise, or conspiracy[] in restraint of trade or commerce."[2] Phillip Areeda and Herbert Hovenkamp (2003, 1) explain that "[t]he three quoted terms are understood to embrace a single concept," which is generally referred to as an agreement. Even though the statutory terms are not usually considered separately, it is worth doing so briefly to see what might be learned.[3]

The first term, contract, has a generally recognized legal meaning that it is not unreasonable to suppose is what the legislature had in mind when including it in Section 1's list. Even in ordinary usage, a contract refers to a binding agreement and usually connotes one that is legally enforceable. As mentioned in section 2.C, this usage is potentially confusing for, once contracts in restraint of trade are deemed illegal, they are no longer legally enforceable, and this result is one effect of the statute. Nevertheless, there seems to be little doubt that the statute was meant to encompass, at a minimum, arrangements that would be contracts but for the nullifying effect of Section 1 itself.

It is plausible that a broader meaning, covering more informal arrangements, was also intended by the term contract. This supposition is

---

[2] 15 U.S.C. §1.

[3] Areeda and Hovenkamp (2003, 16) further suggest, "The several statutory terms for combined action are usually treated interchangeably." This claim does not appear to be correct; for example, a tacit agreement might be referred to as a conspiracy but not as a contract. Of the three terms, the latter, conspiracy, is the one often used generically, which is one of the reasons it receives additional attention in subsection 2.

natural because, with ordinary contracts, parties wishing to enter into agreements wish them to be legally enforceable and thus will undertake efforts to ensure that formalities are satisfied, whereas with contracts in restraint of trade, which the Sherman Act subjects to sanctions, parties would attempt to avoid formalities if such sufficed to avert penalties—and little if anything would be lost since the contracts cannot be enforced in any event.[4] Note further that legally binding contracts can sometimes be rather informal, and that in some contexts binding contracts can be created by actions.

The term combination is used in connection with the elaboration "in the form of trust or otherwise," the concrete reference indicating a common legal form that cartels took at the time the Sherman Act was passed. Combination generally refers to joint action ranging from a formal merger to any sort of acting together, that is, everything from a particular form of express agreement (and one already included in the term contract) to interdependent oligopoly pricing. Adding "or otherwise" seems to invite a broad interpretation, at the least one not dependent on the form that is employed.

Conspiracy, the specific statutory term most often mentioned by courts and commentators alike, also has a range of ordinary meanings. A narrower one would refer to secret agreements to perform an unlawful or wrongful act or an act that becomes unlawful as a result of the secret agreement, which is close to the criminal law definition discussed in subsection 2—although secrecy is not generally required.[5] More broadly, the concept refers to action in harmony toward a common end, readily encompassing interdependent oligopoly pricing. In choosing an interpretation, it does seem highly relevant that conspiracy, like contract, is a legal term of art, which is why subsection 2 considers its standard legal meaning in greater depth.[6]

---

[4] Indeed, merely adding the language "this document does not constitute an enforceable contract"—with perhaps some other adjustments—may be enough to avoid a prohibition on contracts that was narrowly construed to address only formally binding ones.

[5] See note 16 in chapter 2.

[6] Somewhat surprisingly, antitrust commentators tend not to examine (or in many cases even mention) general legal material on conspiracy. Notably, Areeda and Hovenkamp (2003, 227), devote a lone paragraph of a nearly three-hundred-page treatment of horizontal agree-

The three statutory terms, even viewed in isolation and certainly when combined, suggest a range of possible breadths for Section 1's agreement requirement but in many respects signal a broad scope. In considering the clause as a whole, the use of three terms (and the second with an "or otherwise" clause) suggests, as a plausible interpretation, "in any way, shape, or form." Congress used a list of terms rather than a single term; some of these terms are fairly clear (contract), and some are ambiguous; some are narrower and some broader; and they are partially overlapping but not nearly coincident. All of this is reminiscent of a common legal drafting technique that strives to be all-inclusive.[7] Moreover, on its face, there is no attempt to exclude any form of coordinated behavior involving multiple parties.

In considering legislative history and intent, it seems clear that Congress had the trusts themselves most clearly in mind and did not entertain thoughts about modern oligopoly theory.[8] On the other hand, the prohibition is explicitly not limited to trusts and is phrased in a comprehensive fashion. Likewise, the stated legislative purposes, such as promoting competition,[9] do not on their face imply any distinction based on differences in means.

Another question is how much weight should be given to legislative history and intent. The words of Sherman Act Sections 1 and 2 are few, and it has been a century since they have been interpreted literally. Notably, even though Section 1 prohibits "every" agreement "in restraint of trade or commerce," the Supreme Court's 1911 decision in *Standard Oil* interpreted this prohibition to apply only to unreasonable restraints (or, to put it another way, restrictions that are reasonable are not deemed to be restraints).[10] The U.S. Supreme Court's stance toward the antitrust statutes has sometimes been described as one that takes them more as a delegation of common-law-like authority to develop doctrine rather than as a prescription of what that doctrine is.[11]

---

ments to the subject, stating that "a detailed analysis of conspiracy . . . is relevant in principle [but] does not seem promising enough to add to the authors' and readers' burdens here."

[7] It is useful to keep in mind the general caveat that maxims of statutory construction often point in opposite directions. See Llewellyn (1950).

[8] See Kintner (1980, ch. 4).

[9] See Kintner (1980, 145, 242).

[10] Standard Oil Co. v. United States, 221 U.S. 1, 49–68 (1911).

[11] See Leegin Creative Leather Products, Inc. v. PSKS, Inc., 551 U.S. 877, 899 (2007),

Despite this tendency, the Court has not acted as if the statutes give it carte blanche. In particular, it is understood that Sherman Act Section 1 differs from Section 2 in that some sort of group behavior is a prerequisite for application of the former.[12] The question, then, is what sort of group behavior is required to trigger Section 1. The language of the statute readily reaches interdependent oligopoly behavior. Nevertheless, the Court still might choose to define covered activity more narrowly if it believes this course to be prudent in light of current understanding of what constitutes good competition policy. If so, it is difficult to locate such a boundary in the statute itself. In addition, it may be even more difficult to identify any sharp, formal demarcation that corresponds to whatever, upon substantive analysis, the dictates of policy turn out to be.

Accordingly, although it is blackletter law that an agreement must exist in order for Section 1 to be triggered, we have now seen that the concept of agreement, whether viewed by itself or illuminated by the underlying statutory language, does little to indicate what is or should be required, if anything, beyond interdependent behavior. Instead, courts' and commentators' invocation of the term may simply register a conclusion reached on other grounds. If that is the case, however, the doctrine remains obscure because such rationales are not usually elaborated. Nor are they readily inferred because the typical inquiry is presented as the application of a test for whether an arrangement fits within a preexisting, reasonably well defined, and readily understood category.

2. General Law of Conspiracy

Subsection 1 shows that the statutory language can readily be seen as inviting a broad interpretation of the agreement concept yet leaving substantial uncertainty about what Congress really intended, which itself may or may not ultimately be determinative. As also noted,

---

Areeda and Hovenkamp (2003, 226), Baxter (1982, 662–73), and Kintner (1980, 166, 217, 239). For criticism of this approach toward Supreme Court interpretation of the Sherman Act, see Arthur (1986) and Farber and McDonnell (2005).

[12] Even this requirement, central in the present context, is not entirely obvious, for one could imagine deeming any anticompetitive behavior that would be unreasonable under Section 1 if the agreement requirement was satisfied as constituting an act of monopolization or attempted monopolization under Section 2 if the requirement was not met.

however, Congress's intent may be less ambiguous regarding inclusion of the word conspiracy because it was then and continues to be a widely used legal term of art with an established meaning. Moreover, unlike the term contract, it is not as limited and thus is more relevant to determining the reach of the statute.[13] The term is also of particular interest because it—rather than the other two provisions or the term agreement itself—is most commonly mentioned in Supreme Court opinions on the subject.

Under U.S. law, conspiracy refers to "[a]n agreement by two or more persons to commit an unlawful act."[14] This basic formulation has remained largely unchanged over time, being reflective of the common law of conspiracy and the more recent Model Penal Code.[15] Standard definitions' use of the term agreement helps to explain how that term became a common shorthand for the statutory trilogy but may also suggest a dead end in light of the discussion in section 2.B. The previous efforts, however, rely on general understandings. The present question is whether the agreement component of conspiracy doctrine has a more determinate meaning.

Wayne LaFave's (2003, 266 n.11) treatise quotes the Model Penal Code (1985, §5.03, comment, at 419), which states, "It is universally conceded that an agreement need not be express, although whether the idea of an implied agreement connotes only an unspoken, actual consensus or has broader, fictional components is by no means clear." In addition, he observes that the agreement notion with regard to conspiracy law is "more lax than elsewhere," and that "[a] mere tacit understanding will suffice, and there need not be any written statement or even a speaking of words which expressly communicates agreement."[16]

---

[13] One might be concerned that the legal use of conspiracy generally appears in the criminal law; however, Sherman Act Section 1 is a criminal as well as a civil statute (more precisely, it makes violations a felony, while other antitrust provisions add injunctive relief and a private right of action for damages).

[14] Black's Law Dictionary (2009, 351).

[15] See LaFave (2003, 265) and Model Penal Code §5.03(1) (1985).

[16] Similarly, Pollack (1947, 332) states that the pertinent element of conspiracy is that the actor's intention to participate be conveyed "either by words or conduct." Compare ibid. (337), referring to a legislative commission's commentary regarding the overt act requirement of conspiracy law, which speaks of "the formation of this intent by the interchange of

It is of further interest that the Supreme Court case LaFave cites in support of this proposition is *American Tobacco*, an antitrust decision that will be discussed in subsection B.1. LaFave (267) also cites (and partially quotes) another antitrust decision, *Interstate Circuit*, also discussed below, in support of the proposition that "it is thus well established that the prosecution may 'rely on inferences drawn from the course of conduct of the alleged conspirators.'"[17] Although, as chapters 2 and 3 explain, the scope of terms like express, tacit, and communication is quite unclear, the foregoing statements sharply articulate a fairly broad conception of agreement, surely one not limited to direct verbal statements or other highly explicit types of communication.

Furthermore, the use of phrases like "actual consensus" and "mere tacit understanding" reveals a subjective view focused on mental states. Other standard depictions of conspiracy law reinforce this interpretation.[18] For example, *Black's Law Dictionary* (2009, 352) quotes a single court opinion to illuminate its general definition of conspiracy, Justice

---

thoughts." Cousens (1937, 899–90) reviews federal conspiracy law during the period leading up to the passage of the Sherman Act and finds it to be quite broad, allowing that a "common action on a common plan might be plainly shown by actions and circumstances," and he discusses a case in which it was stated that there is no need to show an "explicit or formal agreement," it being sufficient that parties "'positively or tacitly' com[e] 'to a mutual understanding.'" Courts "have emphasized such truths as the lack of necessity for formal or verbal agreement and the possibility of tacit consent and purely circumstantial proof." Ibid. (910). To tighten courts' approach to conspiracy, Cousens proposes that "regardless of the kind of evidence or method of proof [juries] must be convinced of an actual agreement in the sense of a meeting of minds in the pursuit of a course of action according to a common plan." Ibid. (910–11).

[17] It seems standard to cite these Supreme Court antitrust decisions when articulating the blackletter law of conspiracy. For example, 16 Am. Jur. 2d Conspiracy §10 (1998) cites *American Tobacco* as the leading Supreme Court case standing for the proposition that agreements under conspiracy law "need not be formal" (adding further that they need not be "express but may be a tacit understanding; the agreement may be inherent in and inferred from the circumstances[,] especially declarations, acts, and conduct of the alleged conspirators"), and it cites *Interstate Circuit* as the Supreme Court decision supporting the rule that "[t]he agreement need not be entered into by all the parties to it at the same time but may be reached by successive actions evidencing their joining of the conspiracy."

[18] LaFave (2003, 275–76). LaFave further discusses how this central mental state requirement has been difficult to pin down, and concludes that "it may generally be said that the mental state required is an intent to achieve a particular result which is criminal or which though noncriminal is nonetheless covered by the law of conspiracy." See also Pollack

Jackson's concurrence in *Krulewitch*, which concludes with the statement, "It is always 'predominantly mental in composition' because it consists primarily of a meeting of minds and an intent."[19] This subjective notion, in turn, is at the heart of interdependent behavior, including in particular successful coordinated oligopoly pricing.[20]

Before concluding this brief examination of the general law of conspiracy, it is worth commenting on one respect in which Sherman Act Section 1 is atypical of conspiracy prohibitions. For conspiracies like those to rob a bank, the underlying act is itself illegal when undertaken individually. The main relevance of conspiracy law is that it may augment the punishment when individuals act in groups and it may ease proof as a consequence of evidentiary rules. When we see two individuals, each clearly involved in robbing a bank, we have no doubt that each is guilty of bank robbery. Moreover, the odds would usually be overwhelmingly high that, if two or more individuals are observed robbing the same bank at the same time—perhaps each is pointing a gun at a bank teller who is handing over cash—they are part of a conspiracy. It

---

(1947, 329): "Because this crime is so predominately mental, it is very difficult to analyze its elements."

[19] Krulewitch v. United States, 336 U.S. 440, 447–48 (1949) (itself quoting Harno (1941, 632)). The centrality of this feature of conspiracy is reinforced by the fact that Justice Jackson is presenting it (and not any other trait) to pin down what he describes as a seemingly elastic, sprawling, vague, and chameleon-like notion. 336 U.S. at 445–47. In similar spirit, Harno (1941, 631–33) emphasizes the focus of conspiracy law on intent, which he further specifies as determining whether there is "a meeting of the minds," the actor "brings his intention into concurrence with that of the other," or "[t]he evidence . . . establish[es] that there was a unity of intent on the part of two or more persons to accomplish the end charged." English common law preceding passage of the Sherman Act is quite similar. See Williams (1961, 666–68), referring, for example, to whether parties "have put their heads together."

[20] There is another dimension of conspiracy law that is of some interest, that pertaining to who is included in a conspiracy. This question is particularly important for more peripheral participants. Courts "have taken the position that aiding a conspiracy with knowledge of its purposes suffices to make one a party to the conspiracy." LaFave (2003, 270). LaFave indicates that a rationale is that such activity, even if not contributing as much to the danger as central participants do, has nonetheless augmented it. With price fixing, consider the behavior of a firm that is not seen as part of the core conspiracy to raise prices. If it chooses to follow the conspirators' price increase, the assistance is significant, unless the firm is very small: If the firm did not follow and instead undercut the conspirators' price, they might have been forced to respond, thus leading to lower prices in the industry. For further exploration of the question of which firms should be subject to sanctions, see section 12.C.

might be a coincidence, but that possibility is extremely remote. Accordingly, evidence of such parallel behavior would be strong evidence of a conspiracy.

With regard to marketplace activity, by contrast, it is not illegal in a vacuum for a single firm to set a price, even a high one. Thus, Section 1's conspiracy rule makes illegal behavior that otherwise would not be so.[21] This difference helps to explain why the agreement requirement under Sherman Act Section 1 is so important. The distinction does not, however, obviously suggest that the Sherman Act's use of the term conspiracy was meant to convey a notably different reach from that ordinarily associated with this familiar legal term.

B. U.S. Supreme Court

1. Early Decisions

This subsection examines the Supreme Court decisions from more than a half century ago that are still widely cited. The first two, *Interstate Circuit* and *American Tobacco*, were just mentioned as leading cases on the general law of conspiracy that exemplify a broad view of agreement. In *Interstate Circuit*, the Court famously stated,

> While the District Court's finding of an agreement of the distributors among themselves is supported by the evidence, we think that in the circumstances of this case such agreement for the imposition of the restrictions upon subsequent-run exhibitors was not a prerequisite to an unlawful conspiracy. It was enough that, knowing that concerted action was contemplated and invited, the distributors gave their adherence to the scheme and participated in it. Each distributor was advised that the others were asked to participate; each knew that cooperation was essential to successful operation of the plan. They knew that the plan, if carried out, would result in a restraint of commerce . . . .
>
> It is elementary that an unlawful conspiracy may be and often is formed without simultaneous action or agreement on the part

---

[21] On the rationale for structuring the law in this manner, see subsection 8.B.2.

of the conspirators. . . . Acceptance by competitors, without previous agreement, of an invitation to participate in a plan, the necessary consequence of which, if carried out, is restraint of interstate commerce, is sufficient to establish an unlawful conspiracy under the Sherman Act.[22]

This formulation deems sufficient an invitation to act together combined with knowledge that cooperation is essential and the fact of ultimate participation. Many have acknowledged that these factors, taken together, readily encompass interdependent oligopolistic behavior.[23] That is, these requirements are fulfilled by initiation of a price increase from a competitive to a supracompetitive level plus an appreciation that the higher, mutually beneficial price will not stick unless all go along, supplemented by other firms' actually matching and maintaining the higher price. (Recall the two gas stations in section 2.A.)

American Tobacco is cited not for its application of law to fact but rather for several of its general pronouncements on this subject:

It is not the form of the combination or the particular means used but the result to be achieved that the statute condemns. . . . No formal agreement is necessary to constitute an unlawful conspiracy. . . . The essential combination or conspiracy in violation of the Sherman Act may be found in a course of dealings or other circumstances as well as in any exchange of words. . . . Where the circumstances are such as to warrant a jury in finding that the conspirators had a unity of purpose or a common design and understanding, or a meeting of minds in an unlawful arrangement, the conclusion that a conspiracy is established is justified.[24]

The statement that the form of combination and the means used are irrelevant—and particularly that there need not be any exchange of words—rules out interpretations under which words in particular or various modes of communication are determinative.[25] Furthermore, the

---

[22] Interstate Circuit v. United States, 306 U.S. 208, 226–27 (1939).

[23] See, for example, Areeda and Hovenkamp (2003, 191, 193) and Turner (1962, 683).

[24] American Tobacco Co. v. United States, 328 U.S. 781, 809–10 (1946).

[25] A fortiori, it seems clear that no express agreement is required, an inference that seems unmistakable because the Court's description of the facts makes clear that the government did not allege one: "The Government introduced evidence showing that although there was

statement that any of a unity of purpose, common understanding, or meeting of the minds is sufficient echoes the subjective emphasis of the general law of conspiracy. Both features readily encompass interdependent oligopoly pricing behavior, where words may be lacking but a meeting of the minds is central. This interpretation, which fails to exclude a subset of cases having equivalent consequences, is reinforced by the Court's statement that it is "the result to be achieved that the statute condemns."

Theatre Enterprises[26] is seen by some as cutting back on these precedents, especially *Interstate Circuit*,[27] but this view is mistaken: Implicitly, it supposes that the latter case should be interpreted as aggressively as the *Theatre Enterprises* plaintiff sought to do (and failed).[28] This firm complained that the defendant movie distributors jointly refused to deal with its theater. The defendants argued that they each independently found it in their self-interest to abstain because plaintiff's outlet was inferior to downtown theaters for first-run pictures. The jury accepted their explanation. Thus, on appeal, the plaintiff's argument was that it should nevertheless have prevailed; specifically, it insisted "that the trial judge should have directed a verdict in its favor" on liability.[29] To do so would have been to deem purely independent, entirely competitive behavior to be illegal when it involved parallel action. Not only was there no interdependence, but each defendant would probably have been better off had its competitors dealt through an inferior outlet

---

no written or express agreement discovered among American, Liggett and Reynolds their practices included a clear course of dealing." 328 U.S. at 800.

[26] Theatre Enterprises v. Paramount Film Distributing Corp., 346 U.S. 537 (1954).

[27] See, for example, Hylton (2003, 140–41). Areeda and Hovenkamp (2003, 190) label their short subsection on the topic: "*Theatre Enterprises* decision as partial retraction?" They begin by stating that "the Court appeared to retreat from *Interstate Circuit.*" However, they do not find much support for this suggestion because "[e]ven the broad *Interstate Circuit* language would probably not help the plaintiff." Ibid. (191). Regarding the continuing vitality of *Interstate Circuit*, see, for example, Toys "R" Us, Inc. v. Federal Trade Commission, 221 F.3d 928, 935–36 (7th Cir. 2000), which upheld the FTC's horizontal agreement theory as a correct application of that case.

[28] To complete the argument, it supposes that *Interstate Circuit* renders illegal parallel but independent, competitive behavior. Under that view, *Theatre Enterprises* does cut back on *Interstate Circuit*, but this fact would be moot in any event because it would be cutting it back to require the presence of interdependent action—which is what the proper interpretation of *Interstate Circuit* understands it to hold in any event.

[29] 346 U.S. at 539.

such as the plaintiff. This extreme proposition is what the Supreme Court rejected.

> The crucial question is whether respondents' conduct toward petitioner stemmed from independent decision or from an agreement, tacit or express. To be sure, business behavior is admissible circumstantial evidence from which the fact finder may infer agreement. . . . But this Court has never held that proof of parallel business behavior conclusively establishes agreement or, phrased differently, that such behavior itself constitutes a Sherman Act offense. Circumstantial evidence of consciously parallel behavior may have made heavy inroads into the traditional judicial attitude toward conspiracy; but "conscious parallelism" has not yet read conspiracy out of the Sherman Act entirely.[30]

The statement that the "Court has never held that proof of parallel business behavior *conclusively* establishes" a violation hardly constitutes a cutback on its prior decisions. Furthermore, the final sentence—that "'conscious parallelism' has not *yet* read conspiracy out . . . *entirely*"— may constitute one of the most heavily qualified statements the Supreme Court has penned. Perhaps this observation is best understood as a sarcastic reaction to the plaintiff's absurd argument. In any event, the Court explicitly endorsed the inclusion of tacit agreements (whatever that may mean) and distinguished them from independent behavior, which in the context of the plaintiff's argument clearly refers to behavior that is not interdependent (recall section 2.C).[31]

Most other Supreme Court decisions from this time period and in surrounding decades are to similar effect.[32] For example, in its 1969 *Container* decision, the Court stated,

---

[30] 346 U.S. at 540–41.

[31] "Here each of the respondents had denied the existence of any collaboration and in addition had introduced evidence of the local conditions surrounding the Crest operation which, they contended, precluded it from being a successful first-run house. They also attacked the good faith of the guaranteed offers of the petitioner for first-run pictures and attributed uniform action to individual business judgment motivated by the desire for maximum revenue. This evidence, together with other testimony of an explanatory nature, raised fact issues requiring the trial judge to submit the issue of conspiracy to the jury." 346 U.S. at 541–42.

[32] Among the earliest of these decisions is Eastern States Retail Lumber Dealers' Associa-

Here all that was present was a request by each defendant of its competitor for information as to the most recent price charged or quoted, whenever it needed such information and whenever it was not available from another source. Each defendant on receiving that request usually furnished the data with the expectation that it would be furnished reciprocal information when it wanted it. That concerted action is of course sufficient to establish the combination or conspiracy, the initial ingredient of a violation of §1 of the Sherman Act.[33]

Thus, the Court depicted interdependent behavior and deemed the implicit reciprocal understanding to constitute an agreement. In this regard, it found the facts to be "obviously quite different from the parallel business behavior condoned in *Theatre Enterprises*."[34] In this respect and others, all of the foregoing opinions are quite consonant with the

---

tion v. United States, 234 U.S. 600, 612 (1914) ("the conspiracy to accomplish that which was the natural consequence of such action may be readily inferred"), which is cited in *Interstate Circuit*. A seemingly different view, offered in passing in a monopolization case, appears in United States v. International Harvester, 274 U.S. 693, 708–9 (1927) ("the fact that competitors may see proper, in the exercise of their own judgment, to follow the prices of another manufacturer, does not establish any suppression of competition or show any sinister domination"); this part of the opinion is not cited in any of the four cases discussed in the text. The Court in United States v. Masonite Corporation, 316 U.S. 265, 275 (1942), recited much of the language quoted in the text from *Interstate Circuit*, and *Masonite*, in turn, is cited in *Theatre Enterprises*. In United States v. Paramount Pictures, 334 U.S. 131, 142 (1948), the Court cited *Interstate Circuit* and *Masonite* for the proposition, "It is not necessary to find an express agreement in order to find a conspiracy. It is enough that a concert of action is contemplated and that the defendants conformed to the arrangement." *Paramount* is likewise cited in *Theatre Enterprises* on the matter of inferring an agreement from business behavior. Similarly, in Federal Trade Commission v. Cement Institute, 333 U.S. 683, 716 & n.17 (1948), the Court found sufficient an "understanding, express or implied," from firms' practices, citing the formulation of *Interstate Circuit* and *Masonite*. Later, in Norfolk Monument Co. v. Woodlawn Memorial Gardens, Inc., 394 U.S. 700, 704 (1969), the Court found a lack of "letters, agreements, correspondence, or any other testimonials to a conspiracy among the several defendants" not dispositive, citing *American Tobacco* (328 U.S. at 809) for the settled proposition that "[n]o formal agreement is necessary to constitute an unlawful conspiracy," and *Theatre Enterprises* (346 U.S. at 540) for the rule that "business behavior is admissible circumstantial evidence from which the fact finder may infer agreement."

[33] United States v. Container Corp. of America, 393 U.S. 333, 335 (1969). Likewise, Justice Fortas's concurrence found a violation in "defendants' tacit agreement to exchange information about current prices." Ibid. (340).

[34] 393 U.S. at 335 n.2.

general law of conspiracy described in subsection A.2—which should hardly be surprising because, as noted there, some of these antitrust decisions are regarded as exemplars of conspiracy doctrine.

2. Subsequent Decisions

In the past few decades, Supreme Court decisions on the agreement requirement have focused on what is required for a plaintiff to survive dispositive motions.[35] For quite some time, the most important of these cases has been the Court's 1986 decision in *Matsushita*:

> Respondents correctly note that "[o]n summary judgment the inferences to be drawn from the underlying facts . . . must be viewed in the light most favorable to the party opposing the motion." . . . But antitrust law limits the range of permissible inferences from ambiguous evidence in a §1 case. Thus, in *Monsanto* . . . , we held that conduct as consistent with permissible competition as with illegal conspiracy does not, standing alone, support an inference of antitrust conspiracy. . . . To survive a motion for summary judgment or for a directed verdict, a plaintiff seeking damages for a violation of §1 must present evidence "that tends to exclude the possibility" that the alleged conspirators acted independently. [Ibid.] Respondents in this case, in other words, must show that the inference of conspiracy is reasonable in light of the competing inferences of independent action or collusive action that could not have harmed respondents.[36]

Of central importance in interpreting this oft-quoted statement is the meaning of the term independent. As discussed in section 2.B, the most common but not exclusive definition of independent contrasts it with interdependent. This understanding of *Matsushita* is reinforced by the surrounding language, in particular the sentence indicating in essence

---

[35] Subsequent to drafting this subsection, I embarked on a substantial research project on the law and optimal policy for motions to dismiss, summary judgment, and other features of multistage adjudication, aspects of which bear on the present discussion and that on dispositive motions elsewhere in this book. See Kaplow (2013a, 2013b).

[36] Matsushita Elec. Indus. Co., Ltd. v. Zenith Radio Corp., 475 U.S. 574, 587–88 (1986), quoting Monsanto Co. v. Spray-Rite Service Corp., 465 U.S. 752, 764 (1984).

that independent action is taken to be synonymous with competition, which, as previously discussed, generally means rivalry, not mutual understanding and behavior to the contrary.[37] Furthermore, the pertinent context in *Matsushita* is the defendants' argument that the alleged behavior was "economically irrational and practically infeasible,"[38] not that coordinated behavior occurred but did not involve certain sorts of communication.[39] The *Matsushita* decision was generally regarded to be significant not for elucidating the concept of agreement but rather for sending a message to lower courts that summary judgment in favor of defendants should be seriously considered when plaintiffs' cases are insubstantial.[40]

---

[37] Similar language appears later in the opinion: *Monsanto* "establishes that conduct that is as consistent with permissible competition as with illegal conspiracy does not, without more, support even an inference of conspiracy." 475 U.S. at 597 n.21, citing *Monsanto*, 465 U.S. at 763–64.

[38] 475 U.S. at 588.

[39] The Court's quotation from *Monsanto* is not surprising because it was a then-recent Section 1 decision on the evidence required to demonstrate agreement; however, the precise meaning is not obvious because that case involved the qualitatively different setting of a vertical agreement. The *Monsanto* Court's language in the pertinent passage is, in any event, quite similar to that of the earlier Section 1 conspiracy cases: "Thus, something more than evidence of complaints is needed. There must be evidence that tends to exclude the possibility that the manufacturer and nonterminated distributors were acting independently. As Judge Aldisert has written, the antitrust plaintiff should present direct or circumstantial evidence that reasonably tends to prove that the manufacturer and others 'had a conscious commitment to a common scheme designed to achieve an unlawful objective.' . . . [C]f. *American Tobacco* . . . ([c]ircumstances must reveal 'a unity of purpose or a common design and understanding, or a meeting of minds in an unlawful arrangement')." 465 U.S. at 764.

[40] For example, *Matsushita* does not directly discuss the agreement requirement or cite any of the leading Supreme Court cases on the subject, except its then-recent *Monsanto* decision (which, in turn, cites and quotes relevant passages from *American Tobacco*; see note 39). Lower courts frequently cite *Matsushita* for encouragement to grant summary judgment when a plaintiff's case is implausible, which the Court believed to be true in that case, in which a decades-long conspiracy to engage in predatory pricing was alleged. See *Matsushita*, 475 U.S. at 587: "[I]f the factual context renders respondents' claim implausible—if the claim is one that simply makes no economic sense—respondents must come forward with more persuasive evidence to support their claim than would otherwise be necessary."; In re Coordinated Pretrial Proceedings in Petroleum Products Antitrust Litigation, 906 F.2d 432, 439–40 (9th Cir. 1990); and Petruzzi's IGA Supermarkets, Inc. v. Darling-Delaware Co., 998 F.2d 1224, 1232 (3rd Cir. 1993). This particular concern is not seen to be applicable to an ordinary price-fixing case in large part because, in *Matsushita*, which involved a predation claim, the

Before addressing the other major case, it should be mentioned that the Court subsequently made passing reference to the agreement requirement in its *Brooke Group* predatory pricing decision. Specifically, in discussing the plaintiff's claim that the defendant had engaged in predatory pricing in order to discipline the former's low-cost pricing that had disrupted alleged coordinated oligopolistic pricing, the Court described price coordination as a process that is "not in itself unlawful."[41] This comment was unaccompanied by any discussion of Section 1's agreement requirement or of any of the relevant precedent.[42] It should also be remarked that both parties in the case had every reason to characterize the industry's prior behavior as legal; had the plaintiff alleged otherwise, it would have been confessing to a criminal (as well as civil) violation.[43]

Bell Atlantic v. Twombly,[44] although not primarily viewed as an antitrust decision,[45] also merits attention. In it, the Supreme Court gave a negative answer to the question of

---

concern was with chilling low rather than high prices. See also note 35 in chapter 5, on the implications of *Matsushita* in light of the paradox of proof. Nevertheless, *Matsushita*'s broader command to be more willing to grant summary judgment appears to be taken seriously in practice.

[41] Brooke Group Ltd. v. Brown & Williamson Tobacco Corp., 509 U.S. 209, 227 (1993). Elhauge and Geradin (2007, 836) refer to this statement as "dicta and a rather casual aside in a discussion focused on a different issue." Areeda and Hovenkamp (2003, 227) likewise refer to the passage as "dicta."

[42] Elsewhere, the Court extensively discussed *Matsushita*, but for its analysis of predation. The passage in question is accompanied by citations to two academic commentaries, one an economics text and the other the then-Areeda/Turner treatise, identifying the section discussing the economics of oligopoly pricing but not a later volume by Areeda, subsequently revised by Hovenkamp, on application of the law of horizontal agreement to oligopoly pricing.

[43] See Areeda, Kaplow, and Edlin (2004, 231 n.62). Baker (1994, 602 & n.84) points out that the Court did not note, nor did the plaintiff's submissions refer to, modern economics literature on oligopoly theory that was pertinent to the question at hand.

[44] Bell Atlantic Corp. v. Twombly, 550 U.S. 544 (2007).

[45] The characterization of *Twombly*'s breadth has proved controversial. This author, like many, views it as a broader decision if for no other reason than that it reversed such a prominent (general) precedent on the Federal Rules of Civil Procedure, as the text to follow describes; this reading is strongly supported by the Court's subsequent decision in Ashcroft v. Iqbal, 129 S. Ct. 1937 (2009). For an interpretation and analysis of *Twombly* as an antitrust decision, see Klevorick and Kohler-Hausmann (2012).

[w]hether a complaint states a claim under Section 1 of the Sherman Act . . . if it alleges that the defendants engaged in parallel conduct and adds a bald assertion that the defendants were participants in a "conspiracy," without any allegations that, if later proved true, would establish the existence of a conspiracy under the applicable legal standard.[46]

On its face, this question is not about what constitutes a conspiracy under Section 1, it being plain that parallel conduct, which as discussed in section 2.B includes much purely competitive behavior, does not alone suffice, a point firmly established in *Theatre Enterprises*.[47] Instead, as a formal legal matter, the Court's decision is an interpretation of the pleading requirements of the Federal Rules of Civil Procedure. Its holding reverses[48] (at least one important reading of) a fifty-year-old precedent, *Conley v. Gibson*,[49] one of the most cited cases in the federal judiciary, which had held that a complaint is sufficient unless "no set of facts" could support it.[50] *Twombly*'s immediate aftermath reflects this depiction, as it has been heavily cited in all areas of federal litigation, of which antitrust cases are but a small fraction.[51] Thus, somewhat like

---

[46] Petition for a Writ of Certiorari in Bell Atlantic Corporation, et al., Petitioners, v. William Twombly, et al., individually and on behalf of all others similarly situated, Respondents, No. 05-1126 (March 6, 2006, p. i).

[47] The overwhelming (but not exclusive) emphasis of the Brief of Amici Curiae Economists in Support of Petitioners (April 6, 2006) is likewise on the point that the lower court's standard (that was reversed by the Supreme Court) would allow a plaintiff to proceed even when defendants engaged in routine competitive behavior, which by its nature is often parallel. Further suggesting this point, the brief (18–19) endorses a plus-factor approach as a solution, when, as will be discussed in note 53 and in section 5.B, the most commonly cited plus factors are ones indicating that behavior is interdependent rather than independent. This point is also featured in Brief for the United States as Amicus Curiae Supporting Petitioners (August 26, 2006, 31–32).

[48] In the Court's euphemism, the rule in *Conley* was merely "retire[d]." 550 U.S. at 563 ("after puzzling the profession for 50 years, this famous observation has earned its retirement").

[49] 355 U.S. 41 (1957).

[50] Steinman's (2006, 143) data indicate that *Conley v. Gibson* was at that time the fourth most-cited case by federal courts.

[51] "[C]ourts have applied the decision in every substantive area of law governed by Rule 8. Antitrust cases comprised only 3.7% (40 out of 1075) of all cases citing *Twombly* in this study . . . ." Hannon (2008, 1814–15). Interestingly, Hannon's analysis of outcomes before and after

Brooke Group, Twombly is a case that mentions the agreement requirement—in this instance, at much greater length—even though that is not
the core legal focus.[52]

Twombly reveals essentially no measurable impact except on civil rights litigation; with those
cases removed, there was almost no effect in the large sample (for example, motions to dismiss were granted in 37.4% of cases after, compared to 36.9% before). Ibid. (1836–37). Hannon (1836 n.160) further reports that there were too few antitrust cases to meaningfully assess any area-specific impact. Inspection of the partially coded data he shared with this
author indicates that the magnitude of the difference in the antitrust cases that were coded is
negligible. Subsequent data in all areas of law, covering the period before *Twombly* to after
Iqbal, reinforce the view that a sea change has not (yet?) occurred. See U.S. Courts, "Motions
to Dismiss: Information on Collection of Data, http://www.uscourts.gov/uscourts/Rules
AndPolicies/rules/Motions_to_Dismiss_060110.pdf (accessed November 22, 2010), displaying monthly data on motions to dismiss filed, granted, and denied from four months before
Twombly to twelve months after *Iqbal*, with no evident overall trend or breakpoints at the
time of either decision. See also Kuperman (2009, 2): "While more time is needed to allow
the lower courts to flesh out the results of *Twombly* and *Iqbal*, most of the case law to date
does not indicate a drastic change in pleading standards."; ibid. (3): "While there are many
cases supporting the proposition that pleading standards have not changed significantly,
some courts have at least questioned whether there has been a change in the level of detail
required to provide adequate notice. And a few others have indicated that the claims at issue
might have survived before *Twombly* and *Iqbal*, but do not survive under current pleading
standards. At least one court has gone so far as to intimate that *Iqbal* will cause certain plaintiffs to avoid federal court when possible."; Hatamyar (2010, 616–24), reporting regression
results that are mixed and statistically insignificant, including a fall in grants of motions to
dismiss without leave to amend after *Twombly* and *Iqbal*, compared to before *Twombly*; and
ibid. (608–9), finding a fall in grants of motions to dismiss in a very small sample of antitrust
cases, with very few cases involving dismissals without leave to amend. Note that the focus of
these studies on changes in a narrow window around the *Twombly* and *Iqbal* decisions has
strengths and weaknesses. An important strength is that most decisions shortly after these
opinions probably involve complaints filed before them, making it unlikely that changed case
selection (filing behavior) explains the lack of impact. (An explanation for the nonresult is
that *Twombly* and *Iqbal* largely ratified what lower courts were already doing, at least to the
extent that they wished to dismiss cases; failures to dismiss also do not generate a high reversal risk since most such cases will settle.) However, one must also be concerned with whether
more motions to dismiss were filed as a consequence of *Twombly* or *Iqbal*. A serious weakness is that courts may adjust only gradually to these decisions. See Hubbard (2012). Anec-
dotal evidence suggests that many district courts may indeed be requiring more detailed
complaints, which plaintiffs in turn are filing, although the extent to which this merely involves more description up front or also constitutes an important constraint on filings is unclear. For further analysis of the legal meanings and implications of *Twombly* and *Iqbal* with
regard to motions to dismiss, see Kaplow (2013a).

[52] Gavil (2007, 23) states that "*Twombly* should not be interpreted in isolation, however. It

Also, like *Brooke Group*, *Twombly* makes statements reflecting a narrow view of agreement, one that excludes pure interdependent oligopolistic behavior. Most notably, it quotes the previously noted passage in *Brooke Group*.[53] Likewise, in discussing the facts, the Court states that "a

was one of the four cases decided this past term that interpreted Rule 8(a)(2)'s 'short and plain statement' requirement . . . ." In the course of discussing *Twombly*, Gavil does not even mention that it may bear on the interpretation of Section 1's agreement requirement. Although the *Twombly* Court must implicitly have had a legal standard in mind in concluding that it was not met by the plaintiff's complaint, it does not elaborate the standard in a sustained manner, discuss prior precedent as it bears on the question (although, as will be noted, much is cited in passing, unlike in *Brooke Group*), or offer arguments regarding why one or another rule is superior. This trait of the opinion (and of the dissent) reflects the nature of the decision under review, see note 57, and, relatedly, how the case was argued. Neither the parties' briefs nor most of the amicus briefs contained significant discussion of the meaning of the agreement requirement.

[53] 550 U.S. at 553–54, quoting *Brooke Group*, 509 U.S. at 227. The Court cites two other sources in support. The first is Areeda and Hovenkamp (2003, 236): "The courts are nearly unanimous in saying that mere interdependent parallelism does not establish the contract, combination, or conspiracy required by Sherman Act §1." As is already apparent, this is a rather odd statement, for it is clear that Supreme Court precedents themselves were at that time nearly unanimous in embracing a broader view. Indeed, Areeda and Hovenkamp (237) note in the very next paragraph that "[t]here are two groups of precedents that might point toward the opposite conclusion," after which they discuss some of the "older Supreme Court cases" and the point that lower courts' requirement that interdependence be supplemented by so-called plus factors may not in fact require anything more because "[s]ome of those very plus factors . . . seem to describe mere interdependence." In light of what they actually say about all of these cases, a reader not forewarned by the summary quoted in *Twombly* might well have concluded the opposite, that most courts find mere interdependence sufficient. This impression is reinforced by Areeda and Hovenkamp's (¶1434) more in-depth treatment that follows their discussion of the earlier Supreme Court cases, in which they cite numerous plus factors and cases as being incorrect for permitting agreements to be inferred from interdependent behavior (and no more), while identifying few factors or cases in which more than interdependence was indicated. They urge that this large body of case law should not be interpreted as contradicting their view, but they do not identify contrary language or context supporting readings opposite to what the large number of cited courts directly found. See also section 5.B (and note 19 on Areeda and Hovenkamp's discussion of plus-factor cases). A further irony is that the Court did not mention Areeda and Hovenkamp's treatment of *Twombly*'s central question concerning access to discovery, where their view contradicted the course adopted by the Court: "Discovery is most clearly required when the key facts supporting a claim are peculiarly within the other party's knowledge. Because conspiracies, for instance, are usually concealed, conjecture may be inescapable until after the discovery process." Areeda, Hovenkamp, and Blair (2000, 67–68).

The *Twombly* Court also cites Turner (1962, 672) for the proposition: "[M]ere interde-

natural explanation for the noncompetition alleged is that the former Government-sanctioned monopolists were sitting tight, expecting their neighbors to do the same thing."[54]

That said, *Twombly* is limited in a number of respects. The Court did not articulate any concept of agreement or, relatedly, indicate what more a plaintiff had to show. It did not explain how to reconcile its statements with prior precedent, apparently not appreciating that there was any need to do so. And it did not address the rationale for the agreement requirement's existence or its taking any particular form. Instead, the Court focused on erecting a nontrivial hurdle on motions to dismiss that plaintiffs must overcome, and on this central matter its motivation was explicit: The pleading rules should not make it too easy for plaintiffs to instigate discovery that is often highly protracted and costly.[55]

---

pendence of basic price decisions is not conspiracy." However, as the discussion in section 2.B explains, this depiction of Turner is misleading, for he makes clear that there is good (indeed, better) argument for the view that interdependence is conspiracy, but a type that on policy grounds should not be deemed unlawful when the conspiratorial behavior would be difficult to remedy. The distinction is important not only for conceptual clarity but also for practical reasons, for what more Turner would require depends on the policy considerations he identifies, whereas courts that do not see interdependence alone as constituting agreement might require something quite different to deem an agreement to exist. Compare section 3.B on how some commentators, including Turner, would accordingly interpret agreement broadly in order to attack facilitating practices.

[54] 550 U.S. at 568.

[55] "But determining whether some illegal agreement may have taken place between un-specified persons at different ILECs (each a multibillion dollar corporation with legions of management level employees) at some point over seven years is a sprawling, costly, and hugely time-consuming undertaking not easily susceptible to the kind of line drawing and case management that the dissent envisions." 550 U.S. at 560 n.6; see 550 U.S. at 558–60 & n.6, mentioning the "*in terrorem* increment of the settlement value," the "inevitably costly and protracted discovery phase," the problem of "allowing a potentially massive factual controversy to proceed," that "discovery accounts for as much as 90 percent of litigation costs when discovery is actively employed," and that the "threat of discovery expense will push cost-conscious defendants to settle even anemic cases." See also Gavil (2007, 23): *Twombly* "also builds on *Matsushita*'s subtext: the complexity and expense of processing antitrust cases suggests the need for additional judicial controls. Antitrust cases have been transformed from being a protected class to being a suspect one." In failing to discuss the content of the agreement requirement more directly, however, the relationship between the Court's holding and its objective is unclear and potentially problematic. For example, if the agreement re-

For these reasons, it is difficult to read *Twombly* as reversing not only *Conley v. Gibson*'s test on pleading requirements but also, sub silentio, all of the prior Supreme Court precedents on antitrust agree-

---

quirement depends more on subtleties of particular communications than on behavior and economic conditions in the industry, the sort of discovery requiring every external and, importantly, internal communication or notation to be scrutinized and interpreted (the latter potentially requiring depositions of countless employees) may be encouraged rather than dampened, that is, if and when the motion to dismiss hurdle is overcome. An alternative approach would entail district courts allowing discovery on the agreement question prior to deciding a motion to dismiss, either explicitly or simply by refusing to stay discovery and failing to decide the motion promptly. See Page (2009, 466–68). Yet it is not clear how limited such discovery would in fact be, and the *Twombly* majority cited discovery costs and the inability of trial courts to control them as a central motivation for its decision. For a more general treatment of optimal decisions on motions to dismiss in light of discovery costs, see Kaplow (2013a, 2013b).

Although less pertinent for present purposes, it is hard to avoid wondering what sort of factual allegations would be sufficient under *Twombly*. Remarkably, neither the majority nor dissent in *Twombly* addressed this point directly. The closest is a footnote in the majority's opinion. 550 U.S. at 556 n.4. Suppose, for sake of argument, that specific sorts of communications are deemed necessary to constitute an agreement. In that case, *Twombly* could be viewed as requiring allegation of the specific communications (who said what, to whom, and when), which would ordinarily be impossible without discovery in the absence of an informant or perhaps illegal surveillance, with the result that even classic cartel behavior would be close to per se legal, at least in private suits (and also for government investigations, if the probable cause requirement for subpoenas or sting operations was as high as the *Twombly* requirement to survive motions to dismiss). See also note 58 in chapter 6, further discussing the implications of *Twombly* if the agreement requirement is construed narrowly. However, as developed in chapter 6, there is another primary route available: even explicit communications can be inferred from appropriate circumstantial evidence. Hence, it would seem sufficient under *Twombly*, even assuming a circumscribed agreement requirement, for a plaintiff to allege interdependent behavior plus that the degree of conduciveness to coordination placed the case in the liability region rather than the paradox region—that is, that the observed coordination would be unlikely or implausible given the conditions of the industry unless the defendants had engaged in prohibited communications. And if mere allegations to this effect are deemed insufficient, perhaps a plaintiff might append an expert affidavit to that effect, or even incorporate it explicitly in its complaint. Put more abstractly, taking as given that some set of evidence would be sufficient for a plaintiff victory at trial, one presumes that there are some corresponding allegations that would be sufficient to survive a motion to dismiss. Section 6.C advances the further, more specific point that if the paradox region is narrow, as indeed many commentators implicitly assert, then the inference from interdependent behavior to the use of prohibited acts would be powerful, easily enough to survive a motion to dismiss.

ment that are discussed in subsection 1.[56] As mentioned, the question before the Court did not go to the substance of the agreement requirement. Instead, the Court treated it as uncontested and as if it were clear.[57] Moreover, it cited approvingly some of the earlier, broad formulations of Section 1. Indeed, the majority framed its opinion on the legal issues by stating that "'[t]he crucial question' is whether the challenged anticompetitive conduct 'stem[s] from independent decision or from an agreement, tacit or express,' *Theatre Enterprises* . . . ."[58] It further elaborates,

> An antitrust conspiracy plaintiff with evidence showing nothing beyond parallel conduct is not entitled to a directed verdict, see *Theatre Enterprises*, supra; proof of a §1 conspiracy must include

---

[56] It is even more difficult than the text suggests because, as noted, some of the key Supreme Court precedents in question are not just pertinent to Section 1 but they also more broadly define conspiracy for all federal law. If those articulations of the blackletter law of conspiracy were overturned, centuries of conspiracy law would be rejected. Alternatively, the cases could be viewed as reversed only for purposes of federal antitrust law. In any event, given all the attention to whether to overrule a single, widely criticized antitrust precedent by both the majority and the dissent in the nearly contemporaneous decision in *Leegin*, it would be surprising for such a long line of cases to be overturned in passing when no *Twombly* opinion indicates that the underlying legal question was even at issue.

[57] In this regard, it is important to note that the circuit court opinion under review had specifically held that a plaintiff did not have to plead any plus factors to survive a motion to dismiss. See 550 U.S. at 553. The district court had dismissed the complaint for failing to allege any plus factor, and the circuit court reversed, holding that at the motion-to-dismiss stage, plus factors were unnecessary: "[T]he [district] court required the plaintiffs to 'establish[] at least one "plus factor" that tends to exclude independent self-interested conduct as an explanation for defendants' parallel behavior.' [313 F. Supp. 2d] at 179. Such a factor, the court noted, could be, for example, 'evidence that the parallel behavior would have been against individual defendants' economic interests absent an agreement, or that defendants possessed a strong common motive to conspire.'" Twombly v. Bell Atlantic Corp., 425 F.3d 99, 104 (2nd Cir. 2005). Accordingly, under the circuit court's formulation, a plaintiff could proceed without having suggested any basis for ruling out purely independent, competitive behavior. See note 47 and section 5.B.

[58] 550 U.S. at 553. The Supreme Court's subsequent decision in Ashcroft v. Iqbal, 129 S.Ct. 1937, 1950 (2009), characterizes its own recent *Twombly* decision as concerned with the distinction between "agreement" and "unchoreographed free-market behavior," the latter apparently referring to independent, competitive behavior rather than to interdependent, coordinated, anticompetitive behavior.

evidence tending to exclude the possibility of independent action, see *Monsanto* . . . ; and at the summary judgment stage a §1 plaintiff's offer of conspiracy evidence must tend to rule out the possibility that the defendants were acting independently, see *Matsushita* . . . . [59]

Likewise, the dissent opens its opinion citing *Theatre Enterprises* for an authoritative statement of settled law, followed by the declaration that "this is a case in which there is no dispute about the substantive law. If the defendants acted independently, their conduct was perfectly lawful. If, however, that conduct is the product of a horizontal agreement among potential competitors, it was unlawful."[60] Taken together, it seems clear that neither the majority nor the dissent focuses on disputes over the meaning of agreement or deals with the question as one would have expected if the decision were directly addressed to that issue.[61] Furthermore, both their language and the cases cited in these discussions are ones that, as explained in subsection 1, include interdependent behavior.

---

[59] 550 U.S. at 554. The Court goes on to posit, "A statement of parallel conduct, even conduct consciously undertaken, needs some setting suggesting the agreement necessary to make out a §1 claim; without that further circumstance pointing toward a meeting of the minds, an account of a defendant's commercial efforts stays in neutral territory." 550 U.S. at 557; compare section 2.B, on the meaning of "meeting of the minds" and subsection 4.B.1's quotation of the language of *American Tobacco* (including note 39, presenting *Monsanto's* quotation of the pertinent passage of *American Tobacco*).

[60] 550 U.S. at 571 (Stevens, J., dissenting).

[61] See note 52, elaborating on how the Court and the parties did not focus on the legal standard for an agreement. In addition to the Court's seemingly clear but conflicting statements of both a narrow and a broad reading of Section 1's agreement requirement, it also made more confusing comments, such as, "The inadequacy of showing parallel conduct or interdependence, without more, mirrors the ambiguity of the behavior: consistent with conspiracy, but just as much in line with a wide swath of rational and competitive business strategy unilaterally prompted by common perceptions of the market." 550 U.S. at 554. The second part of this statement, taking into account the first part's combining of parallel conduct and interdependence, asserts literally that interdependence is consistent with competitive business behavior, which by ordinary understandings it plainly is not. See section 2.B. For example, in application of Section 1's rule-of-reason test (see subsection 3.B), there is no question that practices that facilitate oligopolistic coordination are deemed suppressions of competition, not as promoting a form of ordinary competitive business behavior.

Regarding both the early and subsequent decisions, some common elements should be emphasized, concerning primarily what they lack in common. None carefully considers well-articulated, competing specifications of the agreement requirement or elaborates on the meaning of the various pronouncements that are made. From some, notably the long line of earlier cases specifically on the agreement requirement, one gets a strong sense of a broad rule that encompasses interdependent oligopolistic behavior. From more recent cases not aimed at interpreting Section 1's trigger, one is told that such behavior in pure form is understood to be excluded, without any indication that a new legal standard is being articulated or reconciliation with the conflicting statements and citations. Furthermore, recent cases offer little hint of what more is required, a matter that chapter 2 indicates to be of great importance and difficult to pin down, especially from formulations using the sort of language that the Supreme Court employs.[62] Repeated demands that there must exist an agreement or a conspiracy are question-begging. Perhaps an express agreement is required. Yet *Twombly*, as noted, quotes *Theatre Enterprises* for the proposition that a tacit agreement is sufficient, as distinguished from independent behavior (which, in the context of *Theatre Enterprises*, refers to purely independent behavior). In any event, as previously discussed, it is difficult to know what express or tacit agreement means.

Finally, one does not find in any of the opinions, early or recent, an explicit discussion of the substantive reasons for interpreting Section 1 in whatever manner each Court imagined itself to be doing. Instead, in each case the Court simply declares what it takes to be self-evident. Reliance on ipse dixit statements is perhaps less surprising in the more recent decisions, in which the question was not formally before the Court and the parties did not contest the matter, but this feature amplifies the uncertainty about the import of the Court's latest pronouncements.

---

[62] For example, Elhauge and Geradin (2007, supp. 106–7) state that *Twombly* is clear that mere oligopolistic coordination is insufficient, so that plaintiffs must demonstrate plus factors. Yet, as will be discussed in section 5.B, many such plus factors merely establish that behavior is interdependent rather than independent.

C. EU Article 101

It is typical of competition policy regulation throughout the world that price fixing and related agreements are illegal, so the question of what constitutes such an agreement is hardly confined to the United States. Therefore, it is natural to suppose that the challenges in defining horizontal agreement are not at all unique to Sherman Act Section 1 but rather are pervasive—that is, if the law attempts to limit the price-fixing prohibition to a narrower class of arrangements than all those involving successful interdependence. After all, the difficulty is not just with the statutory language of Section 1. As mentioned, the term agreement is not even in this statute, and in any event many of the other concepts examined in chapters 2 and 3 are similarly elusive. The difficulty of dealing with the sorts of examples presented there does not arise on account of legal authorities and commentators being confined in their answers and rationalizations to a handful of particular terms in the English language.[63] U.S. law is the focus in this chapter and the next for concreteness and because of the author's familiarity with it. Nevertheless, the main ideas are reinforced when one looks elsewhere. Accordingly, this section briefly and timorously[64] examines the most closely corresponding provision in the law of the European Union.[65]

---

[63] Indeed, a hypothetical involving gasoline stations (but now "petrol" stations) is used to illustrate the challenge in Van Gerven and Varona (1994, 577–78).

[64] The reader is undoubtedly aware that this author is not an expert in EU competition law. As the notes to follow reflect, I have consulted multiple treatises and other sources, and I have also benefited from the input of research assistants from the EU with competition law experience. That said, this section should be viewed as merely suggestive. In any event, the difficulties I identify are highly reminiscent of those in U.S. law, which as explained in the prior sections of this chapter (and in the two chapters to follow) differs importantly from what many commentators suggest. It should further be noted that the problems identified in chapters 6 and 7 do not depend on the particulars of governing law and its interpretation (as long as it does not cover all interdependent behavior), and the policy analysis in parts II and III of the book is likewise independent of the legal regime (although different institutional arrangements may bear on optimal policy, as discussed in section 15.A).

[65] Elhauge and Geradin (2007, 801) remark that "on both sides of the Atlantic [i.e., in both the United States and European Union], the conclusions drawn about this distinction

Article 101(1) (formerly 81(1)) covers "all agreements between undertakings, decisions by associations of undertakings and concerted
practices . . . which have as their object or effect the prevention, restriction or distortion of competition," including "in particular those which:
(a) directly or indirectly fix purchase or selling prices or any other trading conditions."[66] Article 101(1), like Sherman Act Section 1, offers a

---

[between parallel separate action and agreement/concerted action] in the cases often seem
obscure or conclusory."

[66] If firms' relationship does not fit any of the categories, there remains the question of
whether their behavior may be reached under Article 102 (formerly 82), which covers "[a]ny
abuse by one or more undertakings of a dominant position," where the named abuses include
"directly or indirectly imposing unfair purchase or selling prices." (By contrast, Sherman Act
Section 2 is understood not to reach elevated prices charged by a dominant firm.) The European Court of Justice articulated the concept of collective dominance as requiring "that from
an economic point of view [the firms] present themselves or act together on a particular
market as a collective entity." Compagnie Maritime Belge Transports SA, Compagnie Maritime Belge SA and Dafra-Lines A/S v. Commission, [2000] ECR I–1356, at ¶36. It elaborated
(¶45) that "the existence of an agreement or of other links in law is not indispensable to a
finding of a collective dominant position; such a finding may be based on other connecting
factors and would depend on an economic assessment and, in particular, on an assessment of
the structure of the market in question." The 2002 decision of the Court of First Instance in
Airtours, CFI 06–06–2002, T–342/99, as well as discussions in certain previous cases, suggests that successful interdependent oligopoly behavior is reached by Article 102. The case
involved a merger, and the Court overturned the Commission's prohibition; however, its reasoning was that the collective dominance standard was not met on the facts because the
market was not one sufficiently conducive to successful and sustained oligopoly pricing. See
Albors-Llorens (2004, 166–68); Stroux (2004, 109–10, 114–15), suggesting that the *Compagnie Maritime Belge* decision and other sources do seem to support application of Article 102
to oligopolistic interdependence, but questioning the wisdom of this approach; and Whish
(2009, 564). See also European Commission (2005, ¶¶46–47): "However, the existence of an
agreement or of other links in law is not indispensable to a finding of a collective dominant
position. Such a finding may be based on other connecting factors and depends on an economic assessment and, in particular, on an assessment of the structure of the market in question. . . . Undertakings in oligopolistic markets may sometimes be able to raise prices substantially above the competitive level without having recourse to any explicit agreement or
concerted practice. . . . Indeed, they may be able to coordinate their behaviour on the market
by observing and reacting to each other's behaviour. In other words, they may be able to
adopt a common strategy that allows them to present themselves or act together as a collective entity." For a contrary view, see Hawk and Motta (2009, 87–94), arguing that the Commission and courts would not treat oligopolistic interdependence as collective dominance.
To the extent that Article 102 does cover interdependence that effectively sustains joint profit

trilogy of overlapping categories.[67] Interestingly, the first is "agreements," the term used to refer to the requirement under U.S. law even though the term does not actually appear in Sherman Act Section 1. Use of this term, in turn, raises all the problems of interpretation considered thus far. One statement of agreement's meaning under Article 101(1) is that "[a]ll that seems to be required . . . is some form of consensus between two or more undertakings—also referred to as a 'meeting between minds' or a 'concurrence of wills,'"[68] an interpretation that appears to be quite broad, embracing pure interdependence. The second category, "decisions by associations of undertakings," is generally regarded to refer primarily to acts of trade associations.[69]

The third branch, "concerted practices," is (like "agreements") potentially quite expansive,[70] and many of the most important rulings regarding coordinated oligopoly behavior have centered here. In *Dyestuffs*, the European Court of Justice stated that this provision brings within the prohibition "a form of coordination . . . which . . . knowingly substitutes practical cooperation between [undertakings] for the risks of competition. By its very nature, then, a concerted practice . . . may *inter alia* arise out of coordination which becomes apparent from the behaviour

---

maximization, limitations on the ability to reach successful coordinated oligopolistic pricing under Article 101(1) may largely be moot.

[67] As discussed in subsection A.1 with regard to Sherman Act Section 1's trilogy, it is tempting to interpret the overlapping categories in Article 101(1) as an all-encompassing directive meaning "in any way, shape, or form." In fact, perhaps reflecting civil law traditions of statutory interpretation, EU legal authorities give each term or phrase its own construction— although nothing turns on the distinction and "in cartel cases the Commission often states that there is an agreement or a concerted practice, without actually deciding which." Van Bael and Bellis (2005, 61). However, especially given the open-ended nature of the third category, concerted practices, this approach need not imply a limitation on the breadth with which Article 101(1) may be interpreted.

[68] Dabbah (2004, 59), citing Volkswagen AG v. Commission, CFI (2003).

[69] See Dabbah (2004, 69).

[70] Standard meanings of concerted are mutually contrived or agreed on (the former seeming broad enough to embrace interdependent coordination and the latter collapsing back to the definition of agreement) and performed in unison (which could encompass mere parallelism). In interpreting the EU Treaty, however, it seems especially difficult to place much weight on particular definitions of terms that are used in just one of the many languages in which the provisions are translated.

of the participants."[71] The emphasis on cooperation rather than competition and the notion that a concerted practice may be inferred from behavior suggest that interdependent oligopoly behavior (without more) is covered by the prohibition. The Court elaborates the conditions in the *Sugar Cartel* case:

> The criteria of coordination and cooperation ... must be understood in the light of the concept ... that each economic operator must determine independently the policy which he intends to adopt .... Although it is correct to say that this requirement of independence does not deprive economic operators of the right to adapt themselves intelligently to the existing and anticipated conduct of their competitors, it does however strictly preclude any direct or indirect contact between such operators, the object or effect whereof is either to influence the conduct on the market of an actual or potential competitor or to disclose to such a competitor the course of conduct which they themselves have decided to adopt or contemplate adopting on the market.[72]

The Court later states that the firms had violated this prohibition "because they knowingly substituted for the risks of competition practical cooperation between them, which culminated in a situation which did not correspond to the normal conditions of the market."[73]

This final statement bears some resemblance to that offered by the U.S. Supreme Court in *Monsanto* and *Matsushita* in placing emphasis on whether behavior is independent and interprets such behavior as contrasting with that which displaces competition. Accordingly, the problem of the multiple meanings of the term independent is presented, and use of the link to competition may be seen as favoring the narrower meaning, excluding interdependence, as discussed in chapter 2. On the other hand, there is also language stating that it is permissible to adapt

---

[71] Imperial Chemical Industries Ltd. v. Commission, Cases 49, 49, 51–57/69, [1972] ECR 619, at ¶¶64, 65.

[72] Suiker Unie v. Commission, Cases 40–48, 50, 54–56, 111, 113–114/73, [1975] ECR 1663, at ¶¶173, 174.

[73] [1975] ECR 1663, at ¶191.

intelligently to the anticipated conduct of competitors, which might be taken to allow interdependent oligopolistic behavior. Under this interpretation, the risks of competition include oligopoly behavior that is normal under the circumstances. This formulation has a question-begging aspect because in many markets elaborate cartel arrangements would be normal if they were not illegal. Perhaps the line is drawn by the statement that the statute does "strictly preclude any direct or indirect contact [that can] influence the conduct . . . of competitor[s] or . . . disclose to . . . competitor[s] [an actor's] course of conduct."[74] This statement seems like a prohibition on some communications, but which ones are covered is hard to say. Including "indirect" means could encompass just about anything, as the discussion in chapter 3 indicates. Furthermore, disclosing conduct that a firm has decided to adopt covers readily even an announcement of one's current price, which would be broad indeed.

Further amplification is provided by the European Court of Justice's subsequent decision in *Woodpulp II*, which involved, among other practices, advance price announcements.[75] It holds that oligopoly behavior does not establish the use of concerted practices unless, given the nature of the market, the behavior cannot be explained other than by concerted behavior.[76] This rule is in an important sense an empty truism, begging the question of what constitutes a concerted practice under Article 101(1). The Court's discussion of the facts, however, indicates that

---

[74] Commentators have struggled with how the rule might be formulated. For example, Wollmann (2008, 501), after depicting the European Union as tolerant of interdependent behavior, proceeds to explain that "what is severely prohibited is to directly or indirectly liaise with undertakings with the object of influencing the market conduct of actual or potential competitors or to communicate one's own market conduct to such competitors." When we reflect on the fact that liaise means to establish mutual understanding and cooperation or interrelationship, we have that interdependence alone is legal but interrelationship is harshly punished, which is certainly no more illuminating than the semantics often used to describe U.S. law (if it is taken to allow pure interdependence).

[75] A Åhlström Osakeyhtiö v. Commission, Cases C–89, 104, 114, 116–117, 125–129/85 [1993] ECR I–1307.

[76] [1993] ECR I–1307, at ¶71: "parallel conduct cannot be regarded as furnishing proof of concertation unless concertation constitutes the only plausible explanation for such conduct."

it intends to exclude interdependent oligopolistic behavior in the absence of what it called "artificial" modifications to the market.[77] Advance price announcements were deemed to be favorable to buyers in light of their need to plan.[78] It was suggested that the concentrated large buyers contributed to the ease of coordinated oligopoly pricing by sellers because such buyers readily shared price information with each other and with sellers. Additionally, some sellers were also involved in production at the next stage and thus were also buyers and, in that capacity, could learn from the other sellers about their prices. And there were agents who worked for multiple firms and thus could be seen as another conduit for rapid sharing of price information among sellers.

In a sense, the *Woodpulp II* decision adds much clarification because one might view so many of the cited facts as favorable to liability. It is widely known that having concentrated buyers placing large orders makes coordinated price elevation difficult, not easy, and it is surprising to think that a large buyer obtaining a secret price cut would happily offer this information to its competitors so that they too could benefit, depriving the first buyer of any competitive advantage. Perhaps the Court was confused. That it drew much of its analysis from its own appointed experts adds to the mystery.[79] Or perhaps the cited behavior suggests the existence of a cartel among the buyers, operating jointly

---

[77] The Court concludes, "Following that analysis, it must be stated that, in this case, concertation is not the only plausible explanation for the parallel conduct. To begin with, the system of price announcements may be regarded as constituting a rational response to the fact that the pulp market constituted a long-term market and to the need felt by both buyers and sellers to limit commercial risks. Further, the similarity in the dates of price announcements may be regarded as a direct result of the high degree of market transparency, which does not have to be described as artificial. Finally, the parallelism of prices and the price trends may be satisfactorily explained by the oligopolistic tendencies of the market and by the specific circumstances prevailing in certain periods. Accordingly, the parallel conduct established by the Commission does not constitute evidence of concertation." [1993] ECR I–1307, at ¶126.

[78] For critical comments on this frequently expressed idea, see note 56 in chapter 7. In addition, the Court stated that the price announcements made to users do not lessen each producer's uncertainty as to the future attitude of its competitors because, at the time a producer makes its price announcement, "it cannot be sure of the future conduct of the others." Van Bael and Bellis (2005, 58). By this logic, however, even formal cartel agreements would be legal because they in no way bind others' future conduct. See section 2.C.

[79] Serious questions about the reliability of these expert reports have been noted. Harding

with the sellers in some fashion; however, because Article 101(1) explicitly prohibits price fixing by purchasers, the opinion's suggestion that purchasers freely shared their buying prices would seem to describe illegal behavior on their part. Likewise, many of the other practices might be viewed as violations because they are facilitating practices or because they constitute evidence of price fixing itself.[80] Finally, although not particularly relevant in identifying the legal boundary, the Court also chose to ignore what would normally be viewed as smoking-gun evidence of collusion.[81]

In any event, *Woodpulp II* does seem to represent a narrowing of the interpretation of Article 101(1). But the opinion's statements of the rule and applications create much ambiguity and do not resolve apparent contradictions. After all, the Court accepted the broad formulations from the prior cases that appear to have been met or exceeded by many of the cited facts. The practices were nevertheless permitted because they were not "artificial." At this point, however, we have a new ambiguous term that carries all the weight. Furthermore, as mentioned, direct discussions among competitors to fix prices are perfectly normal—as Adam Smith famously proclaimed—and can be expected to occur if not

---

and Joshua (2003, 158 & n.43) describe the Advocate General's analysis thereof as a "mauling."

[80] The idea that it is permissible for competing firms in a concentrated industry to use common agents who transmit pricing information between firms might seem to legalize cartel activity. Also, if buyers may obtain pricing information from all sellers and, moreover, sellers are simultaneously free to act as buyers (perhaps very small buyers), the ruling seems to offer another invitation to circumvention. In both instances and others, the Court offered little detail about what actually transpired, although these activities were cited as key reasons that one could not infer concerted practices—which, recall, the *Sugar Cartel* case deemed to cover all contacts, including indirect ones.

[81] "First of all, the Court summarily excluded the clear evidence of collusion, based on telex communications, meetings, and documents. It did this because it had asked the Commission to indicate between which producers and for what periods each telex and document was proof of collusion. [The Commission argued that such detail was unnecessary.] The Court did not respond to that argument as such (which was partly the 'cartel as a whole' argument) but simply stated in a terse and perplexing non sequitur that 'in the light of that reply those documents must be excluded from consideration.'" Harding and Joshua (2003, 157). In a footnote (n.40), the authors elaborate that "[t]his assertion by the court is one of the most perplexing. The Commission had in fact supplied further tables containing full details of each individual manifestation of the alleged collusion ([citation omitted])."

made illegal. If the practices mentioned in the case were deemed illegal and if the law was enforced, they would cease to be normal. Perhaps, then, it is not surprising that, after this decision, which many see as firmly limiting the reach of Article 101(1), one still finds prominent depictions of the provision that are quite broad.[82]

---

[82] "Indeed, the intention of Article 81 EC is to catch all forms of collusion having the same nature, focusing on the substance and economic reality of the relations between undertakings rather than their form. Thus the concept of collusion under Article 81 EC 'centres around the existence of a concurrence of wills', whereby 'it is necessary that the manifestation of the wish of one of the contracting parties to achieve an anticompetitive goal constitutes an invitation to the other party, whether express or implied, to fulfil that goal jointly." Siragusa and Rizza (2007, 10), quoting Joined Cases C-2 and C-03/01 Bundesverband der Arzneimittel-Importeure and Commission/Bayer, [2004] ECR I-23, ¶¶97, 102. See Van Bael and Bellis (2005, 27): "Article 81 is formulated quite broadly so as to cover not only agreements but all types of collusion between undertakings that restrict competition. Undertakings are to compete with each other, and not cooperate to influence market conditions to the detriment of competition and ultimately of consumers."; ibid. (40): "The term 'agreement' in Article 81(1) is to be interpreted broadly so as to encompass any kind of consensus or understanding between parties as to their future behaviour. . . . [I]t is sufficient that the undertakings have somehow expressed their joint intention to conduct themselves on the market in a specific way. The manner in which such joint intention is expressed (e.g., in writing or orally) does not matter."; and ibid. (44–45), stating that seemingly unilateral actions are covered "if there is a 'concurrence of wills between undertakings', which is the central element of an agreement." Bellamy and Child (2008, 124) suggest that the cases imply that the requirement is of "some positive contact between undertakings, that will often consist of meetings, discussions, disclosure of information, or 'soundings out', whether oral or written," but they fail to explain how the latter does not readily include the sort of advance price announcements allowed in *Woodpulp II*. See also note 66, discussing how Article 102 on collective dominance may reach coordinated oligopolistic behavior even if it is not covered under Article 101(1); Argos Ltd. v. Office of Fair Trading, [2006] EWCA Civ 1318, ¶¶21–27, interpreting U.K. law on concerted practices broadly, citing EU law as being in accord.

5

U.S. Lower Court Practice

Given the uncertainty about how best to interpret the Supreme Court's later pronouncements and the more than half a century since its decisions directly on Section 1's agreement requirement, the lower courts have lacked clear guidance. This chapter examines how these courts confront central legal questions that routinely arise in price-fixing and other horizontal-restraints cases in which the existence of an agreement is in dispute. In light of the discussion in chapters 2–4, it is not surprising that the practice in lower courts is difficult to characterize—although some commentators nevertheless depict a substantially harmonious state of affairs.

The problem begins with the frequent need to make inferences from circumstantial evidence, which all acknowledge to be necessary.[1] As a consequence of the problem of defining agreement, it is difficult to know what one is trying to infer or how inferences can be made even when evidence of agreement appears to be fairly direct. Various seemingly clear rules, such as the demand for so-called plus factors, are unclear upon examination and cast serious doubt on the conventional view of the law. Furthermore, when one looks at what the courts actually do—that is, what sorts of facts they find adequate or insufficient to support a finding of an agreement—the picture becomes even murkier. Sometimes facts wholly consistent with purely interdependent behavior are cited as showing the existence of an agreement, even an express agreement. In addition, when cases get to a jury, standard instructions do not sharply define what concept of agreement the factfinder is supposed to consider and invite a

---

[1] Strictly speaking, it is not. Section 18.B considers a regime that excludes or significantly limits reliance on such evidence.

broad interpretation. Rules governing the calculation of damages are also in tension with leading formulations of the standard for liability. Finally, as introduced briefly in the final section here and elaborated in the next chapter, the conventional, circumscribed view of the agreement requirement gives rise to a paradox of proof that has powerful implications which seem largely inconsistent with practice in lower courts.

A. Circumstantial Evidence

In some cases, such as those challenging open trade association practices, there is no question that an agreement exists, at least regarding the open practices themselves. In others, including a number of notorious price-fixing cases uncovered by government investigations, evidence directly establishes an agreement's existence under any interpretation of the term.[2] However, because some horizontal agreements, notably those involving price fixing, are per se illegal and subject to serious sanctions—including

---

[2] Surprisingly, even in cases with direct evidence, courts do not uniformly find agreements to exist. For example, Petruzzi's IGA Supermarkets, Inc. v. Darling-Delaware Co., 998 F.2d 1224, 1233–35 (3rd Cir. 1993), reversed a district court's grant of summary judgment for the defendant, citing, among other evidence that the trial court found insufficient, a former employee's statement that a superior twice said that there was an agreement and another employee's statement that there were discussions between firms about keeping prices low and that a nonconspirator was solicited to join. In re Baby Food Antitrust Litig., 166 F.3d 112, 118–21, 124–28 (3rd Cir. 1999), deemed insufficient for the plaintiffs to survive summary judgment such evidence as the fact that sales representatives often traded future price information, managers informed sales representatives in advance of competitors' planned price increases, firms possessed competitors' confidential reports about strategies including in some instances about future prices, and an internal email from a defendant manager referred to a "truce" being in effect. (Reasons for rejecting such as insufficient included evidence that much price exchange was by lower-level employees and that defendants did not succeed in oligopoly pricing.) In Blomquist Fertilizer, Inc. v. Potash Corp. of Saskatchewan, Inc., 203 F.3d 1028, 1033–37 (8th Cir.) (en banc), cert. denied, 531 U.S. 815 (2000), a narrow majority found insufficient for plaintiffs to survive summary judgment, among other evidence, proof that high officials verbally verified specific price quotations on completed sales, a variation on the pre-sale verification that the Supreme Court had deemed per se illegal in *Container*; that a foreign cartel memorandum predicted, mostly correctly, future price lists; that there were solicitations to fix prices; and that an internal executive document proposed joint action, which was followed by sudden price changes.

criminal penalties and treble damages in the United States—prospective conspirators attempt to keep their actions secret and, where possible, to rely on more indirect and subtle means of achieving oligopolistic price coordination. Accordingly, it is frequently the case that an agreement must be inferred from circumstantial evidence, and it is an uncontroversial proposition of competition law (and conspiracy law more generally)[3] that this method of proof is available to plaintiffs, including the government.[4]

As a preliminary observation, one obviously cannot know how to infer an agreement from circumstantial evidence without first articulating what an agreement is. If interdependent oligopolistic price setting constitutes an agreement, then firms' coordinated supracompetitive pricing behavior would seem to be direct evidence of agreement. For example, one firm raising its price above competitive levels (that is, not due to a corresponding rise in input prices), followed by other firms matching the price rise and maintaining prices at the elevated level, would be such evidence. Or there might exist internal records indicating that each firm understood itself to be behaving in this fashion. Whether one, the other, or both constituted direct rather than indirect evidence of agreement would depend on whether the acts themselves or the underlying motivations and understandings were deemed to constitute the requisite agreement; it is not clear that any such distinction would matter. Evidence of secret communications between the firms about future pricing might even be regarded as indirect, circumstantial evidence because it is possible that the firms were lying to each other rather than really agreeing to act or that the necessary internal understanding regarding coordination may

---

[3] See LaFave (2003, 267): "[I]t is thus well established that the prosecution may 'rely on inferences drawn from the course of conduct of the alleged conspirators.'" (Quoting *Interstate Circuit*, 306 U.S. at 221.) See also subsection 4.A.2.

[4] See ABA (2007, 5–6 & n.29): "Conspiracies can be proven either by direct or circumstantial evidence. . . . [C]ourts traditionally recognized that '[o]nly rarely will there be direct evidence of an express agreement' in conspiracy cases . . . . Circumstantial evidence as to this element of the offense is . . . not only admissible, but often dispositive." (quoting Local Union No. 189, Amalgamated Meat Cutters v. Jewel Tea Co., 381 U.S. 676, 720 (1965) (Goldberg, J., concurring), and for the latter proposition, citing, inter alia, *Monsanto*); Areeda and Hovenkamp (2003, 2); and Blair (2008, 3), who, in introducing a symposium on *Twombly*, mentions that "plaintiffs may, of course, rely upon circumstantial evidence."

not be formed (due to a lack of trust), and interdependent pricing may not arise. Perhaps such evidence might give rise to a presumption of price fixing or be viewed as attempted price fixing even if the defendants could show that no real meeting of the minds or subsequent coordination ever occurred. In any event, none of these scenarios raise serious conceptual inference problems.

Now suppose instead that more than interdependent oligopolistic behavior is required to constitute an agreement. In that event, it is necessary to specify further the boundary—to state just what additional ingredients are necessary—because one must know what it is that is being inferred in order to assess whether an inference of agreement makes sense. As chapter 3 discusses, many seem to have in mind a demarcation rooted in different sorts of communication. Perhaps words or very close substitutes are impermissible, but subtler signs and signals are allowed. Perhaps it is the mode of communication that matters. Or whether the communications are public. Or whether what is communicated is a prediction or hope rather than intentions, or maybe intentions may be communicated but not assurances. The formulation of the message might matter or only its content. As mentioned, some ways of drawing the line along these and other dimensions are, upon reflection, tantamount to proscribing all interdependent behavior, or very close to it. In any event, as long as the line is drawn at some distance from such a place, there will be communications of type X that are prohibited and fairly similar communications in a category X', which perhaps convey the same content in some settings, that are permitted.[5]

Recognizing the nature of this situation further elevates the problem posed by the agreement requirement. The reason is that the possibly subtle and slight distinction between some elements of X and others of X' may be made by inference from circumstantial evidence. Because it is inevitable that there will be some acts in X and X' that are virtually indistinguishable when viewed directly, clearly, and closely, how are they to be differentiated when viewed indirectly, obscurely, and from afar?

Related, consider the posited theoretical relationship between the use of different means and how the firms' ends are affected. On one hand,

---

[5] Recall from page 52 and note 3 in chapter 3 that the sets X and X' can contain all manner of acts, not just those distinguished by the character of communications involved.

even highly explicit and uninhibited communications can fail: Some firms may not agree, and even if all do think that they have agreed, cheating may nevertheless break out quickly. On the other hand, even communications limited to ordinary pricing behavior in the marketplace might succeed. It is usually believed (but, as will be discussed in subsection 7.B.2, not universally true) that explicit, frequent, and direct communications make success more likely. The hypothesized relationship is probabilistic. On average, the difference in the likelihood of success when using certain elements of X rather than certain others of X' (those near the boundaries) will be small. Oligopolistic coordination may be quite unlikely, but nevertheless more likely when using acts in X. Or it might be highly likely, but even more so when using acts in X. Furthermore, as stated, these relationships are true only on average; in any given case, there may be no discernable effect, and sometimes the effect will be the reverse.

We can see that, if agreement requires more than successful coordination, the routine inference problem in horizontal agreement cases can be daunting. Much of chapter 6 will further elaborate aspects of this challenge. As a logical matter, this problem need not be present in all cases: If observed behavior could have arisen only through the use of prohibited means in X that have no resemblance to any of those in X', then an agreement may readily be inferred. Yet it is unclear whether such confident inferences will often be possible,[6] and the discussion of communications and language in chapter 3 raises significant doubts.

---

[6] Perhaps most often mentioned is the submission of identical, non-round-number, secret bids for made-to-order items. (All of the qualifications are necessary for the claimed inference, which shows how infrequently it would be available.) See, for example, Areeda and Hovenkamp (2003, 168, 243). Even this limited exception, however, has further, unrecognized qualifications. Notably, it must also be true that public price announcements are deemed illegal (which most who offer this sort of illustration do not believe to be the case). To see why, suppose that the use of prohibited communications might otherwise be inferred from the posited identity of secret bids at a price of, say, 3.518 per unit. To break the inference of secret advance communications, all that is required is for one clever firm to announce publicly that it intends to bid (or is thinking of bidding) 3.518, at which point a follow-the-price-leader explanation is a competing inference. Of course, the firms may well have met secretly to agree on the 3.518 price; but as long as, after the meeting, some firm makes the public announcement—and this too can be planned at the meeting—the ability to infer from the pricing coincidence that such a meeting must have occurred would be disrupted. (The

It should also be observed that game-theoretic logic does not offer a simple solution to this inference problem, as elaborated in subsection 6.D.4. To sketch the difficulty, one might initially suppose that firms would be inclined to use acts in X′ rather than those in X, even if the latter are more effective, because the former are legal and thus not subject to a risk of sanctions. If, however, an adjudicator will probably need to rely on circumstantial evidence to infer which type of acts were used, and moreover if it is known that the adjudicator will reason in this fashion, then using acts in X rather than solely ones in X′ may make sense after all. But in that case, the rational inference would be that acts in X were indeed used. Thus, the inference problem is more complicated.

Consider now the sorts of circumstantial evidence that may be relevant for drawing the necessary inferences, continuing to assume a narrower

fact that we never seem to observe this circumvention strategy is suggestive of what firms and their lawyers implicitly believe the law to be. See section 6.F.)

This example also has another serious deficiency: If the firms are secretly meeting to set prices, why should they all submit identical bids that will appear suspicious? See Posner (2001, 87). Instead, they could—and, it appears, do—choose the low bidder in advance and arrange for others to submit plausible-looking-but-higher bids. Porter (2005, 156), in reviewing a study of auctions for oil and gas leases, suggests that bids may have been submitted in such a fashion as "to create the appearance of competition." Porter and Zona (1993) find that non-winning cartel members submitted phony higher bids in highway construction auctions. The U.S. Department of Justice (2005) observes, "Complementary bidding schemes are the most frequently occurring forms of bid rigging, and they defraud purchasers by creating the appearance of competition to conceal secretly inflated prices." Winners might be chosen randomly. However, more often, particular rotations would be more efficient and thus profitable for the conspirators. For example, it would be better to allocate particular bids to firms that have more excess capacity at the moment or are more favorably located. And there is evidence that bidders that meet secretly to plan bids do rotate in this fashion rather than submit identical bids and leave it to the buyer to choose the winner. Comanor and Schankerman (1976) argue that bid rotation is more likely, especially when there are smaller numbers of firms, and they report that, in prosecuted bidding cartels, the substantial majority of cases involving eight or fewer firms employed bid rotation. See also Cook (1963, 68): "In fact, if I were asked, I would certainly bet that most conspiracies involving public tenders are conspiracies to rotate the low bid—and the business. That is, the bidding firms have agreed among themselves who should get the business, and they purposely let that company be low."; and Davis and Wilson (2002, 64–72), who examine the effects of allowing communications on pricing in experimental sealed-bid auctions both when firms' costs are fixed and when they depend on output committed as a result of winning previous auctions. Indeed, McAfee and McMillan (1992, 584) argue that the high prevalence of identical secret bids in government contracting is evidence of less explicit cartel arrangements.

agreement requirement. One type of evidence is from the market, including both firms' pricing behavior and the degree to which their market
conditions are conducive to successful coordination, which chapter 6
considers in depth. Another important sort of evidence, which plays a
significant role in some litigated cases, is internal. For example, there may
be internal communications about price elevation, price leadership behavior, and the degree of homogeneity of competing firms' products.
When internal evidence refers to the same sorts of circumstances as the
external evidence just mentioned, the same analysis is applicable.

In addition to internal circumstantial evidence, there also may be
internal direct evidence that, if sufficiently unambiguous and credible,
would alleviate the need to rely on circumstantial evidence (and that more
broadly may combine with circumstantial evidence in reaching a conclusion, as discussed in subsection 6.D.1). To illustrate, take what may seem
to be an easy case: Each firm's internal documents attest to the fact that
the firms in the industry have an "agreement." Although most courts
would presumably find this to be sufficient evidence from which one
might rationally infer an agreement and might even characterize it as a
direct admission,[7] a moment's reflection suggests a serious difficulty in
reaching such conclusions. As section 2.B indicates and much of this part
of the book elaborates, a common use of the term agreement refers to
interdependence, and in the present discussion we are assuming that
interdependence alone is insufficient for liability. Therefore, even if firms
use the magic words of the doctrine (or of the statute, such as by referring
to their "conspiracy"), they may not mean what the courts mean. And, if

---

[7] Consider, for example, the following evidence that was held to support an inference that
the parties in question acted in concert: "Salisbury signed a written statement stating, 'I did
not bother Darling accounts. Mr. Sage [a high-level Moyer solicitor] told me on at least two
occasions that there was a *mutual agreement and understanding with Darling*, not to bother
their accounts.' . . . When discussing this statement during his deposition, Salisbury stated
that Sage told him: 'there was an understanding.' . . . While Salisbury later testified that he
was not told of any understanding or agreement that Moyer had with any other company . . . ,
he did not retract his statement as to Darling. In fact, Salisbury testified: 'I told [Mr. Rubin
and Mr. Keiser, lawyers for Petruzzi's IGA] that there was an agreement or understanding. I
also explained to Mr. Kaiser (sic) it has been going on ever since I have been in the business.
Ever since 1969. It was something that everybody done (sic).'" Petruzzi's IGA Supermarkets,
Inc. v. Darling-Delaware Co., 998 F.2d 1224, 1234 (3rd Cir. 1993) (emphasis, parentheticals,
and brackets in original).

pressed at a deposition or in court, firms' officials who have used such terms would be strongly motivated (and coached) to suggest the innocent interpretation regardless.

More commonly, cases refer to internal evidence of an "understanding" in an industry, that competitors are viewed as "friends," and so forth.[8] Such documentation seems to be treated as smoking-gun evidence, that is, clear, direct evidence of an agreement.[9] However, all such language is what one would expect to find if rational firms were successfully engaged in interdependent oligopolistic behavior, without regard to the modes of communication that they employed. Courts' willingness to find that such statements nevertheless constitute sufficient evidence of agreement indicates that, whatever they might state the legal test to be, it de facto reverts to interdependence once certain types of evidence of interdependence are presented.

It is perfectly sensible to deem such evidence highly probative of liability if the real problem to be avoided is not penalizing actual coordinated oligopolistic pricing but instead accidently punishing truly competitive behavior that a plaintiff has incorrectly alleged to be coordinated. However, if the law really requires that firms have used means of communication X rather than merely X' in implementing coordinated oligopoly pricing, then such internal evidence is probative only in the same, attenuated manner that external evidence of successful coordinated oligopolistic pricing is probative: Internal evidence of successful coordination may make it somewhat more likely that forbidden means of type X were employed than if such evidence is not present. But if successful coordination is already convincingly demonstrated by marketplace behavior, such evidence would be redundant, and if this is not the case, the evidence would

---

[8] A nice illustration is provided by Judge Posner's widely cited opinion in In re High Fructose Corn Syrup Antitrust Litigation, 295 F.3d 651, 662 (7th Cir. 2002), in which he presents as evidence for the proposition "that there was an explicit agreement to fix prices" such statements from the alleged conspirators as: "We have an understanding within the industry not to undercut each other's prices." "[O]ur competitors are our friends. Our customers are the enemy." A competitor's president is called a "friendly competitor," and mention is made of an "understanding between the companies that . . . causes us not to . . . make irrational decisions."

[9] "Examples of direct evidence include . . . evidence that 'explicitly refers to an understanding' between the alleged conspirators." ABA Model Jury Instructions (2005b, B-5 to B-6 n.4), quoting Viazis v. American Ass'n of Orthodontists, 314 F.3d 758, 762 (5th Cir. 2002).

be useful but not directly probative of whether forbidden acts, those in set X, were employed.

Accordingly, under the posited views of the agreement requirement, it would seem that internal evidence, to be powerful, would have to show specifically that means in X rather than just those in X' had been employed. This standard is much more demanding. There may have to be references to the modes of communication, what content was conveyed, or even how it was phrased (depending on just how the legal rule, and thus the set X, is defined). If one went further and made such proof a prerequisite to finding an agreement, one would have adopted a rule that conspiracies may rarely if ever be inferred from circumstantial evidence,[10] which would be a radical revision in the (at least perceived) understanding of the law. There is little indication that courts or commentators endorse such a restrictive approach. Indeed, as noted, even when internal communications are cited in support of a finding of agreement, they often are consistent with pure interdependent oligopolistic price coordination, suggesting that, regardless of what legal test might be articulated, courts and commentators operate as if interdependence (at least when demonstrated by internal evidence) constitutes agreement.[11] (The problem of inferring agreements from circumstantial evidence will be considered at greater length in chapter 6.)

B. Plus Factors

In cases in which a plaintiff seeks to prove a horizontal agreement by circumstantial evidence, the most common (nearly ubiquitous) formulation refers to a requirement of so-called plus factors:

> The need for additional evidence derives from the same concerns elaborated in *Matsushita*, namely the desire not to curb procompeti-

---

[10] See note 6.

[11] There appears to be little recognition of this conflict—aside from the discussion of plus factors, examined next—despite the frequent apparent contradiction in cases (see, for example, *High Fructose*, discussed in note 8) and by commentators (see, for example, Areeda and Hovenkamp (2003), who repeatedly insist that courts virtually unanimously hold that pure interdependence is not an agreement even while discussing numerous cases finding evidence of interdependence sufficient; see the discussion in note 53 in chapter 4).

tive behavior. Therefore, in addition to establishing consciously parallel behavior by the defendants, a plaintiff also must show the existence of certain "plus" factors, including: (1) actions contrary to the defendants' economic interests, and (2) a motivation to enter into such an agreement.[12]

This requirement is often presented as a direct corollary of *Theatre Enterprises*, which held conscious parallelism by itself to be insufficient because defendants' behavior may be purely independent rather than interdependent (see subsection 4.B.1).

The need to demonstrate plus factors can be understood in two importantly different ways:

- First, the baseline showing—parallel or consciously parallel behavior—might refer, in the price-fixing context, to price comovement supplemented by awareness thereof by the firms, which is wholly consistent with textbook competitive behavior. Under this view, the plus factors must establish at least that the behavior is interdependent rather than purely independent.
- Second, the baseline showing might instead implicitly incorporate interdependent behavior. Under this view, the plus factors must go beyond interdependence in some fashion.

Which of these two views makes sense depends on how each of the features of standard plus-factor formulations is interpreted. When the baseline showing is phrased in terms of parallelism, conscious or otherwise, the first view of the baseline may seem more natural while the second is also possible (see the discussion of terminology in section 2.B). In either case, much of the action lies in identifying which plus factors are sufficient to establish an agreement. Under the first view, if the plus factors require more than interdependence, the result may be equivalent to that under the second, for it does not matter whether the showing of interdependence is part of the plaintiff's baseline requirement or entailed in the necessary plus factors. Furthermore, under the second view, if sufficient plus factors

---

[12] Petruzzi's IGA Supermarkets, Inc. v. Darling-Delaware Co., 998 F.2d 1224, 1242 (3rd Cir. 1993). "The inelegant term 'plus factors' refers simply to the additional facts or factors required to be proved as a prerequisite to finding that parallel action amounts to a conspiracy." Areeda and Hovenkamp (2003, 240).

only (re)establish interdependence, then the net result would be equivalent to that under (the weaker interpretation of) the first view.

If there was a clear, readily articulated understanding of the agreement requirement, the plus-factor formulation would be a mere restatement of what was well settled. But at this point it is apparent that such is not the case.[13] Therefore, it is unsurprising that there is no readily accepted principle that determines what counts as a sufficient plus factor and what does not, or what combinations might be jointly sufficient. At best, we can hope to reason backward. That is, beginning with an understanding of what the leading plus factors actually indicate, we can infer what implicit notion of the agreement requirement is entailed.

When one actually looks at the plus factors frequently identified by the courts, it appears that many are simply alternative ways of describing oligopolistic interdependence, as some commentators have noted.[14] This means that interdependence is de facto sufficient to find an agreement. Perhaps the most-cited plus factor is action contrary to defendants' self-interest.[15] Since firms are presumed to maximize profits, this factor seems mysterious, but the conventional, in-context meaning is that the action would be contrary to self-interest if undertaken independently but would be in firms' interests if undertaken jointly. This interpretation rules out purely independent behavior but readily includes—really, defines—interdependent oligopoly behavior.

---

[13] Accordingly, it is difficult to interpret explorations of plus factors, such as Kovacic et al. (2011).

[14] See, for example, Areeda and Hovenkamp (2003, 245).

[15] See ABA (2007, 12–13): "Among the most important plus factors are those that tend to show that the conduct would be in the parties' self-interests if they all agreed to act in the same way but would be contrary to their self-interests if they acted alone. . . . Conversely, when each defendant has legitimate business reasons that rationally would lead it to engage independently in the challenged conduct, courts do not infer a conspiracy based solely on that conduct."; and Werden (2004, 748–49 n.131), illustratively citing eleven cases, some of which cite or quote additional cases. For example, Merck-Medco Managed Care, LLC v. Rite Aid Corp., 201 F.3d 436 (4th Cir. 1999), 1999-2 Trade Cases ¶72,640 [at 10] (unpublished per curiam opinion), states, "Evidence of acts contrary to an alleged conspirator's economic interest is perhaps the strongest plus factor indicative of a conspiracy." See also City of Tuscaloosa v. Harcros Chemicals, Inc., 158 F.3d 548, 571 n.35 (11th Cir.1998): "[A] showing that the defendant acted contrary to its legitimate economic self-interest . . . is sufficient to satisfy the requirement that the plaintiff show 'plus factors' beyond mere consciously parallel action. Other 'plus factors,' however, may also exist."

Another common plus factor is the requirement of a conspiratorial motivation, which amounts to much the same thing.[16] Yet another plus factor, cited less often but still with some regularity, is evidence of poor economic performance, which likewise would result from successful oligopolistic interdependence, however accomplished.[17] Various other factors are mentioned, some of which include fairly direct evidence of explicit agreement,[18] but it remains the case that many of the plus factors that are identified and relied on serve to establish interdependence but no more.[19] Additionally, as subsection 1 explains, even internal documentation of "understandings" and the like that is readily taken to be direct evidence of explicit agreement may well demonstrate only interdependence.

One way to rationalize this practice is by reference to *Theatre Enterprises*, which substantially motivated the plus-factors formulation, and *Matsushita*, which sought to avoid chilling truly competitive behavior. Given the fact that parallel, even consciously parallel, behavior routinely stems from ordinary competitive interaction, it is important that such behavior not give rise to liability. Emphasizing that there is a further

---

[16] See Elhauge and Geradin (2007, 837): "[A]nother major plus factor is understood to be a 'motivation for common action,' that is, some indication that the firms would have a disincentive to engage in the conduct unless others did the same. The problem is that this plus factor is true for cases of pure oligopolistic coordination, when no conspiracy is inferred."; and Werden (2004, 750–51 n.137), discussing the factor and citing cases.

[17] See Elhauge and Geradin (2007, 837): "Another plus factor sometimes used is evidence of adverse economic performance, like excessive prices or profits. But again this is true in cases of pure oligopoly." The lineage of this plus factor traces to *American Tobacco*, 328 U.S. at 805–6.

[18] It seems odd to view such evidence as a plus factor—the plus meaning that, when joined with parallel pricing, an inference of agreement is supported—because it standing alone constitutes direct evidence of explicit agreement.

[19] For example, in Areeda and Hovenkamp's (2003, ¶1434) nine-page treatment of plus factors, only a single paragraph (243) discusses and cites cases on what they term "[c]ustomary indications of traditional conspiracy," whereas the rest of the section discusses and cites cases on the three factors identified in the text. Regarding the first two, they state (245) that "'conspiratorial motivation' and 'acts against self-interest' often do no more than restate interdependence." See also ibid. (206, 237). What they do not attempt to explain is how this point can be reconciled with their view (206, ¶1433) that courts' insistence on plus factors is what demonstrates that they require more than interdependence.

requirement, met by proving interdependent oligopoly behavior as distinguished from ordinary competitive behavior, is quite sensible from this perspective.

If instead the agreement requirement is definitely understood to require more than interdependence, there are two further possibilities. One is that a large portion of the cases is mistaken. Even courts that explicitly purport to be implementing a tougher test are unaware that they are routinely failing to do so.

Another approach would be to tack a further condition onto the sorts of plus factors just discussed, interpreting them as embedding an additional requirement ruling out interdependence. Thus, a motive to conspire would mean a motive to achieve coordinated high prices by illegal rather than legal means. Yet this variation seems odd because no rational firm would specifically wish to subject itself to sanctions rather than to achieve the same result legally, although this variation could be further elaborated by adding that legal means be ineffective. Actions against self-interest would refer to actions that would not be taken unless other firms' cooperation was specifically obtained by illegal rather than legal modes of communication (note the same reservation). And poor economic performance would mean worse performance than would result from legal interdependence.

Each of these restatements is logically possible. Nevertheless, the formulations seem strained. They also replicate the inference problem stated in subsection 1. Specifically, what evidence would show in a reasonably straightforward fashion that firms intended to use illegal rather than legal means of communication (short of direct evidence of such communications), that firms would rely on others' coordinated actions if such were generated by illegal but not by legal means, and so forth? To be sure, if one could demonstrate that coordinated oligopolistic pricing was possible only through forbidden means and that such pricing did occur, then an agreement would thereby be established, an idea developed at length in chapter 6. But under this approach it is unclear what is added by the plus factors that are so often used to guide the inquiry. It seems that one would first have to prove a violation by other, more subtle methods, and only when that was accomplished would one be able to conclude that any of these oft-cited plus factors were present in this elaborated, more complex form—the latter finding being pointless once the violation had already been proven.

Needless to say, this convoluted method is not the routine practice of lower courts. Accordingly, whatever language these courts use to describe what constitutes an agreement, in practice it seems that interdependence is often sufficient. And, when it is not found to be sufficient, it is unclear what alternative plus factors—or, more broadly, formulations of the agreement requirement (definitions of the set X)—are implicitly being invoked.

C. Jury Instructions

Many court decisions on Section 1's agreement requirement address when a case may reach the factfinder, which under U.S. antitrust law is often a jury. If it does, the relevant legal rule is embodied in jury instructions. Given the elusive nature of a circumscribed agreement requirement—including the difficulty of formulating it in ordinary language while avoiding substantial ambiguity, and the range of possible interpretations of the statute and precedent—as well as the challenge of inferring an agreement (whatever that may mean) from circumstantial evidence, it is important to inquire how these problems are addressed when presenting the matter to juries.

The American Bar Association Antitrust Section's Model Jury Instruction (2005b, B-2 to B-3) on "contract, combination or conspiracy" provides,

> To establish the existence of a conspiracy, the evidence need not show that its members entered into any formal or written agreement; that they met together; or that they directly stated what their object or purpose was, or the details of it, or the means by which they would accomplish their purpose. The agreement itself may have been entirely unspoken. What the evidence must show to prove that a conspiracy existed is that the alleged members of the conspiracy in some way came to an agreement to accomplish a common purpose.

This instruction disclaims the need to demonstrate an express, spoken agreement or any particular sort of communication. Instead it speaks in conclusory terms—it must be proved that the alleged conspirators "came to an agreement"—and it elaborates by focusing on "accomplish[ing] a common purpose," a focus on intent, much like the discussion of the references to a "unity of purpose" or "common design" in *American Tobacco*, as described in subsection 4.B.1.[20] The Model Instruction (2005b, B-3) further elaborates,

> The agreement may be shown if the proof establishes that the parties knowingly worked together to accomplish a common purpose. . . . Direct proof of an agreement may not be available. A conspiracy may be disclosed by the circumstances or by the acts of the members. Therefore, you may infer the existence of an agreement from what you find the alleged members actually did, as well as from the words they used.

This supplement begins by restating a focus on the existence of "a common purpose," presents the standard directive that indirect proof by circumstantial evidence is permissible, and finally instructs that agreement may be inferred "from what you find the alleged members actually did," which emphasizes behavior, perhaps coordinated oligopolistic pricing. After the just-quoted passage, the instruction states (2005b, B-3 to B-4), "Mere similarity of conduct among various persons, however, . . . does not establish the existence of a conspiracy unless the evidence tends to exclude the possibility that the persons were acting independently." Reminiscent of the holdings of *Matsushita* and *Monsanto*, discussed in subsection 4.B.2, this portion presents the now familiar issue (recall section 2.C) concerning the interpretation of the term independent, which most naturally refers to purely independent, competitive behavior as distinct from interdependent behavior but also is sometimes viewed as embracing the latter. One might expect that juries would follow the more common usage. Joined with the preceding components, it appears that this Model Instruction invites juries to find an agreement when there is interdependent

---

[20] It is also of interest that *Interstate Circuit* is cited in the footnote (2005b, B-5 n.2) to the paragraph containing this part of the instruction.

oligopolistic pricing, although this speculation cannot readily be tested. For example, can we really know how juries would address different variations of the two sets of illustrations in section 2.A?[21]

There is an additional Model Instruction (2005b, B-7) specifically on the subject of "conscious parallelism," which reads in relevant part,

> The mere fact that the defendants have [*state nature of conduct*] does not by itself establish the existence of any conspiracy among the defendants. Their behavior may be no more than the result of the exercise of independent judgment in response to identical or similar market conditions. For example, everyone might open their umbrellas on a rainy day, but that similar behavior would not necessarily mean that they had agreed or conspired to open their umbrellas.

It is quite clear that this refinement is designed to exclude from the agreement category purely independent conduct rather than interdependent conduct. The instruction continues (2005b, B-7 to B-8),

> You may consider the defendants' [*parallel conduct*] along with other evidence in deciding whether the defendants' conduct was the result of an agreement, and not the result of separate decisions made by each defendant on its own. To establish the existence of an agreement, the plaintiff must produce evidence that tends to exclude the possibility that the defendants acted independently. . . . [*describe evidence put forward by the plaintiff, such as whether the parallel conduct is contrary to the independent business interests of the defendants*]. . . . [*summarize the defendant's arguments in opposition, . . . such as evidence of . . . competitive conduct inconsistent with conspiracy*]. You should consider all of this evidence as a whole . . . .

In describing the concept of independent action as "separate decisions made by each defendant on its own," the instruction clearly embraces the narrow construction of independent, which contrasts it with interdependent. Furthermore, the example for what a plaintiff might demonstrate refers to conduct "contrary to the independent business interests of the

---

[21] One could imagine performing surveys or various sorts of simulations or attempting to interview actual jurors, but such inquiries would provide an uncertain indication of what juries actually do.

defendants," discussed in section B as a leading plus factor that indicates interdependence (and no more). An illustration of a defendant's rebuttal, correspondingly, is "evidence of . . . competitive conduct," rather than, say, evidence of anticompetitive coordinated oligopoly behavior that may have resulted from recognized interdependence. Thus, again it appears that juries may well understand such instructions as including interdependent oligopolistic coordination within the agreement concept.

Court opinions do not offer substantial further illumination primarily because most address whether a plaintiff is able to survive a motion to dismiss or for summary judgment.[22] Those jury instructions that are occasionally noted are consistent with the foregoing depiction.[23] Accordingly, as best one can tell, cases that reach juries are decided under a broad view of agreement, although as mentioned it remains speculative how juries

---

[22] It is interesting to consider the possibility that the substantive standards would be different. Generally what a plaintiff must show to survive a motion to dismiss or for summary judgment is no more than what is required to prevail at trial. However, given that the Court's more recent decisions, notably in *Matsushita* and *Twombly*, are largely concerned with screening cases from the jury, in order to make it more difficult for plaintiffs with weak or frivolous cases to extract settlements, one can, in theory, imagine a more relaxed approach to the determination of liability once the filtering hurdles have been overcome. See Kaplow (2013a, 2013b) on the relationship between the optimal strength of decision thresholds at different stages of adjudication.

[23] For example, Areeda and Hovenkamp (2003, 59) refer to a case in which "[t]he court upheld an instruction declaring it sufficient 'that a mutual understanding was reached, and that the defendant in fact conformed to the arrangement.'" (quoting Wilk v. American Medical Ass'n, 719 F.2d 207, 231 (7th Cir.1983), cert. denied, 467 U.S. 1210 (1984), and criticizing the *Wilk* instruction on other grounds). This statement's focus on the existence of an "understanding" and whether actions were in conformance to it again readily embraces interdependent oligopoly pricing, yet Areeda and Hovenkamp do not criticize the instruction on this ground even though they repeatedly insist elsewhere that the law is otherwise. (The quoted passage from *Wilk* is not the instruction actually given but instead one that the plaintiff proposed, although the appellate court does indicate that this rejected proposal "correctly states the law." 719 F.2d at 231. The actual instruction, which the court upheld, states, "What the preponderance of the evidence in the case must show, in order to establish proof that a conspiracy existed, is that the members in some way or manner, or through some contrivance, positively or tacitly came to a mutual understanding to try to accomplish a common and unlawful plan." This statement, if anything, is broader; it differs from the former in emphasizing the understanding alone, without the further demand that the defendant acted in accordance with it.)

interpret such instructions (and the extent to which they follow instructions in any event).

D. Damages

When liability is established, damages must be assessed. Under U.S. antitrust law, those who purchase from price-fixing conspirators recover treble damages, and government-imposed fines could be determined so as to reflect to some extent the degree of damage inflicted.[24] Damages, in turn, must in principle be causally related to those actions that gave rise to liability.[25] Hence, this logical nexus implies a direct relationship between the agreement requirement and the determination of damages.

For price-fixing cases, "the usual measure of damage is the difference between the illegal price that was actually charged and the price that would have been charged 'but for' the violation multiplied by the number of units purchased."[26] The concept of the but-for scenario has received significant attention in U.S. antitrust law regarding damages. An important concern arises in cases (generally not involving price fixing) in which a defendant is alleged to have engaged in multiple activities injurious to the plaintiff, but the ultimate finding is that only some of that conduct is unlawful while the other behavior is lawful. In such cases, it is well established that damages may be awarded only for losses attributable to the former, unlawful conduct.[27] This legal rule is reflected in the Model In-

---

[24] For further detail on how government fines actually are determined, see subsection 13.A.3.

[25] "The guiding principle is that the antitrust victim should recover the difference between its actual economic condition and its 'but for' condition." Areeda et al. (2007, 333). See also ibid. (334): "[T]he antitrust damage calculation must isolate the effect of the antitrust violation."

[26] Areeda et al. (2007, 332). It is well known that this measure is conceptually incorrect in omitting deadweight loss (the value in excess of cost of units not purchased due to price elevation), but this discrepancy is tangential to the present discussion and thus will not be considered further.

[27] "Except in circumstances where disaggregation is shown to be impossible or impractical, an antitrust plaintiff challenging a variety of conduct is required to segregate damages attributable to particular business practices or, at a minimum, to distinguish between losses attributable to lawful competition and those attributable to unlawful anticompetitive con-

struction (2005b, F-19 to F-20) on "causation and disaggregation," which states,

> Plaintiff bears the burden of showing that its injuries were caused by defendant's alleged antitrust violation—as opposed to any other factors . . . . If you find that plaintiff's alleged injuries were caused in part by defendant's alleged antitrust violation and in part by other factors, then you may award damages only for that portion of plaintiff's alleged injuries that were caused by defendant's alleged antitrust violation. Plaintiff bears the burden of proving damages with reasonable certainty, including apportioning damages between lawful and unlawful causes.

Consider the implications of this damages rule in price-fixing litigation. On one hand, if successful interdependent oligopolistic price elevation constitutes a violation, then damages per unit of output would be the difference between the price charged and the competitive price, which would then have to be determined.[28] On the other hand, if interdependence is deemed legal and instead illegality rests on a demonstration of the use of communications of type X rather than X' (recall the discussion in section A), then damages per unit of output would be the difference between the price charged and the price that the oligopolists could have charged had they limited their communications to those in category X', which may involve (at least with some probability) a supracompetitive price. Accordingly, a plaintiff hoping to recover nontrivial damages would need to show not only that illegal methods were used but also how much of the price elevation could be attributed to the use of such means.[29]

---

duct. . . . Disaggregation is required because the antitrust laws are only intended to compensate plaintiffs for losses fairly caused by a defendant's unlawful anticompetitive behavior." Litton Systems, Inc. v. Honeywell, Inc., 1996 WL 634213 (C.D. Cal.), 1996-2 Trade Cases ¶71,559, at [2]. See also Areeda et al. (2007, 134–35, 341–42) and Royall (1997). It should be noted that typical cases on disaggregation of damages involve multiple actions that harmed a plaintiff's business, some of which are ruled to be unlawful exclusionary practices while others are not found to be illegal. As this section suggests, the point does not seem to have been addressed with regard to price fixing.

[28] A qualification involves the possibility of uncoordinated interaction that results in supracompetitive prices, the subject of note 16 in chapter 7 and the whole of chapter 14.

[29] Relatedly, it would be insufficient merely to show that at some point some illegal methods had been employed; it would be necessary to have some idea of which methods were

In cases in which proof is by circumstantial evidence and the factfinder might have inferred that the defendants' actions barely crossed the line demarcating liability, damages under this formulation could be quite small. But the implications of having to identify the increment above interdependent oligopoly prices are not so limited. Even in a clear case of express conspiracy—smoke-filled rooms, recorded conversations, and criminal convictions—it would still be possible and sometimes plausible that, but for the prohibited interactions, the firms might still have elevated price above a competitive level, although perhaps not as high, as long, or with as few price wars.

This implication of a narrow agreement requirement conflicts with conventional practice in damages determination, which appears to compare the actual price to a hypothetical competitive price—precisely the correct approach if interdependent oligopoly pricing suffices to establish liability—and not to a hypothetical interdependent oligopoly price. In describing *Chattanooga Foundry*,[30] the Supreme Court's seminal decision establishing the overcharge measure of damages, Areeda et al. (2007, 377) state the damages rule as follows: "The direct loss caused by the price fixing cartel was the increased cost of providing the water service above the cost at which it could have been provided had pipe prices been competitively determined." Even more focused is Hovenkamp's (2005b, 674) comment noting a possible shortcoming of the before-and-after approach to measuring damages:

> If the market in which the cartel occurred is concentrated and conducive to price leadership or tacit collusion, a good deal of monopoly overcharge may be built into the pre-cartel price to begin with. As a result, the before-and-after method may not really measure the difference between the cartel price and a truly "competitive" price at all.

Note that the method is criticized because, in the posited situation, it may capture only the difference between the actual price and the oligopolistic price that would have been charged through interdependence alone, rather than the larger gap between the actual price and the competitive price.

---

used at what points in time to determine what portion of the overcharge at any point in time was attributable to prohibited means.

[30] Chattanooga Foundry & Pipe Works v. City of Atlanta, 203 U.S. 390 (1906).

This criticism is entirely apt if interdependence is sufficient for liability. However, this property is instead a necessary virtue of the approach, not a defect, if interdependent oligopoly pricing is legal (as Hovenkamp elsewhere asserts).

One might rationalize the apparent contradiction between the standard damages formulation and the agreement prerequisite for liability (that is, if oligopoly overcharges through interdependence are permissible) by an infection argument: What otherwise might be seen as legally permissible may be deemed culpable when joined with impermissible activity.[31] Under this view, if defendants had extracted, say, $1 billion in overcharges through tolerated interdependence—using only means of type X′—they would face no liability. But if they were found at any point to have used some means in category X (perhaps a single, poorly supervised subordinate is inferred to have once tip-toed over the line demarcating illegality), they would be liable in the United States for $3 billion in damages (plus treble any increment due to the further overcharge made possible by some use of means of type X). This could be the law, and some hold views regarding the agreement requirement and damages determination under which this implicitly is the law. If so, it is remarkable that this feature seems to have gone largely unnoticed.[32] The seemingly well established

---

[31] This argument is rejected in other antitrust settings, as documented at the outset of this section. A different argument that sometimes might justify a similar result is that, in cases in which it is difficult to segregate the effects of illegal acts, defendants (whose wrong created the situation) rather than plaintiffs should bear the burden of uncertainty. See Bigelow v. RKO Radio Pictures, 327 U.S. 251, 265 (1946), referring to the difficulty of quantifying damages, but only with respect to losses not shown to be attributable to causes other than defendants' illegal behavior. See also Story Parchment Co. v. Paterson Parchment Paper Co., 282 U.S. 555 (1931), permitting recovery of damages when the fact of harm is certain but the extent is uncertain; and MCI Communications Corp. v. American Tel. & Tel. Co., 708 F.2d 1081, 1161 (7th Cir. 1983): "The courts have always distinguished between proof of *causation* of damages and proof of the *amount* of damages. Thus, the courts have been consistent in requiring plaintiffs to prove in a reasonable manner the link between the injury suffered and the *illegal* practices of the defendant."

[32] The assertion in the text is limited by the author's knowledge. However, Areeda and Hovenkamp's failure to mention this juxtaposition despite devoting three hundred pages to the agreement requirement (2003; 2009 supp. 171–87) in the horizontal setting alone, emphasizing throughout their view that the law tolerates interdependent oligopoly pricing, and over one hundred pages to the law of damages (Areeda et al. 2007, 331–437), is rather striking. ABA (1996, 171–98) devotes extensive attention to damages arising in cases of horizontal price fixing and emphasizes the causation point, that damages must be attributable to the

and uncontroversial rule on damages under which one compares the overcharge price to a hypothetically constructed competitive (not interdependent oligopoly) price seems much more in harmony with an agreement requirement that does not freely permit purely interdependent oligopoly behavior.[33]

E. Paradox of Proof: Preliminaries

Although the paradox of proof is explored in depth in the next chapter and beyond, a few comments about lower courts' behavior in this regard are relevant here. As mentioned in section B, one of the plus factors that some courts mention as helping to bridge the gap between parallelism and agreement is the presence of poor economic performance. Relatedly, courts often refer to whether market conditions are conducive to successful coordinated oligopoly pricing.[34] If the law is understood in essence to reach successful oligopolistic coordination, these inquiries make perfect

---

illegal activity (36, 171), but never mentions that damages might sometimes (often) need to be reduced on account of the possibility of legal interdependent price elevation. Interestingly, in one case the defendants' expert argued that the but-for price should be the coordinated (but without express agreement) oligopoly price rather than the competitive price. White (2001, 28). (The court had previously determined that the proposed settlement was in an acceptable range and seems to have finally approved the settlement shortly after competing affidavits were received without addressing whether particular legal or economic arguments were accepted or rejected.)

[33] Under current law, it should also be possible to seek recovery for damages due to successful interdependent price elevation that may be attributable to a prior merger, keeping in mind that the merger itself is a "contract, combination . . . , or conspiracy" and thereby satisfies the agreement requirement of Sherman Act Section 1. If a merger in fact contributes to the feasibility of interdependent pricing, and injured parties can show that prices indeed rose as a consequence, then the merger would have been demonstrated to be anticompetitive and the resulting overcharges, being attributable to the anticompetitive merger, would be recoverable (just as a merger may be blocked by the government as anticompetitive if it would significantly raise the prospects for coordinated pricing, regardless of the means by which such coordination might be accomplished). In such a case, a plaintiff's burden would be to demonstrate interdependent price elevation and causation to the merger. There would be no need to indicate the means by which the price elevation was achieved, even if the price-fixing prohibition was narrowly circumscribed. Therefore, mergers, in principle, constitute another realm in which existing law penalizes interdependent pricing.

[34] See, for example, JTC Petroleum Co. v. Piasa Motor Fuels, Inc., 190 F.3d 775, 777 (7th

sense. If coordinated oligopoly pricing seems implausible in a particular market or if in fact economic performance is competitive, the plaintiff would not have a good case. Even if there were some direct evidence purportedly demonstrating a conspiracy, it would be less credible. At best, there may have been an agreement attempting to fix prices but one that could not or in fact did not succeed, in which case a finding of liability would give rise to little or no damages. Likewise, claims by defendants that their actions were purely independent business decisions reflecting ordinary, rivalrous competitive interaction would be more believable. In light of *Matsushita*'s injunction to avoid chilling procompetitive behavior and thus to require stronger proof when a plaintiff's case seems economically implausible (recall subsection 4.B.2), the argument against finding liability would be strengthened.

Suppose, however, that successful oligopolistic coordination, taken alone, is not deemed to constitute an agreement, and thus condemnation is confined to those defendants who employ particular types of communication. Then the question often will be whether interdependence was achieved only by means of type X' or also, in whole or in part, through means in prohibited category X. On that question, it would seem initially that poor economic performance or evidence that a market is conducive to coordinated oligopoly pricing would not be directly probative. Even worse, as the next chapter elaborates, such evidence will sometimes make it less likely that means in category X were employed.[35] To be sure, there are other instances in which these demonstrations would make the inference regarding prohibited means more likely. As will be seen, determining which case is which depends on complex and subtle factors of a sort not

---

Cir. 1999), explaining that "conditions are thus ripe for effective collusion," and ibid. (778–79), citing evidence suggestive of supracompetitive pricing.

[35] In this respect, the paradox of proof also entails a significant conflict with the just-mentioned thrust of *Matsushita* that lower courts should be more cautious about allowing cases to proceed when the plaintiff's theory is less economically plausible. An agreement requirement more stringent than interdependence will, in the situation described in the text, tend to screen out cases with the greatest danger of oligopolistic coordination while favoring those presenting lower harm—a focus of chapter 17. As section 6.B elaborates, plaintiffs may often need to argue that defendants' coordinated oligopoly pricing is less, not more, economically plausible in order to prevail. Thus, *Matsushita*, which is embraced by *Twombly*, seems to oppose a circumscribed interpretation of Section 1's agreement requirement.

generally considered by courts that refer to poor economic performance or to economic conditions being conducive to coordinated price elevation.

Accordingly, there is yet another important respect in which lower courts' analyses of the existence of a horizontal agreement under Sherman Act Section 1 seem difficult to reconcile with a rule under which interdependent oligopoly behavior, standing alone, is permissible. Taken together, all of the considerations in this chapter pertaining to lower courts suggest that a narrow interpretation of agreement generates substantial inconsistencies, if not outright contradictions with different components of the pertinent legal apparatus. In contrast, all of them are harmonious with a concept of agreement that is understood to encompass all successful interdependent oligopolistic price elevation.

6

Paradox of Proof

꙳

Chapters 2–5 are primarily concerned with articulation of the horizontal agreement requirement. Defining oligopolistic interdependence is not hard, whereas other categories, even that of an express agreement, prove highly elusive. The challenge is compounded by the fact that most view the law as reaching at least tacit agreements, themselves difficult to define in a manner that distinguishes pure interdependence. As explained, drawing on the examples in section 2.A, it is hard to understand how can one demarcate an intermediate category when it is so difficult to distinguish undoubted express agreements from pure interdependence in a coherent fashion.

To set the foregoing complications to the side, this chapter will employ the previously introduced abstraction that seems to capture the essence of what many appear to have in mind: There are some types of communication (modes, settings, messages) or other acts, those in set X, that are prohibited, whereas others, in set X′, are permitted. As mentioned, giving concrete content to this formulation is also precarious, in light of the substitutability among means of communication and the dynamic character of language, but these problems too will be ignored for purposes of the present exploration of the logical implications of such an agreement requirement.

Until now, emphasis has been largely on the conceptual difficulties of stating an agreement requirement under which interdependence is insufficient. Section 5.A, however, raises a different sort of question: How is one to infer which sorts of communication (or whatever) were employed in a given case? This inquiry is particularly important in light of firms' incentives to camouflage or otherwise adjust their behavior in order to avoid sanctions for price fixing, with the result that violations may often have to be proved using circumstantial evidence.

This chapter considers the inference conundrum under a narrow agreement requirement in greater depth. In particular, it examines the relevance of features of the market under scrutiny, notably, the relative ease of oligopolistic coordination and the extent to which such coordinated pricing appears to be taking place.[1] Careful investigation of these matters reveals an important range of situations in which there is a paradox of sorts, as noted briefly at the close of the prior chapter. Although in some settings, greater ease of coordinated oligopolistic behavior and its resulting harmful effects—the basis for the prohibition of price fixing—make liability more likely, in others, specifically those in which the danger is most serious, liability may become less likely. The basic reason for the latter result is that, if successful interdependence is sufficiently easy (think about the two gasoline stations), then firms may find it unnecessary to rely on communications in prohibited category X, so that any inference that they in fact did so is less plausible. As a result, evidence that a market is *less* conducive to successful coordinated oligopolistic pricing may make the inference that firms' actions included at least some falling within set X *more* plausible. While aspects of this paradox have previously been mentioned in the literature,[2] this incongruity has never been explored systematically.

The chapter begins by presenting the logic of the argument verbally and diagrammatically. Next, it elaborates its implications in light of a range of possible variations on the basic story. The chapter finally examines the bearing of empirical evidence and reconsiders the meaning of the law in action in light of the paradox of proof.[3]

---

[1] This book's focus on price fixing is stated in chapter 1, but it is still useful to reiterate the point here because a number of the ideas in this part refer quite specifically to pricing coordination (although, as is true elsewhere in the book, much of the logic applies more broadly, as discussed in section 15.B).

[2] Brief mention appears, for example, in Areeda and Hovenkamp (2003, 221), Areeda and Kaplow (1988, 308 n.54), and Posner (2001, 100). Hay (2006, 898–99) describes some of the circumstances that give rise to the phenomenon but without indicating that there is any paradoxical implication. A lengthier but still rudimentary discussion is offered by Kaplow and Shapiro (2007, 1126–28).

[3] The discussion suggests that the contemplated legal approach is not only strange but undesirable, a subject pursued at length in part III, particularly chapter 17.

Before proceeding, a warning is in order. The discussion in this chapter, until section F, operates on the twin assumptions that the law requires some acts beyond mere interdependent oligopoly pricing as a prerequisite to finding an agreement and that it is permissible to infer the existence of an agreement from circumstantial evidence. As the exposition progresses, it will become increasingly apparent that a number of the implications of the inference process are peculiar in that they differ in substantial, unexpected ways from prior understanding and sometimes seem greatly at odds with how parties and adjudicators view the law. The reader should keep in mind that the present chapter does not purport to describe the law in action but rather to draw out previously unexamined logical implications of conventional views about the law. To the extent that the present reasoning is sound, the conflicts that emerge bear on the validity of the premises, that is, on conventional characterizations of what the law is understood to require.

A. Overview

This section takes a first, somewhat simplified pass at presenting the logic underlying the paradox of proof. To begin the inquiry, note that the inference process cannot be analyzed without saying something about what it is that must be inferred. Under given facts and circumstances, it may make sense to infer the existence of an agreement under some definitions of that term but not under others. As mentioned, the present discussion will be general and abstract, letting X denote the set of acts (modes of communication, perhaps)[4] that, if any are employed, an agreement is deemed to exist, and X' denote the set of all other acts.[5]

---

[4] As explained at page 52 and in note 3 of chapter 3, the sets X and X' can be understood as containing all manner of acts, not just those distinguished by the nature of communications involved, although the language of communications is usually employed here for concreteness and because it seems to capture what most commentators have in mind.

[5] This formulation is not restrictive even if certain combinations of acts may be deemed to be an agreement but not any of the constituent acts taken alone. In that case, the elements of X would be each sufficient combination of such more basic components. Hence, throughout this part, reference to an act or communication in X will be taken to mean a cluster of activities

To further elaborate the background situation, consider that in any case under consideration there will exist various evidence about the likelihood and extent of oligopolistic coordination that is occurring or has occurred. The overall strength of such evidence will be taken as given in this section but explored further in subsection D.1. Likewise for other considerations[6]—except for the present focus, which is on the degree to which the market at hand is conducive to successful coordinated oligopolistic pricing.[7]

Within this specification of the problem, it is now possible to state the core logic.[8] Begin at the extreme end of the spectrum at which circumstances render successful coordination impossible regardless of the means employed. In that case, there is a strong inference that prohibited communications were not used. It is possible that parties misperceive the situation, in which case they may have attempted to implement a price-fixing agreement, but when it is absolutely clear that such would be impossible,

---

(including groups of one) sufficient to be viewed as an agreement, with all other clusters being in X′.

[6] See generally section D. To illustrate, even though this chapter considers inferences from circumstantial evidence, there may be some direct evidence bearing on the existence of an agreement, such as internal documentation of what some of firms' agents said, did, or believed. As noted in section 5.A, however, such evidence is often ambiguous (even misleading) regarding the distinction between interdependence standing alone and whatever more is required to be in category X. Furthermore, even highly direct, unambiguous evidence might present problems of credibility, among others. For example, it may be uncertain whether a clear statement was a careless utterance or writing by someone without relevant authority who is confused about the true state of affairs or instead constitutes a reliable sign of the truth leaking out. Or statements may be made by disgruntled employees. For further discussion, see sections 11.B and 18.B. Attention here is confined to cases in which such other evidence does not render the outcome entirely certain.

[7] For most of this chapter, the focus is on factors that influence the ease of coordination, but not all factors that are favorable to coordinated oligopolistic pricing have this feature. For example, if the product in question is one for which there is greater market power—that is, the profit-maximizing monopoly price is higher—it may not be any easier for oligopolists to succeed in maintaining a supracompetitive price. Nevertheless, their motivation to do so would be greater; hence, as market power rises, throughout the range it might be more rather than less likely that they would employ acts in X that facilitate coordination. See also note 13 and section D.2, both further discussing why the likelihood of use of acts in X need not fall with the ease of coordination even though the ease is high.

[8] See Baker (1993, 185–94) and Fraas and Greer (1977, 29–30).

this outcome seems quite unlikely. (Also, if there were liability, damages or fines based on harm would presumably be zero.) Another reservation is that, even when evidence seems to suggest that coordinated oligopoly pricing is clearly impossible, this assessment might be mistaken. Let us further assume that this is not very likely.[9] In sum, it is supposed that, all things considered, the likelihood that any acts in the set X were employed is small in this extreme case.

Consider next moving from this pole to examine cases in which successful coordination, although still not easy, is increasingly plausible. Along the way, the likelihood that prohibited communications, that is, acts in set X, were employed rises. Firms would not risk such action, the direct detection of which would give rise to liability (including possible criminal sanctions) unless there was at least some likelihood of success.[10] In this range, that likelihood is taken to be increasing, so the plausibility of the use of the necessary actions to achieve success is similarly increasing. Note that it may well be that the likelihoods of acts both in X and in X' that facilitate coordination are rising, but all that matters for the inference of agreement is the former.

In contrast, consider the opposite end of the spectrum, settings in which successful coordination is so easy that firms can accomplish it almost automatically. All that is required is one or two acts in X', and success is immediate, complete, certain, and everlasting. In that case, it is thought to be unlikely that acts in X were employed. Why would firms use such means, with a risk of detection and possibly severe sanctions, when by assumption they can accomplish the same results confining their

---

[9] Recall that the discussion takes as given evidence bearing on what pricing is actually present in the market. If there was, for example, strong evidence of consistent coordinated oligopoly pricing, then the likelihood of a mistake might actually be high. The alternative assumption is that strong evidence that such pricing is nearly impossible in the industry would cast doubt on the evidence that it is occurring. For the present, suppose we are not considering a case in which the evidence of successful oligopoly pricing is extremely strong. On the interaction between these two dimensions, see subsection D.1.

[10] Likelihood of success is taken here as a shorthand for the expected degree of success, which can vary with the extent of price elevation, its duration, and so forth. Complications involving how the mode of inference employed by the decision-maker feeds back on firms' strategic decisions, first mentioned in section 5.A, will be considered further in subsection D.4.

activities to those in X'? (Such extreme cases may not exist, but the present construction is only a theorization.)[11]

If one considers cases just short of this pole, the likelihood of the use of prohibited communications would plausibly be higher. Coordinated oligopoly pricing is taken to be sufficiently easy that there is a substantial chance of success, but as success becomes more difficult to attain, the effectiveness of coordination may well be enhanced by employing a broader set of tools, making it ever more likely that the firms resorted to some acts in X.[12]

Combining the foregoing cases, it seems that the likelihood of the use of prohibited communications (or other prohibited behavior), defined as the use of acts in set X, at first rises and then ultimately falls as the degree to which the market is conducive to coordination increases. This characterization is represented in Figure 1. As one moves from the left to the right along the horizontal axis, the ease of coordination is taken to be increasing, starting with no possibility of coordination (denoted by 0) and ending at extremely easy coordination (denoted by 1). The vertical axis indicates the likelihood (probability, ranging from 0 to 1) of the use of prohibited communications, that is, of at least some act in X. As mentioned, it is supposed that initially, as the ease of coordination rises, starting from zero, the likelihood that some act in set X was employed rises, but, as the ease becomes sufficiently high, this likelihood falls.[13]

---

[11] Likewise, as before we could consider mistakes by firms and by the decision-maker, but we are supposing that they are not sufficient to negate the inference that the likelihood of an agreement is low, well below the standard of proof. There are other possibilities, such as those examined in subsection D.2, where it is explained that the likelihood of agreement might be rising as conditions become more conducive to coordination, even at high levels. As mentioned there, much of the analysis (as well as common claims by commentators and some courts) would be notably altered.

[12] For example, Kaysen and Turner (1959, 109) state, "In general, the more faithful the parallelism, the larger the numbers involved, the more complex the changes through which parallelism has persisted, the greater the number of market variables which have shown parallel behavior, the less easy will it be for the trier of fact to believe that he is witnessing the independent response of several firms to the same market situation; and therefore the more persuasive will parallel action alone be as evidence on which a finding of overt collusion (conspiracy) can be made."

[13] The figure is drawn as if there is a single peak, with the likelihood of an agreement rising monotonically as conduciveness increases up to some intermediate level and falling monotoni-

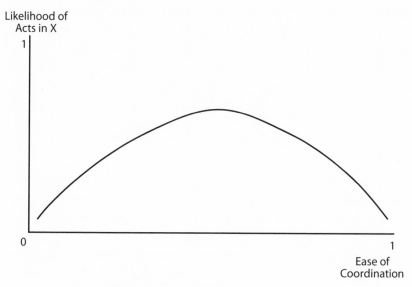

Figure 1. Ease of Coordination and Likelihood of Acts in X

(The smooth, simple, and roughly symmetric character of the curve, as well as its height at various points, should be understood as purely for illustrative purposes, on which more below.)

It is still necessary to translate this inference—from the ease of coordination to the likelihood of the use of acts in X—into a finding on liability. For concreteness, consider the proof standard in U.S. civil cases of more likely than not,[14] in which case one simply needs to consider the portion

---

cally thereafter. This feature is not a logical necessity. As one moves from the left to the right, the likelihood that coordination is successful (and, presumably, the expected profit conditional on some success, because success is a matter of degree) is increasing whereas the need to rely on any specific means, notably, some of those in X, to achieve any degree of expected success is decreasing. There is no guarantee that the first consideration dominates up to some specified point, and then the second dominates everywhere thereafter. Also, it is not obvious that the benefit of using acts in X is falling (they may be less important in achieving some success but may still contribute more incremental value to the expected degree of success), and more broadly account must be taken of firms' reactions to the expectation of liability which itself depends on the inferences that are drawn. See subsections D.2 and D.4. Ultimately, the shape of the relationship—as well as, importantly, the height of the curve at particular points—is an empirical question, explored further in sections D and E.

[14] For other proof standards, it is obvious how the following diagrams would be modified. See section 17.C.

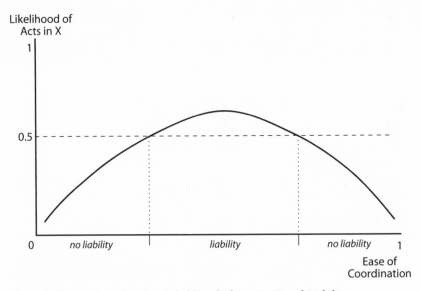

Figure 2. Ease of Coordination, Likelihood of Acts in X, and Liability

of the curve that lies above 0.5 (50%), as depicted in Figure 2.[15] In this figure, we can see the immediate implications for liability. When the ease of coordination is low, there is no liability because the inferred likelihood of the use of prohibited communications is too low. When the ease of coordination becomes sufficiently high, in the middle region, there is liability. As the ease becomes higher still, the likelihood of the use of acts in X begins to fall and eventually becomes low enough that once again the likelihood is insufficient for liability.[16]

As a shorthand, consider the depiction in Figure 3. Here, attention is confined to the horizontal axis. The middle (liability) region is where the

---

[15] Such a liability threshold may well not be optimal, even conditional on the prohibition being defined in this manner, a doubt suggested by the analysis in chapter 9 on the optimal tradeoff of deterrence and chilling costs and examined further in section 17.C. For a general treatment of the optimal burden of proof, see Kaplow (2011, 2012a).

[16] Depending on the height of the curve at various points, there are other possibilities: If the curve always lies above 0.5, an agreement would be inferred regardless; if it is always below 0.5, an agreement could never be inferred; and the curve may cross the 0.5 horizontal line only once, such that the left or right region of no liability does not exist. See also note 13 on possible nonmonotonicity, which under the present analysis could give rise to more than three regions, alternating between no liability and liability. A number of variations will be examined in sections C and D.

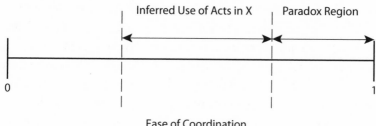

Figure 3. Ease of Coordination and Paradox of Proof

use of acts in X is inferred with the specified probability (taken here to be greater than 0.5). The intuition is that the ease of coordination is sufficiently high that attempts to collude are likely yet the degree is sufficiently low that coordination probably cannot succeed without using at least some act in X. The right (no liability) region is designated as the paradox region. There, the ease of coordination is so great that coordination is imagined to be readily accomplished without having to resort to any means in X.

The existence of this third, rightmost region may be regarded as paradoxical in a number of respects. Perhaps most obvious and important, this formulation makes clear that the legal requirement as conventionally understood carries the implication that there is liability in settings of moderate danger but exoneration in cases in which the expected harm from anticompetitive behavior is at its greatest, a point that is central in chapter 17 of part III, on whether the contemplated narrow agreement requirement can plausibly constitute sound policy—a question set to the side in this part of the book. The remainder of this chapter focuses on how the paradox of proof bears on our understanding of the horizontal agreement requirement.

B. Implications for Adjudication

Using Figure 3 (or Figure 2), it is easy to see the a priori ambiguity of a party in litigation presenting evidence that a given market poses a greater ease of coordination—for example, evidence of higher concentration, more nearly homogenous products, more readily observed prices, and larger numbers of smaller buyers placing more frequent orders. Additional evidence that a market is more conducive to coordination than one might have believed in the absence of such evidence will be helpful to an enforcer (government agency or private plaintiff) toward the left of the horizontal axis. When enough such evidence is shown, the case moves from the left region in which there is no liability to the middle region in which there is liability. Once firmly in that region, additional evidence that the market is even more conducive to coordination first continues to make the probability of the use of some act in X greater and then, eventually, smaller, but is of no consequence, that is, until one approaches the right boundary of the middle region. At that point, further evidence along these lines will ultimately make the conclusion revert to one of no use of acts in X and thus no liability, leading to a victory for the defendants. To summarize, whether evidence indicating a somewhat greater ease of coordination favors the enforcer or the defendants will depend on whether the other facts of the case suggests that it is nearer the left boundary or the right boundary of the middle, liability region.

This point has interesting implications for parties' litigation strategies. Starting with the enforcer at the point of composing a complaint, should it allege that conditions are highly conducive to coordination or the opposite? Regarding the ultimate outcome, convincing a decision-maker that conditions are somewhat more dangerous than what it otherwise would have concluded may be helpful (toward the left of the horizontal axis) or detrimental (toward the right). At the outset, it may not be obvious which situation will prevail, that is, which of the two boundary lines will, after elaborate proceedings, be seen by an adjudicator to be nearer to the case at hand.

Additionally, this uncertainty may arise not only regarding projections about where on the spectrum the case falls but also regarding where the decision-maker will believe that the two boundaries are located. Referring back to Figure 2, the location of the boundaries is determined by the height and shape of the curve relating the ease of coordination to the likelihood of agreement at various points along the horizontal axis, itself a difficult empirical question (on which, see sections C–E). Furthermore, the many variations and complications explored below also bear directly on where these critical points might fall.

In any event, it would seem that we should observe that a number of enforcers (especially in cases where the harm from price coordination and thus fines or damages would be the largest) would find it in their interest to allege that conditions are less conducive to coordination than meets the eye. Defendants' strategic interests are the reverse. Thus, in answers to complaints, they should allege the opposite of what enforcers seek to prove. For example, in cases falling in or near the right, paradox region—including toward the right end of the middle, liability region—they should allege that the industry is highly conducive to coordination.

Of course, each side must not go too far. Enforcers win if the conclusion is that the ease of coordination is moderate, defendants if it is either high or low. In this state of affairs, we also should sometimes find parties arguing on the same side of the issue, for example, when the enforcer is concerned that the decision-maker may find coordination to be fairly difficult but the defendants think that coordination will be found to be fairly easy—or when the parties have different conjectures about where the decision-maker will place the two boundaries. We might also see a party switching its side on these issues midstream, if it senses that the decision-maker is likely to land near a boundary different from the one it originally predicted. Overall, it is unusual that one party needs to show a moderate state of affairs and the other gains by demonstrating either extreme. (The defendants' argument in the alternative is of the form: "Coordination is quite difficult in our market; however, if it isn't quite difficult, it's actually very easy. In any event, it surely isn't anywhere in between.") If interdependence is indeed not sufficient for liability, one might see each of the above possibilities play out regularly in litigated cases, an idea examined further in section F.

In this setting, it also seems difficult ever to grant a motion to dismiss or for summary judgment because a court would have to decide that the allegations, or also the undisputed facts, eliminate any serious question about the region in which the case falls. The problem is that, except in extreme cases, virtually any allegation or fact on these dimensions could cut in either direction on liability, depending on how other facts are weighed, something the court is not supposed to do at these preliminary stages.[17] Furthermore, what range of degrees of ease of coordination are

---

[17] Consider a highly simplified scenario in which there are two things that might be true, A and B: If both are false, the case falls in the left (no liability) region; if one but not the other is true, the case falls in the middle (agreement) region; and if both are true, the case falls in the right (paradox) region. The enforcer must allege: A is true and B is false, or, in the alternative, A is false and B is true. The defendants cannot simply disagree on A and/or B. Rather it

consistent with a victory for the enforcer versus the defendants will itself be contested—and, as will be seen below, it is a priori possible that just about any degree of conduciveness is consistent with a victory for the enforcer or the defendants, depending on the height and shape of the curve in our figures.[18]

C. Breadth of Paradox Region

Figures 1 and 2 depict for illustrative purposes a single, simple, symmetric relationship between the ease of coordination and the likelihood of use of prohibited communications. But the relationship could take other forms as well. This section considers variations influencing the breadth of the paradox region, and section D explores a number of other possibilities.

---

must allege: Both A and B are false, or, in the alternative, both A and B are true. It is hardly clear how to apply either the *Twombly* motion-to-dismiss standard or, at the summary judg-ment stage with possibly accompanying affidavits, the *Matsushita* standard. It would seem that, for the defendants to prevail at the motion-to-dismiss stage, the enforcer may not have to make any allegation regarding these facts, and at the summary judgment stage that it is implausible that either fact is true or that it is implausible that either fact is false. This hypothetical case may seem farfetched, but it is really just a highly simplified version of the generic case consid-ered in this section, in which there may be many facts, with one very large set of possible combinations consistent with being in the left (no liability) region, another with being in the central (agreement) region, and the remaining with being the right (paradox) region. See also note 55 in chapter 4.

[18] To place this problem in the context of U.S. antitrust doctrine, recall the *Matsushita/Monsanto* formulation (quoted at greater length in subsection 4.B.2) that "a plaintiff seeking damages for a violation of §1 must present evidence 'that tends to exclude the possibility' that the alleged conspirators acted independently," and suppose moreover that the term indepen-dently is interpreted (out of context, it would appear) as interdependently. As a matter of logic, any evidence bearing—either way—on the degree of conduciveness to coordination tends to exclude mere interdependence, as long as prior supposition or other evidence places the case in the appropriate segment of the horizontal axis. (Any evidence of greater conduciveness favors liability if the curve in Figures 1 and 2 is upward sloping at the hypothesized location of a case on the horizontal axis, whereas evidence of less conduciveness favors liability if the curve is downward sloping.) Likewise, if the defendants present counterevidence in support of their motion, the enforcer might logically be able to concede it arguendo and say that it too favors liability in light of the proper analysis relating the ease of coordination to the likelihood of agreement.

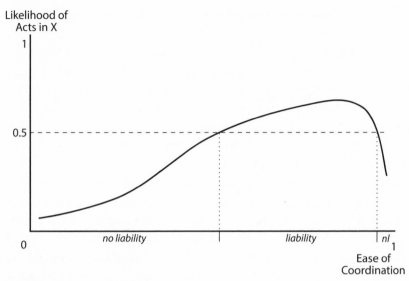

Figure 4. Narrow Paradox Region

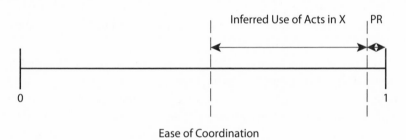

Ease of Coordination

Figure 5. Narrow Paradox Region and Paradox of Proof

Suppose that the relationship between the ease of coordination and the likelihood of use of acts in X instead takes the form depicted in Figure 4. Just as in Figures 1 and 2, the likelihood of use of acts in X first rises and then falls as the ease of coordination increases. The differences here are that it takes a greater ease of coordination for the likelihood of the use of acts in X to exceed 50% and that this likelihood remains over 50% until the ease of coordination is quite high. (Perhaps it is only the two gas stations in section 2.A's example and a few others who are able to collude with any success in the absence of acts in the set X.) The "*nl*" in the figure is an abbreviation for "no liability," the shortened label reflecting that indeed the paradox region is quite narrow in this case, as shown in Figure 5.

This case is particularly interesting because, despite the existence of the paradox of proof, it looks almost like the more intuitive story in which there is no liability when the ease of coordination is low and liability when conduciveness is high. Except in or near a narrow region in which conduciveness is very high, evidence of a greater ease of coordination favors (or at least does not seriously hurt) the enforcer, and contrary evidence helps the defendants. If these figures depict the actual state of affairs (again, for a given legal standard, summarized by X and X', and given evidence on the extent of oligopolistic price coordination), there would be little difference in practice from a legal rule that deemed interdependent oligopolistic coordination sufficient for liability in those settings in which the ease of coordination was sufficiently high, specifically, above the left boundary in Figures 4 and 5.[19] From the perspective that oligopolistic interdependence constitutes agreement, such a rule might be rationalized by the notion that there is not sufficient confidence that interdependence is occurring unless the ease of such coordination is sufficiently high (see section 11.A elaborating how conduciveness bears positively on the optimality of assigning liability).[20]

Of course, there remains a difference between the just-postulated rule, under which oligopolistic coordination is sufficient for liability when the ease of coordination exceeds a threshold, and the rule embodied in X and X' that implicitly lies behind Figures 4 and 5: In those cases in which the danger is especially high (the worst cases), the latter rule would exonerate the defendants rather than finding them liable. That distinction would be the only real stake in the debate between definitions of horizontal

---

[19] This depiction rests on the further assumption that most cases do not fall at the extreme right of the horizontal axis, which supposition is supported by the claims described below in the text. Relatedly, none of these figures are based on a rigorous definition of the units on the horizontal axis, so they all should be seen as illustrating rough characterizations; comparisons between them are more meaningful for the qualitative (relative) differences than for the particular locations of the regions. For example, Figures 1–3 would be consistent with the paradox of proof being rare if very few cases were in the right third of the horizontal axis. In that instance, Figures 4 and 5 would, by comparison, indicate a world in which the paradox was rarer still.

[20] Alternatively, one might take the view that, unless the ease of coordination is high enough, the costs of scrutiny and intervention are not worth the effort.

agreement. A policy-based defense of the X/X' approach would have to be grounded in the desirability of allowing coordinated oligopoly pricing in such cases, on which see section 17.C. It would also have to justify expending the resources necessary to distinguish them from somewhat less extreme cases—keeping in mind that the availability of the defense, even if not often true, may motivate defendants to advance it often, both raising costs and producing some erroneous exonerations in the process.

It remains to ask whether the present depiction is plausible. Discussion of empirical evidence (in many respects, the lack thereof) is deferred until section E. For now, it is worth noting that many legal and economic analysts speak as though this case governs, a claim that also finds some support from the courts. In offering this characterization, writers do not speak directly in these terms, for the paradox of proof is only occasionally recognized and not much analyzed. Instead, what one finds are strong statements regarding the difficulty of any real success at oligopolistic coordination in the absence of fairly explicit means of communication, that is, acts in the set X, even if that set is defined rather narrowly; a number of commentators deem instances of successful plain interdependence to be "rare."[21] Given such beliefs, it follows that something like Figures 4 and 5 describes the regions of liability and of the paradox.

---

[21] See Areeda and Hovenkamp (2003, 215): "The results of perfect express collusion will rarely be achieved by mere interdependence without an express agreement standardizing some product or price terms or relationships."; Hay (1981, 445), suggesting that the dilemma regarding whether to attack all interdependent behavior or just express agreement may not be practically important because pure oligopolistic interdependence is likely to be rare; Motta (2004, 141), offering reasons that it would be difficult for firms to coordinate successfully without talking to each other; Motta (2007, 317): "it is far from clear that tacit collusion can be sustained over time without competitors talking to each other"; Nye (1975, 209): "To put it more forcefully, I believe that pure 'interdependence' without some form of express collusion, however collateral, is a rare case, perhaps almost academic."; Posner (1969, 1574): "[I]t seems improbable that prices could long be maintained above cost in a market, even a highly oligopolistic one, without *some* explicit acts of communication and implementation. One can, to be sure, specify an extreme case in which such acts might be unnecessary. No more than three sellers selling a completely standardized product to a multitude of buyers (none large) should be able to maintain the joint maximizing price without explicit collusion. However, not many industries resemble this model."; ibid. (1575): "Perhaps in an extreme case no explicit acts of collusion or enforcement are necessary for this translation . . . ."; Posner (1976, 904), referring to the fact

This state of affairs is quite surprising in light of the fact that most of the commentators who implicitly assert conditions that imply a narrow paradox region also insist that the law does not and should not make successful interdependent oligopolistic coordination a basis for liability.[22] First, as noted, there is little difference in practice between such a rule and one that carefully delineates a set X if one should virtually always

---

that "one can imagine a group of sellers able to collude without any overt contact or communication" but asserting that "[s]uch a case is probably rare"; Posner (2001, 66–69); Turner (1962, 665): "'some finite minimum of explicit communication, at some time, is involved'" (quoting Kaysen (1951, 268–69)); ibid. (672–73); Werden (2004, 762–63): "it is far less clear that unspoken agreements are a significant phenomenon"; for a "considerable time . . . a widely held view . . . is that 'coordination cannot be simply spontaneous'" (quoting Elzinga (1984, 25)); and Whinston (2006, 26): "most economists are not bothered . . . perhaps because they believe (as I do) that direct communication (and especially face-to-face communication) often will matter for achieving cooperation." In Business Electronics Corp. v. Sharp Electronics Corp., 485 U.S. 717, 727 (1988), a vertical price-fixing case, the Supreme Court stated, "Cartels are neither easy to form nor easy to maintain. Uncertainty over the terms of the cartel, particularly the prices to be charged in the future, obstructs both formation and adherence by making cheating easier." There is, however, the caveat that, because authors do not ordinarily define their terms—such as express agreement, talking, explicit communication, and so forth—or the legal standard (the content of X and X') with any precision, there is substantial ambiguity in what any of these claims mean and how they bear on the breadth of the paradox region. Moreover, the empirical basis for such views is uncertain, particularly because the means employed are not ordinarily observed unless there is a successful prosecution or a legal, publically operating cartel. For further discussion, see section E. Commentary on EU competition law also includes similar suggestions. See Neven (2001, 57): "We review what the economic literature, and in particular the literature in experimental economics, has to say on the matter. We find few reasons to think that collusion is 'easy' to undertake without extensive 'concertation' between firms." He continues (66), "The literature on economic experiments thus does not seem to support the presumption that collusion is 'easy' without communication. In addition, it is found that if communication improves the scope for collusion, its effect is not dramatic unless the environment is very simple . . . ." Of course, it is unclear how behavior in such experiments translates to real-world behavior of firms, run by experienced individuals, that coexist and interact for extended periods of time. See section E for further discussion.

[22] Posner (2001, 97–98), whose academic writing favors reaching successful interdependent oligopoly pricing, has a different take. "Anyway there probably are few cases of purely tacit collusion. What is being proposed is less the alteration of the substantive contours of the law than a change in evidentiary requirements to permit illegal price fixing to be found in circumstances in which an actual meeting of the minds on a noncompetitive price can be inferred even though explicit collusion cannot be proved. In most of these cases there will be explicit although well-concealed collusion that can certainly be deterred by threat of punishment."

infer the use of acts in X when successful coordination is demonstrated. Why is there so much insistence on one rule over another if they differ so infrequently? And why might it be thought that the more restrictive rule would filter out a substantial number of cases, especially at the pleading or summary judgment stages, as is often supposed? After all, if there is basis for supporting oligopolistic interdependence, then sufficiently great ease of coordination is powerful evidence favoring agreement (even when defined as more limited than interdependence); only in exceptional cases would the ease of coordination be so great that liability would be negated. Finally, as noted just above, the little actual difference seems to favor the interdependence rule, for the divergence involves only the cases posing the most extreme danger.

To drive the point home, consider dispositive motions. The U.S. Supreme Court's recent articulation of the legal standard in *Twombly* and *Iqbal* requires plaintiffs to state a "plausible" claim to survive a motion to dismiss. More precisely for present purposes, *Twombly* was quoted in subsection 4.B.2 for the proposition that the plaintiff's alleged facts must "tend to rule out the possibility" of action not based on agreement. Suppose that the plaintiff's only factual allegations indicate the presence of coordinated oligopolistic price elevation, whereas the law we are imagining also requires the use of some acts in X. Under the present (strongly endorsed) assumptions, it would be rare for no acts in X to have been employed, which a fortiori "tend[s] to rule out" that possibility. Hence, surviving the motion to dismiss would be automatic. Indeed, the plaintiff would be entitled to victory at the summary judgment stage if its demonstration of successful coordination was uncontested, even if it had no direct evidence of particular acts in X.[23]

Now suppose instead that the relationship between the ease of coordination and the likelihood of prohibited communications takes the form

---

[23] Since the proof standard at trial merely requires that the use of acts in X be more likely than not, and we are supposing here that the "not" scenario is rare, a verdict for the defendant could not be justified under these assumptions. Of course, these conclusions regarding dispositive motions are opposite to the views of many commentators, including ones advancing beliefs that imply a narrow paradox region. As a further remark on *Twombly* itself, that case involved abstention from entering others' territories, and one might view that sort of coordination to be more sustainable than price coordination without resort to acts in X. For further discussion of nonprice coordination, see section 15.B.

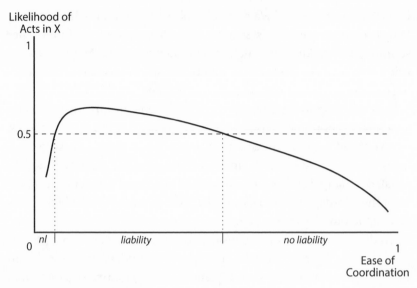

Figure 6. Broad Paradox Region

depicted in Figure 6. Once again, just as in Figures 1 and 2, the likelihood of use of acts in X first rises and then falls as the ease of coordination increases. The differences now are that it takes little danger of coordination for the likelihood of prohibited communications to exceed 50% and this likelihood remains over 50% only until the ease of coordination is moderate. In this instance, the narrow "*nl*" region in the figure is at the left extreme. This scenario can be restated as in Figure 7.

This variation contrasts sharply with that just discussed. Here, the paradox region is quite broad, so we would expect enforcers' and defendants' strategic situations often to be reversed, notably, in all cases in which the ease of coordination was moderate to significant. Rare would be disputes where it was important for an enforcer to establish that the ease of coordination was greater and where defendants would wish to prove the opposite, for few cases would fall in the leftmost region of Figure 7.[24]

---

[24] Just as in the case of a narrow paradox region (see note 19), the statements in the text make implicit assumptions regarding where most cases fall on the horizontal axis. The next footnote considers a different possibility.

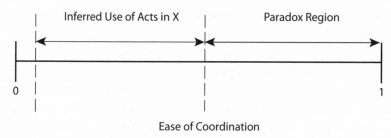

Figure 7. Broad Paradox Region and Paradox of Proof

The present setting, with a broad paradox region, is one in which the choice to define agreement more restrictively, in terms of sets X and X' (where, moreover, the set X is not very inclusive), has great consequences. Most commentators seem to believe that high stakes rest on whether agreements are thus defined, rather than being interpreted to encompass oligopolistic interdependence generally. Accordingly, one might expect to see frequent endorsements of factual propositions consistent with Figures 6 and 7, but (as just mentioned) the opposite is the norm: That is, statements are suggestive of Figures 4 and 5, with a narrow paradox region. Furthermore, because belief that the debate over the meaning of horizontal agreement is important implies that the X/X' implementation involves a broad paradox region, one would expect great attention to be devoted to the sorts of reversed positionings of the parties described in section B. That is, if one were to suppose that most seriously contested cases are not at the far left of the horizontal axis, then it would not merely be possible but typical for enforcers to argue from the outset (the filing of their complaint) that coordination was difficult and defendants that the industry was highly conducive to coordinated oligopolistic pricing.[25] Yet this too does not appear to be so. In sum, it seems that much writing on the subject of horizontal agreement by both commentators and courts, in failing to attend in a sustained manner to the paradox of proof, reflects

---

[25] It is possible that most filed cases would be frivolous, in the sense that there was indeed virtually no prospect of coordination (and, unless factfinders erred significantly, little damages would be awarded even if liability was established). In those cases, the left boundary in Figure 7 would be the operative one, and conventional positionings could be expected.

a lack of appreciation of the implications of different formulations of the legal rule.

It is also useful to consider the differences between Figures 5 and 7—or 4 and 6. As drawn,[26] the outcome in nearly all fact situations (for just about any degree of ease of coordination) is reversed in the two depictions. (The exception is at the extremes.) In other words, for a given legal rule on agreement in the form of X/X', the circumstantial evidence could be completely clear (even stipulated by the parties) and yet, in most cases, opposite results would be possible. A case could be toward the left end of the spectrum (short of the extreme), and either the enforcer or the defendants might be entitled to win; likewise toward the right end. Who should win would depend on which of the two curves relating the ease of coordination and the likelihood of acts in X is the true one, a subject considered further in section E.

An additional implication is that there now is a double strategic paradox. The original one, elaborated in section B, is that the enforcer would wish to argue that the ease of coordination is higher—or lower—than might otherwise appear, depending on where the case falls on the horizontal axis, and the defendants' strategic interest is reversed. The second is that the enforcer would wish to argue that Figures 4 and 5 are correct—if the case is likely to end up on the right half of the horizontal axis—but it would wish to argue that Figures 6 and 7 depict the truth—if the case is likely to end up on the left. And, again, the defendants' position would be the reverse of the enforcer's. Moreover, positions regarding which figures were correct could reverse if it was sensed that the case might end up at a different point on the horizontal axis than anticipated; conversely, parties' positions on where the case fell on that axis might reverse if their predictions on which figures would be deemed to govern were to change. This further strategic paradox, regarding what functional relationship between conduciveness and the likelihood of acts in X prevails, appears

---

[26] The figures could be drawn in any number of ways, with different widths of each of the three regions and, accordingly, varying degrees of overlap or reversal between regions of liability and of no liability. For example, in the middle of the figure, the liability regions might overlap, so enforcers would always win if the ease of coordination was within certain bounds, regardless of which of the two relationships held; or the no liability regions might overlap. For further discussion, see section D.

to be unrecognized, by both commentators and parties in litigation. And, like the initial paradox, it is one that would not arise if the legal rule (perhaps de facto) was one under which successful interdependent oligopolistic pricing was sufficient for liability.

D. Further Variations and Qualifications

This section briefly considers some additional possibilities and complications, leaving more detailed elaboration of some of the points to an addendum (section G). The factors considered are variations in the overall height of the curve in Figures 1 and 2 (and in others), the effects of evidence on the extent of oligopolistic coordination and of direct evidence of agreement, countervailing effects that may reduce or eliminate the paradox of proof, the dependence of the analysis on the legal definition of agreement (that is, some particular delineation of sets X and X′), and how inferences need to be adjusted to take into account that firms' decisions will be endogenous to the legal regime, including the inference process that they anticipate will govern adjudications about their behavior. As will be seen, the paradox of proof is significantly more subtle and elusive than suggested thus far.

1. Evidentiary Variations

The curves in the foregoing figures depend, among other things, on all of the evidence other than that on the ease of coordination. Obviously, the resulting height of the curves matters greatly, for this determines the breadth of the liability ("agreement") region, in contrast to the breadth of the paradox region. If the curve relating conduciveness to the likelihood of the use of acts in X was significantly higher, the liability region would be much wider, potentially reaching one or both extremes on the horizontal axis.[27] See Figures 8 and 9 in section G. Similarly, if the curve was significantly lower, the liability region could be much narrower, even

---

[27] As will become clear from some of the other points discussed below, this result and the next are entirely possible since different other evidence and different legal definitions of agreement (of the sets X and X′) are conceivable.

nonexistent. See Figures 10 and 11 in section G. In the former case, liability would be much easier to establish, perhaps automatic (given other evidence), whereas in the latter, establishing liability would require the enforcer to hit a small target (whose location was in dispute) rather precisely, or it might be impossible (again, in light of the other evidence).

Consider now the relevance of certain types of other evidence that, until this point, have been taken as given.[28] Evidence on the extent of oligopolistic coordination—it's likelihood, magnitude, and duration, as well as the confidence regarding each—might, for example, be substantially stronger than the moderate level stipulated at the outset. Then our curve would be notably higher (see Figure 12 in section G).[29] In particular, we might suppose that the liability region extends further to the left: Previously, the use of at least one act in the set X seemed unlikely due to low conduciveness since we would ordinarily be skeptical that firms would risk sanctions when success was difficult to attain, but when there is strong evidence of actual success, this reservation is less powerful. On the other hand, if evidence on success was quite weak, the curve would be lower (see Figure 13 in section G); indeed, if we were fairly certain that no coordinated elevation was taking place, we would plausibly conclude that the use of any acts in X was fairly unlikely regardless of the degree of conduciveness.

There also may exist direct evidence of agreement, that is, of the use of at least some act in X. If such evidence were decisive, the present inquiry into how to process circumstantial evidence would be moot; if direct evidence were entirely absent, the foregoing analysis would be applicable as is. Sometimes, however, direct evidence will be ambiguous (such as when it refers to an "understanding"), of uncertain import (such as when a subordinate with limited knowledge or authority makes statements), or of questionable reliability (such as when offered by a disgruntled former employee). In these cases, direct evidence of agreement must be combined

---

[28] All types of evidence should be understood broadly and exhaustively. As will be explained, there really is overlap, and a rigorous statement of the inference problem might take each piece of possible evidence as constituting its own dimension. In any event, the categories are employed for purely heuristic purposes.

[29] For a possible contrary effect, generating another sort of paradox of proof, see note 16 in chapter 10 and the accompanying text.

with circumstantial evidence.[30] Specifically, the stronger such direct evidence, the higher our curve would be. The impact need not be uniform: When conduciveness is minimal and there is little evidence of success,[31] ambiguous direct evidence may still leave the likelihood rather low, whereas when conduciveness is fairly high but it is unclear whether or not acts in X would be necessary for success, moderate direct evidence might raise the likelihood more substantially. Accordingly, the division between the liability and paradox regions might shift further to the right than the other boundary shifts to the left.

2. Countervailing Effects

It is also important to reconsider the basic assumptions behind the paradox of proof diagrams, beginning with Figure 1. The standard view implies that the likelihood of the use of prohibited communications falls with the ease of coordination once the ease becomes sufficiently high. This feature, which is necessary to generate a paradox region, can be questioned on two grounds.

First, it is supposed that helpful acts in X become less valuable when conditions are more conducive to coordination, at least once conduciveness exceeds low to moderate levels. This relationship, however, need not be true (ignoring potential liability). Simply put, the value of practices in X may well be increasing, not decreasing, as conditions improve, even at high levels of conduciveness. Certain sorts of communication may raise the expected average markup from, say, 10% to 15% when conditions are moderately conducive but from 30% to 50% when they are very conducive. For example, price wars are far more costly when prices are elevated

---

[30] Direct evidence can well be negative. For example, internal evidence might affirmatively indicate that competitors' reactions are being ignored, or it may negate the presence of coordinated pricing by showing that a price increase was merely passing on a cost increase. Also, sometimes a lack of evidence can constitute evidence, notably when a purported explanation, if true, would likely have been reflected in extensive discussions and internal reports, none of which exist, although there is always the danger that traces are present but were not located because they were hidden or destroyed.

[31] In contrast, if success seems highly likely when conditions are unconducive, the likelihood of the use of acts in X may already be fairly high, as noted just above, and supplemental direct evidence of even modest force might raise the likelihood substantially.

substantially rather than modestly, so avoiding them is more valuable in the former case. Accordingly, even toward the right of the figures, incremental benefits from the use of acts in X may rise rather than fall as the ease of coordination increases—and, if and when they do fall, they may not decline until the ease of coordination is quite high and they may not fall as much as seems generally to be supposed.

Second, the paradox logic implicitly assumes that the risk of sanctions from using acts in X is constant along the horizontal axis. However, some factors that make coordination simpler also make direct detection less likely. When there are fewer firms, coordination is easier, ceteris paribus. But it is also true that explicit communications can be confined to fewer actors, rendering detection more difficult.[32] The probability of leaks and other means by which enforcers may detect the communications falls, making the use of such communications less dangerous. Similarly, if products are homogeneous or the environment is more stable, there is less need for complex and frequent negotiations, which likewise reduces the likelihood of discovery. If the expected sanctions from direct detection consequently fall reasonably rapidly, the likelihood of the use of prohibited communications may be steadily rising as the ease of coordination increases. It might then be true that only permitted means are employed to attempt to achieve modest success when conditions are merely moderately conducive but prohibited means are employed when conditions are more conducive. Again, the result would be no paradox region at all.[33]

For these reasons, suggestions by some commentators and courts that highly conducive conditions negate the inference that prohibited communications were employed might be wrong. Indeed, such conditions may not only fail to negate the inference, but they might instead strengthen it

---

[32] See Hay and Kelley (1974, 20, 23–24 & n.15, 26–27) (portions of which are quoted in note 46) and Masson and Reynolds (1978, 25–26). As is familiar, when there are two players, there needs to be only one line of communication; with three players, there are three connections; four players involves six; five players, ten; and so forth. Hub and spoke systems reduce the required number of linkages, but the number of links as well as the likely volume of traffic still increase with the number of players.

[33] A related point is that, not only does the absence of smoking-gun evidence fail to indicate in general that explicit, secret communications did not occur, but this lack of implication is especially notable in cases in which conditions are highly conducive.

for most or even all of the right portion of the diagrams (see Figures 14 and 15 in section G). Then there would be little qualitative difference between liability triggered by mere interdependence and liability based on a more restrictive rule that confined liability to cases involving the use of prohibited communications (or other specified acts, defining the set X).[34] If instead these countervailing effects were more modest, the consequence might be a narrow paradox region, as depicted in Figures 4 and 5.

3. Dependence on Legal Definition of Agreement

All depictions of the relationship between the ease of coordination and the likelihood of use of acts in X are obviously conditional on the particular legal definition of agreement, that is, a specific stipulation of which acts are deemed to be in set X versus set X'. In each scenario, the ultimate question was of the form: In a given set of circumstances—a given set of evidence on the ease of coordination and on the extent of coordinated oligopoly pricing, and also any direct evidence—how likely was it that an agreement was employed, that is, how likely was it that the defendants used at least some acts in X, rather than confining themselves to acts in X'? If X is limited to highly explicit communications using certain magic words and with assurances signified by a special triple handshake, an agreement could never be inferred from circumstantial evidence. As the definition of X is broadened, the curves in our figures will rise: The likelihood of the use of acts in X will be greater for any given ease of coordination. But how much higher that curve will be as well as its shape—and thus the locations of the liability and paradox regions—will depend on just how X and X' are defined.

Furthermore, it is apparent that a legal rule, and thus the corresponding sets X and X', must be defined rather precisely. After all, the factfinder must infer, often from complex and remote circumstantial evidence, how

---

[34] One possible distinction would arise if, for example, the weaker means employed in situations of moderate danger were sometimes effective and the restrictive agreement definition excludes such means even in cases where they produce successful interdependent oligopoly pricing. Note that, under this difference, the importance to an enforcer of showing that coordination was not too difficult would be greater under a regime requiring proof that acts in X were employed, not the other way around.

likely it is that the defendants confined themselves entirely to acts in X′ rather than having had to use at least one act in X. Knowing that X is narrower than interdependence alone—under which no particular act is required—tells us very little; in a given setting, the likelihood of the use of acts in X might be under 1% or over 99%, depending on how much narrower X is. Likewise, knowing only that X is broader than a very precisely defined sort of explicit agreement—in which case only a few sorts of acts would be in X—provides negligible guidance.

Yet, as the discussion in chapters 2–5 makes clear, little said by courts or commentators gives us much clue of where between these extremes the law currently lies or is advocated to lie. Accordingly, it is hard to know how adjudicators or commentators reach their conclusions about the existence of an agreement in particular cases or hypothetical examples if the requisite inference process is rigorously employed. Furthermore, it is difficult to make sense of statements confined to the probative value of particular pieces of evidence because, as we have seen, many sorts of evidence could cut in either direction, depending on other evidence in a given case—and, as we now can see, on the precise definitions of X and X′.[35] It is also useful to keep in mind many of the points raised in chapter 3 about the substitutability between various means of communication; the flexibility, creativity, and evolution regarding the use of language; and the difficulty those outside the relevant language community have in understanding its operation.[36]

In addition, it is necessary to consider the level of enforcement. The argument that the likelihood of use of acts in X is low when the ease of coordination is particularly low or high presumes that firms would not risk sanctions by employing means that had little prospect of success or when success was likely without resorting to them. However, if expected

---

[35] It is also necessary to determine the level of generality with which the inference process is employed, that is, the extent to which inferences are based on curves implicitly associated with all the facts of a particular case, or an industry, or a type of market structure, and so forth. Additionally, different curves probably need to be applicable at screening stages (in the United States, when considering motions to dismiss or for summary judgment) because less case-specific evidence will be available and that which has been uncovered is not being analyzed fully.

[36] This problem is in addition to the core difficulty of identifying how much information must be transmitted in a given setting to accomplish an effective, successful meeting of the minds, a subject considered further in subsection 7.B.2.

sanctions were sufficiently low, firms would nevertheless employ illegal means in these contexts. Similarly, in the middle region, where the likelihood of the use of acts in X is relatively high, the actual likelihood would be lower if expected sanctions were greater; after all, the main purpose of sanctions is to achieve deterrence.[37]

4. Firms' Behavior, and Hence Inferences, Endogenous to Legal Regime

A legal regime is characterized not only by the formal legal rule and degree of enforcement effort but also by how inferences are made from evidence to conclusions regarding liability. Moreover, the method of inference expected to be employed will, in general, feed back on actors' behavior. This chapter's discussion of making inferences about whether defendant firms were likely to have employed acts in some given set X rather than confining themselves to practices in set X' rests on assumptions about firms' behavior in various circumstances. Specifically, the logic behind the paradox of proof supposes that, when conditions are highly conducive to successful coordination, firms would refrain from acts in X and it is therefore logical to infer that such were not employed. But if the legal regime is understood to operate in this fashion, rational firms would behave differently. Specifically, firms that expect this inference to be made will accordingly be more rather than less inclined to undertake acts in X when the ease of coordination is high.

The analysis underlying this contrary prediction is incomplete, in part because there will sometimes be another route to liability, using direct evidence.[38] For illustrative purposes, think of the possibility that a disgruntled employee becomes an informant and records price-fixing negotiations, or that some participants keep explicit notes that might be uncovered in a criminal investigation or through civil discovery. Even if agreements were never inferred from circumstantial evidence, there would

---

[37] This point is an instance of a more general but insufficiently appreciated phenomenon, that both inferences about likelihoods of violations (using Bayesian reasoning) and optimal evidence thresholds (based on ex ante effects on behavior) depend on enforcement intensity and the magnitude of sanctions. See Kaplow (2011, 2012a).

[38] As discussed at various other points (see sections 5.A and 18.B), in practice there is a substantial blurring of the distinction between direct and circumstantial evidence, and the two types of proof often need to be combined.

be some prospect of liability. This outcome becomes less likely—indeed, its probability might be reduced to near zero—if firms refrain from employing any means in X.[39]

Accordingly, in many settings it would make sense to suppose that firms have some incentive to refrain from employing acts in X even if they otherwise would raise expected profits. If sufficient deterrence could be achieved relying solely on clear, direct evidence, then there would be no need ever to use circumstantial evidence to determine liability, a possibility explored in section 18.B. The present discussion is important only under the standard belief that, given conspirators' incentives to conceal their activity, deterrence would then be insufficient, so that circumstantial evidence must be employed. This desired supplemental deterrence is what can be undermined by the logical inference process described just above.

There is another respect in which the analysis is incomplete. As is, there appears to be a conundrum:[40] If the use of prohibited communications is not inferred because it is reasoned that firms will refrain from acts in X in the stated circumstances, then there is no additional deterrence of such acts and they will tend to be used. If the use of acts in X is inferred in the circumstances, then there would be additional deterrence and the acts would tend not to be used. In either case, the inference would be incorrect. In these sorts of situations, there may instead arise an intermediate outcome in which behavior by firms and adjudicators constitutes a consistent, mixed strategy equilibrium: Some firms might employ means in X and others not, while adjudicators would find liability with a corresponding probability.[41] Perhaps realistically, even modest heterogeneity

---

[39] The risk may not be eliminated entirely due to uncontrollable behavior of employees or other agents and the difficulties a tribunal may have in distinguishing acts in X from similar acts in X'.

[40] This idea was introduced in section 5.A's discussion of circumstantial evidence.

[41] The reader may notice that this sort of inference problem is not unique to the present setting but rather is ubiquitous when factfinders cannot definitively assess behavior. The subject was first explored in the law and economics literature by Ordover (1978) with regard to the negligence rule in tort. A pure, costless, perfectly functioning negligence rule would lead to no prospective injurers behaving negligently; thus, an uncertain factfinder should never infer negligence. But if uncertainty is always present, negligence will never be found, there will be no deterrence, and thus everyone would choose to be negligent. The only equilibrium involves some actors behaving negligently.

would sort firms and factfinders. The firms that choose to employ acts in X rather than abstaining may be in slightly different situations or make somewhat different calculations from those of firms that do not (they may anticipate greater benefits from such acts or believe that it is less likely that they will be caught). Likewise, adjudicators that find liability may be presented with a bit more powerful evidence, be more inclined to believe certain witnesses, or reason somewhat differently from those finding no liability.

The lesson of this subsection is that all of the argument up until this point on the paradox of proof needs to be modified—and, unfortunately, made more complex in yet another manner—as a consequence of the endogeneity of firms' behavior. It is insufficient to reason that firms simply would or would not employ acts in X because of the expected consequences. As a result, the best inference as to the likelihood of the use of prohibited communications is at some intermediate level. Firms' decisions to employ any such acts will depend on how they expect their acts to influence factfinders' inferences regarding that likelihood. The more an act raises the expected likelihood of liability, the more it will be deterred, but such deterrence reduces the likelihood that it is logical for a factfinder to assess. Accordingly, an inference process aimed at determining whether the likelihood of use of prohibited communications exceeds 50% (or any other target probability) will need to find the balancing point (equilibrium) between these forces. (However, as explored at length in parts II and III of the book, it is not generally optimal to determine liability in this fashion.)[42]

E. Empirical Knowledge

This chapter presents a variety of factors and diagrams that bear on the relationship between the ease of coordination and the likelihood that at least some act in the set X was employed. Whether the paradox region is

---

[42] In addition to the core point that one should attend directly to social welfare, it is also true that when, as here, optimal policy depends on ex ante considerations—the balance of deterrence benefits and chilling costs—it is not generally optimal to aim for some stipulated ex post likelihood of undesirable behavior. See section 9.A and Kaplow (2011, 2012a).

narrow (as a number of writers seem implicitly to suggest) or broad and, more directly, what is the location and breadth of the liability region—all for a given definition of agreement (specified sets X and X')—depend on what sorts of acts firms will find it in their interests to employ under various industry conditions. This section briefly considers the empirical basis for making such determinations.

A problem is immediately evident: There does not seem to exist information bearing very directly on the answer to this question in virtually any industry setting. Compounding the difficulty, it is not so obvious at various points in time what the law was (how X was defined), what firms thought the law was, or which acts in X or in X' are ordinarily employed in most settings because many of these acts are not readily observed and firms have a great incentive to hide those even arguably in X. Thus, even if we could catalogue various instances according to market conditions, there would be little basis for drawing the curve relating the variation in any such conditions to the likelihood of the use of at least some act in a specified set X.

Some illumination is provided by studies of litigated (mostly, government prosecuted) cases.[43] In these cases, there typically were highly explicit communications among the defendants. In addition, the industries tended to be concentrated and in some other respects conducive to coordination, and coordinated price elevation was generally achieved. This sort of evidence may provide the basis for some of the conjectures mentioned in section C that successful coordinated oligopoly pricing generally requires direct, even elaborate, communication.[44]

Before proceeding, it is worth reflecting on the point that direct communications have most often been observed when there were few firms. It has also been noted that indirect methods, such as through the use of

---

[43] See Connor (2007a, 2007b), Harrington (2006), and Hay and Kelley (1974).

[44] Motta (2007, 318) supports his claim, previously quoted in note 21, by the observation, "After all, firms have known for a long time that they can sustain collusion without express agreements and yet agencies keep on uncovering documental evidence of meetings and communication among firms' managers. This observation somehow reduces the importance of the question of how to treat tacit collusion, and refocuses our attention on the issue of how to break and deter cartels (i.e., explicit collusion)."

trade associations, were more common when numbers were larger.[45] These findings might seem opposite to what was conjectured in drawing Figure 1, and therefore it may suggest a narrow or nonexistent paradox region. George Hay and Daniel Kelley (1974, 26–27) conclude their study by observing that

> [a] brief summary of our empirical results would be that conspiracy among competitors may arise in any number of situations but it is most likely to occur and endure when numbers are small, concentration is high and the product is homogeneous. We suspect these results will conflict with at least some previously held opinions on the expected locus of conspiracy, and conversely on the ability of oligopolists to regularly attain monopoly profits through tacit collusion.

The pattern might be explained by the ideas articulated in subsection D.2, including that, as conditions become more conducive to successful coordination, fewer and fewer communications are required—assuming that direct, explicit communications are to be employed.[46]

These studies of litigated cases, perhaps the best evidence on the use of various sorts of communication, are limited in many ways. Industry conditions are not very precisely identified. It is difficult to know what

---

[45] See Fraas and Greer (1977, 39–42), Hay and Kelley (1974, 21), and Levenstein and Suslow (2008, 1123).

[46] See Hay and Kelley (1974, 20). They further explain (23–24), "The implications of this result are significant. Despite the writings of Stigler and Posner, it has frequently been assumed that conspiracy would be largely restricted to relatively unconcentrated industries, since high concentration would permit extensive non-collusive coordination through what has been termed 'conscious parallelism.' . . . The results of the present study however, suggest that the low cost of planning and enforcing a conspiracy and the smaller likelihood of being caught in concentrated markets, are equally if not more significant factors in stimulating conspiracy. This is not to suggest that some non-collusive coordination does not take place: but it now appears possible that some of the non-competitive price levels alleged to exist in concentrated industries may be the result not of 'conscious parallelism' but of formal conspiracy."

They add (24 n.15) that "[i]t should be kept in mind that most of the conspiracies were found in concentrated markets even though *a priori* these are the conspiracies which are most likely to escape detection. Thus if there is a bias, it should result in the underreporting of conspiracies in markets with high concentration."

law was de facto applied or what firms thought the law to be. We have only limited knowledge of the acts employed. Some acts may have been clearly detected, either because they were public or because reliable undercover methods (wiretaps, hidden cameras) provided sharp evidence, but we do not know what other acts may also have been used.

But there are even greater shortcomings. First, for the sorts of acts that were proved in those cases studied, we do not know how likely they are to exist conditional on no definitive direct evidence turning up. That is the relevant setting for the use of circumstantial evidence, but in such cases one must wonder what to infer from apparent silence (the dog not barking): Is the lack of direct evidence reflective of effective secrecy or of the fact that the alleged acts never occurred? And with what probability?

Second, regarding acts for which there was no definitive evidence, conclusions may have been reached one way or the other, but they inevitably required use of the very sorts of inferences we are trying to assess. Therefore, we may know that a factfinder deemed some act to have been committed based on circumstantial evidence, but we have no independent basis for confirming whether they were correct.

Third and most significant, we know virtually nothing about other cases: cases with acts in X that were never detected, cases that were not prosecuted because evidence was too weak, and cases that were not prosecuted because the conjectured (or provable) behavior was not deemed to be illegal under the prosecutor's understanding of the definition of X. For example, there is some evidence suggesting that price elevation is present in many oligopolistic industries and in various local markets[47] where there have been few price-fixing challenges. How do we know whether or not acts in X were employed in these situations?[48] Moreover, if some are superficially similar to prosecuted cases regarding the extent

---

[47] See Bresnahan (1989), Scherer and Ross (1990), Schmalensee (1989), and Weiss (1989).

[48] The above discussion of the evidence suggests a narrow paradox region because most prosecuted cases involved rather conducive conditions, but perhaps there are many other industries with even more conducive conditions where acts in X were not employed. (Notably, many prosecuted cases involve sales of intermediate goods, presumably often to large buyers in privately negotiated deals, a factor rendering coordination more difficult.)

to which conditions are conducive to coordination, how can we know the likelihood of the use of acts in X in various settings?[49]

If successful criminal prosecutions, with a "beyond a reasonable doubt" proof standard (in the United States) and a prospect of imprisonment for the individuals involved, are thought to require direct and highly probative evidence of explicit, detailed, face-to-face communications, then the sample of prosecuted cases may well represent a small and possibly highly skewed slice of the total population of possible cases. Thus, studies' findings regarding methods of coordination that are based on this sample depict what may be the tip of a much larger iceberg. The problem is that we cannot readily infer the features of the submerged portion from the small portion in view.

A further challenge is that it is hardly clear where one would look to gather better evidence, either in general or for purposes of a case at hand. One approach is to run laboratory experiments in which volunteer subjects are assigned the role of different interacting firms. Some such studies find that various forms of communication sometimes aid in supracompetitive pricing.[50] But these studies do very little to calibrate the necessary inferences. On one hand, the settings typically are highly simplified in many respects, which may make coordination much easier for any given

---

[49] If one were to assume that most cases involving express agreements are detected and prosecuted, then the aforementioned evidence on oligopolistic price elevation suggests that there may be a broad paradox region, contrary to the oft-stated view; indeed, such an assumption directly implies this result for it means that, in the absence of smoking-gun (direct) evidence, there is no express agreement present. But if most such cases are successfully prosecuted, we might suppose that deterrence would be high, in which event these cases would not exist. So their presence may instead imply inadequate deterrence (a possibility examined further in subsection 13.A.3), which, given high sanctions, may indicate that coordination involving undetected explicit communications is rampant.

To take a concrete example, if we were to determine that in numerous isolated local markets—perhaps small towns where gas station owners may frequently interact outside the business context—neighboring gasoline stations charged supracompetitive prices, should we conclude that successful interdependent oligopoly pricing without secret communications is simple or that it is fairly easy in such settings for such communications to be kept secret from the government and potential plaintiffs?

[50] See Crawford (1998), Davis and Wilson (2002, 64–72), Fonseca and Normann (2012), Holt (1995, 409–11), and Wellford (2002, 28–29).

level of permitted communication.[51] On the other hand, many artificial features may make successful coordinated oligopoly pricing much harder. For example, student subjects, unlike firm decision-makers, do not have relevant training, certain common experiences, possibly years of interaction in their industry, perhaps personal contacts such as through trade association activities, and so forth.[52] These limitations are compounded by the fact that results in laboratory settings are often sensitive to subtle differences in how the experiments are framed, perhaps reflecting their simplicity, lack of real context, and other respects in which student players of artificial games depart from actual business decision-makers.

There are also studies of oligopoly behavior in different market settings.[53] Substantial work has been undertaken on many industries, employing differing methodologies. Such evidence does provide some basis for relating various features bearing on the ease of coordination to interdependent oligopoly pricing. If the test for liability focuses on successful interdependence, this empirical work is highly probative. However, regarding the question of whether, for a given degree of success that has been observed in particular market conditions, the firms were more likely than not to have employed acts in some set X rather than confining themselves to acts in X'—the question at hand—such evidence is essentially silent.

In light of this dearth of evidence bearing on the likelihood of use of acts in X in various circumstances, a number of challenges are immediate. First, how can we run a legal system that routinely must make these sorts of inferences? Relatedly, how have we done so for decades, if the law is indeed what many proclaim it to be? For example, what sort of proof (if

---

[51] Compare Neven (2001, 65): "The first striking observation, which arises from this literature, is that without communication, collusion is difficult to achieve. It is only in very simple market environments and with only two firms and a lot of experience that successful collusion appears frequently. When the number of players is increased, or the environment is made more complicated (for instance with different costs or different demands across firms), firms appear to be unable to sustain collusive outcomes. Interestingly, even a substantial amount of *ex post* transparency does not seem to help firms in sustaining collusion."

[52] Whinston (2006, 24) questions "whether the results of these experiments, usually with college students as subjects, are indicative of the actual market behavior of businessmen and women."

[53] See the references in note 47.

any) has been offered to fill in these gaps, what should have been required at trial or at summary judgment, and what must an enforcer allege in order to show that it would be able to establish the existence of an agreement with sufficient plausibility to avoid having its complaint dismissed? It is also true that, even if we had some evidence on the relevant mapping, it would relate to some particular definition of agreement (specification of the sets X and X'), some understanding thereof by firms, and a conjectured process of inference by factfinders. If we wished to assess legal reform—notably, making the definition of agreement more or less strict—it would be hard either to operate the new system (lacking the data necessary for inferences) or to assess its likely effects and thus its desirability.

Second, how can commentators or courts justify the various claims they have made concerning the likelihood of the need for explicit communication in general or about whether it is plausible to infer the existence of an agreement in various actual cases or hypothetical examples about which they regularly offer opinions? Regarding both parts of this question, recall that the problem is greatly compounded by the failure to specify the definition of agreement with much precision; that single degree of freedom could allow one to rationalize either conclusion with any postulated degree of confidence in a wide range of circumstances. In other words, the implicit empirical claims can be regarded as meaningless due to the lack of specification of what is being asserted.[54] In any event, it is difficult to see even how unambiguous assertions about the pertinent question could have much basis in fact.

F. On the Meaning of the Law

In the course of the foregoing analysis of the paradox of proof, the reader may well have had the reaction that the discourse was somewhat strange, even bizarre. So much of what has been explained, although merely drawing out the logical implications of a posited legal definition of agreement, seems grossly at odds with both conventional accounts of the law (whether

---

[54] Similarly, because we do not know if any writer is implicitly using a consistent definition of agreement or if two different writers have the same definition in mind, it is impossible to compare statements.

espoused by commentators or courts) and the law in action (that is, what parties and courts actually do). Inquiries argued to be necessary in routine cases—if the law is as many allege—do not seem to be contemplated. Implications of evidence are often highly indeterminate, in that they depend in unexpected ways on other evidence, and are possibly contrary to expectation. And the empirical foundation for making most inferences about the existence of agreements, understood as the use of some act in a set X, seems to be nonexistent. Taking the standard account of the law as given and analyzing what it entails seems to have produced conclusions that are more like fantasy than legal exegesis.[55] This section comments on the resulting tension while situating the conclusions of this chapter among those in chapters 4 and 5 on doctrine and juxtaposing all of the foregoing with various additional indicators of the law in action.

To start, it is helpful to consider different senses in which one could identify what is the law of horizontal agreement. One could read the pertinent statutory provisions. One could examine commentary. One could look to courts, which examination might encompass canonical statements of higher courts, the actual decision-making of intermediate appellate courts or of trial courts in granting motions to dismiss or for summary judgment, the instructions given to factfinders, actual liability determinations, and the assessment of sanctions—all subjects of preceding chapters. One could also consider the behavior of firms and their lawyers as well as plaintiffs (including prosecutors) and defendants in the conduct of litigation with regard to the types of allegations, arguments, and evidence they typically present.

Regarding the latter, it seems that, in the simplest setting regarding the paradox of proof, what we typically see is not in accord with what the paradox-of-proof logic predicts. Consider a plaintiff whose allegations and proof consist solely of two points: Pricing exhibits oligopolistic coordination, and collusion is very difficult in the particular industry (in the absence of requisite communications). As explained, this may imply that the existence of an agreement (defined in whatever fashion is deemed

---

[55] A further implication of the analysis of the paradox of proof is to make it difficult to sustain the view that factfinding will be less economically complex and more reliable if the law employs a concept of agreement more restrictive than interdependence, a point developed in section 17.D.

appropriate) is more likely than not. Indeed, such allegations would seem to constitute a standard case built on circumstantial evidence (just as the negation of the second point is increasingly taken to be a defense). Yet it hardly seems that plaintiffs' cases, beginning with their complaints, typically adopt this approach. Furthermore, suppose that one accepts the common conjecture mentioned in section C that implies the rarity of cases in which interdependence alone is sufficient for successful coordination. Then a plaintiff's claim would be provisionally likely even if all that the plaintiff alleges is the existence of coordinated oligopolistic pricing. After all, such is presumed typically to be difficult if not impossible absent the requisite communications. But such a case, rather than being routinely accepted, seems to generate skepticism or even derision from courts and commentators, which logically contradicts conventional statements of what the law requires.[56]

---

[56] Consider also the most straightforward defense that relies on the logic of the paradox of proof. Why don't defendants frequently, beginning with their answers to complaints and running through to closing arguments before a factfinder, argue roughly as follows: "We have been charging a monopoly price for years and expect to do so forever after. We have no price wars, no discord. It's just incredibly simple given how conducive are our industry conditions. Moreover, we all have key employees and consultants trained at the same business schools and who attend the same conferences. They use a well-known playbook, so coordinated behavior is easy as pie." (This query is raised in Kaplow and Shapiro (2007, 1126–28). Elhauge and Geradin (2007, 836) observe: "To this day, one does not see firms proudly proclaiming that they are engaged in oligopolistic coordination. To the contrary, they tend to deny it . . . even in cases where acknowledging it would support their claims.") One possibility is that defendants fear that factfinders and legal decision-makers would be prejudiced (see Baker 1993, 190 n.95), in which event the law arguably is closer de facto to a successful interdependence standard. Another is that, conditional on losing liability, defendants fear higher damages. However, the analysis of section 5.D indicates that damages should approach zero in this case (even if a plaintiff can show that some employee slipped and engaged in forbidden communication)— again, unless the damages rule is more consistent with a liability standard that de facto prohibits interdependence. A simpler explanation is that defendants and their lawyers do not believe that the rule clearly excuses successful coordinated oligopoly pricing when it is so readily accomplished, despite assertions that the law is otherwise. Yet another possibility is that they may find such a defense to be one that would lose on the facts; that is, they expect a persuasive plaintiff's rebuttal proving that effective coordination is sufficiently difficult that it requires the use of prohibited communications. (Perhaps they reserve the paradox-based argument for legal briefs, when it is more difficult for a plaintiff to mount a factual response.) Note that, if the law is indeed such that the paradox of proof strongly holds and if, moreover, defendants

Two observations are apparent. First, as already noted with regard to certain perspectives, what is taken in various settings to be the standard of horizontal agreement may vary, possibly substantially. Second, most of what we observe in these contexts is in sharp tension with the logical implications regarding the paradox of proof. The paradox of proof involves more than the possible existence of a counterintuitive inference in one type of setting. Rather, conflicts may be widespread, and much of the inference process is at odds with what is generally taken to be the statements and operations of most components of the relevant legal environment.

As already suggested at many points in chapters 4 and 5, the legal system broadly operates in many respects as if the legal definition of agreement is akin to successful interdependent oligopoly pricing. From this perspective lower courts' use of plus factors would make sense, jury instructions would reflect the state of the law, and damages determinations would be consistent with the rules governing liability. Regarding the paradox of proof itself, the strange and complex inferences that do not seem to be indulged would no longer arise under an interdependence standard for agreement.[57] And the nonexistence of the empirical evidence that seems necessary to make any headway in determining liability would be irrelevant. By contrast, the more restrictive understanding of the horizontal agreement requirement that is commonly advanced seems to describe the actual law in at most a limited and formal sense: It reflects what many assert the law to be.[58] One consequence is that, if one wished

---

are reluctant to take strategic advantage of what it offers them, then we might expect plaintiffs to be even more aggressive in advancing from the outset the sort of argument sketched in the text.

[57] One might instead rationalize what is observed by granting the importance of the countervailing effects examined in subsection D.2, which imply that the paradox region is small or empty. But then, as discussed in section C, if the paradox region is thought to be narrow (and, a fortiori, if it is nonexistent), it is unclear why so many insist on the importance of imposing a circumscribed agreement requirement (limiting liability to cases in which some act in the set X has been employed).

[58] Going forward, however, one could speculate that everything will change greatly in light of *Twombly*. Such an argument would take an aggressive interpretation of that decision, emphasizing that because the plaintiffs in that case obviously did allege what seems to be required, the outcome implicitly adopts a stricter rule on liability than meets the eye. Specifically, one could assert that the new doctrine is not far from a regime in which no proof by circumstantial

the law in action to implement a more restrictive notion of agreement, substantial reform would be required, and its implementation would need to be informed by new empirical findings.

The reason for this state of affairs has been noted at a number of points. If the agreement requirement rests only on successful interdependence, it is sufficient to assess market conditions, itself a formidable task. However, if more is required to establish an agreement, then it is necessary to make inferences about whether the firms' meeting of the minds was achieved by some means (acts in X) rather than others (acts solely in X'). Because the means employed cannot directly be observed (we are considering cases in which circumstantial evidence is important), and because there are so many sorts of means whose functionality varies greatly by context and in ways that are difficult for factfinders to appreciate, it should not be surprising that requiring this distinction to be made poses tremendous challenges. We have little idea how much communication is required and even less of what means were employed to accomplish it when the most that we can observe (absent direct evidence) is whether the defendants were successful. Recall also that the variety, complexity, and flexibility of means of communication complicate the very effort to articulate a definition of agreement in the first instance.

A complete assessment of the law in action requires that one also look beyond adjudication, the focus until now, to the actors that actually determine the law's everyday influence in the regulated world. First, legal counselors advise their clients on what sorts of activities are legally prudent. Interestingly, some practitioners warn clients against behavior that many academic commentators assert does not give rise to liability; much

---

evidence is permitted (see section 18.B), which would render irrelevant the inference process explored in this chapter. A complicating factor is that much so-called direct evidence is ambiguous or otherwise suspect, raising again the need to make inferences from circumstantial evidence. Note also that, under this aggressive interpretation of *Twombly*, private suits that are not follow-ons to successful government prosecutions would perhaps be almost entirely eliminated, for a plaintiff would have to state, before any discovery, such particulars as what words were said to whom by various of the defendants. With informants, public confessions, or crystal balls, this would be possible, but it is hard to see how one could otherwise make the necessary allegations if direct evidence is demanded. See also note 55 in chapter 4, further discussing how *Twombly*'s requirements might be met if agreement is defined restrictively, and section C, just above, on how a narrow view of the paradox range implies that facts indicating successful coordination are easily sufficient to meet *Twombly*'s articulated standard.

advice seems to operate on the assumption that purely interdependent behavior is legally risky.[59]

Second, it is important to inquire into the beliefs and practices of firms in the marketplace.[60] They, after all, are the real audience for the law because the purpose of the price-fixing prohibition is to deter undesirable

---

[59] See, for example, ABA (2005a, 66), stating that agreements include "written agreements, verbal agreements and even tacit understandings that are reached through a course of conduct or other form of communication"; Fullerton (2011, 34), advising "clients [to] avoid appearing to threaten to reduce prices or resume a price war if competitors fail to respond to an invitation to raise prices," and to be cautious about "public and internal communications to ensure that the company does not appear inadvertently to have accepted a perceived invitation to collude"; Kessler and Wheeler (1993), warning against anticompetitive price signaling, including through advance public pricing announcements, describing press releases and interviews as dangerous, and suggesting that such behavior in concentrated industries is particularly suspect; DaimlerChrysler Corporation (2005, 4): "[a]n agreement need not be written or even spoken," it "may be inferred from the conduct of the parties without showing any direct meeting of the minds," and, "[f]or example, if one company's executives tell a newspaper reporter that they would like to stop giving discounts if their competitors would, the story is printed, and all competitors then simultaneously announce that they are dropping their discount programs, this may be seen as an illegal agreement"; Risk Management Association Antitrust Guidelines (2010): "An anticompetitive agreement need not be formal or even express and can be proven by circumstantial evidence. Thus, if such circumstances as the exchange of pricing plans permit the inference of a tacit understanding to 'act in concert' or 'follow the leader,' a jury may be allowed to find intentional violation of the law."; and John Q. Lawyer (pseudonym) (1963, 98), in advising the use of less explicit forms of interdependence, offers the rule: "Conscious parallelism may be illegal, but it is certainly not as illegal as conspiring. Moreover, it is hard to prove." See also U.S. Department of Justice (2005, 1–2): "Proving such a crime does not require us to show the conspirators entered into a formal written or express agreement."; International Titanium Association (2010): "'Agreements' on such matters are not limited to written documents, and also include informal, unwritten, and even unspoken agreements or understandings."; and Smith (2005, 6), in addressing "What Is An 'Agreement' Among Competitors?," states that agreements in antitrust law are referred to using terms that include "understanding," "meeting of the minds," and "common scheme," that they "need *not* be expressly stated" and "may be found to exist with *no* actual offer or acceptance," and that they "may be proven entirely by indirect or 'circumstantial' evidence."

[60] Anticipating parts II and III, which address what regime is optimal, it is also worth considering what sort of legal command is easier to convey to private actors. One might have thought that a formalistic, communications-based prohibition would be easiest to communicate, but this entire part has explained that this is an illusion; even simple scenarios, like those in section II.A, can readily be characterized in opposite ways. Coordinated oligopolistic price elevation seems more subtle, but as mentioned in the text and note to follow, the subject is

behavior. It may be difficult to ascertain directly what firms generally believe. One plausible conjecture is that their views are in part a product of the just-mentioned advice from their lawyers. Additionally, some managers may have absorbed lessons about the legal risks of various strategies in business school. The advice offered by competitive strategy texts is rather mixed in this regard.[61]

The best source of information on what firms believe, however, is probably what they do—and refrain from doing. On one hand, the use of price signs by adjacent gasoline stations is routine. On the other hand, detailed discussions about prices and other terms of competition via press conferences, with carefully lawyered language and so forth, seem to be rare. In the *Airline Tariff* case (mentioned in section 3.C),

---

routinely taught in business schools. See also section 13.C on how firms might be expected to respond to the prospect of sanctions.

[61] See Dranove and Marciano (2005, 119), suggesting, shockingly, that "[f]irms may . . . privately voice that if their rivals toe the line, they will, too. (Public utterances of that sort would be blatant violations of antitrust law.)"; ibid. (138–39), advising price leadership as the best example of a facilitating device, but warning that "when a preannouncement has no obvious benefit for customers, antitrust agencies are sure to take a close look"; ibid. (143–44), offering a list of dos and don'ts; Garicano and Gertner (2000, 45), in discussing "attempts to create market segmentation, commitments to published price lists, advanced announcement of price changes, and price leadership," caution that "[t]he antitrust treatment of such actions is very complex, so none of them should be taken as a strategic recommendation by the authors."; Heil, Day, and Reibstein (1997, 285–86): "Companies don't have the option of saying to competitors: 'I'm raising my price, and if you follow, we can all enjoy higher margins.' Instead, they must simply raise the price and hope the competitor interprets the move properly."; Porter (1980, chs. 4, 5), in presenting an extensive discussion of market signals and competitive moves, mentions antitrust liability only in a footnote (100 n.6), which warns: "Nevertheless, some modes of signaling and establishing commitments are under review by the U.S. antitrust authorities because of the concern that they may be effective in leading to tacit collusion in industries. Although this interpretation is novel and unproven, managers must be aware of its existence."; and Saloner, Shepard, and Podolny (2001, 206–7, 211–13), offering examples of sequential price announcements in the steel and airlines industries and discussing the ambiguity of antitrust law's agreement requirement. See also Garda and Marn (1993, 97): "But, of course, do not 'price signal' to your competitors. There are laws against it. But if you find yourself taking actions that might be construed by your competitors as price slashing, it is proper to include in your normal price communications to the market a clear description of all qualifiers and limitations and, in some circumstances, an explanation of your action—for instance, 'This price will remain in force until our inventory of obsolete goods is exhausted.'"

airlines went to great efforts to hide their signaling, were the subject of an investigation, and ultimately agreed to cease the practices in question. Why behave secretly, why settle, and why not subsequently resume detailed negotiations, so to speak, in public view? Nor is it common before a secret-bid auction for a firm to suggest publicly what its bid will be, with other firms responding in kind.[62] One might wonder why price signs, like those used by gasoline stations, are not widely employed as signaling devices. The price postings in *Airline Tariff* had this character, but that was exceptional and is not ongoing. Perhaps gasoline stations cannot help but post their prices in such communicative ways, so it is understood to be allowed, whereas anything more contrived is thought to be legally hazardous.

The foregoing suggests that firms perceive the set X of prohibited acts very broadly, or at the least are worried that many acts in the set X' are sufficiently likely to be classified as belonging to set X that they too are excessively risky. Observed behavior seems to be notably more cautious than one might expect if a wide swath of public comment and signaling was generally regarded to be plainly legal. This timidity also helps to explain why price-fixing prosecutions with secret meetings do not vanish: Why do executives risk treble damages and time in prison if they can be protected by moving discussions into the open? Although some of the explanation could be that pressure, political or otherwise, might be expected to follow, it seems we should see substantially more of such activity, even if it is less than completely detailed, given the large gains from doing so—that is, if the law is as many assert it to be.

---

[62] Indeed, as explained in note 6 in chapter 5, such a public announcement may be a clever defensive tactic if firms are actually discussing bid prices secretly, for the public statement of the agreed-upon bid would negate the inference that identical sealed bids could only have been the product of secret discussions. More broadly, any coincidences that prospective defendants are worried might look excessively suspicious and thus be evidence of conspiracy might be "explained" by appropriate unilateral public statements. If such statements are clearly legal, then there is all the more reason we should see them. There is the caveat that this cleverness can be reversed, by a plaintiff arguing that the unilateral statement is suggestive of secret meetings. But if one is inclined to suppose that interdependence alone (where alone is now understood to include quite a bit of public give-and-take) can explain successful oligopolistic coordination, absent strong evidence of the use of prohibited acts (those in set X), and if accordingly such public signaling was widespread, it would no longer be true that one could infer from such statements the existence of secret meetings.

G. Addendum

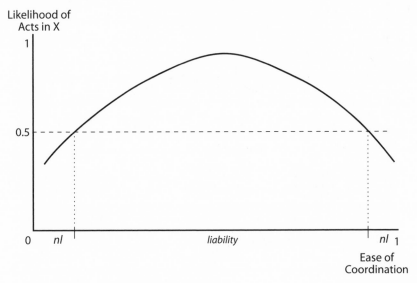

Figure 8. Greater Likelihood of Acts in X

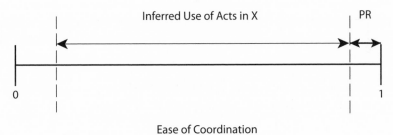

Ease of Coordination

Figure 9. Greater Likelihood of Acts in X and Paradox of Proof

This section expands on section D's abbreviated analysis of additional considerations bearing on the paradox of proof.

BREADTH OF LIABILITY REGION. To illustrate the foregoing points on this subject, consider Figures 8–11.[63]

---

[63] The situation depicted in Figures 10 and 11 is consistent with the combined ideas that, when coordination is moderately to seriously difficult, the firms would be unlikely to attempt it and hence one could not plausibly infer the use of prohibited means (acts in X), and when

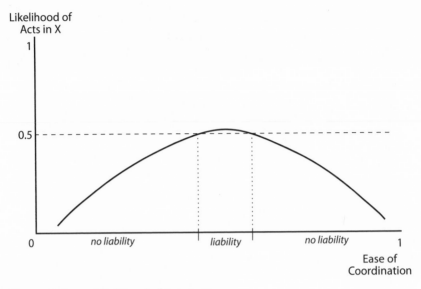

Figure 10. Lesser Likelihood of Acts in X

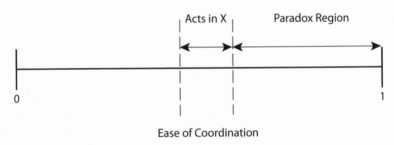

Ease of Coordination

Figure 11. Lesser Likelihood of Acts in X and Paradox of Proof

Viewing these two scenarios together, we can see that, even with a simple, symmetric curve relating the ease of coordination to the likelihood of the use of acts in X, it is possible, for any given point on the horizontal

---

coordination is moderately to very easy, the firms would be able to accomplish it without having to use prohibited means. See Baker (1993, 190–91). Of course, each of these ideas is an empirical conjecture that is a matter of degree, so it is hardly obvious a priori that no middle region exists or, if it exists, that it is very narrow rather than a good deal wider. Furthermore, recalling the situations described in section C, it is also necessary to determine where such a middle region is located; even if it is narrow, if it is located at the point on the horizontal axis where the facts of the instant case fall, there would nevertheless be liability.

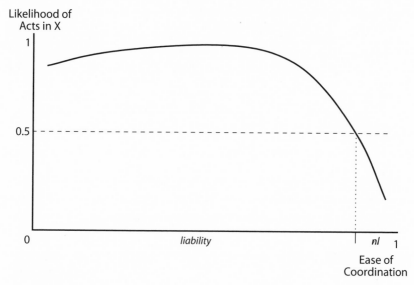

Figure 12. Ease of Coordination, Likelihood of Acts in X, and Liability: Significant Oligopoly Pricing

axis—corresponding to a particular set of evidence adduced by the enforcer and defendants bearing on the ease of coordination in the case at hand—that either outcome could arise. Whether the use of acts in X should logically be inferred with sufficient probability would depend on the height of the curve. Combining this result with those in section C, we can see that both the skewness of the curve and its height are critically important to determine when the use of acts in X may logically be inferred.

EVIDENCE ON THE EXTENT OF OLIGOPOLISTIC COORDINATION.—To illustrate these points, consider Figure 12. Start at the left of the horizontal axis. Even when the ease of coordination is quite low, strong evidence that it is taking place is highly suggestive of the use of some acts in the set X. As the ease of coordination rises, this high probability may approach certainty. Eventually, however, the probability falls, as it becomes increasingly possible that great success was achieved without resort to acts in the set X. However, as Figure 12 is drawn, the ease of coordination must be quite high before the likelihood of the use of acts in X falls below 50%; because the success is so substantial (high in magnitude, long term, and with little interruption by price wars), it is taken to be plausible absent resort to acts in X only when conditions are very conducive to coordination.

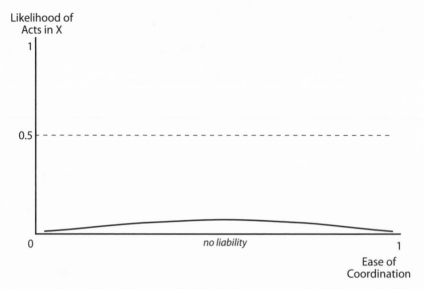

Figure 13. Ease of Coordination, Likelihood of Acts in X, and Liability: Negligible Oligopoly Pricing

Now suppose that the evidence shows little sign that any coordinated oligopoly pricing is taking place. This situation might be represented as in Figure 13. In this figure, the fact that there is almost certainly no oligopolistic price coordination taking place renders the likelihood of the use of acts in X very low. It may not reach zero because it is possible that the evidence is mistaken (but this probability is assumed to be minimal) and, as mentioned in section A, firms might mistakenly attempt price coordination even when there is little hope of success.

Taken together, Figures 12 and 13, when combined with Figure 2—or, more broadly, with all of the previous figures—show that evidence on the extent to which coordinated oligopoly pricing is taking place can have a dramatic effect on whether it makes sense to infer the use of acts in X (continuing to take as given some specification thereof). Roughly speaking, all else equal, it would typically seem that, the stronger is the evidence of actual coordinated oligopoly pricing, the more likely it is that some acts in X were employed. When the ease of coordination is low (when conditions are unconducive to success), the likelihood of the use of acts in X may usually be low, but the discussion of Figure 12 suggests that, as the evidence of actual success becomes increasingly powerful, it is more likely that some acts in X were employed. How else can one explain the observed success under such adverse conditions? Moreover, the evidence of success casts doubt on the demonstration that conditions are so unconducive. (And also conversely, as noted just below.) As the ease of coordination increases, the likelihood of the use of acts in X may well rise and then fall, as in Figures 1 and 2 (and the others). However, taking as given the ease of coordination—even if moderate or fairly high—it seems that greater success renders it more probable that more powerful means were employed, making the use of at least some acts in X more likely.

Many readers will recognize that the foregoing discussion in essence describes a three-dimensional figure. Circumstantial evidence might bear on two dimensions: the ease of coordination (whether conditions are in principle conducive) and the extent of coordinated oligopoly pricing (whether it actually seems to have occurred). These dimensions, taken together, indicate the likelihood of the use of some act in X—the strength of the inference from all of the circumstantial evidence to agreement.

The situation is somewhat more complicated, as already suggested at many points. The reason is that much circumstantial evidence may bear on both of these dimensions. Relatedly, a view on each is probative of the other. If conditions are highly conducive, for example, it is more plausible to construe ambiguous evidence as indicating successful coordinated oligopoly pricing. Put more directly, it is the underlying evidence, all of the relevant bits, that jointly determines whether one should believe that conditions are conducive, the extent to which coordinated oligopolistic pricing has occurred, and the likelihood of the use of acts in X. Since all that matters legally—for liability—is the latter question, what is really needed is a multidimensional diagram relating all manner of circumstantial (and other) evidence to the likelihood that some act in X was employed. Stated in this fashion, the claim is a truism.

Observe that, within this more complete depiction of the situation, we can restate the paradox of proof with regard to types of evidence. Many sorts of evidence, although certainly not all, will have the character that, for some sets of other facts (collections of evidence), stronger proof of the item in question will raise the likelihood of use of acts in X, whereas, for other sets of these other facts, stronger proof will reduce this likelihood. The degree of complexity is now apparent, for this statement will

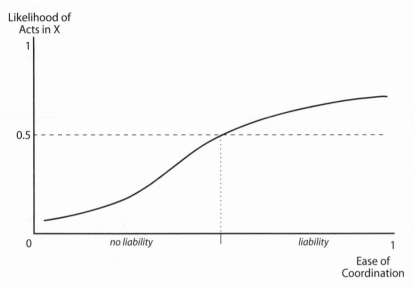

Figure 14. No Paradox Region

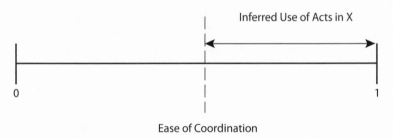

Figure 15. No Paradox of Proof

hold for many pieces of evidence. Moreover, there is a tremendous inter-relationship among items of evidence. Depending on the other evidence, and importantly on how the factfinder interprets it all, many different pieces could help or hurt a given party. Looking at the evidence collectively—and keeping in mind that in an actual case there may be very many items and numerous competing arguments about how they are best interpreted—there may well be myriad scenarios (combinations of which evidence is believed, to what degree, which not, and how they are related) under which the enforcer should prevail and myriad others under which the defendants should. For any given piece of evidence, crediting it more heavily may help the enforcer in some scenarios and hurt it in others. Parties' litigation strategies are highly interrelated, and the direction of effect of any one component may change from moment to moment as a case proceeds. Needless to say, figuring out what is best alleged at the time of filing a complaint, or which components the defendants may be better off conceding or amplifying rather than contesting, should be an extremely challenging strategic problem in many settings.

COUNTERVAILING EFFECTS.—When the countervailing effects are sufficiently strong, one might have a situation like that depicted in Figures 14 and 15.

7

Oligopoly Theory and the
Agreement Requirement

꒢

Preceding chapters have highlighted the horizontal agreement problem, considered definitions of key terms and the role of communications, examined doctrine, and studied the problem of inferring agreements from circumstantial evidence. This chapter concludes the legal-doctrinal inquiry—and transitions to the remaining parts of the book—by examining the relationship, if any, between various notions of horizontal agreement and the modern economic theory of coordinated oligopoly behavior. Especially because enforcement agencies, courts, and commentators increasingly emphasize the central role of economic analysis in formulating competition law doctrine, it is natural to explore the connection with regard to price fixing under Sherman Act Section 1, EU Article 101, and analogous provisions of other jurisdictions' competition regimes. Interestingly, it appears that little prior attempt has been made, perhaps because the prohibition against price fixing is largely uncontroversial from an economic perspective (and others).

The chapter begins by discussing pertinent aspects of contemporary oligopoly theory—material that will be familiar to most economists—although it is worth emphasizing in particular the point that the analysis does not distinguish between coordination achieved purely through recognized interdependence and that arising from secret negotiations. As explained in the first subsection, the importation of language from game theory to the legal arena has, unfortunately, generated some confusion in this regard, including in some writing by economists on competition policy. The remainder of the chapter uses these ideas to illuminate the law's agreement requirement.

A. Theory of Coordinated Oligopoly Behavior

Even though the theories of perfect competition and of monopoly have long been clear, oligopoly theory remained murky well past the middle of the twentieth century. Many conjectured that the results—notably the market price and the quantities supplied—would lie somewhere between those for the two polar cases, but just how these intermediate outcomes would arise was not well articulated. With perfect competition, each firm considers only the market price when making its decisions; with monopoly, the firm takes account of market demand. In neither case is there strategic consideration of competitors' behavior. With oligopoly, by contrast, strategic interaction is central.[1]

For ages, analysis of oligopolistic firms, particularly regarding coordinated behavior, tended to be ad hoc. Some models were static; that is, each firm set prices or quantities once and for all, based on various assumptions about how other firms were expected to behave. Yet it was recognized that, over time, each firm would observe market outcomes and react to them. Other models were nominally dynamic but did not contain coherent assumptions about how firms expected each other to behave. For example, it might be that firms' postulated conjectures about others' behavior were disconfirmed each period, but firms nevertheless were imagined to continue to move forward based on these conjectures.

The situation changed rapidly beginning in the 1970s with the development of the theory of repeated games and its application to the problem of coordinated oligopoly behavior.[2] While these newer models still abstract

---

[1] As the section heading indicates, the present focus is exclusively on coordinated behavior—because the subject at hand is interpretation of the law's agreement requirement. The relevance of unilateral market power to competition policy toward oligopolistic price elevation is explored in chapter 14.

[2] The seminal article is Friedman (1971). On modern game theory in general, see Fudenberg and Tirole (1991) and Osborne and Rubinstein (1994); on the application to oligopoly theory, see Friedman (1986), Shapiro (1989), Tirole (1988, ch. 6), and Vives (1999, 301–23); and on the connection to competition law, see Kaplow and Shapiro (2007, 1103–21) and Whinston (2006, ch. 2).

in many ways from the complex world, they offer explicit and consistent depictions of firms' strategic interactions over time. In part, the motivation was to remove widely acknowledged defects in prior analysis. In addition, rough, intuitive accounts of interdependent oligopolistic price coordination had long been articulated, yet key notions were not well captured by existing models.[3] Accordingly, the new theory aspired to offer a sound logical foundation as well as a framework for explaining and predicting coordinated oligopoly behavior in real markets. Although the underlying story has long played a prominent role in academic commentary and court opinions, the modern theory that makes it more precise has been virtually absent in these arenas.[4]

This section begins by discussing a central distinction in game theory, between cooperative and noncooperative games. Although the distinction is familiar to economists, its relevance to the agreement concept is not appreciated and sometimes has generated confusion on the matter. Next, this section considers briefly how the theory of repeated games captures dynamic interaction that may, under appropriate circumstances, support supracompetitive prices. Finally, it reflects on the notion of equilibrium that is central in game theory because it may inform the challenge of defining agreement under competition law. As mentioned, the core ideas are well understood by economists, but their implications for interpreting the agreement requirement have not previously been developed.

---

[3] See Friedman (1971, 11) and Bagwell and Wolinsky (2002, 1872–73): "Of course, the consideration of the collusive and non-collusive outcomes predated the more recent analyses of the repeated game model. The important contribution of the repeated game framework is in establishing the validity of these as outcomes of rational and far-sighted competition that takes place over time."

[4] Academic commentary by economists makes use of modern oligopoly theory (see the sources cited in note 2), but little attempt is made to draw out implications for delineation of the horizontal agreement requirement (rather than to refine the understanding of what conditions are conducive to successful coordinated oligopoly pricing or how its presence might be detected). When legal academic commentary (for example, Hovenkamp 2005b, 159–65) refers to oligopoly theory, it typically discusses literature of the earlier generation, supplemented as in the past by informal remarks regarding strategic interaction. There are some exceptions (for example, Lopatka 1996, 889–96), although even then modern theory is not used in an attempt to illuminate the agreement requirement.

1. Distinction between Cooperative and Noncooperative Games

From the beginning of modern game theory in the middle of the twentieth century with Nash (1951, 1953), a sharp distinction has been drawn between cooperative and noncooperative games. This distinction both is critical for understanding the relationship between game-theoretic analysis and any notion of agreement and at the same time is potentially confusing. Hence, it is important at the outset to get certain terminology straight.[5]

"The fundamental distinction between cooperative and noncooperative games is that cooperative games allow binding agreements while noncooperative games do not."[6] In what are formally designated as cooperative games, one studies what sorts of agreements parties might enter under the explicit assumption that whatever agreement they choose will definitely be enforced. The precise mechanism by which the implicitly perfect and costless enforcement is accomplished is outside the analysis. The focus instead is on the question: Taking as given that readily enforceable agreements are possible, what agreement would the parties reach?

It is immediately apparent that cooperative games in this formal sense are irrelevant to the main question considered here.[7] Competition law renders all price-fixing agreements nonbinding. Indeed, this is one of the law's most important effects because in many settings price fixing may

---

[5] As will emerge, the possibility for misinterpretation may be due to an unfortunate choice of terminology. See Osborne and Rubinstein (1994, 2): "Sometimes models of the first type are referred to as 'noncooperative,' while those of the second type are referred to as 'cooperative' (though these terms do not express well the differences between the models)."; and Lopatka (1996, 889), who notes that "the terminology can be confusing."

[6] Friedman (1986, 148). Cooperative games are also sometimes referred to as coalitional games. See Osborne and Rubinstein (1994, pt. IV). "[A] coalition is a subset of players that has the right to make binding agreements with one another . . . ." Friedman (1986, 184); see also ibid. (186), formally defining a coalition as "a subset of the set of players, N, that is able to make a binding agreement" (italics omitted), and Friedman (1971, 1).

[7] If the weight of promises and the like, discussed in subsection B.3, were sufficiently strong relative to the stakes involved so that firms would never cheat regardless of the profit from doing so, then cooperative game theory, which does not focus on how coordination can be sustained, would be directly applicable. In most settings regulated by competition regimes, however, this case seems exceptional.

thus be rendered infeasible. The oligopoly problem that is at the center of the horizontal agreement question is the possibly quite significant residual: cases in which firms may nevertheless be able to charge coordinated supracompetitive prices despite their inability to enforce cartel agreements in court.

This remaining problem is the subject of what is called noncooperative game theory, which is defined as addressing all situations in which parties cannot use an outside enforcer to ensure compliance. Notice importantly that this branch of game theory is applicable to express cartels of the extreme form (detailed negotiated agreements signed in blood), to purely interdependent behavior (the two gas stations in section 2.A's example), and to everything in-between.[8] Ultimately, for any such arrangements to be successful, they must be self-enforcing in the sense elaborated in the next two subsections.

A source of confusion is that the terms cooperative and noncooperative are often used to describe *outcomes* of noncooperative games as well as the two *types of games*. Specifically, in a noncooperative game—one in which no binding, externally enforceable agreements are possible—it is common to describe the situation in which firms successfully engage in sustained, coordinated oligopoly pricing as a cooperative outcome and that in which firms charge competitive prices as a noncooperative outcome.[9] Both the cooperative result and the noncooperative result, however,

---

[8] In a report to the European Commission, Kühn and Vives (1995, 43) state: "With tacit collusion we mean any type of cooperation between firms which is not sustained by legally enforceable contracts. The theories do not distinguish between explicit 'agreements' between firms and implicit anticipation of reactions by rivals in dynamic interactions (as for example in what is termed 'conscious parallelism' in the competition policy literature). This is because in theory there is no significant difference between these two types of behaviour." In reviewing Whinston (2006), Hall (2007, 1067) states that the author "starts with the familiar proposition that our leading framework for thinking about collusion cannot distinguish tacit from explicit collusion. The framework of Nash equilibrium describes an equilibrium but often says nothing about how the participants got to the equilibrium."

[9] See, for example, Areeda, Hovenkamp, and Solow (2007, 11–15) and Hovenkamp (2005b, 159–65). Hovenkamp (162 n.15), after using the terms cooperative and noncooperative to refer implicitly to two different types of play of a noncooperative oligopoly game, refers the reader to references on "the difference between non-cooperative and cooperative game theory, and its relevance to antitrust policy," where, as explained in the text, these two branches of game theory refer to the structure of the game, the latter to games with binding agreements,

are outcomes of noncooperative games. The contrast is elaborated by James Friedman:

> There is a cross link between the cooperative game chapters and some of the material on noncooperative games, because a central aspect of the repeated games literature . . . is that a repeated game allows a *cooperative outcome* to be supported by (i.e., be the result of) a *noncooperative equilibrium*. In a way, this causes a blurring of the distinction between cooperative and noncooperative games; however, this blurring need not be confusing if a distinction is kept in mind between cooperative versus noncooperative games (i.e., the structures) on the one hand, and cooperative versus noncooperative outcomes on the other. The presence or absence of binding agreements is the definitive element for cooperative versus noncooperative games. If binding agreements are possible, then the game (structure) is cooperative, otherwise it is noncooperative. A cooperative outcome can be defined as an outcome that is Pareto optimal in a game where not all outcomes are Pareto optimal. A noncooperative outcome is merely an outcome supported by a noncooperative equilibrium. Thus the *cooperative* outcome[s] of repeated games are *both cooperative and noncooperative outcomes*. Such outcomes are noncooperative because they are supported by noncooperative equilibrium strategies and they are the former because they are Pareto optimal. By contrast, a structure is either cooperative or noncooperative but not both. With respect to structure, these properties are mutually exclusive and exhaustive, but with regard to outcomes they are neither.[10]

---

which are not relevant to the subject under discussion. It is interesting that it has become common to describe firms that fail to coordinate effectively as noncooperative rather than using the more familiar term uncooperative. The choice of the former does seem to derive from its use by game theorists; yet, as the text describes, confusion arises precisely because the technical term coined to depict the structure of the game is being used informally to refer to one type of outcome of the game.

[10] Friedman (1986, 20) (emphasis in original; some emphasis omitted). See Fudenberg and Tirole (1991, xviii): "'Noncooperative' does not mean that players do not get along, or that they always refuse to cooperate. As we explain in chapters 5 and 9, noncooperative players, motivated solely by self-interest, can exhibit 'cooperative' behavior in some settings."

As the foregoing quotation indicates, the difficulty of keeping terminology straight is augmented when one adds that the term equilibrium, to be discussed further momentarily, can be characterized either by the structure of the game to which it pertains or by the nature of the outcome it describes. Hence, when oligopolists coordinate successfully, the equilibrium in which firms charge a supracompetitive price might be called noncooperative (because it is the equilibrium of a noncooperative game) or cooperative (because, within the noncooperative game, the equilibrium reflects a cooperative outcome). Accordingly, mention of a noncooperative equilibrium could refer to any equilibrium of a noncooperative game, including one characterized by cooperation (a cooperative noncooperative equilibrium) that results in a supracompetitive price but also one characterized by a lack of cooperation (a noncooperative noncooperative equilibrium) that results in a competitive price.[11]

It is also worth reflecting further on the distinction between game types, specifically as it pertains to the notion of agreement. As stated, a cooperative game is defined as that in which binding agreements are possible, and a noncooperative game as that in which binding agreements are impossible. Given this usage by economists wherein agreement is taken to mean binding agreement, all noncooperative games—regardless of whether the outcome is cooperative or noncooperative—would be described as involving no agreement. After all, if there is an agreement, we by definition have a cooperative game, but it was stipulated that the game is noncooperative. Thus, when using the language of game theory, an economist choosing words carefully will say that noncooperative games with successful coordinated oligopoly pricing never involve an agreement. Furthermore, because noncooperative games, as noted, include the case of a classic cartel, these too would have to be deemed not to involve any agreement.

By contrast, under the law, this latter depiction is patently false, whatever may be the uncertainty and dispute over the legal meaning of the

---

[11] The latter usage (noncooperative equilibrium referring to an equilibrium of a noncooperative game characterized by a lack of cooperation, that is, competitive pricing or, more broadly, Nash reversion in the sense of a one-shot game) is common among economists. See, for example, Shapiro (1989, 364), referring to "swift reversion to a noncooperative equilibrium."

term agreement. Accordingly, this book follows a common usage in formal game theory by using the paired term "binding agreement" to refer to any agreement associated with a cooperative game, and it reserves the single, unmodified term "agreement" to refer to whatever is the notion under competition law. The latter uncontroversially encompasses at least some equilibria of noncooperative games if those equilibria are reached in particular ways—certainly including at least supracompetitive outcomes that are a product of classic cartels. When reading work by economists on oligopoly theory and on competition law, it is worth noting that usage will not always be so clearly demarcated. Furthermore, it is this author's belief that, for quite some time, economists have sometimes misapplied the precise, game-theoretic notion of agreement with which they are familiar (which is limited to binding agreements) to legal settings where they see the term agreement being employed, without always appreciating that it is necessarily being used in a different, indeed conflicting, sense.[12]

A preliminary and straightforward conclusion, therefore, is that modern oligopoly theory does have a well-articulated, formal definition of the term agreement—binding agreement—but one that is utterly useless in addressing the challenge of defining horizontal agreement under competition law. Indeed, the theory's definition is worse than useless because it can readily be misleading if its usage is not fully appreciated. In this latter respect, the reader may note an analogy to the potential for confusion discussed in section 2.C wherein the term independent is used to refer to truly independent (competitive) behavior but is also sometimes used to refer to interdependent (noncompetitive) behavior. With semantic difficulties set aside, it is now possible to consider whether the substance of modern oligopoly theory, as developed in the analysis of noncooperative games, sheds any light on how one might give meaning to the agreement concept in competition law.

---

[12] A related point is that economists' frequent association of communications and agreement (see the sources cited in note 32 in chapter 2) may also relate to the distinction between the two types of games. In cooperative games, because it is binding agreements that are being studied, it is natural to suppose that explicit communications of some sort are necessarily involved. By contrast, in noncooperative games, as will be discussed throughout this chapter, such communications are not theoretically essential and the question of what sorts of communications might be employed is outside most analyses of the problem.

2. Repeated Games and Dynamic Interaction

The motivation for focusing on repeated games is that they allow analysis of the sort of strategic interaction that can make successful coordinated oligopoly pricing possible.[13] The need to examine a dynamic setting is made clear by considering the familiar result in a one-period pricing game, say, between two identical firms that sell homogenous goods that they each produce at the same, constant marginal cost of 10. The competitive price, P_c, would accordingly be 10. Suppose further that the joint profit-maximizing monopoly price, P_m, is 20. Finally, assume that the firm charging the lowest price captures all the sales, whereas if the two firms charge the same price, sales are divided evenly between them.

The only equilibrium of this one-shot game is for each firm to charge P_c, that is, 10. The term equilibrium refers to a situation in which, taking as given the other players' strategies, no player can gain by deviating from its own current strategy.[14] The claim that the competitive price, P_c, is the unique equilibrium might be rationalized by the argument that, if either firm charges more than 10, the other would charge less, capturing all the sales, which would drive the price down to 10. This story, however, is a dynamic one. In the standard formulation of the one-shot game, it is common to suppose that the firms set their prices simultaneously (and, because the game is only for one period, they are understood to stick with those prices).[15] This interaction could be described as a classic prisoners' dilemma. No price above 10 can be an equilibrium because, if either firm is imagined to charge such a price, the other would select a price that was slightly lower. This leaves as the unique equilibrium the competitive outcome, in which each firm charges 10 and neither firm has an incentive to deviate given that the other is assumed to charge 10.[16]

---

[13] See generally the sources cited in note 2, and also Werden (2004, 720–34).

[14] For further elaboration on the meaning of equilibrium, see subsection 3.

[15] If firms instead set their prices sequentially, the first firm would know that, at any price above 10, it would be undercut slightly by the second firm, which would thereby capture the market. (Actually, in this formulation, the first-moving firm is indifferent to the price it selects in that it makes zero profits regardless of whether it selects the competitive price of 10 and shares the market or instead sets a higher price and makes no sales.)

[16] For more formal discussion that raises interesting subtleties not pertinent to the present task, see Shapiro (1989, 344–46) and Tirole (1988, 212–18), who address the nonexistence of

Yet it seems clear that sometimes firms are able to charge coordinated supracompetitive prices (despite the absence of binding agreements), and successful coordinated behavior has been observed in a variety of other settings in which similar logic based on a one-period model suggests that it is impossible. It is not surprising, therefore, that commentators have long offered reasons why firms in an oligopoly setting may indeed be able to sustain coordinated supracompetitive prices.[17] The key intuition is that starting, say, at P_m, a price of 20, no firm will wish to cut its price and steal its rival's business if it expects this act to induce its rival to cut its price as well, perhaps matching the first firm's lower price and perhaps

---

pure-strategy equilibria in one-shot pricing games with rising marginal costs. In addition, it has long been understood that, under certain alternative assumptions, even if the firms are unable to coordinate, the resulting price will exceed marginal cost even though it will continue to fall short of the monopoly level. See Friedman (1986, 54–57), Kaplow and Shapiro (2007, 1083–86), and Shapiro (1989, 333–56), and also Chamberlin (1929), who presents a history of thought on these models. For those unfamiliar, in a model due to Cournot (1838), it is supposed that each firm chooses its quantity rather than its price. In that case, each of our two firms finds it advantageous to supply less than half the competitive output for the industry because reducing supply leads to a rise in price; that is, each firm has some market power. As elaborated in section 14.B, this outcome is best rationalized in a two-period game wherein the quantity selection, in period 1, might correspond to choosing the size of the firm's production facility or a farmer deciding how much crop to plant. Then, in the second period, in which each firm has a limited quantity to sell, it would not find it advantageous to undercut every price above P_c because it would not have the capacity to supply the entire market; as long as it could sell all of its available (and limited) quantity, it would cut prices no further. (Without supposing such a capacity constraint, it is not clear why the Cournot quantity-setting equilibrium would persist in real market settings, for as long as the price exceeds P_c, each firm will have an incentive to reduce price in order to capture business from its rival.)

In another model—which builds on the view associated with Bertrand (1883), that firms set prices, as supposed in the text, rather than quantities—it is assumed that firms' products are differentiated rather than homogeneous (see section 14.C). As a consequence, undercutting one's rival ever so slightly will capture only a modest amount of additional sales. Once again, each firm has some market power. Firms will trade off the profit per unit sold with the quantity of sales. The result is a price above the competitive level, the more so the greater the degree of differentiation. (In the limit, if the products are not substitutes at all, each firm would have a monopoly over its segment of the market.)

Because neither of these models involves the sort of coordination that is the focus in this book, further examination is deferred to chapter 14, which discusses how the possibility of supracompetitive pricing in these sorts of situations is in principle relevant in determining what regime is optimal.

[17] Prominent early works include Chamberlin (1929, 1933).

undercutting it. Whether, when the dust settles, the price is somewhat lower than P_m or all the way down to P_c, a price of 10, the prospective price cutter will be worse off: It will not wish to share the market at a price of 18, 15, or 10 when it can share the market at 20, which is presumed to be the joint profit-maximizing price. As long as the firm does not expect to profit sufficiently in the short run (before the rival cuts its price as well) to make up for the lost profits in the long run, it will adhere to the price of P_m. Note that this logic applies regardless of whether each firm's expectation about the other's reaction arises from their mutual appreciation of the situation or as a consequence of direct discussion of the matter.

Similar logic can explain how the price might rise to P_m in the first place, whether it starts at P_c or some intermediate level. A firm may be willing to brave a price increase if it expects—again, whether by conjecture or as a result of explicit discourse—that its rival will reciprocate. If its rival indeed cooperates by matching the price increase, the firms will both be better off forever after, supposing that, by the logic of the preceding paragraph, the price increase can be sustained. As long as the first firm does not lose much profit in the interim due to any delay in the other's reaction, the long-run gain will make the venture worthwhile. Moreover, the firm will expect its rival to follow quickly because its rival understands—again, either because of its grasp of the circumstances or through prior dialogue—that delay will be taken as defection, leading the initiator quickly to drop its price back to the preexisting level.

This logic, unlike that in earlier oligopoly models, is explicitly dynamic. Each firm's strategy does not consist of a single price at a single point in time. Rather, it involves a price pattern over time that, moreover, is contingent on its rival's behavior. Modern economists, finding loose stories not entirely satisfying and previous accounts that were grounded in static models to suffer from formal inconsistencies, began innovating in the 1970s, quickly reaching the point where dynamic analysis embodied in explicit repeat-play models became the dominant method of analyzing coordinated oligopoly (and other strategic interactions, such as that involved with predatory pricing).[18]

---

[18] See Bagwell and Wolinsky (2002, 1869, 1882): "The earlier literature, which preceded the introduction of the repeated game model, . . . lacked a coherent formal model."; "Noncooperative game theory has become the standard language and the main methodological framework of industrial organization. [The prior gap relating to the need for an oligopoly

The most commonly analyzed model, referred to as a supergame, involves the infinite repetition of a simple, one-period game. In each period, the firms simultaneously choose their prices and, as above, a firm captures the entire market if its price is the lowest and shares the market pro rata in the case of identical prices. Although an infinitely repeated game may strike the uninitiated as complicated, it is actually fairly straightforward to analyze in its most basic form. Moreover, it is a convenient way to capture strategic interaction in a manner that allows for successful coordination in accordance with long-standing intuitions.[19]

---

model] was filled by verbal theorizing and an array of semi-formal and formal models. The formal models included game models like those of Cournot, Bertrand and Stackelberg, as well as non-game models with strategic flavor such as the conjectural variations and the contestable market models."; Friedman (1971, 1), developing a theory of supergames and observing that "[o]ligopoly may profitably be viewed as a supergame"; Kaplow and Shapiro (2007, 1104): "The basic theoretical framework used to evaluate the presence, absence, or efficacy of collusion is that of dynamic or repeated oligopoly, that is, situations in which an identifiable group of suppliers offering substitute products interact over time. This framework includes infinitely repeated oligopoly games, so-called supergames. Cartel theory requires dynamic analysis because the central elements of detection and punishment inherently take place over time."; Motta (2007, 315 n.6): "Modern theory on collusion is based on supergames."; Shapiro (1989, 352 & n.39, 354–56), stating that "it is clear that a serious theory of oligopoly behavior cannot be timeless" as was the case in traditional static models, observing that, "This line of argument suggests that the most appropriate games to study are dynamic ones with price-setting.", and presenting a subsection titled "Can there be reactions in a static model?", a question answered in the negative: "To study reactions, retaliation, price wars, and tacit collusion we require explicitly dynamic models of oligopoly."; and Tirole (1988, 240–45), criticizing the failures of attempts to make traditional static models dynamic, thereby explaining the need for explicit dynamic models. The seemingly excessive quotations in support of this noncontroversial proposition are offered because, as mentioned, the past few decades of game-theoretic work by industrial organization economists has had little penetration in the analysis of competition law and virtually no application to the analysis of the agreement requirement. When economics literature, including game-theoretic work, is mentioned, discussion is still ordinarily based on the prior generation of literature that has been largely displaced in the analysis of coordinated pricing behavior.

[19] In contrast, in simple, finite models, successful supracompetitive pricing is impossible due to the familiar backward-induction argument. If there were two periods, in the second and final period, the situation would be just as in the one-shot game, so a competitive price is the unique equilibrium in period 2. Because that result is not contingent on what occurs in period 1, in the first period also there will be competitive behavior, for there is no sense in which defection can be retaliated against subsequently because competitive pricing prevails later in any event. In simple enough models like the one considered here, this logic applies to any known, finite number of periods, whereas allowing infinite repetition disrupts this chain

To capture the essence of the story, consider the following strategies that firms might employ.[20] Each firm will charge the monopoly price P_m in the initial period and in every period thereafter as long as its rival has done the same in preceding periods. However, if a rival ever charges less than P_m, the firm will charge P_c for the next ten periods, after which it will resume charging P_m with the cycle beginning anew, on a clean slate. That is, it will continue charging P_m indefinitely unless and until there is another defection, which the firm will meet by charging P_c for the next ten periods, and so forth.

If both firms play this strategy, they will share the market and the industry-maximizing monopoly profit indefinitely, which is the best they can do collectively. The question is whether an individual firm ever has an incentive to defect. To see whether it might, suppose that a firm contemplates cheating in the next period. It can, by assumption, take the whole market for that period by pricing just under P_m, which will almost double its profit for that period because it will obtain the whole market rather than half of the market at essentially the monopoly price. However, for the ten periods thereafter, the firm will earn no profits because it expects its rival to charge P_c for those periods. Accordingly, the prospective defector will not wish to cheat as long as it values the gain of one period's profits (the increment in the next period from capturing all rather than half of the market) less than the loss of ten periods' profits spread in the future (from period 2 through period 11 from the present). Even

---

of reasoning because there is no final period from which to work backward. See Selten (1978), offering the seminal articulation of the concept in the predation context, and Shapiro (1989, 357–60). Further exploration of the relevance of infinite periods and of other variations on the basic model (including, for example, when the number of periods is indefinite) that make coordinated pricing possible even without infinite repetition are beyond the scope of the present discussion. See Friedman (1986, 94–103), Kreps and Wilson (1982), Radner (1980), Rosenthal (1981), and Shapiro (1989, 360–61).

[20] For a simple exposition of a more standard variant under which punishment continues indefinitely, see Kaplow and Shapiro (2007, 1104–5). The version in the text, in which punishment is imposed for a finite number of periods, is in the spirit of the models in Green and Porter (1984) and Porter (1983a). See also Fudenberg and Tirole (1991, 185–87). These models were developed for the case discussed later in this subsection in which low realizations of uncertain demand may trigger price wars, a consequence that makes it important for punishment to be limited. MacLeod (1985) examines a different model with price announcements and price leadership in which coordinated oligopoly prices are reached and sustained.

for moderately impatient firms—that is, firms that do discount the future but not very steeply—this tradeoff will be disadvantageous, so they would continue to charge P_m.[21] Accordingly, this set of symmetric strategies constitutes an equilibrium of this repeated game. That is, given these strategies, no firm would ever find it in its interest to behave differently, which would amount to employing a different strategy.

This simple repeated game is therefore able to rationalize successful oligopolistic coordination, indeed, entirely successful in the sense that the firms would perpetually charge P_m, yielding maximal profits. Furthermore, as was true in the preceding, more informal discussion, none of the logic depends on whether firms' strategies are chosen because of spontaneous mutual appreciation of the situation or after engaging in explicit communications. In either situation, this state of affairs is sometimes described as involving a self-enforcing agreement.

Note that, by similar logic, this strategic approach can rationalize (render self-enforcing) other outcomes, including any price between P_c and P_m.[22] If, for example, each firm chose the midpoint, 15 in our example, as the benchmark, we would likewise have an equilibrium. Each firm would charge 15 indefinitely, yielding a positive (supracompetitive) profit, albeit less than the monopoly (maximal) profit. Defection (charging slightly less than 15) would double the (now lower) profit in the defection period and forfeit that (now lower) profit amount for the next ten periods. Thus, we can see that such an intermediate price also constitutes an equilibrium if firms are not too impatient.[23] Indeed, a price of P_c is an equilibrium too. In this case, the reasoning may be short-circuited: No firm would ever wish to undercut this price, for it would incur losses. The

---

[21] For example, a firm would defect if it had a discount rate of 50%, which is to say that it valued each period's profits at only half those of an immediately preceding period. The gain of 1 unit in the next period would be traded off against a loss of $1/2 + 1/4 + 1/8 + \ldots + 1/1024$ from the ten subsequent periods, which sums to slightly less than 1 (approximately 0.999). From this illustration, it is clear that if the firm was even slightly more patient than this, it would not defect.

[22] The text here and afterward indicates that the equilibria include this entire range without stating that they are limited to it; indeed, there exist equilibria in which prices above P_m would be sustained.

[23] A firm would not contemplate raising its price above 15 in the postulated scenario because its rival is assumed to stick with its current price (unless the rival undercuts it, which leads to ten periods of pricing at the competitive level).

result that there can be multiple equilibria is not an artifact of the particulars of the present example but rather arises quite broadly in the theory of infinitely repeated games.[24] Further elaboration, with an emphasis on how an equilibrium might be selected, is one of the topics in the remainder of this chapter.

The foregoing model is by no means the only one in the literature analyzing coordinated oligopoly. Numerous extensions, designed to capture a variety of realistic features, have been introduced.[25] To get the flavor of this large body of work, consider the problem that coordinating oligopolistic firms face in detecting defections in markets where each firm's prices are not readily observed—a challenge first explored in depth by Stigler (1964).[26] Suppose that firms negotiate orders with individual customers, which is common in some intermediate goods markets. If a firm cheats, how are others to know? Firms might be able to infer that someone has cheated from a fall in sales of their own products, and in simple models this information would suffice. But suppose as well that buyers' demand fluctuates in ways firms cannot observe, raising the possibility that a decline in a firm's sales might have been due to another's cheating or instead to less favorable market conditions. In the presence of such uncertainty, firms need to choose a strategy that trades off rapid, sufficiently harsh punishment of actual cheating—in order to deter it effectively—and avoidance of price wars when there was no actual cheating but just a period of unusually low demand. In models of this problem tracing to Green and Porter (1984), coordinated oligopoly pricing is still possible, but it is less effective. Specifically, there will be occasional price wars even when no cheating has occurred. It has also been suggested that this more complicated scenario is more consistent with what has actually occurred in some markets characterized by coordinated oligopoly pricing.[27]

This extension and many others show how repeated games can be used to provide more accurate depictions of oligopolistic markets. These teach-

---

[24] This result is referred to as the "folk theorem" for infinitely repeated games. See Fudenberg and Tirole (1991, 150–60) and Osborne and Rubinstein (1994, 143–53).

[25] See the sources cited in note 2.

[26] See also Spence (1978).

[27] See Baker (1989), Bresnahan (1987), Levenstein (1997), Porter (1983a, 1983b), and Shapiro (1989, 373–79). Perloff, Karp, and Golan (2007, 104) find the evidence to be more mixed. Slade (1990) examines alternative price-war models.

ings facilitate the examination of such questions as whether conditions are conducive to successful coordinated oligopoly pricing and whether it is occurring, both important inputs into inferences about the existence of price fixing, the subject of chapters 10 and 11. Observe, as has been noted at many points throughout, that there is no direct relationship between the analysis of this subsection and the foregoing classifications of firms' interdependence: pure interdependence, highly explicit agreement of a particular type, or any other combination. That is, in this exposition of modern oligopoly theory, it was not necessary at any point to address how the particular interdependent behavior arose.

In this regard, it is important to recall and emphasize a central idea from subsection 1, namely, that both extreme, old-fashioned cartels (stripped only of the ability to legally enforce their agreements) and pure interdependence, along with everything in between, are analyzed as noncooperative games. The current subsection presents the basic contours of that analysis. The core model, the variations mentioned, and many more in the literature are each, on their face, applicable without distinction to any of these sorts of coordination. Whether a pair of strategies constitutes an equilibrium for two gas stations engaged in price signaling with their price postings or having a discussion in a smoke-filled room leading them to charge the monopoly price depends on precisely the same calculation that compares the gain from defection with the lost future profits due to the other firm's anticipated response.[28] Firms are assumed to act in their own best interests, to maximize profits, in either case. If the gains from cheating exceed the costs, it is supposed that a firm will cheat, and otherwise not.

Section B will take up the question of whether, despite this point, anything more can be said about the connection between oligopoly theory and the notion of agreement. In order to do so, it is helpful to contemplate further the concept of equilibrium that is employed in game-theoretic analysis.

---

[28] Whinston (2006, 21), in discussing oligopolists' attempts to collude, even if freely permitted to communicate, states that "[t]he incentive problem can be formally stated as follows: To be credible, any agreement must be a subgame perfect Nash equilibrium. If it were not, then some party to the agreement would find it profitable to cheat. But note that this is exactly the same condition that economic theory uses to identify the set of outcomes that are sustainable without any direct communication . . . ."

3. Equilibrium Elaborated

The structure of the game dictates firms' possible strategies. In the one-period version of the above game, strategies consist of the prices to be charged for that period. In the repeated game, strategies consist of a specification of prices over time, including how such prices depend on rivals' past behavior. One might end the analysis at that point, throwing up one's hands. Firms might be said to be able to do anything that is feasible. But in game theory and in real life, analysts and actual players do more. Thus, in the example with repeated play, we could imagine that one firm would perpetually charge 20 and the other 19.99, with the latter reaping essentially the full monopoly profit from the market and the former earning nothing. Yet it seems implausible that this state of affairs is sustainable. Firms are assumed to be rational profit maximizers. They act and react in light of their self-interest.

Accordingly, it is conventional to confine attention to equilibria of the game under investigation. As mentioned, the standard definition of equilibrium is a situation in which, given the other player's strategies, no player can gain by adjusting its own strategy. This concept, often referred to as Nash equilibrium—or, with play spanning multiple periods, subgame perfect Nash equilibrium—embodies the core of the dissatisfaction with the idea that firms might just do anything.[29]

Subsection 2 illustrated the further idea that some games, including standard repeated games used to model coordinated oligopoly, involve multiple equilibria. In the basic example, any price from P_c to P_m, from 10 to 20, was an equilibrium. This range of possibilities immediately raises the question of which equilibrium the firms will choose.[30] This question

---

[29] See Nash (1950), Fudenberg and Tirole (1991, 73–74), and Osborne and Rubinstein (1994, 14–15, 97).

[30] In most game-theoretic analysis in economics, including applications to oligopoly theory, it is generally supposed that players will be in some (i.e., common) equilibrium. Cases in which some firms play a different equilibrium (each believing, at least initially, that other firms are playing that same equilibrium) have received little attention although they are of interest. Consider, for example, a case in which the competitive price is 10, the monopoly price is 20, and any price from 10 to 20 would be an equilibrium; in the first period, firm 1 prices at 20 and firm 2 at 19. In reflecting on what transpired in the first period, firm 1 must consider whether firm 2 thought it was charging an equilibrium oligopoly price of 19 or imagined that

has received substantial attention, formal and informal, for quite some time.[31] A few intuitive points that are most relevant for present purposes will be mentioned.

Following Schelling's (1960, 54–57) famous exposition, it is often suggested that equilibria that constitute focal points are more likely to be selected than are others. The focal-point notion derives from examples such as the problem of two individuals who have agreed to meet for lunch but have not selected a time. Twelve noon is more likely to emerge in both of their minds than is 12:23 p.m. For prices, round numbers, like 10, 15, and 20, might be focal. Or perhaps 19.95 and 19.99, where such pricing is conventional. Two prices are particularly focal in our example: 10 and 20. Not only are they both round numbers, but one is the worst and the other the best (the Pareto optimal) price for the two firms, and each corresponds to a well-understood concept, competition and monopoly respectively.

The parties may employ other criteria as well. Notably, among all equilibria, or perhaps among focal-point equilibria, parties may well be inclined to select more advantageous equilibria. Thus, in our present example, a price of 20 seems most compelling. Also of great importance, the parties might communicate directly on the subject, a topic to which we will return in subsection B.2. For the present, it is useful to keep in mind that parties' statements may lack credibility and, indeed, might be designed to deceive, such as by stating that one will sell at 20 but immediately cheating by selling at a price just below that, although such would not be an equilibrium in the present example.

Observe that the parties' efforts in arriving at a particular equilibrium (or at *the* equilibrium, when there is only one) involve an intersubjective

---

firm 1 would indeed charge 20 but firm 2 was cheating; firm 1's pricing decision in period 2 might, for example, be more aggressive in the latter case. For formal treatments of the notion that not all players will play the same (or any) equilibrium, see Aumann (1987), Bernheim (1984), Fudenberg and Tirole (1991, 22 & n.12, ch. 2), and Pearce (1984). In such cases, there would not be a meeting of the minds in the sense described below when all play the same equilibrium. Subsection B.2's discussion of communications as potentially influencing equilibrium selection (in the case of multiple equilibria) could also be applied to consideration of the likelihood that all play the same equilibrium from the outset.

[31] See Fudenberg and Tirole (1991, sec. 8.4, ch. 11) and Osborne and Rubinstein (1994, 243–53).

process, the conclusion of which may aptly be described as a meeting of the minds, as elaborated in section 2.B.[32] To be more precise, strategic thinking necessarily involves getting (metaphorically) into other players' heads. One firm needs to think about what the other will do: "If I cheat, the next period my rival will retaliate." Furthermore, to think about what the other will do—because it also is taken to be a strategic player—requires contemplating what it thinks that you will do. Which in turn requires thinking about what it thinks you think it will do. And so forth ad infinitum. As expressed by Drew Fudenberg and Jean Tirole (1991, 13),

> Nash equilibria are "consistent" predictions of how the game will be played, in the sense that if all players predict that a particular Nash equilibrium will occur then no player has an incentive to play differently. Thus, a Nash equilibrium, and only a Nash equilibrium, can have the property that the players can predict it, predict that their opponents predict it, and so on.

To be in an equilibrium is for firms to have engaged in such a thought process and somehow to have reached a common conclusion. It is in this sense that one would say their minds have met.[33] Or, to use another common expression, such a state of affairs might be called getting on or being

---

[32] The topic discussed in the text is one for which the failure of legal analysis to incorporate modern economic theory generates misconceptions. For example, Hovenkamp (2005a, 126–27) asserts that, although "[t]he lawyer's understanding of collusion is fundamentally subjective, . . . the economists is fundamentally objective. . . . Economic theories of oligopoly pricing, such as the one developed by Augustin Cournot in the nineteenth century and widely used, do not depend at all on . . . any knowledge about someone else's subjective state of mind." See also note 16, on how Cournot behavior differs from that examined by modern oligopoly theory involving repeated interaction, and note 18 and the accompanying text, on why it is essential to employ the modern repeated-games approach to study oligopoly behavior. A further irony is that commentators like Hovenkamp, who insist that agreements should not be deemed to exist based on pure interdependence but rather require specific sorts of communications, are the ones that in fact eschew a subjective view of what constitutes agreement.

[33] Players are not actually in each other's minds, which is impossible short of psychoanalysis, hypnosis, or fMRI scans, none of which are taken to be pertinent here or in other settings in which such characterizations are offered. Nor are explicit, detailed communications required. As Posner (1969, 1576 n.39) aptly remarked in his seminal article, "The proposition that a belief in mental telepathy is not necessary to allow one to conclude that there may be a 'meeting of the minds' without verbal interchanges has been illuminated by game theorists."

all on the same page, yet another synonym for agreement.[34] Moreover, an equilibrium entails such a mutual understanding without regard to the manner in which it was reached—that is, without regard to whether there was an old-fashioned cartel, pure interdependence, or some other manner of interaction or communication.

B. Is There a Concept of Agreement in Oligopoly Theory?

As subsection A.1 on the distinction between cooperative and noncooperative games makes clear, there is a concept of agreement in oligopoly theory, specifically, in that of cooperative games. But, as explained, it is equally clear that this concept is irrelevant for present purposes because the agreements that are taken to be feasible in cooperative games are ones that are legally binding. When such agreements are not possible—which is certainly the case given that competition law renders any purported agreement void—we are in the realm of noncooperative games, where by definition there are no such agreements in the game-theoretic sense. And, as mentioned, this conclusion holds equally for traditional cartels, plain interdependence, and everything in between.

Accordingly, the reformulated question becomes whether there is a concept of nonbinding agreement in the theory of noncooperative games that is used to analyze coordinated oligopoly behavior. In light of the foregoing point as well as the fact that no such notion leaped out of the exposition of the applicable modern theory in subsection A.2, one might be skeptical. Indeed, one might wonder why the question should even be asked.

The motivation for the inquiry is based on three observations. First, competition law in the realm under consideration insists that there is a category we are calling agreement that serves as a necessary condition—and, for plain price fixing, a sufficient condition—for liability. The legal doctrine is thus based on the supposition that, in reality, there

---

[34] See Abbreviations.com, http://www.abbreviations.com/b1.asp?KEY=392313&st=All%20 On%20The%20Same%20Page (last accessed November 22, 2010): "ALL ON THE SAME PAGE: To be in agreement with; all of one accord."

is some substantive distinction between nonbinding agreements and nonagreements.

Second, modern oligopoly theory is understood by economists as offering the general toolkit for making sense of firms' interactions in markets. Although no particular model is comprehensive, the theory attempts to be so.[35] Thus, if there is some key distinction that exists between one and another type of coordinated oligopolistic behavior, that distinction should be present in the theory. Moreover, given the importance the distinction plays as a matter of regulatory policy, one would suppose that it would not merely be present but have a central role.

Third, modern competition law and policy, particularly in the United States, affirmatively embraces economics, both for understanding behavior in particular cases and for formulating legal rules.[36] Courts, other government officials, lawyers, and academic commentators all assert that the law is grounded importantly in economics. A leading exemplar of the U.S. Supreme Court's embrace of this view is *Sylvania*'s reversal of *Schwinn*: "The Court's [*Schwinn*] opinion provides no analytical support for these contrasting positions. Nor is there even an assertion in the opinion that the competitive impact of vertical restrictions is significantly affected by the form of the transaction."[37] The Court further observed that "even the

---

[35] It is difficult to view economic analysis of oligopoly as a priori restrictive in any way, all the more so because modern oligopoly theory is an application of game theory, which itself is a highly general set of ideas designed to encompass any manner of strategic interaction involving more than one party.

[36] Although conventional wisdom suggests that this connection has emerged and grown in the past few decades in the United States, Kaplow (1987) suggests that it was central pretty much from the beginning.

[37] Continental T.V., Inc. v. GTE Sylvania, Inc., 433 U.S. 36, 53 (1977), reversing United States v. Arnold Schwinn & Co., 388 U.S. 365 (1967). Some see the roots much earlier; writing shortly after the Court's decisions in *American Tobacco* and *Paramount* (discussed in subsection 4.B.1), Rahl (1950, 768) concluded that, with respect to the conspiracy requirement, "the courts are really attempting to turn the Sherman Act into something of the economic document that it needs to be." See also Rahl (1950, 759–60), arguing that attempting to distinguish coordinated behavior from formal agreements "is 'artificial' in an economic sense" because "the competitive policy of the Sherman Act is as offended [by naturally arising behavior] as when a formal conspiracy exists." However, Rahl (1962, 147–48) asserts that oligopoly behavior in the absence of an agreement should not be addressed by the antitrust rule against price fixing. Writing subsequently, Posner (2001, 53) finds that "the law relating to collusive pricing became emptied of economic content. . . . Since lawyers and judges are more comfortable with con-

leading critic of vertical restrictions concedes that *Schwinn*'s distinction between sale and nonsale transactions is essentially unrelated to any relevant economic impact."[38] The *Sylvania* Court insisted that if Sherman Act Section 1's agreement requirement was to be the basis of a difference in legal treatment, the difference needed to be justified in terms of the contrasting economic effects of the practices under consideration.[39] The Court's *Matsushita* decision (discussed in subsection 4.B.2) is also probative, particularly because it is one of the few modern pronouncements relating to the agreement requirement. The Court was specifically concerned about allegations that made no "economic sense,"[40] notably a situation in which defendants "had no rational economic motive to conspire"[41] in the fashion that a plaintiff suggested; the Court certainly was not worrying about claims that were wholly in accord with economic rationality but failed to satisfy formalistic legal requirements arising from the Court's interpretation of the statute. Even more recently, *Dr. Miles*'s[42] reversal in *Leegin*[43] was defended on the ground that the former "Court justified its decision based on 'formalistic' legal doctrine rather than 'demonstrable economic effect'" (quoting *Sylvania*).[44]

---

spiracy doctrine than with price theory, the displacement of emphasis from the economic consequences to the fact of conspiring was natural. But it was harmful to an effective antitrust policy." (The quotation is from the 2001 edition of Posner's book; similar language appears in the 1976 edition at pages 40–41.) See also note 63, quoting Whinston.

[38] 433 U.S. at 56.

[39] With regard to horizontal price fixing, no one suggests that the distinction between pure interdependence and interdependence resulting from various forms of communications or other interactions produces a different economic effect. For more thorough analysis, see chapter 8 and section 16.B. Note that, if circumstances are not held constant, there may be differences; notably, in light of the paradox of proof, discussed further in chapter 17, successful coordination achieved via pure interdependence may be present in settings posing the greatest danger, not a lesser one.

[40] 475 U.S. at 587.

[41] 475 U.S. at 596.

[42] Dr. Miles Medical Co. v. John D. Park & Sons Co., 220 U.S. 373 (1911).

[43] Leegin Creative Leather Products, Inc. v. PSKS, Inc., 551 U.S. 877 (2007).

[44] 551 U.S. at 887–88. The *Leegin* Court further emphasized that antitrust principles on vertical restraints were to be formulated by reference to "differences in economic effect" so that "it is necessary to examine . . . the economic effects of vertical agreements to fix minimum resale prices" to determine what legal rule should apply. 551 U.S. at 888–89. See also 551 U.S.

These three points, taken together, seem to make it obligatory in interpreting Section 1 of the Sherman Act to find a concept of nonbinding agreement in the heart of the economic theory of oligopoly behavior. Starting with the two examples in section 2.A and running through the discussion of both definitions and doctrine, we have seen that it is fairly easy to distinguish interdependent oligopolistic behavior from purely independent competitive behavior—as a matter of language, actual conduct, and economic consequences—but nearly impossible to make meaningful distinctions within the category of interdependent behavior. This section explores whether an examination of oligopoly theory reveals new possibilities of distinguishing between types of interdependent behavior or mirrors the difficulties that we have previously encountered in attempting to do so. Subsection 1 revisits the concept of equilibrium, the aspect of oligopoly theory that seems most related to the idea of agreement (keeping in mind that neither agreement nor any even loose synonyms appear directly in noncooperative game theory, the pertinent branch). Subsection 2 considers communications (previously addressed in chapter 3), and subsection 3 explores promises and related acts; because both notions appear in legal discussions about agreements and have been increasingly explored by economists, it makes sense to examine what role if any they may have in connecting the agreement requirement to oligopoly theory.

1. Equilibrium

In searching for a concept of legally nonbinding agreement in modern oligopoly theory, it seems appealing to find one, if it is to be found anywhere, in the idea of an equilibrium in dynamic interaction. After all, many sources, including court opinions and dictionaries, define an agreement as a meeting of the minds, and this notion is at the core of the definition of an equilibrium. As discussed in subsection A.3, two or more firms that arrive at and maintain prices at a supracompetitive levels are imagined to have achieved a common understanding—a meeting of the minds—about the current price and the consequences of defection. This

---

at 902: "The *Dr. Miles* rule is also inconsistent with a principled framework, for it makes little economic sense when analyzed with our other cases on vertical restraints."

definition of agreement does not, as the prior exposition makes clear, contain any distinction among modes of interdependence, ranging from plain interdependence to old-fashioned cartel arrangements.[45] To be sure, as chapter 6 considers in depth, under various market circumstances one or another means might be more or less likely, but that inquiry is addressed to how an equilibrium might have come about rather than to whether or what sort of an equilibrium exists.

There are, however, some respects in which equating equilibrium with agreement appears to be problematic. One issue that can be dispensed with quickly concerns the fact that, in any equilibrium of a noncooperative game, including one involving successful coordinated oligopoly pricing, each firm at every point behaves in its own self-interest, taking as given what it expects other firms to do in reaction to its own behavior. Recall the discussion of independent interdependence in section 2.C. As explained there, this is necessarily true of any nonbinding agreement that succeeds, including a traditional cartel. After all, if it is not in every firm's self-interest to abide by the firms' mutual understanding, firms will not do so, in which case the coordinated oligopoly price will not be sustainable—that is, it will not really be an equilibrium. To restate, this point about equilibria is always true in noncooperative games, whether an equilibrium reflects purely interdependent behavior or something else. All nonbinding agreements that work are equilibria, and all equilibria are nonbinding agreements that work.

Another point is that not every equilibrium involves supracompetitive oligopoly pricing. As noted in subsection A.2, in one equilibrium of the repeated-game example, every firm charges the competitive price, P_c, indefinitely. Although such could be viewed as a nonbinding agreement, one would not wish to deem it to be an illegal one.[46] A distinction is that competitive pricing can be seen as resulting from other processes as well. For example, in such an equilibrium, firms' unwillingness to reduce price does not depend on any supposition that others would respond by cutting their prices as well. Instead, this result is no different from that in which

---

[45] Note 8 quotes economists on this point.

[46] Note, however, that, technically, under competition law it is illegal to fix any price, including a competitive one. See United States v. Trenton Potteries, 273 U.S. 392 (1927), and United States v. Socony-Vacuum Oil Co., 310 U.S. 150 (1940).

each firm reasons independently; that is, the result does not require a meeting of the minds.

Another distinction could be based on the process of equilibrium selection. As mentioned, when there are multiple equilibria, as in our simple example, the firms ultimately must arrive at particular equilibrium. The process of equilibrium selection could itself be seen to constitute agreement. Think about a firm that reasons as follows: "Among the many equilibria available, I will choose one with supracompetitive prices, say, that with the monopoly price, because this will be mutually advantageous and accordingly I imagine that my competitors will reason likewise—and they will suppose that I am thinking this way, and so forth." One might use the term agreement to refer to only those meetings of the minds that involve mutually advantageous cooperation.[47]

An equivalent result through somewhat different reasoning could be reached by attending to Sherman Act Section 1's full provision, which prohibits (only) agreements that are "in restraint of trade."[48] A competitive equilibrium would be viewed as not involving any such restraint whereas an equilibrium with supracompetitive pricing would.[49] After all, the purpose of competition law's prohibition on horizontal agreements is to prevent groups of firms from behaving as if they were a single firm rather than as competitors, and it is precisely the decision to play price-elevating equilibrium strategies that brings about the disfavored result.[50]

Each of these modes of reasoning produces the same conclusion: that one could view as agreements firms' mutual understanding that involves supracompetitive pricing. In any event, there are two basic reasons to

---

[47] On the possibility of uncooperative behavior that results in prices above purely competitive levels, see note 16 and chapter 14. Consider also the distinction in the U.S. Department of Justice and Federal Trade Commission's Horizontal Merger Guidelines (2010, §§6, 7) between unilateral and coordinated effects.

[48] Consider, for example, the language from *American Tobacco*, quoted at page 78.

[49] Although price fixing is per se illegal in the United States, its prohibition is understood as a rule that directs the usual outcome that would be expected under the rule of reason, which in turn employs a test that examines whether practices promote or suppress competition. See the cases cited in note 22 of chapter 3.

[50] When the firms charge the monopoly price, P_m, this is clear. When they charge a price between the competitive and monopoly prices, the problem is partial, but price-fixing prohibitions have never been limited to cases in which the conspirators charge the full monopoly price.

connect the agreement concept with the notion of equilibrium. One is the overlap in underlying definitions and ideas: Both terms are fundamentally concerned with a meeting of the minds or mutual understanding. The other is the lack of alternatives. As the introduction to this section emphasizes, modern competition law needs to ground a definition of agreement in some core feature of modern oligopoly theory, and there does not appear to be any other candidate.

The point is not that the language of the economic theory has no corresponding term. As we saw, it does—legally binding agreement—but one that is entirely inapt. Rather, the substance of the theory, which is designed to illuminate the behavior that the law seeks to regulate, does not recognize any other ideas that plausibly relate to a definition of agreement. The proffered resolution works if agreement is defined as interdependence, particularly if it is understood to mean successful oligopolistic interdependence. The present subsection elaborates how this concept is a coherent, central aspect of the pertinent economic theory. And the preceding chapters explain that a wide range of difficulties are due to attempts to define agreement as more restrictive than interdependence. Thus, the economic theory designed to illuminate the oligopoly problem is substantially in harmony with what one learns from other perspectives on the agreement requirement. The theory likewise shares with the foregoing analysis the lack of a coherent, narrower concept that would demarcate a boundary somewhere between classic cartels and pure interdependence.

2. Communications

As remarked in section 2.C, many commentators view communications as central to the existence of a horizontal agreement. We have already seen in chapter 2, however, that communications are not really related to any ordinary meaning of the term agreement (or conspiracy and so on). Nevertheless, perhaps communications can in some fashion be seen as part of the definition given that the law sometimes uses terms in entirely specialized, even fictitious ways, particularly when such an interpretation helps to implement the underlying purpose of a legal rule. Furthermore, the introduction to this section emphasizes that the law seeks to ground competition rules in pertinent economic theory. Accordingly, this subsection asks whether modern oligopoly theory provides a basis for viewing the use of certain sorts of communications—but not others[51]—as agreement.

A review of section A immediately raises a substantial obstacle to any such attempt: Namely, communications do not appear in the pertinent theory of oligopolistic behavior. Therefore, it seems difficult to suppose a priori that communications would be the linchpin of the legal regulation of coordinated oligopolistic pricing. Whether supracompetitive prices are sustainable—that is, constitute an equilibrium—depends most directly on whether firms are sufficiently patient that they are unwilling to defect, which provides short-term rewards at greater long-run sacrifice, and on the magnitude of immediate gains and subsequent losses, which depend on such matters as the ease of detecting cheaters and the efficacy of punishment.

It is hardly the case, however, that communications are unimportant in this realm. Indeed, they might be relevant in a number of ways.[52] First, consider the problem of equilibrium selection, recalling that in basic settings there are multiple possible equilibria, including in our example the range from the competitive price, P_c, to the monopoly price, P_m. In the absence of communications beyond pricing itself, such as in the example in section 2.A with the two gas stations, the firms might well choose the monopoly price because it is a focal point and, among the set of focal points, the one that is mutually most attractive. Or perhaps they will not. In such cases, it might be supposed that more explicit communications would be helpful. The firms might, for example, disagree on the monopoly price because they have differing costs or different views about buyers' demands. More broadly, when firms sell multiple products, some of which may be differentiated, the necessary common understanding will be more intricate than mere assent to a single price. In these and other circumstances, more elaborate negotiations could assist in coming to a common, mutually advantageous conclusion.[53] Of course, they could also interfere

---

[51] Recall from chapter 3 that the concept of communication is broad and includes ordinary marketplace behavior, such as the posting of a price; hence, any rule triggered by communications needs to distinguish some types from others.

[52] See Buccirossi (2008, 311–17), Kaplow and Shapiro (2007, 1106–8, 1124–26), and Whinston (2006, 23–26).

[53] Determination of applicable punishments (notably regarding the magnitude and duration

in some instances. For example, if left to simple price signaling, the firms may quickly reach a common price that is a round number close to what each views to be its ideal price, whereas extended negotiations could break down.[54] A plausible presumption is that firms would attempt more elaborate negotiations only when they expected them to be helpful, although the theory underlying this commonsense view is not well developed.[55]

---

of price cuts) is part of the problem of equilibrium selection because, as subsection A.2 makes clear, the pattern of punishments is part of players' strategies, which are taken to be in some equilibrium. (In this regard, Schelling (1960, quoted at page 67) has suggested that actions may be more important than words in demonstrating that punishment will in fact be employed. Nevertheless, words may help coordinate actions.)

[54] An interesting possibility is that one-way communications might be in a party's interest and also might better facilitate a cooperative outcome than would two-way communications, which are the focus of those seeking to tie the definition of agreement to communications. For example, Schelling (1960, 58–59) discusses how a party may prefer one-way communications; Cooper et al. (1989, 574–78) report results in a coordination game in which a beneficial equilibrium was achieved 48% of the time with no communication, 55% of the time with two-way communication, and 95% of the time with one-way communication; and Cooper et al. (1992) find in a simple coordination game that two-way communication was much more effective than one-way communication, but that in a more complicated coordination game, cooperation was much higher with one-way than two-way communication. In addition, in light of Rosenthal's (1981) demonstration of how uncertainty about whether other players engage in flawless, forward-looking calculation can sustain coordination in a finitely repeated game, it seems that direct, two-way communication could undermine oligopolistic coordination by eliminating this sort of uncertainty about other firms' behavior.

[55] See Whinston (2006, 21): "[E]conomic theory has relatively little to say about the process of coordination among equilibria. It is natural to think that talking may help with this coordination, but exactly to what degree and in what circumstances is less clear."; Kühn and Vives (1995, 43–44 n.12): "Explicit agreements may help in solving coordination problems in selecting an equilibrium. However, this coordination can be achieved by unilateral communication by just one firm . . . . Furthermore, there is no satisfactory economic theory that would explain why communication would resolve coordination problems in a determinate way."; and ibid. (54–55): "However, theoretical research on the subject has not succeeded in sustaining the intuition that communication facilitates coordination. . . . [I]t is hard to find any argument why private communication between firms about future planned prices or production would be beneficial. It appears that despite the lack of formal theoretical support the only way one can explain such behavior is that firms use communication to coordinate their future market conduct." Although any such communications constitute "cheap talk," they may nevertheless be useful, which possibility is suggested by the example on price determination in note 58. For some general reservations about the ability of pre-play "agreements" to facilitate coordination on an equilibrium in a game, see Aumann (1990).

Second, communications may influence the enforceability of an equilibrium. As discussed in subsection A.2, an important difficulty in some settings is that firms' prices may not be observable, leaving firms to infer others' cheating from declines in their own sales; however, such drops could be due to reductions in buyers' demand rather than others' cheating, making accidental price wars possible. Communications might help if firms are able to convey information credibly.[56] For example, firms

---

[56] See, for example, Genesove and Mullin (2001). In this context, the role of information is sometimes misunderstood, a subject elaborated in section 10.C on facilitating practices. Price information that is made public and, in particular, available to all buyers, rather than kept secret, is often viewed as more benign or even desirable from a social perspective, perhaps because secrecy breeds suspicion. This impression seems often to be mistaken, however, because secrecy undermines successful coordination by making cheating more attractive whereas publicity facilitates coordination. This point is familiar from situations like that in the *Container* case, in which firms verified with competitors various assertions by buyers that they had been offered lower prices, and that posed by many government-run auctions in which bidders' prices are made public afterward, thereby alerting firms immediately of any cheating that has transpired. Albæk, Møllgaard, and Overgaard (1997) describe the Danish competition authority's gathering and publishing of prices of concrete, motivated by a belief in the desirability of price transparency, with the result that prices increased due to eased oligopolistic coordination. To be sure, there are other settings in which public pricing can help buyers, such as when each customer is a small, nonrepeat purchaser who finds it costly to determine sellers' prices, which is why some competitors have attempted to suppress price advertising. See, for example, Benham (1972). Note that the spread of the Internet may significantly influence consumers' and firms' behavior, which may alter both the use of various forms of price dissemination and their effects.

As discussed further in section 10.C, another point to keep in mind is that firms' decisions whether to have highly public prices or more private ones, to the extent that the choice is under their collective control, will tend to be made in a way that is contrary to consumers' interests. Relatedly, buyers may individually prefer to have advance notice of their suppliers' price increases, but buyers as a whole will generally be worse off in the long run if advance price announcements facilitate supracompetitive pricing. Regarding sellers' motives, it is noteworthy that, in Porter's (1980, 76–80) text on competitive strategy, giving buyers advance notice is not on his long list of strategic reasons for advance announcements, which is dominated by concerns with communication between competitors. In contrast, Dranove and Marciano (2005, 139) state that "[p]reannouncements often help customers plan their future purchases, such as [by] allowing contractors to better budget." Porter (1980, 80, 103–4) also emphasizes that making statements publically can be a way to enhance the effective commitment: "Declaring commitments to the industry or financial community in public statements, publicizing targets for market share, and a variety of other devices can let competitors know that a firm will be embarrassed publicly if it has to back down. This knowledge will tend to deter them from trying

unconstrained by the law might allow independent audits of invoices or other records to verify that they have adhered to the understood price. More casually, firms might merely inform each other that they have not cheated. This lesser method, which economists refer to as a form of "cheap talk,"[57] is obviously problematic because a firm that has in fact cheated will hope not to be detected and thus will be expected to lie if its statements cannot be validated.[58] Thus, with regard to the detection of cheating, verification rather than communication per se is particularly important.

As is true of equilibrium selection, communications are not unambiguously helpful in enforcing coordinated oligopolistic pricing. For example, when a price war does occur, firms will find it in their ex post interest to shorten it, which negotiations might help to make possible. Quicker restoration of the monopoly price is desirable from the firms' point of view at that moment in time. However, if such negotiations are anticipated, then any firm that contemplates cheating will expect punishment to be brief rather than sustained, and this prospect will make cheating more attractive ex ante. Hence, better communications can make it more difficult to sustain supracompetitive prices.[59]

Communication may be relevant in other ways as well.[60] Suppose, for example, that there is a decline in demand, so that the former monopoly price is now higher than that which is jointly profit-maximizing. It makes sense for firms to reduce their prices. But any firm that does so may fear

---

to force it to do so." Schelling (1960, 29–30) also discusses how publicity rather than secrecy is necessary for reputation to be effective. Heil, Day, and Reibstein (1997, 281) suggest that firms may have their cake and eat it too by making statements that are public to each other yet less likely to be noticed by buyers (such as by making announcements through trade journals).

[57] See Crawford (1998) and Farrell and Rabin (1996).

[58] Cheap talk is more widely regarded to be potentially useful in selecting among equilibria, each of which is, by definition, self-enforcing and thus compatible with parties' self-interest. For example, suggestion of a price—notably, a non-round number, like $3.47, that was not already a focal point—may make it one and thus more likely to be selected.

[59] See Andersson and Wengström (2007) and McCutcheon (1997).

[60] See also Athey and Bagwell (2001), Gerlach (2009), and Harrington and Skrzypacz (2011) on the use of communications to facilitate market sharing and compensatory transfers among coordinating firms.

that its reduction will be viewed by others as cheating rather than as an invitation to all to adjust the industry price.[61] The more the leader can act openly, maybe with an advance public price announcement, perhaps accompanied by an explanation as well, the less likely is misunderstanding.[62] From the perspective of consumer and total social welfare, the present example is ambiguous regarding the virtues of prohibiting facilitative communication. On one hand, if communication is not allowed and a firm nevertheless reduces its price in an attempt to move the industry to a new, superior equilibrium, there is the prospect of a price war, which would tend to be socially beneficial. On the other hand, the prospect of such a price war may delay or deter the attempt to reduce the equilibrium price, which would tend to be detrimental.

The foregoing list is not exhaustive but should be sufficient to reinforce the conventional wisdom that more elaborate communication often is helpful to oligopolistic firms seeking to sustain supracompetitive prices, while at the same time to suggest that standard views are oversimplified and not without important qualifications. Modern oligopoly theory allows various intuitions to be made more precise, which helps to ascertain whether and when they are correct and to determine what sorts of communications may be important in particular circumstances. Unfortunately, modern oligopoly theory has not yet systematically explored the relevance

---

[61] Interestingly, much discussion of the role of communications in facilitating successful coordinated oligopolistic pricing emphasizes future price increases, but in that setting the risk of misunderstanding is less serious. A unilateral unanticipated price increase will not be mistaken for cheating and is likely to be understood as an invitation to follow (and, if it is not, the initiator may lose little if the price increase can be rescinded rapidly). In contrast, once a price war is triggered, even accidently, it may be difficult to put the genie back in the bottle quickly.

[62] See Farrell and Rabin (1996, 116): "Because talk can help avoid misunderstandings and coordination failures, it often improves outcomes (for the players), but even unlimited cheap talk does not reliably lead to a Pareto-efficient outcome." There also exist substitutes for such explicit communications. For example, if an immediately effective price cut is implemented during a period of conspicuously low demand—for some industries, this might be over a weekend or a holiday; see Dranove and Marciano's (2005, 139) description of the airline industry's practice after settling the government's antitrust suit—competitors, upon observing that the initiator is attempting to gain as little as possible, may infer that the move is an invitation rather than a defection.

of communications (although a number of specific studies of limited scope have appeared).[63] In addition, empirical evidence, largely based on volunteer subjects playing simplified games in a laboratory setting, has yielded only modest results of uncertain relevance to actual firm behavior.[64]

What, then, is the implication of the foregoing for the definition of agreement under competition law? As discussed in section 3.A, it is difficult to equate communications with agreement, and the present discussion of the possible relevance of communications to coordinated oligopoly behavior does not provide any reason to revise that conclusion. Furthermore, when one focuses on settings in which communications might be helpful to oligopolistic firms, the form or mode of communication, which seems to be the focus of those who attempt to make the agreement-communications link at all concrete, has no direct role.[65] What sorts of communications will be helpful is an entirely contextual, empirical question, and one that chapter 3 suggests will be difficult to answer and almost certainly cannot be answered by reference to some general, a priori classification.

---

[63] See the sources cited in note 52. Whinston (2006, 26) concludes his discussion of the theory of price fixing by stating, "It is in some sense paradoxical that the least controversial area of antitrust is perhaps the one in which the basis of the policy in economic theory is weakest." In similar spirit, Vives (1999, 321) concludes that "[t]he research on the effect of communication on collusion is not yet conclusive. . . . However, in general, the presumption is that communication abets collusion."

[64] A half century ago, Schelling (1960, 166) stated, "One such question [for research] would be this: by and large, does it appear that the players are any more successful in reaching an efficient solution, that is, a mutually nondestructive solution, when (a) full or nearly full communication is allowed, (b) no communication or virtually none is allowed, other than what can be conveyed by the moves themselves, or (c) communication is asymmetrical, with one party more able to send messages than he is to receive them? There is no guaranty that a single, universally applicable answer would emerge; nevertheless, some quite general valid propositions about the role of communication might well be discovered." Unfortunately, what has been subsequently learned leaves these questions largely unanswered. For surveys, see the sources cited in note 50 in chapter 6. For skepticism about the real-world applicability of such experimental research, see Whinston (2006), quoted in note 52 of chapter 6.

[65] That is, although a case study or a laboratory experiment will involve particular forms of communication, modern oligopoly theory itself—including plausible extensions one might imagine to address the role of communications more explicitly—does not provide any basis for deeming specific modes of communication to be of central importance.

Second, as discussed in section 3.B, various sorts of communications might be viewed as facilitating practices that themselves could be prohibited, that is, independently of whether the underlying price elevation that might be facilitated is deemed illegal. As previously explained, however, there remains the question of whether there is an agreement to use the facilitating practices—the means of communications themselves. An affirmative answer could readily be given only if interdependence is deemed sufficient to constitute agreement.

Accordingly, the present analysis of communications has relevance to price-fixing inquiries, but not because communications constitute agreement or illuminate that concept. Instead, a better understanding of communications is useful if indeed communications are to be attacked directly under competition law. In that case, the central question will be whether the communications at issue in a particular case are more likely to promote or suppress competition, and modern oligopoly theory offers the best set of tools for undertaking that inquiry, although as mentioned the toolkit is limited. In addition, if agreement, however defined, is to be inferred from circumstantial evidence, modern oligopoly theory informs the interpretation of circumstantial evidence, which may include various communications.[66] In sum, communications are important in understanding some aspects of coordinated oligopoly but are not directly pertinent in elaborating the notion of horizontal agreement.

3. Promises

Promises are central to binding, legally enforceable contracts as well as to informal agreements between individuals. If competition law had taken formal contracts as the core model of agreement—which it has not, as discussed in subsection 4.A.1 and section 4.C—then the existence of a promise might have been seen as determinative. The question remains

---

[66] The observation of various forms of communication raises the paradox of proof. Notably, if a certain sort of communication that would facilitate coordination in a given setting is identified, it is more likely that successful oligopolistic coordination is taking place, but the need to resort to such communication, especially if it raises legal risk, indicates that, ceteris paribus, the industry must be less susceptible to successful price elevation.

whether promises and related notions, like assurances or indications of commitment, might nevertheless be important, as a few commentators urge,[67] and how this possibility relates to modern oligopoly theory.[68]

---

[67] The notion of a commitment is central to Areeda and Hovenkamp's view of the law on horizontal agreement. (See also Baker (1996, 47–48), arguing that the law's notion of agreement only includes outcomes reached by "what may be termed the 'forbidden process' of negotiation and exchange of assurances.") Areeda and Hovenkamp (2003, 6–7) see pure interdependence as insufficient and the existence of commitment or assurances as providing the necessary additional ingredient: "The second step . . . is to look for some evidence of commitment, whether weak or strong, among the alleged conspirators." See also ibid. (59–60): "The traditional agreement sought by conspiracy law involves some kind of commitment to a common cause."; ibid. (63): "we know what we are looking for: some level of commitment to a common course of action"; and ibid. (96, 205). They do not insist on the use of magic words expressing commitment. See ibid. (60): "The commitment may be weak or strong, express or implied."; ibid. (63): "reciprocal assurances can be communicated by conduct rather than by words and remain 'agreements' even though vague, incomplete, and riddled with qualifications and exceptions"; and ibid. (64), offering four examples in which an illegal conspiracy would be found, the first and third of which contain no language of assurance or commitment. And sometimes it appears that commitment is not necessary after all, as they do not insist on anything beyond coordination. See ibid. (19): "Although collective decision making *plus* mutual assurance of compliance is the principal vice, *either element alone* may suffice to establish an antitrust agreement." (emphasis added); ibid. (19–20): "An exchange of information, views, or complaints does not necessarily imply any jointly reached decision or assurances on any course of action, *but it may do so when the discussants are competitors.*" (emphasis added); ibid. (20), offering a formulation close to the interpretation of *Interstate Circuit* that encompasses mere interdependence: "To be sure, an addressee of a proposal for common action who behaves in accordance with the proposal may find it difficult, to say the least, to persuade us that it acted unilaterally and without regard to the proposal."; and ibid. (64), observing, in an attempt to distinguish two sets of examples, that the first group has "an advance statement about future behavior and thus something of a commitment," but acknowledging that "undertaking to do as one thinks best is not much of a commitment and may merely verbalize what is implicit in the second group." Nevertheless, they state (65), "Although the line between coordination through recognized interdependence and some commitment is shadowy, the distinction is important so long as antitrust law allows the former but condemns the latter." For the most part, they take it to be self-evident that commitment is central to agreement. Notably, they do not offer a direct justification, quote cases in support of their interpretation, or trace its implications. Surprisingly, despite their insistence that the cases require more than interdependence and that the key additional element is commitment, they rarely mention the notion in their many and often lengthy discussions of Supreme Court and lower court cases, either when they praise a court's reasoning or when they are critical.

[68] The most extensive examination of the problem is probably that of Leslie (2004), a legal

With formal contracts, the existence of a clear exchange of promises plays the important role of triggering legal enforcement, thereby distinguishing suggestions, predictions, statements of intentions, and preliminary indications of an interest in making a binding commitment. Since price-fixing agreements of any form are unenforceable, this function is irrelevant. Nevertheless, promises and related notions do play some analogous roles in informal settings. There is a difference between stating that you expect to be able to attend a meeting or a party and that you promise to attend. With the latter, nonperformance may trigger or heighten informal psychological and social sanctions, such as guilt feelings, shame, and disapprobation by others.[69]

If the law were to make promises, assurances, or other indications of commitment a necessary and sufficient condition (or an important factor) for deeming an agreement to exist, it would be essential to identify when such has occurred. With both formal contracts and informal arrangements, parties often will be clear about their intentions; indeed, clarity and publicity may aid in enforcement, both formal and informal. But if the use of actual promissory language triggers not enforcement of price-fixing promises but rather legal liability and strong sanctions, then parties would be expected to employ carefully lawyered communications in order to provide immunity. In addition, parties engaged in price fixing will seek to keep their intentions secret. Moreover, when such activity is hidden, it will be exceedingly difficult to determine from circumstantial evidence what language parties used in some alleged communication (recall the analysis of the paradox of proof in chapter 6).[70]

---

scholar who argues that interactions that enhance trust increase the likelihood that oligopolies will be successful. Note that this positive inquiry differs from the question of whether the existence of trust or the manner in which it might have come about, such as through an assurance, is consequential for the definition of horizontal agreement.

[69] See generally Hume (1739, 521–23) and Kaplow and Shavell (2002, 204–7). The application to oligopoly theory is made by Friedman (1986, 70–71, quoting Hume).

[70] The discussion of language in section 3.C suggests additional difficulties with an approach linked to magic words. And the point that actions often speak louder than words seems especially pertinent to the force of promises and the notion of commitment. A standard definition of assurance—indeed, the one that seems to motivate Areeda and Hovenkamp's position (discussed in note 67)—refers to something that inspires or tends to inspire confidence, which deeds may do more effectively than assertions. In this regard, it is interesting that Areeda and Hovenkamp (2003, 221), despite their arguing for the centrality of commitment, above and

Alternatively, liability might be made to depend on successfully conveying the idea of a commitment. Here, the problems may be even more challenging. The analysis depends critically on just what one means by an implicit promise or commitment. On one hand, such a mutual understanding might be seen to exist whenever there is successful interdependent behavior, that is, whenever firms are in an equilibrium that supports coordinated supracompetitive pricing. As explored in subsections A.2, A.3, and B.1, there is a meeting of the minds under which each firm expects the others to adhere to the coordinated oligopoly price, the others expect it to comply, and so forth.[71] If this view is accepted, then the idea of agreement as (implicit) promise is equivalent to accepting pure interdependence as agreement.

This view might be rejected, however, because, as explained, in an equilibrium each firm by definition is simply acting in its self-interest given how it expects other firms to react. The idea of an implicit state of commitment might be taken to involve something more: specifically, that parties will stick to the supracompetitive price even when it is in their interest to cheat. But firms are taken to be self-interested, neither moralists nor altruists toward their competitors; competition law generally imputes rational maximization in gauging firms' behavior. If a given elevated price is not in firms' interest to maintain—that is, cheating is profitable, even taking likely reactions into account—then it is not an equilibrium and thus not something we would expect to observe. By this

---

beyond interdependent behavior, acknowledge this sort of qualification: "Stated another way, we can ask whether a history of price leadership or of maintaining noncompetitive price levels is any less of a commitment to continue doing so than is a clearly unlawful exchange of unenforceable express commitments among cartel members, who, after all, remain legally free to defect and often do whenever net self-interest is served (taking prospective rival behavior into account)." See also ibid. (226): "[T]he mind-set of oligopolists who have long followed a pricing leader may approach that of cartel members, especially where many trade association, lobbying, or social meetings have generated mutual trust."

[71] In this regard, it is worth noting that standard definitions of assurance include the state of being assured and being in a certain state of mind, and a common definition of commitment is the state or an instance of being obligated or emotionally impelled. All of these definitions refer to subjective states. A further implication of this point is that there is no necessary connection between promises and commitment on one hand and forms of communication on the other hand. Recall also chapter 3's more general discussion of the relationship between agreement and communications.

account, the posited notion of promise would be a phantom in the relevant context. Therefore, if agreements required the demonstration of operative promissory behavior, they would never be deemed to exist, with the result that price fixing would be per se legal.

Nevertheless, it is possible to augment standard models of oligopoly to make room for an informal notion of promising. In other realms of business behavior, such as contracting with suppliers, it is generally supposed that honor and trust may play a role. Not everything need be in writing. When a party promises to make a delivery, their word may be worth something, particularly if they have behaved well in the past. Observe that promises and commitment can readily be unilateral and that their force is not obviously diminished on this account. Heads of state, businesses, and friends frequently make unilateral commitments or offer assurances without the exchange of promises associated with contracts, or the bidirectional understanding associated with agreements more broadly. Thus, if a firm would take the lead in raising its price only if it had a commitment that its rival would quickly follow, then a one-way assurance from the rival is what is relevant.[72]

An important caveat is that such behavior is often indistinguishable from narrowly self-interested maximizing behavior in a repeated game. Parties who break their commitments will jeopardize future business with their counterparts and may damage their reputation more widely; hence, keeping promises can constitute equilibrium behavior.[73] Even so, sometimes business honor carries more weight. Parties might be trusted even

---

[72] Leslie (2004, 568–73) discusses cartel members' use of goodwill gestures and benevolent moves to build trust.

[73] This familiar maxim is captured by the phrase "Honesty is the best policy." Miguel de Cervantes, Don Quixote, pt. ii, ch. xxxiii (1615). An early modern articulation of this notion is offered by Schelling (1960, 134–35): "While the possibility of 'trust' between two partners need not be ruled out, it should also not be taken for granted; and even trust itself can usefully be studied in game-theoretic terms. Trust is often achieved simply by the continuity of the relation between parties and the recognition by each that what he might gain by cheating in a given instance is outweighed by the value of the tradition of trust that makes possible a long sequence of future agreement." See also Hume (1739, 521–22) and Kaplow and Shavell (2002, 205). The point to follow in the text is likewise distinguished by Hume (1739, 523): "Afterwards a sentiment of morals concurs with interest and becomes a new obligation upon mankind."; and Kaplow and Shavell (2002, 205–7).

when future business and reputational concerns are insufficient in themselves to provide the necessary incentives for reliable behavior.

A question remains whether informal commitments are possible among competitors, whose general interactions are expected to be rivalrous rather than cooperative. Supposing that they are, then promises, even implicit ones, might help support coordinated oligopoly pricing. In particular, assume that, in the sort of repeated game described in subsection A.2, a given elevated price is not quite sustainable. Perhaps firms are a bit too impatient or the possibility of secret defections is just great enough that the mutually desired price is not an equilibrium. In that case, the existence of a psychological or social commitment might be enough to alter firms' calculations about cheating, in which case the posited price would be an equilibrium after all.[74]

This possibility raises a number of issues. First, as already noted, there is an important empirical question of the magnitude of such informal sanctions in the present context. Second and related, what does the weight of such promises (perhaps implicit) depend on? Might it matter how long the particular individuals with relevant price-setting authority have been at a firm?[75] How well they are known to their counterparts at rivals?[76] Whether they interact or have previously met informally in other settings, such as business school, community activities, or trade association meetings?[77] To what extent do firms as distinct from particular individuals have externally identifiable corporate cultures that are associated with trustworthy behavior? What was the nature of firms' interactions that produced the state in which the firms felt committed?[78] Little is known

---

[74] Stated more explicitly, the argument supposes that, when firms cheat, they bear an additional cost due to their violation of their commitment, and that this cost is large enough to tip the balance against defection.

[75] Porter (1980, 90), in discussing how the "*continuity of interaction* among the parties can promote stability since it facilitates the building of trust," notes that such continuity "also is aided by a stable group of general managers of these competitors."

[76] Glaeser et al.'s (2000, 834) experiment on trust and trustworthiness finds that levels are higher when participants knew each other longer. Leslie (2004, 565–68) describes personal relationships among key actors in some notable cartels.

[77] See Leslie (2004, 599, 661).

[78] Hume's (1739, 522) discussion of promises in informal settings refers to conventions under which individuals communicate their intentions through "certain *symbols* or *signs*,"

about the answers to these and related queries. Moreover, one would need to determine how such matters could be assessed in a particular case.

Third, there is the practical question of how one could infer whether such commitments are operative. Once again, commitments could be seen as present whenever there is successful interdependent behavior.[79] When firms engage in coordinated oligopoly pricing, they all recognize their mutual gain from adhering to the supracompetitive price and avoiding cheating. If firms were capable of commitments, one would suppose that they would probably be operative in any such instance. Secret price cuts are ordinarily described as cheating or defections, moralistic language that is undoubtedly appreciated by the relevant actors. That is, when a firm cheats, it probably sees its behavior as such and expects other firms to view it that way. When firms who enjoy supracompetitive profits see that one of their collaborators has cheated, and a price war breaks out, one suspects that they are angry (to the extent such moralistic, emotional responses are pertinent in this setting, and we are for present purposes supposing that they have some relevance). Thus, if commitment is deemed to equal agreement, this route readily leads once again to the conclusion that any successful interdependent behavior is sufficient.[80]

Another possibility would be to deem an agreement qua commitment to exist only when commitment was not merely present but also necessary to sustain the equilibrium involving a coordinated oligopoly price. Why one would embrace this rule, except out of a felt need to avoid the result

---

suggesting a broad array of triggering devices, the particulars of which emerge in specific contexts. In the context of cooperative oligopoly pricing, it is hardly apparent that magic words communicated secretly are essential to create whatever degree of commitment is possible. For example, Porter (1980, 81) notes that one function of public discussions of industry conditions by competitors may be to make "implicit promises to cooperate if others act 'properly.'"

[79] The argument in the text does not rule out its presence as well in cases in which interdependent behavior is unsuccessful, just as there can be elaborate cartel arrangements that fail.

[80] One may suppose that the degree of commitment—in contrast to a mere recognition of being in an equilibrium governed entirely by narrowly viewed self-interest—varies across contexts, depending among other things on the sorts of empirical questions raised previously. The present suggestion is merely that there would be some (perhaps trivial) level in (nearly?) all cases. The text to follow explores the possibility of making the weight of the felt commitment determinative.

that interdependence is enough for liability, is unclear. The approach also clashes with a core conventional understanding, for classic cartels would fail to constitute agreements whenever they were sufficiently solid that the social-psychological force added by the presence of such a commitment was not required for its success.

Moreover, under this approach the proof problem would be severe. Recall the analysis of the paradox of proof in chapter 6. For the legal test now under consideration, a plaintiff would have to show (taking other factors as given) that the ease of coordination was in a quite narrow band. Specifically, the ease of coordination would have to be high enough that the incremental oomph from commitment was sufficient to make a documented price-elevated equilibrium sustainable, but the plausibility of successful coordination could not be so high that such an equilibrium was sustainable without that additional support.[81] Supposing that the psychological and social weight of commitment is modest relative to the direct profit-loss calculus, the plaintiff's case would have to hit a small bull's-eye. (Moreover, the location of that bull's-eye—which would be at the degree of ease of coordination that was the tipping point between the coordinated oligopoly price being unsustainable and sustainable—would itself be in dispute.[82] Accordingly, what the plaintiff would have to show on one dimension would depend on the factfinder's determination on the other. Note further that, if the case were at all close, both the plaintiff and defendants would be quite uncertain regarding which evidence and

---

[81] Although described somewhat differently, this requirement seems to be close to what Areeda and Hovenkamp (2003, 96)—whose general view is described in note 67—have in mind when they refer to acts sufficiently perilous that firms would not undertake them without an exchange of commitments or comforting assurances. The emphasis on two-way communications rather than on unilateral pronouncements (noted previously in the text) or on context is largely taken for granted. To illustrate the importance of unilateral action in this setting, the widespread use of white flags in war and in some other settings involves individuals placing themselves at extreme peril based on an implied commitment that ordinarily is not communicated by the other side.

[82] In finite repeated games, in which backward induction ordinarily disrupts equilibria reflecting cooperative behavior (see note 19), small differences in payoffs can be quite important. See Friedman (1986, 100–103) and Radner (1980). In some such settings, successful interdependence would imply the existence of promises, commitment, or whatever else was hypothesized to make firms somewhat more reluctant to cheat.

arguments favored which party; small shifts in the perceived weight of one item of proof would reverse parties' tactical positions on others.[83])

In principle, promises, like communications, might be relevant to the feasibility of successful coordinated oligopoly pricing in some contexts. It follows that it may be desirable to regulate interactions that facilitate achieving an intersubjective state in which commitments are firmer, just as it makes sense to regulate some forms of communication as facilitating practices.[84] However, once the potential role of promises in oligopoly theory is understood, it is difficult to see them as central to a legal definition of horizontal agreement—that is, as the central pillar that determines liability.

---

[83] This observation provides another reason to be highly skeptical of the claim that the postulated theory accurately describes the (implicit) current state of the law. An additional reason, suggested in note 67, is that if current law depends on the existence and weight of promises, commitments, and the like, one would expect to see them addressed directly in cases on a routine basis rather than being mentioned only occasionally, in passing, and not subject to direct dispute by the parties, including, for example, in the presentation of expert evidence.

[84] Such regulation might include restriction of direct, elaborate interactions in which parties might convey commitments but also of what is usually regarded to be benign activity, such as competitors' agents serving together on trade associations or boards of civic organizations or playing golf, for direct social interactions may be relevant to the feasibility of explicit or implicit commitments and to the strength of their psychological and social pull. Leslie (2004, 656–73) advocates that significant efforts be made to regulate interactions that facilitate trust but otherwise might be viewed as competitively benign. And, although not commenting on the merits of such an approach, Areeda and Hovenkamp (2003, 226) advance a view that suggests the relevance of this sort of intervention in observing that "the mind-set of oligopolists who have long followed a pricing leader may approach that of cartel members, especially where many trade association, lobbying, or social meetings have generated mutual trust." Of course, if the present theory is deemed too far-fetched or insufficiently weighty, these sorts of limitations would not make sense. Likewise, as with other facilitating practices, see section 18.C, heavier regulation tends to be favored the more difficult it is to reach coordinated oligopolistic pricing directly.

PART II

PRICE-FIXING POLICY

8

Social Welfare

Part I probes competition law's horizontal agreement requirement from a range of perspectives. It finds that they all readily support the distinction between coordinated oligopolistic price elevation and competitive interaction whereas none provide any substantial basis for making distinctions within the category of coordinated behavior. In particular, attempts to distinguish mere interdependence from express agreement—or from any other formulation that is significantly narrower than interdependence—fail from every angle and for largely the same reasons.

Despite this convergence of conclusions and rationale, part I does not in itself demonstrate what competition policy toward price fixing is optimal. The coherence of linguistic or conceptual categories is sometimes symptomatic of substance and may well suggest paths of inquiry but cannot suffice to answer normative questions. Accordingly, this part of the book presents a ground-up approach to the policy problem. Part III then uses this analysis to return to the doctrinal debate by systematically comparing the prescriptions derived here to those flowing from the conventionally endorsed view.

A policy-based approach to coordinated oligopolistic price elevation naturally considers three issues, with attention to their interrelationship. First, we should articulate the problem to be addressed with reasonable precision, identifying the key tradeoffs involved. Second, we need to examine methods of detection, including an assessment of how they might optimally be combined in light of the analysis of benefits and costs of attacking coordinated oligopolistic price elevation. Third, we have to determine appropriate sanctions.

This chapter and the next consider the first set of issues, elaborating the social welfare consequences of coordinated price elevation and developing a framework for decision-making that is sensitive to the tradeoff of deterrence benefits and chilling costs—distortions due to the prospect that firms behaving properly anticipate that they might be mistakenly subject to sanctions or in any case be forced to incur expenses due to legal scrutiny. Chapters 10 and 11 address detection, while chapter 12 considers how to assess liability in light of all of the analysis to that point. Sanctions are the subject of chapter 13. Chapter 14 examines the possibility that some oligopolistic price elevation may arise not as a consequence of coordination but instead through the unilateral exercise of market power, a phenomenon largely set aside in the rest of the analysis. Chapter 15 discusses administrative costs and other institutional issues, and it briefly considers the applicability of the analysis to coordination on strategic dimensions other than price.

As mentioned, this chapter examines the effects of coordinated oligopolistic price elevation on social welfare. It first reviews the familiar static effects, noting some generally unappreciated subtleties that may be relevant in formulating policy. Then it explores dynamic effects at greater length because of their importance with regard to the core deterrence benefit of enforcement and the possible cost of chilling desirable conduct.

Before proceeding, it should be noted that, just as with the descriptive theory of coordinated oligopoly behavior in section 7.A, static and dynamic effects on social welfare do not fundamentally depend on the means by which coordinated price elevation is accomplished—that is, whether it arises purely through recognized interdependence or results from secret meetings at which detailed plans are formulated. This rough equation is not particularly controversial; the point is often acknowledged by those who favor a narrow price-fixing prohibition.[1] As will be seen, although a few interesting differences do exist, they do not constitute substantial bases for limiting the social concern about coordinated oligopolistic price elevation to that achieved by particular means.[2]

---

[1] For example, Areeda and Hovenkamp (2003, 226).

[2] Although a given degree of price elevation tends to be associated with the same harm, however the elevation is accomplished, different degrees of price elevation may be associated with different modes of implementation. On one hand, all else equal, giving firms additional tools will tend to make cartel arrangements more effective. On the other hand, as indicated by the paradox of proof discussed in chapters 6 and 17, given a narrow, communications-based

A. Static Effects

The core objection to coordinated oligopolistic price elevation is that prices are higher—higher than the competitive level and also higher than is ordinarily necessary to induce producers to supply goods and services to consumers (a topic examined further in section B). Such high pricing is generally regarded to be undesirable in itself, which makes sense if the objective of competition policy is the maximization of consumer welfare. If the objective is overall efficiency or social welfare—which also includes producers' profits, which ultimately are enjoyed by individuals, perhaps owners or workers—then elevated prices are still objectionable because, despite firms' gain in profits, the excess of price over marginal cost destroys value, resulting in deadweight loss. This loss is associated with sales that would have occurred at the lower, competitive price but are choked off by oligopolistic price elevation. For such forgone sales, buyers' valuations, which by assumption are above the competitive price, exceed marginal cost; hence, what buyers lose exceeds the costs sellers avoid. Thus, from both perspectives, coordinated oligopoly pricing is taken to be undesirable because it involves supracompetitive prices.

Commentators disagree about whether competition policy should maximize total welfare or just that of consumers.[3] Although the former objective seems more compelling for the reasons suggested in the margin and accordingly will be the focus in much that follows, it is worth identifying some of the unappreciated differences in the implications of these competing views.[4] First, for any given price increase, the loss in consumer

---

price-fixing prohibition, there may be a tendency for the most dangerous price elevators to be those who do not engage in secret meetings and the like (because when conditions are most conducive to coordination, such activities may be less necessary).

[3] On the choice between consumer and total welfare as objectives of competition policy, see Kaplow (2012b) and Kaplow and Shapiro (2007, 1165–69), the latter of which focuses on the choice with regard to the efficiencies defense to horizontal mergers. Even if consumers are to be favored on distributive grounds, perhaps because they are on average less well off than beneficiaries of firms' profits, it does not make sense to ignore producer surplus entirely. In any event, it tends to be advantageous to achieve distributive objectives more directly, through redistributive taxation and transfers. See Kaplow (2012b) and Kaplow and Shavell (1994b).

[4] Kaplow (2012b, §3) contains a diagrammatic exposition of the analysis to follow. It is widely accepted that the difference between the two views is important in certain settings,

surplus exceeds the loss in total surplus because the latter subtracts the additional profits accruing to sellers. Second, fairly small price elevations are a significant concern if only consumer surplus counts but not if total welfare is the objective. For example, consider linear demand that has a slope of negative one and intersects a supply curve with a constant marginal cost of 100 at a quantity of 100. A 1% price elevation, from the competitive price of 100 to a price of 101, reduces consumer surplus by 99.5 but total surplus only by 0.5. (Consumers pay 101 rather than 100 for the 99 units they still consume, and there is an additional loss of consumer surplus, equal to the deadweight loss, of 0.5 on the unit no longer consumed, the area of a triangle with a base and height of 1.) For a 5% elevation, price is 105, quantity is 95, lost consumer surplus is 487.5 and total surplus falls by 12.5.[5] And at the monopoly price, which is 150 in this example, quantity is 50, lost consumer surplus is 3,750, and total surplus falls by 1,250.[6] Therefore, the ratio of lost consumer to lost total surplus is nearly 200 to 1 for the 1% elevation, nearly 40 to 1 for the 5% elevation, and only 3 to 1 for the 50% elevation. A corollary of the present analysis is that the incremental loss in consumer surplus as price increases is falling whereas the incremental loss in total surplus tends to be rising.

The basic lesson regarding static effects is that a competition policy concerned with consumer rather than total surplus should optimally be more aggressive and, in a relative sense, this prescription holds particularly for small price increases. Put another way, once one recognizes that there are costs associated with enforcement, as will be discussed in sections 9.A and 15.A, policy based on total welfare would be especially forgiving of small price increases, whereas if consumer surplus is the focus, intervention may be optimal for much smaller elevations.[7]

---

such as mergers, where those concerned with only consumer surplus would disallow an otherwise on-balance efficient merger unless enough efficiency benefits are passed on to consumers that prices do not rise at all. It is not generally discussed, however, that focusing only on consumer surplus has implications with regard to many other areas of competition policy, including price fixing.

[5] At a quantity of 95 and an elevation of 5, consumer surplus of 475 is transformed into seller profits and deadweight loss is 12.5 (the area of a triangle with a base and height of 5).

[6] At a quantity of 50 and an elevation of 50, consumer surplus of 2,500 is transformed into seller profits and deadweight loss is 1,250 (the area of a triangle with a base and height of 50).

[7] A subtle but possibly important qualification is that the weight on each dollar of lost consumer surplus (under the view that only consumer welfare matters) need not equal the weight on each dollar of lost total surplus (under the view that total welfare matters). Never-

Static effects of oligopolistic price elevation are not necessarily limited to allocative inefficiency (deadweight loss) and transfers from consumers to producers. When oligopolistic firms raise price and accordingly reduce output, their output may not be allocated efficiently among them. To see this point, begin with a competitive equilibrium. Each firm sells additional units until the point at which its marginal cost equals price. Since all firms face the same, competitive price, all operate such that their last unit produced has the same marginal cost as the last unit produced by other firms; hence, there is ordinarily production efficiency in the sense that reallocating output among the firms could not reduce and (with rising marginal costs) would instead increase total production costs for the given level of output. When oligopolistic firms coordinate to elevate price, however, they would each like to sell more output than at the competitive price, but instead they must sell less, for otherwise the elevated price could not be maintained. How much of the smaller industry output is supplied by each firm will depend on the circumstances. Perhaps they share output equally, as hypothesized in some simple models. If products are differentiated, consumers will allocate themselves based on how they value particular products. In any event, there is no guarantee that production will be allocated efficiently, which can be a further source of welfare loss.

An interesting related point is that well-organized cartels have the advantage over looser arrangements that this type of loss in production efficiency can be avoided. Firms might agree to let their more efficient members produce more than they otherwise would permit, in exchange for transfer payments.[8] Accordingly, if coordinated price elevation is to occur to a given extent, classic cartels may entail lower efficiency costs than those that arise under pure interdependence or other less formal schemes.

B. Dynamic Effects

Coordinated oligopolistic price elevation and deterrence thereof may also have important dynamic effects. As with static effects, these consequences

---

theless, the point in the text about relative significance holds; that is, the relative importance of large price elevations versus small ones is greater under the total welfare view.

    [8] See Schmalensee (1987b).

do not on their face depend on the means by which coordination is achieved. The dynamic effects considered here pertain to entry and inducing investment more broadly. The latter consideration is also central to understanding the rationale underlying competition law's tendency to prohibit price fixing by groups of firms while (ordinarily, in most jurisdictions) permitting unilateral price elevation by a monopolist, a distinction that has led to some confusion in academic commentary on the appropriate breadth of price-fixing prohibitions.

1. Entry

Regarding entry, the literature identifies two competing effects.[9] First, to the extent that prices are elevated above marginal cost, there tends to be too much entry due to a business-stealing effect: Firms that enter obtain profits in part by diverting customers from incumbents, whose lost surplus is not taken into account by entrants. Therefore, resources wasted on excessive entry are an additional cost of price elevation. Second, to the extent that products are differentiated, there tends to be too little entry because firms offering new products do not capture all of the surplus generated by their contribution to product variety: Firms consider only the revenue they obtain, ignoring inframarginal consumers' surplus. When this effect is sufficiently large, the additional entry induced by price elevation is socially beneficial.

It is useful to elaborate these points separately for industries selling homogeneous goods and those with differentiated products. Homogeneous goods industries are particularly important because coordinated oligopoly pricing is thought to be less difficult when products are homogeneous (see section 11.A), and empirical evidence on price-fixing prosecutions indicates that most serious violations have involved homogeneous products (see sections 6.E and 9.C). In these industries, only the first effect is present, so price elevation would always seem to induce excessive entry.

Consider a simple example of an industry in which actual and prospective entrants face a fixed entry cost and, once that cost is incurred, produce at a common, rising marginal cost. If pricing is competitive, that is, price

---

[9] See, for example, Mankiw and Whinston (1986).

equals marginal cost, firms will enter the industry until the point at which an additional entrant will no longer be able to cover its fixed costs. This state of affairs will be efficient. For the last firm that enters, its entry lowers prices, which benefits consumers, while the business it captures from others involves output that would have sold at marginal cost and hence did not generate a surplus to the sellers.[10] A subsequent firm would not enter because, at the lower price it would induce, it could not cover its fixed costs. This unprofitability implies that consumers' further gain is less than the production cost of generating that gain.

Suppose instead that pricing will be at the monopoly level regardless of how many firms enter; that is, coordinated oligopolistic pricing (however achieved) is perfectly effective. In this case, the higher price induces more firms to enter, and more will enter until the additional entrant could not cover its costs (because its share of the monopoly output would be too small, even given that price exceeds its marginal cost). All of the supplemental entry is a social waste. There is no consumer benefit—for price is assumed to be unaffected—while further production costs are incurred.[11] Indeed, in this case, essentially all of the oligopolists' profits are transformed into production inefficiency.[12] The conclusion is that the

---

[10] The exposition in the text, following Mankiw and Whinston (1986, 50–54), oversimplifies in ignoring the integer constraint (i.e., that in reality, each firm is a discrete unit, so there cannot be an equilibrium with a fractional firm operating). As they show, when the integer constraint is imposed explicitly, it is possible to have one firm too few, rather than too many. (One way to think about part of the implication is that, in moving from zero firms to one firm, the variety available to consumers does increase; hence, the second effect is operative, which implies that too little entry is possible.) They note, however, that in Perry's (1984) simulations, this qualification is important only if the number of firms would be quite small. This case is considered further later in this subsection.

[11] This example is analogous to one presented in Kaplow (1984, 1871–73 n.200), showing how the prohibition of de facto horizontal merger to monopoly among competing patents, with the possibility of new entry, tends to result in lower prices, which improves not only static, allocative efficiency but also dynamic, productive efficiency by reducing entry that would only serve to increase production costs.

[12] In a simple example with linear demand, Mankiw and Whinston (1986, 53 n.10) report that in the limiting case the entry effect dissipates 50% of the total welfare potential in the market. In contrast, the deadweight loss from overpricing would be 25% of total potential surplus in this example. The point that monopolistic profits tend to be converted into resource costs rather than constituting mere transfers is advanced by Tullock (1967) and Posner (1975). Rogerson (1982) and Fisher (1985) argue that Posner's argument is overstated.

total welfare loss from price elevation in homogeneous goods industries could be even larger than the static inefficiency in cases in which there are not effective barriers to entry—to the extent that such entry does not undermine the price elevation. It is also useful to note that the magnitude of the incentive for excess entry is determined by the magnitude of price elevation; when price equals marginal cost, there is no incentive for excess entry. (A further observation is that the common view that more entry is generally desirable on competitive grounds sometimes overlooks that the competitive benefit lies precisely in moving prices downward, closer to a competitive level;[13] to the extent that competition policy better induces that result without the need for as much entry, the reduction in entry is beneficial, not detrimental.)

There is a caveat to the tendency toward excessive entry (aspects of which are discussed in note 10), one that is most likely to be important in industries that might otherwise have difficulty supporting one or two firms due, say, to relatively high fixed costs.[14] One possibility is that even a single-firm industry in which the monopoly price is charged would not yield enough profit to cover fixed entry costs. Then there would be too little entry if total surplus would make it efficient to have a single producer. This problem arises because even monopolists often cannot capture inframarginal consumer surplus (because they cannot perfectly price discriminate). In this instance, a subsidy would be required; permitting price fixing would not help since it is assumed that even the monopoly price is insufficient to induce the entry of a single firm.

Consider also the case in which a monopoly price is sufficient to induce one firm to enter, but that a second firm is deterred from entering because it is supposed that, conditional on entry, competition would be sufficiently aggressive that the prospective entrant's share of the remaining profit would be inadequate to cover fixed costs. The result would be monopoly (and might warrant direct regulation, particularly if the market cannot support a second firm). Again, subsidized entry might be advantageous, in this case because the induced competition may reduce allocative inef-

---

[13] Some of the impetus for the literature assessing the welfare effects of entry was precisely to dislodge what was seen as an overly favorable view about entry. See, for example, von Weizsäcker (1980).

[14] See, for example, Kaplow and Shapiro (2007, 1079–80, 1089, 1093–94, 1098).

ficiency enough to justify the additional production costs. Freely permitting price fixing, however, would be a poor solution because then the additional fixed costs would be incurred but there would be no price reduction and thus no offsetting benefit. If no subsidization were possible, it would sometimes be better than nothing to allow a supracompetitive yet less-than-monopolistic price, which again might require direct regulation. Hence, although in some cases entry might otherwise be insufficient, permitting price fixing is not likely to be an attractive solution.[15]

Turn now to industries with differentiated products. With product heterogeneity, as mentioned, additional entry not only influences price, creating the business diversion effect just discussed, but also enhances

---

[15] Some have suggested to me that a prohibition on interdependent price elevation might be undesirable because of the problem in covering fixed costs. One could imagine that this point might hold in some cases, but it is difficult to see it as a general argument in favor of the proposition. Whenever interdependent behavior cannot succeed without elaborate communications, such as through a classic cartel (which might not succeed in any event), this argument entails allowing explicit price fixing. Perhaps such would be desirable, assuming that somehow price would be elevated only moderately, but no one seems to favor it. If exceptions are required, it is generally thought best to allow them through special legislation, perhaps authorizing price regulation—in part for the reason noted in the text, that price elevation to the monopoly level ordinarily induces excessive entry. In any case, whatever permission, if any, should be offered to cartels would naturally be extended to looser forms of interdependence, which, when successful, may or may not result in a degree of price elevation that produces results superior to those under an unpermissive regime. The core idea is that the fixed-cost problem does not in itself distinguish among the means by which successful oligopolistic coordination may be accomplished. Perhaps there might be cases that could be identified in which pure interdependence would result in modest price elevation, on average—a level that was in the neighborhood of "just right"—whereas a stronger cartel would cause excessive elevation. Of course, there also might be others (ones with less conducive conditions) in which it is the stronger cartel that provided approximately the right inducement whereas pure interdependence would be insufficient. More broadly, a permissive approach tends to allow significant price elevation in some industries, those particularly conducive to coordination, and little or none in others—not an intermediate level in all industries and certainly not an intermediate level in just those industries where such might be desirable.

The view that the difficulty of covering fixed costs justifies legal permission of interdependent price elevation is also inconsistent with standard merger policy, wherein the prospect that mergers may render coordinated price increases more likely is uniformly viewed as a reason for prohibition, never as a defense. Similarly, mergers that significantly increase unilateral market power are condemned for that reason, again with no exception for cases in which price elevation will help cover fixed costs. Such a policy is also applied to facilitating practices, examined further in section 10.C.

product variety, which consumers tend to find valuable. Moreover, since the total value of enhancing variety includes inframarginal surplus that sellers do not ordinarily capture, the incentive to add varieties is socially suboptimal. Combining these effects, entry may be excessive or inadequate relative to the level that maximizes social welfare.[16]

It is useful to consider two of the factors that influence which case is likely to prevail. The first concerns the price level. As price elevation becomes larger, entry and thus variety increase. Note in particular that, starting at a price equal to marginal cost, the business diversion effect is unimportant (as explained above), so the only effect would be increased variety. Some price elevation will accordingly be desirable in terms of total welfare. In this regard, recall from section A that deadweight loss is negligible as price increases just above marginal cost, so the overall trade-off in terms of total welfare would be favorable. (However, the marginal loss to consumer welfare from price elevation is greatest at this point, so the tradeoff would not necessarily be favorable if the social concern is only with consumer welfare.) When price elevation is substantial, the business diversion effect becomes larger; moreover, the marginal benefit from additional variety would tend to be smaller. This combination indicates that significant price elevations will more likely be associated with socially excessive entry, in addition to the allocative inefficiency that results from price being above marginal cost.

The second factor concerns the degree of product heterogeneity, that is, the magnitude of consumers' benefit from product variety. Clearly, the greater this benefit, all else equal, the more likely entry will be insufficient rather than excessive. Put another way, incremental entry, at any given

---

[16] In addition to Mankiw and Whinston (1986), see Spence (1976), Dixit and Stiglitz (1977), Tirole (1988, ch. 7), Vives (1999, ch. 6), and Fershtman and Pakes (2000). Product differentiation and entry have been studied in a variety of models that differ in terms of assumptions about consumer demand, which embody preferences for variety, and about competitive interactions, which influence the degree of price elevation, which in turn can yield quite different results in terms of whether entry is excessive or insufficient. Regarding the latter, some form of monopolistic competition is typically assumed, with price elevated above marginal cost but well short of the collusive optimum. Vives (1999, 176) offers the view that "[i]n summary, and contrary to a tradition in the literature, with excessive reliance on the constant elasticity model, excess entry does appear to be a robust phenomenon arising in a range of very plausible models."

point, will be more valuable. In this regard, it is important to recall that, when differentiation is substantial, successful oligopolistic coordination is less likely, making this case of less practical interest when analyzing price fixing. Of most relevance will be cases with only modest differentiation, where results seem unlikely to diverge substantially from those with homogeneous products, where entry tends to be excessive.[17]

This point is particularly apt with regard to more informal modes of oligopolistic coordination to the extent that the feasibility of such coordination depends even more on there being little or no product heterogeneity. Viewing this point from the opposite perspective, coordination that turns out to be socially desirable due to enhanced product variety will likely involve more explicit and elaborate means of coordination. Hence, banning only such coordination while permitting informal coordination (in accord with the commonly advanced view) can hardly be justified by reference to this dynamic consideration. (See section 16.B.) In other respects, however, the dynamic effects of oligopolistic price elevation on entry are largely independent of whether such elevation is achieved purely through interdependence or through more explicit sorts of communication.

2. Investment

Entry is just one form that investment may take. Viewed more broadly, elevated prices tend to reward whatever activities lead firms to be in a position to charge prices in excess of marginal cost or to capture a larger share of the market when doing so. That the allocative inefficiency of supracompetitive pricing may often be outweighed by the dynamic gains from investment induced by the prospect thereof constitutes the classic justification for intellectual property rights. More broadly, recognizing the function of profits in a market economy, many competition regimes, such as that in the United States, tend to tolerate monopoly pricing as long as the monopoly position was obtained and is maintained through efficient behavior—producing products that consumers value and selling

---

[17] Spence (1976, 234) states, "Given monopolistically competitive pricing, high own price elasticities and high cross-elasticities create an environment in which monopolistic competition is likely to generate too many products."

them at sufficiently attractive prices—rather than through exclusionary practices.[18] Likewise for unilateral market power short of monopoly, as elaborated in section 14.A. This permissive approach is not without costs; ex ante incentives can be excessive,[19] and ex post payoffs, with accompanying allocative inefficiency, may be greater than is necessary to induce investment. Hence, intellectual property rights tend to be limited, and direct regulation of monopoly is sometimes imposed. However, the typical judgment behind competition regimes is that, in typical settings, monopolies or other firms with unilateral market power should be permitted to price as they wish, although the degree to which this view is accepted varies across jurisdictions.

Price elevation achieved by interdependent behavior among oligopolists is qualitatively different in this regard. Such price elevation does not reward firms to the extent that they outperform their competitors but instead bestows profits whose magnitude depends on firms' success in refraining from competition.[20] To be sure, the prospect of such rewards will induce a variety of ex ante investment behavior. In addition to entry, already discussed, firms might expand their production facilities if they expect their capacities to have a positive effect on their share of oligopoly rents,

---

[18] See, for example, United States v. Aluminum Co. of America, 148 F.2d 416, 430 (2nd Cir. 1945): "The successful competitor, having been urged to compete, must not be turned upon when he wins."; and United States v. Grinnell Corp., 384 U.S. 563, 570–71 (1966), which refers to "the willful acquisition or maintenance of that [monopoly] power as distinguished from growth or development as a consequence of a superior product, business acumen, or historic accident."

[19] See note 12. They may also be inadequate: Firms, even monopolies, cannot ordinarily engage in perfect price discrimination (due to difficulties of identifying consumers' valuations and the problem of arbitrage), so they do not capture all consumer surplus, which makes it possible that investments with social benefits to direct consumers that exceed investment costs will be forgone because even the prospect of (non-price-discriminating) monopoly profits is insufficient. Compare the discussion in subsection 1 of insufficient product variety. When there are positive externalities, investment also may be insufficient—but, with negative externalities, there is an additional reason that it may be excessive.

[20] Unilateral market power by oligopolists must be distinguished. See chapter 14. Demsetz (1973, 3) offers a classic statement of the ex ante investment benefits of the prospect of market power and their inapplicability to coordinated oligopolistic pricing: "To destroy such power when it arises may very well remove the incentive for progress. This is to be contrasted with a situation in which a high rate of return is obtained through a successful *collusion* to restrict output; here there is less danger to progress if the collusive agreement is penalized."

and this expansion would be wasteful if the additional capacity would remain idle. Similarly, some activities, like advertising, may be zero-sum to an extent. However, other types of investment are socially valuable, such as product improvements and cost reductions. Yet, even regarding the more useful activities, the reward from oligopoly pricing will substantially reflect the firms' ability to abstain from competition rather than the merits of their prior investments. Thus, although permitting oligopolistic price elevation may produce some dynamic gains, there is insufficient nexus to justify price coordination.[21]

Furthermore, coordinated oligopolistic price elevation reduces potential dynamic benefits. When some oligopolists are more efficient or offer products superior to those of others, successfully coordinated pricing tends to dampen the tendency of better firms to serve an increasing share of consumers. Relatedly, economies of scale are not fully realized by successful oligopolists. Firms also have less incentive to become more efficient and innovative in the first place because they may not greatly benefit from such activity unless they will be willing to defect from the interdependent arrangement, which they will be reluctant to do if the oligopoly profit margin is substantial. Moreover, even when they do defect, they compare their resulting profits to artificially elevated profits in the scenario in which they fail to innovate and do not defect; hence, the ex ante incentive is still reduced. Another point, mentioned in section A, is that successful interdependent oligopoly pricing can be worse than old-fashioned explicit cartels because the latter might be able to rationalize production and thus achieve some efficiencies that will not result from mere coordinated price elevation.

Competition laws may allow competing firms to merge or enter into joint ventures precisely because of the potential to realize efficiencies;

---

[21] Schmalensee's (1989, 989) observation about empirical evidence on oligopolistic industries is not encouraging with regard to the dynamic and productive efficiency consequences of rewarding oligopoly pricing. "The shortcomings of accounting data might account for the apparently stronger association between concentration and price than between concentration and profitability. Another explanation might be that costs in concentrated industries tend to be above minimum levels. This would occur if rent-seeking efforts to attain or protect monopoly power elevated costs in these industries substantially, if non-price competition were generally sufficiently intense to erode profits, or if high prices in concentrated industries tended to attract inefficiently small producers."

however, such actions are subject to review in order to verify that anticompetitive effects are negligible or perhaps are justified in light the efficiency gains. Coordinated oligopoly pricing incurs the costs without
producing these benefits. Finally, note once again that none of the foregoing analysis (except the production rationalization point on explicit cartels) suggests any direct distinction between unaided, albeit successful
oligopolistic interdependence and price elevation achieved through explicit communication.[22]

Before closing the analysis of dynamic effects, a brief comment on the
literature is in order. Some commentators have argued that plain interdependent oligopoly pricing should be permitted because price elevation
by monopolists is legal.[23] This claim is surprising: It overlooks the core
distinction just described. Competition law explicitly distinguishes and
subjects to tough sanctions the efforts by groups of firms to eliminate
competition among themselves, in contrast to the price-elevating behavior
of monopolists. Moreover, as just explained, this differential approach is
well founded.[24] A final reason the argument is puzzling is that the same
logic would legalize classic cartels—indeed, even legally enforced cartel
prices; after all, a monopolist can legally force its employees to charge the
price it commands—yet those advancing the argument roundly condemn
express price fixing.

---

[22] A speculation is that the possible investment benefits from price elevation may tend to
be greater when appropriability is more difficult, which would tend to be true in less concentrated industries, and these are the settings in which more elaborate communications are often
thought more likely to be necessary. See chapters 6 and 17.

[23] See, for example, Areeda and Hovenkamp (2003, 232, 272) and Turner (1962, 668): "It
would make no sense to deprive lawful oligopolists—those who have achieved their position
by accidental events or estimable endeavor—of the natural consequence of their position if
the lawful monopolist is left with his." Turner's argument is criticized in Lopatka (1996,
854–55).

[24] Another important distinction concerns the administrative ability to identify and regulate
price elevation by monopolists versus oligopolists, the latter being the subject of chapters 10
and 11 as well as part III.

9

Framework for Decision-Making

🌿

The problem of controlling coordinated oligopolistic price elevation is, in general terms, little different from that in any other setting in which legal sanctions are employed to regulate harm-causing behavior. However, because there exists only limited systematic analysis of optimal regulation in situations in which decision-making errors are a central concern and there has been essentially none with regard to coordinated oligopoly pricing, this chapter begins by elaborating the appropriate decision-theoretic framework as it applies in the present context. Next, additional attention is devoted to the cost of false positives, namely, the chilling of desirable behavior, a concern that strongly motivates past discussions of price-fixing rules but almost always remains implicit, which makes it difficult to assess its importance and how the magnitude of the problem is influenced by the nature of the rule that is adopted.[1] The foregoing

---

[1] For example, although Posner offers the only substantial direct assessment of competing regimes for addressing oligopolistic price elevation, devotes significant attention to the problem of detection, and seems implicitly concerned about false positives, his latest treatment (like the others) barely mentions what the costs of his proposed regime or others might be. In perhaps his only specific remark on the subject, Posner (2001, 98) mentions without further elaboration that "[a] subtle objection to my suggested approach is that it might discourage entry into monopolistic, duopolistic, or other highly concentrated markets"—not even indicating whether this supposed problem is a possible cost of successfully deterring actual oligopolistic price elevation or arises only if false positives are anticipated to be likely. Turner's (1962, 669–71) seminal article advocating a narrow price-fixing prohibition devotes scant attention to the actual costs of a more encompassing approach. Even more notable, Areeda and Hovenkamp's (2003, 227–34) three-hundred-page treatise volume mentions but does not significantly elaborate the direct or indirect costs of a broader prohibition of the sort Posner advocates. Among the few other direct statements in the literature is Cohen and Scheffman (1989, 352–56), who express concerns about overdeterrence arising from too high a level of sanctions for antitrust

analysis provides a lens through which one can view evidence pertaining to the prevalence of oligopolistic price elevation, a question of clear importance since the empirical magnitude of the problem bears on how aggressive the policy response should be.

A. Elaboration

If detection of successful oligopolistic interdependence was perfect—that is, if all such behavior was detected and no innocent behavior was misclassified—and it also was costless, then the only question would be how to set sanctions optimally, the subject of chapter 13. This proposition does assume that all such behavior is detrimental. The analysis in chapter 8 notes some qualifications; that is, there may be instances in which it would be optimal to permit some coordinated price elevation, assuming such cases could readily be distinguished from others. Most of the discussion in this part of the book, however, sets that concern to the side and proceeds on the supposition that it is optimal to deter coordinated oligopolistic price elevation.

A substantial challenge remains because detection of successful coordination, examined in chapters 10 and 11, is inevitably imperfect. Accordingly, a central question—probably the most difficult and important one regarding coordinated oligopoly pricing—is deciding how much of what sorts of evidence in various contexts should be deemed sufficient for a finding of liability. It is essential, therefore, to specify the proper framework for making this determination. Although the method is largely generic, it is worth spelling it out in order to focus subsequent analysis because it has not been much elaborated in legal or economic literature and because the framework is not straightforward in light of the fact that error costs are primarily in terms of effects on ex ante behavior, which itself is endogenous to the legal regime.[2]

---

violations generally. The first two of their examples—chilling activity such as that in Broadcast Music, Inc. v. Columbia Broadcasting System, 441 U.S. 1 (1979), and discouraging resale price maintenance—seem largely orthogonal to the problem of mistaken application of sanctions (as distinguished from consciously forbidding activity that may have benefits), and their third—reducing pressure on subordinates to maximize profits out of fear that they may do so by price fixing—is not developed.

[2] The analysis in this section draws heavily on Kaplow (2011, 2012a).

First, consider situations in which firms have in fact engaged in coordinated oligopolistic price elevation. The primary benefit of a regime that assesses liability in such circumstances is deterrence. That is, the social benefit derives from such behavior occurring less often in the first place, and the prospect of sanctions for such behavior, taking into account their probability and magnitude, will tend to deter it. That the actual application of sanctions after the fact is not in itself central can be appreciated by considering a perfectly operating regime that succeeds in deterring all such price elevation. No successful prosecutions would occur, yet all the benefits of preventing harmful behavior would be obtained. In contrast, if there was no deterrence, price fixing would be widespread; there might be many successful prosecutions, but to no avail. This state of affairs would prevail if sanctions were sufficiently low that even detected price fixing remained profitable.[3]

Against this background, it is clear that the social cost of false negatives—failures to identify price elevation that has in fact occurred—is the loss of deterrence. That is, deterrence will tend to fall the more one insists on stronger proof, whether by requiring that particular means be employed or by insisting that the degree of confidence, however achieved, be higher. The extent of the deterrence reduction will depend on a number of factors. Suppose, for example, that some essentially random fraction of cases of actual price fixing result in detection failure—whether because no one notices the price elevation or because it cannot successfully be demonstrated in adjudication. In that event, expected sanctions for all oligopolistic price elevation would fall. If sanctions were sufficiently high that such activity was still unprofitable, there would be no welfare loss.[4] Relatedly, if it was possible to raise sanctions to make up for the detection deficit, there again would be no difficulty. Because there are often limits to how high sanctions can be (firms will be judgment proof beyond a certain point, for example) and because there are also costs in trying to identify and prosecute acts of price elevation (so raising the probability is not costless), it seems likely that insisting on greater certainty of proof

---

[3] The possibility of injunctions against future price fixing remains, but, as section 13.C discusses, even these will be ineffective unless the sanctions for violating the injunctions are themselves high enough to deter the behavior, raising the question of why such higher sanctions are not employed in the first instance.

[4] Section 13.A addresses how optimally to set the level of fines and damage awards.

will involve some loss in deterrence due to the larger portion of false negatives that result. Some of the evidence in section C and in subsection 13.A.3 suggests that many regimes currently fall short in deterring price fixing, although the extent to which such could be remedied with stiffer penalties rather than a higher frequency of applying sanctions in adjudication is unclear.

Of additional concern, failures in the detection of oligopolistic price elevation will not be entirely random. Most means of detection will be more effective in some settings than in others. Moreover, firms are likely to have some sense of these differences ex ante. Accordingly, if some methods of proof are readily allowed but others are restricted (they may be disallowed or subject to high proof standards), it may well be that certain groups of firms will be deterred and others not. Further raising the magnitude of sanctions may primarily boost expected sanctions on the former, where there may be little or no deterrence deficit, while having little effect on the latter, which is where the problem lies.[5] Raising deterrence for these undeterred firms may accordingly require permitting more encompassing means of proof.

In assessing the social welfare consequences of deterrence failure, it is necessary to consider not only how frequently oligopolistic price elevation will arise but also the magnitude of price elevations. It is socially more important to deter significant price elevations than small ones. Both deadweight loss and consumer welfare reductions are greater when price is further above marginal cost. And, as the numerical illustrations in section 8.A show, the rate of increase in lost total surplus (deadweight loss) is rising in the extent of price elevation; hence, if total surplus is the social objective, large price increases are disproportionately of concern. Likewise, regarding dynamic efficiency, any marginal benefits from price elevation in terms of increased product variety or otherwise are probably falling in the extent of the elevation, whereas costs of excess entry are rising. (Recall that the business diversion effect depends on the extent to which price exceeds marginal cost.) Hence, it is probably much more

---

[5] This point is particularly relevant to part III, which compares the approach presented in this part of the book to the commonly advocated narrower approach that exonerates oligopolistic price elevation in certain settings. Obviously, raising penalties will not deter groups of firms that are effectively immune from them.

socially important to deter significant price elevations than small ones.[6] Moreover, as will be elaborated in section 12.A, attempting to deter small elevations probably entails relatively greater risks in terms of false positives, the subject considered next.

Second, consider firms that have not engaged in oligopolistic price elevation. The prospect of sanctions may tend to chill (discourage) beneficial activity in settings in which firms anticipate that their actions generate a substantial risk of false positives.[7] It is familiar that, if certain medical procedures involve a high risk of malpractice liability even when doctors behave properly, doctors may refrain from such procedures although they are beneficial. Commentators, courts, and enforcement agencies that have been reluctant to take too aggressive an approach toward coordinated oligopoly pricing seem to have this sort of concern in mind. The point is especially significant if evidence that all firms in an industry engaged in similar or identical pricing behavior is taken to be proof of price fixing, or close to it, for such behavior is the norm even among perfect competitors. Logically, such evidence does not even begin to make the case for coordinated oligopolistic price elevation.[8] What is less obvious is just what chilling effects would look like when more sensible but nevertheless imperfect approaches to identifying oligopolistic price elevation are employed. Accordingly, this subject is examined further in section B and is revisited in section 12.A.

---

[6] A caveat, already noted, is that if concern is limited to consumer surplus, then even though large price increases are worse than small ones, the harm rises less than in proportion (so it would be more important to deter five cases each with a 5% price elevation than to deter a single case with a 25% elevation); however, the point to follow in the text about false positives would remain (although false positives themselves may be viewed as less costly if the concern is limited to consumer surplus).

[7] False positives may also reduce the deterrence of oligopolistic price elevation, which will be discussed at the outset of section B.

[8] Pricing patterns are explored further in section 10.A. Note as a preliminary matter, though, that identical or very similar pricing and price movements are not even suspicious in many instances. What actually requires more explanation are prices that do not move together, for neither perfect competitors nor well-coordinated oligopolists would so behave. Price differences may reflect some combination of product differentiation, cost differences (including cost shocks that affect firms differently), different information, or perhaps deviation from an implicit or explicit price agreement.

The cost-benefit calculus in setting proof burdens involves a tradeoff of deterrence benefits and chilling costs. Requiring more compelling proof as a predicate for assigning liability will tend to reduce both deterrence benefits and the costs of chilling desirable behavior. Likewise, greater openness to less definitive proof will enhance deterrence and amplify chilling effects. The problem is more complex than may be apparent given the variety of types of relevant proof, as will be explored in chapters 10 and 11. Furthermore, the optimal balance depends importantly on empirical questions concerning the extent of the oligopoly pricing problem and its responsiveness to changes in expected sanctions, on which the limited available information is surveyed in section C, and also on the magnitude of chilling effects associated with different regimes, about which little is known.

To further clarify, most of the discussion to follow will assume that the burden of proof is not in a range at which the marginal deterrence benefits of a slightly lower proof burden are negative (which is analytically possible because one sort of chilling effect is the chilling of abstention from coordinated price elevation). Such tends to be suboptimal because raising the proof burden would both enhance deterrence and reduce chilling. It will similarly be helpful to use the term deterrence benefits to refer to net deterrence benefits and to use the term chilling costs to refer to the suppression of other sorts of desirable behavior (that is, other than mere abstention from price elevation).

Note that it is easy to be misled about the effectiveness of a legal regime—for price fixing or any other harmful behavior—if one looks, as is often done, at the systems' outputs, such as the number of successful prosecutions or the fraction of cases that seem to have been correctly decided. Because the most important benefits and costs are in terms of ex ante behavior, it follows that such ex post outcomes provide a highly misleading indicator of whether a system is well designed and effectively functioning. To illustrate this point, consider some simple numerical examples. Suppose that there are 1,000 markets that can generate potential cases. Under one regime, 90% of true instances of price elevation are detected and punished, whereas liability is mistakenly assessed in 2% of cases in which there is no price elevation. Finally, assume that deterrence is quite effective in this regime, so that coordinated oligopolistic price elevation occurs in only 10 of the 1,000 markets. Since 90% of those 10 cases are subject to sanctions, there will be 9 convictions consisting of true positives, and, correspondingly, 1 false negative. In the 990 markets with no price elevation, the 2% error rate suggests that approximately 20 false positives will arise. The small absolute number of successful prosecutions and the ratio of 20 false positives to 9 true positives, more than 2 to 1, may look quite disturbing. Yet deterrence is substantial, and the 2% false positive rate may entail little chilling of desirable conduct.

Suppose next that this high false-to-true positive ratio prompts a tightening of the burden of proof. As a consequence, false positives fall to only 1%, and in cases in which price elevation does occur, the punishment rate falls to 80%. That is, the false positive rate is halved and the false negative rate is doubled. Furthermore, imagine that the lower punishment rate significantly erodes deterrence, such that there are now 100 instances of price elevation. Given the 80% punishment rate, there are 80 true positives (and 20 false negatives). Of the 900 instances with innocent behavior, the 1% false positive rate translates into 9 false positives.[9] The ratio of false to true positives is now 9 to 80, or about 1 to 9—equivalently, 2 to 18, which is 20 times more favorable than before (when it was over 2 to 1).[10] Put another way, initially almost 70% of instances in which sanctions were applied were mistakes; now that percentage is barely over 10%, so the fraction of mistaken convictions in the total has fallen to nearly 1/7 of its prior level.

But is the second scenario substantially better? Or little better? Or even possibly much worse? Deterrence has fallen greatly; there are 100 rather than 10 settings with coordinated oligopolistic price elevation, so harm is on the order of 10 times higher. How about the cost of chilling effects? The number of false positives has fallen from 20 to 9, on a base of nearly 1,000, so there is some gain, but one that may well be small, perhaps negligible, in terms of the welfare loss from the chilling of desirable behavior. Note also that, although not the focus of this chapter,

---

[9] That the number of false positives falls when the burden of proof in adjudication is increased need not hold in general. For example, the resulting decline in deterrence may lead enforcers (public or private) to be more aggressive, sweeping more cases (including more true negatives) into the system, so even if adjudication produces a lower false positive rate per true negative that it processes, the total number of false positives could rise. For other possibilities, see Kaplow (2011, 2012a).

[10] More precisely, it was 20 to 9, which is 2 to 0.9, and 18 is 20 times 0.9.

administrative costs may well be higher under the latter scheme with its tougher burden of proof: Because of the resulting decline in deterrence, the total number of positives, true and false, rises from 29 to 89. Whichever regime turns out to be best, it is clear that the ratio of false to true positive findings—or more broadly any ex post assessment of cases that actually arise—provides a significantly distorted picture of the relative desirability of the two regimes. Instead, the primary determinants are the magnitudes of the favorable and undesirable ex ante effects on behavior.

Accordingly, much of the analysis in the remainder of this book, especially in chapters 10, 11, and 17 on detection, must be understood by reference to the foregoing discussion. All else equal, greater accuracy will be desirable, for it is possible in principle to set the burden of proof so that both false negatives and false positives are reduced, enhancing deterrence and reducing chilling costs. However, references such as to whether one or another inference is more likely, which implicitly refer to the civil burden of proof in the U.S. legal system, should not be interpreted literally. That proof cutoff is both arbitrary and reflects an ex post view rather than considering the ex ante effects regarding deterrence and chilling. Put another way, the commonly held view that it makes sense to try to "get it right" in any given adjudicated case is not a prescription that can be grounded in a decision-making framework concerned with how legal rules affect social welfare. These broader points are the subject of other research.[11] For the present, the central point is that it is necessary to focus on the consequences of choices regarding the mapping from evidence to liability for deterrence and the chilling of desirable behavior, not for meeting target ex post likelihoods that the outcome in a given case is correct.

The approach outlined in this section assesses the importance of errors, both false positives and false negatives, in terms of their effects on social welfare. There are two important respects in which this method departs from most prior analyses of the subject. First, errors are sometimes viewed as if they are intrinsically bad, and the manner of specifying their weight is mysterious. Even if one sets aside the previously described problem—that relative ex post error frequencies provide a highly misleading indication of the effectiveness of a legal system—it remains unclear how most

---

[11] See Kaplow (2011, 2012a).

commentators imagine the importance of either type of error to be determined.

Second, errors are often understood by reference to a formal legal criterion, even when that criterion itself may have been chosen because it is a proxy indicator of which behavior should be sanctioned. Most relevant for present purposes, as parts I and III discuss, many commentators endorse a legal standard that limits punishment to cases in which it can be established that certain forms of explicit communication were employed. Hence, the application of sanctions in a case where this standard is not met is regarded as a false positive. However, if certain classes of such supposedly erroneous findings entail the assignment of liability in settings in which coordinated oligopolistic price elevation in fact occurred—but without the requisite communications, or at least without proper proof thereof—these so-called false positives would be desirable, not detrimental, in terms of their effect on social welfare. The prospect of such liability would deter undesirable activity, not chill desirable behavior. Thus, when errors are viewed in a vacuum, there is the danger that, not only might the weights be wrong, but the sign with regard to welfare effects will sometimes be the opposite of what is denoted by designating the outcomes as erroneous. This hazard constitutes a further motivation for carefully attending to the actual nature of chilling effects, the topic of the next section, rather than thinking abstractly in terms of false positives.

In sum, the framework for decision-making advanced here is qualitatively different in many ways from the apparatus implicit in much prior analysis of the problem. As a consequence, the types of inquiries that are appropriate in evaluating how to detect and punish coordinated price elevation often diverge as well. Even when some of the same information is considered, the use to which it is put may be different. Relatedly, shifting the method of analysis leads one to examine different sorts of empirical evidence in trying to inform the design of an optimal regime.

B. Chilling Effects

The decision-making framework in section A indicates the importance of chilling effects as well as deterrence. Deterrence is familiar and often straightforward, at least conceptually, whereas chilling effects usually are not examined explicitly and sometimes are rather subtle. As further motivation for exploration, it seems that the possibility of chilling effects is a primary basis for the dominant view that price-fixing prohibitions should be narrowly circumscribed (what else might motivate constricting the prohibition?), yet the literature advancing this position had devoted virtually no direct attention to the subject.[12] Accordingly, this section offers a preliminary discussion of a number of possibilities. The overall concern about chilling effects should also be kept in mind when considering any type of evidence used to detect oligopolistic price elevation, the subject of chapters 10 and 11, as well as when examining detection under a communications-based prohibition, in chapter 17.[13] Moreover, because the subject is so central and yet so ignored, it is ripe for further research.

As a preliminary matter, it is useful to state two potentially adverse behavioral effects of enforcement that are not the focus here. First, as explored previously, some price elevation may be desirable—for example, by usefully contributing to product variety—so successful deterrence will sometimes be disadvantageous. As a matter of convenience and clarity, this is subsumed under deterrence, the net benefit of which is accordingly reduced (unless the problem can be avoided by allowing exceptions). This effect does not arise as a consequence of making errors in the detection of coordinated price elevation; rather, it is caused by the prospect of true positives.

Second, some of the cost associated with actual false positives is usefully grouped with deterrence as well. To illustrate, suppose that there is some probability that a firm will bear a price-fixing sanction without regard to how it acts. In this case, the net penalty from actually engaging in oligopolistic price elevation is reduced: This expected random sanction must be subtracted from the expected sanction attributable to true posi-

---

[12] See note 1.

[13] In addition, section 15.A will discuss administrative costs, including the prospect that innocent firms may face costly lawsuits. It is important to think about the chilling effects caused thereby. As a preliminary thought, it may be that the effects would be similar to those of mistakenly assessed liability and thus would depend on what behaviors (sudden, sharp price increases, price wars, and so forth) made such lawsuits more likely or more costly.

tives in order to determine the net expected legal cost of the undesirable activity.[14] Problems of this sort are most likely to arise if adjudication puts heavy weight on whether industry conditions are conducive to coordination and only modest weight on whether successful oligopolistic coordination is actually taking place. Such a strategy, it is clear, would undermine deterrence; insisting on proof of socially detrimental behavior rather than the existence of an opportunity is important, as will be elaborated in section 11.A.[15] Note, however, that the prospect of essentially random sanctions (or ones that are a function merely of background conditions) does not tend to discourage particular alternative behaviors,[16] the subject to which we now turn.

Whether and what sorts of chilling effects arise depend on what forms of proof are employed. Suppose, for example, that sudden, substantial price increases are considered as possible evidence of coordinated oligopolistic price elevation. The inference would, of course, be negated if there had just been a corresponding change in conditions, such as an increase in a common cost. For example, a freeze in Florida that destroys much of the crop of oranges would lead to a corresponding increase in wholesale and retail prices for oranges. But if no such explanation is available, the price increase may give rise to an inference of coordinated oligopolistic price elevation. This prospect, in turn, would discourage such price increases, but this effect is desirable: It is the deterrence achieved when true positives are anticipated.

False positives may occur in such cases, however, particularly when one considers that, in response to the foregoing mode of detection, oligopolistic firms wishing to raise prices might instead increase them

---

[14] See, for example, Png (1986) and Kaplow and Shavell (1994a). The analysis assumes that the expected sanction attributable to true positives is instead of rather than in addition to the random sanction that is independent of behavior. Which characterization applies depends on the source of the random sanction.

[15] Punishment based primarily on conditions is not entirely useless, for its prospect would discourage behaviors that tended to render conditions more conducive to coordination. Many such behaviors may be desirable, of course, but some—which are often discussed under the rubric of facilitating practices; see section 10.C—are not.

[16] It does discourage entry because a prospective entrepreneur who never starts a business will presumably escape sanctions.

gradually, making it more difficult to identify the price change as one due to coordination.[17] Gradual price increases are common, and it may be hard to determine whether they are in response to true cost shocks or instead constitute oligopolistic cleverness. This ambiguity makes false negatives and false positives more likely. The former reduce deterrence, encouraging oligopolistic firms to raise prices. The latter produce chilling effects.

To examine how such chilling might be manifested, suppose that firms in an industry see their costs rising and anticipate that this trend may continue for some time. Furthermore, imagine that this is an industry in which coordinated price elevation is plausible but is not taking place. Firms might fear that passing on their cost increases through price hikes would produce some risk of (erroneous) liability, particularly if their cost increases are hard to document. Rising prices of tangible inputs, like labor, materials, and electricity, would tend to be easy to verify, but perhaps the need to increase reserves for subsequent maintenance that has become more difficult due to heightened regulations would be more difficult to prove.[18] How might such firms react?

Since price increases are assumed to be the basis for the risk of mistaken liability determinations, firms in this predicament may raise prices less than they would otherwise. This moderation will tend to be inefficient because prices were taken to be competitive, not elevated, to begin with. In an industry with rising marginal costs, the need to restrain price increases would induce firms to reduce output relative to the level they would produce if they could increase prices appropriately. If all firms behave in this manner, industry output will be less than total demand, which is unsurprising since price is being set below the competitive equilibrium level. Necessarily, consumers' loss in surplus from the sales reduction exceeds the production cost for these units, so there is a net

---

[17] See note 15 in chapter 10 and the accompanying text.

[18] More broadly, as will be further explored in section 10.B, marginal cost is sometimes difficult for outsiders, including adjudicators, to ascertain. It may be overestimated (such as when fixed or joint costs are inappropriately allocated as marginal costs for the product in question) or underestimated (such as in the case in text or others in which costs are subtle or when joint costs are underallocated). Overestimation will tend to produce false negatives, and underestimation false positives.

social loss.[19] Note that consumer surplus obtained on units still sold would rise on account of the pricing restraint, this gain being a transfer from producers.[20] Another effect of the prospect of such pricing restraint is that entry in the industry would be less attractive because there would be less producer surplus to cover fixed costs. Although entry can be excessive—particularly in homogeneous goods industries, as subsection 8.B.1 explores—such excess arises when price is elevated above marginal cost. When prices are instead suppressed, entry is too little from a social perspective, and all the more so if there is also lost product variety.

Thus, the prospect of false positives from truly cost-justified price increases, when prices are otherwise at competitive levels, may have chilling effects—price and quantity reductions and reduced entry—that are socially detrimental. Nevertheless, as long as the degree of price suppression is small, these losses will be insubstantial: Deadweight loss from price suppression (like that from price increases) is zero at the margin when pricing initially is at marginal cost;[21] likewise, loss from insufficient entry in homogeneous goods industries will also initially be second order (although the loss from reduced variety in differentiated goods industries would be first order). However, if marginal cost was constant rather than rising, the problem could be much worse. The reason is that price suppression, beginning at a competitive level at which price equals marginal cost, would render production entirely unprofitable, inducing exit. At the point at which only a single firm remained—or if only one entered in the first place—this problem would

---

[19] The extent of the loss in consumer surplus would depend on how output was rationed; the lost surplus would be greater, for example, if the deficit was allocated randomly rather than primarily to the lowest-value potential consumers (the latter of which may arise if the highest-value users made the greatest efforts to obtain scarce goods, although such efforts may themselves be socially costly).

[20] Observe that if the social objective is taken to be the maximization of consumer surplus rather than total surplus, this chilling effect could be viewed as a virtue rather than a vice because (depending on the manner of rationing, as mentioned in the preceding note) the gain in consumer surplus due to lower prices could exceed the loss in consumer surplus due to fewer units being supplied.

[21] This statement oversimplifies in a manner suggested by the discussion in the preceding two notes concerning how the induced shortage is rationed. (The characterization is strictly valid only if the marginal units are the first to be forgone.)

vanish because a single firm cannot be guilty of coordinated price elevation. However, as a monopolist, this lone firm would not merely cover incremental costs, including any that may be difficult to document, but also charge a monopoly price.[22]

It is familiar that constant-marginal-cost industries, when there are fixed costs, pose a potential problem of natural monopoly, as do industries in which firms have declining marginal costs. Moreover, this problem exists aside from the present concern with false positives in the enforcement of an anti-price-fixing regime, as subsection 8.B.1 notes. The social response sometimes takes the form of public utility regulation, but it generally is not to permit private price fixing. A laissez-faire approach is not entirely without virtues, for as more firms enter, prices may come down somewhat as price elevation is more difficult to maintain, and it is possible that the benefit from such price reduction would outweigh the waste from excessive entry. But there is no particular reason to expect this scenario to prevail. In any case, it is hardly clear that an optimal response would be to permit whatever price elevation can be achieved without certain forms of explicit communications but to disallow all other price elevation.[23]

Consider next a case in which one or some—but not nearly all—firms in an industry enjoy sustained high profits as a consequence of charging prices that are well above average cost. It might appear that coordinated oligopoly pricing prevails. But another possibility (a false positive if liability were based on such evidence) is that such firms enjoy cost or other advantages over their rivals. If there is no coordinated price elevation, then such firms may be selling at marginal cost, despite appearances to the contrary: They may have rising marginal costs such that the marginal cost of much of their production is below the market price, which would explain why average cost is notably less than price. There may also exist other firms with smaller market shares or with significant sales at higher average cost. The prospect that the more efficient firms might be found

---

[22] As subsection 8.B.1 discusses, this situation would often be better than one with many firms charging an equally elevated price because in the latter case resources are wasted on the additional entry that results.

[23] This point is elaborated in some detail in note 15 in chapter 8.

liable would tend to discourage ex ante investments in cost reduction or quality improvement.[24]

To avoid such chilling effects, it seems important that assessments of cost focus on marginal rather than average costs. Moreover, in the setting just described, firms' costs may differ. If the market were in fact competitive, all firms will be equating the common market price to marginal cost, so marginal costs would be identical. However, since marginal cost may be difficult to measure, leading to the use of various proxies that perhaps more nearly indicate some measure of average cost, costs would appear to be different. In this case, adjudicators should look to the higher-cost firms. If their marginal costs, as best can be determined, more nearly equal the market price, then there may be little concern of coordinated oligopoly pricing. The more profitable firms would owe their success to efficiency, not price fixing.[25] This suggestion, however, poses dangers of false negatives, particularly when most sales are by a number of firms with lower costs—who may be pricing well above marginal cost due to successful oligopolistic coordination among themselves—while some sales are made by a competitive fringe of less efficient firms.[26] The problem is that, if such cases are to be identified and condemned, there may sometimes be false positives, giving rise to the prospect of chilling desirable ex ante investment.[27]

---

[24] For example, Whinston (2006, 54–55) observes, "Second, there is an important issue of ex ante incentives that our discussion has ignored so far. Firms will naturally avoid placing themselves in positions that trigger antitrust intervention, whether monetary damages or restructuring, and this may lead them to shy away from cost reductions or product improvements that might improve their margins." He does not, however, elaborate how it is that the prospect of antitrust intervention, particularly relating to price fixing, would create such perverse incentives.

[25] See Demsetz (1973), quoted in note 20 in chapter 8.

[26] The distinction between these two settings is that the latter involves a number of firms having nontrivial shares charging coordinated, elevated prices (although each may instead have rising marginal costs that limit the profitability of further output expansion), whereas the classic case of the former would be a single firm that is more efficient than all of its rivals. See section 14.A, on dominant firms' exercise of unilateral market power. When products are significantly differentiated, it may be more difficult to distinguish these situations, although the danger of oligopolistic price coordination tends to be notably less in such settings.

[27] Recall from section 8.B that not all reduction of ex ante investment due to the prospect

The most relevant lesson for present purposes is that detrimental chilling effects may arise as a consequence of the prospect of imposing sanctions for price elevation that is not in fact due to successful oligopolistic coordination but instead is in response to industry conditions, such as costs, that are difficult to ascertain. As will be discussed in section 12.A, it tends to be optimal to adjust proof requirements accordingly—perhaps, for example, by crediting ambiguous evidence of higher marginal costs, particularly when the degree of price elevation that must thereby be explained is modest.

There are, of course, other means by which coordinated oligopolistic price elevation might be proved, and it remains to consider whether they too may involve chilling effects. Many proof methods will be explored in chapters 10 and 11, which address various means of detection, but it is useful to mention some of them here to develop a broader view of chilling effects. For example, false positives would arise when a price drop that appeared to be evidence of a price war was in fact a competitive industry's response to a sudden decline in costs. Then there would be a chilling effect; specifically, firms would be reluctant to pass cost reductions on to consumers as quickly as they occurred, which would entail some loss in surplus.

A rather different route of demonstrating oligopolistic price elevation (although complementary to others) involves the use of internal evidence, such as firms' strategy memos that depict the reasons for their pricing behavior or their own measurement of marginal costs. In this instance, the main effect of the prospect of liability may be to induce firms actually engaging in coordinated oligopoly pricing to reduce their paper or electronic trail and to limit discussions to fewer employees.[28] The more murky is the evidence in general or the more an adjudicator must read between the lines of seemingly innocent statements to see if they are a cover for improper behavior, the greater the prospect for false positives. This concern may influence firms' behavior, as discussed previously, and it may also affect their internal practices. In trying to avoid creating possible

of liability is undesirable. Oligopolistic price elevation itself induces excessive investment (rent seeking). Such waste will tend to be discouraged by the anticipation of true positives.

[28] The feasibility of such restraint is discussed in section 11.B.

indicators of forbidden activity, they may say and write less, or they might be more explicit and record more, so that, for example, it will be clear that the reason for a price increase was that costs were higher, not that there was an understanding that a higher price charged by all firms would boost profits.

Evidence of traditional cartel behavior—written interfirm agreements and other focused interfirm communications about price—can involve issues similar to those raised by purely internal documents and statements. The more firms hide their behavior or communicate in code (see section 3.C), the more a factfinder will need to make conjectures about what actually transpired. These phenomena, in turn, raise the possibility of false positives and accompanying chilling effects. In addition to effects on firms' pricing behavior, firms might reduce contacts with competitors that may be mistaken for price-fixing meetings and the like. This avoidance behavior involves effective deterrence—such as when actual price-fixing communications are reduced—and chilling effects—to the extent that firms become reluctant to participate in valuable trade association activity, cooperate in standard setting, or enter useful joint ventures.

Yet another consideration regarding chilling effects is the manner in which sanctions are calibrated, a subject taken up in section 13.A. Briefly, suppose that sanctions are a direct function of the determined severity of the violation. For example, damages owed to injured parties in the United States (before trebling) are based on the product of the price elevation and the quantity sold during the period over which price fixing is demonstrated to have occurred. A consequence of this approach is that small price elevations will be met with low sanctions. Regarding chilling effects that arise when marginal cost is underestimated, the problem may often involve small estimated overcharges, which accordingly would result in small penalties and thus only modest effects on ex ante behavior. In contrast, under an approach that makes the penalty largely independent of the overcharge (a tendency under guidelines for fines in the United States and the European Union), relatively harsher sanctions will be levied in such cases, increasing the magnitude of chilling effects—and also producing less deterrence in cases with unusually large price elevations, which are less likely to involve false positives. The general point is that the magnitude of both chilling costs and deterrence benefits will depend not only on how liability is determined but also on how sanctions are assessed.[29]

The heterogeneity of possible chilling effects is great. Different channels of proof also vary substantially in their effectiveness. Accordingly, the overall problem of setting a proof burden that optimally trades off deterrence benefits and chilling costs is complex and multidimensional. In any particular case, there may be many channels of proof that differ in reliability and in the nature of the costs that may arise from misinterpretation, regarding both false negatives and false positives. The best approach in principle will ordinarily involve combining complementary types of evidence and according different weights to each so as to enhance deterrence while reducing chilling effects.[30] Unfortunately, it is difficult to determine the optimal approach both because of the inherent complexity of the problem and also due to the paucity of empirical evidence on many of the relevant phenomena, a subject to which we now turn. Nevertheless, it guides both present application and future research to have this explicit framework in mind rather than just a vague call for caution.

C. Empirical Evidence

The relevance of empirical evidence to determination of the optimal regime to address oligopolistic price elevation is apparent from the preceding discussion. On one hand, the purpose of such a regime is deterrence, so the extent of such price elevation in the economy and its responsiveness to the prospect of sanctions is central in considering how tough enforcement should be. On the other hand, the main force that optimally limits the intensity of enforcement is the concern for chilling effects, so it is important to know how likely false positives would be under different rules and what would be the behavioral effects from the anticipation of

---

[29] A further point, explored briefly in section 12.A, is that sanctions could, in principle, be scaled not only to the magnitude of the violation but also by the strength and type of proof used to establish it.

[30] Stated more formally, the optimal method of combining evidence is given by likelihood ratios (for true price coordination versus competitive behavior), as indicated by the Neyman-Pearson lemma.

such errors. Unfortunately, despite significant research on oligopoly pricing and studies of prosecuted cases, rather little is known. This section begins by noting some of the main empirical findings and then considers more thoroughly respects in which they do and do not illuminate the issues that need to be understood to formulate policy.

Empirical examination of the extent of oligopolistic price elevation in various industries in the United States peaked in the 1980s. Timothy Bresnahan's (1989, 1052–53) survey concludes that "[t]here is a great deal of market power, in the sense of price-cost margins, in some concentrated industries" and "[o]ne significant cause of high price-cost margins is anticompetitive conduct." A number of the studies reported (1051, tbl. 17.1) show industry price-cost margins in the neighborhood of 0.5, which indicates that price is double marginal cost; other industries have much lower margins. It is explained that the industries studied were not randomly selected but rather often were ones in which elevated pricing was suspected, an important reason for concluding (1051–53, emphasis added) that prices are significantly elevated in "*some* concentrated industries." Other surveys provide further evidence of price elevation in many industries and in various local markets.[31]

More detailed evidence is provided by studies of litigated—mostly government prosecuted—cases.[32] In these cases, there typically were highly explicit communications among the defendants, and coordinated oligopolistic price elevation was usually achieved. John Connor's (2007b, 59, 90, 94–95) broad survey of the literature finds that median measured overcharges, averaged over the period of such price-fixing conspiracies, were approximately 25%, with a mean of about 40%; nearly two-thirds

---

[31] See, for example, Hall (1988), Scherer and Ross (1990, 426–47), Schmalensee (1989), and Weiss (1989). Based on a review of historical evidence in the petroleum, automobile, tobacco, and airline industries as well as brief reports on many others, Brock (2006, 280) concludes, "Considered in this light, perhaps the inordinate degree of solicitude for oligopoly that has arisen in the courts and antitrust agencies is profoundly misplaced." As suggested by the analysis in section 8.B (see especially note 20, quoting Demsetz 1973), the fact that concentration is often associated with price elevation in oligopolistic industries does not negate the idea that the creation of concentration through firm growth may reflect efficient behavior. See, for example, Salinger (1990, 291, 310). As Brock (2006) suggests, concentration attributable to horizontal mergers may be viewed quite differently in this regard.

[32] See, for example, Connor (2007a, 2007b), Connor and Lande (2005), Harrington (2006), Hay and Kelley (1974), and Levenstein and Suslow (2006).

of the episodes had overcharges above 20%.[33] Overcharges were about a quarter lower in the United States and a quarter higher in the rest of the world (59, 90–92). Particularly notable cases involved international vitamins cartels in operation during the 1990s, examined in Connor (2007a, 338, tbl. 12.1), with total overcharges of nearly $9 billion in 2005 dollars, with almost a third in the United States.[34]

What do we learn, and fail to learn, from such studies? This question is best examined against a template indicating what information we in principle need in order to design a legal regime in light of the analysis earlier in this chapter.

Initially, we would like to know the extent of coordinated oligopolistic price elevation and how it varies with enforcement.[35] Even if there were

---

[33] This survey covers 259 publications involving 279 markets and 512 episodes, with 770 observations on average overcharges. In addition, Connor and Lande (2005, 540, 559–60) report mean and median overcharges in all published scholarly economic studies of cartels of 49% and 25%, and for all final verdicts in U.S. antitrust cases of 31% and 22%.

[34] Some have suggested that the inherent instability of cartels means that prolonged overcharges would be rare and thus that enforcement against price fixing may be unimportant and unwise. The figures reported in the text indicate otherwise. In this regard, it is of interest that the vitamins cartels generally ended either because, after many years of substantial overcharges, entry or fringe firm expansion eventually reduced cartel members' market power or, more often, because of enforcement activity; apparently, none of these cartels ended due to an inability to maintain internal cohesion. Connor (2007a, 318–19) notes further that the shorter-lived cartels had a mean duration of nearly four years. Such evidence also casts doubt on earlier studies that failed to find that price-fixing prosecutions led to price reductions in those very cases. For example, Asch and Seneca (1976) found that firms prosecuted in 1958–1967 were largely unprofitable to begin with, and Sproul (1993), in a sample of 25 of the 400 U.S. Department of Justice cases in 1973–1984, found that prices were 7% higher than predicted four years after indictment, a finding that is not reported as statistically significant and appears not to be. These findings and other, more encouraging evidence about the effects of prosecution are discussed in Whinston (2006, 26–38), and Motta's (2007, 315–16) review of Whinston takes a skeptical view of empirical evidence that casts doubt on the efficacy of price-fixing law. One explanation offered by Asch and Seneca (1976, 8) involves sample selection bias, specifically, that prosecutions might be most likely in cases of failed coordination while success remains largely invisible. The findings reported in the text suggest instead that, in broader samples of prosecuted cases, there is much successful coordination. Connor (2007b, 93) also points out that Asch and Seneca's sample period was one with low median overcharges.

[35] It is also necessary to know the resulting social cost: the deadweight loss from static allocative inefficiency, the extent of resources dissipated by excessive entry and other forms of rent-seeking, and also other effects, including positive ones, on firms' incentives. Likewise for chilling effects.

no direct enforcement, oligopolistic price elevation may not be rampant, for theory indicates that coordination is often difficult to effectuate even when sanctions are ignored, and history suggests that many markets seemed to behave fairly competitively despite the absence of competition law. It is also worth keeping in mind that the mere fact that laws make cartel agreements legally unenforceable has some effect, and possibly a significant one, in reducing the amount of coordinated price elevation.

The existing empirical evidence offers some illumination. Given the extent of oligopolistic price elevation and the number of successful prosecutions of explicit price-fixing arrangements involving substantial overcharges, it seems not only that, in the absence of enforcement, there would be a significant problem but that, even with substantial modern enforcement and penalties much stiffer than had existed in the past, the existing level of deterrence may be insufficient. Indeed, even detected and punished cartels may suffer only moderately or realize net gains.[36] Underdeterrence is compounded to the extent that detection is highly incomplete. To test this hypothesis and to estimate the probability of sanctions, a natural inquiry would determine what portion of industries and markets have been subject to prosecution from among those in which elevated oligopoly prices were identified independently of any enforcement activity. That is, much could be learned by combining the empirical industrial organization literature aimed at understanding oligopoly pricing, without attention to the legal regime, with studies of the operation of that regime that focus only on prosecutions. Limited evidence to date suggests that the probability of detection is quite low.[37]

---

[36] This is a theme of Connor (2007a).

[37] See Connor (2007a, 394 n.1), citing informal evidence from forensic economists and antitrust defense counsel speculating "that as few as 10% of all price-fixing conspiracies are investigated or prosecuted"; Bryant and Eckard (1991), estimating the probability of a U.S. federal indictment to be at most 0.13–0.17 per year, although these estimated probabilities are only for those conspiracies eventually caught; Connor (2008, 8–9 & n.20), citing studies supplementing Bryant and Eckard and reaching similar conclusions for the United States during 1990–2004 and for the European Union's prosecution of international cartels from 1969–2003; note 23 in chapter 13, mentioning Assistant Attorney General for Antitrust Ginsburg's estimate in 1986 that the probability is at most 10%; and Combe, Monnier, and Legal (2008), using Bryant and Eckard's method to estimate the probability in Europe to be approximately 0.13. An interesting indication of the detection rate in the early 1990s is suggested by data in Connor (2008, 6), which shows that about 6 international cartels were discovered per year in 1990–1995

To the extent that deterrence may currently be inadequate—and it is unlikely to be optimal in most competition regimes since the scope of laws, level of enforcement, and penalties vary widely—it is also necessary to know how the extent of oligopolistic price elevation varies with enforcement. Since enforcement, as just mentioned, differs across jurisdictions and there also have been important legal changes, particularly in penalties, within jurisdictions, it may be possible to identify incremental deterrence effects, although little such study has been undertaken.[38] One challenge in conducting such an investigation regards ambiguity in the law, particularly the law as actually enforced and as perceived some years beforehand by firms when deciding how to behave, both of which may diverge from hornbook statements.[39] The problem may be less serious regarding legal rules on the level of sanctions, although even on this dimension there is some ambiguity, as elaborated in subsection 13.A.3.

A significant complication is that there are multiple enforcement instruments, so there is no single measure of enforcement intensity that can capture all relevant effects. From a given (nonzero) level of enforcement, one can increase sanctions (within limits of feasibility and with

---

while the rate increased to about 33 per year in 2004–2007. Since the detection rate in the latter period cannot exceed 100%, and most suspect it to be far lower, and, moreover, since both detection efforts and penalties were substantially weaker in the earlier period (implying a far lower level of deterrence and thus a significantly greater incidence, ceteris paribus), a conjecture is that the detection rate in the early 1990s must have been extremely low.

[38] Clarke and Evenett (2003) identify smaller price elevations in jurisdictions with active and effective competition law regimes. Block, Nold, and Sidak (1981) find that increased enforcement intensity and private class actions reduce markups in the bread industry. Symeonidis (2002) analyzes the effects of the introduction in the United Kingdom of the 1956 Restrictive Trade Practices Act.

An observation is that expected sanctions are generally regarded to be higher in the United States than elsewhere, which explains why members of international cartels sometimes avoid the United States. See Connor (2007a, 67) and OECD (2005). The higher U.S. enforcement may make it hard to explain why overcharges are lower in the United States since one might think only very high price elevations would be attempted in light of the high sanctions. One possibility is that U.S. enforcement more heavily targets high-elevation situations. Another is that, as subsection 13.A.3 explains, government fines in the United States and European Union tend not to rise with the magnitude of the price elevation, leaving high-elevation cartels least deterred, which deficit, however, is offset in the United States (only) by private treble-damage suits that do fall heavily on high-elevation cartels.

[39] See section 6.F.

possible other costs, as discussed in section 13.A), which will increase deterrence but only to the extent of the existing probability of being sanctioned, which may well vary across settings. One can also adjust enforcement effort, involving preliminary identification as well as focused investigation aimed at ascertaining the truth and developing evidence in particular cases. Such expenditures will be more effective in some areas than in others, although the payoff may be higher where the challenge is greater because such settings are most likely to suffer from underdeterrence. That is, for given sanctions, deterrence may already be effective (or easy to make effective by raising sanctions) in realms where detection and prosecution are easy, but it may be inadequate (and not remediable simply through further penalty increases) where demonstration of violations is difficult. To assess this dimension (and also the next), it would be useful to identify both where successful coordinated oligopoly pricing now occurs (suggesting a deterrence deficit) and also where there has tended to be little enforcement.

Finally, a central focus of this part of the book is on proof requirements—what must be demonstrated with what degree of confidence to establish a violation—which are important determinants of deterrence. Like enforcement effort, these different dimensions are not perfect substitutes. For example, with regard to forms of behavior that are difficult to detect or are deemed to be immune, only changes in the prerequisites for establishing liability can have an appreciable impact on deterrence. Unfortunately, even if one ascertained which markets involved likely coordinated price elevation yet no enforcement, we would be unlikely to know the methods by which such price elevation was achieved or what evidence might be obtainable, so it would be difficult to gauge how various changes in the legal regime would influence deterrence in these settings.[40]

Studies of prosecuted cases, involving detected explicit communications, do provide some valuable information about the markets involved. As elaborated in section 6.E, most had small numbers of firms in highly concentrated industries selling homogeneous products. As with any

---

[40] Relatedly, some empirical evidence on price elevation does not distinguish unilateral market power from coordinated price coordination, which may be relevant, as chapter 14 elaborates.

evidence drawn from prosecuted cases, however, it does not tell us about other cases. One possibility is that there may be more settings with larger numbers of firms and less conducive conditions, although this possibility does not seem particularly likely unless such cases involve little prolonged overcharging, in which event their omission would be less important.[41]

Another, more important possibility is that there are a number of industries in which conditions are highly conducive to coordinated oligopolistic price elevation—small numbers, homogeneous products, and so forth—yet prosecutions do not occur, either because the behavior was undetected or because it could not be prosecuted due to limited evidence or on account of a view that only informal coordination occurred and such is legal.[42] Consider, for example, industries or markets identified in the empirical literature in which it appears that coordinated oligopolistic price elevation is present but there have not been price-fixing challenges. If indeed there was this sort of price elevation, we do not know how it was achieved, such as by pure interdependence or highly explicit communication. Nor do we know what evidence might have come to light if there had been a serious investigation. Accordingly, it is difficult to know the extent to which the features of prosecuted criminal cases—that were selected (in the United States) to meet a "beyond a reasonable doubt" proof standard and are probably thought to require direct and highly probative evidence of explicit, detailed, face-to-face communications[43]— are representative of the larger, submerged portion of the iceberg. Quite

---

[41] Hay and Kelley (1974, 24 n.15), as quoted in note 46 in chapter 6, explain that such settings require more communications and hence are more likely to be detected; therefore, their low incidence in the sample probably overstates their relative frequency.

[42] The latter possibility may not be empirically important. As elaborated in section 6.E, the finding that most prosecuted cases involve high concentration and homogeneous products seems inconsistent with the paradox of proof being applicable in a wide range of settings, for these are the sorts of industries where coordination is relatively easy and hence those in which firms would be most able to eschew the sorts of explicit communications that might be detected. Nevertheless, there may exist other industries in which coordination is even easier; it may therefore have been accomplished with behavior closer to pure interdependence, and accordingly no prosecution was brought.

[43] As discussed in section 6.E, we do not know what other acts may also have been used, and, perhaps more important, for proven acts, we do not know what their likelihood would be conditional on no such direct evidence being available, which is the relevant setting for interpreting other evidence (the subject of chapters 10, 11, and 17).

possibly, the studied cases constitute a highly skewed sample. Broader analyses of oligopoly pricing in the economy might provide some answers, but probably not regarding the means by which oligopolistic coordination is accomplished and the evidence of such means that might be obtainable.

Turning to chilling effects, the situation with regard to empirical knowledge is far worse. Essentially nothing is known about existing regimes or how changes in enforcement instruments would influence the nature and magnitude of such effects. Nor would it be easy to learn about these questions. It would be necessary to study firms that do not elevate prices, but might be confused for firms that do, in order to see how their behavior may be affected by their perceived probability of mistakenly being subject to sanctions. Some illumination might come from examining areas in which there have been government prosecutions or private cases alleging price fixing but where there does not appear in fact to have been coordinated price elevation.

Further complicating the matter, chilling effects will undoubtedly vary across enforcement dimensions. For example, if the proof standard is high, so that false positives are a negligible problem, raising sanctions will enhance deterrence and involve little cost in terms of chilling desirable behavior. However, as explained previously, deterrence may remain ineffective in areas where detection is more difficult or the means of effectuating oligopolistic coordination are currently deemed legal. When adjusting enforcement so as to increase deterrence there, chilling effects might be more important and need to be quantified in some way.

We have seen that, on many policy-relevant questions, there is little or no empirical evidence. Although this lacuna is due in part to the inherent difficulty of finding answers, it seems that some important issues could be illuminated by combining empirical knowledge across the two literatures, on oligopoly pricing generally and on price elevations in prosecuted cases. These topics, however, do not seem to be on existing research agendas, perhaps in part because of the failure of existing analytical work to identify more systematically what needs to be known in order to formulate intelligent competition policy in this domain.

10

Detection: Market-Based Evidence

✒

The central challenge in addressing coordinated oligopolistic price elevation is detection.[1] Because firms have incentives to hide their behavior to
the extent that it may be illegal, it will often be difficult to identify instances
of successful oligopolistic coordination. Relatedly, because an aggressive
approach may well be necessary, sometimes false positives will occur,
resulting in undesirable chilling effects. As a consequence, it is important
to consider all pertinent means of inference and figure out how to employ
them in complementary ways.

This chapter, as elaborated momentarily, focuses on evidence derived
from the observation of market conditions and behavior that bears on
the presence of successful oligopolistic coordination. In the next chapter,
section 11.A considers the degree to which industry conditions are conducive to successful coordination and also elaborates on the relevance of
this inquiry, which is particularly important in light of the contrast with
how such evidence is employed under a communications-based prohibition, a subject examined in depth in chapters 6 and 17. Section 11.B
explores evidence from within firms—whether records of strategy or
internal indicators of what is actually taking place in the market. Section
11.C discusses evidence on interfirm communications, which when present and sufficiently clear may well be decisive in demonstrating the existence of successful coordinated price elevation although its absence

---

[1] Posner (1969, 1578, 1583, 1593; 2001, 98–99) takes a similar view. He also voices some
optimism on the subject (1969, 1587): "If colluding sellers generate no such evidence, their
collusive efforts will not have amounted to much. Economically significant collusion should
leave some visible traces in the pricing behavior of the market, even granting fully the interpretive difficulties that such behavior presents."

does not negate such behavior because detailed interchanges may be unnecessary and in any event may remain hidden. (As a reminder, this part defers until chapter 14 the question of how the analysis of detection is affected by the possibility that some price elevation in oligopolistic industries is due to the unilateral exercise of market power rather than coordination.)

Taken together, the analysis suggests that confident identification of coordinated oligopolistic price elevation will sometimes be possible, but often the available evidence will be quite murky. In light of the latter possibility, section 12.A considers further how liability should be assessed under the decision-making framework articulated in chapter 9. The tradeoff of deterrence and chilling effects will depend on the types of evidence available, and some suggestions will be made about how to adjust methods of inference and proof requirements accordingly. Unfortunately, simple, across-the-board prescriptions are not possible.[2]

Turning attention now to the specific subject matter of this chapter, there are a number of ways to infer the existence of successful oligopolistic coordination using market-based evidence. The present treatment extends the substantial body of prior work in a number of respects:[3] It devotes greater attention to certain difficulties due to firms' strategic responses designed to mask their behavior, to possible synergies available from combining different indicators with each other and with other types of evidence, and to relative costs in terms of chilling effects, a subject that has been largely neglected. Regarding some factors that imply coordination, it is important to keep in mind that their absence may often negate its existence, where absence should be understood as not merely constituting ambiguity and difficulty of proof but rather demonstration of nonexistence.

Despite the overlap and interrelationship among them, indicators are usefully grouped in two clusters—pricing patterns and price elevation—which will be explored in turn. Certain pricing patterns, such as sharp

---

[2] This conclusion bears on appropriate enforcement institutions, as explored in section 15.A.

[3] See, for example, Baker and Bresnahan (1992, 2008), Bresnahan (1989, 1997), Harrington (2008a), Kaplow and Shapiro (2007, 1087–95), Perloff, Karp, and Golan (2007), Porter (2005), and Posner (2001, 79–93).

price increases unrelated to cost shocks or the sudden outbreak of price wars, may be indicative of oligopolistic coordination rather than competitive behavior. As will be emphasized, mere similarity of price movements and other parallel activity are not suspicious in this regard, a point about which there has been some confusion. Finally, various practices that may facilitate successful coordination will be discussed: They may be further indicators of coordination but also may be given independent legal significance. In particular, one may wish to regulate facilitating practices themselves, without requiring demonstration in a particular case that their use resulted in price elevation.

It is important to elaborate at the outset on the point that the manner in which the legal system is expected to make inferences will have a feedback effect on firms' behavior. The most obvious is deterrence itself: The purpose of punishing oligopolistic price coordination is to discourage firms from attempting it, and to the extent that deterrence is successful, there will be fewer indicia of successful price elevation. The further point is that firms that nevertheless continue to elevate prices will hope to escape detection and accordingly will adjust behaviors that might be held against them.[4] Sometimes, this may not be possible without giving up on or seriously interfering with oligopolistic coordination, in which case deterrence will have been achieved. But in certain instances, firms may be able to alter outward appearances without undermining their objective. Of course, then enforcers and adjudicators should be on the lookout for such modified behavior, leading to further responses. When firms are able to blend in, which is to say, behave in ways that are difficult to distinguish from competition, deterrence may not be possible. Also relevant in assessing a legal regime will be determining whether these behavioral responses themselves are desirable or detrimental.[5]

Finally, note that market-based means of inferring successful oligopolistic coordination do not generally reveal how success was achieved—notably, the existence, extent, and nature of any interfirm communications.

---

[4] See, for example, the sources cited in note 15.

[5] Conceptually, a legal regime can be viewed as assigning sanctions not to behavior, which often is not directly observed, but rather to patterns of evidence, that is, what an adjudicator can observe. See section 12.A. Since underlying behavior is associated (often nondeterministically) with evidence, any given mapping from evidence to sanctions will have a behavioral effect. An optimal regime consists of that mapping associated with the highest social welfare in light of the behavior the mapping induces (as well as administrative and sanction costs).

There may be direct evidence of such interactions and also indirect evidence and inferences, some of which may be based on the factors considered here. Even so, one often cannot directly tell what sorts of behavior contributed to the mutual understanding among the firms that produced price elevation or the conditions preceding the outbreak of a price war, for example.[6] This information limitation is not, however, problematic because, as chapter 8 elaborates, the social consequences of coordinated oligopolistic price elevation do not depend on this. Whether some methods of proof are to be privileged above others should reflect analysis of the pertinent inferences and application of chapter 9's framework. Accordingly, any special or exclusive relevance of interfirm communications, or any other indicator of coordinated pricing for that matter, is not to be determined a priori but instead needs to emerge from the appropriate functional analysis. Part III, especially chapter 17, compares the direct approach developed in this part with the commonly advocated alternative of deeming the use of certain forms of explicit communications to be determinative of liability. As will be seen there, and as already foreshadowed in chapter 6, the detection challenges under the latter, conventionally advocated method are even more daunting than under the direct approach pursued here.

A. Pricing Patterns

Certain pricing patterns may indicate successful oligopolistic coordination or a breakdown that implies its prior existence. Given the long history

---

[6] See, for example, Jacquemin and Slade (1989, 452), who, in discussing certain economic methods of identifying coordination, state: "it is impossible to distinguish pure tacit collusion from . . . explicit cartel agreements. What matters for the empirical estimates is the outcome and not the cause of noncompetitive pricing."; and Porter and Zona (2008, 1071): "As a matter of economics, it is difficult and perhaps impossible to distinguish between [interdependent oligopoly, conscious parallelism, tacit collusion, and explicit collusion] on the basis of outcomes alone." It is sometimes suggested that one occasionally can tell whether elaborate, explicit communications have occurred, particularly when behavior is especially sharp and precise (e.g., secret bids that are identical down to many digits). Even this point is overstated, for often the opposite inference might be made instead because, the more explicit were the communications, the more readily firms could have orchestrated their behavior so as to avoid leaving clear, visible tracks. See note 6 in chapter 5.

of confusion on this subject,[7] it is best to begin by emphasizing that the presence of parallel pricing and other shared behavior is not usually a symptom for the simple reason that ordinary competitive interaction also has this character. Indeed, when competition is vibrant, pricing and other behavior tend to be highly parallel.[8] When firms' costs increase, their prices rise and quantities fall. When demand increases, firms' prices and quantities both rise. When technology changes, consumers' locations or tastes shift, regulations are modified, and so forth, competitors react similarly, even identically. No doctor would view the fact that a patient is breathing as evidence of bronchitis (although it is a necessary condition); only atypical breathing (wheezing, coughing, shortness of breath) would be even prima facie symptomatic, warranting further examination. Likewise, it makes no sense to deem parallel pricing or other commonly undertaken behaviors as even indicative of coordinated oligopolistic price elevation since such activity is ubiquitous and, in particular, characterizes innocent competitive activity.[9]

---

[7] Such confusion may seem surprising because the main point is so obvious from the most elementary economic analysis—at a simple enough level that not even introductory study is required—and also because, in the United States, the Supreme Court emphatically rejected the conflation in Theatre Enterprises v. Paramount Film Distributing Corp., 346 U.S. 537 (1954), as discussed in subsection 4.B.1. Poor use of language may be partly responsible. See note 8. A group of economists filed an amicus brief in Twombly devoted substantially to the point that parallel behavior is commonplace, so that punishing it would be problematic. See Brief of Amici Curiae Economists in Support of Petitioner (April 6, 2006). (Recall that, in Twombly itself, also discussed further in subsection 4.B.2, the dispute involved the standard for surviving a motion to dismiss, which question is intimately related to the substantive legal test for liability—although such was not recognized in the Court's opinions—but involves separate issues as well.)

[8] The term "conscious parallelism" is often used. As explained in section 2.B, to the extent that it refers to parallel behavior of which firms are conscious, it is little different, for each competitor is ordinarily aware that, when it, say, must increase price because of a rise in the cost of some widely employed input, its competitors will behave similarly. But sometimes this terminology, or even parallelism alone, is used as a shorthand for interdependence, which is quite different. Likewise, the term "independent" is usually used to mean the opposite of interdependent but is sometimes used to include interdependence. See sections 2.B and 2.C, and see also section 5.B's discussion of plus factors (specifically regarding the implicitly presumed baseline from which these factors supposedly add).

[9] Contrast pricing that is not merely parallel across firms but identical, which arises, however, in situations in which there exists nontrivial heterogeneity, such as in product quality. As

The goal is to distinguish successful oligopolistic interdependence from competitive, independent, rivalrous behavior. As a logical matter, traits such as parallel pricing that are typically shared by both categories are not useful in drawing the distinction.[10] Instead, analysis should focus on behavior that is consistent with oligopolistic interdependence and inconsistent with competition, which favors liability, and behavior consistent with competition but inconsistent with interdependence, which disfavors liability. In short, we are concerned with the observational differences between competition and coordinated oligopolistic price elevation.

In considering pricing patterns that may support inferences of successful oligopolistic coordination, it is useful to analyze three phases: raising prices from a competitive to a supracompetitive level (or further escalating prices), maintaining elevated prices, and price drops, notably, as a consequence of price wars.[11] Initiation or enhancement of oligopolistic price elevation may be marked by a sharp price increase. However, sudden price increases can also occur in competitive markets, most obviously when there is a cost shock, such as a sudden increase in the price of oranges for grocery retailers or in the price of oil for sellers of gasoline. Accordingly, it is also necessary to check for concurrent cost increases or other changes, like sudden shifts in demand, that may explain the price increase.[12] When price increases are large and sudden and other

---

section C discusses, this pattern may indicate suppression of quality differences, which does tend to indicate coordination.

[10] Traits that appear to be common to neither are perplexing, unless they are shared by some third, omitted category. Because competition and oligopolistic price elevation are often the only two important hypotheses under consideration (putting to the side unilateral market power, the subject of chapter 14), evidence seemingly inconsistent with both may warrant further investigation to ascertain whether it may, after all, be consistent with one or another category of behavior (or perhaps both).

[11] The best methods may differ when detecting coordination in auctions, such as with government procurement. See, for example, Bajari and Ye (2003) and Porter (2005, 159–62). On the difficulty of detecting bid-rigging in auctions, in part because cartel members can submit phantom bids (for all but the member designated to win) that are devised to elude detection by announced techniques, see Porter and Zona (1993) and the discussion in note 6 in chapter 5.

[12] Demand shifts are not ordinarily sudden but they can be, such as in response to sharp price increases of substitutes, perhaps themselves attributable to cost shocks in other markets.

simultaneous changes of corresponding magnitude seem unlikely, coordinated oligopolistic price elevation is plausible.

Note that independent explanations must match the changes that have actually transpired. For example, under competition, increases in demand would ordinarily be associated, at least in the short run, with higher prices (assuming rising marginal cost) and firms each producing more (unless they are capacity constrained). In contrast, oligopolistic price elevation involves higher prices but reduced quantities. Accordingly, it is important to consider changes in output as well as in price when attempting to infer whether price increases are competitive or oligopolistic.

Cost shocks in competitive markets ordinarily result in higher prices and reduced quantities and thus appear more similar to coordinated oligopolistic price increases. Cost increases may be identifiable through examination of input markets and also the markets for other goods. Moreover, some cost shocks will not have common effects across firms and thus should be reflected in differential quantity reactions. For example, some firms may use more of certain inputs than others (transportation costs for certain inputs or for final products are an obvious example) or be subject to different changes in input prices (labor costs and rental prices tend to differ geographically).

There are, however, a number of reasons that coordinated price increases may not be sudden and sharp. One is that oligopolists may increase their prices in smaller steps because they do not fully trust each another. Perhaps a price leader is uncertain whether rivals will follow its moves quickly and completely and does not want to risk losing significant market share, which may be costly to recoup, if they do not. Or firms may be uncertain of what others believe to be the best price, which may be true when coordination is accomplished with little explicit, direct communication.[13] In such cases, coordinated oligopolistic price increases may be

---

[13] It is occasionally suggested that follow-the-leader behavior may be indicative not of coordinated oligopolistic price elevation but rather of competition, wherein other firms follow the more intelligent or informed leader's behavior because it is assumed to know what is best for the industry. The basis for this view is obscure. Many variants seem to suppose at least the existence of unilateral market power, which is consistent with firms reacting to others' changes in price or quantity but not with the informational story under consideration. Consider instead, for concreteness and because of its relevance to the present context, a setting with homogeneous products and no binding capacity constraints. Why would secondary firms match the leader's

harder to detect, but this need not be true. Instead, signaling and jousting about price—such as through sequential price changes, where firms await others' reactions and then proceed—may sometimes provide an even stronger basis for inferring coordinated price elevation.[14] Even if each price adjustment is smaller, there will be more of them, and it may be even clearer that cost or other exogenous changes cannot explain observed patterns.

A greater difficulty is that sophisticated firms, aware of what inferences may be drawn from their price moves, may instead adjust prices strategically in order to disguise their coordinated behavior.[15] Of course, gradual but substantial price increases or occasional smaller jumps in fairly close proximity may also be suspicious. But by spreading out the changes and perhaps timing them with other events—like exogenous changes that

---

price increase rather than undercutting it slightly? Presumably because of the anticipated reaction. But such behavior would be interdependent. And with a price cut, why might it be imagined that secondary firms follow because of the information signaled rather than necessity (to avoid losing all sales)? To be sure, when there is coordinated pricing, one firm may play the role of leader, both because this facilitates coordination and because that particular firm may be perceived as better at determining the industry-profit-maximizing price. Another possibility is that the leader may have lower marginal cost and thus a lower preferred coordinated price that it imposes on the other firms, who prefer to go along rather than start a price war. One can imagine a pure informational story: Perhaps sometimes the cost of an input rises in a manner that most firms will not notice for awhile (they have inventory), but the wiser, more informed firm sees this and raises its price immediately (since current marginal cost is properly understood by reference to the opportunity cost of using inventory, which must be replenished at the higher price). Other firms might imitate such behavior, in which case there may be, for example, cost-induced price increases or decreases that generate follower-like behavior to some extent. Or the leader might recognize an upcoming demand spike before the others, so it raises its price in advance, happy to lose sales in the present knowing it can sell its product for more soon thereafter—all assuming an inability to increase production to meet the full expected demand. (An implausible account sometimes offered is that rivals must follow a firm's price increase lest it alone reaps greater profits that it can use to fund advertising or other activities that will permanently raise its market share at rivals' expense—which assumes that the rivals were previously willing to leave available profits (from unilateral market power, one might suppose) on the table and that they would not otherwise be willing or able to fund long-run maximizing activities).

[14] Closely related are advance price announcements, considered further in section C of this chapter and in section 11.C.

[15] See, for example, Harrington (2005) and Harrington and Chen (2006). Relatedly, Marshall, Marx, and Raiff (2008) found that the vitamins cartel adjusted its pattern of price changes to minimize buyer resistance.

plausibly affect cost, but in amounts that may be difficult to determine with much precision—firms may to an extent render detection through this approach more difficult. Observe that more complex behaviors of this sort might require more elaborate (and thus more explicit) communications that may leave traces. Additionally, more internal evidence of the sort considered in section 11.B may be generated, so this strategy is not without risk to the firms employing it. If such camouflaging strategies are net helpful to firms, an implication is that interdependent behavior involving little or no direct interfirm communication may be easier to distinguish from competitive behavior than is interdependent behavior implemented after more explicit interchanges.[16]

In maintaining elevated oligopolistic prices, it may appear that firms' pricing patterns would differ little from those of aggressive competitors: In the absence of any exogenous changes, prices would remain constant, and in response to changes, prices would change accordingly, rising, for example, if cost or demand increases. As will be discussed in section B, economic theory and econometric methods can, in principle and sometimes in practice, distinguish how price responds to changes in cost or demand as a function of the nature of competitive interaction among firms. These analyses typically imagine immediate responses by oligopolists. For purposes of this section, let us consider a less subtle point that may more readily be detectable in pricing patterns, namely, the possible lack of response or delayed or muted response of coordinating oligopolists, in contrast to competitors, to exogenous changes in market conditions.

The reasonably familiar point is that coordinated oligopoly prices, and perhaps also market shares, tend to be stickier over time than those of competitors.[17] Because coordination is difficult, frequent fine-tuning may be avoided. If frequent adjustments were accomplished through explicit

---

[16] This point supplements the analysis of the paradox of proof in chapters 6 and 17 in that stronger evidence of coordinated price elevation (in contrast to stronger evidence of conduciveness) may make it less rather than more likely that prohibited communications were employed. Contrast the analysis in subsection 6.D.1.

[17] For example, Carlton (1986, 655) presents empirical evidence that price rigidity is greater in more concentrated industries; Levenstein (1997, 122) finds that prices changed much less frequently during cooperative periods in the bromine cartel; Pesendorfer (2000) finds more stable market shares in a bid-rigging cartel that did not use side payments compared to one that did; Abrantes-Metz et al. (2006) use a variance screen to identify price coordination by

negotiations, the likelihood of detection would rise. If accomplished through price signaling behavior, there may be misunderstandings; for example, a firm decreasing price in response to a perceived softening in demand or decline in costs may mistakenly be viewed by others as a cheater, triggering a price war.[18] Consequently, firms may be more reluctant to respond promptly to changes in circumstances. In contrast, competitors do tend to respond quickly, and if changes are frequent, often.

This difference is not always easy to ascertain because there are other explanations for sticky prices, such as menu costs (the cost of changing prices per se). But in some settings, these costs are negligible or insufficient to explain the extent of stickiness. Likewise, menu costs tend to apply symmetrically to price increases and decreases, and their existence may lead firms to change prices at somewhat different times, whereas sluggishness due to problems in coordinating oligopoly pricing does not have these features. Additionally, oligopolists often tend to stabilize cooperating firms' relative market shares for fear that, if they do not, firms with growing shares will be seen as guilty of secret price cutting or other forms of cheating. Competitors also may have stable shares, but, depending on cost structures and other changes in the marketplace, they may be less stable.

Sudden, sharp price reductions are as suspicious as sudden, sharp price increases, again, in the absence of corresponding changes in cost or demand. Oligopolists do not ordinarily wish to drop their price, but sometimes this is unavoidable. Price wars arise to punish cheaters or, as explained in subsection 7.A.2, when firms experience a loss of customers and thus must act on the assumption that cheating occurred even though a decline in demand that is not yet evident might have been the cause. If prices fall precipitously, without any exogenous change of corresponding magnitude, it follows that the preexisting price involved coordinated elevation.[19] Note further that price wars that do not permanently end

---

gasoline stations; and Marshall and Marx (2012, 123–28) discuss the frequent use of market share allocations by cartels.

[18] This notion may also help to explain the sometimes-observed phenomenon that prices rise more promptly following cost increases than they fall following cost decreases. See, for example, Balmaceda and Soruco (2008).

[19] This claim supposes that there is not group predation, which would not ordinarily be likely and, when it occurs, might be illegal for other reasons.

oligopolistic coordination may well be followed by price increases, which themselves may be detected in the manner described previously.

Using price wars to identify oligopolistic price coordination raises an important danger that is not present when targeting price increases. If the direct effect of penalizing price increases is to discourage them, the result is precisely the deterrence that is desired. However, if penalizing price decreases discourages them, we may be concerned that the consequence will be higher, not lower prices. This depiction of a possible problem does, fortunately, involve a crucial omission: Oligopolists rely on the feasibility of price wars in order to establish and maintain supracompetitive prices in the first place. That is, the prospect of punishment is a necessary condition to successful interdependent oligopoly pricing. Hence, if enforcement makes price wars difficult, oligopoly pricing may be discouraged after all.[20]

Although this response provides a more complete picture, the problem is still more complicated. For example, if price wars are rendered more costly, it may be that they would still be employed but with a less sensitive trigger, in which case society may suffer from oligopolistic price elevation in any event but receive somewhat less frequent relief because price wars are rarer or shorter. (A shorter punishment phase may accomplish similar discouragement of cheating because a prospective cheater will reckon that it suffers from not only the periods of reduced profit but also the enhanced likelihood of legal sanctions.) Clearly, the issue is more complex than it may initially appear, and the usefulness of detection through price wars may depend on subtle factors.[21]

Nevertheless, this conundrum might be viewed as presenting an opportunity rather than an obstacle. For coordinated oligopolistic price

---

[20] An interesting variant is explored in Harrington (2003), who models a setting in which firms lower prices more gradually in the punishment phase to avoid detection, but the consequence is to reduce the sustainable coordinated price. In this model, the prospect of legal sanctions reduces oligopolistic price elevation even though actual detection by the enforcement authority never occurs.

[21] Cyrenne (1999) analyzes a model of the phenomenon in which the penalty does not depend on the extent of oligopolistic price elevation and is assumed to be insufficient ever to deter coordinated pricing or the price wars required to sustain it, and he finds for this case that the penalty will not affect price or output and will only shorten the duration of price wars.

elevation detected through price wars, one might provide leniency, immunity, or even some sort of reward to the initial cheater, preserving full legal sanctions for those firms administering punishment in response to the defection. Some interesting arguments and proposals along these lines have been offered.[22] For present purposes, it seems fair to say that,

---

[22] For further discussion of the strategic use of leniency, see section 12.C, and for prior analyses, see Aubert, Rey, and Kovacic (2006), favoring rewards over mere leniency to help break otherwise stable cooperative behavior, and emphasizing how this tactic can usefully create principal-agent conflicts in firms; Harrington (2008b); Miller (2009), providing empirical evidence that the introduction of a leniency program in 1993 in the United States enhanced deterrence; Motta and Polo (2003); and Spagnolo (2008), surveying the literature.

Two interesting proposals that are related in spirit have been put forward. Bishop (1983) suggests that, in industries selected in advance by a regulator, firms would have to submit prices periodically and stick with them for a significant period of time. The impact is that firms that bid lower, essentially the biggest cheaters, would reap substantial gains at the expense of their rivals, the latter of whom would be prohibited from retaliation during the freeze period. The mechanics of selecting eligible industries, running the bidding, enforcing prices, and preventing all manner of indirect shading would be daunting. (Although regulation would cover many dimensions of firms' activities, note that the firms, not the regulators, set the prices each period.) If industries include local, regional, and national markets that were susceptible to coordinated pricing, a large portion of the economy might be subject to ongoing, intrusive regulation. The proposal also could backfire. After all, it publicizes prices, prevents haggling by essentially requiring any cuts to be across the board, attempts to regulate various indirect means of cheating, and so forth. That is, the government is enlisted to prevent many types of behavior that often undermine the efficacy of coordination. If the time periods during which prices stick are short, the net effect may be to make successful elevation easier, not more difficult. So the periods would need to be reasonably long, but in that case the intrusive regulation and related costs of preventing price adjustments for extended intervals would be substantial.

Sagi (2008) offers a different implementation. Again, in a select group of industries, there would be price freezes, but he would have them triggered when (and only when) a firm submits a significant price cut. He suggests a six-month freeze if the cut is at least 20% and a three-month freeze for a cut of at least 10%. The government needs to regulate only when a freeze is triggered; moreover, if the proposal successfully deters initial price elevations, because firms do not want to lose out from a freeze when a rival cheats through official channels, then the actual need for regulation will be avoided. Mechanical challenges similar to those under Bishop's proposal are present along with the possibility of reinforcing oligopoly pricing through the publicity of price cuts (although firms could presumably keep them secret, rendering the proposal moot). Sagi's requirement of substantial price cuts is highly problematic because of the large capacity required to take advantage of one. He notes some ability to ramp up production and draw down inventories but does not seem to appreciate the required magnitude. For

although the optimal legal approach is not obvious, it seems likely that a thoughtful enforcement strategy can be devised that uses detection through behavior involved in price wars as a weapon against coordinated oligopolistic price elevation.

---

example, if a firm is able to fully double output instantly, then, for the 20% benchmark, the initial price elevation must be two-thirds (that is, price 67% above marginal cost, taken to be constant for this illustration) for cheating to be a break-even strategy in the short run, and higher for there to be any short-run gain. (The firm is enjoying some share of an elevation above cost of 2/3. If it cuts price 20%, its price is now only 1/3 above marginal cost—because a 1/5 cut on a price equal to 5/3 of marginal cost yields a price at 4/3 of marginal cost. Twice the sales at half the profit margin just breaks even.) If the prospective cheater can quickly increase production by only 50%, then the short-run break-even price elevation is 150% rather than 67%. Moreover, this is just the short-run impact, which ignores any cost from a post-freeze price war. To consider that effect, suppose that only a 10% cut is contemplated, triggering a three-month freeze, and that the resulting post-freeze collapse will eliminate what would otherwise have been two years of elevated prices (discounting is ignored for simplicity). Hence the price cutter is forfeiting a fraction given by its market share of industry profits over eight calendar quarters for what it hopes is greater profits for a single quarter. It needs eight times the profits, which would require an eightfold output increase at the prevailing price; actually, since it must cut its price at least 10% to trigger the freeze, it needs almost a ninefold output increase (assuming no rise in its marginal cost in doing so). Not only is such vastly beyond capacity in most instances, but if, say, its initial market share was 25%, it also requires a market share of over 200%. (Actually, perhaps not quite so high, for a 10% price cut will plausibly expand the quantity demanded, but obviously not by nearly enough unless the demand elasticity was very high—in which case the initial price elevation would have vastly exceeded the highest price that oligopolists would ever wish to charge.) In short, for Sagi's proposal to have any prospect of working, it appears necessary to trigger very long freezes with very small price cuts. However, in that case freezes would often be triggered, even by minor fluctuations in cost or other factors, and extensive ongoing regulation (and inefficiencies due to long-frozen prices) would be commonplace. Indeed, these sorts of concerns motivate his insistence on large initial price cuts and short freeze periods, which unfortunately do not seem to provide anywhere near the desired incentives to cheat.

Neither proposal is obviously superior to using price wars as evidence of successful oligopolistic coordination while providing generous legal treatment to firms that initiate price cuts. Indeed, Sagi notes the possibility that firms might be reluctant to be price cutters under his proposal for fear of triggering legal liability, and he offers leniency as a possible response. He also suggests reducing the potential regulatory burden by severely limiting the reach of his proposal to markets with known oligopoly pricing problems, but, where we can indeed identify such markets, the detection problem is taken to be solved or at least mitigated, which largely renders his proposal unnecessary. In sum, although one should be skeptical about these particular proposals, the basic ideas of using price wars to trigger a government response and giving some sort of preferential treatment to the initial cheater seem attractive.

B. Price Elevation

Although most of the discussion in section A concerns price elevation, the primary means of inferring the existence of successful oligopolistic coordination under consideration there is to examine major price changes—when substantial price elevations come into existence or evaporate quickly—as well as nonresponsiveness to changes in conditions in the interim. This section looks at means of inferring whether existing prices are elevated by examining the prices themselves, typically under the assumption that they do reflect and respond to existing market circumstances. (Keep in mind that assessment of elevation per se does not distinguish coordinated from unilateral elevation, a subject addressed in chapter 14.)

A logically straightforward way to determine whether price exceeds a competitive level, marginal cost, is to compare price and marginal cost directly.[23] While price is often easy to determine,[24] marginal cost is quite difficult to measure in many settings. This challenge is familiar in competition law enforcement, often being confronted when measuring market power[25] and also at issue in predatory pricing disputes[26] and in some other contexts.

---

[23] A closely related approach would be to measure profits to see whether they are above a competitive (risk-adjusted) return on capital. In addition to difficulties similar to those associated with measuring marginal cost—see, for example, Fisher (1987) and Fisher and McGowan (1983)—profits reflect average cost, which the text to follow explains may provide a misleading indicator of supracompetitive pricing in some settings.

[24] There may be complications when goods are bundled (including, for example, with delivery or other services) or customized and also limitations of data, such as when many transactions are privately negotiated at off-list prices, although the latter information may well be available to an enforcer even if not to academic researchers. A different challenge is that, when products are differentiated, there is no single price (and no single marginal cost), but rather one for each product. In these instances, however, oligopolistic coordination is more difficult and hence less likely in any event.

[25] If measuring existing (that is, exercised) market power, the problem is tantamount to measuring price-cost margins. See Kaplow and Shapiro (2007, 1079–80). Measuring unexercised or prospective market power may be more difficult.

[26] It is common to inquire whether price is below cost, although the relevant notion of cost is not always defined. Notably, Brooke Group Ltd. v. Brown & Williamson Tobacco Corp., 509 U.S. 209, 222 (1993) (emphasis added), requires somewhat opaquely that "the prices complained

Leading difficulties involve the determination of which costs are variable over what time period and the allocation of joint or common costs to particular products.[27] It also may often be easier to measure average cost even though marginal cost is more relevant for determining whether pricing is supracompetitive. An example of where problems may arise is the case in which a firm's marginal cost is low through much of its output range but rises rapidly as production approaches full capacity. If the firm is producing near capacity and pricing near marginal cost, its price may be significantly above average cost and thus may appear to be elevated well above marginal cost. Thus, when firms produce close to capacity, one must be particularly cautious about making inferences of supracompetitive pricing.[28] Indeed, in the short run, firms operating at capacity could not behave so as to reduce industry price significantly in any event.[29]

Underestimating marginal cost and thus producing false positives can occur as a consequence of treating costs as fixed that are really variable (perhaps equipment could be rented or sold), ignoring common costs (which may actually need to be raised to support additional output of the product in question), or failing to recognize that marginal costs may rise steeply when output is close to capacity, as just described. In response, enforcers could consciously err in the opposite direction (treating more costs as variable, for example) and require demonstration of a more significant elevation of price above measured marginal cost. Whether direct measurement of the gap between price and marginal cost will often be

---

of are below an *appropriate* measure of its rival's costs." Note that if true marginal cost is above measured cost, which as the text to follow indicates is the more likely error, predation tests are too lax but price elevation determinations are too strict.

[27] See Kaplow and Shapiro (2007, 1087–88).

[28] Compare the discussion in section 9.B of the case in which one or more firms have costs below those of others, at least over much of the production range, but nevertheless charge a price equal to the higher marginal cost at the actual level of output. It was suggested that looking to industry marginal cost, by examining competitors, was appropriate. As noted previously, an important caveat is that, if a group of leading firms significantly elevates price, there may well be a competitive fringe, with different products or technology, that is selling at marginal cost, and this fact would not negate the existence of coordinated price elevation.

[29] In the long run, if average cost is far below marginal cost and price, one would expect the firm to expand production capacity, competitors to expand, new entry to take place, or some combination—that is, unless firms are coordinating their capacity decisions.

useful is hard to say. For some products, presumably, marginal cost will be fairly easy to measure or the magnitude of elevation will be sufficiently great that there is little doubt of supracompetitive pricing. Often, significant uncertainty will remain, and inquiries of this sort may provide little illumination. In all cases, it will be useful to examine as well other evidence bearing on the presence of coordinated price elevation.

Another approach to measuring price elevation compares prices for the same product sold to different purchasers. Prices might be compared across markets; notably, geographical price differences may indicate supracompetitive pricing in regions with higher prices.[30] The logic is that price is at least as high as marginal cost in all markets, so higher prices must to that extent be supracompetitive. The limitation to such inferences is that markets may exhibit cost differences as well. Indeed, the prices of many competitively supplied products differ across regions. Accordingly, it is necessary to establish that cost differences are relatively small or to control for these differences when making comparisons. This need recreates the problem of measuring marginal cost directly, but the challenge may be less severe when attention is limited to factors that make marginal cost for a given product differ across regions.[31]

Similarly, different prices charged to different customers in a single market—that is, the presence of price discrimination—indicate the exercise of market power.[32] The lower price must be at least as high as marginal cost, for otherwise those units would not be sold, so it follows that a higher price must exceed marginal cost by at least the extent to

---

[30] It is also sometimes useful to compare prices across products that may have similar cost structures but face different degrees of competition.

[31] This method of estimating price elevation was employed in the FTC's challenge to the merger of Staples and Office Depot. See Ashenfelter et al. (2006). Note that cross-market techniques can be combined with others. For example, if there is a common cost shock (see the discussion in the text to follow) but prices react differently in different markets, inferences about noncompetitive pricing may be possible.

[32] "It is well known that price discrimination is only feasible under certain conditions [including that] firms have short-run market power. . . ." Stole (2007, 2226). "[W]hen markets are perfectly competitive and firms have neither short-run nor long-run market power, the law of one price prevails and price discrimination cannot exist." Ibid. (2224). "It is straightforward to construct models of price discrimination in competitive markets without entry barriers in which firms lack long-run market power . . . providing that there is some source of short-run market power that allows price to remain above marginal cost . . . ." Ibid. (2224 n.2).

which it exceeds the lower price.[33] There are, however, complications, including that not all differential pricing constitutes price discrimination in the sense just described.[34] Here, confounding cost differences may exist but would be more circumscribed, as they are limited to differential costs of serving different customers, which often would be negligible.[35] Note that if the existence of price discrimination was known by firms to be used by competition law enforcers as an indicator of oligopolistic price coordination, price discrimination may be discouraged without deterring (average) price elevation. Static, allocative efficiency may rise or fall as a consequence.[36] Producer surplus would fall, which may often but not always be socially advantageous in such settings as a consequence of the reduced incentive for entry and other rent-seeking investments, as discussed in section 8.B.

---

[33] This logic applies not only to posted price differentials but also to unposted prices, including prices determined through buyers' haggling. In such contexts, it is often overlooked that, if some buyers are thus able to obtain significant discounts, other buyers are at least to that extent paying a price in excess of marginal cost. Similar analysis applies when some buyers obtain nonprice concessions. Note that offering nonprice concessions that are less valuable to buyers than equally costly price concessions may indicate coordinated pricing, as sellers attempt to circumvent the agreed price without visibly cheating.

[34] Some variation in the price paid by different buyers may be explained by buyers' imperfect information about prices rather than (or in addition to) coordinated pricing. See, for example, Burdett and Judd (1983), Salop and Stiglitz (1977), Shilony (1977), Varian (1980), and Wilde and Schwartz (1979). Indeed, if coordinated oligopolistic price elevation is highly successful, such as when a cartel succeeds almost completely in preventing secret discounts, price dispersion may be smaller than under more competitive conditions with imperfectly informed purchasers. See Connor (2005). Borenstein and Rose (1994) found greater price dispersion on more competitive airline routes, grounding the explanation in a model with differentiated products, but Gerardi and Shapiro (2009) subsequently present evidence that increased competition reduces price dispersion and argue that Borenstein and Rose's contrary result was due to omitted-variable bias. See also Gaggero and Piga (2009), finding that competition reduces fare dispersion on routes between Ireland and the United Kingdom. Yet another possible source of price dispersion arises when firms set prices in advance (that cannot later be modified) when the magnitude of future demand is uncertain. See Dana (1999) and Eden (1990).

[35] Measuring such cost differences can pose difficulties, as evidenced in some disputes under the Robinson-Patman Act in the United States, where demonstrated cost differences provide a defense, but one that has sometimes been difficult to establish even where it may plausibly be present. See Areeda, Kaplow, and Edlin (2004, 821–23 & n.2).

[36] See Varian (1989, 619–22).

A different method of identifying successful oligopolistic coordination is to examine whether ordinary pricing behavior (that is, aside from episodes of commencing or terminating coordination) responds to changes in demand and cost in the same manner as would pricing by competitors or somewhat (or entirely) like pricing by a monopolist.[37] Such analysis sets aside the point in section A that, by comparison to monopolists, coordinated oligopoly pricing may be sticky, which itself differentiates coordinated pricing patterns from competitive ones. A substantial body of econometric research since the 1980s is designed to measure the exercise of market power using such an empirical strategy.[38]

To illustrate some of the intuition behind these methods, consider an upward shift in demand in an industry with common, constant marginal cost. Perfect competitors would expand output, but price would not rise (it would continue to equal the preexisting marginal cost). A monopolist generally would increase price (not necessarily, because it would depend on how the elasticity of demand changed as well, but this would be a typical response, and demand elasticity would also be estimated). Therefore,

---

[37] See Bresnahan (1989, 1012): "As a result, the nature of the inference of market power is made clear, since the set of alternative hypotheses which are considered is explicit. The alternative hypothesis of no strategic interaction, typically a perfectly competitive hypothesis, is clearly articulated and is one of the alternatives among which the data can choose."; and Bresnahan (1997, 71): "There are some first-order implications of oligopoly theory that are quite testable in real-world data environments. Collusive oligopolies will have monopoly-like pricing behavior (i.e., pricing behavior that depends on marginal revenue) in their cartel regime." It may be tempting to examine just the elasticity of demand since a monopolist or fully successful oligopoly will elevate price until the elasticity is not very low (for, if it were, further elevation would be profitable). But demand elasticity is difficult to interpret in a vacuum. Perfect competitors may sell at a market price at which demand is quite elastic (because industry marginal cost may intersect the demand curve at such a point). Also, if elasticity is observed to be low, this level may rule out monopoly pricing, but some coordinating oligopolists may be able to enforce only an equilibrium involving lesser price elevations. Ultimately, one must consider additional information to determine whether and to what extent price is elevated.

[38] In addition to the sources cited in note 3, see Bresnahan (1982), Hall (1988), and Lau (1982). However, Corts (1999) argues that the common method of estimating a conduct parameter, which indicates where an industry falls between perfect competition and monopoly, can be misleading in certain settings, and Nevo (1998) explains that the conduct parameter is difficult to identify in differentiated products industries, although it is possible to compare particular models of industry behavior.

if price rises in an oligopolistic industry with constant marginal cost, this would be evidence of price coordination. Cost shifts allow similar analysis. With constant marginal costs, a common cost increase will be fully passed on by perfect competitors, and idiosyncratic cost changes will cause large shifts in production across competitors. But if there is coordinated oligopoly pricing, the passing on of a common cost increase will depend on the curvature of demand, which would be estimated, and firm-specific cost shifts would involve less reallocation of production.

More broadly, these econometric techniques entail simultaneous estimation of demand and firms' costs. Such methods do not assume that firms' marginal costs are directly measurable; these costs are implicitly estimated from the data.[39] This work represents a significant advance in market power measurement, but it is hardly a panacea. The techniques often require strong assumptions about the structure of demand and cost that it may not be possible to test directly.[40] The central question for present purposes concerns the reliability of such techniques given the data that would be available when investigating a particular group of firms. These methods are increasingly used to predict the effects of horizontal mergers, where agencies are often attempting to determine whether a price elevation of at least a few percent is likely to result.[41] Allowing for some (perhaps significant) margin of error, a similar approach could be employed to detect coordinated oligopolistic price elevation.[42]

Entry also provides a window on the existence of successful oligopolistic coordination. First, entry itself may be a clue. For example, if in-

---

[39] See Bresnahan (1989, 1012) and Perloff, Karp, and Golan (2007, 5, 42).

[40] See, for example, Perloff, Karp, and Golan (2007, 42, 70–71, 91), who conclude: "That said, the fundamental problem of estimating market power remains. As in the one-sector structural model, reliability depends critically on identifying both market power and costs. Many researchers have identified these parameters within their models by making heroic assumptions about costs, such as constant returns to scale, because they lacked detailed data on costs."

[41] See Baker and Bresnahan (1985), Epstein and Rubinfeld (2001, 2004), and Werden and Froeb (2008).

[42] As mentioned previously with regard to the direct measurement of marginal cost, one might require demonstration of larger price elevations the more uncertain the method of estimation appears to be. Just how one would calibrate such margins of error in particular cases requires further work.

cumbent firms have unused capacity yet new firms enter the industry (or fringe firms expand), it is plausible that prices are elevated.[43] Recall the discussion in subsection 8.B.1 of how oligopolistic price elevation induces (often socially excessive) entry. Second, incumbents' response to entry may be revealing. If pre-entry behavior is competitive, a new entrant will draw sales from other firms, prices will tend to fall, and the other firms' quantities will fall. The same may occur if the industry exhibits coordinated oligopoly pricing, but it is also possible that incumbents' output would stay constant or even rise, depending on how the operative understanding about industry price is affected by entry. A move to a substantially more competitive environment, indicated by a steep decline in price and increase in quantities, would evidence preexisting supracompetitive pricing much as would the outbreak of a price war in response to perceived cheating by incumbents.[44]

The foregoing list is hardly exhaustive.[45] It is clear that successful oligopolistic coordination resulting in price elevation has a number of features that distinguish it from ordinary competition and that there exist techniques for identifying these differences. On the other hand, these differences will not always be apparent, and sometimes alternative explanations will be available that themselves may be difficult to assess. Accordingly, it is also important to consider other sources of information that bear on whether oligopolistic coordination took place.

---

[43] An important implicit assumption is that entrants' marginal costs are not lower than those of incumbents, which would be true if marginal cost was reasonably constant, similar technologies were employed, and similar input costs were faced. Also, excess capacity is a vague notion. The main idea is that fixed entry costs are already sunk and that the firms are producing at marginal costs that are low (whereas marginal cost may rise as capacity is approached, as discussed previously in the text). Note that even if there are no particular capacity constraints, leading firms' consistent loss of market share to entrants or fringe firms suggests that those firms' prices are elevated; competing explanations are, again, that the others may have lower costs, or that they offer differentiated products.

[44] See Nye (1975, 220).

[45] See the sources cited in note 3. For example, the failure of price to fall upon expiration of a key patent may indicate coordinated oligopoly pricing. A competing hypothesis would be that the patent was not significant in that it conveyed little market power; the extent of a patent's market power might be measured by the level of the royalty that had been charged. Also, even if price falls, this change may involve a decline from the monopoly price to the highest price an oligopoly can sustain rather than to the competitive price.

C. Facilitating Practices

Facilitating practices are acts that make it easier to engage in oligopolistic coordination. Typically, they address the challenges of determining a mutually acceptable oligopoly price and deterring cheating through the prospect that defection will be detected and punished quickly. Because coordinated oligopoly pricing is often difficult to accomplish, facilitating practices may be important and thus have long been a focus of policy analysis of the oligopoly problem.[46] Indeed, explicit interfirm communications, taken by many to be determinative of what constitutes a price-fixing agreement, can also be viewed as facilitating practices, as discussed in section 3.B.

Facilitating practices may be relevant under competition law in two ways. First, their use provides a basis for inferring the existence of oligopolistic coordination. This inference is sensible when there exists no other plausible explanation for the practice.[47] In contrast, practices that may facilitate oligopolistic interdependence but would likely be employed regardless are not directly probative.

Second, facilitating practices may themselves be made a basis for liability.[48] One rationale would be that it often makes sense to punish attempts even when they are unsuccessful, a subject explored in section 12.B. Of particular importance in the present context, punishing attempts is good policy when it is difficult or costly to determine whether they are successful. As when using facilitating practices as a diagnostic for the existence of coordinated oligopoly pricing, one must determine whether there are other plausible explanations for the practice, and, if there are,

---

[46] See Posner (2001, 86–87, 88–89, 91–93); Buccirossi (2008) and Marshall and Marx (2012, ch. 6), providing surveys; and Kaysen and Turner (1959, 150–52), offering an early discussion.

[47] As explained in section 11.A, the nature of facilitating practices is also relevant to whether conditions are conducive to coordination, which in turn bears on the inference of coordination.

[48] If liability is to be found under Sherman Act Section 1 or EU Article 101, there must be some sort of agreement, and as discussed in section 3.B, commentators are often inconsistent on this point. In contrast, if facilitating practices are taken as signals of the existence of coordinated price elevation, the agreement question may be irrelevant with regard to the facilitating practices, although it would be concerning the pricing.

any benefits must be weighed against the competitive risks.[49] The remainder of this section considers a number of facilitating practices without much attending to whether any given practice should be viewed primarily as a symptom of coordinated oligopoly pricing or also as an act that might be directly condemned.

An important way to facilitate oligopolistic interdependence is through improved mutual understanding of relevant circumstances. Most obvious are direct interfirm communications about price, which will be explored further in section 11.C. Advance price announcements that on their face are directed at the world are also important.[50] Firms hoping to increase the industry price may wish to convey their beliefs without taking the risk of raising prices unilaterally, possibly alienating customers and losing interim sales without being confident about whether and how quickly rivals will follow. Perhaps more important, if a firm believes that the industry price should be reduced because it perceives falling demand or because of cost reductions, it faces the danger that a unilateral price cut will be perceived as a defection, thereby triggering a price war, which risk may be alleviated by an announcement.

Both concerns can readily be overstated and may be unimportant in some markets. For example, price changes might be initiated during periods when sales are unlikely, when the moves will be quickly observed by competitors, and where they can be rescinded almost immediately if not promptly matched. Nevertheless, advance price announcements, which may be followed by rivals' responsive announcements and further modifications by the initiator, in as many rounds as necessary, may reduce risks attendant with changing prices, consequently facilitating coordinated oligopoly pricing.[51] Such announcements could be quite detailed,

---

[49] See also section 18.C, discussing how a more limited prohibition on coordinated oligopoly pricing may require stricter and thus more costly regulation of facilitating practices.

[50] For significant further discussion, including criticism of some common views, see note 56 in chapter 7.

[51] In addition, it is usually overlooked that, if advance price announcements are deemed to be a permissible means of coordination, they may serve as cover for secret interfirm communications that are outlawed. Suppose, for example, that firms agree at a clandestine meeting to increase price to 100 at the stroke of midnight a week later. Such simultaneous activity by itself may be highly suspicious, serving as an indicator of the meeting. However, the firms could further plan that, shortly after the meeting concludes, one of them will publicly announce

indicating price moves, dates, and so forth, or they may be more vague, such as a statement that the firm believes that demand has fallen, after which its price decrease may be more likely to be interpreted as an industry-wide invitation rather than a unilateral defection.

Firms might also share information about prices and other matters through trade associations. Possibilities include broad discussions about industry trends as well as precise, exhaustive information about actual prices, such as by having the association audit invoices, reporting transaction prices to other members.[52] In this regard, it is interesting to note that the enactments of anti-price-fixing regimes in the United States and in Britain were each followed by a surge in trade association activity.[53] Furthermore, in some notorious price-fixing cartels, secret discussions were held in conjunction with trade association gatherings, which provided a cover for the relevant players regularly happening to be at the same hotels on the same dates.[54] Also, in those prosecuted price-fixing cases that do

---

a supposed unilateral intention to start pricing at 100 at the prescribed time. Others could publicly respond, indicating their similar (also purportedly unilateral) intentions, or they could simply remain silent and act likewise as planned; if they were investigated, they would point to the first announcer's statement and deny any secret meetings. The interim advance announcement would accordingly disrupt an inference that forbidden meetings likely occurred. By contrast, if successful oligopolistic coordination subjects firms to sanctions, such action may instead tend to trigger liability. This problem is discussed further in note 6 in chapter 5.

[52] See American Column & Lumber Co. v. United States, 257 U.S. 377 (1921). A rarely mentioned but possibly important alternative means of obtaining information about rivals' pricing, including cheating, is for each firm to investigate rivals' prices carefully and continuously, including possibly through the use of secret buying agents. See Porter (1980, 96): "From a defensive point of view perceptual lags may be shortened by having a competitor monitoring system in place which continually assembles data from the field sales force, distributors, and so on." Porter further observes that "[i]f systems for competitor monitoring are known to competitors, all the better for deterrence."—although to be effective it would be necessary for competitors to know merely of the existence of the system but not its details, so that it could not readily be circumvented.

[53] Heath (1960, 475) shows that more than 150 price exchange agreements arose within a few years of Britain declaring overt price fixing to be illegal, and a similar rise in trade associations occurred in the United States in the decades following passage of the Sherman Act. In Britain, it appears that information sharing arrangements were often successful, especially before they were subject to stricter scrutiny. See Swann et al. (1974, 158–63).

[54] See Connor (2007a, 11, 143–44, 295–96).

not involve a fairly small number of firms, use of trade associations seems common.[55]

A major reservation regarding such information-sharing activities is that they may also have redeeming virtues. These benefits might provide an innocent explanation, thereby negating the inference of oligopolistic coordination, and they also mean that it would be socially costly to prohibit or chill the activities. While these points are important, they are subject to a significant qualification that is not always appreciated: In determining whether a possibly ambiguous facilitating practice should be viewed positively or negatively, it is necessary to consider the cooperating firms' incentives. That is, it is necessary to consider whether, under relevant alternative hypotheses, firms in fact gain from sharing the information. As a general matter, one may note that sellers' interests will often be opposed to buyers' and society's interests, for sellers are better off the more successful are their attempts at price elevation.

For example, regarding the common suggestion that firms engage in various open pricing practices in order to help buyers, it must be asked why sellers have an incentive to do so. If firms are colluding, then making it easier for buyers to find discounts—i.e., firms that are cheaters—will tend to undermine coordinated oligopoly pricing. In contrast, making it easier for sellers to identify cheaters will make punishment swift and thereby deter defection. Hence, if firms in an industry conducive to coordinated price elevation act to make pricing more open, the logical inference would be that the latter, socially undesirable effect is dominant in their actions.[56] To be sure, if firms are able to share the information secretly, they avoid any tradeoff.[57] However, if that is difficult (at least without

---

[55] See Fraas and Greer (1977, 39–42), Hay and Kelley (1974, 21–22), and Levenstein and Suslow (2008, 1123).

[56] This idea is discussed further in note 56 in chapter 7. Among other points, it is noted that, in Porter's (1980, 76–80) text on competitive strategy, giving buyers advance notice is not on his long list of strategic reasons for advance announcements, which is dominated by concerns with communication between competitors, although Dranove and Marciano (2005, 139) do offer aiding customers as a reason. Porter (1980, 80, 103–4) and Schelling (1960, 29–30) also discuss that publicity may make effective commitment more possible, which also facilitates coordination.

[57] This point is familiar from situations like that in United States v. Container Corp. of

being caught by enforcers) and if public sharing is viewed as benign, then they may well prefer public dissemination. An individual buyer in the short run will be happy to learn where lower prices might be obtained. But, in the long run, buyers as a whole are worse off if the result is more elevated prices with fewer, if any, discounts.[58]

The point in this example about firms' incentives is reinforced by considering a more (but not perfectly) competitive setting. When it is costly for buyers to learn about the prices offered by different sellers, there tends to be price dispersion, with buyers engaging in costly search activity to discover lower prices but also finding it optimal not to search indefinitely, often settling for prices above the lowest that may be available.[59] Likewise, unsophisticated customers may pay higher prices than others do. In this situation, firms developing a mechanism to make price information readily available to buyers may be socially desirable. The problem is that the firms' joint incentive may be the opposite. Hence, we should be skeptical of group information dissemination that is claimed to assist buyers in generally obtaining lower prices from the firms involved.[60]

America, 393 U.S. 333 (1969), discussed in subsection 4.B.1, in which firms verified with competitors various assertions by buyers that they had been offered lower prices. See also Heil, Day, and Reibstein (1997, 281): "Announcing plans is particularly effective when it is conducted outside the public eye (in a trade journal, for example). This way, the announcements will not delay consumers' purchases or damage consumers' willingness to pay." Another forum might be meetings with stock analysts that cover an industry, the subject of one of the FTC's actions against Valassis Communications for inviting its competitor to collude. See "FTC Consent Order Protects Competition in the Market for Free-Standing Newspaper Inserts," http://www .ftc.gov/opa/2006/03/valassis.shtm (accessed March 23, 2011), which is discussed along with related cases in Fullerton (2011).

[58] A further complication regarding buyers' incentives is that, if they are intermediate purchasers rather than final, individual consumers, they may suffer little from common price elevation because their competitors are in the same situation. In contrast, a buyer who is able to obtain a concession unavailable to others benefits, and one unable to obtain concessions received by others suffers.

[59] See note 34.

[60] This skepticism does not mean that there cannot be exceptions, particularly regarding particular firms as distinguished from joint activity. Firms introducing a new product or operating in a new location may wish to attract customers. Likewise, certain firms may wish to advertise prices to draw business from incumbents, who themselves may attempt to suppress such efforts. Benham (1972).

Now consider what may appear to be a more innocuous situation that does not involve pricing information: Firms at trade association meetings may wish to share information about future demand because demand is uncertain and difficult to predict.[61] If all firms can better plan capacity decisions, inventories, and the like, production will tend to be more efficient, a social gain. An important question, however, is whether individual firms gain, and what other consequences may flow from such sharing. Recall from subsection 7.A.2 that uncertain demand is a significant threat to coordinated oligopoly pricing in settings where transaction prices are secret, which is typical in many industries selling intermediate goods to large buyers, where sales are individually negotiated. In that case, firms' inability to distinguish sales lost to demand fluctuations from those lost to cheating can trigger price wars and thus may constitute the greatest threat to the sustainability of coordinated oligopoly pricing. Accordingly, in such industries there may be reason for society to fear information exchanges that reduce future demand uncertainty.[62] Moreover, firms may have a strong incentive to share this information precisely when this threat to their elevated prices is present but not otherwise.[63] It might be socially advantageous for more information to be shared if it is possible independently to prevent it from being employed to facilitate price elevation, but that raises different questions.[64]

------

[61] Exchange of cost information may be different. Shapiro (1986) finds that oligopolists, in a model with Cournot behavior, have an incentive to share cost information, which raises their profits, reduces consumer surplus, and increases total welfare.

[62] For example, Levenstein and Suslow (2008, 1121–23) describe efforts of international cartel members to avoid price wars by sharing information about market conditions, including through trade association activity. Likewise, inventories can be used strategically (for example, buildups can enable more profitable defection), so firms desiring to facilitate oligopolistic price elevation may benefit from sharing inventory information and coordinating inventory decisions. See Rotemberg and Saloner (1989).

[63] This result is obtained, for example, in the model in Clarke (1983).

[64] See Clarke (1983). Note that if firms have incentives to share even if there is no price elevation, and if expected sanctions for price elevation are sufficiently high in the industry in question, then it would not make sense to infer successful oligopolistic coordination from voluntary information sharing. And if firms do not have such incentives, it may be optimal for the government to provide for or subsidize information, but, again, perhaps only if enforcement against price elevation is sufficiently strong. Consider that the Danish competition authority gathered and published prices of concrete, motivated by a belief in the desirability of

Another set of facilitating practices is addressed to product standardization. The introductory analysis of coordinated oligopoly behavior
imagines that firms produce a single, homogeneous product, and it is
familiar that successful coordination is most likely when products are
homogeneous or nearly so. Heterogeneity raises a number of challenges.
First, it is more difficult to coordinate on an industry price. Indeed, if
heterogeneity is substantial or even if goods differ only modestly but vary
along a single dimension that consumers rank similarly (so-called vertical
differentiation), it may be necessary for an array of prices to be charged.
Moreover, this set of prices needs to be changed over time as industry
conditions evolve, resulting in a more complex problem that may generate
more disagreement than caused by the need to adjust a single price for a
homogeneous good.

Accordingly, standardization facilitates coordination. If firms could
create or gravitate toward a common template indicating relative values,
then perhaps they would need to adopt—and, over time, adjust—only a
single index value, with other prices following in line. To illustrate, it is
often suggested that basing-point pricing facilitates coordination. The
problem arises when transportation costs are nontrivial and rivals' plants
are significantly dispersed. It might be difficult for all firms to agree on
prices at each of many locations, but perhaps they could limit themselves
to one or a few basing points, each with a single price, with prices at all
other locations determined by adding some standardized freight rate to
the price at the (nearest) basing point.[65] In other settings, where heterogeneity concerns quality differences, firms might attempt to suppress

---

price transparency, with the result that prices increased due to eased oligopolistic coordination.
See Albæk, Møllgaard, and Overgaard (1997).

[65] See, for example, Scherer and Ross (1990, 502–8). Basing-point-pricing patterns can also
arise without coordination. For example, if most producers are at the same location and one
small producer is elsewhere, the latter may take advantage of the fact that the price others
charge at its location reflects production costs plus a significant transportation cost, if it can
sell all of its output without lowering the price. However, when substantial capacity is widely
dispersed, such patterns would not arise through competition. Also, significant cross-hauling
(shipping large quantities in opposite directions) may indicate that oligopolistic coordination
is taking place. Relatedly, a firm's failure to charge lower prices near its plant in order to capture
more of the market, when it also makes significant sales at a distance at a lower profit margin—which occurs when the plant is not at a basing point—suggests interdependent pricing
rather than competitive rivalry.

information about this variation so they can utilize a uniform price. A firm with a slight quality advantage might go along because it prefers to sell at an elevated oligopoly price rather than enjoying a somewhat higher market share at a more nearly competitive price.

A second problem is that one form of cheating on an elevated price consists of improving quality or offering additional services or better terms, while adhering to the nominal coordinated price. Oligopolists therefore wish to suppress all manner of quality competition as well.[66] Note that, in these instances, a competitive firm that took its rivals' actions as given would have an incentive to differentiate its product, emphasize the advantages of its own wares over those of competitors, adjust its price to reflect differences in quality, and otherwise act in ways that divert business from rivals to itself.

A rather different type of facilitating practice is aimed at altering firms' direct payoffs from raising or cutting prices. One means is cross-ownership: If firm A owns a fraction of firm B (setting to the side mergers or other transfers of control), A has less incentive to cheat if the result will hurt B's profits.[67] Another mechanism is the use of side payments, for example, to share industry profits more equally when some firms need to make greater sacrifices or when it turns out ex post that one firm sold more than its allotted share of output (whether due to cheating or luck; rivals may be unable to tell which). Side payments are widely accepted as evidence of coordinated oligopolistic price elevation, for why else would a competitor make a payment to a rival for no consideration. A more subtle form of the practice involves cross-purchases. That is, a firm that sold more than its allotted share might buy from firms that sold less; if such purchases are at the elevated oligopoly price, compensation will have been accomplished.[68]

A more direct way to reduce incentives to provide selective price reductions is through most-favored-customer clauses that bind a seller to give all of its customers retroactive price cuts if it is found to have sold to

---

[66] For example, Catalano, Inc. v. Target Sales, Inc., 446 U.S. 643 (1980), holds illegal an agreement not to offer credit to buyers.

[67] See Gilo, Moshe, and Spiegel (2006) and Reynolds and Snapp (1986).

[68] This practice has been employed by firms in some prosecuted cartels. See Connor (2007a, 143), referring to the citric acid conspiracy, and Harrington (2006, 57–62), discussing forms of compensation, including buybacks, in a number of conspiracies.

anyone else at a lower price.[69] For such clauses to be effective, there must be a sufficient chance that, at least eventually, other customers would detect the secret price cut. Additionally, it is necessary for firms to coordinate on the adoption of such restrictions, for, if some firms abstain, their incentive to cut price is increased because contractually obligated rivals may find punishment too costly.[70]

It has also been suggested that an industry might employ resale price maintenance to facilitate coordination. When it is in force, upstream price cuts cannot be passed along to consumers, so they do not generate as much gain in market share. On the other hand, price cuts still induce retailers to steer customers, perhaps aggressively, toward the price cutter's product. Moreover, since the retailer is prevented from passing any of the reduction to consumers, the upstream price cut may be less visible to rivals.

A different approach is the use of meeting-competition clauses to reduce rivals' incentives to cut prices.[71] These might promise customers that the offeror will meet or undercut by some margin any lower price of a competitor. Such clauses may be effective particularly when customers have some switching costs: If they are offered a price reduction by a rival, they would prefer to stick with their existing supplier, using the rival's offer to extract a lower price. It follows that rivals would be less inclined to reduce prices in the first place. Note, however, that even without any price-matching promise, a customer can always convey the rival's price cut to its regular supplier, and if the price cut involves cheating, as we are currently supposing, that supplier would be inclined to respond even without being obligated to do so.[72] These guarantees nevertheless have

---

[69] See Cooper (1986) and Salop (1986).

[70] A further, underexplored complication is that, even if adoption is industry wide, such contracts nevertheless make punishment, not just cheating, more costly. See Buccirossi (2008, 340).

[71] See Edlin (1997), Edlin and Emch (1999), Moorthy and Winter (2006), and Salop (1986).

[72] A related question under both scenarios is whether the rival's price cut can credibly be conveyed to the original seller. This problem gave rise to the *Container* case, mentioned in note 57 and also discussed in subsection 4.B.1. Note that, if rivals indeed are cheating, they would not cooperate with the buyer wishing to stay with its regular supplier. Meeting-competition clauses are readily triggered when rivals' price cuts are public, but in those cases it seems that secret defection is not what is taking place.

communications value, both alerting buyers of a willingness to respond to competitors' price cuts and also signaling intentions to competitors.

As suggested at the outset, it often will be ambiguous whether a posited facilitating practice is being employed (and how broadly in the industry), what are its actual effects, and therefore how strongly it supports an inference of oligopolistic price elevation or a conclusion that the practice is undesirable and thus should be prohibited. Some practices are more probative or problematic than are others, and for many of them the conclusion will depend very much on the circumstances of the particular case. Another important consideration concerns how reliable is the implication of the facilitating practice in comparison to that of other sorts of evidence bearing on the existence of successful coordination. Once again, different types of proof are best employed in a complementary fashion, although the particular mix will be context specific.

Detection: Other Types of Evidence

❦

A. Conduciveness of Conditions

An assessment of the degree to which industry conditions in a particular setting are conducive to successful oligopolistic coordination can sharpen the accuracy of inferences on the ultimate question of whether such coordination is occurring. This section begins by elaborating on this idea because of its importance and because the relevance of conduciveness under the commonly advocated communications-based prohibition may be radically different—arguably the opposite in many settings, as explored in chapters 6 and 17.[1] Then attention turns to factors bearing on the conduciveness to coordination. Last, the section reflects on the weight that should be given to these structural factors in light of doubt cast on the structure-conduct-performance paradigm by decades of empirical research.

The social cost of errors and thus the importance of their reduction is emphasized in section 9.A, and the (sometimes significant) uncertainty about inferences regarding whether coordinated oligopolistic price elevation took place was the subject of the preceding chapter and will recur later here. It remains to consider precisely how evidence bearing on the conduciveness of conditions improves the inference process. First, in a crude sense conduciveness is a necessary condition for successful coordination.[2] If coordinated oligopoly pricing is impossible under the cir-

---

[1] To remind, under the latter approach, it is often suggested that conditions highly conducive to successful coordination—rather than merely moderately conducive—favor a finding of no liability because the likelihood that explicit communications were used is considered to be lower when they are less essential.

[2] For this reason, conduciveness may seem to be a candidate for a procedural screen (see

cumstances, we can confidently infer that it is not taking place. Similarly, if conditions are unconducive, success seems unlikely.

One reservation to this argument concerns ill-conceived attempts. As will be discussed in section 12.B, it is often helpful to punish attempts even if they fail—or, importantly, when it is difficult to know whether they have succeeded. Nevertheless, the deterrence benefit of such punishment is likely to be limited when considering realms in which success is difficult or impossible in any event, and we should also be more skeptical that an attempt occurred in unconducive circumstances.[3]

The more important qualification is that the investigator or adjudicator may be mistaken about how unconducive the conditions actually are. Particularly in large industries with significant stakes, the firms involved will ordinarily have a better grasp of industry conditions and of their own ability to succeed in spite of them than will an outsider.[4] Thus, if one sees clear attempts to coordinate or strong evidence that oligopolistic coordination is successful, the better inference is that the mistake lies not with the firms' analysis of conditions but rather with the enforcer's.

It should be clear as well that inferences about conditions should influence inferences about successful coordination and vice versa. If we are highly confident about one set of inferences, then we should adjust, perhaps significantly, our inferences about the other. As mentioned, if conditions seem quite unconducive, we should be more skeptical of

---

section 15.A), just as market power is a prerequisite for some competition law violations. One difficulty with this approach, just as with market power, is that substantial evidence and analysis may be required to make the assessment.

[3] It is commonly argued in standard criminal law contexts that punishment of attempts is still important in such cases because actors may try more efficacious means in the future. For example, if someone believes he can use a voodoo doll to kill someone else, but the government is certain he is mistaken, failure to prosecute involves the risk that, when initial attempts have failed, the perpetrator may use a gun next time, which may well succeed. Firms attempting coordinated price elevation in structurally competitive markets where successful coordination is essentially impossible do not have the option of switching industries. They may, however, resort to facilitating practices, discussed in section 10.C, in order to increase their subsequent odds of success.

[4] This point did not prevent the Supreme Court majority in Brooke Group Ltd. v. Brown & Williamson Tobacco Corp., 509 U.S. 209 (1993), from stating that the cigarette companies could not succeed at coordinated oligopoly pricing, against the dissent's criticism that the Court should not substitute its judgment for that of the defendant firms, who had long done so in the past.

evidence that may otherwise lead us to believe that coordinated oligopolistic price elevation took place.[5] However, if evidence on the latter is quite strong, then we should doubt evidence that conditions are highly unconducive. Often, there will be nontrivial uncertainty surrounding both matters. In addition, even when there is reasonable confidence regarding conduciveness, it may be that it is at an intermediate level, readily admitting the possibility that coordination would succeed and that it would fail. In such cases, we would need to rely primarily on the strength of the evidence bearing on success to determine whether oligopolistic coordination took place.

To round out consideration of the relevance of conduciveness, it is also important to emphasize that although, at some level, it is a necessary condition to success, it is not a sufficient condition, and this is so even when conditions are extremely conducive. First, the characterization may be incorrect. In addition, high conduciveness is no guarantee: Even tasks properly assessed to be easy may not be doable by certain actors in some settings.

There is, however, a more serious reservation on account of the fact that deterrence may be effective. Even the simplest activity will not be undertaken if the expected penalty for doing so is sufficiently great. In a well-functioning regime, coordinated oligopolistic price elevation may be deterred in most instances,[6] a point noted in section 9.A's elaboration of the framework for decision-making. Put another way, unless one believes that the legal system is a substantial failure, one cannot assume that highly conducive conditions in and of themselves imply a significant likelihood of coordinated price elevation.

---

[5] Posner (2001, 69) remarks: "The reader may wonder whether the first stage is either necessary or appropriate: one could hardly punish firms simply for finding themselves in a situation where collusion would appear to be an advantageous strategy; and if they *are* in fact colluding, why worry whether the circumstances in the market are favorable to collusion? The answer is twofold: first, to enable enforcers to concentrate their resources in markets where those resources are likely to be employed most productively; second, to enable ambiguous conduct to be evaluated."

[6] Indeed, this may be especially so when conditions are highly conducive to successful coordination if enforcers focus on such industries. On the other hand, under an approach that limits liability to cases in which certain communications have been employed, oligopoly pricing may be de facto permissible when conditions are highly conducive as a consequence of the paradox of proof, explored in chapters 6 and 17.

Turning next to the conditions themselves, the present discussion will be brief since the subject has received extensive attention in the literature and is not particularly controversial.[7] First, numbers and market concentration, two closely related factors, are important for many reasons. When the number of firms is larger, coordinating on a common price and punishment strategy tends to be more difficult, and cheating may be harder to detect because there will be smaller firms whose defection may be more difficult to identify. There may be more asymmetry when numbers are larger, which, as just indicated and will be discussed further momentarily, inhibits coordinated price elevation. Accordingly, it is unsurprising that, in most prosecuted cases, the number of firms in the industry was low and concentration high.[8]

Firms' capacities are also relevant. Greater capacity is two-edged: A cheater may be able to grab more of the market if its capacity is larger, but other firms have a greater ability to punish, keeping in mind that the industry price can be driven down only if firms as a whole can supply a sufficient quantity.[9] Asymmetries in capacity make coordination more difficult: A firm with substantially more excess capacity may gain much from cheating, whereas the others with limited additional capacity may find it difficult to impose punishment.

Another important factor is the transparency of prices and the structure of the buyer side of the market, two dimensions that are often interrelated. Cheating is easiest to detect when prices are open.[10] When there are large numbers of small buyers (consider markets for many consumer goods), public pricing is common, which should make coordination easier. In contrast, when there are a few large buyers, who have the ability to make

---

[7] See Connor (2007a, 32–42), Hay and Kelley (1974, 14–17), Kaplow and Shapiro (2007, 1108–21), Levenstein and Suslow (2006, 57–75), Posner (2001, 69–79), and Vives (1999, 306–10).

[8] See Hay and Kelley (1974, 22 tbl. 2, 23–24 & tbl. 3, 27). Concentration was extremely high for the large international cartels examined in Connor (2007a, 123, 174, 249–52, 261).

[9] See Brock and Scheinkman (1985).

[10] Furthermore, recall from the discussion of facilitating practices in section 10.C that many of these pertain to making price information more available. More generally, most facilitating practices have the characteristic that they aim to operate on one of the factors identified in this section in such a way as to make conditions more conducive to coordination; conversely, for any factor noted here that is subject to firms' control, one can imagine corresponding facilitating practices.

infrequent large orders, the terms of which are privately negotiated, coordination tends to be more difficult. (In this respect, the evidence that
many prosecuted price-fixing cases involve sales of intermediate goods[11]
may seem surprising, although there are other factors that may explain
this fact.)[12] An interesting and important setting concerns public auctions,
where governments ordinarily publish winning bids; this practice makes
cheating particularly easy to detect, which may help to explain why so
many price-fixing prosecutions involve bid rigging.[13] Yet another relevant
aspect of the buyer side of the market concerns changes in demand over
time. As noted in subsection 7.A.2, demand uncertainty inhibits coordination by making cheating more difficult to identify when prices are not
public. Additionally, anticipated changes in demand can affect incentives
to cheat by altering the ratio of cheaters' current gains from defection to
their future losses during punishment.[14]

Product heterogeneity also makes oligopolistic coordination more
difficult, which is consistent with the fact that most prosecuted cases
involve homogeneous products.[15] First, reaching consensus on price and
other terms is more complex when the problem is multidimensional, as
discussed in section 10.C. Relatedly, when there is significant potential
for differentiation, cheating is more likely because it may be more difficult

---

[11] This point is apparent from examination of the lists of industries in Connor (2007b,
136–53), Harrington (2006, 98–102), and Hay and Kelley (1974, 29–38).

[12] First, intermediate goods are more often homogeneous whereas consumer products are
often differentiated (including by location and format of retail outlet). Second, if prosecutions
have been limited to cases of explicit communications, it may be that such are less necessary
or at least less frequent when prices are more open.

[13] See Connor (2007b, 79, 88–89). Note that even if bids are not published, knowing who
won may well be sufficient, particularly if the firms arranged in advance that only one of
them would put in a lowest bid, rather than all placing identical bids, as discussed in note 6
in chapter 5.

[14] Cheating is also more likely when it has a lasting impact on demand, such as when there
are customer switching costs or network effects, although these factors also make it more difficult for the cheater to increase market share quickly. Cheating could also have a more durable
impact if long-term contracts at favorable prices are signed, although buyers anticipating price
cuts from others might be reluctant to do so.

[15] Examination of the lists of industries in Connor (2007b, 136–53), Harrington (2006,
98–102), and Hay and Kelley (1974, 29–38) strongly suggests this to be true (see also Hay and
Kelley 1974, 24–25, 27), and it is certainly true of the large international cartels examined in
Connor (2007a).

to police product quality, subtle terms of sale (such as being more prompt and helpful in dealing with buyers), and other features. When products are differentiated, the cheating calculus also differs in two opposed respects: On one hand, a small price cut is less attractive because it will draw fewer customers from rivals, but on the other hand, punishment from rivals' price cuts will be less painful.[16]

Greater similarity on virtually any dimension is helpful to oligopolistic firms seeking to coordinate on elevated prices. It was already suggested that smaller firms and those with relatively more excess capacity are more inclined to cheat. Firms with shorter time horizons also are more prone to defection: Consider a firm in temporary financial distress that needs additional cash quickly. Firms with more similar production costs will more readily be able to agree on a particular elevated price and none will gain disproportionately from cheating.[17] More extensive contacts and more similar backgrounds of key decision-makers may make mutual understanding easier and enhance trust. Such might include educational and social backgrounds, longevity in the industry, and participation in joint ventures and trade association activities (even if no secret discussion about pricing takes place).[18] Multi-market contact may have similar benefits and also enlarges the strategic space in which punishment may occur.[19]

A final set of considerations involves group market power, which is indicated by the industry elasticity of demand and also the ability of others to increase supply through entry or expansion by fringe firms not part of the group understanding. In the extreme, if there is little or no ability for even a hypothetical monopolist to increase price, then an oligopoly will fare no better. However, if there is some industry-wide market power, albeit limited in degree, oligopolistic firms will still wish to elevate price

---

[16] See Deneckere (1983) and Ross (1992).

[17] Relatedly, Crawford, Gneezy, and Rottenstreich (2008) offer experimental evidence suggesting that even small degrees of asymmetry in payoffs can inhibit coordination on focal points. However, this result is in a game with no communication whatsoever and no repetition, so even the ability to react, say, to another firm's price is absent.

[18] See the related discussion in subsection 7.B.3 and Glaeser et al. (2000), Leslie (2004), and Porter (1980, 90).

[19] See Bernheim and Whinston (1990) and, for further discussion, Kaplow and Shapiro (2007, 1116).

to that extent. Observe that, when the best coordinated oligopolistic price is lower, both the gain from cheating and the cost of punishment are each proportionately lower as a first approximation. Hence, if a coordinated oligopolistic price was otherwise sustainable, the same tends to be true in a market where power is less. The major caveat is the existence of fixed costs of coordination. Some may involve time and effort. Others may relate to the structure of penalties, which will be elaborated in chapter 13. In brief, for fines or damages that are proportional to the price elevation, lower profit potential implies correspondingly lower penalties, so the deterrence calculus would be largely the same. However, there may be fixed punishment costs, including the costs of responding to investigations and participation in adjudication and also some penalties that even if not fixed do not rise in proportion to the magnitude of the violation, which is common for prison terms and also for government fines in many jurisdictions. In that case, deterrence will be more powerful when industry market power is lower. A countervailing factor is that enforcement may be less likely for smaller elevations because they are harder for enforcers to detect and prove and also because enforcers may choose to devote fewer resources to such cases.

At this point, it is useful to reflect further on the importance of these conditions bearing on the feasibility of coordination in different markets. In addition to the already-noted logical relevance of conduciveness to inferences about whether successful oligopolistic coordination took place, empirical evidence on the correlation between various indicia of conduciveness and industry profitability or price elevation is also pertinent. After all, the weight that should be accorded this type of evidence depends importantly on how predictive it is of the problem we seek to detect. To take as an extreme, a sometimes-mentioned view is that oligopolistic price coordination is inevitable, even through pure interdependence, when conditions are favorable;[20] but this view seems quite inconsistent with existing empirical work.[21]

Since the 1980s (if not earlier), industrial organization economists have become quite skeptical of what is referred to as the structure-conduct-

---

[20] See note 43 in chapter 13.

[21] It is also inconsistent with the evidence presented in section 6.E indicating the frequent use of explicit communications—thereby risking heavy sanctions—even when conditions are conducive.

performance paradigm that, in its simplest form, holds that market structure dictates conduct, which in turn dictates performance.[22] In the present
setting, the proposition would be that conduciveness determines whether
firms behave interdependently which in turn determines whether prices
are elevated and thus whether firms realize supracompetitive profits.

Reservations about the relationship between structure (industry conditions) and performance are due in significant part to cross-sectional
studies of different industries in which structural factors such as industry
concentration explain little if any of the variation in profitability. In addition, to the extent that there is some relationship, there are competing
explanations, notably, that concentration is often due to one or a few firms
being highly efficient, which is the basis for their profitability, rather than
its being caused by industry-wide price elevation. Evidence for this interpretation derives from some studies showing that higher profits are
only enjoyed by the largest firms. That claim, in turn, is contested on the
ground that smaller firms may operate largely in different market seg-
ments (strong product differentiation) or that lesser efficiency of fringe
producers is not inconsistent with the large firms collectively elevating
price. Resolving this debate has waned in importance as studies have
failed to find a substantial relationship between concentration and profits
in any event, although there is evidence of some correlation.[23]

Stronger evidence consistent with the importance of structural conditions is that they, notably concentration, correlate with price, as distinguished from profits. Such findings are more common in intra-industry
studies, often comparing price across regions where concentration varies.
On one hand, such studies are more powerful because many problems in
measuring profits are avoided, more factors are implicitly controlled since
only a single industry is considered, and price is more relevant because
a lack of high profits may arise even with elevated prices if nonprice

---

[22] See Baker and Bresnahan (2008, 24–26).

[23] Schmalensee (1987a, 420) offers the following view of the competing hypotheses: "At
any rate, there is no support here for the use of the DEH [differential efficiency hypothesis],
the DCH [differential concentration hypothesis], or the DEH/DCH hybrids as maintained
hypotheses in policy analysis or the study of individual industries. It would appear likely that
the relative importance of collusion and differential efficiency vary considerably among industries and over time." See also Perloff, Karp, and Golan (2007, 33–34) and the sources cited
in note 26.

competition erodes margins. There are also limitations: Costs may vary across regions and in ways related to concentration; that is, higher costs may lead to both higher concentration and higher price. Accordingly, it is important to control for costs. More broadly, regressions relating concentration or other features of industry structure to price or to profits suffer from endogeneity, so greater effort is required to identify causation and measure the magnitude of any effects.[24]

Another source of evidence not as often considered in the industrial organization literature is that discussed in sections 6.E and 9.C deriving from enforcement against price fixing. As mentioned, these cases are typically in industries with high concentration, few firms, and homogeneous products, precisely the structural conditions believed to be conducive to successful oligopolistic coordination.[25]

Taken together, there certainly is justification for paying attention to the conduciveness of industry conditions in examining particular cases. Nevertheless, empirical evidence gives us reason not to place excessive weight on this factor.[26] It probably remains true that highly unconducive

---

[24] Evans, Froeb, and Werden (1993) discuss the issues and implement a solution for the airline industry, finding that an unbiased estimate of the effect of concentration on price exceeds ordinary least squares estimates by 150–250%.

[25] These prior discussions also raise some caveats on the interpretation of such evidence.

[26] Some views of the literature expressed in leading surveys are as follows: "The current state of affairs is quite encouraging: we know that there is market power out there, and need to know a lot more about exactly where. We know essentially nothing about the causes, or even the systematic predictors of market power, but have come a long way in working out how to measure them." Bresnahan (1989, 1055). Schmalensee (1989, 952) suggests that empirical studies rarely will yield consistent estimates of structural parameters but can produce useful stylized facts to guide theory construction and the analysis of particular industries. Among the stylized facts he identifies (971, 976, 988) are the following: "4.3 At the firm or business unit level in the United States, industry characteristics account for only about 10–25% of the cross-section variation in accounting rates of return. . . . 4.5 The relation, if any, between seller concentration and profitability is weak statistically, and the estimated concentration effect is usually small. The estimated relation is unstable over time and space and vanishes in many multivariate studies. 5.1 In cross-section comparisons involving markets in the same industry, seller concentration is positively related to the level of price." Scherer (1977, 982–83), in reviewing the first (1976) edition of Posner (2001), offers a highly discouraging view: "First, I doubt that the power of economic analysis has advanced so far that his two-stage determination is feasible. The first stage depends on our limited ability to predict the likelihood of supracompetitive prices from the kinds of structural indicia identified by Posner . . . . While I was with the FTC we had an active effort to identify potential price-fixing cases using only such structural

conditions strongly negate the plausibility that firms successfully elevate price. Given the noisy relationship, however, strong evidence of success should usually be regarded as convincing. On the other hand, high conduciveness is a weak basis for assuming success, particularly in light of the point emphasized at the outset of this section that, if deterrence is strong, coordinated price elevation should be infrequent even when conditions are ideal.[27]

Conduciveness is also important with regard to the magnitude of deterrence benefits and chilling costs. When conditions are quite unconducive, any successful oligopolistic coordination is likely to result in price elevations that are small and short-lived. On the other hand, chilling costs are likely to be greater in such situations because these industries are reasonably likely to be competitive. There are a large number of markets where conditions are quite unconducive to successful coordinated price elevation. If such cases are not screened out, they might give rise to many false positives. On the other hand, when conditions are highly conducive, undeterred firms may succeed in significant, long-lasting price elevations, whereas chilling costs may be less worrisome because, even in the event of error, highly competitive behavior is less likely to have been taking place. Accordingly, insisting on moderately or perhaps highly conducive conditions seems sensible.

B. Internal Evidence

The discussion throughout chapter 10 and section A of this chapter, like much prior literature, proceeds implicitly as if evidence bearing on

---

evidence. The kindest thing I can say about the effort is that it was a resounding flop—partly because of severe data limitations and partly because our staff lacked the insight or imagination to hold its conceptual divining rod in the right position." See also Abrantes-Metz and Froeb (2008), suggesting that recent efforts at screening have been largely unsuccessful; Grout and Sonderegger (2007), advocating the use of structural screening by enforcement agencies as a component of cartel detection; and Harrington (2007), advocating greater use of behavioral rather than structural screening by enforcement agencies.

[27] A concern with empirical studies of the relationship between structural conditions and price elevation is that they do not take into account the deterrent effects of anti-price-fixing laws. If deterrence is substantial, this could help to explain the weakness of the observed relationships.

successful oligopolistic coordination will largely be external to the firm. However, for virtually any factor and channel of inference, there is corresponding internal evidence. In addition to hard evidence—for example, invoices or other records indicating prices charged and quantities sold—there is a variety of other information. Some of it may directly indicate firms' thinking (strategy or decision memos, notes of meetings, internal policy pronouncements), and much more will convey aspects indirectly (cost and marketing data being suggestive of firms' beliefs about marginal cost and demand). This section first considers more fully how various sorts of internal evidence may be relevant to inferences about oligopoly behavior, on the assumption that reliable internal information can be obtained, and then takes up two important reservations: the difficulty of discerning what a firm "knows" and the problem that firms may sanitize or otherwise pervert records of internal understandings in order to avoid liability.

Confining attention to larger firms,[28] a substantial portion of higher-level managers' time, as well as efforts throughout particular departments, is devoted to information gathering, analysis, and decision-making. Sometimes there are outside consultants and industry-wide information agencies as well. These activities generate all manner of notes, reporting up and down chains of command, memos, communications, meetings, and so forth. They relate to what firms know or believe as well as to the reasoning behind their decisions.

It follows that there may often be significant internal evidence bearing on every consideration identified in chapter 10 and section A of this chapter. Consider pricing patterns: When a firm suddenly (or otherwise) increases its price, it will have reasons, usually supported by its own evidence. If there is a corresponding increase in cost, this will be seen in the firm's internal cost data as well as in its decision-making process. When the price suddenly drops, similar internal information and activity will also be involved. Whether the firm is a secret price cutter, is responding

---

[28] If adjacent, owner-operated gasoline stations coordinate their prices, the only internal source of information about their thinking is likely to be the owners' own statements upon questioning (unless perhaps they keep journals, confide in spouses, or are talkative at bars after work). Large organizations are quite different in this regard.

to perceived cheating by others, or is reflecting changes in cost or demand, the information and rationale will be reflected internally. Likewise for more modest price adjustments. More broadly, if firms are interacting interdependently, playing the sort of repeated game described in subsection 7.A.2 involving a consensus price elevation and punishment strategy, we would expect internal discussions and other traces to differ from the situation in which firms behave as competitors who take rivals' behavior as given.[29]

Regarding the existing degree of price elevation, one would expect firms to have knowledge of their own prices and marginal cost and thus an estimate of price-cost margins.[30] Firms think about which costs are fixed and variable and how joint costs are properly allocated. They know when production is at or near capacity and if marginal cost is rising sharply. When they price discriminate or grant a price concession to a large buyer, they presumably are aware of their costs and their reasons for charging different prices to different customers. If their prices vary across geographic markets, they again have reasons and information on which their reasoning is based. In deciding how much of a cost shift to pass on to consumers or how to respond to demand fluctuations, they are thinking about whether their marginal costs are constant over the relevant output range, what is the elasticity of the demand they face, and (certainly if they are coordinating) possible interactions with competitors.

---

[29] For example, in some court cases, as discussed in section 5.A, there is evidence of firms' "understanding" with others, viewing competitors as "friends," and so forth, all of which suggest interdependence. See also Kessler and Wheeler (1993, 26): "internal company documents about a price change in a concentrated market will quite naturally often speculate about the possible reaction of rivals to the price change."

[30] Farrell and Shapiro (2010, 18) argue that, although "gross margins are hard to measure using public data . . . and methods sufficiently standardized for cross-sectional studies[,] . . . firms have an incentive to keep track of their cost functions via managerial accounting tools, for instance to know how far they can profitably cut prices. Such information . . . normally is available to antitrust agencies and courts." Others are more skeptical. See Motta (2004, 116): "Determining the impact of a marginal change in the quantity produced by a firm on the total cost of production is often beyond practical feasibility even with the best knowledge of the technological conditions under which a firm operates. Indeed, there might be large differences in the estimates of marginal costs even within the management of the same firm."; Baker (2007, 142–43); and Werden (1998, 394).

If they have excess capacity, they have thought about using more of it, which probably involves reducing price, and presumably have decided against it, again, for a reason.

Facilitating practices may be adopted to ease oligopolistic coordination or, in many cases, for additional or alternative reasons. If firms announce prices in advance, they know why they do so. If they voluntarily share sensitive information through a trade association or otherwise, they anticipate gaining something in return and have a sense of what the benefit will be. If a firm's product is superior to others, those in marketing and sales departments will want to take advantage of this fact, and if they are ordered not to do so, there will be indicators of that restriction as well as of the reasoning behind the decision; likewise if they desist from offering new products, enhancing service to buyers, and so forth.[31] If they have adopted most-favored-customer clauses, price-matching guarantees, or resale price maintenance, they will have considered the pros and cons in reaching a decision.

One particular facilitating practice that is mentioned in section 10.C and will be revisited in the next section concerns interfirm communications. These will also tend to leave internal tracks. Not only may there be direct evidence of such communications—such as email, notes, and explicit mention thereof—but there also might exist other evidence indicating that such communications have been made, such as analyses or discussions premised on knowledge obtained thereby. In addition, evidence may clarify why they were made, which is particularly important when the competitive effects of the communications seem to be ambiguous. Consider again the example of advance public price announcements.

Similar reasoning applies to the conduciveness of conditions. Firms know their production capacities and have at least an educated guess about those of competitors. Similarly, they have views about cost asymmetries and the degree of homogeneity of their products, including, importantly, how salient are any differences to buyers. They have a sense of how well they know and can trust counterparts at rival firms. And they

---

[31] See Posner (2001, 97).

have a view on industry market power, including demand elasticity and prospects for entry and fringe expansion.

In sum, regarding every question considered in chapter 10 on market-based evidence and section 11.A on the conduciveness of conditions, there often will exist traces and sometimes a rich vein of pertinent material inside the firm. Note that omissions can also be revealing. For example, a lack of new data or of discussion about changes in demand makes a sharp demand shift an unlikely explanation for a price move. In contrast, if a new product proposal is shot down because studies detail how the firm lacks production capability or show that consumers are uninterested, suppressing heterogeneity is an unlikely explanation.

Such internal evidence is underplayed in the analysis of competition policy, including importantly that directed toward what might be provable in an enforcement action.[32] It sometimes seems as if firms are personified to such an extent that they are treated as if they were a single person whose mind cannot be fathomed by an outsider. An individual might be called to testify, but it may be supposed that the person would lie and that, lacking other evidence, perjury could not be deterred or overcome.

Consider now two important limitations in relying on internal evidence from firms. First, since a large firm is a group of many individuals with complex, overlapping, and sometimes conflicting duties, it can be difficult to determine what a firm knows or what reasoning explains its actions. Many decisions are based on soft information or are made despite seemingly contradictory information, perhaps because the information is seen to be unreliable, because there are overriding considerations, or because of incompetence. There may exist internal disagreement or misunderstanding. Firm politics may also play a role, reflecting that employees are not perfect agents of the owners. Reasons may be clear in the minds of some, but they may not be the individuals with decision-making authority.

In addition, there remains the question of how such views and intentions will be reflected in firms' records and other indicators. There may be omissions, incompleteness, and ambiguity. And individuals who tes-

---

[32] It is important to distinguish this setting from enforcers who are viewing the economy as a whole in search of markets in which violations might be taking place. See section 15.A.

tify when the firm is subject to an enforcement proceeding may have strong incentives to bend the truth, selectively recall events, and the like. Disgruntled employees may tilt in the opposite direction, perhaps attributing nefarious motives for price changes that are innocuous. To top it off, in an adversary proceeding, in which an outsider—the government or a private plaintiff—seeks to present a reconstruction of firms' knowledge and thinking by creating a mosaic that selects from myriad fragments, the potential for misapprehension and conscious obfuscation by both sides is vast.

That said, it seems plausible that some substantial and fairly reliable conclusions will be possible to reach. Firms cannot operate while lacking even an approximate sense of their costs and market demand, without any rationale for their actions. If successful oligopolistic coordination significantly elevates prices for extended periods of time, there may well be substantial internal indicators. Similarly, if no such behavior has occurred, there may be evidence inconsistent with hypothesized coordinated price elevation.

A second concern is that lawyers or others will anticipate the liability implications of firms' knowledge, decision-making, and actions and therefore will distort the various clues to be found within the firm.[33] Some may believe that this sort of adjustment is not very difficult to accomplish, but it is not clear that experience bears this out.[34] Moreover, we should be skeptical that a cleansing process can be highly effective.

Initially, it is difficult for a team of lawyers or others to reach broadly and deeply into a large corporation, controlling how myriad individuals speak, write, email, and otherwise behave. Furthermore, any such process

---

[33] For example, the ABA (2010) compliance guide for corporate counselors contains a chapter titled "Internal Communications: What Not to Say and How Not to Say It."

[34] For example, then-Judge Breyer, in Barry Wright Corp. v. ITT Grinnell Corp., 724 F.2d 227, 232 (1st Cir. 1983), states, "[I]f the search for intent means a search for documents or statements specifically reciting the likelihood of anticompetitive consequences or of subsequent opportunities to inflate prices, the knowledgeable firm will simply refrain from overt description." There are, however, glaring contrary examples. In early U.S. enforcement actions against Microsoft, it is notorious that the leader of the company (among others) sent (and retained record of) numerous emails that strongly indicated anticompetitive purpose. See Heilemann (2000). Likewise with the more recent Whole Foods Merger. See ABA (2010, 132–34) and Levy (2007).

that is not limited to a handful of key agents may itself leave incriminating tracks. Relatedly, aggressive destruction of electronic and physical documents is often prohibited, is difficult to implement (since so many copies will exist in so many places), and leaves its own traces that can be highly incriminating.

Furthermore, even if firms succeeded in ensuring that no individuals made explicit reference to forbidden activity, most of the information described in this section would remain. That is, none of the foregoing depends on finding documents in which firms admit to price fixing. Instead, it refers to all manner of data and documentation regarding firms' costs, demand, strategic decision-making, and so forth. It seems rather implausible that all such information could be eliminated, kept fully hidden, or elaborately concocted to present a reasonably consistent picture that departs radically from the truth. And if such was attempted, the inevitable lapses—as well as the attempts at orchestrating the charade—may well belie what was happening.

The firms' task is even more daunting in the present context because we are examining the possibility of coordinated behavior. Suppose, for example, that a group of firms significantly elevates price to a supracompetitive level. Consider how difficult it would be for all of them to fabricate consistent stories about a cost shock that had not in fact occurred. Each would need relevant departments to invent data, produce reports, and so forth, and this fabricated information would have to largely coincide across the firms and yet appear to have been independently generated. All of this would need to happen quickly and be documented before the pricing decision is implemented. And no one at any of the firms could leave traces or subsequently be induced to testify about any of it. Finally, the fabricated cost shock would have to be consistent with external evidence. In contrast, if there really was a cost shock, and accordingly the price increase was an ordinary response of competitors, substantial corroborating material would likely have been generated in the ordinary course of business by each of the firms, and it would be consistent with external indicators.

Sometimes covering tracks may be possible. When there is a simple, standardized product sold in a stable market, perhaps only a few individuals who have price-setting authority at each firm need to be involved in pricing decisions, and they may be able to operate secretly, leaving no recorded clues. Such seems to have been the case in a number of prose-cuted price-fixing cases, although some traces may ultimately have surfaced. But there, internal searches often focused on admissions of explicit, clandestine price-fixing communications between firms. It is quite another matter for such firms to hide all cost and demand information or, as just described, to concoct in parallel elaborate, phony information that appears to have been collected and disseminated throughout each firm.

In all, internal evidence is no panacea, but it seems to have substantial potential.[35] Moreover, as with the other bases for inference considered previously, different means can be employed together. Thus, if the question is whether a price increase can be explained by a common cost shock, one would look to external evidence, such as market data and information from suppliers, and also to internal evidence from the firms in the industry. Using both together, a more reliable conclusion can be drawn.

C. Interfirm Communications

Interfirm communications—particularly explicit ones, often taken to be secret—are the focus of many commentators' views of what the regulation of coordinated oligopolistic price elevation is or should primarily be about, a subject explored in depth in parts I and III. The question for present purposes is how interfirm communications are relevant in making inferences about whether successful oligopolistic coordination has taken place. To a substantial extent, the answer is already incorporated in the preceding discussion of detection, and in any event the answer is often obvious.

First, interfirm communications contribute to our understanding of what firms have done and why. In that respect, they are much like some of the other types of internal evidence just considered. Thus, when there is evidence not just on the existence of interfirm communications but

---

[35] It also has costs, both adjudication costs and ex ante costs implicit in what has just been discussed in that firms may undertake some efforts at subterfuge, which may entail direct expenditures of effort as well as losses from reductions in internal operational efficiency. Moreover, innocent firms may feel the need to engage in precautions to avoid even the accidental generation of fragmentary evidence that, taken out of context or otherwise misinterpreted, might give the impression of coordinated behavior.

also on their content,[36] they may provide a strong basis for inference if they are sufficiently explicit and reliable,[37] especially when they refer to prior, successful price elevation. Of course, the same is true of some other types of internal evidence. Likewise, the caveats concerning internal evidence are relevant, some with particular force. In addition to problems of authority, ambiguity, and conflicts, the concern that firms may hide their tracks is particularly great because interfirm contacts may, as noted, be confined to a few individuals whereas much other internal activity is more ubiquitous.

Note that public interfirm communications, ranging from advance price announcements to commentary on industry conditions, are not hidden and may be as revealing as secret discussions. Indeed, if public interchanges were per se legal, firms could simply move their meetings from hotel rooms to joint press conferences (recall the second example in section 2.A). Even when purportedly directed toward the public, sequential advance announcements arriving at a consensus price may indicate what firms are doing. In this respect, communications may supplement information from price moves themselves. For example, if an industry-wide price increase is due to a common cost shock and firms are behaving competitively, they will have less of a need to feel out their rivals before raising their prices.[38] Of course, to the extent that public

---

[36] When all we know, for example, is that secret meetings took place, we may still be quite suspicious of firms' activities, which can be useful in making inferences for purposes of liability. However, as will be discussed in section 13.A, if we wish to levy sanctions that are based on the level of price elevation, it will be necessary to rely primarily on other evidence for that purpose, although our confidence that such other evidence is not entirely mistaken may be greater. See also section 12.B, discussing the punishment of attempts to elevate prices.

[37] Interfirm communications pose an additional issue concerning reliability because they may be designed to mislead competitors. For example, a firm may try to convince others it will go along with price elevation because it intends to cheat from the outset, hoping to gain at others' expense. One would often need further evidence to know whether firms actually engaged in price elevation, and such other evidence would often be sufficient in itself. More to the point, interfirm communications may nicely complement such evidence if the latter does not, standing alone, resolve all doubt as to what transpired. Another, perhaps more farfetched, possibility is that firms would orchestrate discussions designed to mislead enforcers, perhaps by having a discussion about a supposed cost shock, as suggested in note 38.

[38] Firms might still seek to learn from their competitors, for example, if the magnitude of the cost shock is somewhat uncertain, which in some instances complicates the inference process. See the discussion in note 13 in chapter 10, suggesting reasons to be skeptical of this

communications are understood to provide a basis for inferring a violation, they would be discouraged, possibly being driven underground.

Second, as already mentioned in section 10.C, interfirm communications can serve as an important facilitating device and thus support an
inference of coordinated oligopoly pricing. These might include not only
secret meetings but also many sorts of public statements: advance price
announcements, predictions about industry demand or costs, and open
discussions of various matters at trade association meetings. Such communications may help firms reach a consensus, which can be challenging
when there are multiple equilibria and there may be disagreement about
which is best, and also when more complex understandings are required,
perhaps because of product heterogeneity. In addition, direct interchange
may help identify and coordinate the punishment of cheaters, although
there are problems regarding the credibility of firms' statements in this
context, as discussed in subsection 7.B.2.

Relatedly, as previously mentioned, some forms of interfirm communications are an attractive enforcement target because there is little social
cost if firms are deterred from engaging in them. Secret meetings in hotel
rooms come to mind. For other communications, such as public price
announcements, trade association activities, and participation in standard
setting or joint ventures, there are varying degrees of possible benefits
that need to be considered, and the risks obviously vary depending on
the content of the communications and the nature of the industry.[39]

Interfirm communications of all sorts can be important in making
reliable inferences. It is also clear that their reliability may be enhanced,
perhaps significantly in many instances, by combining them with the
other evidence considered throughout. Accordingly, evidence of interfirm
communications should be viewed as a weapon in the detection arsenal
but not as the be-all and end-all.

---

explanation in many settings. Note that, if one gives sufficient credence to this qualification
and wishes to avoid any interference with this interfirm learning process, one might then be
excusing explicit discussions couched in terms of purported cost changes, which could readily
cover for direct discussion of prices.

[39] In this regard, as section 18.C explains, a legal regime that is more aggressive toward
successful oligopolistic coordination may be able to be more relaxed about activities that both
have social benefits and also might facilitate price elevation; the latter can be downplayed if it
is independently deterred.

A related question is how probative is the lack of explicit, detailed interfirm communications. First, because firms attempt to keep these secret and may succeed in doing so, a failure to find such communications is hardly conclusive that they did not occur. Second, successful oligopolistic coordination is sometimes possible without elaborate communications. Regarding both points, there is an important interaction with the conduciveness of conditions, discussed in section A: When conditions are most conducive—particularly when the number of firms is small— explicit interfirm communications may be less essential and also more difficult to detect.[40] This suggests that, when the danger of coordinated oligopolistic price elevation is greatest, we should be less bothered by the lack of such evidence. Similarly, when firms' coordination problem is highly complex and likely to require extensive, explicit communications among large numbers of individuals, the absence of direct (or strong indirect) evidence that any such communications took place would make an inference of successful oligopolistic coordination notably weaker. As seen in chapter 6 and pursued in chapter 17, the logic in this paragraph differs greatly from that implied under the commonly advanced view of the appropriate standard for liability.

An additional point explored in those chapters is that it generally makes little sense in cases where no secret interfirm communications are directly detected to attempt to infer whether they have taken place through the use of circumstantial evidence. Since the reason we care about these communications is not for their own sake but instead because evidence thereof contributes to an ultimate inference about coordinated oligopolistic price elevation, nothing is added by this process. Stated abstractly, if evidence E1, E2, and E3 give rise to a probabilistic inference that secret communication C occurred (it not having been observed directly), then any implication from the set E1, E2, E3, and C about successful oligopolistic coordination can be no stronger than what one could have inferred directly from E1, E2, and E3 alone.[41] As discussed in chapters 6 and 17, the

---

[40] See the elaboration and qualifications in subsection 6.D.2. Regarding detection, see Hay and Kelley (1974, 20, 23–24 & n.15, 26–27)—portions of which are quoted in note 46 in chapter 6—and Masson and Reynolds (1978, 25–26).

[41] Even though direct evidence of C would strengthen the ultimate inference, the point is that, if the only evidence of C is due to the inference from E1, E2, and E3, nothing is added.

process of attempting to infer specific sorts of communication from circumstantial evidence is complicated and uncertain,[42] and it generally entails having already reached a judgment on whether coordinated oligopolistic price elevation has occurred.[43] Thus, the supplemental inference about communication is of little use, very costly, and also highly distracting.

---

[42] Because the approach generally requires inferring whether particular sorts of interfirm communication occurred, the process is especially difficult, and any conclusion is even less plausible as a source of illumination of the present question.

[43] The ultimate irony arises when defendants grant this point—that is, that they are collectively elevating price—and use the ease of coordination to negate the existence of particular sorts of communication in order to escape liability for admitted harmful behavior. Such is the paradox of proof.

12

Liability Assessment

❦

A. Probability and Magnitude of Coordinated Price Elevation

Few simple lessons can be drawn from the foregoing examination of the many types of evidence that may be used to support or negate inferences of successful oligopolistic coordination, particularly in light of the nature of the optimal decision-making framework discussed in chapter 9 with its emphasis on ex ante effects on deterrence and the chilling of desirable behavior.[1] This section nevertheless offers some observations on the relationship between avenues of proof and the social problem at hand.[2]

First, it is useful to reflect on why the probability of coordinated oligopolistic price elevation is important. In some basic models of optimal sanctions, all that matters is the expected harm. Here, further

---

[1] Among other points, it is important to keep in mind the significant contrast with traditional thinking that, here, error costs are identified and measured by reference to effects on social welfare and not by reference to deviations from some stipulated test (such as a particular, formal definition of agreement) that may itself be chosen on pragmatic grounds to serve as a proxy. The central example given was that false positives by reference to such a standard that arise when coordinated oligopolistic price elevation took place, perhaps through pure interdependence, produce desirable deterrence benefits rather than costly chilling effects.

[2] This section sets to the side questions of liability for the use of facilitating practices—that is, the condemnation of facilitating practices as such rather than making inferences about oligopolistic coordination from their use—as will much of the discussion in the following two sections, although liability for attempts does bear on the matter. One point in common with attempts is that liability assessed directly for the use of facilitating practices poses a question regarding the setting of sanctions because it may not be true that (and in any case may not be proved whether and to what extent) price elevation took place, so sanctions would need to reflect expected rather than actual harm.

decomposition is necessary, in part because the social consequences of errors may well be asymmetric. In particular, section 9.B's discussion of chilling effects suggests that significant social costs may be incurred if highly competitive industries with constant marginal cost face a non-trivial prospect of sanctions for price elevation. Accordingly, it is important that competitive firms, especially in such settings, not be subject to even moderate expected sanctions,[3] which implies that the uncertainty in any estimate of price elevation is important.[4]

Specifically, it matters how much of the distribution of possibilities involves no price elevation. Different forms of proof, viewed individually and in various combinations, may differ substantially in the likelihood of false positives. For example, some forms of proof may be highly probative of the magnitude of price elevation, yet admit a nontrivial risk of outright error. In contrast, other sorts of evidence—perhaps certain internal evidence or interfirm communications[5]—may be highly probative of whether there is coordinated oligopoly pricing (greatly reducing the likelihood of a false positive) without necessarily giving much indication of the extent of price elevation.

It is also worth reflecting further on the importance of the conduciveness of conditions with regard to the avoidance of false positives so as to reduce chilling effects. As mentioned, markets with quite unconducive conditions are ubiquitous, so false positives could be excessive if such cases are not effectively immune from liability (in the absence of powerful contrary evidence on coordinated price elevation). In addition to the adjudication costs that would be involved, there is the danger that the distribution of such cases would not be seen as random ex ante, but instead certain groups of firms in particular circumstances might have significant

---

[3] It may not be sufficient for such firms to treat the prospect of expected sanctions as a current marginal cost (which they would) because they would then need to raise price as a consequence, which itself could further raise expected sanctions.

[4] Observe that the nature of the cost of false positives is assumed throughout this section to concern cases of no actual price elevation from a competitive level with price equal to marginal cost. As chapter 14 explores, with regard to price elevation attributable to the unilateral exercise of market power rather than to coordinated price elevation, the chilling costs from errors in assessing the existence of price elevation beyond that due to unilateral market power would be different (generally, much less, and possibly even benefits).

[5] As discussed in chapter 11, these types of evidence are by no means uniformly reliable.

reason to fear that their actions would be mistaken for oligopolistic co-ordination, producing serious chilling effects.[6] Moreover, when coordinated oligopolistic price elevation does occur in industries that are unconducive, the elevations will, on average, tend to be small in magnitude and duration, so deterrence will be less valuable. Accordingly, insisting on moderately or perhaps highly conducive conditions seems sensible.[7] Recall from section 11.A, however, that high conduciveness is not sufficient, particularly if deterrence is reasonably effective.

Other features of industries bear on the risk of chilling effects that may be associated with one or another type of evidence.[8] For example, regarding demonstrations of price elevation that involve direct attempts to measure marginal cost, firms in some industries may each produce a single product with a simple cost structure whereas other industries may be inhabited by firms that produce multiple, related products with complicated technologies and substantial costs that may not obviously be fixed or variable in a relevant time frame. Accordingly, the optimal weight to give to such evidence will depend on whether a specific sort in a particular type of industry is likely, viewed ex ante, to pose a problem of

---

[6] It is not obvious that random chilling effects are innocuous whereas concentrated ones are costly. The core rationale that supports this view is based on the conjecture that chilling effects rise disproportionately in the expected sanction (they are nonlinear) at low levels. For example, if 1,000 markets are each subject to an expected sanction of 1, firms in these markets might each, in anticipation, elevate price slightly to cover the expected liability costs, which would not materially raise the likelihood of detection and may have little social cost (since marginal deadweight loss is zero when price elevation is zero). In contrast, if expected sanctions are concentrated—perhaps 10 markets each face an expected sanction of 100—distortion might be great and some might become monopolized, as discussed in section 9.B. For a formal statement and qualifications (pertaining to the density function for the distribution of private benefits of benign acts that may be chilled), see Kaplow (2012c).

[7] As discussed in chapter 17, some views of more traditional approaches to liability, which emphasize explicit interfirm communications, may have the opposite implication regarding conduciveness, which for the reasons just given in the text (and others, including the argument to follow on the magnitude of elevation) serves to reduce rather than maximize social welfare.

[8] Additionally, the analysis in section 9.B suggests that the social costs attributable to a given prospect of error will depend on industry conditions. Notably, if marginal costs are rising, competitive firms might be able to avoid false positives (with little attendant social cost) by somewhat reducing price, but if marginal costs are constant, false positives can be more problematic.

chilling effects or to enhance deterrence substantially. Regarding the latter, note that the importance of any type of evidence is a function of what other forms of proof are likely to be present if coordinated price elevation is indeed taking place. If some type of evidence is unreliable and involves chilling costs but other, superior evidence is likely to be available under the circumstances—conditional on undesirable behavior actually having occurred—then the former evidence might optimally be given little weight. In contrast, if the problematic evidence is likely to be the only type of evidence in such an industry, it may need to be given greater emphasis.

A final point in considering the probability of oligopolistic coordination is that, as section 9.A explains, a high proportion of actual positives will be false in a well-functioning system because successful deterrence greatly reduces true positives. This notion is not inconsistent with the need to avoid chilling effects because this other phenomenon concerns the ratio of false to total positives ex post, in the context of adjudication, whereas chilling effects are primarily determined by the absolute level of false positives anticipated ex ante.

A second observation is that the analysis in chapter 8 indicates the importance of the magnitude of oligopolistic price elevation. Not only is harm rising with this magnitude, but efficiency costs generally rise non-linearly. Marginal deadweight loss rises, beginning from zero, as price is elevated above marginal cost. (In contrast, it was mentioned that marginal forgone consumer surplus is falling with price elevation, even though the total sacrifice in consumer surplus is rising.) Waste due to excessive entry in the homogeneous goods case similarly is zero at the margin when price equals marginal cost and increases nonlinearly thereafter. When product variety is valuable, it is plausible that gains are greatest at the margin for small elevations, with the marginal benefit falling thereafter.[9]

This observation suggests that it may be best in many settings to require evidence of a significant price elevation. A simple and familiar reason for

---

[9] An interesting implication of this point combined with the preceding one on chilling effects is that a mean-preserving increase in the variance of the distribution of possible price elevation has ambiguous welfare consequences. For positive values of price elevation, greater variance implies greater social loss. But greater variance also implies a greater likelihood of false positives (no price elevation) and thus of chilling effects as well. Thus, the shape of the distribution matters, an aspect of which forms the basis for the next point in the text.

such a conclusion is that, in light of adjudication costs, it may not be worthwhile to pursue small cases. This basic claim may not, however, be true. One may not know that the elevation is small until most of the investigative costs are sunk. In addition, due to the prospect of deterrence, it may well be optimal to have a policy of pursuing cases with small elevations even if, ex post, the litigation costs exceed the harm in the case at hand.[10]

A further and probably more important reason that it may often be appropriate to require proof of significant price elevation concerns the tradeoff of deterrence benefits and chilling costs. When the price elevation is large, not only are deterrence benefits particularly great but it is also probably true that chilling costs are low because the likelihood of a false positive is small. In contrast, when the price elevation is very small, not only are deterrence benefits insignificant but chilling costs are probably a larger concern because a nonexistent elevation has a nontrivial likelihood of being misperceived as a small elevation. As mentioned, the prospect of false positives will depend on the type of evidence, some of which indicates the magnitude of price elevation (price wars, price discrimination, direct measurement of marginal cost) and some of which may not (the existence of interfirm communications, internal references to the existence of an industry understanding, the use of facilitating practices). But, for certain types and combinations of evidence, it seems useful to require that a substantial oligopolistic price elevation be demonstrated.[11] This suggestion is reinforced when considering that there exist many market settings in which there is not in fact coordinated price

---

[10] This point is standard in the economics of law enforcement, which suggests further that the difficulty can be too little rather than too much enforcement if society relies on private enforcement motivated by the prospect of recovering damages or public enforcers who are rewarded in ways leading them to focus on high-stakes cases. See Shavell (1982).

[11] Regarding evidence indicating the magnitude of price elevation, it was explained in chapter 10 that the risk of error varies greatly, being most significant when attempting to measure marginal cost directly in certain types of industries but less significant when using price wars or price discrimination to indicate successful oligopolistic price elevation. Even regarding the latter sorts of proof, however, larger elevations tend to involve less risk of false positives. For example, what appear to be price wars involving small price cuts may really be competitive reactions to changes in cost or demand that are too small to measure, and small price discriminations are more likely to be attributable to undetected cost differences in serving different groups.

elevation. Indeed, when deterrence is reasonably effective, such elevation is unlikely even when conditions are fairly conducive to successful coordination. Finally, if private lawsuits are permitted, the concern for meritless (or low-merit) litigation designed to extract settlements may further counsel in favor of setting a higher threshold.[12]

Anticipating some of the analysis in section 13.A, it is interesting to consider briefly the extent to which the operation of sanctions may be a partial safety valve in cases with low price elevation.[13] If penalties are limited to fines or damages that are themselves proportional to the magnitude of price elevation, then the prospect of sanctions being imposed when no price elevation is mistaken for small price elevation may not cause very serious chilling effects. In contrast, if there are significant sanctions even for small elevations, which seems to an extent to be the practice in some jurisdictions, then the problem would be much more serious. Clearly, the threshold for liability and level of sanctions need to be optimized together.

The foregoing point combined with the analysis in recent chapters suggests that it is conceptually useful to view the problem of designing a legal regime as one of determining how evidence maps into sanctions.[14] Ordinarily, laws contain elements of liability, each of which must be met by some standard of proof. Liability often exhibits an all-or-nothing character. If there is no liability, there are no sanctions. If there is liability, then we separately assess sanctions by some other set of criteria, perhaps with its own proof burdens. What results from this or any other regime can be described equivalently by a composite function that, for any set of evidence that might be adduced, simply assigns certain sanctions. In a standard regime, all combinations of evidence that yield no liability map to sanctions of zero. For sets giving rise to liability, one can combine as well the evidence used to assign penalties to determine what sanctions attach to the complete set of evidence.[15]

---

[12] So-called strike suits may nevertheless arise. Even if they cannot be dismissed quickly under an elevated standard, such suits may be less credible if the liability standard is tougher to meet, in which case plaintiffs would be in a weaker position to extract significant settlements, which in turn would deter suits in these circumstances.

[13] This point was also mentioned in section 9.B.

[14] This perspective is employed in Kaplow and Shavell (1990).

[15] This function, call it $f(x)$, is simply the composite function $h(g(x), x)$, where x describes

More generally, sanctions could in principle be any function of the full set of conceivable evidence. For example, instead of absolute liability thresholds, one might assign higher sanctions not only when the extent of price elevation seems to be greater but also when the probability is higher. Small or uncertain elevations might be assigned low rather than zero sanctions. Given administrative costs, however, such graduated fine-tuning may not be optimal. In any event, sanctions are considered further in chapter 13; for the present, the point is that both the probability and magnitude of detected oligopolistic price elevation are important in assigning sanctions, whatever their optimal level may be. And, as this section has emphasized, it is necessary to consider explicitly the significance of deterrence benefits and chilling costs when deciding, for example, how high a probability of price elevation or how great a magnitude should be required. Finally, it is important to keep in mind that the process of liability assessment will be anticipated by firms. Therefore, in addition to straightforward deterrence and chilling, there will be other adjustments in behavior—for example, as noted in section 10.A, coordinating firms may

---

the complete set of evidence (only some of which may bear on liability and only some of which may bear on sanctions), g is the function determining liability, and h is the function determining sanctions. For typical legal rules, $g(x)$ could be set equal to 1 if there is liability and 0 if not, and for all pertinent x in the latter case, we would have $h(0, x) = 0$.

Another way to describe conventional on-off liability, setting to the side the question of sanctions, is to conceive of x as an n-dimensional vector and consider the simple case in which stronger evidence along each dimension raises the desirability of liability, holding evidence along all other dimensions constant. (To a degree this does require simplifying assumptions, but to some extent this can be a naming convention, so that if some type of evidence, when stronger, negated liability, one could redefine it with a negative sign so that higher values favored liability.) Then a liability rule could be understood as an $n-1$ dimensional surface in n-dimensional space; all points above the surface (with all components of the vector greater than or equal to those of some point on the surface and at least one component strictly greater) would be associated with liability and all points below with no liability. (For a piece of possible evidence to always be ignored would mean that there did not exist any possible sets of values for all of the other evidence such that varying the strength of the piece of evidence in question made any difference. Put another way, in a case that was a tie or arbitrarily close to a tie, the piece of evidence in question could not break the tie or influence the outcome no matter how much the strength of that evidence varied.) Within this framework, choosing an optimal legal rule would correspond to choosing the $n-1$ dimensional surface that minimized the loss function or, equivalently, that maximized social welfare. The fact that behavior is endogenous to the legal rule greatly complicates this task.

raise prices gradually so as to render detection of oligopolistic elevation more difficult—which further complicates the problem of how best to combine various types of evidence in making judgments about liability.

B. Liability for Attempts

In some instances, the available evidence may establish that firms attempted to coordinate their behavior to elevate price but not show that they succeeded. Proof regarding success may be ambiguous even though the attempt is fairly clear, or coordination may be demonstrated to have failed. Many sorts of evidence, including much of that discussed in chapter 10 and sections 11.A and 11.B, bear directly on the occurrence of successful oligopolistic coordination. However, certain evidence, including some involving the existence of interfirm communications addressed in section 11.C, may relate directly to firms' attempts.[16] For example, evidence of a secret meeting at which it was decided that the firms would jointly elevate price does not establish that they succeeded (and there may be evidence that they did not).[17] Such cases raise the question of whether it is optimal to punish attempts.[18]

---

[16] Also related is the treatment of facilitating practices, addressed in section 10.C, particularly if they are themselves to be subject to sanctions—that is, independent of their providing a basis for inference regarding successful coordination. In a sense, facilitating practices can be seen as attempts or as evidence that an attempt is contemplated.

[17] However, when there is evidence of ongoing meetings—to discuss cheating, price and market share adjustments, and the like—it may be clear that successful oligopolistic coordination has characterized the past and present, in which case the meetings would constitute evidence of success.

[18] See Shavell (1990). This section, like most of this part, does not examine whether the law is or could be interpreted to be congenial with what is socially optimal. In the United States, the monopolization statute, Sherman Act Section 2, explicitly includes attempts, whereas Section 1, the provision applicable to horizontal restraints of trade, does not. However, acts involving attempts could be judged as restraints themselves, subject to the rule of reason. (It would be difficult, however, to apply Section 1 to unilateral attempts such as that in United States v. American Airlines, Inc., 743 F.2d 1114 (5th Cir. 1984), cert. dismissed, 474 U.S. 1001 (1985), where an executive of one firm contacted his counterpart at another to suggest fixing prices, and the latter rebuffed the overture.) Pushing from the opposite side, Posner (2001, 53–55) criticizes the commonly advanced view that the law should focus on explicit communications

At first, it may seem that punishing attempts is unnecessary and possibly undesirable, and sometimes this view is correct. Such punishment is costly, which cost may be unproductive in light of the fact that no harm occurred. Furthermore, there may be mistakes in identifying attempts, the prospect of which could chill desirable behavior. Indeed, if there is no evidence of success or if there is affirmative evidence of failure, perhaps we should be skeptical that there really was an attempt. When masked individuals enter a bank with guns drawn, but ultimately need to flee without any money in hand, we have little doubt about what they were attempting to do. However, when attempts are inferred from ambiguous internal documents or from meetings whose existence seems likely but whose content is unknown, the prospect of error may be significant. Of course, sometimes there will be fairly clear evidence of an attempt, perhaps a tape of the secret price-fixing session.

The benefits of penalizing attempts—which are widely punished in the criminal law—typically concern deterrence. An alternative to punishing attempts would be to raise sanctions for success. However, when success is difficult to prove, as it often is for price fixing, and when there are limits to sanctions that can be imposed, punishment of attempts helpfully augments deterrence. It may also reduce costs: If some attempts cases are easy to establish, enforcers might be able to forgo other more difficult and expensive cases involving apparent success while still maintaining deterrence. In addition, when attempts are clear and sufficient for liability, costly inquiries into success may be avoided—although evidence of success may nevertheless be needed to set sanctions.

Another important consideration involves chilling costs. All else equal, it is optimal to raise penalties for more clearly undesirable acts while reducing sanctions for more ambiguous ones. If sometimes attempts are clear and they are subject to significant penalties, lower sanctions can be applied in more ambiguous cases of success, or some might be excused as a consequence of an elevated burden of proof made possible (while maintaining deterrence) by the punishment of attempts. Taken together, these reasons suggest that the punishment of attempts at oligopolistic

---

(which are a means to an end, with evidence thereof often proving an attempt but not success) rather than on the undesirable outcome (coordinated oligopolistic price elevation) as one that punishes attempts while excusing success itself.

price coordination probably makes a good deal of sense, particularly when the evidence is strong.

An important caveat, previously suggested by the discussion of the relevance of the conduciveness of conditions,[19] is that imposing sanctions on attempts that fail (or where success is unknown but seems unlikely) may not much enhance deterrence in realms where it is most socially valuable, while still imposing chilling costs. The point is that deterrence is not very important in industries where success is highly unlikely. Few firms would attempt oligopolistic price elevation in any event, and even those that do so may be almost certain to fail. Moreover, given that few will try, it may be more likely that findings of apparent attempts involve false positives. The strength of this reservation depends on the quality of the evidence bearing both on attempts and on failure. Thus, when conditions are conducive and success is merely hard to prove, punishing attempts is probably valuable. Moreover, even when the foundation is weaker, there may be some deterrence benefits because firms uncertain about success will be better deterred. In addition, deterrence may suffer from the prospect that firms that make undesirable attempts might be exonerated when success cannot be established and defendants might convince an adjudicator that success was unlikely or absent. After all, the firms themselves may have a better view about the ex ante likelihood of success, and their very attempt may attest to their belief that it was at least plausible that they would succeed. Put another way, firms' attempts, when they are subject to the risk of sanctions, themselves provide evidence of the plausibility of success, assuming of course that the evidence on the attempts themselves is substantial.

Another question concerns sanctions for attempts. Ordinarily, penalties should be set to reflect the harm caused, as will be discussed in section 13.A. For failed attempts, harm is zero, and for attempts of ambiguous outcome, harm is uncertain. Sanctions for attempts, accordingly, will need to reflect prospective harm. More precisely, one should consider the preceding analysis of the benefits of punishing attempts in augmenting deterrence while reducing chilling costs and set penalties, for both attempts and cases involving demonstrated success, to maximize social welfare in light of these considerations. Although a mere truism, it does

---

[19] See note 3 in chapter 11.

guide thinking: We know which factors make punishing attempts more valuable, and these same factors tend to favor stronger sanctions as well.

C. Which Firms Should Be Held Liable?

Consider an industry with five symmetrically situated firms where it is clear that they have engaged in successful oligopolistic coordination that has raised prices significantly. There is little question that all of these firms should be found liable.[20] The many sorts of evidence and analysis considered so far in chapters 10 and 11 concern making inferences about whether such has occurred. The null hypothesis is one of rivalrous, competitive behavior, which involves no price elevation. The issue in a typical case is whether the *firms* were behaving in one fashion, or instead *they* were behaving in another. If some of the firms tried to elevate price and others refused to go along, it is ordinarily supposed, with good reason, that price elevation by the subset of firms would have failed.[21]

---

[20] There are important questions of whether, when there are fines or damages imposed, firms should be jointly and severally liable (such that each is responsible for others' payments); whether, if such liability is allowed and plaintiffs or the government are permitted to collect from whichever firms they choose, those firms should have a right of contribution against other firms; and, perhaps most important, whether some firms might be given immunity, leniency, or even rewards in exchange for offering evidence useful in proving others' violations. See section 10.A (and note 22 for references) regarding the latter issues and also, on contribution in particular, Easterbrook, Landes, and Posner (1980) and Polinsky and Shavell (1981). An aspect of strategic exoneration is considered later in this section. Other issues pertaining to fines and damages are taken up in section 13.A.

[21] See, for example, Posner (1969, 1592). In this section, attempts are being set to the side. It can readily be imagined that some firms might attempt to elevate prices, whether through pricing moves or by first engaging in various forms of direct communications, with others not going along (as occurred in *American Airlines*). In any event, it is uncontroversial that firms that reject invitations to participate and never do so will not be held liable.

A mixed outcome is not inconceivable when coordinated oligopoly pricing is subject to sanctions (which are omitted in most literature on oligopoly behavior). For example, suppose that the firms charging lower prices had capacity constraints and thus could not prevent the price-elevating firms from making significant sales. (An intermediate case is where there is no literal constraint but rising marginal costs make it unprofitable for nonparticipating firms to capture the entire market. Blair and Romano (1990) argue that such firms should not be held liable and that they can empirically be distinguished from participants, whose quantities fall rather than rise as price is elevated.) Another possibility involves differentiated products. The

In less simple settings, it is necessary to consider liability for fringe firms. Assume, for example, that in addition to the five large firms in our hypothetical industry (which have indeed been demonstrated to have elevated prices significantly), there are a number of small producers, each with a limited capacity. It is less obvious whether and when they should be held liable.[22]

To begin, suppose that fringe firms would be held liable.[23] If this liability were applied regardless of their behavior, it might be point-

firms charging lower prices could earn more by raising prices, but we might imagine that they are deterred from doing so by the prospect of penalties. The puzzle is why the high-pricing firms would not be similarly deterred; possibilities are that they may be judgment proof (not have assets sufficient to pay the fines) or be difficult to reach legally (they operate in another jurisdiction) or have a view that detection is unlikely.

[22] See also section 14.A, discussing fringe firms when there is a single, dominant firm elevating price. The present analysis, like that in most of this book, examines the consequences of different legal regimes for behavior and thus social welfare. Some might instead ask whether such small firms are culpable in some other sense. Or, following approaches to liability that emphasize certain forms of explicit communications, the question would be whether those communications included the firms in question, which would formally establish whether they were part of the agreement, conspiracy, concerted action, or whatever other term might be employed. Under this approach, issues related to those addressed in the text would arise. Thus, in addition to establishing that prohibited communications were employed, for example (which might be done using circumstantial evidence, as discussed in chapters 6 and 17), one might need to inquire further to determine which firms (even among the five major firms) were included. Without knowing all of the communications, including their content, this might sometimes be difficult because there may be ambiguity about certain firms' participation. For example, one firm's reference to an "industry understanding" could refer to an implicit one with regard to some of the firms. Indeed, it is possible for some firms to be part of an explicit agreement and others only to be part of an implicit understanding, with all of the firms nevertheless having a complete meeting of the minds and thus successfully elevating price. Regarding the discussion of leniency and its strategic use to disrupt oligopolistic coordination (for references, see note 22 in chapter 10), similar considerations would apply under this alternative legal approach.

[23] One could also consider simply exempting such firms (which may be close to the result of the second approach described in the text to follow). Posner (1969, 1592) suggests that such would be the practice under his favored approach but does not elaborate the point. Areeda and Hovenkamp (2003, 229–31) give some consideration to how a firm (in their example, a large firm) might attempt to avoid liability under a rule that reached coordinated oligopolistic price elevation (without requiring more explicit communications, for example) and suggest that it might be difficult because the firm can do little more than price at marginal cost and produce what it can at the market price, but it may have difficulty proving that it is doing so. Regarding their concern and the related points discussed in the text, it is worth keeping in

less.[24] One approach would be to exempt fringe firms that price nontrivially below the industry price.[25] If this induces the leading firms to lower price, thereby removing the defense and encouraging further price reductions by fringe firms, all the better. If the leading firms stick to their price, there are a number of effects, some subtle, that do not yield a clear assessment.[26]

---

mind the types of evidence that may be available. For example, if one of a few large firms consistently behaved independently, pulling the industry price down to the point where it equaled its own marginal cost, leaving the other firm(s) to sell correspondingly lower quantities if they wished to maintain elevated prices, it is not clear the situation could be sustained and, if it was, one might imagine there to be internal evidence suggesting that the deviant firm was an open, continuous cheater. To take another type of evidence, suppose that a number of large firms elevate the industry price in order to earn a supracompetitive margin, but one large firm is indeed outside the group. When the price is elevated, the outside firm will raise its output and the coordinated firms will all be reducing their output, so it may be quite apparent which firms are in the coordinated group and which, if any, are outside of it.

[24] It could also be worse if it discouraged entry, although the analysis of subsection 8.B.1 indicates that additional entry is not obviously desirable. The costs could exceed any benefit from raising consumer surplus; relatedly, as discussed in section 8.A, reallocating some sales from firms with low marginal costs to firms (the entrants) with high marginal costs is inefficient. (Note that if it was desirable to encourage entry, such as in an industry with only one firm—where the entrant would be concerned that the prospect of liability for successful oligopolistic coordination would induce a competitive post-entry equilibrium and thus insufficient profits to recover its fixed costs—it would be possible to strategically exempt entrants in such settings from liability for a period of time or perhaps only if price falls significantly even if not all the way to marginal cost. Such decisions might better be made through expert regulation than case-by-case adjudication. See section 15.A.)

[25] The analogue when there is product differentiation is more difficult, leading to a greater focus on the following point in the text. In many respects, inferences are harder when variety is substantial and important to consumers, although successful oligopolistic coordination is less likely in such situations in any event.

[26] If fringe firms' marginal costs are rising and they charge somewhat less to avoid liability, their quantities will fall. Some consumers gain from buying at a lower price, but producers lose surplus. The net effect would depend on rationing: All consumers would prefer that their purchases be from the fringe firms; if some consumers who would not buy at the oligopoly price are able to purchase from the fringe, there would be a welfare gain. There is also a gain in production efficiency from the fringe producing less because the marginal cost of the output they no longer produce approximately equals the oligopoly price, and if the oligopolists now sell more, they incur a marginal cost that we are assuming is significantly less than the price they charge. Finally, since the coordinating firms now face a somewhat stronger residual demand, they would raise the price a bit more, which would be detrimental.

If we consider instead the case of constant marginal cost, then the fringe cannot lower

In addition or instead, firms could be exonerated if they charge a price equal to (or, perhaps more plausibly, close to) their own marginal cost.[27] Hence, if fringe firms have rising marginal cost that they are equating to the coordinated oligopoly price (the colluders' marginal costs being lower), they would not be held liable. This would tend to exonerate most fringe firms since such behavior is optimal for them and thus expected in the absence of liability. Proving marginal cost might be difficult, but it also may be unnecessary since we would infer such behavior absent evidence to the contrary. Note furthermore that the foregoing discussion oversimplifies by ignoring the role of sanctions. Notably, if fines or damages for a particular firm are proportional to its own overcharges, then being subject to liability encourages the firm to lower any elevated price. However, if the fringe is already pricing at marginal cost, its sanction would then be zero, making the question of liability moot to that extent.

These conclusions presuppose that we know which firms are the competitive fringe, with one technology, selling at price equal to marginal cost, and which firms are the large players who are the colluders that are charging supracompetitive prices. Sometimes this will be clear, but other times it will not.[28] This challenge and the need to focus on each firm's marginal cost rather than some average industry marginal cost are discussed above, in section 9.B, regarding the measurement of marginal cost as a means of inferring successful oligopolistic coordination. Relatedly,

---

price. Hence, they would exit (or not enter in the first place). This may or may not be desirable in itself. See note 24. However, if there is, say, a readily available technology to entrants at a common, constant marginal cost and none would enter, then the incumbent oligopolists would no longer face pricing pressure from them and might charge a higher price, which would reduce welfare. In equilibrium one would not expect to see such a constant-marginal-cost fringe in operation (with the posited price configuration). After all, if they did enter, incumbents could reduce price slightly (from a post-entry equilibrium with a price equal to entrants' marginal cost), eliminate the fringe, suffer negligible inframarginal loss on any existing sales, and earn positive profits on the market share regained from the fringe.

[27] Exonerating fringe firms that charge a price (approximately) equal to their marginal cost who match the oligopoly price, without requiring them to undercut any elevated price, does forgo the possible benefits of the first approach, if indeed net benefits would be likely.

[28] Also, it may be clear which are which for some firms, perhaps the largest and smallest, but uncertain for some firms of modest size. See also section 14.A, discussing a case with a dominant firm, a few firms each having a nontrivial but not huge market share, and additional fringe firms that are quite small.

if we require, as section A suggests, that price be shown to be significantly above marginal cost when using this sort of evidence of price elevation, and if that test is applied to each firm, the problem may be substantially addressed.

Aside from the treatment of fringe firms, it is worth considering strategic exemption or leniency regarding the magnitude of sanctions for the more substantial, coordinating firms—that is, favorable treatment designed to induce one or more of them to behave disruptively. An example was given in section 10.A, where it was explained that exonerating a firm that initiates a price war might be helpful because cheating is made relatively more attractive. Similarly, firms that fail to follow price increases quickly or completely, firms that aggressively pursue nonprice competition, and perhaps others might receive less harsh treatment. This approach may discourage firms from attempting coordinated price elevation and interfere with the success of those who continue to try. The subject of leniency has received some attention in the literature and also relates to some previous proposals to address coordinated oligopoly pricing, and it clearly is a fruitful channel for further study.[29]

---

[29] See the sources cited in note 22 of chapter 10.

13

Sanctions

𝓇

Detection must be combined with sanctions in order to reduce the extent of coordinated oligopolistic price elevation in the economy. Section A explores fines and damages, section B adds imprisonment, and section C discusses injunctions.

Although there is a substantial literature on the economics of law enforcement addressed to the choice among types of sanctions and their optimal magnitude, work on competition policy has devoted only modest attention to these questions.[1] Much existing analysis is incomplete or misleading as a consequence of this omission. For example, literature on rules of liability for price fixing is often significantly guided by the implicit or explicit assumption that injunctions will be a central or the sole remedy when this may well not be optimal and also is not in accordance with existing practice. And some work on the magnitude of penalties finds those under consideration, usually government-imposed fines, to be too low but does not take into account that those sanctions may be in addition to others, such as private damages and imprisonment. Accordingly, it is valuable to sketch at the outset some of the considerations that bear on the choice among types of sanctions before considering each in greater depth.

Discussion throughout this part of the book takes fines or damages to be central. Such sanctions are widely used to penalize price fixing. Moreover, basic law enforcement theory suggests that their use is often desirable, for monetary sanctions tend not to be costly in themselves (in

---

[1] For a survey of the general problem, see Polinsky and Shavell (2007), and for discussion of the application to cartels, see Werden, Hammond, and Barnett (2011) and Wickelgren (2012).

contrast to imprisonment and injunctions), they deter behavior (which injunctions alone do not), and they may be calibrated to the extent of harm caused and the likelihood of detection. Regarding the latter, the general prescription is that, ideally, expected sanctions should be set equal to expected external harm, so fines or damages should equal actual harm multiplied by the inverse of the likelihood of successful detection. Because oligopolistic firms attempt to keep their price coordination secret, this latter point is important in the present setting, and it constitutes the rationale for employing treble damages in private lawsuits in the United States—which, note, are in addition to any fines and prison terms imposed by government enforcers.

Because imprisonment is socially costly—resources are consumed in running the system and the loss to imprisoned individuals is not matched by any direct social offset (unlike fines, which are transfers)—it tends to be optimal not to use it unless monetary sanctions are insufficient. Imprisonment, which is employed in price-fixing enforcement especially in the United States, can nevertheless be important on account of the difficulty of detection, which may require for adequate deterrence a level of fines that exceeds firms' assets, and also because of agency problems within firms.

Injunctions are notably different from the other two types of sanctions. Most importantly, they do not by themselves achieve deterrence. Firms would be happy to elevate prices for as long as they could get away with it—which may be a long time given detection difficulties and also the time delay involved in adjudication—if the only cost upon being found liable is the need to abstain in the future. Furthermore, if fines and damages (and imprisonment) are to be employed, it is unclear why there is any further need for injunctions. When the other sanctions succeed at deterrence, whether to impose injunctions becomes moot. Also, injunctions are parasitic on the other sanctions because firms have little incentive to comply unless they fear penalties from failing to do so. If those penalties, in turn, are essentially the same as those for the underlying violation, it is not clear what an injunction adds with regard to deterring future violations. A higher sanction or more summary proceedings for repeat violations might be employed, but such could be done in any event. Injunctions can differ from other remedies in that, instead of attempting to induce compliance, they may implement it directly, such as by an agency regulating firms' prices going forward or restructuring an industry so as to make conditions no longer conducive to successful oligopolistic coordination.[2] Such remedies, of course, are often quite costly in themselves.

A complete analysis of optimal enforcement must consider additional issues as well,[3] but they are set aside for present purposes (except for some brief mentions, notably, in section 15.A). Among them are whether private suits should be used instead of or in addition to public enforcement, how private enforcement should be operated (permission of class actions, allocation of attorneys' fees, determination of who should be permitted to sue), and how obligations for fines or damages should be allocated among the firms (particularly if the defendants do not constitute the entire market or if some are judgment proof). Some additional dimensions, such as the strategic use of leniency policy, liability for attempts, and deciding which firms should be liable at all, have been discussed previously (in sections 10.A, 12.B, and 12.C, respectively). Finally, analysis of detection and sanctions should not, in principle, be compartmentalized, a point elaborated in section 12.A.

A. Fines and Damages

The use of fines or damages—monetary sanctions—is generally desirable, as the introductory remarks suggest. The guiding principle is that fines or damages (which for the most part will not be distinguished in this section, with fines often used as a shorthand) should equal external harm times a probability multiplier, in the simplest case equal to one divided by the probability that sanctions will be imposed. For example, if firms contemplating price fixing anticipate that there is only a 50% chance of being caught and fined, fines should be twice the harm, for otherwise their activities may well be profitable even taking into account expected sanctions.[4]

---

[2] Imprisonment also directly restricts the future behavior of incarcerated individuals. But if ex ante incentives are inadequate to deter, firms might replace such individuals, and the replacements, having the same incentives as those replaced, would likewise not be deterred.

[3] See Polinsky and Shavell (2007).

[4] Except for occasional notes, the analysis throughout simplifies by abstracting from risk aversion. In addition, with price fixing, expected fines equal to harm are sufficient to deter,

The logic of deterrence is simple and familiar but is worth emphasizing because it seems that many competition law commentators fail to appreciate it, as discussed in section C, despite Posner's (1969, 1588–93) clear presentation of the basic idea in his seminal article decades ago. Whatever methods firms might use to achieve coordinated oligopolistic price elevation—and whether or not the particular means ultimately will be discovered—firms' decision-making calculus changes if they expect to be subject to sanctions. If they anticipate a large gain from successful oligopolistic coordination and no penalties, they will expend great effort to accomplish it. However, if there are fines, and if the expected level of fines exceeds expected profits from coordination (each properly discounted),[5] then they will voluntarily forgo such efforts and aim to ensure that their employees do not engage in this activity. The reasoning is no different for, say, the application of a corrective tax to firms that pollute. In imposing the tax, the government simply charges firms for the external cost of their pollution. How pollution is reduced is up to the firms: They may change their production methods, seek to invent new technologies, improve training and supervision of employees, or reduce output. The government does not need to know which techniques are employed or in what combination. As long as pollution is detected and firms are fully charged for the harm attributable to it, they will control it to an optimal extent. With price fixing, the optimal degree is ordinarily zero, and if expected sanctions are equal to harm to others and thus exceed any profits, this is the level that firms will choose.

Subsection 1 further explores the harm component of the basic formula for optimal fines. To simplify the exposition, it ordinarily assumes that

---

but smaller sanctions may also be effective if they are large enough to disrupt the stability of coordination on price. See, for example, Allain et al. (2011) on how cartel continuation becomes less profitable over time (and thus cheating more attractive) because the increasing accumulation of prior overcharges (that determine the penalty) raises the cost of the increment to the detection probability due to continuation. See also note 22 of chapter 10 and section 12.C on leniency and other methods of disrupting coordination.

[5] An interesting point is that greater patience tends to make it easier for oligopolistic firms to succeed because their punishment of cheaters becomes relatively more weighty in cheaters' calculations, see subsection 7.A.2, whereas greater patience also makes competition law penalties more effective in achieving deterrence for similar reasons, see Harrington (2005, 155–56).

the probability of sanctions is one, so that expected sanctions simply equal the stated sanction. Subsection 2 elaborates on the probability multiplier. Finally, subsection 3 briefly discusses the law on fines in the United States and European Union, which, as will be seen, does not closely match what seems to be optimal. Much of the discussion sets to the side other sanctions, although they will occasionally be noted because of their significance and the fact that the theory of optimal sanctions encompasses the entirety of sanctions as well as having implications for particular components.

1. Determination of Harm

What counts as social harm is controversial in the present setting. As section 8.A explains, total social welfare is an appealing objective to maximize, but many would consider only consumer surplus. As an initial matter, this difference is not important for present purposes because the harm component of the standard optimal sanction prescription refers to all harm that is external to the firm, which is lost consumer surplus in any event. Thus, crudely speaking (specifically, with constant marginal cost), if a group of firms elevates price, reaping 100 of profits and causing deadweight loss of 25, the harm component of the sanction is 125, which is the total loss in consumer surplus.[6] The point is that firms will in general be induced to behave optimally when they bear the full social costs of their actions. The 100 in profits is directly matched by a loss of 100 to consumers, and sanctions must include the latter to achieve deterrence. Clearly, if the expected sanction was only 25 rather than 125, the firm would not be deterred.

---

[6] If marginal cost is rising, then the deadweight loss from reduced output exceeds the loss in consumer surplus from output reductions. Nevertheless, it is the consumer surplus component of the deadweight loss that, in principle, should be used in calculating the fine because the producer surplus component is already borne by the firm. Likewise, the relevant profit in calculating the fine should be that from the overcharge—the price increment times the quantity still sold—without subtracting this forgone producer surplus. As the text states, the core idea is that the consumer surplus loss equals that which is external to the firms and thus what must be internalized by the fine. This qualification will be ignored for ease of exposition in the discussion to follow.

It is also dangerous to set expected sanctions simply equal to firms' profits, or, equivalently, a measure of lost consumer surplus that omits deadweight loss. Firms that compare a profit of 100 to an expected sanction of 100 would be indifferent about price elevation. We might hope that they would refrain from the activity, perhaps because there are additional expenses of undertaking it and on account of adjudication costs not included when stating that the expected sanction is 100.[7] The problem is that there will inevitably be errors in setting the sanction, so if the system aims at setting an expected sanction that just equals firms' expected profits, sometimes the actual sanction will be too high and other times too low.[8] If firms do not anticipate what errors will be made in particular cases, they would still bear an expected sanction of 100. However, if they do anticipate them—for example, they may have knowledge of aspects of their industry that lead adjudicators to systematically underestimate harm, or to overestimate it—then some will be underdeterred, and the additional fines on other firms in different circumstances provides no consolation.[9] Accordingly, brinkmanship is not good policy. Expected sanctions need to exceed expected profits from harmful activities. As a first cut, one can follow the general prescription that the target should be expected external harm. Alternatively, one could, for example, omit deadweight loss but otherwise augment profits from overcharges in determining this component of the formula for the optimal sanction.

The analysis to this point places a floor on the magnitude of the optimal expected fine. There should also be a ceiling that ideally is no higher than necessary to deter. (The foregoing point about measurement errors indicates that this suggestion is overly simple. In general, there will be a

---

[7] Since adjudication costs (both direct expenses and disruption) are nontrivial, it is indeed the case that they enhance deterrence somewhat. For cases involving large overcharges, however, such may not be that important. In addition, the prospect of such costs augments chilling effects. Indeed, even firms confident that, at the end of the day, they would be subject to no explicit sanctions might anticipate significant expected costs in an expensive system of adjudication. Such costs may encourage settlement, which is still costly, and in a system with private suits might tend to encourage meritless litigation, further adding to the problem. See section 15.A.

[8] Even if a system makes no errors, firms' ex ante expectations may be subject to some error, which would produce much the same problem.

[9] See Kaplow and Shavell (1992, 312–16; 1996a, 194, 204–5).

tradeoff; higher fines will usefully augment deterrence in some instances, presumably less and less so as fines rise to ever-higher levels.) A standard reason in the optimal law enforcement literature concerns overdeterrence, which is to say deterring even those acts with social benefits in excess of social costs. For actual coordinated price elevation, there may be few such acts—and, when there are, which section 8.B indicates is possible, there is no particular reason to believe that such would be the cases where further increments to already high fines would make the difference.

More importantly, as emphasized throughout this part of the book, chilling costs need to be taken into account. The prospect of false positives tends to discourage some desirable behavior. For a given probability of false positives, the problem will be worse when sanctions are higher. Accordingly, lower sanctions tend to be beneficial, all else equal. More broadly, the analysis at the close of section 12.A indicates that optimal sanctions should not be viewed independently of optimal liability rules. For example, it may be that sanctions should be greater when proof is more certain, in significant part because the chilling costs are lower when false positives are less likely.[10]

Relatedly, section 12.A suggests that it may well be optimal when successful oligopolistic coordination is established by direct measurement of marginal cost to limit liability to cases in which price is significantly in excess of marginal cost. If that is done, there remains the question of whether, once liability is thereby demonstrated, sanctions should reflect the full difference between price and marginal cost, only the extent to which price exceeds the higher threshold, or somewhere in between. The full difference (or perhaps even more, if there is then particularly high confidence) seems best for deterrence since expected sanctions need to exceed expected profits.

Therefore, it is important to attempt to measure harm reasonably well when determining the magnitude of fines or other sanctions. Obviously, this task will often prove difficult for many of the same reasons that the

---

[10] Indeed, as mentioned, it may tend to be optimal to raise sanctions when proof is particularly strong and to lower them (including to zero, that is, exonerating firms) when proof is weak. This combination works well if firms do not know in advance in which situation they will be. If they do, those in the latter situation would be underdeterred, and the higher sanctions applied to firms in the former situation will not rectify the deterrence deficit.

accurate determination of liability is challenging. Indeed, some of the evidence is basically the same. When liability is established by pricing patterns or price elevation, as described in chapter 10, a measure of harm is the basis for finding liability, that is, that some harm due to successful oligopolistic coordination has occurred. This measure, in turn, can provide the benchmark for assessing sanctions.[11] Some internal evidence and interfirm communications, discussed in chapter 11, may similarly indicate the magnitude of the overcharge. However, other evidence is more ambiguous. Price stickiness may indicate coordination without demonstrating the extent of price elevation. The existence of interfirm communications may likewise fail to reveal the size of overcharges, although they may if sufficient content is revealed. Similarly, the use of some facilitating practices may signal coordination, or perhaps attempted coordination, but not indicate the degree of success, if any. In the latter sorts of cases, it is necessary to inquire directly into the magnitude of price elevation for purposes of setting the level of sanctions. And once such evidence is examined, it makes sense to use this information to refine inferences regarding liability as well.[12]

Another question concerns the baseline against which overcharges are determined. It is ordinarily assumed that the benchmark is competitive interaction, with price equal to marginal cost. That baseline may pose problems, particularly when using direct measurements of marginal cost (rather than, say, the degree to which price rose at the onset of coordinated pricing or fell during price wars). In addition to the usual difficulties, there is a further complication if marginal cost rises significantly with

---

[11] See Baker and Bresnahan (1992, 15). Price elevation for purposes of assessing sanctions is sometimes determined by comparing prices charged during the period of illegal price elevation to those before or after it. The "before" comparison corresponds to detection by attempting to identify a price jump at formation. The "after" comparison assumes that at some point, perhaps when an investigation commences, price will drop to the competitive level. This latter measure, however, creates perverse incentives because firms that fail to reduce their prices not only continue to earn supracompetitive profits but also reduce their sanctions for past actions. See Harrington (2004).

[12] Relatedly, there is no reason to be reluctant to include such evidence when considering liability on the ground that the evidence is costly or potentially ambiguous, in light of the fact that it is necessary to use it in calibrating sanctions. If proceedings were bifurcated (see section 15.A), so that liability is determined first, then there may be some cost savings in ignoring such evidence until there is an affirmative finding of liability.

output. Since successful oligopolistic coordination elevates price and concomitantly reduces quantity, marginal cost at the price-elevated equilibrium will be lower than marginal cost at the competitive equilibrium, so a measure based on marginal cost in the former setting will exaggerate the overcharge.

There is an additional baseline issue raised by the analysis in the following chapter on unilateral market power. Consider a case in which there is both some unilateral market power and some coordinated elevation of price. If price elevation due to the former is legal and thus sanctions in principle should only reflect the latter increment, it will be necessary to ascertain not the hypothetical competitive equilibrium but the hypothetical equilibrium with the exercise of unilateral market power but no further price elevation. The techniques will sometimes be similar. If interdependence is demonstrated by a sharp price increase or the outbreak of price wars, those price changes provide a basis for estimating the pertinent elevation. However, if there is a need to determine marginal cost directly, then even after overcoming other obstacles it would still be necessary to assess the degree of unilateral price elevation that would otherwise have occurred. In principle, this measurement can be made with information about demand, marginal cost, and the nature of firms' unilateral interactions. But, in practice, the task will often prove difficult.[13]

2. Probability Multiplier

When sanctions are not imposed with certainty, higher sanctions are necessary to achieve a given level of deterrence.[14] A central difficulty in

---

[13] As noted in section 5.D and elaborated in section 18.A, there is an even more daunting problem of assessing the but-for scenario if the law is deemed to forgive even interdependent price elevation as long as that elevation is achieved by some means rather than by others, for there do not exist either models or data from which the appropriate decomposition may be made.

[14] As discussed in subsection 1, higher sanctions also lead to greater chilling effects. However, chilling effects depend on expected sanctions: A sanction of 100 imposed with certainty and a sanction of 200 imposed with a 50% probability would have the same consequence (abstracting from risk aversion). Of greater importance is the relative rate of the two types of error as one shifts the types of evidence required and burden of proof, as discussed in section

determining the appropriate probability multiplier is that it is necessary to know what the probability of detection is in a given enforcement regime. This probability, in turn, is the ratio of cases in which sanctions are (correctly) imposed to the total number of violations, but since the violations are largely secret, it is quite difficult to know what the multiplier should be. The empirical evidence surveyed in section 9.C indicates that there are many successful prosecutions of cases that seem fairly clearly to have involved significant price elevations, and they resulted in large sanctions. As long as those sanctions were notably greater than firms' profits—a point that is subject to dispute, as discussed in subsection 3—it would follow that there must be a significant number of undetected violations since not all prospective violators are deterred. With some laws, like those against murder and automobile theft, it may be fairly straightforward to measure, at least approximately, the number of unsolved cases. But individuals who pay elevated prices are often unaware of this fact, for what is difficult for enforcers or experts to determine is beyond the reach of individual consumers, although large buyers of intermediate goods may have some direct knowledge and an incentive to learn about and report violations. What limited information exists on this question suggests that the detection probability is rather low.[15]

In addition, the probability of sanctions is not simply fixed. Instead it depends, as noted, on the substantive law and the rules of proof, and also on enforcement effort. Regarding the latter, public enforcers are given budgets and then set priorities, which could be modified. It is commonly suggested that current prosecutions usually follow from customer complaints (presumably the sorts of large customers just mentioned, especially given the intermediate-goods industries in which most prosecutions occur) and from informants. If these cover most actual instances of price elevation, they may suffice. However, if there indeed is significant undetected price elevation,[16] then one option is to employ other enforcement

---

12.A. Reducing deterrence deficits through heightened sanctions is especially problematic with regard to chilling effects when the low probability of sanctions is due primarily to the low quality of evidence—rather than to a low initial detection rate but with resulting prosecutions based on reliable evidence.

[15] See the sources cited in note 37 in chapter 9, which suggest the probability may be in the 10–20% range.

[16] One reason for the existence of price elevation that is not effectively prosecuted is that

methods that require greater initial effort, such as using econometric methods to identify plausible instances of price fixing, followed by more targeted investigations. Alternatively, it may be cheaper simply to raise sanctions, achieving the same increment to the expected sanction while economizing on enforcement effort, a standard prescription in the literature on the economics of law enforcement. Reasons to increase effort in the present setting are limits on sanctions (such as caused by the judgment-proof problem, which may be significant for single-product firms that substantially elevate price), problems of selective targeting (if firms in certain settings know they will not be prosecuted using current means, raising sanctions on firms in other settings does not help), and concern about chilling costs (greater effort, by yielding more cases with true positives that can be demonstrated, may enable an increase in proof burdens that reduces false positives and thus expected sanctions on firms that behave properly).[17]

Private enforcement, allowed in some jurisdictions, also deserves mention.[18] In this setting, enforcement effort is endogenous, determined by the expected payoffs from litigation compared to litigation costs. Higher damage awards,[19] more relaxed proof burdens, and other measures encourage litigation, which itself can be costly, although to the extent that it sufficiently augments deterrence, it may reduce costs because there

some may be deemed legal or not generate the sort of evidence that a circumscribed legal proscription may require—as explored in parts I and III.

[17] See Kaplow (2011, 2012a).

[18] On the less developed use of private damages in the European Union, see Sorinas (2007, 584–86), who notes that private damages are not allowed in Community courts but are left to member states, and that they have been rather limited, with the law highly varied and underdeveloped. For a proposal to allow actions for single damages, see European Commission (2008).

[19] The fact that the level of damages directly affects private incentives to sue, but may not so directly affect government enforcement incentives (depending on how government enforcers are rewarded)—and, relatedly, that the resulting probability of sanctions differs in the two cases—constitutes one of the two central reasons that optimal damages may differ from optimal fines. The other is that victims ordinarily receive damages awards but not fine proceeds (although neither is inherent, as decoupling or nondisbursement of class action proceeds is possible and governments could distribute fine proceeds to victims if they wish). As a consequence, victims' incentives to avoid harm are influenced, and some have suggested that this may be an important adverse effect of private damages actions for price fixing. See Baker (1988), Besanko and Spulber (1990), Breit and Elzinga (1974), and Salant (1987).

would be fewer defendants whom it would make sense to sue. In practice, many (but not all)[20] private suits in the United States for price fixing constitute follow-on litigation to successful government prosecutions, the effect of which is to augment government sanctions with private damage awards. Some further discussion of private litigation appears in section 15.A.

As mentioned, sanctions may fail to be imposed both because of difficulty in initial detection and also because of difficulties of proof. Regarding the latter, raising sanctions to enhance deterrence is more problematic because, as noted, this policy also tends to increase chilling effects.[21] This point essentially restates the question of how optimally to determine both liability and sanctions when proof is uncertain to varying degrees.

3. Law on Fines

In the United States, private suits for damages measure harm as the overcharge—relative to a competition benchmark—times the quantity sold,[22] which omits deadweight loss. Injured victims then receive three times this amount, along with attorneys' fees. The multiplier, established over a century ago, might be rationalized primarily in light of the difficulty of

---

[20] See note 27, discussing facts about private antitrust enforcement in the United States, including the importance of private damage suits relative to government enforcement actions.

[21] Consider in this light Posner's (1969, 1590–91) suggestion that, if anything, sanctions for more subtle forms of successful oligopolistic coordination should be higher, not lower (or zero, as many commentators advocate), because more subtle methods are harder to detect. Perhaps the main reason this point is likely to be valid is that coordination achieved with the aid of highly explicit interfirm communications can be detected not only through such means but also through other observations, such as of price wars, price elevation, and the like, which can also be employed with respect to more subtle forms of coordination. However, if proof in cases involving more subtle methods tends to be more uncertain, there is a greater concern for chilling effects, which tends to favor moderated sanctions. It is unclear which factor is usually greater, and it is easy to imagine instances going in both directions: Evidence of secret communications could itself be quite murky, as mentioned: Internal evidence may be ambiguous, disgruntled employees may distort, and, perhaps most important, the process of inferring particular interfirm communications from circumstantial evidence is incredibly difficult and subject to error, as chapters 6 and 17 explore. And evidence from price movements or internal evidence of successful oligopolistic coordination will sometimes be quite clear and reliable.

[22] See Areeda et al. (2007, ¶¶392, 395).

detection but also in part by the omission of deadweight loss, although the magnitude of other sanctions, notably government-imposed fines and imprisonment, needs to be accounted for as well.

One might have thought that government fines would ordinarily be determined similarly, in accordance with the analysis in subsections 1 and 2. That is, the magnitude would be based on some fairly direct measure of harm—proportional to the magnitude of the overcharge times the units sold, perhaps with an addition for deadweight loss—and then multiplied by some factor reflecting the probability of sanctions. One could also imagine that there may be offsets allowed for other penalties so that sanctions as a whole met such a target.

In fact, the normal determination of fines in the United States and the European Union works rather differently. Although subject to reservations and some ambiguity, it appears that both law and practice base the fine on something closer to a fixed fraction of firms' revenues in the affected markets, with little or no adjustment to reflect the actual price elevation.[23]

---

[23] Fines for violations of U.S. competition law are governed by the Sentencing Guidelines (U.S. Sentencing Commission 2008), on which see ABA (1999). Harm is measured by taking 20% of the volume of commerce involved. This figure is rationalized on the asserted ground that the usual markup is 10%, but using that figure would understate harm by omitting the effect on discouraged buyers (deadweight loss). Other factors enter into the determination of fines under the Guidelines, and even regarding this factor, there can be adjustments (but not taking the factor below 15%). Use of the 20% factor, making no adjustment for higher or lower overcharge increments, seems to be widespread. ABA (1999, 43). The 10% markup assumption is attributed by some (see Connor and Lande 2005, 524–26) to Assistant Attorney General Ginsburg's (1986, 13–16) testimony before the Sentencing Commission, although his emphasis on the need for a multiplier of at least tenfold to account for a probability of detection he speculated to be under 10%, producing a baseline of over 100%, seems to have had no impact on the Commission's determination. (In addition, the FTC (2008, §II.B.2) claims the authority to disgorge what it terms unjust enrichment, and it has successfully done so in some cases.)

EU law is unclear regarding the extent to which the magnitude of the overcharge (however defined) is relevant in setting fines, either under the European Commission Fining Guidelines or in practice. European Commission (2006, §1.B.21) states as the general rule that "the proportion of the value of sales taken into account will be set at a level of up to 30% of the value of sales." In describing previous practice, Sorinas (2007, 578) explains: "However, as of the end of 2005, the Commission had not adopted any decision where the need to confiscate the profits of the infringement was specifically referred to as a factor justifying an increase in the amount of the fine. This was no doubt due to the practical difficulty of assessing gain with any degree

Although motivated on grounds of simplicity, this approach seems surprising in light of the huge variation in overcharges across cases.[24] Accordingly, setting to the side other penalties (which may be substantial in the United States because of private suits and imprisonment, but less so elsewhere), deterrence is likely to be inadequate when large overcharges occur since fines will be less than firms' profits, even ignoring any probability discount. This point may help to explain why, as section 9.C presents, there are numerous prosecuted cases, many of which involve substantial price elevation.

The analysis of subsection 1 indicates that this approach is also highly problematic in cases involving small overcharges. The concern is not so much with overdeterrence per se as with chilling effects. The excessive application of fines is unnecessary to deter true violations involving small overcharges, and some such cases may involve false positives because, as discussed in section 12.A and elsewhere, cases not involving actual violations are more likely to present evidence of small price elevations than of large ones. Indeed, it was previously mentioned that low sanctions for small overcharges provide a partial safety valve against chilling costs by reducing the magnitude of expected sanctions in settings in which false positives are more likely. These considerations suggest that, if anything, it might be best to moderate sanctions—relative to the best estimate of harm and an appropriate multiplier—when overcharges are low rather than imposing relatively high sanctions (that is, high relative to apparent harm) in such cases.

Another question of interest is how the current, standard level of fines relates to typical overcharges. Some argue that fines are too low

---

of precision. The commission has been acknowledging repeatedly that it is often impossible to isolate precisely the effects of a cartel on the level of prices from the impact of external economic factors." See also ibid. (534): "However, the 2006 Fining Guidelines make clear that cartel-type agreements . . . will 'as a matter of policy, be heavily fined'. . . . Therefore, in cartel cases the percentage level can be expected to be equal or close to 30%, and the other factors mentioned in the 2006 Fining Guidelines will probably come into play and lead to a lower percentage only in exceptional circumstances."; Van Cayseele, Camesasca, and Hugmark (2008), critiquing the Guidelines for not proportioning fines to expected harm, as economic theory prescribes; and Veljanovski (2011), providing evidence on cartel fines under the 2006 Guidelines.

[24] See, for example, the sources cited in note 32 of chapter 9.

on average, a position that is consistent with the aforementioned evidence of a high rate of detected and prosecuted violations.[25] As a consequence, collusion may indeed be profitable in some cases.[26] Keep in mind, however, that analyses limited to fines alone can be misleading if other sanctions, notably damages in private suits and imprisonment, are substantial.[27]

---

[25] Connor (2007a) and Connor and Lande (2005). See also Sokol (2012), presenting results from a practitioners' survey suggesting that existing penalties in the United States provide inadequate deterrence. Previously, some commentators had expressed concerns about U.S. fines being overly severe. See Cohen and Scheffman (1989) and Connor and Lande (2005, 526–27 & n.79), discussing the literature. (It seems apparent from Connor and Lande (2005, 532, tbl. 1) that Cohen and Scheffman examined an unusually small number of cartels and found mean and median overcharges that are well below those reported in other surveys.) It must be acknowledged that much of the empirical evidence, even in the more recent surveys, is from past time periods and other jurisdictions, both involving lower sanctions. But some is also fairly recent and in high-sanction jurisdictions like the United States. Note that, in equilibrium, given the nature of fines (and that prison terms, discussed in section B, have ceilings), one might expect firms capable of only low or moderate price elevations to be deterred, with the result that high-overcharge cases would predominate in actual prosecutions. A countervailing factor is that the probability of detection may be greater when overcharges are larger. Yet another consideration is that many assessments look at authorized sanctions, whereas fines actually imposed often involve significant discounts as a consequence of plea bargaining or leniency provisions. Connor (2008, 48, 56).

[26] See Combe and Monnier (2011) on fines in the European Union and also the conflicting claims of Connor (2004) and White (2001), who were, respectively, experts for plaintiffs and defendants in the lysine case.

[27] Lande and Davis (2008, 880) find "that almost half of the underlying violations were first uncovered by private attorneys, not government enforcers, and that litigation in many other cases had a mixed public/private origin," and they conclude that "private litigation probably does more to deter antitrust violations than all the fines and incarceration imposed as a result of criminal enforcement by the DOJ." See also ibid. (893–95), reporting that total payouts in just the cases in their sample exceeded total fines in all cases by more than four to one, and that limiting their sample of forty large cases just to those in which there were both private recoveries and criminal fines, the former were larger than the total of the latter for all cases, not just those in their sample; ibid. (897, 909 tbl. 5), showing that, of the approximately $18 billion in total private recoveries, about $8 billion were not from follow-on actions and an additional $4 billion were from cases of mixed origin; and ibid. (901), indicating that just over half of the forty cases in the private suit sample involved naked price fixing or bid rigging. For arguments that Lande and Davis overstate the relative importance of private enforcement, see Werden, Hammond, and Barnett (2011).

B. Imprisonment

As mentioned in the introduction to this chapter, nonmonetary sanctions, notably imprisonment, tend to be inferior to fines or damages because of their greater social cost, and thus they are optimally used primarily when monetary sanctions are insufficient. When an individual or firm pays a fine or damages award, the funds are transferred to the government or plaintiffs (often victims), so the sanction is not socially costly in itself.[28] With imprisonment, the utility loss suffered by those incarcerated—the prospect of which provides the deterrent effect—is a social loss not otherwise offset. In addition, it is socially costly to operate prisons. Despite these substantial disadvantages, imprisonment is increasingly used in the United States for price-fixing violations and has recently received greater attention in other jurisdictions.[29]

Two key rationales for the use of nonmonetary sanctions are relevant in the present context. The first is to make up for sanction insufficiency, notably, when defendants may be judgment proof. If fines or damages were limited to firms' profits, there would not often be a problem. But, as explained in section A, monetary payments should exceed profits and, moreover, they need to reflect a probability multiplier in light of the difficulty of detection, with treble damages being the norm in private suits in the United States. Accordingly, it seems plausible that firms that

---

[28] This statement abstracts from the administrative costs of the system, including extracting the payments—the former of which are substantial for imprisonment and the latter of which are often negligible relative to the costs of prison—and also from risk aversion. Regarding the latter, an expected monetary sanction of 100 imposes a utility cost greater than 100 if there is uncertainty and the prospective payor is risk averse. This effect does increase the deterrence from a given sanction, but to that extent a fraction of the utility lost to the payor is not a transfer but a pure social loss. See Polinsky and Shavell (1979).

[29] For data on practice in the United States, see Hammond (2008): Total imprisonment rose from an average aggregate of nine years per fiscal year in the 1990s to a record high of eighty-six aggregate years in 2007 (4). Average sentence length was eight months in the 1990s and has (roughly) trended upward, reaching a record of thirty-one months in 2007 (6). See also Connor (2008, 91–92, tbl. 1). Outside the United States, however, imprisonment is ordinarily not authorized and is rarely used, and fines against individuals are also quite limited. See OECD (2002, 10–12). However, such policies are increasingly being revisited.

significantly elevate prices for years may not, when ultimately detected, have sufficient assets to pay the full fine or damages award, particularly for firms elevating price on their only product or products.[30]

The second rationale, which is especially relevant to sanctions levied on particular individuals, relates to the agency problem within a firm.[31] Most obviously, the threat of imprisonment (or fines on individuals) can usefully introduce a divergence between a firm's and its agents' incentives. In cases in which the firm is not adequately deterred, the prospect of imprisonment may nevertheless deter key employees, making it difficult for firms that wish to violate the law to do so.

Also important is the reverse situation, where the agent rather than the firm may be the one who is inadequately deterred. Managers or sales personnel may receive compensation, including bonuses, and have promotion prospects tied to measures of performance. In such cases, they may have an incentive to engage in price fixing even when it is against the firm's interest. The reason for this possible divergence is that, even if expected sanctions are adequate to deter the firm, making it affirmatively in its interest to quash improper behavior, the firm may not be able to induce its agents to comply. They, in turn, may calculate that there are large personal gains from violations, with low chances of detection. Moreover, if they are detected, such as when the firm is successfully prosecuted, the firm may not be able to heavily sanction the individuals. Usually, the most it can do is fire them, which may cost them future earnings as well as unvested deferred compensation. But these costs may not always be sufficient to deter the relevant individuals. In such cases, the firm would like to be able to sanction its misbehaving employees more severely, but

---

[30] I am unaware of data indicating how often firms are judgment proof in price-fixing cases. In many jurisdictions, this problem may not often arise because required payments are much lower than theory suggests may be appropriate, but the situation might change if sanctions were increased significantly.

[31] In the absence of agency problems and the judgment-proof problem, it tends not to matter in theory whether sanctions are levied on an entity or its agents, who can rearrange any such allocations by contract (such as indemnity provisions), unless those are outlawed. See generally Kraakman (1984), and also Ginsburg and Wright (2010), who advocate a greater emphasis on penalizing responsible individuals rather than heightening fines on firms, and Sokol (2012), who emphasizes the relevance of looking inside the firm to identify determinants of the behavior of individual employees.

it cannot legally do so. Thus, the prospect of government-imposed sanctions may provide a useful supplement.[32]

To use a sanction of imprisonment (or fines levied directly on individuals), particular culpable individuals must be identified.[33] This need raises two challenges: determination of who in principle should be subject to imprisonment and detection of any such individuals in a particular case. These issues are generally present when attempting to sanction specific individuals in a legal entity for actions as agents in serving that entity. Accordingly, similar problems arise when firms illegally dispose of toxic waste, bribe government officials, violate safety regulations, and so forth.[34]

Because the cost of sanctions is greater and because the nature of chilling effects may differ when it is particular agents who are faced with sanctions—and their interests can diverge from firms' interests—different proof burdens may be optimal.[35] And, of course, significantly higher proof burdens are ordinarily employed. This and other dimensions regarding

---

[32] See Polinsky and Shavell (1993). As noted, the logic in the text justifies individual sanctions but not necessarily imprisonment; its justification will, again, typically be the judgment-proof problem, in this case with regard to individuals rather than firms.

[33] There is also the possibility of criminal liability imposed on the firm, but since imprisonment of a firm is not coherent and fines (whether or not deemed criminal) are already addressed, it is unclear how much independent significance remains. See Khanna (1996). A criminal conviction may, due to other rules, have independent consequences; for example, a firm convicted of bid rigging might be barred from future bidding, although such a prohibition could also follow as a result of civil liability.

[34] Even if price-fixing liability is confined to a narrow, precisely defined set of interfirm communications, there will be important questions of individual liability concerning those who are not, say, caught on tape in the hotel room discussing prices, but who instead are the pertinent superiors or are others engaged in price setting or strategizing who have knowledge of such behavior. See section 18.A. Acts that seem as simple as illegally discharging toxic substances into the sewage system can be quite complicated once the black box of the firm is opened. For example, it may be unclear whether individuals doing the actual disposal are aware that the materials are toxic, and centrally responsible individuals may be those who knowingly failed to take certain precautions or relay certain information.

[35] A particular concern is that, if individuals face a significant risk of heavy sanctions on account of false positives, chilling effects could be large. Even if the firm could absorb a certain level of expected sanctions imposed by mistake, risk-averse individuals with more limited assets may not be able to do so. For this reason, individuals are often indemnified by firms, but some risk may remain (depending on the conditions of indemnification) and, if imprisonment is to be employed, financial indemnification may not be an entirely effective substitute (perhaps unless it is quite large).

the use of imprisonment warrant further study in the present context, and with regard to sanctions applied to agents more generally.

C. Injunctions

As the chapter's introduction notes, injunctions are not obviously important in the present setting.[36] Moreover, it is not apparent that they are heavily used.[37] Nevertheless, many commentators seem to be fixated on their centrality—often implicitly, in arguing against a price-fixing rule on the ground that it would be difficult to fashion an injunction commanding compliance.[38] Accordingly, it is important to examine injunctions further.

Injunctions, as was explained, do not deter violations. If the only legal consequence of theft, murder, or tax evasion was the possibility of being ordered not to repeat the violation in the future, crime may become

---

[36] Discussion is confined to orders to cease price fixing and related behavior. Structural remedies are discussed briefly in note 39 and in section 18.C (primarily with regard to stricter merger control).

[37] Exploration of the web site and publications on workload and enforcement of the U.S. Department of Justice Antitrust Division reveals substantial information on fines and imprisonment, but not (that this author could readily locate) on injunctions. Examination of competition law treatises in the United States and other research does not reveal significant attention devoted to injunctions for price fixing. It appears that injunctions are used with regard to explicit, open practices, such as when an organization requires price fixing or employs particular facilitating devices. For example, in civil antitrust actions against the airlines industry (*Airline Tariff*, for sending coded messages through the electronic price-posting service (U.S. v. Airline Tariff Publishing Co., et al.)), NASDAQ market makers (for activity designed to maintain supracompetitive bid-ask spreads (U.S. v. Alex Brown & Sons, et al.)), and a firm engaged in FCC license auctions (for using price digits to send messages (U.S. v. Mercury PCS II, L.L.C.)), defendants were enjoined from the specific challenged practices (and also in general terms from agreeing to fix prices). For documents on the pertinent cases, see Antitrust Division, Antitrust Case Filings, http://www.justice.gov/atr/cases.html (accessed April 7, 2011). Most U.S. Department of Justice cases that involve price fixing are criminal, and injunctions do not appear to be employed.

[38] See the statements in the seminal writing of Kaysen and Turner (1959, 143–44): "By the very fact that we are dealing with practices—that is, conduct—the appropriate remedy is always the injunctive remedy: cessation of the practice."; and Turner (1962, 669); and also Baker (1996, 47).

rampant. Oligopolists would hardly be encouraged to forgo large profits by the prospect that, if they were caught, they might have to desist from continuing to earn supracompetitive rewards in the future. Instead, deterrence is accomplished through the use of fines and damages, along with imprisonment, if necessary. Once they are in place, the supplemental role of injunctions is unclear. Injunctions themselves could also be punitive, but injunctions are not ordinarily designed in this way and such an approach tends to be inefficient.[39]

Ordinarily, injunctions are used to help ensure prospective compliance. With regard to coordinated oligopolistic pricing, it is unclear why injunctions are important for this purpose either.[40] Why not simply rely on fines and damages, and imprisonment if necessary, in order to deter future violations? The basic logic is the same as that regarding ordinary deterrence: If the expected cost of a violation exceeds firms' expected profits, they will be induced to comply. Indeed, even if there is an injunction against future violations, it too must be enforced. Presumably, firms will be led to comply with the injunction under the same conditions: when the expected sanction for violation is greater than the expected gain therefrom.

The foregoing raises the question of what, if anything, injunctions add to the preexisting legal command. Perhaps sanctions were previously insufficient to accomplish deterrence, and the penalties for violating an injunction are greater. But if this is so, one should ask why sanctions are

---

[39] Sanctions generally are more efficient and effective when designed directly as such. The threat that firms might, for example, be forced by an injunction to deliver their goods through circuitous routes in the future would accomplish deterrence, but it would be better to fine them an amount equal to the cost of complying with the injunction and not require them actually to waste the resources. Some injunctions may impose costs indirectly, such as structural relief in the competition law setting. But, for the reason just given, this result tends to make sense only as a side effect. For example, if oligopolists were forced to deconcentrate, they would bear costs (in addition to forgone supracompetitive profits) if they lost scale economies, but that would be an undesirable rather than beneficial consequence of the relief, which would need to make sense in spite of this effect.

[40] More generally, in contexts in which behavior generates negative externalities, fines or damages tend to be more efficient than injunctions because the government needs to know about (or to estimate) only the level of harm (which information is required for any remedy) and not also compliance costs. See Kaplow and Shavell (1996b).

not higher in the first instance. Also, if there is some good reason, sanctions could be raised for repeat offenders—which is often done in the criminal law[41]—without any separate need for an injunction.[42] Another aspect of the problem is that coordinated pricing may be undeterred when it is particularly difficult to detect. It is again unclear how an injunction would help; the industry could be subject to greater scrutiny in the future, but this could be done by enforcers and private plaintiffs in any event. Or one might reduce proof burdens and provide for expedited adjudication for the violation of an injunction, but these procedural adjustments, if optimal, could be employed for alleged recidivism that was punished by ordinary sanctions. Perhaps instead, firms might be subject to ongoing internal monitoring, making future furtive behavior more difficult. Note that in such cases the key difference made by the injunction would not be in the acts it prohibits or the sanctions it sets, but rather in the information it generates. Yet another possibility is that a government agency might set firms' prices or directly control other aspects of their behavior; that is, direct government regulation might be substituted for decentralized marketplace decision-making that operates under the threat of competition law's sanctions.

Supposing that more ordinary injunctions were to be employed, consider what they might require. In other realms, injunctions and government regulations sometimes dictate specifics of behavior and in other settings focus primarily on results. Thus, a factory might be required to adopt a particular pollution-control technology or it might be ordered to meet a stated emissions target in any way it can. If the problem is waste discharges that contaminate groundwater, particular disposal techniques may be commanded or firms might be ordered to cease certain types of discharge, which they might choose to accomplish by changing technology, improving maintenance and monitoring, or halting production in a vulnerable location. With respect to coordinated oligopolistic price elevation, firms could be commanded what prices to charge (that is,

---

[41] For a survey of the theoretical literature, see Polinsky and Shavell (2007, 438–39).

[42] Regulatory commands can be useful when firms may be judgment proof, but such commands must be enforced directly, such as through ongoing monitoring, discussed in the text to follow, rather than relying solely on probabilistic, after-the-fact detection.

something akin to public utility regulation) or to cease coordinating their behavior.

This latter possibility has caused great consternation among commentators. The objection is that abstention from coordinated behavior, when conditions are conducive to success, would somehow be unnatural or irrational and hence futile to require, and the asserted implication is that liability must be limited to the commission of specified acts, such as particular forms of interfirm communication.[43] This complaint, however,

---

[43] See Areeda and Hovenkamp (2003, 150): "In the preceding hypothetical, however, we cannot reasonably expect firm L to refrain from increasing its prices when it feels that the market would accept them, or the others to refrain from following."; ibid. (231): society cannot employ "a legal rule [that] tells the oligopolist to close its eyes to the immediate and direct market impact of its own output choices, as well as to the subsequent market impact of its rivals' probable responses to its own output decision"; ibid. (232): competition law cannot have a rule that "tells each firm to ignore the profit-maximizing signals emitted by the market"; Chamberlin (1929, 65): "Each is forced by the situation itself to take into account the policy of his rival in determining his own . . . ."; Dabbah (2004, 268), who argues that we cannot make illegal firms' behavior that constitutes profit maximization; Elhauge and Geradin (2007, 801–2), who refer to "the problem that firms [in] oligopolistic markets cannot avoid knowing their prices are interdependent when they set their prices, so that it would be hard to define any prohibition in a way that tells firms how to behave"; ibid. (835): "If so, how could one define the offense in a way that oligopolists could avoid behaving illegally? Is it practicable to ask them to ignore the reality of their price interdependence when making their pricing decisions?"; Hovenkamp (2005a, 128), who objects to the condemnation of interdependent behavior standing alone because "implicit in condemnation of any practice under the antitrust laws is that the defendant was obliged to behave in some other way than it did"; Monti (2001, 145), who asserts that remedies are infeasible as long as there exists a rational economic explanation for the oligopolists' behavior; Scherer and Ross (1990, 342): "How should oligopolists change their behavior so as to avoid breaking the law? Must they begin ignoring their interdependence in pricing decisions, when to do so would be irrational?"; Stroux (2004, 114): "Imposing competitors to disregard their rival[s'] behaviour would obviously be nonsense, as it would require them to behave irrationally."; Turner (1962, 666): "Particularly is this so when the behavior involved, setting the 'profit-maximizing' price in light of all market facts, is not only legally acceptable but vitally necessary to make competitive markets function as they are supposed to function."; Van Bael and Bellis (2005, 51): "[S]ometimes it is only rational commercial behaviour which makes competitors align their conduct. In such a case undertakings should not be punished for doing what makes sense commercially."; and White House Task Force on Antitrust Policy (1968, 5): "antitrust law . . . cannot order the several firms to ignore each other's existence." Interestingly, most of these references postdate Posner's work (in one case, co-authored) that is cited in the note to the following paragraph, yet they seem to overlook its

is quite puzzling since the response is both obvious and has been offered before: What is natural and rational depends on whether sanctions are imposed. It may be natural and rational for a hungry shopper to steal an apple, for a youth with public artistic impulses to create graffiti, or for a greedy manager to embezzle funds—that is, if such were legal. However, if these activities are illegal and subject to heavy sanctions, engaging in them becomes irrational. Such individuals may continue to contemplate antisocial behavior from time to time but would be disinclined to translate their thoughts into action.

Oligopolistic price coordination is no different. If there are no sanctions, a firm may find it attractive to follow a leader's price increase and to avoid undercutting the industry's supracompetitive price because of the allure of sustained supracompetitive profits if cooperation continues. But if such acts are associated with sufficiently high penalties, then the firm would find it irrational to follow the leader's price increase and profitable to undercut elevated prices. Regarding the later, subsection 7.A.2 describes firms' calculus in deciding whether to cheat; if one adds a sufficient penalty to the choice involving cooperative behavior, cheating becomes more appealing. Therefore, the question of whether a command to refrain from coordinated oligopolistic pricing—whether issued through a particular injunction or by the law more generally—will succeed depends on the adequacy of expected sanctions. This adequacy, in turn, depends

---

basic point with regard to the deterrent effect of sanctions altering what firms would find it rational to do.

Even ignoring that sanctions change firms' incentives, the sometimes-expressed position that interdependence is inevitable that is reflected in the aforementioned views—see also, for example, Kaysen and Turner (1959, 27), suggesting that recognized interdependence is "extremely likely" when concentration is even moderately high—is not empirically well grounded. Evidence on successful prosecutions, discussed in sections 6.E and 9.C, reveals the use of explicit and sometimes highly elaborate direct communications even in very concentrated industries, and industrial organization research for decades on the structure-conduct-performance paradigm, discussed in section 11.A, implies that successful coordination often fails even in highly concentrated industries. Moreover, most commentators who have offered an opinion on the subject (overlapping in part with those cited just above in this note) assert that coordination is actually quite difficult in the absence of explicit communications. See section 6.C and note 21. Accordingly, both the empirical basis and apparent consensus behind the premise for this common argument seem on reflection to be lacking. See also Posner (1969, 1566–69), critiquing Turner's view that oligopolistic coordination is inevitable.

on detection and on the magnitude of penalties.[44] It does not depend on firms' managers possessing some mystical ability to engage in a form of reasoning heretofore unknown to humankind.

---

[44] See Posner (1969, 1592 n.80): "All I am arguing is that a deliberate restriction of output by competitors is conduct that rational men can avoid—and will avoid if it is made sufficiently costly to them to engage in it."; Posner (2001, 97–98): "Tacit collusion is not an unconscious state. . . . The threat of a damages judgment for supracompetitive pricing will influence their pricing decisions; what would be irrational would be for the oligopolists to ignore such a threat."; and Posner and Easterbrook (1981, 333): "The defendants can alter their behavior even if the behavior was once in their interest. Sanctions for disobedience change the incentives."

14

Unilateral Market Power

꙰

The analysis thus far focuses on distinguishing two categories of behavior: purely independent behavior—taken to be synonymous with competition, where firms take prices as given—and interdependent behavior—where firms take rivals' reactions into account and thereby are able to elevate price.[1] Analysis may further divide the category of interdependent behavior based, say, on whether particular types of explicit interfirm communication occurred, a distinction that is not under examination in this part but is the focus of parts I and III.

This chapter examines a further distinction within the category of independent behavior: between competitive behavior—where rivals select quantities so as to equate marginal cost to a given price—and interactions in which firms, although taking rivals' behavior as given, nevertheless elevate price through what is referred to as the unilateral exercise of market power. In the latter case, firms find it profitable to sell at a price above rather than equal to marginal cost, without assuming that other firms will respond by raising their prices, and to maintain price in excess of marginal cost rather than slightly undercutting others' prices, even if they do not take into account any retaliation by rivals. This characterization merely restates the point that the exercise of unilateral market power entails price elevation without the sort of coordination (interdependence) described in subsection 7.A.2.[2]

---

[1] On terminology, see section 2.B.

[2] The use of the term unilateral market power and its contrast to coordinated oligopolistic behavior (interdependence) on one hand and competition on the other hand is conventional in economics but, as section 2.C elaborates, is often confused in competition law commentary (including some written by economists), where the term "independence" is sometimes used to encompass interdependence—thereby including not only behavior in which rivals' actions

Until now, this part of the book has largely proceeded as if such unilateral market power did not exist. When it might, a number of questions arise. First, what treatment of unilateral price elevation maximizes social welfare? This topic is the analogue to that addressed in chapter 8, where it is implicitly assumed that oligopolistic price elevation is due to coordination.

Second, how can we distinguish price elevation attributable to the exercise of unilateral market power from that due to successful oligopolistic coordination? The answer to this question is important if the response to the first question implies that different treatment is optimal in the two cases. As will be discussed, many of the methods of detection considered in chapters 10 and 11 specifically identify interdependence whereas others identify price elevation without necessarily suggesting what mode of interaction produced it.

Third, in situations in which it is difficult to distinguish the two causes of price elevation, what approach to liability makes sense in light of the social costs arising from the possibility of misclassification? These errors are different from errors of mistakenly treating competitive behavior, with price equal to marginal cost, as if there was coordinated oligopolistic price elevation. Accordingly, ex ante behavioral effects tend to differ as well, and sometimes the effect of anticipating mistaken liability in this setting is to raise rather than lower social welfare.

These questions have received virtually no attention in the competition policy literature on price fixing and related matters,[3] although there is an extensive industrial organization literature on unilateral market power and consideration of such power plays a significant role in deciding which horizontal mergers should be challenged.[4] Accordingly, the analysis in

---

are taken as given and but also strategic behavior that takes into account rivals' anticipated reactions.

[3] Markovits (1974, 1975)—in a series of papers that, to a significant extent, are critiques of Turner (1962) and Posner (1969)—emphasizes that price can exceed marginal cost without coordination. Posner's (1976, 911–13) otherwise critical reply accepts this point. But neither author substantially illuminates the questions considered here.

[4] Both the U.S. Horizontal Merger Guidelines (2010, §§6, 7) and European Commission Horizontal Merger Guidelines (2004, ¶¶24–28) distinguish between unilateral and coordinated effects. See also section 18.C, discussing the tension between prohibiting mergers that augment unilateral market power and allowing unilateral price elevation more generally.

this chapter is preliminary, focusing mostly on relating the three aforementioned questions to the analysis in the rest of this part of the book,
emphasizing the problem of detection in light of error costs. The analysis
first briefly considers the case of a dominant firm that elevates price. This
case, common with monopoly, usefully introduces the subject of unilateral
market power and helps create a bridge between most of the discussion
in preceding chapters and that which immediately follows. Also, it has
some relevance because it is not always easy to distinguish dominant firm
pricing from coordinated oligopoly pricing, notably, when the leading
firm is not completely dominant and there are substantial rivals. Next
considered are industries with multiple leading firms for cases with homogeneous goods and with differentiated products, the latter corresponding to the form of interaction often referred to as monopolistic competition.
Each of these settings is examined separately because it may be that ideal
treatment, problems of detection, and related error costs differ according
to the context in which unilateral market power is exercised. Finally,
concluding comments are offered on the implications of the present
analysis for competition policy toward oligopoly pricing.

A. Dominant Firm

A dominant firm, whether the sole producer or somewhat constrained
by a group of fringe firms that behave competitively (aspects of which
were addressed in section 12.C), is ordinarily free as a matter of general
competition law to elevate price to its profit-maximizing level. As discussed in subsection 8.B.2, this approach is justified on grounds of dynamic efficiency: the belief that on average the prospect of such monopoly
profits will induce socially desirable ex ante investments sufficient to
outweigh the costs of subsequent allocative inefficiency. When a single
firm can successfully elevate price substantially above marginal cost, this
ordinarily is taken to reflect the superiority of its product, assuming that
the firm's market power is not attributable to exclusionary practices or
unwarranted government protection. Moreover, as explained in that
subsection, coordinated oligopolistic price elevation does not typically
produce such dynamic benefits (and when it does so, they are not well
correlated with firms' ability to elevate price) and may be accompanied

by additional efficiency costs. These differences explain why monopoly pricing is ordinarily legal (in the absence of direct regulation, often employed for natural monopolies) whereas coordinated oligopolistic price elevation is condemned (although prohibitions, as many would interpret them, may reach only a subset of such behavior).

Monopolists elevate price unilaterally. When there are no other producers, there is no one to coordinate with. When there are small firms comprising a so-called competitive fringe, it is normally supposed that the dominant firm chooses the supracompetitive price that is best for itself on the assumption that fringe firms will produce whatever quantity they profitably can at that price.[5] That is, fringe firms are understood to set their marginal cost equal to the price, which they take as given, and they accomplish this equation by increasing quantity until marginal cost rises to equal the price. In such markets, it is conceivable that the price would be even higher if the firms coordinated on price. That is, all firms could profit by reducing quantity and raising price. It is imagined, however, that such coordination is not sustainable because of free riding by the small firms, each of which has a negligible effect on industry price.

Proceeding on the assumption of no coordination, a dominant firm and an oligopoly involve two distinct settings subject to two different regimes. Complications may arise, however, because it is not always so obvious when a dominant-firm situation exists. Instead of, say, a single firm with a 90% market share and dozens of firms, none with a share exceeding 1%, consider an industry with a leading firm having a 60% share, a few firms with shares of 10% each, and perhaps additional very small firms. In this case, one could try to distinguish price elevation due to the leading firm's unilateral market power (if indeed it has any of note, which would depend on the elasticity of market demand and rivals' cost structures) from that (possibly further increment) due to coordinated behavior between the leading firm and the few larger firms. Such distinction would be necessary if unilateral price elevation by a dominant firm is permissible whereas coordinated oligopoly pricing is not. If elevation above the unilateral, dominant-firm price (that is, the price the dominant

---

[5] See, for example, Kaplow and Shapiro (2007, 1081) and Landes and Posner (1981, 944). This approach derives from Forchheimer (1908), on which see Reid (1979).

firm would set if it took all of the other firms' behavior as given)[6] is established, there would be liability. Moreover, to the extent that sanctions
are based on the magnitude of the violation, the relevant price increment
would presumably be the difference between the coordinated price and
the dominant-firm price (rather than the difference between the former
and a competitive price)—a subject that was mentioned in subsection
13.A.1 and will be revisited in section D of this chapter.

Consider how one would use the types of proof examined in chapters
10 and 11 to determine whether there is coordinated oligopolistic behavior
that further elevates price above the dominant firm's best unilateral price.
Some types of evidence examined there concern interdependence per se
and thus provide a basis for inferring that coordinated pricing took place.
These would include advance price announcements and price jousting,
secret meetings to discuss pricing, sudden price elevations unexplained
by cost or demand shocks, price wars, sustained price discrimination of
the relevant sort, and price stickiness. In contrast, direct measures of the
dominant firm's marginal cost provide little basis for distinguishing the
two situations. However, evidence on the 10% firms' marginal costs could
be quite illuminating, for whether they were pricing at (or near) versus
significantly above their marginal cost bears on whether dominant firm/
competitive fringe behavior or oligopolistic coordination took place. (The
10% firms may elevate price somewhat above marginal cost on account
of their own unilateral market power—see the cases examined in sections
B and C—but significantly elevated prices by them would indicate coordinated oligopoly pricing.)

Finally, some evidence may or may not bear on whether elevation is
accomplished by interdependence. Internal evidence could be of just
about anything. For example, internal memos of the dominant firm could
reveal pricing strategy based on the assumption that the leading rivals
behave reciprocally, or that they will equate marginal cost and price, which
behavior needs to be taken as given. Likewise, the leading rivals' internal
evidence could be quite probative. Much internal evidence may bear on

---

[6] There is some ambiguity here because, although the other larger firms with the 10% shares
might be supposed to behave as competitors, setting price equal to marginal cost, they may
themselves have some unilateral market power. Cases in which multiple firms each exercise
unilateral market power are examined in sections B and C.

optimal pricing or marginal cost, considered just above. Regarding evidence on the conduciveness of conditions, this too will vary in relevance. Whether goods are homogeneous, prices are open, and numbers of key players are small, all bear on the ability to coordinate successfully but not directly on the extent to which a dominant firm can unilaterally raise price.[7] But evidence on overall market power in the industry, such as the elasticity of industry demand and ease of entry, bears on the ability to elevate price through coordination or unilaterally, without directly distinguishing the two.[8]

As is generally true regarding the problem of detection, often inferences will be uncertain, raising the prospect of errors. False negatives will tend to undermine deterrence much as when attempting to distinguish successful oligopolistic coordination from competitive interaction. The importance of this reduction, however, may be less because achieving full deterrence only reduces price from the monopoly price to the dominant-firm price, not all the way to the competitive benchmark of marginal cost.

False positives are qualitatively different in this context. Consider a dominant firm, like that in the preceding example, that faces some prospect of liability for oligopolistic price elevation even if it is merely charges the unilateral, dominant-firm price. Perhaps such an error will be due to underestimation of the key firms' marginal costs. The dominant firm might then react by moderating its price. As discussed in section 9.B, when highly competitive firms, particularly ones with constant marginal cost, are faced with such a prospect, the result could be quite problematic. But in the present context, the social loss may be small, or there may even be some social gain. Ordinarily, a dominant firm can reduce its price moderately without being induced to exit the industry since its price is well above marginal cost. Moreover, this price reduction reduces deadweight loss, raising social welfare. The main social detriment is that the expectation of reduced profits diminishes prospective or actual dominant

---

[7] An important contrast for the following sections is that small numbers do importantly increase the magnitude of unilateral price elevation by groups of firms, in addition to making oligopolistic coordination more feasible.

[8] These factors will be relevant indirectly because they bear on how much price elevation we might expect for both the unilateral exercise of market power and coordinated price elevation, and in the situations examined in the subsequent sections, these elevations may be quite different, especially when there are more than a few significant firms.

firms' ex ante investment incentives. Note, however, that the reduction in profits (and thus the sacrifice in socially valuable investment) may be small compared to the gain in allocative efficiency. The reason is that, at the profit-maximizing price, the marginal profit is zero (this feature characterizes the firm's optimum); hence, modest reductions result in little diminution in profit, despite causing a notable social welfare gain (marginal deadweight loss is given by the extent to which price exceeds marginal cost, which is assumed to be substantial, not negligible, at the dominant firm's profit-maximizing price).[9] Also, as discussed in subsection 8.B.2, a dominant firm's incentives may be excessive even if the unconstrained unilateral exercise of market power is superior to having price equal to marginal cost.

Accordingly, the relative concern with false positives seems less, perhaps significantly less, regarding the prospect of mistakenly finding that a dominant firm has engaged in interdependent price elevation. It is also relevant that, to the extent sanctions are based on the degree of the violation (a point discussed in sections 12.A and 13.A), any problem is likely to be moderate (or a net benefit), as long as much of the dominant firm's price elevation is properly attributed to the unilateral exercise of market power, if such is indeed the case. In contrast, if all price elevation, perhaps demonstrated and measured using evidence that marginal cost is much less than price, is ascribed to interdependence when much of it is not,

---

[9] To elaborate slightly for those less familiar with the economics of firms' optimizing behavior, a dominant firm continues raising price above marginal cost as long as the marginal profit (marginal revenue minus marginal cost) from doing so is positive, and it stops when marginal profit is zero (marginal revenue equals marginal cost). Accordingly, a small reduction from the dominant firm's profit-maximizing price, at the first instant, involves no loss in profit and, as the price falls further, the marginal profit reduction is increasing. If the price-moderation chilling effect is small, the profit loss will be small, not only in absolute terms but also relative to consumers' gains. Accordingly, it is familiar that it would be ideal in a basic setting if monopolists' (dominant firms') prices were pushed down at least somewhat below their profit-maximizing level. If regulation designed to accomplish that task would be costly and the social gains modest, laissez-faire on this dimension makes sense. However, when considering the social cost of false positives in terms of chilling effects that entail some price moderation, it is relevant to recognize that the social cost may be negative (that is, a benefit) or, even if a net cost (perhaps because the chilling effect is fairly large), it may be more modest than in other settings.

significant chilling costs, in terms of reduction in socially valuable ex ante investment incentives, could ensue.[10]

B. Homogeneous Goods

Section A considers the unilateral exercise of market power by a single firm. Because this book focuses on oligopoly, we wish to consider markets in which there are a number of firms other than mere fringe firms. Accordingly, suppose that a market is inhabited by five symmetric firms, each having a 20% market share (implying that there are no fringe firms, the analysis of which would be similar to that just presented). Even though there are five firms rather than a single, dominant firm, each firm might be able to exercise some market power, with the result that price will be elevated above the competitive level—although still below the monopoly level, that is, unless the firms also successfully coordinate their behavior. In examining this issue, it is conventional and useful to distinguish the case of homogeneous goods from that involving differentiated products, recognizing that few goods are perfectly homogeneous and that some obviously differentiated products are not that different from each other in consumers' minds. In these cases, our questions remain the same: What is ideal treatment? Can we distinguish the unilateral exercise of market power from successful oligopolistic coordination? And, if we wish to do so but it is difficult, what are the social costs from misclassification?

This section examines the homogeneous goods case, which is most relevant for the analysis of interdependent oligopolistic price elevation

---

[10] A concern worth further study is the case of a firm that, due to a sequence of investments or perhaps significant initial investments that take a long time to fully materialize, has a gradually increasing market share and, as its unilateral market power increases, raises price ever further above marginal cost. Although the prospect of false positives may be socially costly in such settings, it seems that they may be infrequent because the behaviors are not that difficult to distinguish. The fact that a firm's share is growing larger and larger at the expense of rivals is itself strong evidence of growing dominant-firm strength accompanied by the unilateral exercise of market power rather than interdependence (for rivals would not continue to cooperate if one member of the price-elevating group was continuing to grow at their expense).

because coordination is more difficult when products are differentiated. In analyzing this setting, it is useful to make a further distinction between whether firms are understood to compete on price or on the quantity of goods sold.[11] Put another way, when we imagine that firms are acting unilaterally, taking their rivals' actions as given, which rivals' actions are we referring to? Since each rival has a nontrivial presence in the market, it is unreasonable to suppose that, if one firm significantly changes its behavior, rivals would be expected to keep both price and quantity the same, for the market would no longer clear. If a firm raises its price, for example, and other firms keep both price and quantity constant, there will be excess demand for their wares. If the other firms keep price constant, it would suggest that they are increasing their quantity to meet the additional demand. If they keep quantity constant, then they must increase price somewhat (even though not as much as did the initiator of the price increase), to the point at which the reduction in the quantity demanded is so as to equate consumers' resulting demand for their product with the stipulated quantities.

Suppose first that the initiating firm assumes that other firms keep their prices the same. If firms have constant marginal cost, the result will be competitive, which is to say that there can be no unilateral exercise of market power. If prices are at the competitive level, any firm that raises price loses all of its sales to rivals, who sell the identical good and maintain their lower prices. And if prices were ever elevated, a firm that cut its price slightly would take the entire market, greatly increasing its profit at the others' expense. This result should not be surprising; after all, it is believed that many markets with at least a few firms do behave quite competitively, and that coordination would be required if the firms are to do better for themselves.

While not widely appreciated, it has long been understood in the technical literature that the foregoing result depends on the assumption of constant marginal cost. If marginal cost is increasing or if there are capacity constraints (which can be described as marginal cost rising to infinity at full capacity), the outcome may be different. Capacity constraints will be discussed momentarily, under the rubric of competition

---

[11] See Friedman (1986, 54–57), Shapiro (1989, 333–56), Tirole (1988, ch. 5), and Vives (1999, chs. 4, 5).

in quantities rather than price. More broadly, rising marginal costs may make possible some price elevation. The reason is that, when our initiating firm raises its price, rivals who keep their prices constant will not wish to increase their quantities to meet demand, for increasing output implies a higher marginal cost, which in turn would exceed the price that they are keeping constant (assuming that we began from a point at which price equaled marginal cost). However, no supracompetitive price can be an equilibrium either.[12] Starting from such a price, where each firm is pricing above its marginal cost, each has an incentive to cut its price slightly if the others maintain price. Even though it may not be able to profitably supply the whole market as a consequence of its rising marginal cost schedule, it can increase its market share and thus its total profit.

The literature offers a formal answer to this conundrum, one that involves mixed strategies (each firm randomly selecting its price each period from within a band of supracompetitive prices), but many analysts find this solution unsatisfactory as a depiction of real-world pricing behavior.[13]

---

[12] The equilibrium existence problem is originally raised in Edgeworth (1925).

[13] Formal solutions using mixed strategies are presented in Dasgupta and Maskin (1986) and Maskin (1986). However, some analysts find the mixed-strategy solution inapt in terms of understanding actual strategic interactions among firms. Friedman (1988, 608) explains: "I restrict attention to pure-strategy equilibria because I do not find mixed-strategy equilibria behaviorally plausible. . . . It might be argued that mixed strategies represent some uncertainty in the minds of decisionmakers. . . . This may be plausible in a one-shot model, but a deep understanding of oligopolistic behavior cannot be achieved by means of single-period models with results that are unreasonable in a multiperiod setting. This article is intended as a prelude to a study of dynamic models. Mixed strategies, under which prices and outputs are randomly selected in each period, seem bizarre in an infinite-horizon oligopoly." He further notes (616 n.13): "The latter belief is based on my conviction that single-period oligopoly models are almost exclusively of interest as elements of many-period models, and my conviction that mixed actions make no behavioral sense in many-period models." The main problem is that, in the hypothesized mixed-strategy equilibrium, each of, say, two firms, after announcing different prices, would immediately wish to change them: The firm with the lower price, which captures the market, would prefer to raise price (while still keeping it below the other firm's price), so as to further increase profits. The firm with the higher price, in contrast, would prefer to move its price below that of the other firm. See Shapiro (1989, 346 & n.30). Davidson and Deneckere (1986, 412 n.1) note: "An anonymous Associate Editor has raised the following objection to the mixed strategies employed in this article and in Kreps and Scheinkman (1983). In any pure-strategy equilibrium firms never 'regret' the price they charge ex post. . . . [But here, once] firm i finds out what price its competitor is charging, it may want to change its own price (under the assumption that its competitor's price will not change). It can be argued,

Therefore, although price competition with homogeneous goods seems natural, it is not clear if, without any further coordination, we should expect significant, sustained price elevation to take place. Some suggest that prices may exhibit cycling behavior, at least some of the time being supracompetitive, and there is some empirical evidence indicating that this may occasionally be observed.[14]

Accordingly, economists generally focus on quantity competition, drawing on Cournot's seminal discussion.[15] In the most plausible formulation of this story, a two-stage process is envisioned. Firms choose their quantities in an initial period, after which these quantities are sold in a subsequent period, in which price is determined to clear the market. The total quantity is given by the sum of the firms' quantity choices, and the price is then given by the corresponding point on the market demand curve. When each firm chooses its quantity, it is assumed to take other firms' quantity choices as given. This formulation implies some price elevation. To begin, suppose that all quantities were at the competitive level (which is to say, firms' aggregate quantity choices would lead to a second-stage price equal to that which would result from perfect competition). If a firm considers reducing its quantity somewhat, this deviation would decrease the total quantity supplied (other firms, recall, are assumed to keep their quantities constant), which in turn implies a higher market-clearing price. If initially the firm was behaving competitively, so that

---

therefore, that we are assuming that consumers can respond to market prices faster than firms." Their use of the term "may" regarding the wish to change its price is a notable understatement, and the assumption about consumers is that all purchases are made, by individuals who all are aware of the firms' prices, before any firm can realize what the different prices are and make any adjustments. Tirole (1988, 215 n.6) also suggests that the mixed-strategy feature makes this static model of price choice "particularly suspect," and that, ex post, a firm "may" wish to adjust its price.

[14] Shapiro (1989, 345) and Tirole (1988, 234) discuss Edgeworth's posited price cycles, and empirical evidence is offered by Noel (2007a, 2007b), Wang (2009), and Zimmerman, Yun, and Taylor (2010).

[15] See, for example, the sources cited in note 11 and, for a brief introduction, note 16 in chapter 7. Interestingly, the articles that provide a more rigorous foundation for the two-stage version of the Cournot model elaborated in the text, Kreps and Scheinkman (1983) and Davidson and Deneckere (1986), also show that it does not necessarily solve the problem of the nonexistence of a pure-strategy equilibrium, requiring resort to mixed strategies.

price equaled marginal cost, this higher price will increase its profits. All firms are assumed to behave likewise, resulting in a supracompetitive equilibrium price. This elevated price, however, is below the monopoly price because, at the monopoly quantities, each firm would have a strong incentive to sell more. This action does cause the price to fall, but the firm that raises its quantity bears the cost of that price reduction only with regard to its own share of the output, whereas a monopolist would bear losses on output for the entire industry.

In this model, the equilibrium price is elevated, but the exercise of market power is unilateral. If the firms coordinated their behavior, price would be elevated further, perhaps to the monopoly level, but even with no coordination—unilateral action, taking other firms' quantities as given—there is some price elevation.

Although this model is commonly used, there are questions about its realism. Specifically, once firms are in the second stage, why do they not raise their quantity, reducing their price somewhat, to increase their profits? After all, the supposed equilibrium has price in excess of marginal cost, so this action would be profitable. And if all firms reason and act accordingly, we would be back to a competitive equilibrium with price equal to marginal cost and no exercise of market power. The firms may all choose to abstain from such competition because of anticipated retaliation by others, but then the price elevation would be a product of oligopolistic coordination—that is, interdependence, not independence.

The strongest answer is that there are some settings—and therefore, the Cournot model should be viewed as apt only in those cases—in which such second-stage quantity increases cannot take place.[16] Specifically, these involve capacity constraints, which make price cuts unattractive because each firm is unable to sell more, so the price cut can only reduce its profits.[17] Consider two reasons that such constraints might exist.

---

[16] In a model, one can also rule out second-stage competitive behavior by assumption, but such analytical fiat does not provide a reason for believing that the model explains real-world behavior.

[17] See Tirole (1988, 218, emphasis omitted): "More generally, what we mean by quantity competition is really a choice of scale that determines the firm's cost functions and thus determines the conditions of price competition. This choice of scale can be a capacity choice, but more general investment decisions are also allowable."

First, it may be necessary to make long-term investments in capacity, perhaps by constructing manufacturing facilities. At any given moment, each firm has a given number of plants of particular sizes, which limits total feasible output. Note that, in this case, evidence that each firm was producing at full capacity would imply that any implied exercise of market power was unilateral.[18] If firms instead have excess capacity, then sustained supracompetitive prices would be attributable to interdependence.[19]

Next, consider a second stage involving the sale of perishable goods at a market, perhaps the day's catch of fresh fish. When fishing boat owners send out their fleets each morning, they must decide how long to work, which determines the size of their catch.[20] Once the boats come in and

---

[18] Observe there is also a sense in which firms are equating marginal cost and price in this case. In a common formulation of the Cournot model, firms have constant marginal costs up to their capacity constraint, at which point we might conceive of marginal cost as rising to infinity for higher quantities. Precisely at the quantity constraint, marginal cost jumps from some level less than price to infinity; thus, marginal cost at that one point is undefined, although one could take it to equal price (as well as any other particular value). If capacity is difficult to observe, however, detection of price elevation through the comparison of price and marginal cost could be problematic. Average variable cost would be equal to the marginal cost up to the capacity constraint in this case, and it may be difficult for a firm to prove that, if it sold more, its marginal cost would skyrocket.

More realistically, capacity constraints often are not absolute, but rather marginal cost begins rising more steeply as one tries to squeeze additional output from a given facility. In this case, we might suppose that each firm is in fact equating price and marginal cost in the second stage—that is, unless there is also coordinated price elevation. Nevertheless, for the reason just given (that average variable cost will be well below marginal cost), this fact may be difficult to establish unless one could identify that indeed firms' outputs are close to full capacity. If we do know that firms are operating near capacity, it may be difficult to know whether there is additional price elevation due to interdependence through measurement of marginal cost since that may be hard to pin down very precisely if quantities are at a level where marginal cost is rising steeply. Other techniques of identifying interdependence remain available, although such identification may be unimportant because by assumption firms could not significantly increase quantities and thereby notably reduce the market price in any event.

[19] Firms also might coordinate in the first stage on capacity reduction, the feasibility of which may be eased by the fact that capacity expansions are often difficult to keep secret and take time to implement, although some firms may also try to preempt others, undermining coordination. In any case, coordinated capacity reduction may be more difficult to detect than stage-two price coordination. See section 15.B.

[20] Realistically, there is also uncertainty due to weather and about the location of the fish, but the basic idea remains valid.

the market opens for business, the total quantity of fish is taken to be fixed for that day.[21] Accordingly, the price that clears the market will reflect this quantity. Moreover, the previous analysis indicates why this quantity is plausibly below the competitive quantity—significantly so if there are few firms—and thus the resulting price above the competitive price. These markets should also be fairly easy to distinguish from others.[22] Note that price could be still higher, through interdependence, in which case there would remain unsold fish. (Or, with ex ante coordination on quantities, there would be further price elevation without excess production.)

Viewing each of the above cases, with competition in prices and in quantities, it is not evident how often there will be significant unilateral exercise of market power with homogeneous goods. Supposing, however, that such price elevation does occur, let us return to our main questions. Initially, we can inquire into whether such price elevation is socially valuable. In the cases posed, it would seem that it is not. Static, allocative efficiency suffers. Regarding dynamic efficiency, we can consider whether such supracompetitive pricing is necessary to induce entry. As explored in subsection 8.B.1, with homogeneous goods entry tends to be excessive when prices are elevated, with the degree of excess rising with the extent of the elevation.[23] The optimal amount of entry ordinarily arises when

---

[21] It is assumed that the fish are perishable, fresh for only a short period of time, so the possibility of stockpiling an inventory of fish is ruled out. Likewise, it is supposed to be too costly or too slow to send a boat back out for additional fish if there is a desire to sell more. Of course, these assumptions significantly limit the domain in which this model is applicable.

[22] Further limiting the range of application of the standard, two-stage Cournot model, observe that unilateral price elevation in this context may not be easy to sustain over time. A regular buyer of fish could approach a particular seller and make an advance contract for part or all of tomorrow's catch at a somewhat reduced price, offering that seller the prospect of additional sales. Such arrangements would erode supracompetitive pricing. Analogous behavior is possible as well in the first example involving investment in capacity. For example, if the price of coal was elevated through unilateral market power, a large buyer such as an electric utility might enter into a long-term contract with a supplier to sell it a large quantity at less than the prevailing price, which the supplier would find attractive in connection with a con-comitant capacity expansion.

[23] The present question differs from that considered in the literature on excessive entry that is discussed in subsection 8.B.1. In that literature, it is taken as given that there will emerge an equilibrium price that is a declining function of the number of firms, where that function is implicitly determined by some game between the firms that operates in the background. The

price equals marginal cost. The main exception is when fixed costs make it difficult to sustain even one or two firms in an industry, in which case, as noted, some price elevation may be socially desirable.

The prospect of supracompetitive pricing might also encourage other sorts of investment that perhaps reduce production costs or improve product quality or service,[24] as discussed in subsection 8.B.2. If one of our five firms makes such investments, however, it will tend to be rewarded without regard to the sort of price elevation under discussion. For example, a firm with lower costs can reduce price below that of its higher-cost competitors, gain market share, and earn positive margins on such additional sales as well as on sales it previously enjoyed. To be sure, it might profit even more if prices are elevated further—or it may not, if price elevation serves to protect its rivals and thus limit the firm's ability to increase market share.[25] If the firm is sufficiently successful, it may become a dominant firm, in which case it would be able to elevate price unilaterally, and in a manner that would generally be permitted. It would, however, be restrained in how much it could elevate price, for a higher price, as just mentioned, may retain or resurrect its rivals' abilities to be significant

---

question addressed is whether, taking as given the function relating the number of firms to price, it would be optimal for a social planner to raise or lower the number of firms relative to that which would arise in equilibrium. In contrast, the present question supposes that entry will not directly be regulated and instead asks—when entry is determined by firms' profit-maximizing decisions—whether it would be optimal to reduce the price from what would otherwise be the outcome of the game that the firms would play.

[24] The latter possibilities may transform the analysis to that of differentiated products, the topic of section C.

[25] There remains an incentive problem with regard to subsequent firms' motivation for cost reduction that is analogous to that associated with entry by a second firm into a monopolistic industry, discussed in subsection 8.B.1. If the second innovator expects to have a fully competitive interaction with the first, it may not earn enough to recoup the expense of its cost-reducing investment. Even though its innovation would have been duplicative of that of the first, it would have eroded that firm's unilateral market power, which is the cause of reduced allocative inefficiency. On the other hand, if the two firms each are able to elevate prices somewhat, whether through coordination or through exercise of their own unilateral market power (which the text suggests may or may not be possible), there may be sufficient reward to induce the second innovator to proceed. Depending on the cost of the innovation and magnitude of the price reduction, there may be a net social gain or loss as a consequence. This assessment is further complicated by the need to consider the ex ante effect on the first firm's behavior from its anticipation of imitative cost reduction by other firms.

players in the market. But the social benefits of, say, its cost reductions do not exceed the amount of those reductions, so the existence of such a constraint on the firm's rewards does not inefficiently discourage investment.

In sum, it seems that the exercise of unilateral market power by multiple firms in homogeneous goods industries tends to be detrimental, in contrast to the conclusion with dominant firms. One might therefore wish to condemn such supracompetitive pricing along with that due to successful oligopolistic coordination. Suppose, however, that for one reason or another, such behavior does not give rise to liability. (It generally does not under existing competition law, although horizontal mergers that enhance such market power are condemned on this account.)

Next, can we identify cases in which the unilateral exercise of market power is taking place? For each situation, comments were already offered suggesting that such identification may often be feasible (pricing cycles if prices are firms' strategic variable, selling at capacity if firms compete in quantities). Furthermore, the timing of the two-stage process indicates the plausibility of the posited interaction that takes quantities as given.[26] Because these methods of identification may be imperfect, however, we can also consider how interdependence itself may be identified—as distinct from the unilateral exercise of market power. Although this question was substantially examined in section A,[27] some additional observations can be offered in the present setting. Notably, if firms are engaged in the two-stage quantity-setting interaction described above,

---

[26] For example, if producers negotiate contracts, perhaps for customized orders, before production (and capacity is not fully constrained), then firms are able to reduce price to particular buyers in order to increase the quantity they produce. Note, however, that if secret price negotiations and large orders are involved, conditions will be less conducive to successful coordination.

[27] Among other points, it was explained that direct measurement or other evidence of marginal cost indicating that it is below price does not distinguish interdependence from unilateral price elevation. However, if in such cases one insists that price be shown to be substantially in excess of marginal cost, for the reasons adduced in section 12.A, then one may have de facto exempted much unilateral market power in industries in which there are more than a few firms since unilateral market power in such settings is likely to be modest. Relatedly, this latter observation indicates that one can distinguish coordinated oligopoly pricing that is highly successful because it will result in prices significantly higher than those that would result from unilateral behavior alone.

additional leverage can be derived from the fact that, in the second stage during which price is determined, firms are imagined to sell all of their quantities. Accordingly, within a significant range, quantities would not respond to stage-two cost or demand shocks. With interdependence, in contrast, there may be some short-run price stickiness, but quantities might still adjust promptly (and perhaps additionally or differently if prices adjust incompletely). In sum, it seems that it often will be possible to distinguish coordinated from unilateral price elevation.

Finally, consider cases in which there is nontrivial uncertainty about whether price elevation is unilateral or due to successful oligopolistic coordination. The anticipation of occasional false positives—deeming to be interdependent instances of price elevation that are really unilateral, and the resulting tendency to reduce prices and raise quantities ex ante—may actually be beneficial rather than socially costly: As mentioned above, unilateral price elevation with homogeneous goods tends to involve both allocative inefficiency and dynamic inefficiency by inducing excessive entry. Accordingly, when the competing hypothesis for coordinated oligopolistic price elevation is not highly competitive behavior but rather the unilateral exercise of market power in the manner under consideration in this section, there is less reason to err on the side of caution in assessing liability.

C. Differentiated Products

Suppose now that the five firms in our previous example, each with a market share of 20%, produce differentiated rather than homogeneous products. Analysis of firms' interactions in this case differs because it is no longer true that pricing slightly below rivals can capture the entire market.[28] Instead, as one firm reduces its price, taking rivals' prices as

---

[28] See the sources cited in note 16 of chapter 8. An exception arises if product differences are such that all consumers are indifferent between any given product pair at the same price ratio and wish to purchase only whichever is cheaper (quality-adjusted). Then the market is as if products were homogeneous, where prices are interpreted on a per-equivalent-quality-unit basis.

given, consumers only gradually substitute toward that firm's product, away from those of rivals.[29]

It follows that some unilateral market power exists in this setting, which is to say that firms will elevate their prices above marginal cost even when they take rivals' prices to be constant. To see this, suppose that all firms initially price at marginal cost. A firm that increases its price slightly does lose some sales to rivals, but it also earns more on those customers it retains. Since it was previously assumed to be pricing at marginal cost, the lost sales at first entail no sacrifice in profit, so at least some price increase will be profitable. At some point, however, additional price elevation will become unprofitable. The situation is similar for the other firms, and their price increases in turn tend to make it profitable for the initial firm to increase its price further, and so on. At the resulting equilibrium, all firms charge prices above marginal cost.

Nevertheless, firms still charge less than the monopoly (or jointly maximizing oligopoly) price. That price is such that any price reduction is barely unprofitable to the industry as a whole. However, when a single firm contemplates reducing its price, taking others' prices as given, to some extent it gains at others' expense, as some customers switch from rivals' products to its own. Since it ignores rivals' lost profits (unlike a monopolist that sells all the products), some price reduction will be profitable. And if there are many rivals, this process will result in an equilibrium substantially below the monopoly price (and when the number is very large or differentiation is small, price will approach marginal cost).

---

[29] Section B mentioned at the outset that the cases of homogeneous goods and of differentiated products are not entirely distinct, but blend. This point is reinforced by the analysis in Benassy (1989), who allows the degree to which products are substitutes to vary, and he finds, not surprisingly, that results with differentiated products approach those in the homogeneous goods case as substitution becomes more nearly perfect. One consequence is that the problem of the nonexistence of any pure-strategy equilibrium when price is the strategic variable (requiring resort to mixed strategies, which may be unrealistic) that was discussed in section B is applicable with differentiated products when substitution is not very imperfect. Ibid. (232). Moreover, such cases with differentiated products are important for present purposes because successful oligopolistic coordination is most likely when differentiation is minimal (or, of course, nonexistent).

Our first question is whether such price elevation is desirable. As usual, there is allocative inefficiency due to the fact that price exceeds marginal cost. An important dynamic effect is to encourage entry. In the homogeneous-goods case, this effect is undesirable, but, as explained in subsection 8.B.1, with product differentiation there is the benefit of increased product variety. When price equals marginal cost, variety tends to be too low. In the equilibrium involving firms' unilateral exercise of market power, variety could be either too high or too low. (In particular settings it may be possible to tell which.) The previous analysis explained why variety tends to be too little at the competitive price, with the benefits of variety falling and the degree of inefficiency rising as price is elevated further and further above marginal cost. Thus, it is probably unwise to adopt a broad rule condemning unilateral price elevation in this context, and it is ambiguous in the general case whether some reduction in price (say, through a chilling effect) would be desirable or detrimental.

Second, consider whether it is possible to distinguish the unilateral exercise of market power from elevations that may be due to successful oligopolistic coordination. As mentioned in section A, many means of detection identify interdependence per se and thus do distinguish the cases. Again, other sources of evidence (such as on marginal cost[30] or internal documents) may or may not be helpful, depending on the particulars.[31]

One of the main criteria helping to distinguish the sources of price elevation in this situation is the assumption of differentiated products itself. When differentiation is low, unilateral market power will tend to be negligible from this channel. Moreover, interdependence may well be feasible. When differentiation is high, unilateral market power will be more substantial on this account, but interdependence tends to be infea-

---

[30] It is again worth recalling that if, as section 12.A suggests, liability based primarily on evidence of marginal cost being below price would be assigned only in cases of significant elevation, unilateral market power would be de facto exempted when product differentiation was not too large—which involves precisely the cases that would be targeted, as noted in the text to follow. In addition, it was already explained that the benefit of price elevation in reducing any product variety deficit is likely to be small (or reversed, a cost of excess variety) when the price elevation is large.

[31] For econometric studies that distinguish unilateral from coordinated exercise of market power, see Baker and Bresnahan (1988) and Nevo (2001).

sible. In other words, this particular dimension of conduciveness will be particularly probative of which explanation governs.

Finally, if we try to distinguish the two sources of price elevation and might err, particularly by producing false positives, we should consider the social costs entailed because these will bear on how we should set proof burdens. As explained, some reduction in price when the true source of elevation is the exercise of unilateral market power tends to have ambiguous welfare effects in this case. Accordingly, it may be important to attempt to distinguish among settings involving product differentiation to see whether a positive or negative effect is more plausible. In any event, observe that the typical social cost of this sort of false positive does seem to be less (if indeed it is a net social cost) than that of errors in settings in which the market is fully competitive, with no actual price elevation taking place.

D. Implications for Liability

It might have initially appeared that unilateral market power is irrelevant to price-fixing prohibitions precisely because the behavior involved is unilateral whereas jurisdictions ordinarily require the existence of a "conspiracy," "concerted action," and the like—as explored at length in part I. As should be apparent from the foregoing, however, analysis of unilateral market power is relevant for a number of reasons, corresponding to the three questions considered throughout this chapter.

First, the desirability of the exercise of unilateral market power may bear on what the law should prohibit. As elaborated in parts I and III, competition regimes tend not to be highly formalistic, and rules are increasingly interpreted in light of economic analysis, particularly in the United States. Furthermore, reform of competition policy should be guided by an understanding of how various types of firm and industry behavior affect social welfare.[32] The analysis in this chapter suggests that the exercise of unilateral market power tends to be desirable in the case of dominant firms, undesirable with multiple firms and homogenous

---

[32] Also recall the point that horizontal mergers are condemned when they are likely to increase unilateral market power, a point related to the discussion in section 18.C.

goods, and desirable with multiple firms and differentiated products, although in the first case and sometimes in the last, optimal elevation may be less than that which occurs. In any event, most of this book, both before and after the present chapter, sets unilateral market power to the side, although occasionally noting appropriate qualifications in light of its possible presence.

Second, if there is to be a legal distinction between the unilateral exercise of market power and coordinated oligopolistic price elevation—specifically, permitting the former while prohibiting the latter—it is necessary to distinguish these categories in particular cases. Different methods might best be employed at the investigative stage (notably, when agencies survey the marketplace for possible violations or pursue leads indicating potential wrongdoing), when screening suits filed by private parties at early procedural stages, when adjudicating liability, and when assessing the magnitude of harm for purposes of determining sanctions. As discussed, some detection methods focus on interdependence and accordingly distinguish successful oligopolistic coordination from the unilateral exercise of market power, but others indicate price elevation per se and thus may not, without further analysis, readily differentiate the two categories. Regarding detection, it is worth keeping in mind that successful oligopolistic coordination is most likely and tends to cause the most social harm when products are homogeneous or at least not highly differentiated, and it is not apparent that significant unilateral price elevation is very probable in a broad range of these settings unless there is a dominant firm.

Third, this part of the book emphasizes, beginning in chapter 9, the need to consider error costs explicitly and systematically, keeping in mind the importance for deterrence of avoiding false negatives and the point that false positives are not costly in the abstract but rather on account of various chilling effects. False positives might ordinarily be understood to refer to cases in which firms' actual behavior was competitive. But when the alternative hypothesis to coordinated oligopoly pricing is the unilateral exercise of market power—not competitive behavior with price equal to marginal cost—the chilling effects caused by the prospect of false positives may be qualitatively different, and in some cases these effects may even involve benefits. This consideration bears on how to weight different types of evidence and how to set proof burdens in cases where it is not obvious whether price elevation was unilateral or coordinated.[33]

---

[33] To further suggest the importance of attending to error costs, consider settings in which distinguishing unilateral market power from coordinated oligopolistic price elevation is extremely difficult. If the cost of false positives was sufficiently low, it may well be optimal to make the unilateral exercise of market power de facto illegal in such cases (including disallowing or placing a high burden on any defense that the price elevation was unilateral). In contrast, if false positives were extremely costly and the unilateral exercise of market power was sufficiently frequent, it may instead be optimal to make oligopolistic coordination de facto legal in those instances.

Additional Considerations

A. Institutional Issues

The analysis throughout this part largely abstracts from the administration of competition law. Enforcement institutions vary widely across jurisdictions and sometimes within them—especially in the United States, which has public and private suits, state and national enforcement, and two distinct systems at the national level. These differences may influence what rule is optimal and vice versa, which is to say, if certain rules are notably better in principle, it may accordingly be desirable to make institutional choices that best facilitate their implementation.

This section is confined largely to identifying issues rather than resolving them, both because there exist independent literatures on institutional design and because the control of successful oligopolistic coordination is but one of the tasks of a competition regime. It is useful to organize thinking around three features of the administrative apparatus: enforcement effort, error rates, and cost.

Enforcement effort is particularly important in the present setting because of the difficulty of detection and resulting concerns about underdeterrence, as suggested by the evidence reviewed in section 9.C and discussed further in subsection 13.A.3. As mentioned, higher sanctions are a substitute for enforcement effort, but there are important limits. In the United States, where enforcement is generally thought to be the strongest, there are private suits for treble damages as well as public enforcement, potentially by numerous government entities, with the possibility of significant fines and imprisonment. Allowing private damages suits motivates victims who may have access to information not readily available to the government; such information could be conveyed to officials, but the incentive to develop the information may be less without the prospect of compensation.[1] Private suits are also useful because they provide a check against laxity[2] or industry capture of government enforcers. Government enforcement has its own advantages, such as those due to economies of scale and scope, a potential willingness to investigate when private parties may not be in a position to capture enough reward to motivate them, and the ability to employ certain enforcement instruments (for example, wiretaps and the use of informants) and sanctions (notably, imprisonment).

Each approach also has costs, an important one being the possibility of overzealous enforcement. Private parties have incentives to bring unmeritorious cases if there is a sufficient probability of factfinder error or, in some circumstances, if adjudication costs are sufficiently high, in both cases in an attempt to extract significant settlements.[3] Likewise, government enforcers, eager to advance their careers or augment their agencies' budgets through high-visibility prosecutions, can be overly aggressive.[4] For these reasons, the best choice among possible enforcers and the optimal way to incentivize them are hardly obvious.[5]

Error rates and costs are determined both by who brings enforcement actions (and how they are motivated) and by the system of adjudication.

---

[1] See also note 27 in chapter 13, presenting facts about private enforcement in the United States.

[2] One difficulty, hardly unique to competition law, is that government enforcers may be rewarded more for successful prosecutions, which are visible, than for deterrence, which is invisible for certain types of violations. Considering extremes, perfect deterrence would yield no enforcement actions (barring errors), whereas a state of affairs generating no deterrence (which might arise if sanctions, although seemingly high, are systematically insufficient) can result in numerous victories for enforcers, which may in turn be used to support larger budgets.

[3] The main restraint concerns the credibility of going forward, which may not be present if prospects of success are low and the plaintiffs themselves would bear significant litigation costs. See Spier (2007, 305–7).

[4] Overenforcement can also arise due to protectionism when defendants are from other jurisdictions.

[5] See Becker and Stigler (1974), Landes and Posner (1975), Polinsky (1980), and Shavell (1993). An additional issue, raised at the outset in chapter 13, is the need to coordinate sanctions, which is rendered more complex when sanctions may result from actions of different enforcers operating through different systems. For example, in the United States, treble damages are not reduced if defendants have already paid substantial fines to the government.

In most countries (and in the United States for actions by the Federal Trade Commission), expert agencies are employed, typically with appeals brought in generalist courts. Direct enforcement in generalist courts is another possibility, employed in the United States for private plaintiffs and for the Antitrust Division of the Department of Justice—with the further idiosyncratic feature that juries are often used as factfinders.[6] It is worth noting that none of these match-ups is inevitable: One could, for example, use expert agencies to adjudicate private suits, or have government enforcement actions adjudicated by the same entity as the initiator, a distinct agency, a specialized court, or a generalist court.

The virtues of expert adjudication of one sort or another are obvious.[7] In most areas of competition law, and certainly including oligopolistic coordination, complex economic issues are involved, and the mass of relevant information that must be assessed in a given case is often vast. There is frequent but not widespread use of specialized adjudicators, but often not with the relevant expertise. In particular proceedings, decisionmakers may be guided by parties' (partisan) experts or by adjudicator-appointed (neutral) experts.[8] Use of the latter, in whole or in part, seems highly advantageous in light of the potential for bias by paid experts,[9] yet

---

[6] U.S. courts' distrust of juries, whether on account of a pure inability to understand the complex subject matter or also due to a fear of anti-defendant bias, helps to explain the tendency in recent decades to raise procedural hurdles for plaintiffs and, relatedly, to substitute judges' decisions for juries' by resolving more cases through legal motions decided by the court. Similar concerns may also help to explain Supreme Court reversals of jury verdicts in fully tried cases. See, for example, Brooke Group Ltd. v. Brown & Williamson Tobacco Corp., 509 U.S. 209 (1993), and Spectrum Sports v. McQuillan, 506 U.S. 447 (1993). One of the difficulties posed by this approach is that the judges are themselves generalists, often with negligible relevant experience, and trial judges in particular may be biased in favor of defendants regarding dispositive motions because of the significant effect on their workload caused by even a single, significant antitrust case. Or they may err in favor of plaintiffs at preliminary stages, hoping that cases will settle, thereby avoiding appellate review of their decisions.

[7] Note that expert tribunals could take many forms. They could be composed of lawyers, economists, individuals with knowledge of business, or various combinations. They could specialize in competition regulation or be somewhat more general. Likewise, adjudicators may not so much be trained subject-matter experts as individuals with significant experience in such adjudication.

[8] For example, in the United States, Federal Rule of Evidence 706 authorizes court-appointed experts.

[9] Consider, for example, Scherer's (1977, 983) criticism of Posner's more direct, economi-

such use seems atypical in U.S. adjudication. When a single agency serves as investigator, prosecutor, and adjudicator, their experts have a mixed character, perhaps fairly neutral at the outset when attempting to identify whether an investigation should be pursued (although maybe not if the political stakes are high), but possibly partisan once in adjudication.

The nature of the tribunal as well as the selection of experts should have a direct and, one would suppose, substantial impact on the quality of outcomes: Greater and more neutral expertise should enhance deterrence and reduce chilling effects because both false negatives and false positives would be fewer. The main potential tradeoff concerns cost, for higher expertise is often more expensive. However, the opposite may be true in the present context. A battle of purely partisan experts before a decision-maker with little or no expertise may, in addition to being less accurate, be more costly as each party invests substantially in attempts to sway the tribunal and presentations are drawn out because even basic concepts must be explained rather than taken as part of presumed knowledge. Moreover, the greater unpredictability that may arise and resulting higher costs can have the further undesirable consequence of encouraging meritless challenges, which itself worsens the problem of chilling effects.

It is also useful to examine the particular problem of controlling coordinated oligopoly pricing with attention to different enforcement stages. For initial identification of cases to investigate more thoroughly, agencies might, in addition to relying on buyer complaints and informants, employ

---

cally oriented approach toward oligopoly pricing. "Granted, with *enough* strong evidence of this type, a competent economist could in good conscience testify that even though no meetings in smoke-filled rooms were proved, it was quite unlikely prices could have been set as observed had there been no tacit restrictive understanding. The trouble is, economic analysis is an elastic instrument and, I am sorry to report, some economists' consciences are also elastic, so one can find economists who with apparent conviction will explain away any pattern of behavior, however bizarre, as the consequence of special but highly competitive industry circumstances. Sometimes they may even be right, if there exists any absolute measure of 'right' in such complex matters. Every tacit collusion case under Posner's scheme would be a 'big case,' drawing teams of economists to ply the courts with their expert but conflicting opinions. In the end, the decision would turn significantly upon whose experts were more credible. It would not, I fear, be a system highly likely to yield either truth or justice . . . ." As chapters 6 and 17 explain, however, a communications-based prohibition is heavily (if not more) reliant on economic expertise, including on questions for which there is less basis for the required judgments.

economists who would study industry data on pricing, market shares, and the like, as well as features bearing on the ease of coordination, to identify where violations are most likely to be present—and this is so independently of what ultimately must be proved in an adjudication to establish liability.[10] There is, however, an important caveat relating to the paradox of proof. If the law limits liability to cases in which a prescribed set of communications is demonstrated to have been employed (acts in a set X), then, as explained in chapters 6 and 17, it may be that industries that a priori are most susceptible to significant oligopolistic price elevation are ones in which liability cannot readily be found, with the implication that agencies should avoid rather than emphasize truly high-danger industries in their investigations.[11]

Another stage-related challenge involves the formal screening of cases by an adjudicator. Because of the aforementioned concerns about overzealous enforcement, with concomitant litigation costs and chilling effects, it is desirable for meritless cases to be eliminated before undertaking long, expensive proceedings—involving both pretrial work, including investigation or discovery and preparation of expert reports, and trials themselves. This consideration explains the increasing emphasis in the United States on granting motions to dismiss at the outset of case filings in court and motions for summary judgment before proceeding to trial.[12] Unfortunately, this task is far easier said than done precisely because of the elaborate and complex nature of the evidence and analysis involved.[13]

---

[10] See Abrantes-Metz and Bajari (2009), Harrington (2008a), and also Posner (2001, 55, 64, 69), who emphasizes that, even if the law is interpreted narrowly, enforcement agencies should use broader economic criteria to decide where to focus their investigations. For skepticism about the prospects for economic screening by agencies, see the sources cited in note 26 in chapter 11.

[11] An important qualification is that they still might expect to find direct evidence of prohibited communications. Even though prospects for a provable case may be low, since the danger is so much higher investigation might nevertheless be justified as long as the likelihood of finding powerful, direct evidence is modest rather than remote. Of course, if that likelihood is sufficiently high, the paradox of proof would not hold (although it is a separate question of whether the agency is confident it can convince the adjudicator that this is so).

[12] The most pertinent cases are *Twombly* (on motions to dismiss) and *Matsushita* (on summary judgment), both discussed with regard to the agreement requirement in subsection 4.B.2.

[13] For analysis of how such decisions are optimally made, see Kaplow (2013a, 2013b).

Because so much of the total expense of adjudication is borne before an actual trial commences (investigation, discovery, experts), the greatest benefits are realized if meritless cases can be dismissed up front. The problem is that, at the outset, there is very little basis for ascertaining whether cases of the sort examined here have merit. The relevant sorts of evidence, examined in chapters 10 and 11, are varied and complex, need to be interpreted together, and may be available only after significant inquiry, often involving review of material solely in the possession of the defendants. (Furthermore, section 6.B explains that, even under the communications-based prohibition examined in parts I and III, as long as proof by circumstantial evidence is allowed, a private plaintiff or government agency would be in a position to allege that, taking into account all manner of evidence concerning whether the market in question is conducive to oligopolistic coordination and whether successful coordination is taking place, the use of at least some act in the prohibited set X is sufficiently likely under the prevailing legal standard. Without reviewing all of the pertinent evidence—which the enforcer is presumed not to have expended much effort in gathering at the motion-to-dismiss stage—how is an adjudicator to assess such a claim? To further complicate matters, under the communications-based prohibition many types of evidence and thus many factual allegations could favor a finding either of liability or of no liability, depending on the strength with which the allegation is deemed to hold as well as the strength of other allegations and evidence.)[14]

The difficulty of rendering a judgment at so preliminary a stage is part of what lends appeal to the alternative discussed in section 18.B of prohibiting all circumstantial evidence—requiring direct evidence of prohibited communications, and possibly even smoking-gun evidence. However, in the absence of an informant who comes forward early in the process,[15] it is difficult to see how even this narrower question can be

---

[14] Recall further that, as section 6.C observes, under often-expressed views that imply a narrow paradox region, allegations and proof of successful interdependence would be sufficient to infer the use of acts in X even if that set is defined in a circumscribed manner.

[15] Importantly, a significant impetus to informers coming forward is the fear of successful prosecution. But if prosecution is rendered essentially impossible without informants, and if prospective informants know this, informants would be harder to come by. Offering rewards rather than mere leniency or immunity could help overcome this problem and in any event has significant appeal in light of difficulties in detection.

resolved at the beginning. After all, we are considering whether a case can be removed from the system before any discovery or extensive investigation by an enforcer. But if cases rise or fall primarily on the sort of evidence that can be gleaned, not from pricing or other behavior that might be publicly observable, but only from internal evidence hidden deeply in the defendant firms, it would seem that either all cases (except those with an informant) would need to be dismissed, or that essentially none could be disposed of at this preliminary stage.[16] An alternative approach would be to rely more on market-based evidence, some of which is publicly available, at this preliminary stage, switching to the other evidence at later stages, such as judgment just before trial or in the adjudication itself.[17]

Because of these inherent difficulties with early dispositions, it is appealing to consider some more explicit sequencing of litigation than is ordinarily undertaken.[18] For example, if it is desired, on one hand, not to dismiss nearly every case at the outset, and, on the other hand, not to allow highly costly proceedings when cases may well be meritless, a compromise might be struck under which there is some preliminary, partial factfinding, perhaps based largely on publicly available information. Parties (or the tribunal) might engage the services of a limited number of experts to offer initial opinions on the likelihood of successful oligopolistic coordination and on the conduciveness of industry conditions. If the initial showing is sufficiently weak, the case would be dismissed, but if it is reasonably strong, the case would be permitted to proceed. It is speculative how reliable an assessment could be made based on limited evidence, and in designing such a system, it would have to be decided just how much or little effort—use of experts, access to defendants'

---

[16] The U.S. Supreme Court in *Twombly* acted as if it had an answer, but what it might be does not seem possible to extract from the opinions in that case (which do not directly consider the dilemma discussed in the text). See also subsection 4.B.2. For further analysis of *Twombly*, see Kaplow (2013a).

[17] Intelligibly assessing the former at a highly preliminary stage (or even on the eve of trial, as discussed later in this section) seems quite difficult, unless the sort of hybrid procedure sketched next is employed. Yet similar demands are made in other areas of competition law, such as when market power screens are employed. It would seem that, except when an enforcer's claim is transparently weak (which may depend on poor lawyering as well as a lack of factual basis), it would be almost impossible to dispose of a case without some (and possibly significant) assessment of parties' competing factual claims.

[18] For a general analysis of this problem, see Kaplow (2013a).

pricing data, and so forth—would be permitted. However, it might be possible to eliminate a significant portion of meritless cases at well under the full cost of complete proceedings. Moreover, in systems allowing private suits, if such incremental proceedings are indeed possible, merit-less cases would be less attractive to initiate if their threat value in extract-ing significant settlements would be reduced, in comparison to a regime in which dismissal was difficult.

For competition regimes that rely on specialized agencies, it would seem that such procedural reform may well be possible. Indeed, more incremental approaches are already employed: Competition enforce-ment agencies ordinarily begin with preliminary inquiries that are ex-panded or terminated depending on what is learned along the way. It may still be useful, however, to permit defendants—parties under in-vestigation—to instigate such a preliminary determination, particularly in light of the potential problem of overzealous government enforcers. For proceedings in court, it may require more substantial reform to en-able such an approach, although aspects might be implemented through more subtle means.[19]

It remains to consider the disposal of cases after all investigation, discovery, and preparation of expert reports, but before formal adjudi-cation. This possibility is especially important when the just-described, more preliminary proceeding cannot screen very powerfully. However, even on the eve of trial, screening is challenging. Unless a party's case has negligible evidentiary support, it seems difficult for an adjudicator to find that a trial is unnecessary without in essence conducting a par-tial trial to determine whether the evidence is sufficiently strong. In the United States, courts often grant defendants' pretrial motions for sum-mary judgment in antitrust cases, and a reading of the opinions sug-gests that some do resolve substantial factual disputes that, under stan-dard articulations of procedural law, they are "supposed" to avoid (by

---

[19] In the United States, Federal Rule of Civil Procedure 42(b) allows for separate trials of different issues, and Rule 52(c) for partial findings as a trial proceeds (when a judge is the factfinder). Both, however, contemplate already being at the trial stage. It may still be possible, however, through deft use of pretrial conferences and by requiring plaintiffs to make more substantial showings as a prerequisite to obtaining fuller discovery from objecting defendants, for judges to manage cases and provide periodic indications of their leanings in response to information that is presented. It also seems possible that the use of court-appointed experts or special masters could help perform similar functions.

denying the motion and allowing trial to proceed). One limitation on achievable cost savings is that such decisions come only after many costs are sunk. Also, because judges are not supposed to resolve cases in this manner, they cannot organize proceedings in a way that best enables them to make the requisite decisions.[20]

In sum, issues of institutional design are quite important for competition regulation because of the scope and complexity involved. Costs are high and the risk of false positives producing chilling effects and false negatives undermining deterrence is great. Moreover, there is a tension between enforcement intensity, which is necessary to address the deterrence problem, and both the high administrative costs and the chilling effects that arise when well-behaved firms can effectively be threatened with protracted litigation. As mentioned at the outset of this section, these issues are relevant to the choice of legal rule. Also, if one legal rule is in principle substantially superior to another, that preference may bear on how the supporting institutions and procedures should be designed.[21]

B. Nonprice Coordination

The analysis throughout this book considers the problem of oligopolistic coordination of pricing behavior. Legal prohibitions, however, typically have a broader scope than price fixing, reaching as well other means by

---

[20] Sometimes courts also dismiss cases at the outset when factual disputes exist, essentially inferring from the weakness of a plaintiff's complaint that its case is unlikely to be substantial. To the extent that this practice becomes more common after *Twombly*, perhaps plaintiffs will begin to offer expert reports and other evidence at this early stage, even though such proffers are supposed to be unnecessary. At that point, the motion to dismiss would itself, to an extent, become somewhat like the compromise procedure discussed just above in the text. Preliminary studies of the effects of *Twombly* are reported in note 51 in chapter 4.

[21] To restate one aspect of this point in the U.S. context, there is, to a degree, a choice between employing highly simplified but necessarily poor rules in order to adapt to the use of lay juries (and, arguably, generalist judges) or instead crafting more sensible rules that may require restructuring how enforcement takes place. Also of great importance in the United States, the allowance of private treble damages actions, even if helpful for deterrence, adds greatly to potential administrative costs as well as to concerns about chilling effects. It may make more sense to limit or abolish private suits, making up the slack with substantially higher fines (see subsection 13.A.3) than to adopt a legal rule that renders permissible much of the most socially damaging oligopolistic price elevation out of the concern that a direct approach would induce excessive private litigation.

which prospective competitors might substitute cooperation for competition. For example, it is generally illegal for firms to agree to stay out of each other's territories or to refrain from launching new products or advertising campaigns. It is thus natural to inquire whether and how the analysis of the optimal regime differs when interdependence concerns nonprice dimensions of competition.

On one hand, it seems clear that the broad analytical framework is the same: We are concerned with the same social objective—the goal is to optimally trade off deterrence benefits and chilling costs—and the chief practical challenges are accurate detection and application of effective sanctions.[22] On the other hand, many particulars, especially concerning detection, seem likely to differ. This section sketches some key similarities and differences, but the discussion should be viewed as highly preliminary and incomplete, mainly suggesting avenues for further thought.

First, although it is familiar in rough terms, it is useful to state the present concern clearly.[23] Territorial division and other forms of mutual nonprice restraint are damaging in significant part because they facilitate firms' charging higher prices. That is, they are facilitating practices that themselves might appropriately be prohibited, as discussed in section 10.C. Additionally some practices may have direct efficiency consequences, such as by reducing consumers' product choices. Section 8.B discusses how firms' activities in this regard may, however, be socially excessive when prices are elevated, but incentives for variety may also be too low, in which case further coordinated reductions would be particularly detrimental.

If the central cost of nonprice restraints is elevated prices, then highly effective deterrence of successful oligopolistic price coordination would render further regulation largely unnecessary. One caveat would be where nonprice coordination creates effective, perhaps localized, monopoly power or other significant unilateral market power (on which, see chapter 14),[24] the exercise of which we are supposing is not

---

[22] Likewise, the legal analysis in part I pertaining to the agreement requirement is almost entirely applicable to nonprice coordination.

[23] Despite the familiarity of this story, it has been subject to little explicit analysis. For an interesting recent investigation, see Byford and Gans (2010).

[24] For example, it was noted in section 14.B that, in a two-stage strategic interaction in markets for homogeneous goods, firms find it in their interest to reduce capacities in the first stage through coordinated action—that is, to reduce capacities to a lower level than would

reached by competition law. Another qualification is explicit in the stated condition: Even an optimal regime may, due to limits on feasible detection or otherwise, leave some possibly substantial room for price elevation, in which case facilitation would be detrimental. For these reasons, it is important to consider how successful nonprice coordination may be detected and sanctioned.

Detection poses difficult challenges, just as with price coordination, but the best sorts of evidence and manner of inference differ in some notable respects.[25] To begin, echoing one of the preceding points, we should consider why nonprice coordination needs to be detected at all. Why not limit detection to successful oligopolistic coordination on price, which in turn would be identified in the manner discussed in chapters 10 and 11? If there is success, sanctions may be applied without untangling what practices contributed to it. And if there is none, there is no social harm and thus no need for punishment. Some answers have also been given: concern for creation of monopoly or other unilateral market power plus the obvious problem that price coordination sometimes escapes detection and thus may be insufficiently deterred. Also relevant is the discussion in section 12.B of the value of punishing even unsuccessful attempts, particularly when detection of completed acts is difficult. Even so, it should be kept in mind that a more effective regime against price coordination reduces the need for as stringent an approach toward nonprice coordination, allowing, for example, for tighter burdens of proof when chilling effects are a particular concern.[26]

---

result from unilateral quantity competition, where firms take others' capacities as given—although such might be difficult for the firms to accomplish. See note 19 in chapter 14.

[25] Following the analysis of price coordination throughout this part of the book, the discussion in the text is concerned with the detection of successful oligopolistic coordination, not with the existence of an express or explicit or other specific concept of agreement, however it may be defined (again, some set X of prohibited acts). As mentioned in section 3.B, many commentators who insist on a restrictive definition of agreement seem to switch (implicitly) to something close to pure interdependence with regard to some facilitating practices. In any event, if one were to analyze the application of a narrower agreement requirement to nonprice coordination, many issues similar to those examined in part III would likely arise, but particulars could differ significantly.

[26] See also section 18.C, discussing the need for more aggressive regulation of facilitating practices if liability for oligopoly pricing itself is more limited.

For price coordination, market-based evidence plays a central role. The analysis of conduciveness of conditions seems equally apt, with the adjustment that here we are interested in not only conduciveness to price elevation but also conduciveness to coordination on the particular nonprice dimension. Some features, such as territories, may be fairly easy targets for oligopolists since entry tends to be a highly visible act. The same is true of new product launches and large advertising campaigns, although in those cases it is far more complex to define the cooperative benchmark from which a firm might be deemed to have defected. Other adjustments, such as in product quality, may be harder for other firms to detect, but this point has limits since a firm can attract significant business from rivals on this account only if customers appreciate the differences. Improvements in delivery and other services may be more difficult for competitors to observe and identify as deviations than are changes in products' tangible characteristics. In some cases, it may be possible for firms to cheat not because of secrecy in implementation but due to stealthy preparation: Designing new products, entering new markets, and even crafting new advertising campaigns involve significant lead time, so a cheater may have a first-mover advantage even if rivals observe the defection once implementation commences.[27] In these instances, nonprice coordination might be quite difficult.[28]

There is another important factor regarding conduciveness. Namely, it matters how much the effective coordination on the nonprice feature would contribute to the feasibility of price coordination. If it would not help much, regulation would not be worthwhile, especially given possible chilling costs. When it would enhance price coordination substantially, further scrutiny and possible stiff sanctions may well be valuable.

Market-based means of inferring successful nonprice coordination pose a significant challenge in most instances. Many of the factors mentioned in chapter 10—relating to pricing patterns and price elevation—are relevant to price coordination but bear only indirectly on nonprice

---

[27] Rivals could, however, respond immediately by cutting their prices.

[28] Other features of the situation may modify this judgment. For example, with territorial invasion, if there are many small territories and only a few would be entered at a time, then only small defections may be possible secretly (in the sense of advance preparations), so it might be fairly easy to effectuate cooperative restraint.

coordination.[29] Furthermore, nonprice coordination typically involves inaction: failure to enter new territories or product lines, abstention from rapid product improvement, or maintaining only a moderate advertising budget. It is very difficult to know when firms' merely continuing to behave as they have in the past constitutes coordination rather than ongoing rivalry that is in a state of equilibrium. Likewise, it is hard to figure out when various investments and marketing efforts are meek or moderate rather than appropriately aggressive—that is, competitive.

In many cases, it may be that the only way to determine from external evidence whether nonprice coordination is taking place is to generate independent cost-benefit analyses that indicate whether firms on various dimensions are leaving profits on the table (that is, short-run profits from defection). If abstention is due to coordination, we would expect that all leading firms are acting similarly, not only in outward behavior but in terms of forgoing individually profitable competitive moves. Such would be quite difficult to determine reliably in most settings. The ever-present alternative hypothesis is that the opportunities all firms choose to forgo are unprofitable after all. Costs may be higher, demand less promising, and difficulties of internal expansion (management, supply chains, and so forth) more daunting than meets the eye. Across the economy, every firm in each market it occupies is constantly failing to do any number of things that some outsider might imagine would be in its interest. Overwhelmingly, inaction or moderation will be efficient.[30] Hence, chilling costs of overly aggressive enforcement on these grounds seem likely to be unusually large. Taken together, it

---

[29] One may combine price and nonprice evidence, and one may look for patterns in nonprice behavior. Suppose, for example, that firms all reduce capacity at about the same time. Such behavior might reflect coordination, but it could (and often would) reflect common responses to common stimuli, such as rising costs or falling demand. Falling demand would be associated with price declines, whereas coordinated capacity restriction and rising costs would both lead to higher prices. Regarding the latter possibilities, there still may be differences. If costs are rising, one might expect prices to rise even before capacity reductions, unless capacity reductions are due entirely to the anticipation of future cost increases, in which case one would expect prices to rise over a period of time after the capacity reductions.

[30] Undoubtedly, firms also make countless mistakes and miscalculations, and such may occur in patterns. For example, no firm may appreciate the viability of a new sort of competitive opportunity. Of course, competition agencies and courts are hardly in a good position to second-guess and redirect routine firm decision-making.

would require very convincing evidence of this sort to establish liability, and such may rarely exist.[31]

Accordingly, internal evidence and interfirm communications may be particularly important in this context. The former seems potentially promising. As section 11.B explains, firms usually do have reasons for what they do and what they choose not to do. Moreover, firms' reasoning will often be apparent from internal evidence, even allowing for attempts at "lawyering" recorded communications, because firms cannot effectively operate on many dimensions without performing analyses that leave significant traces. In the present setting, if firms make explicit decisions regarding entry into new territories, designing and launching new products, and so forth, a great deal of preparation would be involved.

Of course, myriad forms of inaction will leave few tracks. This point corresponds to the aforementioned ubiquity of all manner of inaction and moderation by firms. Nevertheless, important coordinated abstention may well differ in this regard. If entry into another territory or product redesign really is unilaterally attractive—and, moreover, if this is true for most or all firms in the industry—one would expect many to have examined the possibility, perhaps in detail, in order to decide whether it might make sense to go forward regardless of rivals' responses. The main exception would be where firms really do have a solid mutual understanding to abstain, and this understanding is disseminated to the relevant analysts and decision-makers at each firm.[32] In this case, however, one might discover evidence that such is the case. As described in section 11.B, a major limitation in interpreting internal evidence is ambiguity, but one

---

[31] These points may help to explain the U.S. Supreme Court's hostility toward the plaintiffs' complaint in *Twombly*, where defendants were alleged to have agreed not to enter each other's territories, the alleged profitability of such actions being the primary support for the plaintiffs' claim that the defendants' behavior was coordinated.

[32] This latter point is significant. When there are profitable opportunities for expansion, increased sales through marketing, and so forth, there often will be individuals at the firm who might expect to gain personally if the firm pursues them, so their efforts may need to be suppressed for coordination to be successful. And such suppression may leave tracks. A difficulty is that there are countless overzealous individuals in firms that are not engaged in coordination—people who are overly optimistic or simply wish to get ahead and may be less concerned if an initiative ultimately fails—and their activities will need to be curtailed by higher management, perhaps in ways that leave tracks similar to those one would expect if truly profitable initiatives were resisted to maintain coordination.

central type of ambiguity need not concern us here, namely, regarding the means by which firms have reached a mutual understanding to restrict nonprice competition.[33] Therefore, if there is clear reference to an understanding not to invade each other's territories, that would demonstrate oligopolistic coordination on the nonprice dimension. To be sure, not all evidence will be very clear (much will not), and not all will be reliable, as previously discussed. The point is that, at least sometimes and perhaps often (conditional on the existence of an actual understanding), internal evidence will provide a significant basis for determining liability.[34]

Evidence of interfirm communications has a standing similar to internal evidence relating directly to the existence of an understanding (in contrast to that pertaining to whether, say, entry in others' territories would be individually profitable). Accordingly, the discussion in section 11.C seems largely applicable. Just as with internal evidence, communications will vary in their clarity and relevance.

In sum, the problem of detection, which is the greatest challenge regarding oligopolistic price coordination, may be even steeper for nonprice coordination. Specifically, market-based evidence on nonprice coordination, at first glance and standing alone, seems to be unpromising in most instances, particularly in light of chilling costs. Hence, greater reliance on internal evidence and direct proof of interfirm communications is probably necessary. Conduciveness is quite important, both for the usual

---

[33] As mentioned there and in section 17.A, this ambiguity is, in contrast, an important limitation in implementing a communications-based prohibition.

[34] Another important qualification concerns causation, which may be more relevant to sanctions, as discussed in section 18.A. Suppose, for example, that internal evidence or direct proof of interfirm communications—even tape recordings—reveals an understanding not to invade each other's territories. Defendants could still argue that, on reflection, such would have been unprofitable and, if attempted, ultimately unsuccessful in any event. One might be skeptical of such a claim, especially in light of the firms risking liability for no gain. However, the possibility exists and sometimes may not be remote. Indeed, even many good ideas for product launches or territorial expansion fail. If in fact entry would not have taken place or succeeded, there would be no actual harm, and thus fines or damages based on harm might be zero (or low). There could still be punishment for the attempt. Note that this issue also relates to the point in the text on the subject of conduciveness, that is, how much the nonprice dimension contributes to the potential for successful price coordination. Perhaps territorial exclusivity itself contributes significantly, but if cross-entry is unprofitable regardless, then a mutual understanding on the subject does not.

reasons and due to the need to assess the potential contribution to price coordination of the nonprice dimension under scrutiny.

The subject of sanctions raises a few distinctive issues for nonprice coordination. One is the measurement of harm that, as discussed in subsection 13.A.1, is central in properly gauging penalties. As noted above, much of the justification for assigning liability for nonprice coordination is that the price coordination it may facilitate is often hard to detect. For that very reason, quantification of harm can be difficult. If nonprice coordination makes possible monopoly (perhaps local monopoly, due to territorial coordination) or otherwise enhances unilateral market power, then in principle harm could be determined. Even then, some of the techniques for measuring price effects, such as before-and-after comparisons, may be unavailable. In these sets of cases, the problem can be viewed as one of causation, the difficulty of attributing particular consequences in the market to the practices in question. Finally, to the extent that liability is predicated on attempts-related reasoning, the usual challenge in determining how to calibrate sanctions will exist.

The use of injunctions seems to be particularly problematic in this context. If, for example, it is determined that firms coordinated on failing to enter each other's territories or to launch new products, one might think an injunction should command these affirmative acts. This approach raises obvious challenges, such as determining the prices, timing, magnitude of action, and so forth. Note that cases involving highly express agreements on territories or products would raise the same issues. That is, the problem is due to the nature of the practices and to the use of injunctions that mandate specific behaviors, not to the means by which the understanding that resulted in effective coordination was accomplished. In any event, as section 13.C emphasizes, it is not clear that injunctions are needed at all.[35]

---

[35] It is also explained that one could simply enjoin coordination itself, but once one addresses enforcement of such a command, the original problems of detection and sanctions are largely re-created, so having such an injunction may change little.

PART III

COMPARISON OF APPROACHES

16

Communications-Based Prohibition

✺

As this book's introduction suggests, the need for this third part is not immediately apparent in light of what has come before. To motivate and guide the present inquiry, it is helpful to expand on this proposition before proceeding.

Part II analyzes how to construct a regime to address coordinated oligopolistic price elevation. The problem is a challenging one because it is difficult to detect successful coordination with sufficient frequency to achieve substantial deterrence while limiting false positives so as to contain the cost of chilling desirable behavior. There are a variety of techniques available, some focused on market conditions and behavior and others on internal evidence thereof and on interfirm communications. It seems best to employ these methods in combination, with the relative importance of each determined by the strength of particular evidence and the other circumstances of a given case or type of case.

The approach that emerges appears to be quite different from what most commentators believe that the law does and should require. As part I develops at length, that alternative, often characterized as involving a requirement of express or explicit agreement, tends to focus on a subset of interfirm communications in determining liability.[1] A priori, this scheme seems unlikely to be best or even nearly so.[2] Because it asks the wrong question—whether there exists an "agreement" rather than whether

---

[1] See sections 2.C and 3.A.

[2] Compare Posner (2001, 94): "If the economic evidence presented in a case warrants an inference of collusive pricing, there is neither legal nor practical justification for requiring evidence that will support the further inference that the collusion was explicit rather than tacit. From an economic standpoint it is a detail whether the collusive pricing scheme was organized and implemented in such a way as to generate evidence of actual communications."

harm is likely—it ignores or misuses many types of evidence that are probative of the existence of the social harm in question, privileging a small portion that will often be unavailable and sometimes be unreliable. (Of course, when it is available and reliable, it receives heavy weight under the more catholic approach toward evidence presented in part II.) Moreover, as will be developed in chapter 17, which expands on chapter 6's exposition of the paradox of proof, it takes one significant category of evidence, on the conduciveness of conditions, and gives it negative weight—that is, opposite to what is implied by the objective of minimizing social harm—in the most consequential settings (if one accepts commonly advanced views, although these have already been called into question). Accordingly, it is hard to defend this approach even as a proxy technique that might be rationalized by the difficulty of detecting successful oligopolistic coordination.

Because the key elements of defining the social harm, detecting its presence, and determining the appropriate sanction have already been considered, there is a fundamental sense in which the analysis in part II is complete. Indeed, the whole point of that part was to provide a comprehensive, ground-up analysis of the problem at hand. Having done so, there is no logical necessity to consider why one or another approach that fails to emerge from a systematic analysis of the problem might not be superior after all. This conclusion is all the more compelling with regard to commentators' favored alternative given the prima facie basis just offered for doubting its sensibility. Finally, one should also recall part I's demonstration that a direct approach focused on successful interdependent behavior, involving a meeting of the minds and common understanding among coordinating firms, is in many respects more in accord with competition law's agreement requirement than is commentators' circumscribed proscription, so use of the latter is hardly dictated by rigid doctrinal constraints.

Nevertheless, a communications-based prohibition has nearly monopolized analysts' attention for decades—the main exception being Posner's (1969, 2001 [first edition, 1976]) writing that preceded this long period.[3] In this light, it is fitting to undertake a thorough, side-by-side

---

[3] Both editions of Posner's book contain a chapter building on his 1969 article. The later edition does not, however, offer a substantial reworking of the problem or present a direct, systematic critique of what by then had become the dominant contrary view.

comparison, which is the task of this part of the book.[4] This investigation will highlight what is lost under the conventional method and reinforce some of the key lessons of part II's direct analysis of the problem.

This chapter begins by defining this alternative. Although familiar in a rough sense and examined in painstaking detail in part I, a concrete restatement helps sharpen the comparison between methods. Then the chapter briefly examines the nexus—really the lack thereof—between the communications-based approach and the social harm that motivates the prohibition, which heightens the a priori sense that the standard view is misguided. Chapter 17 explores the sharpest differences, which concern detection, elaborating the important and unappreciated manner in which the most commonly advanced method, if consistently pursued, is not merely incomplete and off target but potentially perverse: Rather than being simpler than the direct inquiry presented in part II, the inference process is more complex and, of greater concern, in stark conflict with the social objective of the legal prohibition. Finally, chapter 18 considers a number of additional topics, including the determination of sanctions under the communications-based prohibition, a legally radical alternative that eschews all but smoking-gun evidence in the determination of liability, implications of the difference in approaches for other competition law rules, and how recent and future evolution in electronic communications bears on the detection problem. It closes by commenting on the main arguments offered in prior literature.

A. Definition of the Approach

As the analysis in part I makes abundantly clear, the commonly favored view of the determinant of liability for oligopolistic coordination is difficult to articulate despite being long discussed and widely endorsed. Most commentators, regulators, and courts offer neither a canonical statement nor a series of well-constructed illustrations from which one can infer the scope of the contemplated prohibition. In writing on the U.S. rule, the modal statement by commentators is that there must be an express

---

[4] Because prior work does not develop or analyze the direct approach and devotes only the briefest attention to criticism of such an alternative (see section 18.E), it goes without saying that the content of this part is almost entirely absent in existing scholarship.

or explicit agreement—although many reject this formulation and indicate that the breadth is at least somewhat greater, perhaps including tacit agreements, whatever they might be.[5] This choice of language as well as the archetypical example of secret meetings to discuss future prices suggests an emphasis on particular sorts of interfirm communication.[6]

A close consensus on the criterion for liability may not exist.[7] In any event, even if one or more crisp articulations could be identified, it is better to explore the approach broadly, not dwelling on particular variants. We wish to know whether strengths and shortcomings are generic rather than possibly idiosyncratic to one or another formulation and thus perhaps avoidable with some appropriate minor adjustment. Accordingly, it is helpful to state the communications-based prohibition in an abstract and general fashion, which will be done by reintroducing the formulation from section 3.A.

The set X, we said, comprises only (but all of) those communications (or other acts)[8] that are deemed to constitute agreements, or conspiracies, or concerted actions, and thus to give rise to liability. All other communications are deemed to fall in the permitted set X'. That is, any acts or clusters of acts[9] that are deemed legally sufficient for liability are elements

---

[5] Moreover, as noted in subsection 4.B.2, even the latest and arguably narrowest U.S. Supreme Court opinion, *Twombly*, specifically includes tacit agreements. More broadly, some authoritative pronouncements fairly clearly embrace all interdependent behavior in the prohibition; others just as clearly rule it out; elaborations are intermittent and inconsistent; and key elements of practice (the use of plus factors, jury instructions on liability, and the rule for determining damages—and also the absence of many of the litigation behaviors implied by the paradox of proof; see section 6.B) implicitly adopt the broad approach that requires only interdependence, even when employed by courts that purport to take a narrower view. And, as section 4.C indicates, EU law, although less elaborated, is similarly murky.

[6] For further discussion, see sections 2.C and 3.A.

[7] Recall from chapter 2 that the problem is compounded by a failure to define key terms as well as by the use of language susceptible to significantly differing and even opposite meanings.

[8] As mentioned previously, it is convenient and seems in accord with practice to use the language of communications when referring to the sorts of acts that are in set X, although the analysis does not depend on this interpretation: The set X is more precisely taken to refer to acts, which may but need not be restricted to communications, however that term may itself be defined.

[9] The reference to clusters of acts, introduced in section 6.A, indicates the flexibility of this formulation. If some acts taken alone do not give rise to liability but in combination they do,

of set X, and all others, set X'.[10] As stated previously, communications in set X might be limited by mode: Face-to-face meetings, letters, phone calls, and emails count, whereas hand or smoke signals—deemed to be in the set X'—do not. Or they might be limited by content: Future prices may be a forbidden subject whereas present prices would be permissible; assurances might be prohibited whereas declarations of intentions or predictions would be allowed. Or they might be limited by the setting: Statements in smoke-filled rooms could be prosecuted whereas public announcements would be tolerated; permissible methods of price announcements may be more circumscribed when there are a few large buyers that occasionally place large orders than when there are significant numbers of small, nonrepeat purchasers. Or these and further dimensions might be combined.

As explained before, the central reasons for focusing on some delimited set of communications rather than on commonly used terms like agreement, conspiracy, and concerted action are that the latter are vague, their scope is contested, and they are most plausibly understood as close synonyms for interdependence. The latter point means the prohibition would be of the sort examined in part II, which interpretation is rejected by most commentators and would render further comparison unnecessary. To illustrate the predicament, recall the first example in section 2.A of two gasoline stations on adjacent corners in a remote location that successfully coordinate their behavior to charge a significantly elevated price. If they achieve this objective through sequential price jousting involving responsive posting of price signs, most would deem there to be no agreement, but if they accomplish it through a secret discussion having precisely the same sequence and content, all would deem there to exist an express

---

then the acts individually would be in set X', but the combination of the acts would be a single element of the set X.

[10] Because this approach essentially targets particular acts, those in set X, that have a tendency to facilitate successful oligopolistic coordination, while not targeting successful price elevation itself, one might describe the approach as one that renders price fixing, standing alone, per se legal (that is, legal in and of itself) and deems illegal only certain types of attempts or the use of certain means of accomplishing it, which amounts to deeming illegal certain facilitating practices. Viewed this way, there arises the further doctrinal question whether there must exist an agreement (or conspiracy, concerted action, or whatever) concerning the use of acts in X. The ideas in this note are elaborated in section 3.B.

agreement. Suppose, indeed, that identical information is conveyed, identical states of mind are produced (achieving a so-called "meeting of the minds"), and identical actions result, having identical consequences. The sharply and unambiguously opposite legal outcomes must be due to the nature of the interfirm communications, not the substance of the resulting consensus between the firms.

More broadly, as already suggested, one might imagine distinctions that look not only to form but to content, setting, and other factors. Note further that what matters is the character rather than the existence of communications. As chapter 3 explains, in the example just given, communication is present in both cases. More broadly, firms set prices, issue public statements, and engage in trade association activity that involves communication, much of which is not and would not sensibly be prohibited. In any event, the present formulation of the sets X and X′, with the generality it encompasses, does capture much of what seems to be envisioned by those who would reach different outcomes in the hypothesized example and, notably, who would describe or advocate that the legal prohibition be significantly more limited than one on any oligopolistic coordination that succeeds in elevating price.

Before proceeding with the analysis in this part, it is worth contemplating further the contours of this sort of communications-based prohibition. It is natural to inquire into the grounds for singling out some types of communication while excluding others. Even though most commentators seem to favor a rule that does just this, essentially no attention has been devoted to the question of how one would decide which sorts of communication (or acts more generally) should be deemed to be in the set X and which in X′.[11] The most plausible approach would involve balancing

---

[11] This gap is remarkable. It may be partially explained by the earlier observation that commentators have not done much even to define the approach that they claim is embodied in existing law and/or should be. In attempting to articulate a more precise definition, the question of why some acts are included in the prohibition and others excluded from it would become more salient.

There has also been only a modest amount of analysis and little highly probative empirical evidence (that is, in realistic, relevant settings) on the role of communications in facilitating oligopolistic coordination, and relatedly on the implicit assumption that communications are more useful than actions (such as price moves) in sending credible messages (contrary to the

the benefits against the costs of including particular acts in the prohibited set. However, the benefits would presumably be those of better deterring coordinated oligopolistic price elevation and the costs those of greater chilling of desirable behavior. Hence, consistently pursuing this route replicates the method developed throughout part II of this book.[12] This point merely restates what is mentioned at the outset of this chapter: the suggestion that, once the analysis in part II has been performed, the task is complete. The result would not be sets X and X' of the sort commentators generally envision. Rather, it would be the approach of part II itself.

Suppose that one sticks with a prohibition that is limited to the types of communication sometimes described as involving express or explicit agreement. A further difficulty in any communications-based prohibition is posed by the flexibility and substitutability of modes of communication, a point elaborated in section 3.A. Specifically, recall the problem of functional equivalents: If set X is confined to a prespecified list of modes, content, or various combinations, then circumvention is invited, but if functional equivalents are included in set X, then there is no real limita-

---

familiar maxim that "actions speak louder than words"). For further discussion, see section 3.C and subsection 7.B.2.

[12] A more simple-minded approach that may have some appeal (and that may capture some of what commentators perhaps believe) would involve prohibiting those communications that seem to be of a type that both facilitates coordination and also can be forbidden at negligible cost. Secret meetings in hotel rooms seem to fit whereas posting prices, which may be unavoidable if one is to sell at all, does not. An obvious problem is that many sorts of communications involve tradeoffs. Advance price announcements are not strictly necessary but might sometimes have social benefits. Rapid price changes greatly enhance signaling ability, but freezing prices for long periods limits flexibility in responding to changing conditions. Even secret (private) meetings (chats after dinner at a trade association meeting held in a hotel) can have value in developing working relationships that are useful in standard setting or other socially productive activities, and much discussion of future market conditions can help reduce uncertainty about demand or share information about cost, which can have social benefits in some circumstances but also may facilitate coordination. See section 10.C. Accordingly, some sort of cost-benefit balancing seems unavoidable. Another difficulty is that the communication-focused prohibition tends to punish means in and of themselves whereas the approach pursued in part II addresses more directly the socially undesirable consequence, successful oligopolistic coordination, without disallowing means that may be socially beneficial in other respects. See also section 18.C.

tion. Because the function in question is to communicate sufficiently well to enable successful interdependent behavior, it follows that, when coordinated pricing is achieved, the function has been served and liability would be triggered. That is, a functional approach dispatches with any limit to the inclusion of all successful interdependent oligopolistic behavior, which is directly contrary to what those who insist on a communications requirement have in mind.

Put another way, it is difficult to conceive of commentators' communications-based approach to liability except as one entailing a substantial degree of formalism in defining the sets X and X'. This approach to liability also creates serious proof problems when inferences are to be made using circumstantial evidence, a difficulty explored in chapter 6 on the paradox of proof and expanded in chapter 17 on detection, which emphasizes the policy implications for the choice of legal rule.[13]

B. Social Welfare

The key point about the relationship between a selective communications prohibition and social welfare is that the connection is indirect, the rule focusing on a subset of means that are related to adverse effects on social welfare rather than seeking directly to ascertain whether behavior is socially detrimental. Questions addressed in section A concerning the difficulty of articulating this approach—defining which acts are in X rather than X'—reinforce the point that the method is significantly detached from the social objective. Indeed, the more one attempts to define which acts are in prohibited set X with the objective of the prohibition in mind, such as by employing a cost-benefit test or by including functional equivalents, the more the approach tends to dissolve into the direct inquiry pursued in part II.

---

[13] The difficulty of proof in particular cases also suggests challenges in defining the sets X and X' in the first place, assuming that they are to be delineated in terms of types of communication. It would be necessary to know which particular types of communication are most likely to enable interdependence that was otherwise impossible, either in general or in identifiable classes of cases, under the assumption that other types, those in X', are already assumed to be available.

More broadly, as mentioned, a large portion of probative evidence would not seem to be directly relevant under the communications-focused prohibition. As will be explored in chapter 17, such evidence is still considered, but it is ultimately legally relevant to making inferences about the likelihood that acts in set X were employed—which bears only indirectly on whether liability would be socially desirable—rather than to making inferences about whether undesirable behavior has occurred. Moreover, this will be so even when the latter inference is more straightforward and reliable than is the former inference.

Although this mismatch between approach and objective is fairly plain, it is worth revisiting the social welfare consequences of oligopolistic coordination to sharpen our understanding of the gap. Successful interdependence generates losses in static (mainly allocative) efficiency and dynamic efficiency (particularly involving excessive entry), or, under a common view, losses in consumer surplus. These adverse effects are caused by price elevation. On their face, they seem to be neither more nor less severe when the means by which such elevation is coordinated happen to involve one or another type of communication or other facilitating practice.

Section 8.B did identify some possible benefits of oligopolistic price elevation, such as in industries where fixed costs cannot otherwise be covered, or relatedly when there are significant gains due to product variety that is usefully increased by the prospect of supracompetitive pricing. As mentioned there, however, these benefits depend on certain industry traits—the cost structure, the nature of consumers' demands for different products—but not directly on whether communications (or other acts) in some set X need to be or are in fact employed in elevating price.

Considering the matter further, one can imagine that there might sometimes be a connection. Notably, when product differentiation is particularly important, coordination is much more difficult, so one might suspect that it would be feasible (if it is at all) only when frequent, explicit communications are employed. In this instance, the need for such communications is associated with a below-average net social benefit of limiting price elevation, so perhaps a more permissive approach could be justified in such circumstances. This implication runs directly counter to that of the communications-based prohibition, which confines liability to situations involving fairly explicit communications.[14] This particular observation is speculative and possibly of limited importance, and there may exist other settings in which the need to use acts in some set X in achieving price elevation is instead positively correlated with the likelihood or magnitude of social harm. Nevertheless, the relationship seems in most instances to be highly attenuated and not nearly of sufficient strength (even if of the right sign) to warrant an across-the-board, exclusive focus on the use of acts in set X.

Social welfare analysis is also importantly concerned with chilling effects. Perhaps substituting a selective communications prohibition has advantages in this regard. A possible influence on chilling costs depends on how high the burden of proof is set. One might suppose that it would be set quite high. In that case, there would be few false positives—and significantly diluted deterrence as well. Of course, one might set the proof burden high under the direct approach, similarly reducing false positives. Indeed, much of the discussion in part II is about how it probably makes sense to elevate proof burdens when key evidence is associated with significant chilling costs. For example, large price elevations proved by evidence of price wars might entail a lower risk of false positives than small price elevations proved by direct evidence of firms' marginal costs, suggesting the value of an elevated proof burden in the latter case.

The more relevant question is whether placing exclusive reliance on evidence of the use of practices in X would better distinguish true coordinated price elevation from actual competition than would the alternative of considering all the relevant evidence, focusing directly on how it illuminates this distinction rather than a qualitatively different one, and giving the greatest weight to the types of evidence that are most reliable in a given context. The question largely answers itself. This subject should be kept in mind in the analysis that follows, particularly the discussion in chapter 17 on detection and in section 18.B, which introduces a more radical approach that eschews any use of circumstantial evidence.[15]

---

[14] This limitation arises both de jure, by the nature of the prohibition on its face, and de facto, in that credible evidence of use of such communications is more likely to appear when they are more frequent and elaborate.

[15] See also section 15.A on institutional issues.

A further point suggesting an a priori basis for skepticism about the communications-based prohibition concerns the relationship between social welfare and the likelihood of finding liability by type of industry. Chilling effects are most likely, and the benefits of deterrence are least important, in industries that appear to be fairly competitive. However, because these industries tend to be less conducive to coordination, they are the ones—under the (possibly mistaken) views of many, as discussed in chapter 17—in which the use of acts in X and thus a finding of liability are relatively more likely under the communications-based prohibition than under the approach developed in part II. Therefore, upon further analysis, a communications-based prohibition seems to be even more poorly matched with the social objective than might first appear.

The comparison of approaches is also helpfully viewed from another, complementary perspective—one focused on the use of evidence and the setting of the burden of proof. As a general proposition, it would seem that a concern for chilling effects is best addressed through a combination of utilizing as much probative evidence as possible, in a manner that reflects complementarities and risks of error, and of setting an appropriately high proof requirement.[16] Precisely these considerations dominate the analysis in part II, particularly chapters 9 through 12. The communications-based approach embodies a qualitatively different strategy: Instead of elevating the burden of proof directly, it changes what it is that must be proved. In doing so, the relevance and weight of evidence is determined by considerations that have a looser relationship to the social objective, and arguably a strong negative connection in important instances. This fundamental strategic difference explains why commentators' preferred method is likely to constitute an inferior, perhaps significantly deficient, alternative.[17]

---

[16] Posner (2001, 99) suggests that "the problem of legal error . . . can be dealt with in this context by a variety of means, such as by placing a higher burden of proof on the government in cases in which the only evidence of collusion is economic."

[17] On the general choice between adjusting proof burdens versus altering the substantive legal prohibition, see Kaplow (2013a).

Detection of Prohibited Communications

❦

Detection of prohibited communications—determining whether firms used any acts in X or confined themselves solely to acts in X'—is considered at length in chapter 6, on the paradox of proof. The focus there, within part I, which analyzes the law of horizontal agreements, is on the sharp disjunction between the implications of the paradox and current practices in adjudication. This chapter revisits the paradox in some detail because it bears even more importantly on the policy comparison that is the focus of this part of the book. Some key background conditions and features will be reviewed, but the reader should consult chapter 6 for further details along a number of dimensions.

We know that detection of prohibited communications will be difficult for the usual reason that firms try to hide actions that are deemed to be illegal and subject to significant sanctions. In this respect, the challenge is similar to that in chapters 10 and 11, addressed to the detection of successful oligopolistic coordination. It is important to keep in mind, however, that what we are seeking to detect here is qualitatively different from what it was in that prior discussion. Even when considering the same sort of evidence, we are not using it to answer the same question. Recalling the bank robbery example from section 3.A, the issue at hand is not whether individuals acted interdependently in robbing a bank but instead whether their planning process involved communications of a particular sort. Obviously, which evidence is relevant, and in what manner, will differ. In the first case, we are asking what they were thinking and what they did, in order to ascertain interdependence; in the second, we need to know what specific communications (or other actions) led them to think and act as they did. Moreover, this example makes apparent the greater difficulty of detection in the latter context: It will generally be harder, often much harder, to ascertain what sort of communications preceded a bank robbery than whether the robbery took place, who the perpetrators were, and whether they had a mutual understanding about their robbery.[1]

To begin, consider the relevance under a communications-based prohibition of whether successful oligopolistic coordination has taken place. Under one approach, liability would arise only when acts in X were employed and they succeeded in achieving price elevation. In that case, one would have to undertake the analysis in chapters 10 and 11 and also that necessary to detect the use of prohibited communications. Under another approach, demonstration of the use of acts in X would be sufficient to establish liability. This regime would differ in that it would punish attempts (of a certain type), the desirability of which is examined in section 12.B. Making the use of prohibited communications sufficient for liability may also be justified on the ground that direct proof of successful coordination is difficult while success may be inferred from the attempt, presuming that firms would not undertake the effort and risk liability unless they thought that success was likely.

Most commentary does not mention this distinction, much less explore which approach is thought to be embodied in existing law (if either is) or constitutes better policy. In any event, as discussed at length in section 13.A, a sensible sanctioning regime tends to base penalties in significant part on the extent of success, in which case the magnitude of coordinated oligopolistic price elevation, if any, will be relevant even under the view that attempts are enough to establish liability. Moreover, as will become apparent, inferring from circumstantial evidence whether acts in X were used involves a preliminary determination of the existence of successful coordination. For these reasons, the analysis in this chapter will ordinarily assume that proof of success is required, one way or another, although the discussion will bear on failed attempts and on those whose success cannot be ascertained. Even so, the focus of this chapter will be on how evidence affects the inference that acts in X were employed—rather than

---

[1] Recall further that, under the general law of conspiracy in the United States, examined in subsection 4.A.2, particular communications are not per se relevant: It is blackletter law that no explicit agreement is required, only the meeting of minds that is associated with interdependence.

solely acts in X'—for the problem of detection of success was examined previously.

This chapter's inquiry begins by briefly considering internal and other direct evidence of proscribed communications. Then, the paradox of proof is reintroduced and employed to compare the communications-based prohibition with the direct approach developed in part II—both in terms of outcomes and administrability.

A. Internal and Other Direct Evidence

With regard to proving that competitors met secretly in hotel rooms to discuss future pricing, direct evidence might consist of a recording of a meeting, witnesses to its occurrence, or internal documents referring to the event. Such proof is often referred to as "smoking-gun" evidence, and, when it is available, unambiguous, and reliable, the inquiry may well be complete. Due to firms' interests in maintaining secrecy, however, this type of proof often will be inaccessible. Additionally, as discussed in sections 11.B and 11.C, such evidence may be ambiguous and some, notably testimony of informants who may be disgruntled employees, may be unreliable. Also, the evidence may implicate particular individuals, but to establish the firm's culpability it may also be necessary to consider the individuals' authority in the firm, who else knew about their activities, and whether the firm likely acted in light of the communications.

As suggested by the prior discussion in section 11.B, internal evidence should also be considered much more broadly—and it ordinarily is in cases that lack smoking-gun evidence. Thus, all manner of internal evidence—planning documents, emails, data-gathering activities—may provide a basis for inferring whether acts in X were employed. In addition to direct, detailed references, there may also be indirect indicators, such as internal exchanges that may have been impossible in the absence of the prohibited interfirm communications. For example, there may be expression of knowledge about other firms' future behavior, or discussions of strategies that would not make sense without such specific understandings. As mentioned previously, firms may attempt to avoid creating internal evidence or to distort its appearance, but such efforts are not invariably successful.

With much internal evidence, the inference process is far more treacherous than is usually recognized, a point elaborated in section 5.A. The reason is that the communications-based prohibition is premised on the view that interdependence may be possible without having to rely on acts in X and that such is legal. Keep in mind that the set X' is large, and it specifically includes many means by which firms might communicate with each other. To illustrate the difficulty, consider internal documents that make explicit, repeated references to the firms having an agreement or engaging in concerted action. While these may be taken as admissions of liability, such would be a mistake under the proffered, restrictive view of the law. As noted, these terms are readily defined as interdependence and do not in ordinary usage convey information about the means by which such agreement or concert was accomplished. In some settings they do: A seller of a house saying that the property is under an agreement clearly conveys a conventional understanding of an explicit, typically legally binding, contract. But outside such contexts, a broader set of implications is possible. Accordingly, even direct statements of the existence of an agreement may in themselves do little to indicate whether such agreement was reached using at least one act in X or only acts in X'.

More often, as section 5.A explains, one might see internal evidence of the existence of an understanding in an industry, that a firm does not want to behave aggressively because such action would upset rivals, and so forth. Such evidence may likewise be silent on how any such understanding came about.[2] Therefore, much internal evidence may be highly probative of the existence of oligopolistic coordination (the question in part II), but not, standing alone, very probative of whether communications in the prohibited set X were employed. In such cases, proof of successful interdependence would be easier and more reliable than proof of the use of prohibited communications.[3] Section 11.B in-

---

[2] This point does not seem to be well appreciated. See, for example, note 8 in chapter 5.

[3] An implication, relevant to section 15.A's discussion of institutional factors, is that the breadth of discovery and extent of any ultimate trial may be larger under the present approach than under one where interdependence is sufficient. Regarding discovery, however, most evidence relevant under one approach is also relevant under the other, although the intensity of inquiry about particular sorts of evidence will vary between the approaches. At trial, if there is no smoking-gun evidence (or anything close to it), the discussions in chapter 6 and in this

dicates that substantial evidence may often be present on the former, even though we can now appreciate that it may provide little illumination of the latter.[4]

To overcome this obstacle, it is necessary to make the further inference that the agreement or understanding that is demonstrated through internal evidence could not, under the circumstances, have come about unless the firms engaged in prohibited communications. In this respect, once one moves past crisp, smoking-gun internal evidence (e.g., a document referring to the meeting at the Sands Hotel on April 7, 2010, at which a firm's vice president discussed and agreed with counterparties Smith from Rival 1 and Jones from Rival 2 to raise prices on May 1, 2010, from 100 to 120), one begins to enter the territory where one is also employing other evidence in attempting to make the requisite inference. This supplemental evidence may also be internal in nature. Often, however, internal evidence plus any direct proof of prohibited interfirm communications themselves will not be sufficiently powerful. In such cases, one must rely in varying degrees on market-based evidence, the subject of the remainder of this chapter.

B. Paradox of Proof Revisited

In cases in which internal or other direct evidence does not definitively establish liability—the use of at least some act in the set X—inferences must be made from circumstantial evidence. Recall that it is a basic maxim of competition law that circumstantial evidence may indeed be employed.[5] Moreover, it is widely accepted that, once acts are made illegal and subject to heavy sanctions, they will be driven underground and accompanied by concealment, so circumstantial evidence may need to be employed if adequate deterrence is to be attained. This proposition is especially applicable in the present setting since the prohibition under discussion is

---

chapter suggest that more (and more difficult) questions need to be answered under the communications-based prohibition (which might in turn require additional experts, which also adds to discovery costs).

[4] It is as if the social objective is concerned with the presence of hay, but the rule forces us to wade through a substantial haystack in order to ascertain whether or not some needles might be hidden inside.

[5] See section 5.A.

directed at particular communications and the like. The relevant contrast is with a prohibition aimed at successful oligopolistic coordination, where the act in question, coordinated price elevation, is more public—even though, as chapters 10 and 11 indicate, it is nevertheless often difficult to identify.

Chapter 6, which introduces the paradox of proof, elaborates on the difficulty of making inferences about the use of prohibited communications from circumstantial, market-based evidence. Some acts in the set X will be hard to distinguish from some in X′ even when observed directly, so the task will be especially formidable when indirect methods are required. One must search for symptoms, but such will often be noisy signals. The hypothesized relationship between the use of various acts and successful coordination is probabilistic and varies greatly with the setting. In order to make the necessary inferences, one will have to view all the facts and circumstances bearing on conduciveness to successful coordination, supplement these findings with knowledge of which means of coordination are associated with what probabilities of success in the identified type of setting, and also consider the degree of success that has been achieved.

The analysis begins by considering whether successful oligopolistic coordination is likely to be taking place. If it is very unlikely, then an inference that it is being attempted through improper means, that acts in X are being employed, is unwarranted, which is to say that the probability is low. (It is not zero because the evidence on successful coordination may be mistaken and because attempts may fail.) Since cases that involve no apparent coordination are ubiquitous—all the more so if deterrence is reasonably successful—the probability is presumably too low to justify a positive inference.

Now suppose that successful oligopolistic coordination is established with some requisite likelihood—and the present analysis will largely take the degree of demonstrated success as given. Under the direct analysis considered in part II, the inquiry would be complete. However, under a communications-based prohibition, we must ask a second question: whether, under the circumstances of the market in question, such success is sufficiently unlikely in the absence of the use of prohibited communications (acts in X) to warrant an inference that such acts were used. This inference process is obviously more involved than that required under a prohibition on successful oligopolistic coordination since an additional

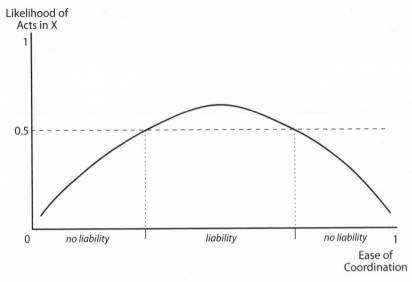

Figure 2. Ease of Coordination, Likelihood of Acts in X, and Liability

inquiry is necessary. Moreover, as we saw in chapter 6, this second question is more difficult to answer than is the first.

The basic logic of the paradox of proof concerns the relationship between the degree to which the market at hand is conducive to successful
coordinated oligopoly pricing and the likelihood with which one can infer
that at least some prohibited means were employed. As explained in section 6.A, it is generally supposed that the likelihood that some act in X
was used is low when conditions are highly unconducive (because firms
would not risk liability in such circumstances), is rising as conditions
become more conducive, but eventually falls as the means become highly
conducive (because firms are imagined to forgo legally risky methods
when success is sufficiently likely without them).[6] This relationship was
depicted in Figure 1, to which was added—purely for illustrative pur-

---

[6] Numerous further complications were explored in chapter 6, particularly in section 6.D,
but will not be repeated here. Also, firms may find it optimal to employ illegal types of communication that are further from the line because they are more effective, or legal types that
are further from the line in the opposite direction because they are less likely to be mistaken
for illegal forms. The latter strategy is problematic, however, because one of the most important
ways that firms can avoid liability in a world governed by inferences from circumstantial evidence is to be unsuccessful.

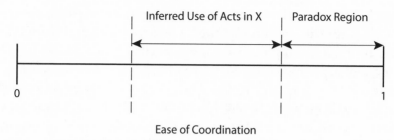

Figure 3. Ease of Coordination and Paradox of Proof

poses—a more-likely-than-not proof burden, which generated Figures 2 and 3, reproduced here for convenience.

Chapter 6 examined the implications of this depiction, particularly regarding the rightmost paradox region, for adjudication and our understanding of the law of horizontal agreements. In this chapter, we are stipulating the use of this commonly advocated legal rule—without regard to the validity of most commentators' claim that it accurately depicts existing legal regimes—for purposes of assessing how well it would control coordinated oligopolistic price elevation compared to the results produced by the direct approach outlined in part II.

In considering this question, we can see from the outset (and recognized previously) that the communications-based prohibition is indeed paradoxical in the sense that it assigns liability to cases of moderate danger while exonerating defendants in cases posing the highest threat: where the expected likelihood, magnitude, and longevity of price elevation are the greatest. For this reason, the commonly advocated approach seems prima facie to be inferior to a direct one. The next section elaborates this problem.

C. Comparison of Outcomes

To compare the direct approach to liability developed in part II with the communications-based prohibition considered here, it is useful to specify the former in terms of the above diagrams. Suppose that the direct approach would find liability when the ease of coordination is at least at the left boundary of the liability region in those figures, or perhaps starting somewhat further to the right. Any outcome is a priori possible: Selection of the optimal boundary point, which can be understood as the optimal proof burden on conduciveness taking as given other evidence, including that on successful coordination, would be determined as discussed in chapters 9 and 12, on which more in a moment.

Regarding deterrence, the communications-based prohibition would be weaker (even nonexistent, depending on how well firms can predict factfinding) in the right, paradox region. Because this region is where the social danger—the expected harm from oligopolistic price elevation—is the greatest, this disadvantage of basing liability on the presence of particular communications is substantial. In this regard, one should also keep in mind that, as explained in chapter 8, net expected harm from oligopoly pricing rises disproportionately with the magnitude of price elevation; for example, when elevations are likely to be twice as great, social harm will be significantly more than double.[7] Likewise, under the communications-based prohibition, deterrence is maintained in the middle region, and (depending on how proof burdens are set under the direct approach) may be, in comparison, relatively strongest toward the left of that region, which is where expected harm per event is lowest.

Consideration of chilling costs also seems adverse to the communications-based prohibition if one considers the costs per unit of enforcement or deterrence. In an absolute sense, if liability is reduced—say, the prospect is the same in the middle region and negligible in the paradox region—total chilling costs will fall.[8] But we should be concerned with the significance of chilling costs relative to deterrence benefits. Toward the middle of the diagrams, where conduciveness is moderate (including cases toward the left of that region, where it is not very high), errors in identifying successful coordination are greatest. All else equal, it is less plausible that coordination is taking place when conditions are relatively unconducive. Moreover, any success achieved is likely to be smaller in magnitude, and the analysis in chapter 9 and section 12.A suggests that mistakes are more likely when elevations are small. Similarly, error seems

---

[7] However, the loss in consumer surplus, although still increasing, does so at a decreasing rate.

[8] One might further argue that even this point is less favorable to the communications-based prohibition if one accepts advocates' commonly stated (although empirically dubious) view that successful oligopolistic coordination is inevitable when the ease of coordination is high (see note 43 in chapter 13), for if that were so, false positives would be impossible. As explained in section 13.C, however, that view ignores deterrence.

less likely as one moves toward the right in the diagram and least likely in the paradox region. In sum, the communications-based prohibition aims at cases where coordination is not as easy, which will tend to include a relatively higher fraction of cases in which coordination is less likely to exist, so false positives that produce chilling costs will tend to be relatively more frequent. Furthermore, it is explained in sections 9.B and 12.A that chilling costs are most serious in industries that are truly competitive, or very nearly so, which will be more likely to be true as one moves toward the left along the horizontal axis. That is, relatively speaking, chilling costs will be both more frequent and more severe under this circumscribed rule of liability.

Combining these two observations suggests that a communications-based prohibition exonerates firms in cases in which the tradeoff of deterrence benefits and chilling costs is most favorable to liability and imposes sanctions when the tradeoff is relatively less favorable. To dramatize this point, compare this prohibition to a direct one that imposes a particular burden of proof on conduciveness: specifically, such that liability begins at the border between the middle and right regions, that is, at the left border of the paradox region. In other words, liability in the middle and right regions is the opposite of what would prevail under the communications-based prohibition. And, to ease the exposition, suppose that there are the same number of cases in the middle and right regions.[9] Compare Figure 3A, slightly altered from the original Figure 3, to Figure 3B, reflecting the just-described modification.

This comparison provokes a simple question: All else equal, how do we feel about imposing liability just in cases that pose moderate danger (Figure 3A)—the situation under the communications-based prohibi-

---

[9] This assumption is unrealistic; it would only hold by chance. Moreover, the number of cases in each region depends on the liability rule, and what we care about for ex ante effects are the number of settings influenced rather than the number of cases, as elaborated in section 9.A. In any event, the discussion in the text is merely suggestive and one could modify the burden of proof to produce the desired comparison. For example, to get the same number of affected markets under each rule, the proof burden under the direct approach of part II might turn out to be further to the left. Then we would have an intermediate region—from that point on the horizontal axis up to the border with the paradox region—where the treatment under the two rules was the same, and the difference would be between the remaining regions, which by construction would affect the same number of settings.

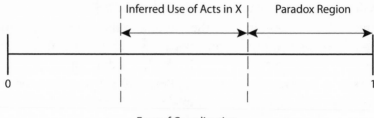

Ease of Coordination

Figure 3A. Ease of Coordination and Paradox of Proof (Modified)

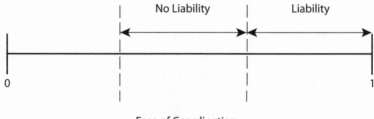

Ease of Coordination

Figure 3B. Reversing Liability and Paradox (Rightmost No Liability) Regions

tion—or just in cases that pose high danger (Figure 3B)—as under this particular implementation of the direct approach of part II? Since deterrence benefits are higher and chilling costs are lower under the direct approach, and possibly to a great degree, it would obviously be superior. That is, there exists a way to set the proof burden under the approach of part II such that it clearly, and perhaps overwhelmingly, dominates the communications-based prohibition.[10]

More broadly, the concern with chilling costs due to the prospect of false positives is optimally confronted directly, as suggested at the close of the preceding chapter. Notably, it may make sense to increase the proof burden on whether successful oligopolistic coordination has taken place rather than focusing only on conduciveness, which is but

---

[10] The proof burden that gives rise to this sharp comparison will, of course, be best only by chance. The optimal burden, discussed in section 12.A, might be higher or lower; but, in any case, since it is optimal, the results would necessarily be superior to those under the burden stipulated here for ease of comparison. See also Kaplow (2013a), exploring generally the tendency for heightened proof requirements to dominate adding additional elements to be proved when the supplemental requirements merely serve as proxies for social harm.

one consideration bearing on the central question of concern. Likewise, it may be appropriate to give less weight to particular types of evidence of more questionable reliability. In contrast, it is not optimal to exonerate defendants in a wide range of cases that pose the greatest danger and least chilling cost, including those in which the overall proof is strongest. Put another way, because a greater ease of coordination tends to be associated with both greater deterrence benefits and lower chilling costs—which is why it is identified in section 11.A as a consideration favorable to liability—it is truly perverse to count it backward in the strongest cases for liability.[11]

The preceding point focuses on setting the proof burden under the direct approach. It is also revealing to consider adjusting the burden of proof under the communications-based prohibition. To see the effects, recall the horizontal dotted line in Figure 2 that indicates where the probability of use of acts in X is 0.50, so that above that line such use is more likely than not. Raising the proof burden would involve setting a higher probability threshold and thus raising the horizontal line; conversely for a lower burden.[12] The resulting tradeoff from either adjustment has a mixed quality. For example, raising the burden slightly may well be desirable with regard to the left boundary between liability and no liability because those cases in which liability is no longer deemed to exist pose a relatively low danger of social harm and a relatively significant possibility of chilling costs—that is, compared to the group of scenarios in which liability was initially assessed. However, the effect may be adverse at the right boundary, between the liability and paradox regions, because those now-exonerated cases involve relatively high danger and low chilling

---

[11] Another perverse effect concerns firms' incentives to influence the ease of coordination. Under a direct approach, if firms seek to increase conduciveness, liability is more likely, but under the communications proscription, when conduciveness is moderate to high, the incentive is to further increase conduciveness—firms are more likely to succeed at price elevation (as always) and (contrary to under the direct approach) less likely to be held liable. For example, a firm considering defection through quality competition (increasing product differentiation) would have less incentive to do so under the prohibition on communications than under the direct approach.

[12] There exist subtle but possibly significant qualifications; however, they are ones that generally disfavor ex post likelihood standards of the sort employed under a communications-based prohibition. See Kaplow (2011, 2012a).

costs—compared to cases in the interior of the middle region, where liability is retained. That is, raising the proof burden under a communications-based prohibition exonerates both the weakest and strongest cases, defined in terms of the social welfare consequences of liability.

This unfortunate—indeed, anomalous—tradeoff is, however, readily avoidable. Under the depicted circumstances, moving each boundary toward the right would be a better way to improve social welfare—supposing that liability is indeed desirable for some of the cases in the liability region. Doing so would entail a relatively higher burden toward the left of the horizontal axis—exonerating the weakest cases, as with a straightforward rise in the burden of proof—and a relatively lower burden toward the right—now resulting in broader liability rather than greater exoneration for the strongest cases.

Similar logic favors moving the right boundary all the way to the right—eliminating the paradox region—and setting the left boundary of the liability region wherever the tradeoff between deterrence benefits and chilling costs is optimized. But, of course, this realignment would abandon the communications-based approach embodied in the sets X and X' and replace it with the direct approach from part II. This conclusion is hardly surprising; the reasoning merely recasts the logic developed earlier in this section.

This point restates the theme with which this part opens, namely, that part II states the nature of the social problem and then considers how to go about detection and setting sanctions in an optimal fashion, that which maximizes social welfare. Since nothing like the communications-based approach emerged from that analysis, we knew from the outset that such a liability regime would not be optimal. Moreover, if we state some liability regime that differs from what is optimal and ask how it can be improved, we might expect that reshaping its boundaries to move it toward the previously identified optimal regime would make sense. The present analysis makes this idea concrete by articulating the initial differences and explaining how the deterrence and chilling effects change as one liability regime is morphed into the other.

In this regard, recall from chapter 9 that the welfare-based approach does not define false positives and false negatives relative to some formal statement of a liability rule but rather in terms of how findings of liability and of no liability in various settings will influence firms' behavior, for better or worse, in terms of effects on social welfare. Commentators who favor a communications-based approach object to liability in the paradox region and thereby view liability in such cases as involving false positives. But such false positives are defined by reference to this formal standard for liability, whose desirability is in question. As discussed throughout this section, the prospect of liability in the paradox region tends to be especially valuable in terms of deterrence and less costly in terms of chilling effects than is liability in the middle region, where the posited approach would hold firms liable. The core "chilling effect" of liability in the paradox region consists of deterrence of coordinated price elevation, and it is deterrence in settings involving the greatest social harm. Hence, when the social objective motivating the legal prohibition is front and center in the analysis, the error tradeoff is assessed quite differently—and properly. This divergence between a rule based on the use of acts in a set X and one designed in light of the social objective, the focus of section 16.B, is also what explains why the simple device of adjusting the proof burden upward or downward (raising or lowering the horizontal dotted line in Figure 2) is such a blunt—and odd—way to fine-tune a legal regime.[13]

D. Comparison of Administrability

The analysis in section C indicates that a direct approach with an appropriately calibrated burden of proof dominates a communications-based prohibition. In that light, it seems unlikely that administrative considerations could swing the balance. Yet it is worth considering the differences along this dimension, especially because a (perhaps the) central concern

---

[13] Another perspective on the contrast in approaches focuses on the different uses of evidence, a point emphasized from the outset of this chapter. Recall from the discussion of interfirm communications in section 11.C that the direct approach uses all manner of evidence to draw the best inference regarding the social welfare consequences of liability whereas the communications-based prohibition uses the evidence to infer whether prohibited communications occurred. As a matter of logic, there is no way that this latter inference can help with the former because the inference itself contains no information not already reflected in the evidence from which it was drawn. Hence, it is not possible to improve the mapping from evidence to liability that is determined without regard to consideration of the likelihood that acts in some set X were present.

with the direct approach that focuses on detecting successful oligopolistic coordination is that it involves too complex an inquiry requiring extensive and subtle expert economic evidence that is subject to manipulation, particularly by financially motivated private parties. The analysis of the paradox of proof—both here and in chapter 6—suggests a strongly contrary conclusion in this respect as well.

As already explained, an approach to liability that depends on detection of prohibited communications through circumstantial evidence requires answering both the central question under the direct approach—whether successful coordination appears to have taken place—and also the one focused on here—whether any success is best attributed to the use of at least some act in the set X or entirely to acts in X'. Almost by definition, the communications-based prohibition seems to be more difficult to apply because it subsumes what must be demonstrated under the direct method and requires additional, complex analysis.

This conclusion would not follow if the supplemental question could often readily be answered in the negative, even in cases in which the former question is difficult to address. However, this scenario seems unlikely: When conduciveness is sufficiently low that we can be fairly confident that firms would not even attempt to coordinate on price, we can likewise conclude that success is unlikely to be present. Indeed, this was a key part of the analysis in section 11.A explaining that conduciveness was close to a necessary condition for liability under the direct approach. That leaves cases in which conduciveness is obviously so high that it is quite unlikely that any acts in X would be necessary to achieve success. As suggested previously and elaborated just below, such cases also seem unlikely.[14]

Therefore, the communications-based prohibition is almost surely more difficult to apply in cases involving circumstantial evidence.[15] To see how much worse, consider the problem confronted by experts

---

[14] It may also seem that such cases fail to satisfy the stated condition, for if success is indeed virtually automatic, we are not in a situation in which success is difficult to determine. However, under the direct approach, effective implementation may result in significant deterrence, in which event success would no longer be likely, as previously explained. Note that, in any event, as section C implies, if there were many such cases, this fact would be a telling objection to the communications-based prohibition with regard to outcomes.

[15] As previously stated, in cases with unambiguous direct evidence of highly explicit com-

attempting to offer guidance on liability. A significant challenge is posed by the need to determine the height[16] and shape[17] of the curve in Figure 2, which in turn determine the boundaries between the no liability and liability regions in Figures 2 and 3. As section 6.E discusses, empirical evidence bearing on this relationship—which is contingent on both the strength of evidence that successful coordination is taking place and on the legal regime, that is, the definition of the set X—seems nonexistent and difficult to develop. Moreover, the nature of the relationship will depend on facts of the case at hand: Particular features of markets will affect the probability of success that may be achieved using various combinations of acts and thus the likelihood that at least some act in X was employed. Accordingly, witnesses, expert or otherwise, will have to rely substantially on conjecture when supporting the requisite conclusions.

In comparing the direct approach with the communications-based prohibition, we can ask which question economists—whether working within an enforcement agency or supplying reports to and testifying before an adjudicator—can know more about: whether successful oligopolistic coordination is taking place or whether any observed pricing could have come about only using at least some act in a legally specified set X or may instead have come about using solely means in X'.[18] However difficult is the first question in various settings, it is a subject of decades of theoretical and empirical research, whereas little is known about the second question, and even less with regard to any particular legal definition of the sets X and X'.[19] (Of course, regarding outcomes, the subject

---

munications that produce successful coordinated elevation, liability is clear under both approaches.

[16] See subsection 6.D.1 and section 6.G. For example, if the curve in Figures 1 and 2 was substantially higher, the liability region would correspond to much of the horizontal axis. (In principle, it could reach either or both ends. Keep in mind that the curve is drawn taking as given evidence on the demonstrated likelihood and degree of success in oligopolistic coordination, which might be quite high.) Alternatively, the curve could be much lower, in which case the liability region would be thinner or even nonexistent. (Suppose that other evidence showed that the industry was probably exhibiting competitive pricing.)

[17] Variations were presented in sections 6.C and 6.D, some of which are revisited below.

[18] See section 6.E.

[19] That is, any expert opinion on the likelihood of use of some acts in X given some set of facts will depend on precisely which acts or combinations of acts are deemed to be in set X versus in X', a matter that itself will be disputed. See subsection 6.D.3.

of section C, it is obvious which question has greater relevance to social welfare.)

Further confounding the inference process are a number of simplifying assumptions employed in section 6.A and here that need to be relaxed to apply the framework in practice. One already alluded to is that a given set of diagrams is based on a particular finding about the degree of achieved success in oligopolistic coordination. Different degrees imply different curves and thus different regions for liability and no liability. And the degree of success will, of course, be contested. Thus, in principle, an adjudicator needs to know the proper curves for each possible finding that may be reached. Furthermore, evidence bearing on the ease of co-ordination may also bear on the extent to which success has been achieved, and vice versa. Indeed, each conclusion is related to the other: If success seems highly likely and substantial, it is implausible that the ease of co-ordination is very low; if the ease of coordination is low, then one would be more skeptical of evidence demonstrating success; and so forth. Section 12.A describes how, viewed broadly, one can consider a mapping from all the evidence to a finding of liability and setting of sanctions, abstracting from separate, intermediate conclusions—a viewpoint applicable to the present inquiry into the likelihood of use of prohibited communications, acts in X.[20] This perspective is reinforced by considering that there also may be some internal or other direct evidence of the use of prohibited communications that needs to be incorporated in reaching an ultimate decision on liability.[21]

Note further that all of the variations and complications examined in sections 6.C and 6.D bear on the shape of the curve relating the ease of coordination to the likelihood of the use of some act in the set X and thus on the locations and breadths of the liability and paradox regions—and, as explained there, scenarios exist in which either of the regions may be empty. For example, recall from section 6.C the examination of different possible locations along the horizontal axis for the higher portions of the curve and thus different possible breadths of the paradox region. Narrow and broad paradox regions were depicted in Figures 4–7. As drawn, for virtually any ease of coordination—all but at either extreme—opposite

---

[20] For elaboration, see section 6.G.

[21] See subsection 6.D.1.

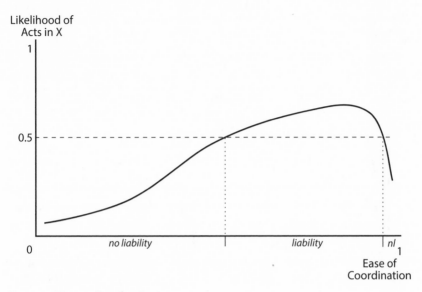

Figure 4. Narrow Paradox Region

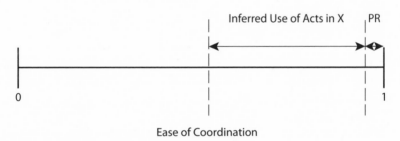

Ease of Coordination

Figure 5. Narrow Paradox Region and Paradox of Proof

outcomes are possible depending on which of the two curves governs. Although these are just possibilities, given the dearth of evidence about the pertinent curve we can see how daunting is the prospect of attempting to apply a communications-based prohibition in adjudication. Even stipulating outcomes on many other issues, liability remains highly indeterminate unless the pertinent curve can be established, which may be the most difficult issue of all.

The discussion of these figures in section 6.C raised some additional points of relevance for present purposes. First, the case depicted in Figures 4 and 5, with the narrow paradox region, implies outcomes fairly similar

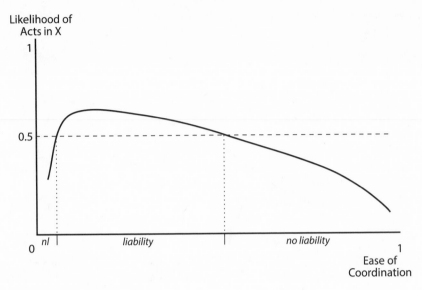

Figure 6. Broad Paradox Region

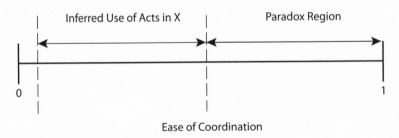

Figure 7. Broad Paradox Region and Paradox of Proof

to those under a direct approach—the latter with a proof burden set so as to provide liability in (roughly) the right half of the figures. As noted, the analysis in section 11.A explains how conduciveness favors liability, and in this case it generally does even under a communications-based prohibition, except at the right extreme. Of course, this residual discrepancy favors the direct approach because it hardly makes sense to exonerate defendants in a small slice of the cases posing the greatest danger and least chilling costs. Moreover, even though such cases may be exceptional, allowing for the possibility might induce defendants to raise the argument often, which would add to adjudication costs and also give rise to some false negatives, most likely in cases near the right extreme and thus involving high danger and low chilling costs.

Second, remarks were offered concerning the irony of the fact that those analysts who address the matter, albeit indirectly, advance empirical conjectures suggesting that this case generally depicts reality—by suggesting that successful coordination in the absence of highly explicit communications is rare.[22] Given such views, it is hard to understand why commentators would so strongly believe that the law should not (and does not) deem successful interdependent oligopolistic coordination to be sufficient grounds for liability. It was explained that, given a narrow paradox region, plaintiffs should survive motions to dismiss and even win at summary judgment if they allege sufficient facts and (at summary judgment) present sufficient and uncontested evidence of successful coordination, even if they have no direct evidence of particular acts in X, because the inference that such were used is so powerful. For these reasons, we would have imagined that these commentators would believe that the scenario in Figures 2 and 3—or perhaps the quite broad paradox region in Figures 6 and 7—depicts reality, for then the choice between these contrasting approaches to liability would be more consequential.[23] This incongruity reinforces the sense that existing commentary has not systematically analyzed the implications of its preferred legal rule or alternatives.

In this regard, it is also useful to revisit another of the many other variations examined in chapter 6, that in subsection 6.D.2 on countervailing effects. Specifically, it was questioned whether the core empirical assumptions underlying the paradox of proof were valid: Even if the use of acts in X is less necessary to achieve a given degree of success as the ease of coordination rises, the value of enhancing coordination may nevertheless be increasing (because success is more valuable when condi-

---

[22] As discussed in section 6.E, empirical evidence from prosecuted cases—most of which involve small numbers of firms and homogeneous products, yet highly explicit communications—is consistent with this supposition.

[23] As mentioned, in that event, the sorts of strategic reversals of positions elaborated in section 6.B would be frequent, even typical, rather than exceptional, which seems contrary to what ordinarily occurs in adjudication.

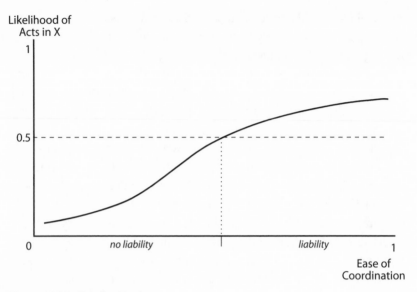

Figure 14. No Paradox Region

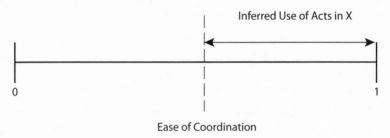

Figure 15. No Paradox of Proof

tions are conducive). Also, many factors that make coordination easier also make direct detection of explicit communications more difficult, so the use of acts in X may be less legally risky as conduciveness rises. Taken together, it is possible that one would have the results depicted in Figures 14 and 15 (of section 6.G).

In this scenario, there may be little real difference between the two approaches to liability. Conduciveness now can favor only liability under both approaches, and if the burdens of proof—the minimum degree of ease of coordination required, taking other evidence (such as on success) as given—resulted in the same dividing line between the two regions, outcomes would be the same as well.[24] Hence, it is possible that the debate over what rule should govern coordinated oligopolistic price elevation is not merely of limited significance—as suggested when there is only a narrow paradox region—but entirely moot. This conclusion, of course, is true only in principle, even granting the factual assumptions underlying Figures 14 and 15. Because the height and shape of the curve would be in dispute under a communications-based prohibition, outcomes could differ due to errors, and adjudication would be more complex because an additional and difficult question would be germane to liability.

This section reminds us of the many complications adduced in chapter 6 concerning the inference process logically entailed by a prohibition on selected communications (or other specified acts). The level of complexity and lack of an empirical basis for making the requisite determinations are difficult to overstate. Taken together, the analysis in chapter 6 and in this chapter indicates that implementation of a communications-based prohibition is immensely more challenging than is appreciated by its advocates and also notably more so than entailed by the direct approach considered in part II, which itself is often quite difficult to apply. This hurdle is distinct from the problem identified in section C: that, even if well implemented, the communications-based prohibition is likely to be clearly inferior in terms of its effects on social welfare.

---

[24] Regarding how one should, in principle, set the proof burden under the communications-based approach, compared to under the direct approach, see the latter portion of section C.

18

Further Topics

❧

A. Sanctions

The subject of optimal sanctions is considered in chapter 13. Discussion here focuses on differences that arise when employing a communications-based prohibition rather than when basing liability on the presence of successful oligopolistic coordination.

First, as discussed before, many (but not all) of the methods of demonstrating successful oligopolistic coordination also indicate the magnitude of price elevation and thus provide a basis for setting fines and damages. When liability is triggered by the use of some prohibited act rather than proven price elevation, additional inquiry for purposes of calibrating sanctions will often be necessary. One implication of this point is that, even in cases in which there is decisive internal or other direct evidence of prohibited communications, the expense and complexity involved with assessing market-based evidence will not be avoided.[1]

Second, with a communications-based prohibition, there is an additional problem that concerns the pertinent baseline. As subsection 13.A.1

---

[1] The analysis in the text assumes that sanctions will be based on an estimate of the actual price elevation, which section 13.A explains should be done but, under existing law in many jurisdictions, often may not be. In addition to the previously noted reasoning in favor of employing sanctions that reflect actual harm, there may be an additional concern with a communications-based prohibition relating to chilling costs due to the fact that evidence of liability less often requires demonstration of nontrivial oligopolistic price elevation, whereas evidence directed toward such elevation tends to screen out industries that are actually operating competitively, where the chilling effects of false positives tend to be most severe. This point is most pertinent when internal or other direct evidence is at least somewhat ambiguous, otherwise weak, or largely nonexistent.

discusses, the benchmark for setting fines and damages is (in principle) related to the extent of firms' overcharge. Under the direct approach, the overcharge is the difference between the actual price charged and a competitive price. However, if the violation is defined in terms of the use of prohibited communications, the use of acts in a set X, then, as section 5.D elaborates, it may seem logical for the benchmark not to be the competitive price but rather the possibly elevated price that the firms could have charged had they confined their behavior to acts in the set X'. After all, such price elevation is deemed to be legal under this regime, so the incremental harm attributable to the firms' illegal activity is limited to the magnitude of the further price increase made possible by using acts in X. It is not the entire gap between price and marginal cost at the competitive level of output.[2]

Accordingly, a government intending to levy a fine that was a function of harm caused by the violation or a plaintiff hoping to recover damages would need to show not only that illegal methods were used but also how much of the price elevation could be attributed to the use of such means. In cases in which proof is by circumstantial evidence and the factfinder infers that the defendants' actions barely crossed the line demarcating liability, damages under this formulation could be quite small. But the implications of having to identify the increment above plain, interdependent oligopoly prices are not so limited. Even in a clear case of express conspiracy—smoke-filled rooms, taped conversations, and criminal convictions—it is possible that, but for the prohibited interactions, the firms would have elevated price above a competitive level, although perhaps not as high, for as long, or with as few price wars.[3]

This additional requirement could prove quite challenging.[4] First, one would have to determine which of the acts the defendants employed are

---

[2] As section 5.D further explains, use of the full gap between the price charged and the competitive price seems more in accord with current practice in damages assessment in the United States, thus constituting one of the respects in which existing law in action is more consistent with successful oligopolistic coordination being sufficient for liability.

[3] See also section 5.D for discussion of an infection argument that would hold defendants responsible for the full overcharge above the competitive level rather than the possibly lesser increment due to their illegal activity.

[4] As subsection 13.A.1 and chapter 14 explain, if the unilateral exercise of market power is deemed legal and is present, the overcharge would be relative to a supracompetitive baseline

in set X and which other acts they might have used in addition or could have used instead are in the set X'. Then, one would have to assess the degree of price elevation under both scenarios. That is, one would need to know the extent of successful price elevation in fact (even if this is not required for liability, established perhaps by evidence of interfirm communications) as well as what it would have been if the defendants had confined themselves to acts in X'. In determining the latter, there may be dispute over which acts, not necessarily ones actually used, would be legal (in addition to expected disputes over which acts actually found to have been employed were legal, even granting that some were illegal). And, of course, there would be significant disagreement about the extent to which prices might have been elevated if only such legal means had been employed. Given how little is understood about this sort of question and the hypothetical nature of the inquiry, the need for this additional determination is problematic.[5] Furthermore, even if this determination can be made well, deterrence of socially harmful price elevation is undermined thereby—although this problem is better attributed to the rule of liability that permits successful (even, and perhaps especially, very successful)

---

even under the direct approach. The point that there may be interdependence relying solely on acts in X' that results in further price elevation applies with respect to this higher initial baseline as well. That is, when there is unilateral market power, its extent would not determine the baseline, which would instead be given by the higher price achieved through legal means of producing interdependence.

[5] Similar challenges would be posed in determining overcharges in standard ways, which often involve comparisons to other markets or to behavior before or after the period of illegal activity. Notably, there may be disputes about whether acts in X or solely acts in X' were employed in those comparison markets or time periods. To be sure, challenges arise with these comparisons under both approaches to liability because it may be necessary to determine the extent of interdependence (however accomplished) in the comparison markets.

One question specific to the communications-based prohibition arises when defendants continue to price interdependently after suit is filed, concede that this is so, and argue that this is done without the use of any acts in X and hence demonstrates that such were not needed in the first place, disproving liability or showing that damages were zero. Suppose, however, that it is argued by an enforcer that this subsequent success is possible only because of the relationships and understandings reached through the initial use of illegal means, that is, acts in X. Then it becomes necessary to decide as well whether liability should be found and thus sanctions imposed for the subsequent behavior. As a matter of internal logic, the answer may be affirmative since the later behavior is caused, at least in part, by illegal activity (prior use of acts in X). See also the further discussion in the text at the end of this section.

coordinated price elevation as long as prohibited communications are not (and we can now add, need not be) employed.

The main point with regard to fines and damages is that further complication is introduced by the communications-based prohibition, in addition to the detection difficulties that are the focus of chapter 17. The social consequence is a more costly and error-prone adjudication process in addition to one that is less effective in advancing social welfare even without regard to administrative concerns.

In contrast, the analysis of imprisonment of individuals, usually within a firm, for violation of a selective prohibition on communications is fairly similar to that under the direct approach, outlined in section 13.B. One difference might concern the relative importance of imprisonment as a supplemental sanction. As previously explained, a key rationale involves remedying any deterrence deficit present when only fines (and private damages) are employed. Because firms may be sanctioned in a narrower class of circumstances when liability requires proof of the use of an act in set X, there may be less deterrence due to a lower probability of sanctions and thus arguably a reason to employ higher sanctions, possibly including imprisonment. However, what matters is whether firms know ex ante the situation they will be deemed ex post to occupy. Perhaps some firms that would have anticipated sanctions under a prohibition on successful oligopolistic coordination will expect sanctions under the narrower prohibition with a positive—because they are using acts in X, or might be found to have done so—but lower probability. The aforementioned point applies to them. Others, those well into the paradox region, may expect to be found liable with a very low probability under a communications-based prohibition, so raising sanctions may not have much deterrent effect on them. A possibly countervailing consideration concerns chilling costs. Although there may be negligible cost from chilling acts in X, the communications-based prohibition disproportionately targets settings with a lower danger of coordination and therefore poses a correspondingly greater likelihood of striking competitive behavior (as explained in section 17.C), so lower sanctions than otherwise might be optimal.

Another difference concerns the evidence required to identify the particular individuals who are to be subject to imprisonment (or personal fines). First, this process may seem easier under the communications-based prohibition since the prohibited class of acts might be defined more clearly—although the opposite is also possible, as suggested by the lack of a sharp definition of what such a prohibition entails, the focus of part I of this book. Second, some evidence that might be clear under a broader prohibition may be ambiguous under a narrower one. Except for individuals caught on tape, it may be difficult to prove that others, such as their supervisors or other individuals who may have acted on the achieved interfirm understanding, knew that the resulting meeting of the minds was obtained using means in the set X rather than solely through acts in X′. It seems that it would be especially difficult to identify particular individuals with the requisite knowledge in a case proved primarily by circumstantial evidence. Of course, under the direct prohibition on successful oligopolistic coordination, it was likewise suggested that determination of the responsible individuals would be difficult, and it might primarily be accomplished when there is powerful internal evidence or proof of specific, explicit interfirm communications linked to the individual defendants in question.

The analysis of injunctions in section 13.C establishes a number of propositions that are also pertinent to a communications-based prohibition. First, it is not obvious that injunctions are important (or that they are frequently used). This point is especially significant with regard to deterrence but also has implications for subsequent compliance because fines and imprisonment could likewise be employed without any need for an injunction, and, when there is an injunction, it is still necessary to use other sanctions to ensure that firms have an incentive to comply with it.

This latter point is not obviously much different when the prohibition applies to particular communications rather than to successful oligopolistic coordination. Suppose that firms are caught having used some acts in X and that an injunction proscribes future use of those acts (or perhaps a broader set than those demonstrated to have been used, such as all acts in X). Proving the original violation may have been difficult, as suggested by the analysis in chapter 17. If it was proved by catching individuals on tape, one might have to catch them again, in the future, to show that they violated the injunction. Even if violations continue, they might be difficult to detect because of inherent obstacles as well as the fact that firms will be extremely cautious, having been caught once. As section 13.C mentions, internal monitoring might be imposed, but this supplement would aid future deterrence regardless of the type of sanction employed. Alternatively, future violations might be established by circumstantial evidence. In either case, just as before, it would be necessary to replicate the detection and sanctioning process, which is little different from what must be done in the absence of an injunction.[6]

Consider the case in which the available proof of a continuing violation consists primarily of ongoing successful oligopolistic coordination. Should it be inferred that some acts in X were employed? If such was previously inferred from this type of evidence, on the grounds that the conduciveness of conditions placed the case in the liability region rather than the paradox region (see chapter 17), the same inference might be drawn again. At that point, there may be little difference (going forward) between a communications-based prohibition and a broader proscription on coordinated pricing. This result should not be surprising since the two rules tend to reach similar outcomes in such settings.

Alternatively, defendant firms might argue that, even if it was appropriate to infer their use of prohibited communications in the past, such should not be inferred in the future because, having learned well about each other's predilections and methods of signaling, elaborate coordination is now possible without resort to acts in X.[7] In such cases, one might associate the future behavior with the prior use of acts in X and thus deem it to be attributable to illegal activity under the communications-based prohibition, which would constitute a further move in the direction of a broader prohibition on successful oligopolistic coordination. As discussed in section 13.C, many commentators would be bothered by such a regime since they seem not to comprehend how rational agents could desist from profitable behavior (price elevation). But it was explained there how, once sanctions are contemplated, the behavior is no longer profitable (if expected sanctions are sufficiently high), so self-interest would produce the desired effect on firms' behavior.

---

[6] It might seem appealing to switch the burden of proof to the defendants once they have been demonstrated to have committed a violation, but it is not clear how this would function. After all, there is no direct way to demonstrate the relevant negative—that the firms are no longer using any acts in X—except by a failure to prove the positive directly or through circumstantial evidence.

[7] This possibility relates to the discussion in note 5.

B. Alternative: Disallowance of Circumstantial Evidence

Much of the difficulty with a communications-based prohibition arises in connection with the use of circumstantial evidence, which gives rise to the paradox of proof. Inferences are complex, costly, and error-prone, and, even when the process works well, the results are problematic in that cases posing the greatest danger lead to no sanctions whereas liability tends to be concentrated on cases involving less social harm but greater chilling costs. Accordingly, it may make sense to consider an alternative formulation of the communications-based prohibition that seeks to avoid some of these problems by disallowing the use of circumstantial evidence—that is, a regime that still requires proof of the use of an act in some specified set X (rather than solely the use of acts in X') but imposes the further requirement that such use be demonstrated entirely through the use of direct evidence. (One could likewise consider a variant of the direct approach that requires proof by smoking-gun evidence, a rule that will implicitly be illuminated by much of the discussion in this section.)

On one hand, such a limitation is radical in a formal, legal sense. As mentioned in section 5.A, it is a central tenet of competition law and conspiracy law more broadly that circumstantial evidence may be employed. Moreover, use of such evidence is generally thought to be particularly important in realms such as the present one in which parties hide activities that give rise to liability. On the other hand, criminal price-fixing prosecutions (that occur mainly in the United States), which target individuals for incarceration, seem to require direct, explicit, even smoking-gun evidence of prohibited communications, presumably due in significant part to high proof burdens and perhaps also the exercise of prosecutorial discretion. In any event, this more restrictive approach to liability (for all sanctions) deserves some attention.

First, chilling effects tend to be lessened when a legal prohibition is narrowed. Reducing the use of less reliable evidence is particularly likely to be helpful in this regard. Indeed, this factor—along with savings in administrative costs—is the chief motivation for considering this more restrictive alternative. This benefit, however, may require that the range of permissible evidence be sharply limited. False positives and concomitant chilling effects may still arise due to the ambiguity and unreliability of direct evidence that is not of a smoking-gun variety. For example, an enforcer may identify various internal fragments, such as from emails, that can be interpreted to demonstrate illegality, even though defendants offer contrary interpretations. Furthermore, exclusion of circumstantial, market-based evidence may raise the pressure to accept dubious but direct proof and will also sometimes undermine defendants' attempts to demonstrate that they actually behaved competitively. Nevertheless, if a sufficiently tough limitation is imposed, false positives would be less likely, possibly by a substantial margin compared to the unrestricted communications-based prohibition analyzed until this point.

Second, disallowance of circumstantial evidence would presumably reduce deterrence because liability could no longer be successfully established in certain settings. One could attempt to remedy the shortfall through higher sanctions.[8] There are, of course, limits to this stratagem, including its selectivity: Across-the-board increases in penalties may be adequate or excessive in some settings (where firms believe that discovery of their use of acts in the set X is reasonably likely) but remain insufficient in those in which firms know in advance that their actions are unlikely to give rise to liability under the circumscribed rule.

Successful oligopolistic coordination may not involve any acts in X, and, for that which does, it is unknown what portion generates the sort of direct evidence that a highly restricted prohibition would credit. For the former group, we already know that a communications-based prohibition, requiring proof of acts in X, exonerates firms in cases involving the greatest social danger and relatively low chilling concerns. Among those cases that remain, there is the further point raised in subsection 6.D.2 that detection tends to be most difficult when there are few firms and the coordination problem is easiest, that is, the cases involving relatively large harm within the group of cases that actually involve acts in X. Furthermore, empirical evidence does not give us confidence that existing deterrence is adequate, both because there appears to be significant oligopolistic

---

[8] In addition, one might increase enforcement intensity, such as by undertaking more undercover operations, employing a lower threshold for wiretapping, pursuing weaker leads, and so forth. The extent to which this alternative is feasible or desirable depends on the aggressiveness of preexisting enforcement, among other considerations.

price elevation in many parts of the economy and because the very number and magnitude of price elevations in prosecuted cases suggest a deterrence shortfall, indicating that the probability of detection may be quite low[9] (in addition to sanctions possibly being too low, as discussed in subsection 13.A.3).

For this circumscribed communications-based prohibition to be on a par with the direct approach of part II, it would have to be that market-based and other circumstantial evidence—when used correctly—adds little to the ability to achieve deterrence of coordinated oligopolistic price elevation[10] while notably raising the likelihood of false positives that generate chilling effects and also augmenting administrative costs. If this is true, note that it is the drastic reduction in admissible evidence—rather than the fact that one is generally looking for the use of acts in X rather than evidence of oligopolistic coordination—that generates the alternative rule's possible advantages. It follows, therefore, that if such limited evidence sufficed to achieve substantial deterrence, other reliable evidence rarely existed, and the chilling costs of allowing further channels of proof (relaxing the proof burden) were great, essentially the same result would be obtained under the direct approach. The main difference is that sharp, direct evidence of the socially undesirable phenomenon—successful coordinated price elevation—rather than powerful evidence of a symptom that is not a necessary condition to harm—the use of an act in some set X—would be the trigger for liability. The difference would be small if virtually any evidence unambiguous enough to be admitted demonstrated both.[11]

---

[9] See note 37 in chapter 9.

[10] See also section D, which discusses the possible erosion of smoking-gun evidence due to innovation in electronic communications.

[11] If a highly circumscribed approach to addressing price elevation by direct competitors was optimal, in significant part due to doubts about factfinders' abilities, it would seem that the law on monopolization, vertical practices, and mergers—areas that rely much more heavily on complex economic evidence and circumstantial evidence more broadly—should be extremely restrictive if not a nullity. After all, the social dangers in these other areas are often more ambiguous. Some commentators skeptical of the value of competition regimes endorse such a view. See Bork (1978, 405–7); Crandall and Winston (2003, 24): "Until economists have hard evidence that the current antitrust statutes and the institutions that administer them are generating social benefits, the Federal Trade Commission and the Department of Justice should focus on the most significant and egregious violations, such as blatant price fixing and merger-

Finally, having examined at a general level the apparent effects of this alternative approach on deterrence and chilling, it is useful to examine its inner workings more closely. To begin, there are some challenges in specifying the approach beyond those of defining the sets X and X'. At a conceptual level, there is no clear distinction between circumstantial evidence and direct evidence. For example, strictly speaking, a signed price-fixing agreement is direct proof only of the document's existence. One has to make a further inference from the circumstances—including that parties subject to sanctions for price fixing would not likely sign such documents purely for entertainment purposes—that it is likely that the signatories indeed are fixing prices (or are attempting to do so). The inference may be extremely strong, but it does require a further step that draws on other information about the circumstances.[12] In addition, short of strong smoking-gun evidence—like a signed agreement or tapes with explicit, detailed communications among clearly identified individuals who certainly have price-setting authority—there will often exist ambiguity, as discussed in sections 11.B and 11.C. There are also important boundary issues. For example, is internal evidence that refers to or strongly implies that acts in X were used circumstantial evidence of the use of acts in X or direct evidence? Under a narrow definition of direct evidence, one would exclude much of the potential pool. However, under a broader (even if not capacious) approach, significant difficulty would remain

---

to-monopoly and treat most other apparent threats to competition with benign neglect."; and Easterbrook (1984, 3): "But suits against mergers more often than not have attacked combinations that increased efficiency, and the dissolution of mergers has led to higher prices in the product market. There are good theoretical reasons to believe that the costs of other enforcement efforts have exceeded the benefits." How restrictive a skeptic should be will depend on institutional considerations, such as whether adjudication is by expert tribunal, generalist judge, or lay jury, and on whether prosecutorial discretion can be relied on to help moderate possible excesses of broader prohibitions. (For the latter to be effective, the prosecutor may need a monopoly on enforcement authority, for if private parties or numerous enforcers in other jurisdictions may each independently decide whether to bring a case, then it is the behavior of the most aggressive enforcer that will determine the actual scope of application.)

[12] In case this point is not self-evident, consider defendants offering evidence that they are students in a business school class that is engaged in a simulation exercise, where they were asked to draft and sign a mock price-fixing agreement. Further evidence shows that none of these students work for or are in communication with any firm identified in the document.

because interpretation would inevitably require the use of other (circumstantial) evidence.[13]

Next, observe that even a narrow direct-evidence requirement may not greatly reduce the cost and scope of adjudication due to the need to gauge sanctions, notably fines and damages. As section 13.A explains, these penalties are central and really do need to reflect the extent of actual harm in a given case. This requirement, in turn, means that the extent of oligopolistic price elevation must be measured, which in most cases will require considering much or all of the market-based evidence and also internal evidence bearing on the question, as section A of this chapter notes. Even though such evidence may only be relevant conditional on finding liability, costs of assembly and presentation will nevertheless be incurred in the absence of sequenced (bifurcated) proceedings, under which discovery, investigation, and expert analysis of marketplace behavior would not commence until after a liability determination is made.

It is also important to inquire further into the reliability of inferences made solely on so-called direct evidence and the sensibility of ignoring other evidence. Market-based evidence is sometimes highly probative standing alone and even more often significantly informative considered in combination with other evidence. In proving violations, ignoring even clear market-based evidence could substantially erode deterrence. Likewise, when defendants seek to disprove violations, ignoring such evidence—for example, strong evidence that pricing is indeed competitive or that successful coordination is unlikely to be feasible—could increase chilling effects, unless the range of admissible direct evidence is quite narrow. To take another example, suppose that the direct evidence—a few internal emails, the meaning of which is disputed—considered alone

---

[13] An interesting variation would be to employ a direct-evidence trigger requirement. That is, circumstantial evidence could not be the sole basis for a finding of liability, but once sufficient direct evidence was presented, circumstantial evidence might then be allowed to aid in the inference process. Such an approach would place heavy weight on what is deemed to be a sufficient trigger, which itself would add pressure to the circumstantial/direct evidence boundary. Also, the approach may (for better or worse) skew outcomes toward defendants, who would win both when direct evidence was weak and also when it was strong but sufficiently weakened by circumstantial evidence. Finally, once circumstantial evidence is admitted, the paradox of proof would reappear—although it is present already with direct evidence because such is more likely to exist in the middle region of the figures in chapters 6 and 17.

would lead a factfinder to find liability, just barely. Yet there exists other reliable evidence that the price increase in question matches in timing and magnitude an increase in the cost of a common input. Could it really be optimal to exclude the latter evidence?

The same general conclusion holds for internal indirect evidence, which in some cases would be powerful (alone or in combination with direct evidence) in establishing or negating liability. In this respect, it is also important to recall the initial point in chapter 17 that, with a communications-based prohibition, it is necessary to address a different and sometimes more difficult question: not (only) whether successful oligopolistic coordination has occurred, but (also) whether it was accomplished using some act in X or only acts in X'. Thus, even when internal evidence is murky on the X/X' issue—requiring a good deal of reading between the lines and thus risk of error—it may be clear on successful coordination, suggesting that this alternative communications-based prohibition similarly suffers from a disadvantage relative to the direct approach.

Accordingly, it seems more sensible to address the risk of errors by adjusting proof burdens.[14] As developed in sections 9.A and 12.A, this calibration would optimally be done in light of deterrence effects and chilling costs. If incremental deterrence gains are small and chilling losses large, it may turn out that a high proof burden is optimal. In that case, however, one would limit consideration to highly credible evidence—actually, to combinations that taken together were very reliable—rather than categorically ignoring large portions of evidence, even when strong, and making conclusions based entirely on a subset of evidence, even when what is available in that subset is limited. If it turned out that a communications-based prohibition—or, more relevant for present purposes, one that significantly restricts admissible evidence—was optimal, then (echoing the point in the introduction to this part III) that conclusion would emerge from the analysis in part II. Throughout that part, consid-

---

[14] Many of the points in this section derive from the central, a priori problem with the communications-based prohibition identified in section 17.C: It raises the hurdle by adding an additional element (one that, it turns out, may be negatively correlated with the social objective) rather than by insisting on stronger proof of socially harmful conduct. See Kaplow (2013a) on the general tendency for direct adjustments of proof burdens to be optimal.

eration is given to whether particular types of evidence in various settings are more or less attractive in light of deterrence and chilling effects and to what implications follow regarding the use of evidence and the establishment of proof burdens. It is important to keep in mind that, even if a very high proof burden is optimal, we should still focus on the question of *what* it is that must be demonstrated with high confidence: successful oligopolistic coordination or the use of acts in some set X. How could it be sensible to find liability when successful coordination is unlikely, simply because acts in X seem likely,[15] while finding no liability when successful coordination is extremely likely, because the use of acts in X is unlikely or unknown?[16]

Institutional considerations of the sort considered in section 15.A may also bear on the relative merits of an evidence-limited communications-based prohibition. One possibility is that a factfinder may be distrusted. For example, if a system uses lay juries who might readily be confused or who might be feared to have anti-defendant biases, complex evidence might best be limited. Given that motivation, a very narrow rule might be necessary, allowing only strong smoking-gun evidence that a judge has in essence already determined demonstrates liability with reasonably high confidence. If, instead, more ambiguous communications or evidence of communications—notably, from internal evidence, where interpretation is required—is allowed, similar problems with factfinders might arise.

A final challenge is posed if there is a desire to screen cases at an early stage. If strong, explicit proof is required, then it may be that no case could proceed, particularly if discovery or continuing investigation requires a preliminary determination of sufficient cause.[17] Exceptions might be allowed for government investigations, if they are not themselves subject

---

[15] As discussed in section 12.B, liability for attempts may be useful, which would justify liability in the former case, although it is questionable whether the optimal regime would be concerned primarily with attempts.

[16] This point is reinforced by the difficulty of defining a set X, discussed in section 16.A and throughout part I. Why entertain interminable debate over whether an act is or should be in set X (e.g., constitutes an "agreement") if it is clear that coordinated price elevation took place—or that it did not?

[17] The U.S. Supreme Court's decision in *Twombly* wrestles with this issue, but fails to provide a definition of the legal standard or an indication of how in principle a plaintiff might state a case sufficient to survive a motion to dismiss. See subsection 4.B.2 and also Kaplow (2013a).

to threshold demonstrations, or cases proved through the use of informants who come forward before investigative pressure is applied. Alternatively, screening may be done with broader evidence. For example, market-based evidence of successful coordination might be deemed to constitute a sufficient basis for going forward in search of the smoking-gun evidence that may ultimately be required to establish liability. This approach might, however, require elaborate preliminary factfinding[18] or, if a modest offer of proof is sufficient, fail to provide much of a screen against weak cases—a predicament that does not distinguish the restricted approach from that considered previously.

To summarize, a doctrinally radical alternative of disallowing all circumstantial evidence has a prima facie plausibility that the commonly advanced version lacks, although the approach is difficult to define and is subject to various shortcomings. If it happens to be true that smoking-gun evidence would usually turn up when successful oligopolistic coordination took place, then a highly circumscribed approach may be adequate, but the direct approach would produce this result under such an assumption. However, widespread beliefs and existing evidence suggest that this detection strategy by itself is insufficient, and the cases it tends to miss may be those involving the greatest expected social harm. If so, a wider range of detection methods needs to be permitted, and in any event the choice of methods and setting of proof burdens should grow out of a decision-making framework aimed at maximizing social welfare, not at meeting some formalistic requirement.

C. Implications for Other Competition Law Rules

It is understood that different aspects of competition policy are interrelated; what is optimal in one area may depend on how other rules are set. The most important application of this principle concerns the oligopoly problem. It is generally believed that the difficulty of directly attacking interdependent oligopoly pricing warrants a tougher policy toward hori-

---

[18] See section 15.A. If such factfinding were done, the presently contemplated approach would then ignore such evidence, however powerful, once in the later stage at which liability is determined.

zontal mergers in order to render markets structurally less conducive to coordinated price elevation.[19] Of course, greater strictness comes at a cost in terms of forgone gains in productive efficiency, inhibition of the market for corporate control that provides important discipline for managers, reductions in opportunities for entrepreneurs to exit (the prospect of which influences desirable ex ante behavior), and so forth.

Conversely, to the extent that competition law is more aggressive against successful oligopolistic coordination, interdependent price elevation is more broadly and effectively deterred. Moreover, as emphasized in the analysis of the paradox of proof in section 17.C, the difference under a direct approach is greatest in industries that are most conducive to substantial price elevation. This beneficial result would, accordingly, make it sensible to pursue a somewhat more relaxed approach toward horizontal mergers, with concomitant gains.[20]

There is another possible and previously unappreciated implication relating to the paradox of proof. Notably, some assert that, when conditions are highly conducive, successful oligopolistic coordination (without any resort to acts in the set X) is inevitable; oligopolists cannot help but recognize their interdependence and charge the profit-maximizing price.[21] If so, it seems to follow that current analysis of horizontal mergers in such an industry would be misguided. If concentration was already sufficiently great that conditions were highly conducive to successful coordination, further mergers, even to monopoly, would seem to be permissible: They may generate efficiencies,[22] and there is no prospect for an anticompetitive

---

[19] See Baker (1993, 199–207), Brock (2006, 280), and Kaysen and Turner (1959, 44–45, 127–41). Similar logic also applies to proposals to deconcentrate existing industries.

[20] A central thrust of Posner's (1969, 1566, 1598–1605) criticism of Turner, who pushed for a strongly prophylactic merger policy both in his writing and as chief of the Department of Justice Antitrust Division, is that the resulting inefficiency was a further cost of lax treatment of oligopoly pricing. Demsetz (1973, 3) also suggests a preference for attacking coordination over tough anti-merger policies that would decrease efficiency.

[21] This view is implicit or explicit in some arguments that oligopolists cannot help but behave interdependently. See the sources cited in note 43 in chapter 13.

[22] Indeed, if one really accepted the premise, one would find firms' representations of efficiencies credible, for why else would they wish to merge? Ordinarily, we are worried that efficiencies are modest or entirely pretextual, and that the firms' true motivation for merger is price elevation, but if that ulterior motive is ruled out, there is no longer grounds for suspicion.

effect because it is supposed that firms already charge a fully elevated price. Moreover, the heavy focus of existing merger policy on unilateral effects[23] would make little sense in such industries because that analysis presumes the absence of any coordination rather than the preexistence of full cooperation.[24]

In practice, one does not find firms arguing[25] or regulators accepting the view that lenient treatment is appropriate with regard to highly concentrating mergers in already heavily concentrated industries that are very susceptible to coordination. Quite to the contrary. Similarly, under this view, the most dangerous mergers would be those that occur in industries that are only moderately concentrated, given the need to stop rising concentration before it is too late. This view held sway decades ago, whereas most now believe that such an approach was excessively stringent and not focused on where the most serious competitive dangers are likely to lie.

This state of affairs probably reflects that few if any really believe the premise that coordination is so easy—and without the use of any practices in set X—in many industries.[26] Such an outlook is consistent with statements favoring a narrow (or nonexistent) paradox region, as explained in sections 6.C and 17.D. Another important argument is that highly concentrating mergers should be opposed even if firms already coordinate on price because the prospect that new entrants or the growth of fringe firms might restore a less concentrated and thus less conducive state would become more remote if not eliminated altogether.[27] In any case, the point

---

[23] See Stroux (2004, 187–88).

[24] It would, however, make sense to focus on unilateral effects in industries with significant product differentiation that renders coordination unlikely. By contrast, in (nearly) homogeneous goods industries—specifically, those not yet sufficiently concentrated for coordination to be inevitable—agencies should (contrary to current practice) focus more on coordinated effects.

[25] Firms would be reluctant to advance such an argument if indeed successful oligopolistic coordination, without demonstrable use of any acts in X, was thought to be illegal rather than legal—contrary to what most commentators assert to be the law.

[26] As a matter of logic, one could hold an intermediate view: When conditions are highly conducive, successful coordination is quite likely, so that use of acts in X cannot be inferred (hence the paradox of proof), but it is not nearly a certainty, so further mergers do entail some probabilistic cost.

[27] See Posner (2001, 151–52): "a market in which prices are already above the competitive

of raising this issue is not to advocate the permissibility of mergers to monopoly but rather to identify another tension in existing understanding of the subject, further indicating a lack of sustained reflection on commonly advanced views.[28]

The legal approach toward successful oligopolistic coordination also has implications for competition law rules that relate even more directly to coordinated oligopoly pricing. By analogy to tougher merger enforcement, many likewise advocate an aggressive approach toward facilitating practices.[29] The same tradeoff is evident: If interdependent pricing cannot be reached directly, it becomes necessary to make more practices illegal—whether per se illegal or subject to stricter scrutiny under a rule of reason (stricter because the competitive danger is presumed to be greater). The problem is that there exists, for example, much exchange of information that generates efficiencies, such as in standard-setting and other trade association activities concerned with technological developments, forecasts of demand, and predictions of costs.[30]

The second point about mergers, relating to further implications of the paradox of proof, can also be applied to price-fixing rules themselves. Specifically, if coordination is indeed essentially automatic in an industry, why not permit an explicit, classic cartel? The social cost in terms of elevated pricing is by assumption little or nothing since prices are high in

---

level, presumably as a result of tacit collusion, should not be allowed to congeal in an anticompetitive mold through the merger of the tacit colluders, which would make it much easier to maintain the supracompetitive price"; and U.S. Horizontal Merger Guidelines (2010, §4.1.2): "If prices are likely to change absent the merger, e.g., because of innovation or entry, the Agencies may use anticipated future prices as the benchmark for the test. If prices might fall absent the merger due to the breakdown of pre-merger coordination, the Agencies may use those lower prices as the benchmark for the test."

[28] Relating merger law to price-fixing law raises additional conundrums, at least under a regime like that in the United States which permits private suits for damages. See note 33 in chapter 5.

[29] See, for example, Baker (1993, 207–19). The subject is addressed briefly, mostly with regard to detection, in section 10.C, and also in section 3.B—both of which contain further references to the literature.

[30] Note further that, as one expands the set of facilitating practices that are made illegal, which can be seen as broadening the set X, the paradox region (e.g., in Figures 2 and 3) shrinks, but, as explained in section 6.C, once the paradox region becomes narrow, it is hard to understand why one would insist on the acts-based prohibition.

any case. Furthermore, as explained in section 8.A, cartels can be more efficient than mere coordinated pricing because cartels are able to realize production efficiencies by reallocating output among their members, providing side payments as compensation. The per se rule against price fixing makes this argument legally irrelevant, but this treatment requires justification. The rationale for the per se rule is that the practice in question is almost never desirable. But the working premise here is that there exists an important class of cases in which successful oligopolistic price elevation is inevitable, and it is also assumed, if the communications-based prohibition is workable, that we can identify this class of cases. After all, under the logic of the paradox of proof, it is supposed that such defendants will be exonerated, and that they can be distinguished from those whose price elevation requires the use of acts in X. Once again, this contrived argument is offered to note the existence of unappreciated (and thus unresolved) inconsistencies in conventional views about competition policy toward coordinated oligopolistic price elevation.

D. Electronic Communications

Advances in communications technology may alter the detection problem. Indeed, changes in recent decades have already changed the landscape.[31] One problem is that new technologies make rapid, highly detailed price signaling easier. Prices, or elaborate price schemes, can be posted, modified, and rescinded at little cost and in ways that few would notice aside from onlooking competitors (thereby avoiding interim sales transactions). In addition to prices themselves, other product attributes, views about future trends (that may be code for pricing invitations and responses), and other information can be posted on web sites. Firm representatives can participate in (possibly facially anonymous) blogs, chat rooms, and the like. And even old-fashioned press conferences can be replaced with or supplemented by webcasts, greetings, and other online messages.

---

[31] Although not drawing the implications considered here, concerns are noted in Baker (1996) and Borenstein (2004). Both authors discuss the *Airline Tariff* case, which in a sense involved a precursor to the Internet. Borenstein suggests that the remedies obtained, involving the prohibition of certain practices, were not effective. For similar findings, see Miller (2010).

If much of this behavior is to be permitted—that is, not included in the set X of prohibited acts—then successful oligopolistic coordination through legally privileged means becomes easier. One implication might be a broader paradox region. On the other hand, if all such behavior is reached, then it is hard to see the limit short of prohibiting all interdependence. It seems difficult to chart a middle course of attempting to delineate a substantial portion of such activity as included in the set X while placing the rest in X′—and perhaps pointless, as long as enough is in the latter. Furthermore, the speed and unpredictability of future developments may cause newly refined rules tied to particular sorts of communication to be obsolete on arrival.

A second problem concerns detection. To the extent that one does not rely much on inferences from circumstantial evidence—raising the paradox of proof, or being disallowed under the alternative approach sketched in section B—and thus depends primarily on obtaining smoking-gun evidence or near equivalents, the task may become more difficult over time. Detailed codes might be communicated through delays of various numbers of milliseconds in price or other web postings. And the use of VOIP (voice over Internet protocol) or other developing technologies may allow direct communications that are nearly impossible to trace; cell phones already pose significant challenges for law enforcement.

The more public methods discussed just before are also relevant. Currently, many attempts at coordination require multiple meetings over time to account for various complications and changing conditions. But with new technology, it may be possible to have very few initial meetings to choose legally permitted (or illegal but extremely difficult to trace) ways to conduct future interchanges. By greatly reducing more detectable forms of contact, the likelihood of discovery could fall substantially.

Not all advances in communications, however, make detection more difficult. As email use has become compulsive for many people, individuals engaged in questionable or illegal activity may leave more traces, ones that advanced search algorithms may be able to locate afterward.[32] For example, in the Microsoft cases in the 1990s, despite presumably sophisticated legal advice, many damaging emails were created—and ultimately

---

[32] See ABA (2010, 128).

discovered—whereas in the past such communications might have been primarily oral.[33]

It is unclear which of these features will become more important in the future. If permitted methods of communication become sufficient or if prohibited communications can readily be routed through undetectable channels, the already serious problem of detection—which evidence noted in section 9.C and subsection 13.A.3 indicates may already result in underdeterrence—could become worse. This concern is especially great if increasingly elaborate legal channels become available, because even finding email trails documenting their use would be to no avail.

Note, in contrast, that direct targeting of successful oligopolistic coordination tends to mitigate these problems. Market-based evidence will continue to be available. Internal evidence may be somewhat harder to come by, but it may still be very useful as long as large numbers of employees (and sometimes consultants or other agents) need to be involved in planning, making, and executing firms' decisions. Indeed, the main force easing detection—the growth of email and other channels that are difficult to erase—may enhance the power of internal evidence in determining whether coordinated oligopoly pricing took place, overcoming efforts by lawyers and others to mask firms' analysis and decision-making. As a result, these technological developments may, as a whole, make a selective communications prohibition even less attractive over time.

E. Comments on Prior Literature

It is surprising that most prior commentary seems to have reached a consensus in favor of a communications-based prohibition without defining it—see part I of the book—or attempting to derive an approach directly from the core concerns about coordinated oligopolistic price elevation— the subject of part II—or systematically comparing it to such a direct approach—as is done in the present part. Indeed, there is very little overlap in content between most prior analysis of how competition policy should

---

[33] See Heilemann (2000), and also ABA (2010, 132–34) and Levy (2007) on the Whole Foods merger.

address coordinated oligopoly pricing and the present treatment. The most notable exception, as mentioned, is Posner's writing from decades ago, whose existence is frequently acknowledged but whose substance is usually ignored. For the most part, commentators rely on three arguments:[34] It is infeasible to command irrational behavior (abstinence from coordinated price elevation); a direct prohibition would be inconsistent with the legality of price elevation by monopolists; and injunctive relief would be tantamount to price regulation. Even in extensive treatments of competition law toward price fixing, these points are usually asserted in a few sentences or at most a couple paragraphs.[35] Although these claims have been addressed previously at various points in the book, it is useful to collect here the primary reasons that these objections are misconceived.

The argument that a prohibition on successful oligopolistic coordination—without a further requirement that particular acts were employed—would entail commanding firms to behave irrationally is addressed in section 13.C. The simple response is deterrence: The threat of sanctions changes what firms find to be in their interest to do (as long as the expected punishment exceeds the profits from oligopolistic price elevation). In this respect, coordinated pricing is little different from unsafe disposal of toxic waste or cheating on taxes, activities that profit-maximizing firms find it in their rational interest to undertake, that is, unless there are substantial penalties.[36]

The second argument is that prohibiting oligopolistic coordination and thus the resulting price elevation is inconsistent with permitting

---

[34] Aside from arguments that competition law should not as a matter of policy punish successful oligopolistic coordination unless certain acts are employed, there is the separate question, addressed in detail in part I, regarding what existing law may require.

[35] See, respectively, the sources cited in note 43 in chapter 13, note 23 in chapter 8, and note 38 just below.

[36] A related objection is that some commentators, at least since Turner (1962, 665–66), seem to be taken by the idea that firms engaging in simple interdependent oligopoly pricing are morally pure because they cannot help but be rational, whereas if they communicate in particular ways, we can then identify evil acts for which we can hold them accountable. See Areeda and Hovenkamp (2003, 227–35). This claim is question-begging. If interdependent oligopolistic pricing can practically be identified and made subject to effective penalties, then it no longer would be the case that interdependent oligopolistic pricing would be either profitable or beyond whatever moral opprobrium accompanies violations of the law.

monopolists to charge supracompetitive prices. Subsection 8.B.2 explains the rationale for differential treatment. Indeed, the justification for permitting firms unilaterally to reap the rewards of dynamically efficient behavior while denying them profits from higher prices attributable merely to their refraining from competition is entirely familiar. Moreover, the logic of this objection, as noted before, applies equally to classic cartels. That is, if oligopolists should be free to raise prices because monopolists are permitted to do so, the logic applies not only to purely interdependent coordination but also to that facilitated by additional means of communication such as meetings in hotel rooms. Of course, none who offer this argument favor making cartels legal.[37]

The third objection is that remedies, with a focus on injunctive relief, would entail all the difficulties associated with price regulation.[38] As just mentioned, this claim is confused because it overlooks deterrence through the prospect of penalties.[39] Also, as explained in section 13.C, it is unclear

---

[37] This argument's suggested equivalence between what behavior should be permitted to groups of firms acting together and to monopolists is even more puzzling because it is a signal feature of competition regimes throughout the world that substantially tougher restrictions are imposed on group activity as distinguished from single-firm conduct. If limitations on group behavior are to be construed as no broader than those applicable to individual firms, the former prohibitions would be redundant. Moreover, given the standard, strong basis for differential treatment, acceptance of this proffered equivalence would foreclose an interpretative approach to competition law that is grounded in economic substance. This implication may help to explain why commentators on price-fixing rules seem attracted to a formalistic approach based on attempts to define agreement in a nonfunctional manner—a subject greatly elaborated in part I (see especially section 3.A's discussion of functional equivalents to forbidden modes of communication).

[38] See Turner (1962, 669), referring to a "purely public-utility interpretation of the Sherman Act"; Areeda and Hovenkamp (2003, 206), noting "the absence of a practical remedy other than judicial price control"; ibid. (232–33), suggesting that the required injunction would be "equivalent to . . . compelling marginal-cost pricing" which "puts the antitrust tribunal directly in the price-control business"; ibid. (273), describing the FTC's view in *du Pont*; Baker (1996, 47): "the only remedy is judicial price regulation—a complete non-starter"; Elhauge and Geradin (2007, 835): "Could courts figure out whether they had done so other than by asking whether the prices were reasonable?"; and Scherer (1977, 984).

[39] Furthermore, as discussed in section A, penalties are also required under a communications-based prohibition, and fines (and/or private damage awards) really should be geared to the magnitude of oligopolists' price elevation, so the need for measuring the excess of defendants' prices over a competitive level is not avoided, only deferred (and limited to cases that happen to involve demonstrable prohibited acts).

that injunctions have an important role to play in attacking successful oligopolistic coordination. Instead, the real question involves the feasibility of detection: If detection is highly imperfect and involves a substantial risk of false positives, socially costly chilling effects will ensue.

Of course, the concern about detection and chilling effects—and related matters of the appropriate burden of proof and the use of varying types of evidence of differing reliability—has consumed much of the attention in this book, beginning with chapter 9, developed throughout part II, and applied to a communications-based prohibition in chapter 17 of this part. Among the highlights are these: Chilling effects indeed constitute one of the two central concerns (along with deterrence) in designing a legal regime addressed to coordinated oligopoly pricing; as a consequence, it is important to consider the full range of types of evidence, employing appropriate mixes in particular cases rather than arbitrarily confining attention to a subset that may or may not be reliable in a given application; and evidentiary standards should depend on the nature of proof (for example, if direct evidence of marginal cost is to be used to demonstrate successful oligopolistic coordination, a significant elevation should probably be demanded and corroborating evidence may be required). Moreover, systematic comparison with commentators' preferred communications-based prohibition is not favorable to it in this regard, which nearly everyone seems to take for granted: Defendants are exonerated in situations in which the social danger is greatest and chilling costs are likely to be low, whereas they may be found liable when the danger is modest and the risk of chilling desirable behavior is high—the reverse of what would be optimal. Additionally, a communications-based prohibition seems more difficult to administer, perhaps substantially so. These matters are not examined in prior treatments of the subject that advance the objection under consideration.

19

Conclusion

A direct approach toward the problem of coordinated oligopolistic price elevation involves articulation of the social benefits and costs, assessment of methods of detection with attention to the deterrence gains and chilling effects of different techniques, and analysis of sanctions. This direct method is superior to commentators' preferred alternative that focuses on the presence of particular means of coordination rather than on the ends to be achieved. Regarding outcomes, the direct approach dominates the more circumscribed one, concentrating liability on situations involving both greater deterrence benefits and lower chilling costs. In addition, it is more administrable because the conventional prohibition necessitates an additional inquiry that is complex and requires empirical knowledge that is largely nonexistent. Finally, a direct, economically based approach is actually more in accord with governing legal provisions, doctrine, and practice than is the favored formalistic formulation.

The greatest gulf between the present study and prior scholarship, however, is not in the conclusions reached but in their contrasting methodologies. Legal academics and economists have almost entirely eschewed analysis and development of a direct approach to the problem of coordinated oligopolistic price elevation, which is at the center of this investigation. This omission means that prior work also fails to undertake a systematic, side-by-side comparison of its favored method of regulation with one directly derived using economic analysis. Additionally, as a matter of legal exegesis, consensus has dulled critical inquiry into the core concepts, actual practice, and the relationship (if any) between endorsed criteria and economic principles. In all, many of the subjects explored in this book are largely absent in prior competition policy literature on price fixing, and others are not probed from many of the relevant angles.

These themes are developed in three parts, the first primarily legal and the latter two economic. Part I examines the notion of horizontal agreement in competition law from a diverse range of perspectives. What emerges is a remarkable consilience under which agreement understood as interdependence is broadly sustainable whereas commentators' attempts to define agreement more narrowly pose fundamental difficulties.

Two opening illustrations—neighboring gasoline stations whose owners may converse or price signal, and price-fixing negotiations that may be conducted in a hotel room or through press conferences—foreshadow what follows and in themselves cast serious doubt on notions of agreement that are narrower than interdependence. In these canonical settings in which the agreement requirement is conventionally understood to provide sharp distinctions between polar opposite cases, further examination reveals that it may fail to provide any plausible distinction at all. Archetypal instances of express agreement readily blur into pure interdependence. This difficulty, in turn, both mirrors and helps us understand why conventional definitions of key terms as well as theories and studies of human language suggest the incoherence of the proposed distinction.

The gist of the problem is that the terms like agreement, conspiracy, and concerted action convey a meeting of the minds or subjective understanding—in the present context on charging elevated prices—which is precisely what is meant by interdependence but is exactly what most commentators reject as the meaning of these terms. Narrower constructions seem to entail a further requirement that some particular means have been used in accomplishing coordinated oligopolistic price elevation. Most often mentioned is the use of communications, but communication is ubiquitous—including, for example, neighboring gasoline stations' iterative price postings, which interchange commentators intend to exclude. A circumscribed view, therefore, must incorporate some further limitation, such as by prohibiting the use of language while permitting signs and symbols. But such a distinction misunderstands language, which is defined as the use of signs and symbols to communicate. This point is driven home by the existence of rich sign languages: Under commentators' formulations, would their use lead to imprisonment (because it is language) or exoneration (because it is mere signs and symbols)? Presumably the former, but if symbolic expression is reached after all, what isn't?

The problem is not merely one of finding the right locution or making subtle distinctions between shades of gray. It is that no robust concept underlies commentators' proffered subdivision of interdependence.

Competition law doctrine reflects this deficiency. Statutes in the United States and European Union use the terms agreement, conspiracy, and concerted practice, which as just mentioned align comfortably with interdependence, not some delimited subset thereof. The term conspiracy in particular has a long-established legal meaning that is consonant with interdependence: U.S. law defines conspiracy to require a meeting of the minds and rejects any demand that understandings be express or otherwise constituted in particular, restrictive ways. For a century after the Sherman Act's passage, Supreme Court opinions almost uniformly embraced this view. In addition, the Section 1 cases most known for articulating a broad interpretation of the agreement requirement, *Interstate Circuit* and *American Tobacco*, are taken to be definitive articulations of the agreement element in conspiracy law more generally. Although two recent cases state differing views, in neither was the meaning of horizontal agreement before the Court. Finally, lower courts, which of late often portray agreement narrowly, at the same time make their decisions using "plus factors" that are tantamount to defining agreement as interdependence, and both jury instructions and damages doctrine seem to embody this broader definition. Neither lawyers' advice to clients nor firms' routine behavior reflects the belief that only something close to an express agreement, approaching the secret negotiations associated with classic cartels, is legally problematic. Thus, a mass of subsidiary legal doctrine and practice in the United States contradicts commentators' narrow view of agreement but is harmonious with agreement encompassing interdependence.

Subsequent analysis develops what is referred to as a paradox of proof, under which a narrow agreement requirement may imply that a greater ease of oligopolistic coordination and thus a higher danger of social harm from price fixing favor exoneration rather than condemnation. The uncontroversial principle of blackletter law, under which conspiracies can be—and due to parties' efforts to maintain secrecy, often must be—inferred from circumstantial evidence, is demonstrated to have remarkably complex and startling implications for the course of adjudication. The empirical basis for the required inferences seems nonexistent, difficult to imagine uncovering, and absent from plaintiffs' or defendants' offers of proof in litigated cases. Furthermore, many commentators believe that successful interdependence without explicit communications is rarely possible in any event, in which case their insistence on a narrow agreement requirement seems inexplicable: It would hardly ever warrant exonerating defendants, by contrast to demanding only interdependence, yet it would complicate litigation and risk false negatives that undermine deterrence, all in the course of seeking to excuse defendants in those few industries in which the social harm from oligopolistic pricing is greatest.

These consistent conclusions from diverse perspectives also align with modern oligopoly theory. Courts and commentators alike broadly endorse grounding competition policy in economic understandings rather than formalistic maxims. Therefore, we should expect any sensible limitation incorporated in the agreement requirement to align with some central, substantive distinction in the pertinent economic analysis. Yet the modern theory of repeated games, which forms the core of contemporary oligopoly theory regarding coordinated behavior, does not distinguish at all between express agreements and pure interdependence: There is no concept in the relevant theory that might support the distinction at the heart of conventional views. The notion closest to agreement is an equilibrium involving coordinated supracompetitive pricing, but that corresponds to successful interdependence, nothing more.

As is generally true with triangulation, the whole is greater than the sum of its parts. Although qualifications are noted at many points in the analysis and some readers may find particular arguments less convincing, it is difficult to see how all of the divergent inquiries could be largely negated, much less in a fashion that directed one to a common conclusion supporting the conventional, narrow view of agreement. The economic analysis is perhaps most damaging to such an endeavor because it goes to the purpose of the prohibition. Also telling is courts' and commentators' inability to delineate the category of acts they deem to constitute agreements with any precision, whether through canonical statements or a collection of examples that might provide an operational definition. Their inarticulateness is best explained by the absence of any relevant concept to be elaborated.

Even though virtually every consideration indicates that agreement and cognate terms can be understood only as interdependence, the design of optimal policy is dictated not by definitions but rather by direct assessment of the consequences of different regulatory approaches. Part I does, however, have important implications in this regard. First and most directly, its legal analysis should free both legal scholars and economists to explore, openly and on the merits, the challenge of optimally controlling coordinated oligopolistic price elevation. Second, many of the results cast strong prima facie doubt on the consensus view that holds we should heavily punish all horizontal price-fixing agreements but exonerate all so-called nonagreements that have the same consequences. Under it, everything turns on what the term agreement is taken to mean, but the proposed line of demarcation is demonstrated to be incoherent, an inauspicious indicator of its usefulness for competition policy. In any event, it is implausible that contorting some word is likely to be a fruitful fulcrum for substantive analysis. It is useful to recall that Turner's (1962) seminal paper endorsed the equation of agreement with interdependence as a matter of statutory language even while rejecting it as a matter of policy. Although his orientation toward terminology versus substance is correct, his policy analysis is highly incomplete and largely unsound as far as it went, as first suggested by Posner (1969) and developed throughout the remainder of this book.

Part II is devoted to the constructive task. Determination of an optimal regime to combat coordinated oligopolistic price elevation requires attention to the social objective, the problem of detection, and the specification of sanctions. The purpose of the regime is to deter such price elevation, both because of the direct, static costs of supracompetitive prices and because of dynamic effects, notably, inducing excessive entry in homogeneous goods industries, which is where substantial coordinated price elevation is most likely to be found. Because of difficulties with detection, achieving effective deterrence is not easy, and empirical evidence suggests that deterrence may well be inadequate even in the United States, which is regarded to have the toughest enforcement in the world in terms of both overall effort and the magnitude of penalties.

The appropriate framework needs to be attentive not only to errors of omission—false negatives, where violators are not sanctioned—but also to mistakes of commission—false positives, where innocent firms are sanctioned. This tradeoff is considered explicitly, with special attention to the nature of chilling costs, that is, the undesirable ex ante effects on behavior attributable to the prospect of false positives. Because the likely magnitude of such costs varies by industry and the type of proof, this consideration has important qualitative implications for system design.

Successful oligopolistic coordination may be detected through a number of methods, ideally considered in combination. Its presence or absence may be demonstrated by market-based evidence, notably pricing patterns and indications of price elevation, and by the use of facilitating practices. The degree to which industry conditions are conducive to coordination is also highly relevant. Conduciveness is largely a necessary condition but not a sufficient one—because of the possibility that deterrence is effective, among other reasons. Explicit interfirm communications, the emphasis of much prior analysis of the subject, can be highly probative, but demonstration of their presence is unnecessary as a logical matter and proof may be unavailable even when they are present. All bases for assessment may be established, reinforced, or negated by evidence internal to firms, including many sorts that do not speak directly to coordination.

Because detection is the central challenge in addressing coordinated oligopolistic price elevation, this subject receives the most attention, with a particular focus on the reliability of various types of proof and their risks of chilling effects. For example, due to the danger of underestimating marginal cost, establishing price elevation through a comparison of price to marginal cost is more precarious than are some other methods; hence, when employing this technique, it may be appropriate to require stronger evidence or proof of a greater magnitude of price elevation, as well as corroborating evidence. Another factor examined extensively is the possibility that price elevation in an oligopolistic industry is due to firms' exercise of unilateral market power. Coordinated elevation is most likely in homogeneous goods industries, so this case is particularly relevant. In this setting, it is not clear that significant unilateral market power simultaneously exercised by multiple firms is frequent, and it may be possible to identify when its exercise is plausible. Moreover, the potential chilling costs from misclassification may not be that great—and may even be negative (that is, benefits) because moderating unilateral market power can be desirable in such industries.

The analysis of sanctions focuses on fines and private damage awards because monetary penalties are heavily used throughout the world and they tend to be the most efficient tool to the extent feasible—subject, notably, to the limit of firms' assets. As in most areas of law enforcement,

sanctions should reflect harm. Large price elevations, which are disproportionately harmful, need to be adequately deterred, which requires high
sanctions because firms' profits are great. Cases that appear to exhibit
small price elevations are both less harmful and also more likely to involve
false positives and thus generate chilling costs, so moderating expected
sanctions is sensible. Government fines in the European Union and the
United States do not reflect either prescription very well, although private
damages do. Furthermore, because the detection rate is low, multipliers
need to be large, raising the possibility that the optimal magnitude of
sanctions may be higher than present levels.

Imprisonment, used increasingly and chiefly in the United States,
provides a helpful supplement in achieving deterrence due to the possible
inadequacy of fines and damages. Furthermore, because of agency problems in firms, sanctions, including imprisonment, applied to individual
violators may be valuable. Injunctions do not seem to be widely used and
are not important in principle because they fail to generate deterrence
and must be enforced through other sanctions in any event.

The foregoing analysis bears little resemblance to that in the competition policy literature on price fixing. Most commentators—legal analysts
and economists, in the European Union and the United States—believe
that current law is best described as, and should be, a communications-
based prohibition, interpreting notions of agreement, conspiracy, and
concerted action so as to limit liability to cases in which the use of particular, explicit forms of communication have been employed. Part I
demonstrates serious deficiencies in this view from a legal perspective
and exposes internal incoherence. Part III, in contrast, focuses on whether
the conventional policy prescription makes any sense with regard to its
effects on social welfare.

To begin, one might wonder why this third part of the book is necessary. Part II's systematic examination of the social objective, the problem
of detection, and the matter of appropriate sanctions does not generate
anything like the commonly favored rule. As a consequence, we already
know that it is not optimal. Nevertheless, because the more circumscribed
proscription has been the near-exclusive focus of attention, there is value
in undertaking a systematic comparison.

The defining feature of the communications-based prohibition is that
it considers only a subset of means to a socially undesirable end rather

than focusing on the end itself or on other matters of direct concern, notably, chilling effects. Its main defects can be traced to this core trait. When one focuses on the wrong question, one is unlikely to obtain a good answer, much less the best one—and this is so even when the correct answer is difficult to ascertain due to limited empirical knowledge and the complexity of the task. The communications-based prohibition is defined in a formalistic manner that is significantly removed from the statement of the social objective and the basic framework for optimal rule formulation. Furthermore, this formalistic character is inherent, for under a functional analysis it would dissolve into the direct approach, which proponents of the narrower prohibition reject.

The means-based aspect of the limitation has crucial implications regarding the central challenge of detection. We can set aside cases with sharp, smoking-gun evidence (tapes of secret meetings that detail firms' behavior), for both the direct approach and the circumscribed one would readily assign liability. The differences lie in all those cases in which circumstantial evidence must be employed, a domain widely regarded to be large in the present context because firms naturally attempt to hide their actions and empirical evidence suggests that they often succeed in doing so. In this realm, one needs to assess the presence of successful coordinated oligopolistic pricing under both formulations, but under the communications-based prohibition one also must ascertain whether such was accomplished through the use of forbidden means of interaction or only using those deemed to be legal. The actual methods that firms used, moreover, are not directly observable in such cases.

This latter, supplemental inquiry is complicated. Worse, its focus is counterproductive: A large body of relevant evidence is used indirectly, even when it is highly probative of the ultimate social question, and another portion of evidence (on conduciveness of conditions) arguably bears on liability in a manner opposite to what is indicated by its implications for social welfare. Hence, even before undertaking a detailed inquiry, the standard view appears dubious.

Building on part I's exposition, it is explained how the paradox of proof has startling implications for social welfare that are not well appreciated. Under standard views of how inferences should be made, it turns out that the communications-based prohibition is relatively more likely to find liability when deterrence benefits are low and chilling costs are high, while it exonerates defendants when deterrence benefits are greatest and chilling costs are low. Accordingly, it is not even a sensible proxy criterion for determining when sanctions should be applied. Indeed, one can establish a dominance relationship between the two approaches. Suppose that, under part II's direct approach, one calibrates the burden of proof to provide a rate of applicability to potential cases equal to that prevailing under a communications-based prohibition. Then, the former finds liability in cases characterized by both larger deterrence benefits and smaller chilling costs than under the latter. Also, as mentioned, the direct approach is more administrable because it renders unnecessary the additional, troublesome inquiry into the means of coordination.

Another perspective on the contrast between the two approaches is provided by focusing on the most plausible welfare-based motivation for a narrow prohibition: the problem of chilling effects that may result from false positives. If that concern is weighty, the natural implication is that the burden of proof should be elevated, as part II's analysis of the direct approach develops at length. One would concentrate cutbacks on less reliable types of evidence and on settings in which forgone deterrence benefits are low whereas risks from chilling desirable behavior are high. The communications-based prohibition instead imposes a supplemental requirement without regard to the quality of available evidence and tends to exonerate defendants in precisely those cases in which deterrence benefits are greatest and chilling costs lowest. In substituting a formalistic exercise for explicit, welfare-based analysis, conventional thinking has gone seriously awry. A direct approach to the problem of coordinated oligopolistic price elevation, wherever it may lead, is markedly superior.

In spite of the book's extensive investigation, which generates a number of strong claims and criticisms, any policy lessons must be viewed as quite tentative. First, there has been little prior elaboration of the social objective, including the development of chilling costs and the framework for trading off errors; rather incomplete assessment of the many avenues of detection, with almost no attention devoted to certain forms of evidence, how chilling costs vary across modes of proof, or the relevance of unilateral market power; and only limited consideration of the choice among types of sanctions and the determination of their magnitude. When so much of the territory has not previously been explored in depth, any initial survey will inevitably be incomplete, so the resulting map should be viewed as suggestive, a guide for further research.

Second, the questions of how aggressive enforcement should be and which strategies are most effective have substantial empirical dimensions, many of which have received little scrutiny. Although relevant evidence is examined here, on key dimensions quite little is known. In part, this neglect is due to the difficulty of the task, but it also reflects past failure to frame the policy problem properly.

Third, the interplay with enforcement institutions requires further study. A rule's desirability depends on the accuracy and cost of its application, which in turn depends on the administrative apparatus that is employed. For example, the optimal legal rule for a system with exclusive government enforcement using an expert agency may diverge from that for a regime that allows private suits adjudicated by generalist judges and lay juries. Conversely, the optimal design of competition law institutions depends on what sorts of rules need to be implemented.

Granting these significant reservations, wholesale rethinking is nevertheless in order. Existing formulations of the legal prohibition are substantially incoherent, conflict with much doctrine and practice, and have implications that differ greatly from what many advancing them seem to contemplate. More relevant for policy formulation, this book's systematic, ground-up analysis of the social problem differs from most prior work even in basic subject matter coverage. And the bottom lines differ as well: Comparison of the direct approach to the commonly supported communications-based prohibition shows the latter to have much backward.

This work constitutes a strong critique of existing modes of thought even though it does not advocate a particular prescription for the reasons just mentioned. It attempts to construct a sound framework for analysis and to contribute to our understanding on many subsidiary questions. It also highlights areas where further empirical research could valuably illuminate the subject and thus better guide future competition policy in this realm.

As a final note, it should be mentioned that the criticism offered here is not primarily directed at courts—and is only secondarily aimed at enforcement agencies—even though the analysis suggests that their current approaches are misguided. It is principally the responsibility of academics and other analysts to assess policy, at which point it is their role and that of government agencies and advocates to bring the teachings to bear in implementation. Accordingly, the present project seeks to rekindle and advance a long-dormant policy debate on perhaps the most important subject of competition regulation.

References

ABA (American Bar Association) Section of Antitrust Law. 1996. *Proving Antitrust Damages: Legal and Economic Issues.* Chicago, IL: American Bar Association.

———. 1999. *Sentencing Guidelines in Antitrust: A Practitioner's Handbook.* Chicago, IL: American Bar Association.

———. 2005a. *Antitrust Compliance: Perspectives and Resources for Corporate Counselors.* Chicago, IL: American Bar Association.

———. 2005b. *Model Jury Instructions in Civil Antitrust Actions.* 2005 ed. Chicago, IL: American Bar Association.

———. 2007. *Antitrust Law Developments.* 6th ed. Chicago, IL: American Bar Association.

———. 2010. *Antitrust Compliance: Perspectives and Resources for Corporate Counselors.* 2nd ed. Chicago, IL: American Bar Association.

Abrantes-Metz, Rosa M., and Patrick Bajari. 2009. Screens for Conspiracies and Their Multiple Applications. 24 (Fall) *Antitrust* 66–77.

Abrantes-Metz, Rosa M., and Luke M. Froeb. 2008. Competition Agencies Are Screening for Conspiracies: What Are They Likely to Find? Section of Antitrust Law, 8 (Spring) *Economics Committee Newsletter* 10–16.

Abrantes-Metz, Rosa M., Luke M. Froeb, John Geweke, and Christopher T. Taylor. 2006. A Variance Screen for Collusion. 24 *International Journal of Industrial Organization* 467–86.

Albæk, Svend, Peter Møllgaard, and Per B. Overgaard. 1997. Government-Assisted Oligopoly Coordination? A *Concrete* Case. 45 *Journal of Industrial Economics* 429–43.

Albors-Llorens, Albertina. 2004. Collective Dominance in EC Competition Law: Trojan Horse or Useful Tool? 5 *Cambridge Yearbook of European Legal Studies* 151–72.

Allain, Marie-Laure, Marcel Boyer, Rachidi Kotchoni, and Jean-Pierre Ponssard. 2011. The Determination of Optimal Fines in Cartel Cases: The Myth of Underdeterrence. CIRANO Working Papers 2011s-34.

Andersson, Ola, and Erik Wengström. 2007. Do Antitrust Laws Facilitate Collusion? Experimental Evidence on Costly Communication in Duopolies. 109 *Scandinavian Journal of Economics* 321–39.

Areeda, Phillip E., and Herbert Hovenkamp. 2003. *Antitrust Law*, vol. 6. 2nd ed. New York: Aspen.

———. 2009. *Antitrust Law*, supp. New York: Aspen.

Areeda, Phillip E., Herbert Hovenkamp, and Roger D. Blair. 2000. *Antitrust Law*, vol. 2. 2nd ed. New York: Aspen.

Areeda, Phillip E., Herbert Hovenkamp, Roger D. Blair, and Christine Piette Durrance. 2007. *Antitrust Law*, vol. 2A. 3rd ed. New York: Wolters Kluwer.

Areeda, Phillip E., Herbert Hovenkamp, and John L. Solow. 2007. *Antitrust Law*, vol. 2B. 3rd ed. New York: Wolters Kluwer.

Areeda, Phillip E., and Louis Kaplow. 1988. *Antitrust Analysis*. 4th ed., and Teacher's Manual. Boston, MA: Little, Brown.

Areeda, Phillip E., Louis Kaplow, and Aaron Edlin. 2004. *Antitrust Analysis*. 6th ed. New York: Aspen.

Arthur, Thomas C. 1986. Farewell to the Sea of Doubt: Jettisoning the Constitutional Sherman Act. 74 *California Law Review* 263–376.

Asch, Peter, and J. J. Seneca. 1976. Is Collusion Profitable? 58 *Review of Economics and Statistics* 1–12.

Ashenfelter, Orley, David Ashmore, Jonathan Baker, Suzanne Gleason, and Daniel Hosken. 2006. Empirical Methods in Merger Analysis: Econometric Analysis of Pricing in *FTC v. Staples*. 13 *International Journal of the Economics of Business* 265–79.

Athey, Susan, and Kyle Bagwell. 2001. Optimal Collusion with Private Information. 32 *Rand Journal of Economics* 428–65.

Aubert, Cécile, Patrick Rey, and William E. Kovacic. 2006. The Impact of Leniency and Whistle-Blowing Programs on Cartels. 24 *International Journal of Industrial Organization* 1241–66.

Aumann, Robert J. 1987. Correlated Equilibrium as an Expression of Bayesian Rationality. 55 *Econometrica* 1–18.

———. 1990. Nash Equilibria Are Not Self-Enforcing. In *Economic Decision-Making: Games, Econometrics and Optimisation*, edited by Jean J. Gabszewicz, Jean-Francois Richard, and Laurence A. Wolsey, pp. 201–6. Amsterdam: Elsevier Science.

Bagwell, Kyle, and Asher Wolinsky. 2002. Game Theory and Industrial Organization. In *Handbook of Game Theory with Economic Applications*, edited by Robert J. Aumann and Sergiu Hart, vol. 3:1851–95. Amsterdam: North-Holland.

Bajari, Patrick, and Lixin Ye. 2003. Deciding between Competition and Collusion. 85 *Review of Economics and Statistics* 971–89.

Baker, Jonathan B. 1988. Private Information and the Deterrent Effect of Antitrust Damage Remedies. 4 *Journal of Law, Economics & Organization* 385–408.

———. 1989. Identifying Cartel Policing under Uncertainty: The U.S. Steel Industry, 1933–1939. 32 *Journal of Law & Economics* S47–76.

———. 1993. Two Sherman Act Section 1 Dilemmas: Parallel Pricing, the Oligopoly Problem, and Contemporary Economic Theory. 38 *Antitrust Bulletin* 143–219.

———. 1994. Predatory Pricing after *Brooke Group*: An Economic Perspective. 62 *Antitrust Law Journal* 585–603.

———. 1996. Identifying Horizontal Price Fixing in the Electronic Marketplace. 65 *Antitrust Law Journal* 41–55.

———. 2007. Market Definition: An Analytical Overview. 74 *Antitrust Law Journal* 129–73.

Baker, Jonathan B., and Timothy F. Bresnahan. 1985. The Gains from Merger or Collusion in Product-Differentiated Industries. 33 *Journal of Industrial Economics* 427–44.

———. 1988. Estimating the Residual Demand Curve Facing a Single Firm. 6 *International Journal of Industrial Organization* 283–300.

———. 1992. Empirical Methods of Identifying and Measuring Market Power. 61 *Antitrust Law Journal* 3–16.

———. 2008. Economic Evidence in Antitrust: Defining Markets and Measuring Market Power. In *Handbook of Antitrust Economics*, edited by Paolo Buccirossi, pp. 1–42. Cambridge, MA: MIT Press.

Balmaceda, Felipe, and Paula Soruco. 2008. Asymmetric Dynamic Pricing in a Local Gasoline Retail Market. 56 *Journal of Industrial Economics* 629–53.

Baxter, William F. 1982. Separation of Powers, Prosecutorial Discretion, and the "Common Law" Nature of Antitrust Law. 60 *Texas Law Review* 661–703.

Becker, Gary S., and George J. Stigler. 1974. Law Enforcement, Malfeasance, and Compensation of Enforcers. 3 *Journal of Legal Studies* 1–18.

Bellamy, Christopher, and Graham Child. 2008. *European Community Law of Competition*, edited by Peter Roth and Vivien Rose. 6th ed. New York: Oxford University Press.

Benassy, Jean-Pascal. 1989. Market Size and Substitutability in Imperfect Competition: A Bertrand-Edgeworth-Chamberlin Model. 56 *Review of Economic Studies* 217–34.

Benham, Lee. 1972. The Effect of Advertising on the Price of Eyeglasses. 15 *Journal of Law & Economics* 337–52.

Bernheim, B. Douglas. 1984. Rationalizable Strategic Behavior. 52 *Econometrica* 1007–28.

Bernheim, B. Douglas, and Michael D. Whinston. 1990. Multimarket Contact and Collusive Behavior. 21 *Rand Journal of Economics* 1–26.

Bertrand, Joseph. 1883. Review of *Théorie Mathématiques de la Richesse Sociale* and of *Recherches sur les Principes Mathématiques de la Théorie des Richesses*. 67 *Journal des Savants* 499–508.

Besanko, David, David Dranove, Mark Shanley, and Scott Schaefer. 2007. *Economics of Strategy*. 4th ed. Hoboken, NJ: John Wiley.

Besanko, David, and Daniel F. Spulber. 1990. Are Treble Damages Neutral? Sequential Equilibrium and Private Antitrust Enforcement. 80 *American Economic Review* 870–87.

Bickerton, Derek. 1990. *Language and Species*. Chicago, IL: University of Chicago Press.

Bishop, William. 1983. Oligopoly Pricing: A Proposal. 28 *Antitrust Bulletin* 311–36.

Black, Oliver. 2005. Communication, Concerted Practices, and the Oligopoly Problem. 1 *European Competition Journal* 341–46.

Black's Law Dictionary. 2009. Edited by Bryan A. Garner. 9th ed. St. Paul, MN: West.

Blair, Roger D. 2008. Introduction to Symposium: The Economics of the Roberts Court. 53 *Antitrust Bulletin* 1–4.

Blair, Roger D., and Richard E. Romano. 1990. Distinguishing Participants from Non-participants in a Price-Fixing Conspiracy: Liability and Damages. 28 (Spring) *American Business Law Journal* 33–57.

Block, Michael Kent, Frederick Carl Nold, and Joseph Gregory Sidak. 1981. The Deterrent Effect of Antitrust Enforcement. 89 *Journal of Political Economy* 429–45.

Bonvillain, Nancy. 2003. *Language, Culture, and Communication: The Meaning of Messages.* 4th ed. Upper Saddle River, NJ: Prentice Hall.

Borenstein, Severin. 2004. Rapid Price Communication and Coordination: The Airline Tariff Publishing Case (1994). In *The Antitrust Revolution*, edited by John E. Kwoka, Jr. and Lawrence J. White, pp. 233–51. 4th ed. New York: Oxford University Press.

Borenstein, Severin, and Nancy L. Rose. 1994. Competition and Price Dispersion in the U.S. Airline Industry. 102 *Journal of Political Economy* 653–83.

Bork, Robert H. 1978. *The Antitrust Paradox: A Policy at War with Itself.* New York: Basic Books.

Breit, William, and Kenneth G. Elzinga. 1974. Antitrust Enforcement and Economic Efficiency: The Uneasy Case for Treble Damages. 17 *Journal of Law & Economics* 329–56.

Bresnahan, Timothy F. 1982. The Oligopoly Solution Concept Is Identified. 10 *Economics Letters* 87–92.

———. 1987. Competition and Collusion in the American Automobile Industry: The 1955 Price War. 35 *Journal of Industrial Economics* 457–82.

———. 1989. Empirical Studies of Industries with Market Power. In *Handbook of Industrial Organization*, edited by Richard Schmalensee and Robert D. Willig, vol. 2:1011–57. Amsterdam: North-Holland.

———. 1997. Testing and Measurement in Competition Models. In *Advances in Economics and Econometrics: Theory and Applications*, Seventh World Congress, edited by David M. Kreps and Kenneth F. Wallis, vol. 3:61–81. Cambridge: Cambridge University Press.

Brock, James W. 2006. Antitrust Policy and the Oligopoly Problem. 51 *Antitrust Bulletin* 227–80.

Brock, William A., and José A. Scheinkman. 1985. Price Setting Supergames with Capacity Constraints. 52 *Review of Economic Studies* 371–82.

Bryant, Peter G., and E. Woodrow Eckard. 1991. Price Fixing: The Probability of Getting Caught. 73 *Review of Economics and Statistics* 531–36.

Buccirossi, Paolo. 2008. Facilitating Practices. In *Handbook of Antitrust Economics*, edited by Paolo Buccirossi, pp. 305–51. Cambridge, MA: MIT Press.

Burdett, Kenneth, and Kenneth L. Judd. 1983. Equilibrium Price Dispersion. 51 *Econometrica* 955–69.

Byford, Martin C., and Joshua S. Gans. 2010. Collusion at the Extensive Margin. Unpublished manuscript, September.

Carlton, Dennis W. 1986. The Rigidity of Prices. 76 *American Economic Review* 637–58.

Carlton, Dennis W., Robert H. Gertner, and Andrew M. Rosenfield. 1997. Communication among Competitors: Game Theory and Antitrust. 5 *George Mason Law Review* 423–40.

Chamberlin, Edward. 1929. Duopoly: Value Where Sellers Are Few. 44 *Quarterly Journal of Economics* 63–100.

———. 1933. *The Theory of Monopolistic Competition.* Cambridge, MA: Harvard University Press.

Clarke, Julian L., and Simon J. Evenett. 2003. The Deterrent Effects of National Anticartel Laws: Evidence from the International Vitamins Cartel. 48 *Antitrust Bulletin* 689–726.

Clarke, Richard N. 1983. Collusion and the Incentives for Information Sharing. 14 *Bell Journal of Economics* 383–94.

Cohen, Mark A., and David T. Scheffman. 1989. The Antitrust Sentencing Guideline: Is the Punishment Worth the Costs? 27 *American Criminal Law Review* 331–66.

Comanor, William S., and Mark A. Schankerman. 1976. Identical Bids and Cartel Behavior. 7 *Bell Journal of Economics* 281–86.

Combe, Emmanuel, and Constance Monnier. 2011. Fines Against Hard Core Cartels in Europe: The Myth of Overenforcement. 56 *Antitrust Bulletin* 235–75.

Combe, Emmanuel, Constance Monnier, and Renaud Legal. 2008. Cartels: The Probability of Getting Caught in the European Union. Bruges European Economic Research Papers No. 12. College of Europe.

Connor, John M. 2004. Global Cartels Redux: The Amino Acid Lysine Antitrust Litigation (1996). In *The Antitrust Revolution: Economics, Competition, and Policy*, edited by John E. Kwoka, Jr. and Lawrence J. White, pp. 252–76. 4th ed. New York: Oxford University Press.

———. 2005. Collusion and Price Dispersion. 12 *Applied Economics Letters* 335–38.

———. 2007a. *Global Price Fixing.* 2nd updated and revised ed. Berlin: Springer.

———. 2007b. Price-Fixing Overcharges: Legal and Economic Evidence. 22 *Research in Law & Economics* 59–153.

———. 2008. The United States Department of Justice Antitrust Division's Cartel Enforcement: Appraisal and Proposals. American Antitrust Institute Working Paper 08-02. Washington, DC.

Connor, John M., and Robert H. Lande. 2005. How High Do Cartels Raise Prices? Implications for Optimal Cartel Fines. 80 *Tulane Law Review* 513–70.

Cook, Paul W., Jr. 1963. Fact and Fancy on Identical Bids. 41 (January–February) *Harvard Business Review* 67–72.

Cooper, Russell, Douglas V. DeJong, Robert Forsythe, and Thomas W. Ross. 1989. Communication in the Battle of the Sexes Game: Some Experimental Results. 20 *Rand Journal of Economics* 568–87.

———. 1992. Communication in Coordination Games. 107 *Quarterly Journal of Economics* 739–71.

Cooper, Thomas E. 1986. Most-Favored-Customer Pricing and Tacit Collusion. 17 *Rand Journal of Economics* 377–88.

Corballis, Michael C. 2003. From Hand to Mouth: The Gestural Origins of Language. In

Language Evolution, edited by Morten H. Christiansen and Simon Kirby, pp. 201–18. Oxford: Oxford University Press.

Corts, Kenneth S. 1999. Conduct Parameters and the Measurement of Market Power. 88 *Journal of Econometrics* 227–50.

Cournot, Augustin. 1838. *Recherches sur les Principes Mathématiques de la Théorie des Richesses*. Paris: L. Hachette.

Cousens, Theodore W. 1937. Agreement as an Element in Conspiracy. 23 *Virginia Law Review* 898–912.

Crandall, Robert W., and Clifford Winston. 2003. Does Antitrust Policy Improve Consumer Welfare? Assessing the Evidence. 17 (Autumn) *Journal of Economic Perspectives* 3–26.

Crawford, Vincent. 1998. A Survey of Experiments on Communication via Cheap Talk. 78 *Journal of Economic Theory* 286–98.

Crawford, Vincent, Uri Gneezy, and Yuval Rottenstreich. 2008. The Power of Focal Points Is Limited: Even Minute Payoff Asymmetry May Yield Large Coordination Failures. 98 *American Economic Review* 1443–58.

Cyrenne, Philippe. 1999. On Antitrust Enforcement and the Deterrence of Collusive Behavior. 14 *Review of Industrial Organization* 257–72.

Dabbah, Maher M. 2004. *EC and UK Competition Law*. New York: Cambridge University Press.

DaimlerChrysler Corporation, Office of the General Counsel. 2005. Corporate Guide for Antitrust Compliance. In ABA Section of Antitrust Law, *Antitrust Compliance*, Manual 2. Chicago, IL: American Bar Association.

Dana, James D., Jr. 1999. Equilibrium Price Dispersion under Demand Uncertainty: The Roles of Costly Capacity and Market Structure. 30 *Rand Journal of Economics* 632–60.

Dasgupta, Partha, and Eric Maskin. 1986. The Existence of Equilibrium in Discontinuous Economic Games, II: Applications. 53 *Review of Economic Studies* 27–41.

Davidson, Carl, and Raymond Deneckere. 1986. Long-run Competition in Capacity, Short-run Competition in Price, and the Cournot Model. 17 *Rand Journal of Economics* 404–15.

Davis, Douglas D., and Bart J. Wilson. 2002. Experimental Methods and Antitrust Policy. In *Experiments Investigating Market Power*, edited by Charles A. Holt and R. Mark Isaac, pp. 61–94. Amsterdam: Elsevier Science.

Demsetz, Harold. 1973. Industry Structure, Market Rivalry, and Public Policy. 16 *Journal of Law & Economics* 1–9.

Deneckere, Raymond. 1983. Duopoly Supergames with Product Differentiation. 11 *Economics Letters* 37–42.

DeSanti, Susan S., and Ernest A. Nagata. 1994. Competitor Communications: Facilitating Practices or Invitations to Collude? An Application of Theories to Proposed Horizontal Agreements Submitted for Antitrust Review. 63 *Antitrust Law Journal* 93–131.

Dixit, Avinash K., and Joseph E. Stiglitz. 1977. Monopolistic Competition and Optimum Product Diversity. 67 *American Economic Review* 297–308.

Dranove, David, and Sonia Marciano. 2005. *Kellogg on Strategy: Concepts, Tools, and Frameworks for Practitioners.* Hoboken, NJ: John Wiley.

Easterbrook, Frank H. 1984. The Limits of Antitrust. 63 *Texas Law Review* 1–40.

Easterbrook, Frank H., William M. Landes, and Richard A. Posner. 1980. Contribution among Antitrust Defendants: A Legal and Economic Analysis. 23 *Journal of Law & Economics* 331–70.

Eden, Benjamin. 1990. Marginal Cost Pricing When Spot Markets Are Complete. 98 *Journal of Political Economy* 1293–1306.

Edgeworth, Francis Y. 1925. The Pure Theory of Monopoly. In Francis Y. Edgeworth, *Papers Relating to Political Economy*, vol. 1:111–42. London: Macmillan.

Edlin, Aaron S. 1997. Do Guaranteed-Low-Price Policies Guarantee High Prices, and Can Antitrust Rise to the Challenge? 111 *Harvard Law Review* 528–75.

Edlin, Aaron S., and Eric R. Emch. 1999. The Welfare Losses from Price Matching Policies. 47 *Journal of Industrial Economics* 145–67.

Elhauge, Einer, and Damien Geradin. 2007. *Global Antitrust Law and Economics.* New York: Foundation Press.

Elzinga, Kenneth G. 1984. New Developments on the Cartel Front. 29 *Antitrust Bulletin* 3–26.

Epstein, Roy J., and Daniel L. Rubinfeld. 2001. Merger Simulation: A Simplified Approach with New Applications. 69 *Antitrust Law Journal* 883–919.

———. 2004. Merger Simulation with Brand-level Margin Data: Extending PCAIDS with Nests. 4 *B.E. Journal of Economic Analysis & Policy: Advances,* article 2.

European Commission. 2004. Guidelines on the Assessment of Horizontal Mergers under the Council Regulation on the Control of Concentrations between Undertakings. Official Journal C 31/03.

———. 2005. DG Competition Discussion Paper on the Application of Article 82 of the Treaty to Exclusionary Abuses. DG Competition, Brussels.

———. 2006. Guidelines on the Method of Setting Fines Imposed Pursuant to Article 23(2)(a) of Regulation No 1/2003. Official Journal C 210.

———. 2008. White Paper on Damages Actions for Breach of the EC Antitrust Rules. Brussels: Commission of the European Communities.

Evans, William N., Luke M. Froeb, and Gregory J. Werden. 1993. Endogeneity in the Concentration–Price Relationship: Causes, Consequences, and Cures. 41 *Journal of Industrial Economics* 431–38.

Farber, Daniel A., and Brett H. McDonnell. 2005. "Is There a Text in This Class?" The Conflict between Textualism and Antitrust. 14 *Journal of Contemporary Legal Issues* 619–68.

Farrell, Joseph, and Matthew Rabin. 1996. Cheap Talk. 10 (Summer) *Journal of Economic Perspectives* 103–18.

Farrell, Joseph, and Carl Shapiro. 2010. Antitrust Evaluation of Horizontal Mergers: An Economic Alternative to Market Definition. 10 (no. 1) *B.E. Journal of Theoretical Economics: Policies and Perspectives,* article 9.

Federal Trade Commission, Office of General Counsel. 2008. A Brief Overview of the

Federal Trade Commission's Investigative and Law Enforcement Authority. Washington, DC: Federal Trade Commission.

Fershtman, Chaim, and Ariel Pakes. 2000. A Dynamic Oligopoly with Collusion and Price Wars. 31 *Rand Journal of Economics* 207–36.

Fischer, Susan D., and Patricia Siple. 1990. Introduction. In Susan D. Fischer and Patricia Siple, *Theoretical Issues in Sign Language Research*, vol. 1, *Linguistics*, pp. 1–6. Chicago, IL: University of Chicago Press.

Fisher, Franklin M. 1985. The Social Costs of Monopoly and Regulation: Posner Reconsidered. 93 *Journal of Political Economy* 410–16.

———. 1987. On the Misuse of the Profits-Sales Ratio to Infer Monopoly Power. 18 *Rand Journal of Economics* 384–96.

Fisher, Franklin M., and John J. McGowan. 1983. On the Misuse of Accounting Rates of Return to Infer Monopoly Profits. 73 *American Economic Review* 82–97.

Fisher, Simon E., and Gary F. Marcus. 2006. The Eloquent Ape: Genes, Brains and the Evolution of Language. 7 *Nature Reviews: Genetics* 9–20.

Fonseca, Miguel A., and Hans-Theo Normann. 2012. Explicit vs. Tacit Collusion—The Impact of Communication in Oligopoly Experiments. Unpublished manuscript, January.

Forchheimer, Karl. 1908. Theoretisches zum Unvollständigen Monopole. 32 *Jahrbuch für Gesetzgebung, Verwaltung und Volkswirtschaft im Deutschen Reich* (Gustav Schmoller, ed.) 1–12.

Fraas, Arthur G., and Douglas F. Greer. 1977. Market Structure and Price Collusion: An Empirical Analysis. 26 *Journal of Industrial Economics* 21–44.

Friedman, James W. 1971. A Non-cooperative Equilibrium for Supergames. 38 *Review of Economic Studies* 1–12.

———. 1986. *Game Theory with Applications to Economics*. New York: Oxford University Press.

———. 1988. On the Strategic Importance of Prices versus Quantities. 19 *Rand Journal of Economics* 607–22.

Fudenberg, Drew, and Jean Tirole. 1991. *Game Theory*. Cambridge, MA: MIT Press.

Fullerton, Larry. 2011. FTC Challenges to "Invitations to Collude." 25 (Spring) *Antitrust* 30–35.

Gaggero, Alberto A., and Claudio A. Piga. 2009. Airline Market Power and Intertemporal Price Dispersion. Department of Economics, WP 2009–10. Loughborough University.

Garda, Robert A., and Michael V. Marn. 1993. Price Wars. *McKinsey Quarterly* (issue 3, September) 87–100.

Garicano, Luis, and Robert Gertner. 2000. The Dynamics of Price Competition. In *Financial Times, Mastering Strategy: The Complete MBA Companion in Strategy* 39. Harlow: Financial Times Prentice Hall.

Gavil, Andrew I. 2007. Antitrust Bookends: The 2006 Supreme Court Term in Historical Context. 22 (Fall) *Antitrust* 21–26.

Genesove, David, and Wallace P. Mullin. 2001. Rules, Communication, and Collusion:

Narrative Evidence from the Sugar Institute Case. 91 *American Economic Review* 379–98.

Gerardi, Kristopher S., and Adam Hale Shapiro. 2009. Does Competition Reduce Price Dispersion? New Evidence from the Airline Industry. 117 *Journal of Political Economy* 1–37.

Gerlach, Heiko. 2009. Stochastic Market Sharing, Partial Communication, and Collusion. 27 *International Journal of Industrial Organization* 655–66.

Gilo, David, Yossi Moshe, and Yossi Spiegel. 2006. Partial Cross Ownership and Tacit Collusion. 37 *Rand Journal of Economics* 81–99.

Ginsburg, Douglas H. 1986. Testimony on Sentences for Criminal Antitrust Violations. In *United States Sentencing Commission: Unpublished Public Hearings 1986*, pp. 4–20. Buffalo, NY: William S. Hein Company, 1988.

Ginsburg, Douglas H., and Joshua D. Wright. 2010. Antitrust Sanctions. 6 (Autumn) *Competition Policy International* 3–39.

Glaeser, Edward L., David I. Laibson, José A. Scheinkman, and Christine L. Soutter. 2000. Measuring Trust. 115 *Quarterly Journal of Economics* 811–46.

Green, Edward J., and Robert H. Porter. 1984. Noncooperative Collusion under Imperfect Price Information. 52 *Econometrica* 87–100.

Grout, Paul A., and Silvia Sonderegger. 2007. Structural Approaches to Cartel Detection. In *European Competition Law Annual 2006: Enforcement of Prohibition of Cartels*, edited by Claus-Dieter Ehlermann and Isabela Atanasiu, pp. 83–103. Oxford: Hart.

Hall, Robert E. 1988. The Relation between Price and Marginal Cost in U.S. Industry. 96 *Journal of Political Economy* 921–47.

———. 2007. Review of Michael D. Whinston, *Lectures on Antitrust Economics*. 45 *Journal of Economic Literature* 1066–70.

Hammond, Scott D. 2008. Recent Developments, Trends, and Milestones in the Antitrust Division's Criminal Enforcement Program. ABA Section of Antitrust Law Spring Meeting (March 26), Washington, DC. http://www.usdoj.gov/atr/public/speeches/232716.htm (accessed March 31, 2009).

Hannon, Kendall W. 2008. Much Ado about *Twombly*? A Study on the Impact of *Bell Atlantic Corp. v. Twombly* on 12(b)(6) Motions. 83 *Notre Dame Law Review* 1811–46.

Harding, Christopher, and Julian Joshua. 2003. *Regulating Cartels in Europe: A Study of Legal Control of Corporate Delinquency.* New York: Oxford University Press.

Harno, Albert J. 1941. Intent in Criminal Conspiracy. 89 *University of Pennsylvania Law Review* 624–47.

Harrington, Joseph E., Jr. 2003. Some Implications of Antitrust Laws for Cartel Pricing. 79 *Economic Letters* 377–83.

———. 2004. Post-Cartel Pricing During Litigation. 52 *Journal of Industrial Economics* 517–33.

———. 2005. Optimal Cartel Pricing in the Presence of an Antitrust Authority. 46 *International Economic Review* 145–69.

———. 2006. How Do Cartels Operate? 2 (no. 1) *Foundations and Trends in Microeconomics* 1–105.

———. 2007. Behavioral Screening and the Detection of Cartels. In *European Competition Law Annual: 2006—Enforcement of Prohibition of Cartels*, edited by Claus-Dieter Ehlermann and Isabela Atanasiu, pp. 51–68. Oxford: Hart.

———. 2008a. Detecting Cartels. In *Handbook of Antitrust Economics*, edited by Paolo Buccirossi, pp. 213–58. Cambridge, MA: MIT Press.

———. 2008b. Optimal Corporate Leniency Programs. 56 *Journal of Industrial Economics* 215–46.

Harrington, Joseph E., Jr., and Joe Chen. 2006. Cartel Pricing Dynamics with Cost Variability and Endogenous Buyer Detection. 24 *International Journal of Industrial Organization* 1185–1212.

Harrington, Joseph E., Jr., and Andrzej Skrzypacz. 2011. Private Monitoring and Communication in Cartels: Explaining Recent Collusive Practices. 101 *American Economic Review* 2425–49.

Hatamyar, Patricia W. 2010. The Tao of Pleading: Do *Twombly* and *Iqbal* Matter Empirically? 59 *American University Law Review* 553–633.

Hauser, Marc D. 1996. *The Evolution of Communication*. Cambridge, MA: MIT Press.

Hauser, Marc D., Noam Chomsky, and W. Tecumseh Fitch. 2002. The Faculty of Language: What Is It, Who Has It, and How Did It Evolve? 298 *Science* 1569–79.

Hawk, Barry E., and Giorgio A. Motta. 2009. Oligopolies and Collective Dominance: A Solution in Search of a Problem. In *Antitrust between EC Law and National Law*, edited by Enrico A. Raffaelli, pp. 59–104. Brussels: Bruylant.

Hay, George A. 1981. Oligopoly, Shared Monopoly, and Antitrust Law. 67 *Cornell Law Review* 439–81.

———. 2006. Horizontal Agreements: Concept and Proof. 51 *Antitrust Bulletin* 877–914.

Hay, George A., and Daniel Kelley. 1974. An Empirical Survey of Price Fixing Conspiracies. 17 *Journal of Law & Economics* 13–38.

Heath, J. B. 1960. Symposium on Restrictive Practices Legislation: Some Economic Consequences. 70 *Economic Journal* 474–84.

Heil, Oliver P., George S. Day, and David J. Reibstein. 1997. Signaling to Competitors. In *Wharton on Dynamic Competitive Strategy*, edited by George S. Day and David J. Reibstein, pp. 277–92. Hoboken, NJ: John Wiley.

Heilemann, John. 2000. The Truth, the Whole Truth, and Nothing But the Truth: The Untold Story of the Microsoft Antitrust Case and What It Means for the Future of Bill Gates and His Company. *Wired*, November. http://www.wired.com/wired/archive/8.11/microsoft.html (accessed March 23, 2011).

Holt, Charles A. 1995. Industrial Organization: A Survey of Laboratory Research. In *The Handbook of Experimental Economics*, edited by John H. Kagel and Alvin E. Roth, pp. 349–443. Princeton, NJ: Princeton University Press.

Hovenkamp, Herbert. 2005a. *The Antitrust Enterprise: Principle and Execution*. Cambridge, MA: Harvard University Press.

————. 2005b. *Federal Antitrust Policy: The Law of Competition and Its Practice.* 3rd ed. St. Paul, MN: Thomson/West.

Hubbard, William H. J. 2012. The Problem of Measuring Legal Change, with Application to *Bell Atlantic v. Twombly.* University of Chicago Law and Economics Working Paper 575.

Hume, David. 1992 [1739]. *Treatise of Human Nature.* Amherst, NY: Prometheus Books.

Hylton, Keith N. 2003. *Antitrust Law: Economic Theory and Common Law Evolution.* New York: Cambridge University Press.

International Titanium Association. 2010. Antitrust Guidelines. http://www.titanium .org/Category.cfm?CategoryID=161 (accessed November 22, 2010).

Jackendoff, Ray. 2002. *Foundations of Language: Brain, Meaning, Grammar, Evolution.* New York: Oxford University Press.

Jacquemin, Alexis, and Margaret E. Slade. 1989. Cartels, Collusion, and Horizontal Merger. In *Handbook of Industrial Organization,* edited by Richard Schmalensee and Robert D. Willig, vol. 1:415–73. Amsterdam: North-Holland.

Jones, Alison. 1993. *Woodpulp*: Concerted Practice and/or Conscious Parallelism? 6 *European Competition Law Review* 273–9.

Kaplow, Louis. 1984. The Patent-Antitrust Intersection: A Reappraisal. 97 *Harvard Law Review* 1813–92.

————. 1987. Antitrust, Law & Economics, and the Courts. 50 (Autumn) *Law & Contemporary Problems* 181–216.

————. 2011. On the Optimal Burden of Proof. 119 *Journal of Political Economy* 1104–40.

————. 2012a. Burden of Proof. 121 *Yale Law Journal* 738–859.

————. 2012b. On the Choice of Welfare Standards in Competition Law. In *The Goals of Competition Law,* edited by Daniel Zimmer, pp. 3–26. Cheltenham, UK: Edward Elgar.

————. 2012c. On the Optimal Burden of Proof. National Bureau of Economic Research Working Paper No. 17,765.

————. 2013a. Multistage Adjudication. 126 *Harvard Law Review* 1179–1298.

————. 2013b. Optimal Multistage Adjudication. Unpublished manuscript.

Kaplow, Louis, and Carl Shapiro. 2007. Antitrust. In *Handbook of Law and Economics,* edited by A. Mitchell Polinsky and Steven Shavell, vol. 2:1073–1225. Amsterdam: North-Holland.

Kaplow, Louis, and Steven Shavell. 1990. Legal Advice about Acts Already Committed. 10 *International Review of Law and Economics* 149–59.

————. 1992. Private versus Socially Optimal Provision of Ex Ante Legal Advice. 8 *Journal of Law, Economics & Organization* 306–20.

————. 1994a. Accuracy in the Determination of Liability. 37 *Journal of Law & Economics* 1–15.

————. 1994b. Why the Legal System Is Less Efficient Than the Income Tax in Redistributing Income. 23 *Journal of Legal Studies* 667–81.

———. 1996a. Accuracy in the Assessment of Damages. 39 *Journal of Law & Economics* 191–210.

———. 1996b. Property Rules versus Liability Rules: An Economic Analysis. 109 *Harvard Law Review* 713–90.

———. 2002. *Fairness versus Welfare.* Cambridge, MA: Harvard University Press.

Kaysen, Carl. 1951. Collusion under the Sherman Act. 65 *Quarterly Journal of Economics* 263–70.

Kaysen, Carl, and Donald F. Turner. 1959. *Antitrust Policy: An Economic and Legal Analysis.* Cambridge, MA: Harvard University Press.

Kessler, Jeffrey L., and Ronald C. Wheeler. 1993. An Old Theory Gets New Life: How to Price without Being a "Price Signaler." 7 (Summer) *Antitrust* 26–29.

Khanna, V. S. 1996. Corporate Criminal Liability: What Purpose Does It Serve? 109 *Harvard Law Review* 1477–1534.

Kintner, Earl. 1980. *Federal Antitrust Law.* Cincinnati, OH: Anderson.

Klevorick, Alvin K., and Issa B. Kohler-Hausmann. 2012. The Plausibility of *Twombly*: Proving Horizontal Agreements after *Twombly.* In *Research Handbook on the Economics of Antitrust Law*, edited by Einer R. Elhauge, pp. 201–45. Cheltenham, UK: Edward Elgar.

Kovacic, William E. 1993. The Identification and Proof of Horizontal Agreements under the Antitrust Laws. 38 *Antitrust Bulletin* 5–81.

Kovacic, William E., Robert C. Marshall, Leslie M. Marx, and Halbert L. White. 2011. Plus Factors and Agreement in Antitrust Law. 110 *Michigan Law Review* 393–436.

Kraakman, Reinier H. 1984. Corporate Liability Strategies and the Costs of Legal Controls. 93 *Yale Law Journal* 857–98.

Kreps, David M., and José A. Scheinkman. 1983. Quantity Precommitment and Bertrand Competition Yield Cournot Outcomes. 14 *Bell Journal of Economics* 326–37.

Kreps, David M., and Robert Wilson. 1982. Reputation and Imperfect Information. 27 *Journal of Economic Theory* 253–79.

Kühn, Kai-Uwe. 2001. Fighting Collusion by Regulating Communication between Firms. 16 *Economic Policy* 169–204.

Kühn, Kai-Uwe, and Xavier Vives. 1995. *Information Exchanges among Firms and Their Impact on Competition.* Luxembourg: Office for Official Publications of the European Communities.

Kuperman, Andrea. 2009. Application of Pleading Standards Post-*Ashcroft vs. Iqbal.* Memorandum to Civil Rules Committee, Standing Rules Committee, November 25. http://www.uscourts.gov/uscourts/RulesAndPolicies/rules/Memo%20re%20plead ing%20standards%20by%20circuit.pdf (accessed November 22, 2010).

LaFave, Wayne R. 2003. *Substantive Criminal Law.* 2nd ed. Eagan, MN: Thomson/West.

Lande, Robert H., and Joshua P. Davis. 2008. Benefits from Private Antitrust Enforcement: An Analysis of Forty Cases. 42 *University of San Francisco Law Review* 879–918.

Landes, William M., and Richard A. Posner. 1975. The Private Enforcement of Law. 4 *Journal of Legal Studies* 1–46.

———. 1981. Market Power in Antitrust Cases. 94 *Harvard Law Review* 937–96.

Lau, Lawrence J. 1982. On Identifying the Degree of Competitiveness from Industry Price and Output Data. 10 *Economics Letters* 93–99.

Lawyer, John Q. (pseudonym). 1963. How to Conspire to Fix Prices. 41 (March–April) *Harvard Business Review* 95–103.

Leslie, Christopher R. 2004. Trust, Distrust, and Antitrust. 82 *Texas Law Review* 515–680.

Levenstein, Margaret C. 1997. Price Wars and the Stability of Collusion: A Study of the Pre–World War I Bromine Industry. 45 *Journal of Industrial Economics* 117–37.

Levenstein, Margaret C., and Valerie Y. Suslow. 2006. What Determines Cartel Success? 44 *Journal of Economic Literature* 43–95.

———. 2008. International Cartels. In *Issues in Competition Law and Policy*, edited by Wayne Dale Collins, vol. 2:1107–26. Chicago, IL: ABA Section of Antitrust Law.

Levy, Judith. 2007. FTC: Whole Foods–Wild Oats Merger Would Thwart Competition. *Seeking Alpha*, June 20. http://seekingalpha.com/article/38876-ftc-whole-foods-wild-oats-merger-would-thwart-competition (accessed March 23, 2011).

Llewellyn, Karl N. 1950. Remarks on the Theory of Appellate Decision and the Rules or Canons about How Statutes Are to Be Construed. 3 *Vanderbilt Law Review* 395–406.

Lopatka, John E. 1996. Solving the Oligopoly Problem: Turner's Try. 41 *Antitrust Bulletin* 843–908.

MacLeod, W. Bentley. 1985. A Theory of Conscious Parallelism. 27 *European Economic Review* 25–44.

Mankiw, N. Gregory, and Michael D. Whinston. 1986. Free Entry and Social Inefficiency. 17 *Rand Journal of Economics* 48–58.

Markovits, Richard S. 1974. Oligopolistic Pricing Suits, the Sherman Act, and Economic Welfare: Part I: Oligopolistic Price and Oligopolistic Pricing: Their Conventional and Operational Definition. 26 *Stanford Law Review* 493–548.

———. 1975. Oligopolistic Pricing Suits, the Sherman Act, and Economic Welfare: Part III: Proving (Illegal) Oligopolistic Pricing: A Description of the Necessary Evidence and a Critique of the Received Wisdom about Its Character and Cost. 27 *Stanford Law Review* 307–31.

Marshall, Robert C., and Leslie M. Marx. 2012. *The Economics of Collusion: Cartels and Bidding Rings*. Cambridge, MA: MIT Press.

Marshall, Robert C., Leslie M. Marx, and Matthew E. Raiff. 2008. Cartel Price Announcements: The Vitamins Industry. 26 *International Journal of Industrial Organization* 762–802.

Maskin, Eric. 1986. The Existence of Equilibrium with Price-Setting Firms. 76 *American Economic Association, Papers and Proceedings* 382–86.

Masson, Robert T., and Robert J. Reynolds. 1978. Statistical Studies of Antitrust Enforcement: A Critique. In American Statistical Association, *1977 Proceedings of the Business and Economics Statistics Section*, Part 1:22–28.

McAfee, R. Preston, and John McMillan. 1992. Bidding Rings. 82 *American Economic Review* 579–99.

McCutcheon, Barbara. 1997. Do Meetings in Smoke-Filled Rooms Facilitate Collusion? 105 *Journal of Political Economy* 330–50.

Miller, Amalia R. 2010. Did the Airline Tariff Publishing Case Reduce Collusion? 53 *Journal of Law & Economics* 569–86.

Miller, Nathan H. 2009. Strategic Leniency and Cartel Enforcement. 99 *American Economic Review* 750–68.

Monti, Giorgio. 2001. The Scope of Collective Dominance under Articles 82 EC. 38 *Common Market Law Review* 131–57.

Moorthy, Sridhar, and Ralph A. Winter. 2006. Price-Matching Guarantees. 37 *Rand Journal of Economics* 449–65.

Motta, Massimo. 2004. *Competition Policy: Theory and Practice.* New York: Cambridge University Press.

———. 2007. Review of Michael Whinston, *Lectures on Antitrust Economics.* 3 *Competition Policy International* 313–20.

Motta, Massimo, and Michele Polo. 2003. Leniency Programs and Cartel Prosecution. 21 *International Journal of Industrial Organization* 347–79.

Nash, John F., Jr. 1950. Equilibrium Points in *N*–Person Games. 36 *Proceedings of the National Academy of Sciences* 48–49.

———. 1951. Non-Cooperative Games. 54 *Annals of Mathematics* 286–95.

———. 1953. Two-Person Cooperative Games. 21 *Econometrica* 128–40.

Neven, Damien J. 2001. "Collusion" under Article 81 and the Merger Regulation. In Konkurrensverket, Swedish Competition Authority, *Fighting Cartels—Why and How?*, pp. 56–77. Stockholm: Konkurrensverket.

Nevo, Aviv. 1998. Identification of the Oligopoly Solution Concept in a Differentiated-Products Industry. 59 *Economics Letters* 391–95.

———. 2001. Measuring Market Power in the Ready-to-Eat Cereal Market. 69 *Econometrica* 307–42.

Noel, Michael D. 2007a. Edgeworth Price Cycles, Cost-Based Pricing, and Sticky Pricing in Retail Gasoline Markets. 89 *Review of Economics and Statistics* 324–34.

———. 2007b. Edgeworth Price Cycles: Evidence from the Toronto Retail Gasoline Market. 55 *Journal of Industrial Economics* 69–92.

Nye, Stephen A. 1975. Can Conduct Oriented Enforcement Inhibit Conscious Parallelism? 44 *Antitrust Law Journal* 206–30.

OECD (Organisation for Economic Co-operation and Development), Directorate for Financial, Fiscal and Enterprise Affairs, Competition Committee. 2002. Report on the Nature and Impact of Hard Core Cartels and Sanctions Against Cartels under National Competition Laws. http://www.oecd.org/competition/cartelsandanti-competitiveagreements/2081831.pdf.

OECD. 2005. Hard Core Cartels: Third Report on the Implementation of the 1998 Council Recommendation. http://www.oecd.org/competition/cartelsandanti-competitiveagreements/35863307.pdf.

Ordover, Janusz A. 1978. Costly Litigation in the Model of Single Activity Accidents. 7 *Journal of Legal Studies* 243–61.

Osborne, Martin J., and Ariel Rubinstein. 1994. *A Course in Game Theory*. Cambridge, MA: MIT Press.

Page, William H. 2009. *Twombly* and Communication: The Emerging Definition of Concerted Action under the New Pleading Standards. 5 *Journal of Competition Law & Economics* 439–68.

Pearce, David G. 1984. Rationalizable Strategic Behavior and the Problem of Perfection. 52 *Econometrica* 1029–50.

Perloff, Jeffrey M., Larry S. Karp, and Amos Golan. 2007. *Estimating Market Power and Strategies*. Cambridge: Cambridge University Press.

Perry, Martin K. 1984. Scale Economies, Imperfect Competition, and Public Policy. 32 *Journal of Industrial Economics* 313–33.

Pesendorfer, Martin. 2000. A Study of Collusion in First-Price Auctions. 67 *Review of Economic Studies* 381–411.

Pinker, Steven. 1994. *The Language Instinct*. New York: W. Morrow and Co.

———. 2007. *The Stuff of Thought: Language as a Window into Human Nature*. New York: Viking.

Png, I. P. L. 1986. Optimal Subsidies and Damages in the Presence of Judicial Error. 6 *International Review of Law and Economics* 101–5.

Polinsky, A. Mitchell. 1980. Private versus Public Enforcement of Fines. 9 *Journal of Legal Studies* 105–27.

Polinsky, A. Mitchell, and Steven Shavell. 1979. The Optimal Tradeoff between the Probability and Magnitude of Fines. 69 *American Economic Review* 880–91.

———. 1981. Contribution and Claim Reduction among Antitrust Defendants: An Economic Analysis. 33 *Stanford Law Review* 447–71.

———. 1993. Should Employees Be Subject to Fines and Imprisonment Given the Existence of Corporate Liability? 13 *International Review of Law and Economics* 239–57.

———. 2007. The Theory of Public Enforcement of Law. In *Handbook of Law and Economics*, edited by A. Mitchell Polinsky and Steven Shavell, vol. 1:403–54. Amsterdam: North-Holland.

Pollack, Benjamin F. 1947. Common Law Conspiracy. 35 *Georgetown Law Journal* 328–52.

Porter, Michael E. 1980. *Competitive Strategy: Techniques for Analyzing Industries and Competitors*. New York: Free Press.

Porter, Robert H. 1983a. Optimal Cartel Trigger Price Strategies. 29 *Journal of Economic Theory* 313–38.

———. 1983b. A Study of Cartel Stability: The Joint Executive Committee, 1880–1886. 14 *Bell Journal of Economics* 301–14.

———. 2005. Detecting Collusion. 26 *Review of Industrial Organization* 147–67.

Porter, Robert H., and J. Douglas Zona. 1993. Detection of Bid Rigging in Procurement Auctions. 101 *Journal of Political Economy* 518–38.

———. 2008. Collusion. In *Issues in Competition Law and Policy*, edited by Wayne Dale Collins, vol. 2:1069–84. Chicago, IL: ABA Section of Antitrust Law.

Posner, Richard A. 1969. Oligopoly and the Antitrust Laws: A Suggested Approach. 21 *Stanford Law Review* 1562–1606.

———. 1975. The Social Costs of Monopoly and Regulation. 83 *Journal of Political Economy* 807–28.

———. 1976. Oligopolistic Pricing Suits, the Sherman Act, and Economic Welfare: A Reply to Professor Markovits. 28 *Stanford Law Review* 903–14.

———. 2001. *Antitrust Law.* 2nd ed. Chicago, IL: University of Chicago Press.

Posner, Richard A., and Frank H. Easterbrook. 1981. *Antitrust: Cases, Economic Notes, and Other Materials.* 2nd ed. St. Paul, MN: West.

Radner, Roy. 1980. Collusive Behavior in Noncooperative Epsilon-Equilibria of Oligopolies with Long but Finite Lives. 22 *Journal of Economic Theory* 136–54.

Rahl, James A. 1950. Conspiracy and the Anti-Trust Laws. 44 *Illinois Law Review* 743–68.

———. 1962. Symposium on Price Competition and Antitrust Policy: Price Competition and the Price Fixing Rule—Preface and Perspective. 57 *Northwestern University Law Review* 137–50.

Reid, Gavin C. 1979. Forchheimer on Partial Monopoly. 11 *History of Political Economy* 303–8.

Reynolds, Robert J., and Bruce R. Snapp. 1986. The Competitive Effects of Partial Equity Interests and Joint Ventures. 4 *International Journal of Industrial Organization* 141–53.

Risk Management Association. 2010. RMA Antitrust Guidelines. http://www.rmahq.org/ (accessed November 22, 2010).

Rogerson, William P. 1982. The Social Costs of Monopoly and Regulation: A Game-Theoretic Analysis. 13 *Bell Journal of Economics* 391–401.

Rosenthal, Robert W. 1981. Games of Perfect Information, Predatory Pricing and the Chain-Store Paradox. 25 *Journal of Economic Theory* 92–100.

Ross, Thomas W. 1992. Cartel Stability and Product Differentiation. 10 *International Journal of Industrial Organization* 1–13.

Rotemberg, Julio J., and Garth Saloner. 1989. The Cyclical Behavior of Strategic Inventories. 104 *Quarterly Journal of Economics* 73–97.

Royall, M. Sean. 1997. Disaggregation of Antitrust Damages. 65 *Antitrust Law Journal* 311–52.

Sagi, Guy. 2008. The Oligopolistic Pricing Problem: A Suggested Price Freeze Remedy. 2008 *Columbia Business Law Review* 269–359.

Salant, Stephen W. 1987. Treble Damage Awards in Private Lawsuits for Price Fixing. 95 *Journal of Political Economy* 1326–36.

Salinger, Michael. 1990. The Concentration-Margins Relationship Reconsidered. 1990 *Brookings Papers on Economic Activity: Microeconomics* 287–321.

Saloner, Garth, Andrea Shepard, and Joel Podolny. 2001. *Strategic Management.* New York: John Wiley.

Salop, Steven C. 1986. Practices That (Credibly) Facilitate Oligopoly Co-ordination. In

New Developments in the Analysis of Market Structure, edited by Joseph E. Stiglitz and G. Frank Mathewson, pp. 265–90. Cambridge, MA: MIT Press.

Salop, Steven C., and Joseph Stiglitz. 1977. Bargains and Ripoffs: A Model of Monopolistically Competitive Price Dispersion. 44 *Review of Economic Studies* 493–510.

Sandler, Wendy, Irit Meir, Carol Padden, and Mark Aronoff. 2005. The Emergence of Grammar: Systematic Structure in a New Language. 102 *Proceedings of the National Academy of Sciences* 2661–65.

Schelling, Thomas C. 1960. *The Strategy of Conflict.* Cambridge, MA: Harvard University Press.

Scherer, F. M. 1977. The Posnerian Harvest: Separating Wheat from Chaff. 86 *Yale Law Journal* 974–1002.

Scherer, F. M., and David Ross. 1990. *Industrial Market Structure and Economic Performance.* 3rd ed. Boston, MA: Houghton Mifflin.

Schmalensee, Richard. 1987a. Collusion versus Differential Efficiency: Testing Alternative Hypotheses. 35 *Journal of Industrial Economics* 399–425.

———. 1987b. Competitive Advantage and Collusive Optima. 5 *International Journal of Industrial Organization* 351–67.

———. 1989. Inter-Industry Studies of Structure and Performance. In *Handbook of Industrial Organization,* edited by Richard Schmalensee and Robert D. Willig, vol. 2:951–1009. Amsterdam: North-Holland.

Selten, Reinhard. 1978. The Chain Store Paradox. 9 *Theory & Decision* 127–59.

Senghas, Ann, Sotaro Kita, and Aslı Özyürek. 2004. Children Creating Core Properties of Language: Evidence from an Emerging Sign Language in Nicaragua. 305 *Science* 1779–82.

Shapiro, Carl. 1986. Exchange of Cost Information in Oligopoly. 53 *Review of Economic Studies* 433–46.

———. 1989. Theories of Oligopoly Behavior. In *Handbook of Industrial Organization,* edited by Richard Schmalensee and Robert Willig, vol. 1:329–414. Amsterdam: North-Holland.

Shavell, Steven. 1982. The Social versus the Private Incentive to Bring Suit in a Costly Legal System. 11 *Journal of Legal Studies* 333–39.

———. 1990. Deterrence and the Punishment of Attempts. 19 *Journal of Legal Studies* 435–66.

———. 1993. The Optimal Structure of Law Enforcement. 36 *Journal of Law & Economics* 255–87.

Shilony, Yuval. 1977. Mixed Pricing in Oligopoly. 14 *Journal of Economic Theory* 373–88.

Siragusa, Mario, and Cesare Rizza, eds. 2007. *EU Competition Law,* vol. 3, *Cartel Law: Restrictive Agreements and Practices between Competitors.* Leuven, Belgium: Claeys & Casteels.

Slade, Margaret E. 1990. Strategic Pricing Models and Interpretation of Price-War Data. 34 *European Economic Review* 524–37.

Smith, Tefft W. 2005. Kirkland & Ellis LLP: A Businessperson's Guide to the Antitrust Implications of Mergers, Acquisitions, Joint Ventures, and Strategic Alliances. http://www.kirkland.com/siteFiles/kirkexp/publications/2354/Document1/Business_persons_guide.pdf (accessed November 22, 2010).

Sokol, D. Daniel. 2012. Cartels, Corporate Compliance, and What Practitioners Really Think about Enforcement. 78 *Antitrust Law Journal* 201–40.

Sorinas, Sergio. 2007. Remedies and Fines. In *EU Competition Law*, vol. 3, *Cartel Law: Restrictive Agreements and Practices between Competitors*, edited by Mario Siragusa and Cesare Rizza, pp. 477–627. Leuven, Belgium: Claeys & Casteels.

Spagnolo, Giancarlo. 2008. Leniency and Whistleblowers in Antitrust. In *Handbook of Antitrust Economics*, edited by Paolo Buccirossi, pp. 259–303. Cambridge, MA: MIT Press.

Spence, Michael. 1976. Product Selection, Fixed Costs, and Monopolistic Competition. 43 *Review of Economic Studies* 217–35.

———. 1978. Tacit Coordination and Imperfect Information. 11 *Canadian Journal of Economics* 490–505.

Spier, Kathryn E. 2007. Litigation. In *Handbook of Law and Economics*, edited by A. Mitchell Polinsky and Steven Shavell, vol. 1:259–342. Amsterdam: North-Holland.

Sproul, Michael F. 1993. Antitrust and Prices. 101 *Journal of Political Economy* 741–54.

Steinman, Adam N. 2006. The Irrepressible Myth of *Celotex*: Reconsidering Summary Judgment Burdens Twenty Years after the Trilogy. 63 *Washington & Lee Law Review* 81–145.

Stigler, George J. 1964. A Theory of Oligopoly. 72 *Journal of Political Economy* 44–61.

Stole, Lars A. 2007. Price Discrimination and Competition. In *Handbook of Industrial Organization*, edited by Mark Armstrong and Robert H. Porter, vol. 3:2221–99. Amsterdam: North-Holland.

Stroux, Sigrid. 2004. *US and EC Oligopoly Control*. The Hague: Kluwer Law International.

Swann, Dennis, Denis P. O'Brien, W. Peter J. Maunder, and W. Stewart Howe. 1974. *Competition in British Industry: Restrictive Practices Legislation in Theory and Practice*. London: George Allen & Unwin.

Symeonidis, George. 2002. *The Effects of Competition: Cartel Policy and the Evolution of Strategy and Structure in British Industry*. Cambridge, MA: MIT Press.

Tirole, Jean. 1988. *The Theory of Industrial Organization*. Cambridge, MA: MIT Press.

Tullock, Gordon. 1967. The Welfare Costs of Tariffs, Monopolies, and Theft. 5 *Western Economic Journal* 224–32.

Turner, Donald F. 1962. The Definition of Agreement under the Sherman Act: Conscious Parallelism and Refusals to Deal. 75 *Harvard Law Review* 655–706.

U.S. Department of Justice, Antitrust Division. 2005. Price Fixing, Bid Rigging, and Market Allocation Schemes: What They Are and What to Look For. http://www.justice.gov/atr/public/guidelines/211578.pdf (accessed December 7, 2010).

U.S. Department of Justice and Federal Trade Commission. 2010. Horizontal Merger Guidelines. http://www.justice.gov/atr/public/guidelines/hmg-2010.html.

U.S. Sentencing Commission. 2008. *2008 Federal Sentencing Guidelines Manual* (November). Washington, DC: U.S. Sentencing Commission. http://www.ussc.gov/Guide lines/2008_guidelines/Manual/GL2008.pdf.

Van Bael, Ivo, and Jean-Francois Bellis. 2005. *Competition Law of the European Community.* 4th ed. The Hague: Kluwer Law International.

Van Cayseele, Patrick, Peter D. Camesasca, and Kristian Hugmark. 2008. The EC Commission's 2006 Fine Guidelines Reviewed from an Economic Perspective: Risking Overdeterrence. 53 *Antitrust Bulletin* 1083–1126.

Van Gerven, Gerwin, and Edurne Navarro Varona. 1994. The *Wood Pulp* Case and the Future of Concerted Practices. 31 *Common Market Law Review* 575–608.

Varian, Hal R. 1980. A Model of Sales. 70 *American Economic Review* 651–59.

———. 1989. Price Discrimination. In *Handbook of Industrial Organization*, edited by Richard Schmalensee and Robert D. Willig, vol. 1:597–654. Amsterdam: North-Holland.

Veljanovski, Cento. 2011. Deterrence, Recidivism, and European Cartel Fines. 7 *Journal of Competition Law & Economics* 871–915.

Vives, Xavier. 1999. *Oligopoly Pricing: Old Ideas and New Tools.* Cambridge, MA: MIT Press.

Von Weizsäcker, C. C. 1980. A Welfare Analysis of Barriers to Entry. 11 *Bell Journal of Economics* 399–420.

Wade, Nicholas. 2006. *Before the Dawn: Recovering the Lost History of Our Ancestors.* New York: Penguin Books.

Wang, Zhongmin. 2009. (Mixed) Strategy in Oligopoly Pricing: Evidence from Gasoline Price Cycles before and under a Timing Regulation. 117 *Journal of Political Economy* 987–1030.

Watkins, Boyce. 2010. DEA Seeks Ebonics Experts to Help with Cases . . . Seriously. *BlackVoices*, August 23. http://www.bvblackspin.com/2010/08/23/dea-may-hire -ebonics-translators-to-solve-crime/ (accessed November 23, 2010).

Weiss, Leonard W., ed. 1989. *Concentration and Price.* Cambridge, MA: MIT Press.

Wellford, Charissa P. 2002. Antitrust: Results from the Laboratory. In *Experiments Investigating Market Power*, edited by Charles A. Holt and R. Mark Isaac, pp. 1–29. Amsterdam: Elsevier Science.

Werden, Gregory J. 1998. Demand Elasticities in Antitrust Analysis. 66 *Antitrust Law Journal* 363–414.

———. 2004. Economic Evidence on the Existence of Collusion: Reconciling Antitrust Law with Oligopoly Theory. 71 *Antitrust Law Journal* 719–800.

Werden, Gregory J., and Luke M. Froeb. 2008. Unilateral Competitive Effects of Horizontal Mergers. In *Handbook of Antitrust Economics*, edited by Paolo Buccirossi, pp. 43–104. Cambridge, MA: MIT Press.

Werden, Gregory J., Scott D. Hammond, and Belinda A. Barnett. 2011. Deterrence and Detection of Cartels: Using All the Tools and Sanctions. 56 *Antitrust Bulletin* 207–34.

Whinston, Michael D. 2006. *Lectures on Antitrust Economics.* Cambridge, MA: MIT Press.

Whish, Richard. 2009. *Competition Law*. 6th ed. New York: Oxford University Press.

White, Lawrence J. 2001. Lysine and Price Fixing: How Long? How Severe? 18 *Review of Industrial Organization* 23–31.

White House Task Force on Antitrust Policy. 1968. Task Force Report on Antitrust Policy. Reprinted in *Antitrust & Trade Regulation Report* (BNA) no. 411, spec. supp. II (May 27, 1969).

Wickelgren, Abraham L. 2012. Issues in Antitrust Enforcement. In *Research Handbook on the Economics of Antitrust Law*, edited by Einer Elhauge, pp. 267–82. Cheltenham, UK: Edward Elgar.

Wilde, Louis L., and Alan Schwartz. 1979. Equilibrium Comparison Shopping. 46 *Review of Economic Studies* 543–53.

Williams, Glanville. 1961. *Criminal Law*. 2nd ed. London: Stevens.

Wollmann, Hanno. 2008. Horizontal Restraints of Competition. In *Competition Law: European Community Practice and Procedure*, edited by Günther Hirsch, Frank Montag, and Franz Jürgen Säcker, pp. 492–526. London: Sweet & Maxwell.

Zimmerman, Paul R., John M. Yun, and Christopher T. Taylor. 2010. Edgeworth Price Cycles in Gasoline: Evidence from the U.S. FTC Bureau of Economics Working Paper No. 303. Washington, DC.

Index

adjudication: in communications-based approach, 15, 372, 373, 401n3, 414–15, 423, 432, 445–46; costs of, 15, 327n7, 368, 369, 372, 373, 376, 423, 430; dispositive motions, 82, 141, 372, 375–76; litigated cases, research on, 154–57; litigation strategies, 7–8, 134–36, 142–45; non-standard procedures in, 375–76; and paradox of proof, 133–45, 414–15, 417, 445–46; partial trials, 375; pleading requirements, 85, 88, 141; proposed reforms in, 375–76; screening of cases, 117n22, 366, 372–73, 375, 432–33; sequencing or stages of litigation, 117n22, 366, 371–76, 430. *See also* administration; enforcement; lower court practice; Supreme Court

administration: costs and difficulty of, 2, 15, 240n13, 258n5, 313, 337n28, 368, 369, 371, 376, 423, 426, 428; in direct and communications-based approaches, compared, 2, 15, 411–19, 442, 443, 451, 452; enforcement effort, 368–69, 331–32, 427n8, 452; error rates and, 368, 369, 376, 423; experts and generalists in, 370–71, 370nn6–8, 428–29n11, 452; optimal policies and, 258n5, 368, 376 and n21, 452; stages in enforcement, 371–76, 430. *See also* adjudication; enforcement

agreements, generally: binding agreements, 8, 23–24, 31, 70–71, 177, 180, 181, 193, 208; collusion as, 34 and n17; commitments and, 207 and n67, 208, 212; common purpose and, 114, 115; communications and, 5, 50–51, 56, 58, 75, 109, 159, 193, 196, 199–200, 205, 206, 276, 318n22, 387, 390, 393, 444; concept of, 4, 5, 21, 28–29, 58, 68n54, 73, 75,

88; conspiracy and, 74–75, 75n17, 81, 92, 103, 109, 114–15, 399n1, 445; defined, 21, 30–33, 51, 149, 162–63, 181, 196–97, 199; definition, problems of, 4, 6, 16, 21, 26, 29n11, 30–33, 44, 58–60, 68n54, 101, 125, 145, 149–51, 159, 180–81, 199, 441n37, 444, 447; direct evidence of, 102n2, 103, 107–9, 146; equilibrium and, 8, 196–99; in EU law, 93–95, 100n82, 178n8, 445; express agreements, 27, 34–36, 44, 45, 48, 50, 65n44, 92, 125, 157n49, 101, 112, 217, 387, 389–90, 393, 444, 446; inferences about, 7, 24n4, 51, 101, 103, 105, 109, 114, 115, 127, 149, 159, 160, 171, 189, 206, 402; interdependent behavior and, 4, 9, 31–33, 44–46, 48, 56–57, 68n54, 73, 92, 81, 91, 101, 103, 107, 108, 109, 114, 115, 124, 125, 138, 143, 162, 199, 206, 209, 212, 217, 388, 391, 444–45, 446–47; as meeting of the minds, 31, 33, 34, 51, 68n54, 95, 196, 198, 199, 209, 318n22, 388, 392, 444; narrow and broad interpretations of, 31, 33, 45, 75, 92, 109, 124, 143–44, 149, 159, 162–63, 389–90, 390n5, 444–45; non-binding agreements, 177, 193, 194, 196; in oligopoly theory, 174, 176, 177, 180, 181, 187, 189, 193–214, 446; promises and, 196, 206, 208, 209, 214; related terms for, 4, 33–43, 164n59, 193, 444; self-enforcing agreements, 187; Sherman Act and, 6, 56, 69, 70, 73, 77, 84, 93, 101, 114, 122n33, 124, 196, 198, 276n48; tacit agreements, 36, 45, 92, 125, 164n59, 390 and n5; and understandings, 4, 68n54, 81, 103, 108, 112, 146, 164n59, 193, 196, 198–99, 318n22, 388, 444. *See also* agreements to fix prices; conspiracy; meeting of the minds